Current Developments in Slavic Linguistics. Twenty Years After
(*based on selected papers from FDSL 11*)

POTSDAM LINGUISTIC INVESTIGATIONS
POTSDAMER LINGUISTISCHE UNTERSUCHUNGEN
RECHERCHES LINGUISTIQUES À POTSDAM

Vol./Bd 29

Zu Qualitätssicherung und Peer Review der vorliegenden Publikation

Die Qualität der in dieser Reihe erscheinenden Arbeiten wird vor der Publikation durch einen externen, von der Herausgeberschaft benannten Gutachter im Double Blind Verfahren geprüft. Dabei ist der Autor der Arbeit dem Gutachter während der Prüfung namentlich nicht bekannt; der Gutachter bleibt anonym.

Notes on the quality assurance and peer review of this publication

Prior to publication, the quality of the work published in this series is double blind reviewed by an external referee appointed by the editorship. The referee is not aware of the author's name when performing the review; the referee's name is not disclosed.

Teodora Radeva-Bork / Peter Kosta (eds.)

Current Developments in Slavic Linguistics. Twenty Years After (*based on selected papers from FDSL 11*)

PETER LANG

Bibliographic Information published by the Deutsche Nationalbibliothek
The Deutsche Nationalbibliothek lists this publication in the Deutsche Nationalbibliografie; detailed bibliographic data is available in the internet at http://dnb.d-nb.de.

Library of Congress Cataloging-in-Publication Data
A CIP catalog record for this book has been applied for at the Library of Congress.

Cover illustration:
Cornelia Scheide: Lightnings (2008).

ISSN 1862-524X
ISBN 978-3-631-67673-8 (Print)
E-ISBN 978-3-653-07147-4 (E-PDF)
E-ISBN 978-3-631-70974-0 (EPUB)
E-ISBN 978-3-631-70975-7 (MOBI)
DOI 10.3726/978-3-653-07147-4

Peter Lang – Berlin · Bern · Bruxelles ·
New York · Oxford · Warszawa · Wien

This publication has been peer reviewed.

www.peterlang.com

Contents

Preface

The 11th European Conference on Formal Description of Slavic Languages (FDSL 11) took place at the Slavic Department of the University of Potsdam from December 2nd through 4th 2015. The organisers gave the conference the motto *20 years after,* since the first founding conference took place exactly 20 years ago at the University of Leipzig, in December 1995.

The idea for this conference was born out of the fact that especially the West German part of Slavic linguistics did not have a tradition of generative grammar compared to the GDR, but rather sought its theoretic homeland in different areas of functional linguistics of different colours and orientations. In contrast, the Leipzig Slavic School, the Karl-Marx University Leipzig and the Centre for General Linguistics in Berlin East had dedicated a part of their research to generative syntax with names such as Rudolf Růžička, Anita Steube, Gerhild Zybatow or Uwe Junghanns in Leipzig (just to mention some out of many), or Manfred Bierwisch, Ilse Zimmermann and Brigitte Haftka at ZAS Berlin.

The present volume is therefore a jubilee volume because it is closely linked to a success story not only of generative grammar, but in general of the blossoming and stabilization of formal models in the field of phonology, morphosyntax and syntax, as well as the digitization of corpora, psycholinguistics and computational linguistics of Slavic languages. The volume contains contributions from the FDSL 11 conference that were chosen and selected according to high standards on quality passing a double-blind review procedure. The volume also features a guest paper by Noam Chomsky which gives the basics of the-state-of-the-art and reviews the generative power of I-languages. Major notions such as hierarchy (instead of linear order), Merge and Recursion are discussed in the context of internal data and external proofs from L1-acquisition, artificial language computations, etc.

Profitable for the revival of the traditional grammar of descriptive-functional schools through formalization, generalization and theory formation combined with a strict attention to the empirical situation and development of the individual Slavic languages is in these years, above all, the inclusion and continuation of recent approaches to formal (mostly generative) language theory, language acquisition theory, biolinguistics, but also to further models as continuation and modification of Strict Minimalism (Chomsky 1995 passim).

At the end I (Peter Kosta) have to thank those, without whose help and financial support this volume would not have seen the light of this world. First,

Teodora Radeva-Bork, the co-editor of the volume, whose lion's share lies in the first stage of the editorial work, while the reading of the proofs and the final stage goes to my assistant student Anastasiya Bortnikova whose support in reading the proofs of 502 pages remains invaluable.

Thirdly, I am grateful to my secretary Monika Kruschinski for typesetting the first draft of the book and delivering a useful model for the typesetter. And finally, we would like to stress the importance of what the reviewers proposed to improve. Without their scrutiny and professional judgments no improvement of the submitted articles would have been possible.

Finally, I would like to thank the German Research Foundation (DFG) for the cost subsidy for the funding of the FDSL 11 conference. May the reader now decide on the success or failure of this book. All formal or substantive, still existing deficiencies I take on my account.

The present volume is dedicated to the memory of Susan Rothstein who passed away on July 30, 2019. Her contribution in this volume represents an important theoretical approach on aspectual semantics of Russian eventive and resultative verbs.

Peter Kosta
Potsdam, September 2019

List of Contributors

Tania Avgustinova
Saarland University

Boban Arsenijević
Karl-Franzens-University of Graz

Julia Bacskai-Atkari
University of Konstanz

Joanna Błaszczak
University of Wrocław

Anna Bondaruk
John Paul II Catholic University of Lublin

Željko Bošković
University of Connecticut

Noam Chomsky
University of Arizona

Miloje Despić
Cornell University

Margarita Dimitrova
University of Lisbon

Elena Dimova
Université de Montréal

Mojmír Dočekal
Masaryk University

Andrea Fischer
Saarland University

Ana Werkmann Horvat
University of Oxford, Institute of Croatian language and linguistics, Zagreb

Klára Jágrová
Saarland University

Keren Khrizman
Heinrich-Heine-University of Düsseldorf

Peter Kosta
University of Potsdam

Marijana Marelj
UiL OTS, Utrecht University

Franc Lanko Marušič
Univerza v Novi Gorici

Olav Mueller-Reichau
Leipzig University

Andrew Murphy
University of Leipzig

Nikola Paillereau
Laboratory of Phonetics and Phonology, CNRS Paris, Charles University Prague

Hagen Pitsch
University of Goettingen

Gergana Popova
Goldsmiths, University of London

Susan Rothstein
Bar-Ilan University

Jelena Runić
Johns Hopkins University

Andrew Spencer
University of Essex

Adrian Stegovec
University of Connecticut

Irina A. Sekerina
College of Staten Island, New York

Radek Skarnitzl
Charles University Prague

Irina Stenger
Saarland University

Christine Tellier
Université de Montréal

Aida Talić
University of Illinois at Urbana-Champaign

Neda Todorović
University of British Columbia

Egor Tsedryk
Saint Mary's University

Susi Wurmbrand
University of Vienna

Marcin Wągiel
Masaryk University in Brno

Jacek Witkoś
Adam Mickiewicz University, Poznań

Jana Willer Gold
University College London

Noam Chomsky

Minimal Computation and the Architecture of Language

From the early days of the modern scientific revolution, there has been intense interest in human language, recognized to be a core feature of human nature and the primary capacity distinguishing modern humans from other creatures. In a contemporary interpretation, Ian Tattersall, one of the leading students of human evolution, writes that "the acquisition of the uniquely modern [human] sensibility was instead an abrupt and recent event.... And the expression of this new sensibility was almost certainly crucially abetted by the invention of what is perhaps the single most remarkable thing about our modern selves: language."[1]

Centuries earlier, Galileo and the seventeenth century Port Royal logicians and grammarians were awed by the "marvelous invention" of a means to construct "from 25 or 30 sounds that infinity of expressions, which bear no resemblance to what takes place in our minds, yet enable us to reveal [to others] everything that we think, and all the various movements of our soul." Descartes took this capacity to be a primary difference between humans and any beast-machine, providing a basic argument for his mind-body dualism. The great humanist Wilhelm von Humboldt characterized language as "a generative activity [*eine Erzeugung*]" rather than "a lifeless product" [*ein todtes Erzeugtes*], *Energeia* rather than *Ergon*, and pondered the fact that somehow this activity "makes infinite use of finite means."[2] For the last great representative of this tradition, Otto Jespersen, the central question of the study of language is how its structures "come into existence in the mind of a speaker" on the basis of finite experience, yielding a "notion of structure" that is "definite enough to guide him in framing sentences of his own," crucially "free expressions" that are typically new to speaker and hearer. And more deeply, to go beyond to unearth "the great principles underlying the grammars of all languages" and by so doing to gain "a deeper insight into the innermost nature of human language and of human thought" – ideas that sound much less strange today than they did during the structuralist/behavioral science

1 Tattersall (2012).

2 For sources, see Chomsky (1966, 2009).

era that came to dominate much of the field through the first half of the 20th century, marginalizing the leading ideas and concerns of the tradition.[3]

Throughout this rich tradition of reflection and inquiry there were efforts to comprehend how humans can freely and creatively employ "an infinity of expressions" to express their thoughts in ways that are appropriate to circumstances though not determined by them, a crucial distinction. However, tools were not available to make much progress in carrying these ideas forward. That difficulty was partially overcome by mid-20th century, thanks to the work of Gödel, Turing, and other great mathematicians that laid the basis for the modern theory of computability. These accomplishments provided a very clear understanding of how "finite means" can generate an "infinity of expressions," thereby opening the way to formulating and investigating what we may consider to be the Basic Property of the human language faculty: a finitely-specified generative procedure, represented in the brain, that yields a discrete infinity of hierarchically structured expressions, each with a determinate interpretation at two interfaces: the sensorymotor interface SM for externalization in one or another sensory modality (usually, though not necessarily, sound); and the conceptual-intentional interface CI for reflection, interpretation, inference, planning, and other mental acts. Nothing analogous, even remotely similar, has been discovered in any other organism, thus lending substance to the judgments of the rich tradition.

It is important to recognize that the unbounded *use* of these finite means – the actual production of speech in the free and creative ways that intrigued the great figures of the past – still remains a mystery, not just in this domain, but for voluntary action generally. The mystery is graphically described by two of the most prominent scientists who study voluntary motion, Emilio Bizzi and Robert Ajemian, reviewing the state of the art today: "we have some idea as to the intricate design of the puppet and the puppet strings," they write, "but we lack insight into the mind of the puppeteer."[4]

That is not a slight problem. It lies at the borders of feasible scientific inquiry if not beyond, in a domain which human intelligence cannot penetrate. And if we if we are willing to accept the fact that we are organic creatures, not angels, we will join leading thinkers of the past – Descartes, Newton, Locke, Hume and others – in recognizing that some problems may be permanent mysteries for us.

3 Jespersen (1922).

4 Bizzi and Ajemian (2015).

The study of the finite means that are used in linguistic behavior – the puppet and the strings – has been pursued very successfully since the mid-twentieth century in what has come to be called the "generative enterprise" and "biolinguistic framework," drawing from and contributing to the "cognitive revolution" that has been underway during this period. The kinds of questions that students are investigating today could not even have been formulated not many years ago, and there has been a vast explosion in the languages of the widest typological variety that have come under investigation, at a level of depth never before contemplated in the long and rich history of investigation of language since classical Greece and ancient India. There have been many discoveries along the way, regularly raising new problems and opening new directions of inquiry. In these respects, the enterprise has had considerable success.

Departing from the assumptions of the structuralist/behaviorist era and returning to the spirit of the tradition in new forms, the generative/biolinguistic enterprise takes a language to be an internal system, a "module" of the system of human cognitive capacities. In technical terms, a language is taken to be an "I-language" – where "I" stands for internal, individual, and intensional (meaning that we are concerned with the actual nature of the biological object itself rather than with some set of objects that it generates, such as a corpus of expressions or set of behaviors). Each I-language satisfies the Basic Property of human language, formulated above. Jespersen's "great principles underlying the grammars of all languages" are the topic of Universal Grammar (UG), adapting a traditional term to a new framework, interpreted now as the theory of the genetic endowment for the faculty of language, the innate factors that determine the class of possible I-languages.

There is by now substantial evidence that UG is a species property, uniform among humans apart from severe pathology, and with no close analogue, let alone anything truly homologous, in the rest of the animal world. It seems to have emerged quite recently in evolutionary time, as Tattersall concluded, probably within the last 100,000 years. And we can be fairly confident that it has not evolved at least since our ancestors began to leave Africa some 50–60 thousand years ago. If so, then the emergence of the language faculty – of UG – was quite sudden in evolutionary time, which leads us to suspect that the Basic Property, and whatever else constitutes UG, should be very simple. Furthermore, since Eric Lenneberg's pioneering work in the 1950s,[5] evidence has been accumulating that the human language faculty is dissociated from other cognitive

5 Lenneberg (1967), Curtiss (2012).

capacities – though of course the use of language in perception (parsing) and production integrates the internal I-language with other capacities. That too suggests that whatever emerged quite suddenly (in evolutionary time) should be quite simple.

As the structuralist and behavioral science approaches took shape through the first half of the 20th century, it came to be generally assumed that the field faced no fundamental problems. Methods of analysis were available, notably Zellig Harris's *Methods in Structural Linguistics*, which provided the means to reduce a corpus of materials to an organized form, the primary task of the discipline. The problems of phonology, the major focus of inquiry, seemed to be largely understood. As a student in the late 1940s, I remember well the feeling that "this is really interesting work, but what happens to the field when we have structural grammars for all languages?" These beliefs made sense within the prevailing framework, as did the widely-held "Boasian" conception articulated by theoretical linguist Martin Joos that languages can "differ from each other without limit and in unpredictable ways," so that the study of each language must be approached "without any preexistent scheme of what a language must be."[6]

These beliefs collapsed as soon as the first efforts to construct generative grammars were undertaken by mid-20th century. It quickly became clear that very little was known about human language, even the languages that had been well studied. It also became clear that many of the fundamental properties of language that were unearthed must derive in substantial part from the innate language faculty, since they are acquired with little or no evidence. Hence there must be sharp and determinate limits to what a language can be. Furthermore, many of the properties that were revealed with the first efforts to construct rules satisfying the Basic Principle posed serious puzzles, some still alive today, along with many new ones that continue to be unearthed.

In this framework, the study of a specific language need not rely just on the behavior and products of speakers of this language. It can also draw from conclusions about other languages, from neuroscience and psychology, from genetics, in fact from any source of evidence, much like science generally, liberating the inquiry from the narrow constraints imposed by strict structuralist/behavioral science approaches.

In the early days of the generative enterprise, it seemed necessary to attribute great complexity to UG in order to capture the empirical phenomena of languages. It was always understood, however, that this cannot be correct. UG must meet

---

6 Joos (1957).

the condition of evolvability, and the more complex its assumed character, the greater the burden on some future account of how it might have evolved – a very heavy burden in the light of the few available facts about evolution of the faculty of language, as just indicated.

From the earliest days, there were efforts to reduce the assumed complexity of UG while maintaining, and often extending, its empirical coverage. And over the years there have been significant steps in this direction. By the early 1990s it seemed to a number of researchers that it might be possible to approach the problems in a new way: by constructing an "ideal solution" and asking how closely it can be approximated by careful analysis of apparently recalcitrant data, an approach that has been called "the minimalist program." The notion "ideal solution" is not precisely determined a priori, but we have a grasp of enough of its properties for the program to be pursued constructively.[7]

I-languages are computational systems, and ideally should meet conditions of Minimal Computation MC, which are to a significant extent well understood. I-languages should furthermore be based on operations that are minimally complex. The challenges facing this program are naturally very demanding ones, but there has been encouraging progress in meeting them, though vast empirical domains remain to be explored.

The natural starting point in this endeavor is to ask what is the simplest computational operation that would satisfy the Basic Property. The answer is quite clear. Every unbounded computational system includes, in some form, an operation that selects two objects X and Y already constructed, and forms a new object Z. In the simplest and hence optimal case, X and Y are not modified in this operation, and no new properties are introduced (in particular, order). Accordingly, the operation is simple set-formation: Z = {X,Y}. The operation is called *Merge* in recent literature.

Every computational procedure must have a set of *atoms* that initiate the computation – but like the atoms of chemistry, may be analyzed by other systems of language. The atoms are the minimal meaning-bearing elements of the lexicon, mostly word-like but of course not words. Merge must have access to these, and since it is a recursive operation, it must also apply to syntactic objects SO constructed from these, to the new SOs formed by this application, etc., without limit. Furthermore, to satisfy the Basic Property some of the SOs created by Merge must be mapped by fixed procedures to the SM and CI interfaces.

---

7 Chomsky (1995).

By simple logic, there are two cases of Merge(X,Y). Either Y is distinct from X (*External Merge EM*) or one of the two (say Y) is a part of the other that has already been generated (*Internal Merge IM*). In both cases, Merge(X,Y) = {X,Y}, by definition. In the case of IM, with Y a part of X, Merge(X,Y) = {X,Y} contains two *copies* of Y, one the SO that is merged and the other the one that remains in X. For example, EM takes the SOs *read* and *books* (actually, the SOs underlying them, but let us skip this refinement for simplicity of exposition) and forms the new SO {*read, books*} (unordered). IM takes the SOs *John will read which book* and *which book* and forms {*which book, John will read which book*}.

In both cases, other rules convert the SOs to the SM and CI forms. Mapping to CI is straightforward in both cases. The IM example has (roughly) the form "for which x, x a book, John will read the book x." Mapping to SM adds linear order, prosody, and detailed phonetic properties, and in the IM example deletes the lower copy of *which book*, yielding *which book John will read*. This SO can appear either unchanged, as in *guess* [*which book John will read*], or with a raising rule of a type familiar in many languages, yielding *which book will John read.*

It is important to note that throughout, the operations described satisfy MC. That includes the deletion operation in the mapping to SM, which sharply reduces the computational and articulatory load in externalizing the Merge-generated SO. To put it loosely, what reaches the mind has the right semantic form, but what reaches the ear has gaps that have to be filled by the hearer. These "filler-gap" problems pose significant complications for parsing/perception. In such cases, I-language is "well-designed" for thought but poses difficulties for language use, an important observation that in fact generalizes quite widely and might turn out to be exceptionless, when the question arises.

Note that what reaches the mind lacks order, while what reaches the ear is ordered. Linear order, then, should not enter into the syntactic-semantic computation. Rather, it is imposed by externalization, presumably as a reflex of properties of the SM system, which requires linearization: we cannot speak in parallel or articulate structures. For many simple cases, this seems accurate: thus there is no difference in the interpretation of verb-object constructions in head-initial or head-final constructions.

The same is true in more complex cases, including "exotic" structures that are particularly interesting because they rarely occur but are understood in a determinate way, for example, parasitic gap constructions. The "real gap" RG (which cannot be filled) may either precede or follow the "parasitic gap" PG (which can be filled), but cannot be in a dominant (c-command) structural relation to the PG, as illustrated in the following:

(1) Guess who [[your interest in PG] clearly appeals to RG].
(2) Who did you [talk to RG [without recognizing PG].
(3) *Guess who [GAP [admires [$_{NP}$ your interest in GAP]]].

Crucially, grammatical status and semantic interpretation are determined by structural hierarchy while linear order is irrelevant, much as in the case of verb-initial versus verb-final. And all of this is known by the language user even though evidence for language acquisition is minuscule or entirely non-existent.

The general property of language illustrated by these cases is that linguistic rules are invariably *structure-dependent*. The principle is so strong that when there is a conflict between the computationally simple property of minimal linear distance and the far more complex computational property of minimal structural distance, the latter is always selected. That is an important and puzzling fact, which was observed when early efforts to construct generative grammars were undertaken. On the surface, it seems to conflict with the quite natural and generally operative principles of MC.

To illustrate, consider the following sentences:

(4) Birds that fly instinctively swim.
(5) The desire to fly instinctively appeals to children.
(6) Instinctively, birds that fly swim.
(7) Instinctively, the desire to fly appeals to children.

The structures of (6) and (7) are, roughly, as indicated by bracketing in (6') and (7') respectively:

(6') Instinctively, [birds that fly] [swim]]
(7') Instinctively, [[the desire to fly] [appeals [to children]]]

In both cases, "fly" is the closest verb to "instinctively" in linear distance, but the more remote in structural distance.

Examples (4) and (5) are ambiguous ("fly instinctively", "instinctively swim/appeal"), but in (6') and (7') the adverb is construed only with the remote verb. The immediate question is why the ambiguity disappears; and more puzzling, why is it resolved in terms of the computationally complex operation of locating the *structurally* closest verb rather than the much simpler operation of locating the *linearly* closest verb? The property holds of all relevant constructions in all languages, in apparent conflict with MC. Furthermore, the knowledge is once again acquired without relevant evidence.

There have been many attempts by linguists and other cognitive scientists to show that these outcomes can be determined by some kind of learning mechanism from available data. All fail, irremediably, which is not surprising, as the simple example just given indicates.[8]

There is a very simple and quite natural solution to the puzzle, the only one known: languages are optimally designed, based on the simplest computational operation, Merge, which is order-free. Equipped with just this information, the child acquiring language never considers linear order in determining how to account for the data of experience; this is the only option open to the I-language satisfying the Basic Property, given that the general architecture of language established by UG satisfies MC.

The strongest thesis we can formulate about human language is that MC holds quite generally: the Strong Minimalist Thesis SMT. Not many years ago it would have appeared to be so absurd that it was never even contemplated. In recent years, evidence has been mounting that suggests otherwise.

Assuming SMT we at once have an explanation for a number of quite puzzling phenomena. One is the ubiquity of displacement – interpretation of a phrase where it appears as well as in another position in which its basic semantic role is determined, a phenomenon that appeared to require mechanisms that are an "imperfection" of language design. Under SMT, as we have seen, displacement should be the norm (namely, by IM) and would have to be blocked by some arbitrary stipulation. Hence a barrier against displacement would be an "imperfection." Correspondingly, any approach to language that bars IM has a double burden of justification: for the stipulation blocking the simplest case, and for any new mechanisms introduced to account for the phenomena. Furthermore, SMT yields at once the "copy theory" of displacement, which provides an appropriate structure for interpretation at CI, dispensing with complex operations of "reconstruction." And as we have just seen, it provides a solution to the puzzles of structure-dependence, an overarching principle of language design. These are, I think, quite significant results, of a kind hitherto not attained or even contemplated in the rich tradition of linguistic inquiry.

Further inquiries, which I cannot review here, carry the account further.

Note again that while MC yields appropriate structures at CI, it poses difficulties at SM. Looking further, there is substantial evidence that externalization to SM is the primary locus of the complexity, variability, and mutability of language, and that, correspondingly, mastering the specific mode of externalization is the main task of language acquisition: mastering the phonetics

---

8 For review, see Berwick et al. (2011).

and phonology of the language, its morphology, and its lexical idiosyncracies (including what is called "Saussurean arbitrariness," the specific choice of sound-meaning correspondences for minimal word-like elements).

We might proceed to entertain another bold but not implausible thesis: that generation of CI – narrow syntax and construal/interpretive rules – is uniform among languages, or nearly so. In fact, realistic alternatives are not easy to imagine, in the light of the fact that the systems are acquired on the basis of little or no evidence, as even the few simple examples given earlier illustrate. The conclusion also comports well with the very few known facts about origin of language. These appear to place the emergence of language within a time frame that is very brief in evolutionary time, hardly more than an instant, and with no evolutionary change since. To be Hence we would expect what evolved – UG – to be quite simple.

Note that to be seriously considered, any speculation about origin of language must account for the emergence of the Basic Property, which cannot be approached in small steps, just as evolution of the arithmetical capacity is not facilitated by ability to deal with small numbers. The leap from 4 or 1 million to an unbounded number system is no easier than the leap from 1 to that goal.

The considerations just reviewed are a sample of those that suggest that the Basic Property is not quite as formulated so far in this discussion. Rather, the Basic Property of I-language, determined by UG, is a finitely-specified generative procedure, represented in the brain, that yields a discrete infinity of hierarchically structured expressions, each with a determinate interpretation at the CI interface. Ancillary principles may externalize the internally-generated expression in one or another sensory modality.

There is neurological and psycholinguistic evidence to support these conclusions about the architecture of language and the ancillary character of externalization. Research conducted in Milan a decade ago, initiated by Andrea Moro, showed that nonsense systems keeping to UG principles of structure-dependence elicit normal activation in the language areas of the brain, but much simpler systems using linear order in violation of UG yield diffuse activation, implying that subjects are treating them as a puzzle, not a language. There is confirming evidence by Neil Smith and Ianthi-Maria Tsimpli in their investigation of a cognitively deficient but linguistically gifted subject; he was able to master the nonsense language satisfying structure-dependence, but not the one using the simpler computation involving linear order. Smith and Tsimpli also made the interesting observation that normals can solve the problem of the UG-violating language if it is presented to them as a puzzle, but not if it is presented as a language, presumably activating the language faculty. These studies suggest very intriguing paths that can be pursued in neuroscience and experimental psycholinguistics.[9]

Note that these conclusions about language architecture undermine a conventional contemporary doctrine that language is primarily a system of communication, and presumably evolved from simpler communication systems. If, as the evidence strongly indicates, even externalization is an ancillary property of language, then specific uses of externalized language, as in communication, are an even more peripheral phenomenon – a conclusion also supported by other evidence, I think. Language appears to be primarily an instrument of thought, much in accord with the spirit of the tradition. There is no reason to suppose that it evolved as a system of communication.

A reasonable surmise today, I think, is that within the narrow time frame suggested by the available facts, some small rewiring of the brain yielded the modified Basic Property – of course in an individual, who was then uniquely capable of thought: reflection, planning, inference, and so on, in principle without bounds. It is possible that other capacities, notably arithmetical competence, are by-products. In the absence of external pressures, the Basic Property should be optimal, as determined by laws of nature, notably MC, satisfying SMT, rather as a snowflake takes its intricate shape. The mutation might proliferate to further generations, possibly coming to dominate a small breeding group. At that point, externalization would be valuable. The task would be to map the products of the internal system satisfying SMT to sensorimotor systems that had been present for hundreds of thousands of years, in some cases far more; thus there is evidence that the auditory systems of apes are very much like those of humans. That mapping poses a hard cognitive problem, which can be solved in many ways, each of them complex, all of them mutable – very much what we observe, as noted earlier. Carrying out these tasks might involve little or no evolutionary change.

If these reflections are on the right track, then the primary task for linguistic research is to fill in the huge gaps in this picture, that is, to show that the vast array of phenomena in the humanly accessible languages can be explained properly in something like these terms. And remaining in the domain of mystery for the moment – perhaps forever – is the origin of the atoms of computation and the nature of the "puppeteer," the creative aspect of language use that was the prime concern of the long and rich tradition that has been revived in a new form in the generative/biolinguistic enterprise.

---

9 Musso et al. (2003); Smith and Tsimpli (1995); Smith (1999).

I remarked earlier that in my student days in mid-20th century, it seemed as though the major problems of the study of language had been pretty much solved and that the enterprise, though challenging, was approaching a terminal point that could be fairly clearly perceived. The picture today could not be more different.

References

Berwick, Robert C., Paul Pietroski, Beracah Yankama and Noam Chomsky. 2011. "Poverty of the Stimulus Revisited." *Cognitive Science* 35: 1–36.

Bizzi, Emilio and Robert Ajemian. 2015. "A Hard Scientific Quest: Understanding Voluntary Movements." *Daedalus* 144/1: 83–95.

Chomsky, Noam. 1966. *Cartesian Linguistics* (Harper & Row). Third edition (2009, revised, edited with an introduction by James McGilvray; ebooks, Cambridge University).

Chomsky, Noam. 1995. *The Minimalist Program*. MIT.

Curtiss, Susan. 2012. "Revisiting Modularity: Using Language as a Window to the Mind." In Robert Berwick and Massimo Piattelli-Palmarini (eds.) *Rich Languages from Poor Inputs*. Oxford University.

Jespersen, Otto. 1922. *Philosophy of Grammar*. Chicago University.

Joos, Martin, ed. 1957. *Readings in Linguistics*, Washington: American Council of Learned Societies.

Lenneberg, Eric H. 1967. *Biological foundations of language* (John Wiley and Sons, 1967).

Musso, Mariachristina, Andrea Moro, Volkmar Gluache, Komma statt Punkt verwenden, Michel Rijntjes, Jürgen Reichenbach, Christian Bücheli and Cornelius Weiller. 2003. *Nature Neuroscience* 6/774–781.

Smith, Neil. 1999. *Chomsky: Ideas and Ideals*. Cambridge.

Smith, Nail and Ianthi-Maria Tsimpli. 1995. *The Mind of a Savant: Language Learning and Modularity*. Blackwell.

Tattersall, Ian. 2012. *Masters of the Planet*. Palgrave Macmillan.

General and Comparative Research on Slavic

Željko Bošković

On the Impossibility of Moving IPs and V-2 Clauses and Labeling

1. Introduction

There are a number of cases where certain phrases have been noted to be unable to move for no apparent reason. One such case involves IPs not dominated by CPs. Another one concerns V-2 clauses in German. The goal of this paper is to provide a unified account of a number of such cases, including these two. In particular, it will be argued there is a larger generalization underlying all these cases which can be deduced within the labeling system (Chomsky 2013).

The point of departure in the discussion will be the ban on moving IPs, including IPs not dominated by CP (Abels 2003). It will be shown that Bošković's (2016a) labeling account of the traditional ban on movement from moved elements provides a new perspective on the ban on moving IPs. The account, however, has broad consequences, generalizing the ban on moving IPs to a number of cases involving phrases other than IPs. In particular, the ban on moving IPs will be seen as an instance of a broader ban on moving phrases with feature-sharing Specs, hence will be unified with several cases that involve phrases other than IPs, including the ban on moving V-2 clauses in German (Reis 1997, Wurmbrand 2014). The ban on moving phrases with feature-sharing Specs will be shown to follow from independent assumptions regarding phases/labeling. Although the account relies on several mechanisms from Bošković's (2016a) account of the ban on movement out of moved elements, and in fact in a sense unifies the ban on the movement of IPs and more generally, phrases with feature-sharing Specs with the ban on movement out of moved elements, it relies on different assumptions regarding the timing of labeling from those adopted in Bošković (2016a); as a result, it requires re-examination of several constructions discussed in Bošković (2016a).

The paper is organized as follows. Section 2 discusses the ban on moving IPs. Since the account of the ban will be stated within Bošković's (2016a) approach to the ban on movement from moved elements, in section 3 I discuss the ban in question. Section 4 discusses timing of labeling, departing from Bošković (2016a) here. Section 5 returns to the impossibility of moving IPs, providing an account of the ban, which is extended to movement of other phrases (like German V-2 CPs) in section 6. Section 7 discusses more general consequences of the account for the structure and movement of other phrases. Section 8 concludes the paper.

2. The ban on moving IPs

A straightforward illustration of the impossibility of moving IPs is provided by (1).

(1) *[$_{IP}$ His$_i$ brother likes Mary]$_j$ everyone$_i$ believes [$_{CP}$ that t$_j$]

Abels (2003) provides an account of (1) in terms of his generalization that complements of phase heads cannot move, which follows from the PIC, which requires movement from phase XP to pass through the edge of XP, and antilocality, the ban on movement that is too short (I will adopt Bošković's 2013a approach to antilocality, which requires movement to cross a phrase). CP being a phase, the PIC forces IP to move to SpecCP, which violates antilocality.

There are also other ways of ruling out (1). As Bošković (2013b) notes, we may have here a *that*-trace effect. If local subject movement across *that* leads to a locality violation, it does not seem implausible that even more local movement of IP across *that* also leads to a violation. Further, as discussed in section 3, a number of authors have argued that only phases can move. The embedded CP in (1) is a phase, but the embedded IP is not – it is a complement of a phase head. If only phases can move, the embedded IP in (1) then cannot move.

There is then no shortage of ways to rule out the illicit movement of the IP in (1). What is important here is that the IP in (1) is dominated by a CP. However, Abels (2003) shows that even IPs not dominated by CPs are immobile (see also Bošković 2013b). Consider (2).

(2) *[$_{IP}$ morgen zu reparieren] hat ihn der Hans beschlossen
tomorrow to repair has it the Hans decided
'Hans decided to repair it tomorrow.' (Abels 2003: 151)

(3) weil ihn der Hans [$_{IP}$ morgen zu reparieren] beschlossen hat
because it the Hans tomorrow to repair decided has

Following Wurmbrand (2001), Abels shows the infinitive in (2) is an IP. Briefly, the adverb indicates the presence of IP and pronominalization ensures the lack of CP since it is not allowed from CP infinitives. (2) then indicates that even IPs not dominated by a CP cannot move (for more evidence, see Bošković

2013b).[1] The mechanisms discussed regarding (1) are irrelevant to (2). The *that*-trace effect and Abels's generalization are obviously irrelevant since the moved IP is not dominated by CP. As for the assumption that only phases can move, Bošković (2014, 2015) and Wurmbrand (2013) argue that the highest clausal projection is a phase, providing a number of arguments to that effect. When the highest clausal projection is a CP, the CP is a phase; when it is an IP, then IP is a phase. In this approach, which will be adopted below, the assumption that only phases can move cannot help in accounting for (2) since the moved IP is a phase, in contrast to the IP in (1). Why is then (2) ill-formed? In section 4 I will show that a modified version of Bošković's (2106a) account of the ban on movement from moved elements can account for such cases, making them part of a more general effect not limited to IPs. Thus, I will show the account provides an explanation for the immobility of V-2 clauses in German (4), as well as a number of other cases. (The V-2 clause is moved to SpecIP in (4a) and the sentence initial position in (4b); in (4c), it stays in situ.)

(4) a. *weil [$_{CP}$ den Peter mag niemand] allgemein bekannt ist.
since the$_{ACC}$ Peter likes nobody$_{NOM}$ commonly known is
'since nobody likes Peter is commonly known' (Wurmbrand 2014: 155)

b. *[Er$_i$ sei unheimlich beliebt] möchte jeder$_i$ gern glauben
he is$_{SUBJ}$ immensely popular would.like everyone like to believe
'Everyone would like to believe he is immensely popular.'
(Wurmbrand 2014: 155)

c. Sie sagte den Peter mag niemand t$_{ob}$ t$_V$
she said the$_{ACC}$ Peter likes nobody$_{NOM}$ (Wurmbrand 2014: 153)

I will, however, first make a digression to discuss the ban on extraction from moved elements.

3. On the ban on movement out of moved elements

Numerous works have argued that (5) holds (see the references in Bošković 2016a).

(5) Movement is not possible out of moved elements

1 Abels (2003) gives an account of the case where IP moves to SpecCP. However, it doesn't extend to movement to other positions (Bošković 2013b) or the cases from section 6. (Bošković 2013b gives cases that he *analyzes* as involving very short IP-movement; however, they seem analyzable in terms of base-generation or PF movement).

The Subject Condition provides one illustration of (5) since under the VP Internal Subject Hypothesis extraction out of a subject in SpecIP involves extraction out of a moved element.[2]

(6) ?*I wonder [$_{CP}$ who$_i$ [$_{DP}$ friends of t_i]$_j$ [$_{vP}$ t_j hired Mary]]

Turning to objects, Lasnik (2001) argues that the object in pseudogapping undergoes object shift, which is followed by VP ellipsis. Crucially, such objects cannot be extracted from, as (7) shows. Particle constructions where the object precedes the particle also involve object shift (see Lasnik 2001, Johnson 1991). Again, (8a) is degraded.

(7) ?*Who will Bill select a painting of, and who$_j$ will Susan [a photograph of t_j]$_i$ ~~[$_{VP}$ select t_i]~~

(8) a. ?*Who$_j$ did you call [friends of t_j]$_i$ up t_i?
b. cf. Who$_i$ did you call up friends of t_i

Torrego (1998) shows Spanish *a*-marked objects must move. They also disallow extraction.

(9) ?*[De quién]$_j$ has visitado [$_{DP}$ a muchos amigos t_j]$_i$ [$_{VP}$ .. t_i]
of whom have.2sg visited many friends
'Who have you visited many friends of?' (Gallego and Uriagereka 2007)

(5) also holds for elements undergoing A'-movement (10) and traditional rightward movement (11). P-stranding is also not possible out of moved PPs, as in (12).

(10) ?*Vowel harmony$_i$, I think that [articles about t_i]$_j$ you should read t_j

(11) ?*What$_i$ did you give t_j to John [a movie about t_i]$_j$?

(12) *Which table$_i$ did you think that [on t_i]$_j$ John put the book t_j?

---

2 Extraction is allowed from subjects in SpecvP, as in Spanish (i) (it's disallowed if the subject moves to SpecIP).

(i) ¿De qué conferenciantes$_i$ te parece que me$_z$ van a impresionar$_v$ [$_{vP}$[$_{DP}$
of what speakers cl-2sg seems that cl-1sg go-3pl to to-impress
las propuestas t_i][t_z t_v]
the proposals
'Which speakers does it seem to you that the proposals by will impress me?
(Uriagereka 1988)

(5) thus has strong motivation.[3] Bošković (2016a) deduces (5) from the phase/labeling system. The former concerns phasehood criteria, namely (13) (see Chomsky 2000, 2001, Rackowski and Richards 2005, Cheng 2012, Matushansky 2005, Harwood 2013, Bošković 2015).

(13) Only phases can undergo movement.

Chomsky (2013) proposes a system that allows unlabeled objects during the derivation, but not final representations. There, when a head and a phrase merge, the head labels the resulting object. When two phrases merge, there are two ways to label: through prominent feature sharing or traces, traces being ignored for labeling. (14) illustrates the former with the merger of *which book* and wh-C (CP at the relevant point). Both the wh-phrase and the CP have the Q-feature–what is projected (i.e. determines the label of the resulting object) is the Q-feature.

(14) I wonder [$_{CP}$ which book$_i$ [$_{C'}$ C [John bought t$_i$]]]

Turning to (15), Chomsky assumes successive cyclic movement does not involve feature sharing, which follows Bošković (1997a, 2002, 2007, 2008). There is then no feature sharing between *that* and the wh-phrase passing through its edge. Since labeling via feature sharing is not an option the embedded clause cannot be labeled when *what* moves there (15b). Since traces are ignored for labeling, ? is labeled as CP only after *what* moves to the matrix clause.

(15) a. What$_i$ do you think [$_{CP}$ t'$_i$ [$_{C'}$ that [he bought t$_i$]]]
b. [$_?$ what [$_{CP}$ that [John bought t$_i$]]]

Bošković (2016a) shows this treatment of successive-cyclic movement and (13) deduce (5). Consider (16a), where YP moves from moved XP. Before these movements, we have (16b).

(16) a. YP$_i$ [$_{XP}$ ... t$_i$ ...]$_j$ ... t$_j$
b. [$_{XP}$ ... YP ...]

Recall only phases can move: for XP to move it must be a phase. Given the PIC, for YP to move out of XP, YP must move to the edge of XP, which must precede the movement of XP itself given the cycle. As is always the case with successive cyclic movement, the merger of YP and XP yields an unlabeled object. Now, for

3 There have been claims that (5) doesn't hold; for relevant discussion, see Bošković (2016a). Note, however, that under Bošković's (2016a) account movement is not always expected to be disallowed from moved elements.

Chomsky, phases are CPs, vPs, and DPs (see Bošković 2013a, 2014 on APs and PPs). However, the result of the merger of YP and XP is none of these; it in fact does not have a label at all, hence it does not count as a phase (in other words, phases require label-determination, hence unlabeled objects cannot be phases).

To illustrate with the Subject Condition, consider (17a), with the structure in (17b).

(17) a. *I wonder who$_i$ [friends of t$_i$] left Mary
b. $[_{IP}$ I… $[_{vP}$ $[_{?}$ who $[_{DP}$ subject]]]]

Subjects being phases, what moves out of it must move to its edge. Given the cycle, this happens before the subject moves from vP. Merger of *who* and DP yields an unlabeled object, which, not having a label, is not a phase. The phrase marked with ? in (17) then cannot move.

Note the account allows remnant movement, where YP moves from XP before XP moves. Consider vP fronting (18a). The result of the merger of the subject and vP cannot be labeled (Chomsky 2013), as in (18b). The subject moves to SpecIP; its trace being ignored for labeling, the relevant element is labeled as vP (18b). Since vP is a phase it can move (18a).

(18) a. $[_{vP}$ t$_i$ kiss Mary]$_j$$[_{TP}$ she$_i$ did t$_j$]
b. $[_{?}$ She $[_{vP}$ kiss Mary]]
c. $[_{IP}$ She$_i$ $[_{vP}$ t$_i$ kiss Mary]]

The above provides a new perspective on (5), where the problem with movement of YP out of moved XP does not arise when YP moves out of XP; it arises already with movement of XP, i.e. XP itself cannot undergo movement here. Movement of XP then does not freeze the internal structure of XP; rather, movement of YP to the edge of XP prevents movement of XP.

All the cases from section 3 involve successive-cyclic movement via the edge of XP, hence they also involve movement of the Spec itself (it's the very nature of successive-cyclic movement that YP undergoing it cannot stay in an intermediate Spec for independent reasons), which means they also involve movement from a moved element. This has led to the 'illusion' that this later movement is responsible for the ungrammaticality of the relevant constructions.

4. On the timing of labeling

In the above cases where XP with YP at its edge couldn't move YP undergoes successive-cyclic movement through the edge of XP, which means it does not undergo feature-sharing at the XP edge. What would happen if YP does undergo feature-sharing? With successive-cyclic movement labeling of the YP-ZP merger was not possible (due to the lack of feature-sharing); YP had to move away. However, with feature-sharing merger labeling is in principle possible at the merger itself. The issue is then whether there are other factors that would delay labeling beyond the creation of the relevant structure with feature-sharing merger. The resolution of the issue affects the answer to the question we are interested in: whether an element that moves to the edge of XP, or is base-generated at its edge, and undergoes feature-sharing at the edge of XP would freeze XP for movement. If feature-sharing labeling must be delayed, this would be the case. However, XP would not be frozen for movement if feature-sharing configurations can result in immediate labeling. The issue is then when labeling via feature sharing occurs.

Several proposals have been made regarding this issue. In Chomsky (2013), all labeling, including feature-sharing labeling, occurs when the structure is sent to the interfaces. This approach has several problems, noted in Bošković (2015, 2016b). Thus, to determine that a phasal level has been reached (which in turn determines the points of spell-out, i.e. when the structure is sent to the interfaces), some labeling is necessary. E.g., we cannot determine whether a phasal level has been reached with [$_?$ X Y] before the labeling of this object. But if labeling is done only when a phasal level is reached, we have an obvious chicken-or-the-egg problem here. Another problem arises when both elements, e.g. both the complement and the head of a phrase, move, given that traces are ignored for labeling (see also Shlonsky 2014).

Bošković (2016b) proposes an approach to the timing of labeling that resolves these problems. In Chomsky (2013), labeling with a head-phrase merger is done rather differently from a phrase-phrase merger: with the former, labeling occurs via minimal search (MS), the same operation as Agree Closest, a syntactic mechanism falling under minimal computation. MS does not determine the label when two phrases merge. Given the difference, Bošković (2016b) argues for a timing difference in labeling, referring to it as TOL. Since the labeling of the head-complement merger is done through essentially a syntactic mechanism, it occurs when the relevant configuration is created. On the other hand, labeling with the merger of two phrases occurs when the structure is sent to the interfaces, given Chomsky's assumption that unlabeled objects are uninterpretable. Under this approach, labeling in the case of a head-complement merger in fact occurs for a strictly syntactic reason, namely, subcategorization, the underlying assumption being that satisfying subcategorization requires that the element with the requirement to take a complement projects, otherwise, there would be no head-complement relation here. This concern does not arise with feature-sharing Spec labeling.

TOL resolves the problems with Chomsky (2013) noted above. No problem arises when both the complement and the head of a phrase move although traces are ignored for labeling since the result of head-complement merger is labeled immediately: the head determines the label before it moves. The spell-out issue is also resolved. Recall phases determine spell-out points (when the structure is sent to the interfaces). If labeling occurs for interpretive reasons it should occur at this point. A chicken-or-the-egg style problem then arises. Phasehood determination requires labeling: to know whether something is a phase we need to know its label (Bošković's 2016a account of (5) in fact confirms unlabeled objects cannot be phases). Since phases determine spell-out points, without any labeling structure cannot be sent to the interfaces, which in turn is needed for labeling to occur under a purely interpretative approach to labeling. The issue doesn't arise if head-complement merger is labeled immediately since this is all we need to determine spell-out points. Moreover, Bošković (2016b) gives an account of a number of locality effects that is crucially based on TOL, in particular, the Subject Condition, the Adjunct Condition, Richards's (2001) tucking, the full range of Comp-trace effects (in declarative, relative, and extraposed clauses), and the effect wh-movement has on agreement in languages like Kinande. I will then adopt here this approach to the timing of labeling.

What is important for our purposes is that under TOL, labeling with feature-sharing Specs is delayed – it does not take place immediately but only when the structure is sent to the interfaces. As a result, labeling at the phasal edge is quite generally delayed beyond the creation of the relevant structure. In the next section I will explore the consequences of adopting this approach to the timing of labeling, where with feature-sharing Specs labeling takes place when the structure is sent to spell-out, for the issues this paper is concerned with.[4]

---

4 This differs from Bošković (2016a), who assumes all labeling may occur as soon as possible. I return to this below. A word of caution is in order. As Bošković (2016a) notes, Bošković's (2016a) treatment of the timing of feature-sharing labeling is in fact consistent with Chomsky (2013) as well as Bošković (2016b) if we interpret labeling taking place when the structure is sent to the interface as labeling taking place at the phasal level for the whole phase, as Chomsky (2013) does. However, since what is sent to the interfaces is the phasal complement, not the whole phase, if labeling is driven by interface considerations, taking place for interpretive reasons, as Chomsky (2013) suggests, labeling should take place at the phasal level but only for the phasal complement, which is what I will assume here. I will take this to determine the timing of labeling of a phrase-phrase merger.

5. Deducing the immobility of IPs

An immediate consequence of this approach to labeling is that the above account of the ban on extraction from moved elements extends to the ban on moving IPs. Recall that IPs are immobile, even IPs not dominated by a CP. As a reminder, (19) provides evidence for the immobility of IPs not dominated by CP (as discussed in section 2, the infinitive here is an IP).

(19) *[$_{IP}$ morgen zu reparieren] hat ihn der Hans beschlossen.
tomorrow to repair has it the Hans decided
(Abels 2003:151)

As discussed above, the standard accounts of the immobility of IP dominated by CP do not extend to such cases. E.g. Abels' generalization that phase head complements do not move is irrelevant here since the moved IP is not dominated by CP. ((13) is also irrelevant since, as the highest clausal projection, this IP is a phase.) However, Bošković's (2016a) account of the ban on movement out of moved elements extends to (19) under TOL. Recall that the problem with movement of YP out of moved XP does not arise when YP moves out of XP; it arises already with movement of XP – XP itself cannot move, i.e. movement of XP does not freeze XP for subextraction; rather, movement of YP to the edge of XP prevents movement of XP. It turns out that under TOL, the IP in (19) is prevented from moving for exactly the same reason.

Recall labeling with feature-sharing occurs when the structure is sent to spell-out. The relevant IP being a phase, its complement is sent to spell-out early in the derivation. However, under the standard assumption that the complement of phase α is sent to spell-out only <u>after</u> movement to the edge of α (the final structure is also sent to spell-out), the IP itself will not be sent to spell-out until the full structure is built in (19) (the IP will move to the edge of matrix vP before matrix VP is spelled out). The IP then moves before it is sent to spell-out. Given the standard assumption that such cases involve PRO in the Spec of the infinitive, the infinitival IP is labeled through feature sharing, which means the labeling of this IP would occur only <u>after</u> it moves. In other words, we are moving here an unlabeled element, which is disallowed. We then have an account of the immobility of IPs not dominated by CP. Such IPs are phases. However, they still cannot undergo movement because they are labeled through feature-sharing. Given that labeling through feature-sharing is delayed until the structure is sent to the interfaces, the labeling of such IPs takes place too late for them to be able to move.[5]

The account extends to the distribution of embedded declarative clauses not headed by *that* in English, which, as is well-known, cannot undergo movement.

(20) a. *[John likes Mary]$_i$ is widely believed t$_i$.
b. cf. That John likes Mary is widely believed.
c. *[John likes Mary]$_i$ Jane believed t$_i$.
d. cf. That John likes Mary, Jane believed.

A number of works have argued the moved clause in (20a,c) is an IP (see Bošković 1997a and references therein). As discussed, the highest clausal projection functions as a phase, which makes this IP a phase (due to the absence of CP). In principle, the IP can then move. However, the problem is that it is labeled via feature-sharing. Under the above approach to the timing of labeling, it would be labeled too late, i.e. after movement, which means IP movement in (20) violates (13) (the moved element is in fact not an IP at the point of movement). In other words, the above account of (19) extends to (20), under the IP account of the moved clauses in (20).

Note, however, that the account is more general. It does not only ban movement of IPs in the constructions under consideration but it quite generally bans movement of phases with feature-sharing Specs. There is evidence that the effect is indeed more general. There are CP accounts of *that*-less declaratives, where they are headed by a null C. Under one such account, the above analysis of (20) can be maintained. Pesetsky and Torrego (2001) argue the clauses in question are CPs, with the subject located in SpecCP. The above account of the immobility of *that*-less clauses can then be maintained under Pesetsky and Torrego's CP analysis.

I conclude therefore that Bošković's (2016a) account of the ban on movement out of moved elements can be extended to account for the immobility of IPs not dominated by CP under the approach to the timing of labeling from Bošković (2016b). The account is more general: it rules out movement of the IPs in question because such cases involve movement of phases with feature-sharing Specs. Such movement is disallowed; as a result, the account can be maintained under Pesetsky and Torrego's CP analysis of *that*-less declarative clauses.

5 Bare IPs with no Spec could then in principle move. However, I am not aware of any uncontroversial cases of this type, where we can be sure that there isn't even a null expletive in SpecIP (the thorny EPP issue arises here).

6. Additional cases

Above, I have interpreted the unacceptability of (19)-(20) as an indication that phrases with feature-sharing Specs cannot move, which follows from (13) if labeling is delayed with feature-sharing. This section discusses additional cases of this effect which do not involve IPs.

Consider first V-2 clauses in German. As discussed in section 2, they cannot move.

(21) *weil [$_{CP}$ den Peter mag niemand] allgemein bekannt ist.
since the$_{ACC}$ Peter likes nobody$_{NOM}$ commonly known is
(Wurmbrand 2014:155)

From the current perspective the immobility of such CPs is not surprising; the system in fact provides a straightforward account of the immobility of V-2 clauses. They involve movement to SpecCP, with the moved phrase undergoing feature sharing in the moved position (this is the labeling update of the Spec-Head agreement analysis.) Movement of the V-2 CP in (21) is then another case of movement of a phrase with a feature-sharing Spec, which is disallowed.

Consider now the mysterious ban on raising the wh-clause in specificational pseudoclefts (Higgins 1973, Bošković 1997b). (22) is unambiguously specificational (suppose the relevant property for the predicational reading is that John is a doctor; John can be proud, but being a doctor can't be). Importantly, the wh-clause in such pseudoclefts cannot undergo raising (23).

(22) [What John is] is proud.
(23) *[What John is]$_i$ seems t$_i$ to be proud.

(23) involves movement of a CP phase with a feature-sharing Spec. Its unacceptability then provides additional evidence that such phases cannot undergo movement. The above account of the immobility of IPs not dominated by CP and V-2 CPs can thus be extended to capture the otherwise mysterious ban on raising the wh-clause of specificational pseudoclefts.[6]

Note that the corresponding element can move in predicational pseudoclefts, as in (24), which is unambiguously predicational (being a doctor can be

6 The counterweight of reverse specificational pseudoclefts can move, as *in [Proud of his job]$_i$ seems t$_i$ to be what John is* (see Bošković 1997b). This is not surprising since the problem from (23) does not arise here.

worthwhile but John cannot be worthwhile). However, the element in question in predicational pseudoclefts is standardly analyzed as a free relative, free relatives in turn being analyzed as DPs, not as CPs with a wh-phrase in their Spec; see here Donati (2006), where the wh-phrase actually heads the DP.

(24) [What John is]$_i$ seems t$_i$ to be worthwhile.

Indirect questions are also relevant here. The unacceptability of passivizing indirect questions can in fact be interpreted as providing additional evidence that phrases with feature sharing Specs cannot move. (I use passivization to minimize the possibility of analyzing what follows the clause as an adsentential, but Nordström 2010 notes topicalization is also disallowed here.)

(25) *Who John hired$_i$ was asked t$_i$ (by Mary).

There is, however, an interfering factor when checking movement of this kind of clauses more broadly. Many languages do not front wh-phrases to the highest clausal projection; in fact, in many languages, for example Spanish, an overt C element can precede a fronted wh-phrase.

(26) Julio preguntó que qué$_i$ íbamos a comprar t$_i$
Julio asked that what.(we) were.going to buy

This effect may be more general, with additional structure present above a fronted wh-phrase in indirect questions even when it is not manifested overtly. In fact, in Rizzi's (1997) split CP, wh-phrases do not move to the highest clausal projection. Under the current analysis of (25), a language that allows (25), or more generally, movement of such clauses, would be analyzed in these terms, as involving additional structure above the wh-phrase (which may be null).

There may in fact be some variation here. French speakers generally disallow cases like (27) and more generally non-complement embedded questions (Hout 1981, Pesetsky 2008).

(27) *Quand Pierre viendra est inconnu.
when Pierre will-come is unknown

However, some speakers do accept such examples (Hout 1981, Pesetsky 2008). The pattern where they are disallowed can be easily explained from the current perspective, providing additional evidence that phrases with feature sharing Specs cannot move. For speakers who allow such cases, it may be that there is additional structure above the wh-phrase along the lines suggested above, or that we are dealing with some kind of nominalization here (e.g. *time when he will come*, with a null nominal; see Huang 1982, Bresnan 1994, for such proposals).[7]

7. Some consequences of the proposed account

A number of cases thus fall into place under the approach to labeling from Bošković (2016b), given (13). However, the proposed account makes a strong prediction: phrases with feature-sharing Specs should never be allowed to move. This will call for a reanalysis, or provide evidence for particular accounts, of a number of constructions. E.g., the DP in (28) cannot be analyzed as having *John('s)* in SpecDP since (28) would then involve movement of a phase with a feature-sharing Spec. However, an account along the lines of Kayne (1994), where the possessor is located in SpecPossP, PossP being dominated by DP, is fully consistent with the above analysis: what is moved in (28) is a phase, but not a phase with a feature-sharing Spec.

(28) $[_{DP}$ John's picture$]_i$ was sold t_i

To illustrate the effects of the above system with another case, consider German (29), where a phrase containing a nominative subject not moved to SpecIP is fronted (see Wurmbrand 2006).

---

7 There may be some variation in English too. Pesetsky (2008) finds (27) acceptable in English and Wurmbrand (2014) gives (i) (see also this work for German). However, Troy Messick (p.c) finds (i) unacceptable.
(i) Which book Mary read yesterday is not known
If there is variation here, it can be handled as suggested above regarding French, the unacceptable cases involving movement of phrases with feature sharing Specs, and the acceptable ones additional structure above the fronted wh-phrase, either within split-CP or some kind of nominalization. The issue may also be whether speakers who find (i)/(27) acceptable, find such examples acceptable only with verbs that need not take questions as complements; if so, indirect questions may be immobile even for these speakers (but note that in Spanish such verbs <u>must</u> have *que* 'that' (i.e. additional structure) above the wh-phrase on the question reading, see Villa-García 2012. Another possibility is that speakers who accept examples like (i) or (27) parse them as involving a relative clause (*which book that Mary read…*) or kind of a cleft (*when it is that Pierre will come…*); Pesetsky (2008) in fact suggests such cases involve *that* which is deleted in PF, which would fit such a treatment (the possibility of a free relative also needs to be quite generally controlled for when considering this type of examples).

(29) [$_{vP}$ Ein junger Hund einen Briefträger gebissen] hat hier schon oft
a_{NOM} young dog a_{ACC} mailman bitten has here already often
'It has happened here already that a young dog has bitten a mailman.'
(Wurmbrand 2006:198)

Assuming that, in contrast to English, a subject in SpecvP can undergo feature-sharing in German, hence subjects need not move in German (Chomsky 2013, Bošković 2016a), (29) cannot be analyzed as involving vP fronting, since then it would involve movement of a phrase with a feature-sharing Spec. However, Wurmbrand (2013) and Bošković (2014) argue the middle-field phase is not vP but AspectP (the highest projection in the extended domain of V being a phase). (29) is then analyzed in accordance with (13) as involving AspectP fronting.

I will not discuss here other cases where the above account has an effect on particular constructions, except to note a couple of cases from Bošković's (2016a), the reason being that Bošković's (2016a) account of these cases crucially relies on the possibility of immediate labeling with feature-sharing (see fn 4), hence cannot be maintained here. Consider (30).

(30) [Jovanovu sliku]$_i$ on prodade t_i
Jovan's picture he sold (Serbo-Croatian (SC))

(30) cannot be analyzed like English (28) for at least two reasons. There is strong evidence that the possessor is located in the highest phrase in the traditional NP (TNP) in SC.[8] One such argument concerning binding is provided by Despić (2013), based on (31). (31c–d) contrast with English (31a–b) in displaying Condition B/Condition C violations. This indicates that, in contrast to English possessors, SC possessors c-command out of their TNPs, which would not be possible if there is a phrase above the phrase where they are located in the SC TNP.

(31) a. His$_i$ latest movie really disappointed Kusturica$_i$.
b. Kusturica$_i$'s latest movie really disappointed him$_i$.
c. *[$_{NP}$ Kusturicin$_i$ [$_{NP}$ najnoviji film]] ga$_i$ je zaista razočarao.
Kusturica's latest movie him is really disappointed
d. *[$_{NP}$ Njegov$_i$ [$_{NP}$ najnoviji film]] je zaista razočarao Kusturicu$_i$.
his latest movie is really disappointed Kusturica

8 The term TNP is used neutrally, for whatever the categorial status of the relevant element is. Note that Bošković (2013a, 2014) argues that the highest projection in the TNP (i.e. the extended domain of N) is a phase.

(31) indicates that SC possessors are located in the highest projection in the TNP, in fact, they are not even Specs, but adjuncts of that projection, given that they bind out. Within a more general approach where the SC TNP has less structure than the English TNP due to the lack of articles, Bošković (2013a, 2014) argues SC TNPs are NPs (though not always), with the possessor adjoined to the NP. Given the standard assumption that XP adjoined to YP c-commands everything YP does, the possessor then c-commands out of its TNP in (31c–d).[9]

The other reason why SC possessors cannot be analyzed like English possessors is that, in contrast to English possessors, SC possessors can undergo movement. Furthermore, as Bošković (2016a) shows, they can even move out of moved elements. Thus, in (32a), the possessor is extracted out of a fronted object, and in (32c) out of a fronted passive subject.

(32) a. Jovanovu$_i$ je on [$_{NP}$ t$_i$ sliku]$_j$ vidio t$_j$
John's is he picture seen
'He saw John's picture.'
b. cf. Jovanovu$_i$ je on vidio [$_{NP}$ t$_i$ sliku]
c. Jovanova$_i$ je [$_{NP}$ t$_i$ slika]$_j$ ukradena t$_j$
John's is picture stolen
'John's picture was stolen.

If there were a phrase, say DP, above the phrase where the possessor is base-generated in (32), this phrase would be a phase as the highest projection in the TNP. The possessor would then need to move to its edge prior to movement out of it. Movement of the possessor to the edge of the phrase in question would "delabel" it, so that it could not undergo movement.

Bošković (2016a) argues movement in violation of (5) can occur if the element undergoing it is base-generated at the edge of the moved phrase, i.e., if it is a feature-sharing edge of the moved phrase, the analysis being crucially based on the assumption that labeling with feature-sharing is not delayed – it can occur when the structure is created (fn. 4). Consider how (32a) is then derived. The possessor undergoes feature sharing with its sister (the possessor agrees with the noun), which results in immediate labeling (33a). Being labeled, the relevant phrase can move (33b), which is followed by the movement of the possessor out of it (33c).

9 Poss must be an adjunct to the highest TNP projection (whatever that is), or (31c–d) could not be accounted for.

(33) a. vidio [$_{NP}$ Jovanovu sliku]
b. [$_{NP}$ Jovanovu sliku]$_j$ vidio t$_j$
c. Jovanovu$_i$ je [$_{NP}$ t$_i$ sliku]$_j$ vidio t$_j$

The account cannot be maintained here. There is, however, a way of accommodating such cases. As discussed, the possessor is actually adjoined to NP. Strictly speaking, when it enters the structure, there is then no projection, only segmentation. In other words, a new category is not created, all that is happening is the segmentation of an existing category. The labeling algorithm is then not relevant here, since nothing is actually happening here from the point of view of the labeling algorithm in the sense that no new category is projected. The label here is the segmented NP. What is important for our purposes is that the TNP in (33) is still labeled. It can then undergo movement in accordance with (13), which is followed by poss-extraction.

There is also an alternative that relies on the standard assumption that adjuncts can be merged acyclically. Given this possibility, the possessor in (32a) can be merged acyclically after the object TNP moves. No labeling problem then arises with the object TNP movement.

Now, adopting an approach where labeling with feature-sharing edges can take place immediately, Bošković (2016a) argues that extraction from moved elements is quite generally allowed with feature-sharing edges, providing several cases of this sort. From the current perspective, the window for such extraction is much smaller: it is allowed for base-generated adjuncts.[10] The relevant cases from Bošković (2016a) should then be re-analyzed from this perspective, or a different account would be needed. Some cases can in fact be quite easily handled from the current perspective. This e.g. holds for left-branch extraction of adjectives.

(34) Skupe$_i$ oni kupuju [t$_i$ automobile].
expensive they are.buying cars

Bošković (2013a) argues APs are NP-adjoined; this is in fact crucial to his account of the SC/ English contrast regarding (34), which is disallowed in English. DP being a phase in languages like English where it is present, AP must move to SpecDP. The movement violates antilocality since it crosses only a segment, not a full phrase. Note also that as Bošković (2013a, 2014) argues, adjectives project

10 I assume phrasal successive-cyclic movement doesn't involve intermediate adjunctions, as standardly assumed.

phases. More precisely, Bošković argues the highest projection in the extended domain of A is a phase (I use traditional AP (TAP) for AP and any functional projections in its extended domain.) What's important here is that AP extraction is also allowed from moved elements. (35) can be handled in the same way as possessor cases like (33a).

(35) Lijepu$_i$ je on [$_{NP}$ t$_i$ [$_{NP}$ sliku]$_j$ vidio t$_j$
beautiful is he picture seen

Another relevant case involves extraction of intensifiers out of attributive APs.

(36) ?Izuzetno$_i$ su kupili [t$_i$ skup] automobil
extremely are bought expensive car
'They bought an extremely expensive car.'

Talić (2015) gives an account of the SC/English contrast regarding such extraction where it is crucial that the intensifier is adjoined to AP. Talić argues the intensifier is generated as AP-adjoined in both English and SC, but there is a functional projection above the base position of the intensifier in the TAP in English, but not SC. More generally, Talić argues that just like the structure of the TNP is richer in English than in SC, the structure of the TAP is richer in English than in SC, the same factor being responsible for both differences. Talić then gives a unified account of the SC/English contrast regarding (36) and AP extraction cases like (34) (see the above account of (34), which extends to (36)). What is important is that Talić (2015) analyzes (36) as the intensifier being adjoined to the edge of the TAP phase prior to extraction.

Crucially, intensifier extraction is possible from moved APs.

(37) ?Izuzetno$_i$ su [t$_i$ skup]$_j$ kupili [t$_j$ automobil].
extremely are expensive bought car
'They bought an extremely expensive car.'

This is then another acceptable case of movement out of a moved element that is captured under the current analysis, which allows movement from moved XP for XP-adjuncts.

8. Conclusion

Adopting the approach to labeling where labeling with feature-sharing Specs occurs when the structure is sent to the interfaces, I have shown that Bošković's (2016a) account of the ban on movement out of moved elements can be extended to the immobility of IPs not dominated by CP. Under this approach to movement out of moved elements, the problem with movement of YP from moved XP doesn't arise when YP moves out of XP; it arises already with movement of XP since XP itself cannot move: movement of XP does not freeze XP for subextraction, rather, movement of YP to the edge of XP prevents movement of XP. Under Bošković's (2016b) approach to the timing of labeling, IPs not dominated by CP are prevented from moving for the same reason. The immobility of such IPs was seen as an instance of a more general effect where movement of phrases with feature sharing Specs is disallowed. It was extended to other cases, like the ban of moving V-2 CPs in German and the wh-clause of specificational pseudoclefts. The impossibility of movement of phrases with feature-sharing Specs was shown to follow from independent assumptions regarding labeling and phases.

References

Abels, Klaus. 2003. Successive cyclicity, anti-locality, and adposition stranding. PhD thesis, University of Connecticut.

Bošković, Željko. 1997a. *The syntax of nonfinite complementation*. Cambridge: MIT Press.

Bošković, Željko. 1997b. "Pseudoclefts." *Studia Linguistica* 51: 235–277.

Bošković, Željko. 2002. "A-movement and the EPP." *Syntax* 5: 167–218.

Bošković, Željko. 2007. "On the locality and motivation of Move and Agree." *Linguistic Inquiry* 38: 589–644.

Bošković, Željko. 2013a. "Phases beyond clauses." In *The nominal structure in Slavic and beyond*, Lilia Schürcks, Anastasia Giannakidou and Urtzi Etxeberria (eds.), Berlin: de Gruyter, 75–128.

Bošković, Željko. 2013b. "Traces do not head islands: What can PF deletion rescue?" In *Deep insights, broad perspectives*, Yoichi Miyamoto, Daiko Takahashi, Hideki Maki, Masao Ochi, Koji Sugisaki and Asako Uchibori (eds.). Tokyo: Kaitakusha, 56–93.

Bošković, Željko. 2014. "Now I'm a phase, now I'm not a phase: On the variability of phases with extraction and ellipsis." *Linguistic Inquiry* 45: 27–89.

Bošković, Željko. 2015. "From the complex NP constraint to everything: On deep extractions across categories." *The Linguistic Review* 32: 603–669.

Bošković, Željko. 2016a. "The ban on movement out of moved elements in the phasal/labeling system." Ms., University of Connecticut. http://ling.auf.net/lingbuzz/002851.

Bošković, Željko. 2016b. "On the timing of labeling: Deducing comp-trace effects, the subject condition, the adjunct condition, and tucking in from labeling." *Linguistic Review* 33:17–66.

Bresnan, Joan. 1994. "Locative inversion and the architecture of UG." *Language* 70: 72–131.

Cheng, Hsu-Te. 2012. "Ellipsis: its correlates with phases and movement." Presented at GLOW 35.

Chomsky, Noam. 2000. "Minimalist inquiries." In *Step by step*, Roger Martin, David Michaels and Juan Uriagereka (eds.). Cambridge MIT Press, 89–155.

Chomsky, Noam. 2001. "Derivation by phase." In *Ken Hale: A life in Language*, Michael Kenstowicz (ed.). Cambridge: MIT Press, 1–52.

Chomsky, Noam. 2013. "Problems of projection." *Lingua* 130: 33–49.

Despić, Miloje. 2013. "Binding and the structure of NP in Serbo-Croatian." *Linguistic Inquiry* 44: 239–270.

Donati, Caterina. 2006. "On Wh-head movement." In *Wh-movement: Moving on*, Lisa Cheng and Norbert Corver (eds.). Cambridge: MIT Press, 21–46.

Gallego, Ángel and Juan Uriagereka. 2007. "Conditions on subextraction." In *Coreference, modality, and focus*, Luis Eguren and Olga Fernández-Soriano. Amsterdam: John Benjamins, 45–70.

Harwood, Will. 2013. Being progressive is just a phase. PhD thesis, University of Gent.

Higgins, Roger. 1973. The pseudocleft construction in English. PhD thesis, MIT.

Hout, Hélène. 1981. *Constructions infinitives du français*. Geneva: Librarie Droz.

Huang, C-T James. 1982. Logical relations in Chinese and the theory of grammar. PhD thesis, MIT.

Johnson, Kyle. 1991. "Object positions." *Natural Language and Linguistic Theory* 9: 577–636.

Kayne, Richard. 1994. *The antisymmetry of syntax*. Cambridge: MIT Press.

Lasnik, Howard. 2001. "Derivation and representation in modern transformational syntax." In *The handbook of contemporary syntactic theory*. Oxford: Blackwell, 62–88.

Matushansky, Ora. 2005. "Going through a phase." *MIT Working Papers in Linguistics* 49:157–181.

Nordström, Jackie. 2010. *Modality and subordinators*. Amsterdam: John Benjamins.

Pesetsky, David. 1998. "Some optimality principles of sentence pronunciation." In *Is the Best Good Enough*, Pilar Barbosa, Danny Fox, Paul Hagstrom, Martha McGinnis and David Pesetsky (eds.). Cambridge: MIT Press and MITWPL, 337–383.

Pesetsky, David and Esther Torrego. 2001. "T-to-C movement." In *Ken Hale: A life in language*, Michael Kenstowicz (ed.). Cambridge: MIT Press, 355–426.

Rackowski, Andrea and Norvin Richards. 2005. "Phase edge and extraction." *Linguistic Inquiry* 36: 565–99.

Reis, Marga. 1997. "Zum syntaktischen Status unselbständiger Verbzweit-Sätze." *Sprache im Fokus*, Christa Dürscheid, Karl Heinz Rahmers, Monika Schwarz (eds.). Tübingen: Niemeyer, 121–144.

Richards, Norvin. 2001. *Movement in language*. Oxford: Oxford University Press.

Rizzi, Luigi. 1997. "The fine structure of the left periphery." In *Elements of Grammar*, Liliane Haegeman (ed.). Dordrecht: Kluwer, 281–337.

Shlonsky, Ur. 2014. "A note on labeling, Berber states and VSO order." *The form of structure, the structure of form*, Sabrina Bendjaballah (ed.). Amsterdam: John Benjamins, 349–360.

Talić, Aida. 2015. "Adverb extraction, specificity, and structural parallelism." *Canadian Journal of Linguistics* 60: 417–454.

Torrego, Esther. 1998. *The dependencies of objects*. Cambridge: MIT Press.

Uriagereka, Juan. 1988. On government. PhD thesis, University of Connecticut.

Villa-García, Julio. 2012. The Spanish Comp system. PhD thesis, University of Connecticut.

Wurmbrand, Susi. 2001. *Infinitives: Restructuring and clause structure*. Berlin: de Gruyter.

Wurmbrand, Susi. 2006. "Licensing Case." *Journal of Germanic Linguistics* 18: 75–234.

Wurmbrand, Susi. 2013. "QR and selection." *Proceedings of NELS* 42: 277–290.

Wurmbrand, Susi. 2014. "The Merge Condition." In *Minimalism and beyond*, Peter Kosta, Lilia Schürcks, Steven Franks, Teodora Radeva-Bork (eds). Amsterdam: Benjamins, 139–177.

Neda Todorović and Susi Wurmbrand

Finiteness across domains

1. Introduction

The notion of finiteness has traditionally been related to tense. However considering semantic tense properties, neither a [+FINITE] ≈ [+TENSE], nor a [−FINITE] ≈ [−TENSE] correlation can be maintained since finite clauses can be tenseless (as in *sequence of tense* contexts), and non-finite clauses can be tensed (see Stowell 1982, Pesetsky 1992, Bošković 1997, Wurmbrand 2001, 2014b, among others). In cartographic approaches (Rizzi 1997), finiteness is typically encoded in the C-domain, and restricts (morphological) options for T. In this paper, we propose, based on the distribution of different types of complementation contexts in English and Bosnian/Croatian/Serbian (BCS), that finiteness is neither associated with tense nor necessarily with a CP. Instead we propose that (non-) finiteness is a morphological feature which can appear either in the C-, T- or *v*-domains.

The tense properties split embedded complement clauses into three broad groups as in (1): tenseless (typically restructuring), irrealis future, and propositional clauses. In Wurmbrand (2001, 2014a, b, 2015a, b), it is argued that the minimal structures these types of embedded clauses can have are different: the former can be just *v*Ps, future contexts require a TP/ModP, and propositional clauses project full CPs. If English allows such size restructuring (see Wurmbrand 2015a for evidence) and the embedded complement in (1a) can be a TP/CP-less *v*P, then the infinitival marker cannot solely be a T or C element; instead, the realization of a [−FINITE] feature would have to be associated with a *v*P-head in (1a).

(1)	a. *Leo tried/began/managed*	$[_{vP}$ *to eat (*tomorrow)*].	tenseless: *v*P
	b. *Leo decided/planned*	$[_{TP}$ *to eat (tomorrow)*].	irrealis future: TP
	c. *Leo claimed*	$[_{CP}$ *to be eating (*tomorrow)*].	propositional, simultaneous: CP

The distribution of complement clauses in BCS leads to a similar conclusion, however, for the feature [+FINITE]. As shown in (2), all three types of embedded clauses can be expressed via (morphologically) finite clauses.

(2) a. *Jovan je pokušao da čita knjigu.*
Jovan AUX tried DA read.3.SG.PRES.IMPFV book
'Jovan tried to read the book.'

b. Jovan *je odlučio da čita knjigu.*
Jovan AUX decided DA read.3.SG.PRES.IMPFV book
'Jovan decided to read the book.'

c. Jovan *je tvrdio da čita knjigu.*
Jovan AUX claimed DA read.3.SG.PRES.IMPFV book
'Jovan claimed to be reading the book.'

If finiteness were (solely) a matter of the CP domain, BCS embedded clauses should be non-transparent and behave like the 'strongest' boundaries, finite CPs. However, this is not the case. As shown in Progovac (1993a, b, 1994, 1996), Stjepanović (2004) (P/S), tenseless and future complements (their *S-complements*) show certain restructuring (i.e., size reduction) effects, whereas propositional complements (their *I-complements*) are non-transparent full clausal complements (see Table 1; for the properties marked P/S see the works cited).

In this paper we argue that BCS does not only distinguish between transparent and non-transparent complement clauses, but also makes the three-way distinction as indicated in the table. This then means, however, that reduced clauses—TPs and *v*Ps—can nevertheless be marked as finite, which is possible if,

Table 1: Properties of clausal complements in BCS

Table 1	***Claim***	***Decide***	***Try***
Tense	propositional, [+TENSE]	future irrealis, ***woll***	Tenseless
Clitic climbing [P/S]	No	Yes, marginally	Yes
NPI/NC licensing by matrix NEG [P/S]	No	Yes	Yes
wh ordering [P/S]	Matrix » embedded	Free	Free
da V.PRES	*perfective	✓perfective	✓perfective
Infinitive possible	No	Yes	Yes
Long passive (with INF)	No	No	Yes
Adverb positions	{*da*} ADV {**da*}	{*da*} ADV {*da*}	{?-**da*} ADV {*da*}
Size	CP	TP/ModP	*v*P

as we suggest, (non-)finiteness is not a property of a particular domain but can be marked in any clausal domain.

2. Aspect—A window into the composition of the tense domain

The first indicator of different compositions of clausal complements in BCS and English is the distribution of perfective/non-progressive aspect. In particular, in present tense contexts, episodic interpretations are not available with perfective/non-progressive verbs, as shown in (3) for both languages.

(3) a. *Mary *sleeps/✓is sleeping right now.* *non-progressive (E)
b. *Milan prevodi / *prevede*
Milan translate.3.SG.PRES.IMPFV / *translate.3.SG.PRES.PFV
pesmu. *perfective
poem (BCS)
'Milan is translating a poem.'/*'Milan has translated a poem (just now).'

In embedded contexts, future and tenseless complements allow perfective/non-progressive aspect even under episodic interpretations in English (4a,b) and in BCS (4c,d).

(4) a. *John decided to eat a frog tomorrow.* future
b. *John tried to eat a frog yesterday.* tenseless
c. *Odlučila sam da sutra prevodim / prevedem*
decided AUX.1SG DA tomorrow translate.1.SG.PRES.IMPFV / PFV
pesmu.
poem
'I decided to be translating a poem tomorrow.' (imperfective)
'I decided to translate the (entire) poem tomorrow.' (perfective)
d. *Pokušala sam juče da prevodim / prevedem*
tried AUX.1SG yesterday DA translate.1.SG.PRES.IMPFV / PFV
pesmu.
poem
'I tried to be translating a poem yesterday.' (imperfective)
'I tried to translate the (entire) poem yesterday.' (perfective)

However, as shown in (5a–c), non-progressive is not possible in propositional complements, whether finite or non-finite in English, and perfective is excluded in BCS (5d).

(5) a. *John believes/claims that Mary *sleeps/✓is sleeping right now.*
b. *John believes Mary to *sleep/✓be sleeping right now.*
c. *John claims to *eat/✓be eating right now.*
d. *Verujem da Jovan prevodi / *prevede pesmu.*
believe.1.SG.PRES DA Jovan translates.3.SG.PRES.IMPFV / *...PFV poem
'I believe that John is translating a poem (right now).' (imperfective)
Intended perfective interpretation: 'I believe that John has translated a poem (just now).'

To account for the aspectual distribution in simple and embedded clauses, Todorović (2015b), Wurmbrand (2014b), argue that the restrictions are the result of incompatibilities of perfective aspect[1] and the temporal domain above aspect. In particular, a perfective event, as per (6a), needs to include the event time within the reference time. This predicts that whenever the reference time for the perfective is too short an interval, the requirements of the perfective cannot be satisfied, rendering the perfective infelicitous in such environments, and only allowing imperfective/progressive as in (6b).

(6) a. PERFECTIVE: $\lambda P.\lambda t.\lambda w.\exists e\ [\text{time}(e) \subseteq t\ \&\ P(w)(e)]$ [Kratzer 1998]
Informally: event time must be included in the reference time
b. IMPERFECTIVE: $\lambda P.\lambda t.\lambda w.\exists e\ [t \subseteq \text{time}(e)\ \&\ P(w)(e)]$
Informally: reference time must be included in the event time

Given that the availability of aspect depends on the reference time interval introduced by the clausal temporal components, the (un)availability of the perfective in clausal complements in turn can provide insight into the composition of the temporal-modal domain above it.

Since the reference time intervals introduced by past, future, and perfect are indefinitely long (unless further restricted), the event time interval can be included in the reference time interval and perfective events are allowed in such contexts. We propose that this is also what happens in the embedded future contexts in (4a,c): a silent future element WOLL (see Abusch 1985, 1988) is projected, which extends the reference time, thereby allowing perfective.

On the other hand, the reference time intervals introduced by semantic present tense, as in (3), is a very short interval. Since the event time cannot be included

1 According to a common view, progressive can be treated as imperfective aspect, and non-progressive as perfective, at least for the purpose of this paper.

in this short interval, perfective is impossible. In the works mentioned, we propose that propositional complements in (5) also introduce a very short reference interval—the attitude holder's (AH) 'now', i.e., the time which the speaker believes to be his/her 'now'. In complements with a simultaneous interpretation (which is the only interpretation in propositional infinitives in English, unless perfect *have* is added), there is a present (finite) or *zero* (non-finite) tense, which is ordered with respect to the AH now and introduces an interval identical to the AH now, making this short interval also the reference time for the perfective. Since the reference time is too short to include the event time, perfective is correctly predicted to be impossible in these complements in both languages. Lastly, although tenseless complements also trigger a simultaneous interpretation in (4b,d), embedded perfective is possible, in contrast to propositional infinitives since they are entirely tenseless and aspect is determined by the temporal domain of the matrix predicate (see Todorović and Wurmbrand 2015, Wurmbrand 2014b).

Considering the distribution of the three classes of complements cross-linguistically, we find a wide range of syntactic and morphological properties which distinguish between propositional, future, and tenseless complements. In addition to the aspectual differences, which could be seen as mere semantic effects, there are properties such as clitic climbing (for BCS see Table 1) which indicate different degrees of transparency and cannot (or are very unlikely to) be accounted for solely by a semantic account. In Wurmbrand (2014b) the correlation between syntactic transparency and the semantic type of complement is taken as evidence for a difference in structure as in (7): propositional complements involve an AH (Attitude Holder) 'now' and *zero* tense, future infinitives involve a modal WOLL (and can be CP-less), and tenseless complements are TP- and CP-less altogether (see the works cited for further details and motivation).

(7) a. *believe, claim* [CP AH NOW [TP PRES/∅ $[_{vP}\ldots]]]$
b. *decide, expect* [TP WOLL $[_{vP}\ldots]]$
c. *try, begin* $[_{vP}\ldots]$

A semantically informed syntactic structure as in (7) captures the cross-linguistic implicational hierarchy of restructuring (see Wurmbrand 2014a, 2015b). Although there are language-specific differences, the distribution of clitic climbing and other transparency properties follows a clear implicational dependency: whenever clitic climbing out of a future complement is possible, it is also possible out of a tenseless complement, or in other words, there is no language in which future complements are more transparent than tenseless complements. The conclusion is that there is an implicational transparency scale of the form: attitude/speech (least/not transparent) » future » tenseless (most transparent). In what follows we will see that BCS also shows properties indicating syntactic size differences that are captured by the implicational transparency scale and the interplay of syntax and semantics as in (7).

3. Propositional complements

In order to integrate finiteness into the structure of clausal complements in English and BCS, we start with a discussion of the temporal properties of propositional complements in the two languages. In English, embedded finite propositional complements can typically occur with any temporal orientation, as in (8a). Infinitives, on the other hand, show temporal restrictions imposed by the matrix verb: specifically, propositional verbs cannot combine with future infinitives, as in (8b,c).

(8) a. *John believes/claims that Mary slept well/will sleep well/is sleeping right now.*
b. **John believes Mary to sleep well tomorrow.* *FUT
c. **Leo claims to sleep/be sleeping in the garage tomorrow.* *FUT

Unlike English, BCS observes no such restrictions — propositional *da* complements allow overt future, as in (9a). Note that this is not simply a general property of *da* complements, since tenseless *da* complements (9b) cannot involve a future interpretation.

(9) a. *Jovan veruje/tvrdi da će sledeće godine sagraditi kuću.*
Jovan believes/claims DA will next year build.INF.PFV house
'Jovan believes/claims that he will build a house next year.'
b. **Jovan pokušava da će sledeće godine sagraditi kuću.*
Jovan tries.3.SG.IMPFV DA will next year build.INF.PFV house
*'Jovan tries to build a house next year.'

When it comes to non-finite complementation, BCS still allows infinitives (with frequency and preferences varying in different regional varieties). Crucially, infinitives are impossible in propositional contexts, as in (10a), whereas they can occur in future and tenseless contexts, as in (10b,c). The distribution is summarized in Table 2.

(10) a. *Tvrdim {da čitam / *čitati } ovu knjigu.*
claim.1SG {DA read.1SG / *read.INF.IMPFV } this book
'I claim to be reading this book.' [Vrzić 1996: 305, (22a,b)]

b. *Odlučila* *sam* {*da* *čitam* / *čitati* } *ovu knjigu.*
decide.SG.FEM AUX.1SG {DA read.1SG / read.INF.IMPFV } this book
'I decided to read this book.'

c. *Pokušala* *sam* {*da* *čitam* / *čitati* } *ovu knjigu.*
tried.SG.FEM AUX.1SG {DA read.1SG / read.INF.IMPFV } this book
'I tried to read this book.'

Table 2: Temporal properties of propositional complements

Table 2	**Finite**	**Non-finite**
claim, believe (E)	no temporal restriction	simultaneous; *zero* tense
tvrditi, verovati (BCS)	no temporal restriction	*

The structure we propose for propositional complements is given (11). In both finite, (11a), and non-finite complements, (11b), a CP hosting the context variable and speaker coordinates is projected. In English, C can be specified for [+FINITE] or [−FINITE], where [−FINITE] selects a *zero* tense. In BCS, on the other hand, where infinitives have been disappearing, as a language-specific property, C can only be [+FINITE] (see section 6 for some remarks on the typology of finiteness). This restriction in BCS and the complementation structures in (7) then capture the lack of infinitives with propositional, but not future and tenseless complements: only propositional complements require a CP, and CP must be finite in BCS.

(11) a.
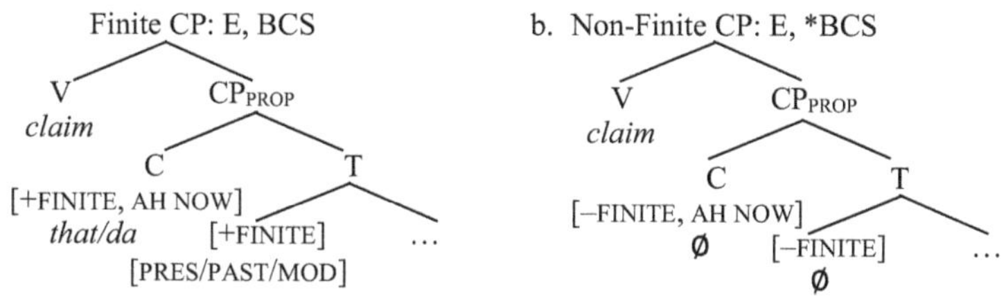

Note that this morpho-syntactic property is unlikely to be the sole result of the semantics of propositional complements since propositional complements can, in principle, be non-finite, as we see in English. Our account establishes a link between the semantics of propositional complements (attitude, speaker/addressee properties) and the syntax (presence of a C-domain). Morpho-syntactic restrictions on (non-)finiteness can then be formulated as, possibly language-specific, spell-out or feature inventory options for the syntactic structure, in the case at hand, the C-domain. Importantly, no direct link exists between the semantics and the morpho-syntactic property of finiteness, which has the advantage that the semantics and basic syntax (the presence of CP) can remain cross-linguistically uniform, with variation occurring only in the morpho-syntactic component (where variation is common and frequent). Furthermore, in our account it is not accidental that it is only the propositional complements that must be finite in BCS, whereas a semantic account (without mediating syntax) may have to stipulate this. If the lexical entry for C comes with an obligatory [+FINITE] feature, only complements that must contain a CP will be subject to this finiteness restriction. Thus, given this account, the possibility of infinitives in future and tenseless complements serves as an indicator of the possible lack of a CP in BCS (but when future complements do project a CP they are again obligatorily finite; see (16c)).

4. Future complements

We continue the discussion with complements of verbs like *decide*, which require an embedded future interpretation, as shown in (12) for English and (13) for BCS. In both cases, the embedded event must occur in the future with respect to the matrix event.[2]

(12) a. *Leo decided to sleep in the garage tomorrow.* FUT
b. **Leo decided to have slept in the garage.* *PERFECT
c. **Leo decided to be eating a frog right then.* *SIMULTANEOUS

(13) a. *Jovan je odlučio da spava / spavati*
Jovan AUX.3.SG decided DA sleep.3.SG.PRES.IMPFV / sleep.INF.IMPFV
u garaži.
in garage
'Jovan decided to sleep/that he would sleep in the garage.' ✓FUT
*'Jovan decided to be sleeping in garage right then.' *SIMULTANEOUS
b. *Jovan je odlučio da je spavao u garaži.*
Jovan AUX.3.SG decided DA AUX.3.SG slept.3.SG.MASC in garage
'Jovan decided to have slept in the garage.'

Such mandatory future-orientation, we propose, stems from a selectional property of certain matrix verbs, which is implemented structurally via a covert

2 In some contexts 'decide' may also allow a perfect interpretation as in *He decided (to pretend) to have slept in the garage*. However, in this example, the meaning of 'decide' has been coerced to that of 'pretend'.

modal WOLL quantifying over possible future world-time pairs. The distribution of such a covert modal is not free, however, but requires special licensing. Specifically, we claim that WOLL needs to be licensed (e.g., valued) by either tense or an irrealis element, as in (14).

(14)

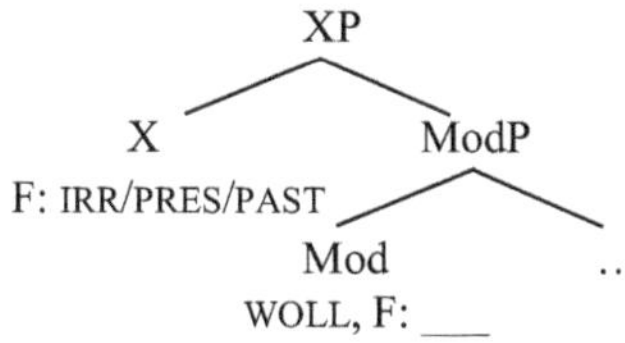

Spell-out
PRES, WOLL → *will* (E), *će* (BCS)
PAST, WOLL → *would* (E), *će* (BCS)
IRR, WOLL → Ø (E, BCS)

Before providing further evidence for such licensing, let us return to examples such as (12) and (13). We assume that verbs which select a future complement have an irrealis feature which must match with an irrealis/future complement. Assuming selection is a local process, the matrix verb has to combine directly with the projection hosting the future element as in (15a), thus, typically future complements lack the CP. While CP-less future infinitives as in (15b) have been proposed in several works (see for instance Bošković 1997), CP-less *da* complements may appear peculiar, since *da* is usually treated as a complementizer. Yet, as shown in (15c), a CP-less structure is exactly what we propose for (13a). Future complements, even when finite, do not involve *semantic* present tense since, as shown in section 2, future and propositional complements differ regarding the availability of perfective aspect and we attribute this difference to the absence/presence of semantic present tense. In BCS, complements of *decide*, can, however, involve a [+FINITE] feature on T (in addition to WOLL), and, as shown in (15c), the spell-out of this feature is *da*. Lastly, a verb selected by a [+FINITE] T, in the absence of semantic tense, is realized as morphological present tense, the default finite form. We thus treat the overt present tense we see in future infinitives as a semantically vacuous morphological form (see also Progovac 1993a, b, 1994, 1996, Stjepanović 2004).

(15) a. *decide* [IRR] [$_{\text{TP/ModP [IRR]}}$ WOLL]

b. *decide* [IRR] [$_{\text{TP/ModP}}$ WOLL [IRR, –FINITE] → Ø V.INF] E, BCS

c. *decide* [IRR] [$_{\text{TP/ModP}}$ WOLL [IRR, +FINITE] → *da* V.PRES] BCS, *E

Evidence for the option of a CP-less structure of future infinitives comes from syntactic transparency effects which are observed for finite future but not propositional complements. This is illustrated in (16) with clitic climbing [CC] (for a full list of transparency properties and evidence that future complements can lack a CP, see Progovac 1993a, b, 1994, 1996, Stjepanović 2004, Todorović and Wurmbrand 2015). While CC is considered marked by many BCS speakers, a clear contrast is nevertheless observed between (16a) and (16b): future complements allow CC whereas propositional complements never do. In Wurmbrand (2014a, 2015b), it is argued that CC is blocked across CPs. The difference between (16a) and (16b) then follows, if, as we suggest, future complements can lack a CP, whereas propositional complements always project a CP.[3] Lastly, when a future complement does include a CP, as in (16c) where T is occupied by an overt future modal (which is the realization of semantic present tense plus WOLL) and hence *da* must be in C, CC becomes impossible.[4]

(16) a. *Ona ga je odlučila / planirala da posjeti.*
she him AUX decided / planned DA visit.3.SG.PRES
'She decided/planned to visit him.' [Stjepanović 2004: 197, fn. 14, (ia)]

b. *Milan {*ga} kaže da {✓ga} vidi.*
Milan {*him} says DA {✓him} see.3.SG.PRES
'Milan says that he can see him.' [Progovac 1993a: 119, (12–13), among others]

c. **Petar ga je odlučio da će da vidi.*
Peter him AUX decided DA will DA see
'Peter decided to see him.'

In addition to future selecting verbs (verbs that semantically require an irrealis complement), we argue that there are additional licensors of WOLL, such as irrealis C, which occurs in exclamatives/wishes, as in (17a), and in questions,

3 This property (as well as some of the others discussed in Progovac 1993a, b, 1994, 1996, Stjepanović 2004) again point to the relevance of a syntactic correlate of the different semantic types of complements. The fact that transparency shows cross-linguistic differences along the implicational hierarchy of restructuring (e.g., some languages allow clitic climbing out of future and tenseless complements, others only out of tenseless complements, but as mentioned above, there is no language that shows the opposite behavior) would be difficult to handle under a pure semantic approach without recourse to different syntactic structures for these complements.

4 A question arising is how is future selected in cases like (16c). We tentatively assume that in these cases, future is transmitted via an irrealis C (Pesetsky 1992).

as in (17b–d). All these environments are future-oriented and crucially have modal flavor (see also Todorović 2015a).

(17) a. *Da ti se sve želje ostvare!*
DA you.DAT SE all wishes come.true.3.PL.PRES
'May all your wishes come true!'
b. *Da Vesna pročita ovu knjigu?*
DA Vesna read.3.SG.PRES this book
'Should Vesna read this book?' [Vrzić 1996: 292: (2a)]
c. *Da li da Vesna pročita ovu knjigu?*
Q DA Vesna read.3.SG.PRES this book
'Should Vesna read this book?' [Vrzić 1996: 292: (2b)]
d. *Koju knjigu da Vesna pročita?*
which book DA Vesna read.3.SG.PRES
'Which book should Vesna read?' [translation corrected]
[Vrzić 1996: 292: (2c)]

Declaratives without exclamative/imperative force, on the other hand, do not license WOLL; instead, an overt modal is required, as illustrated in (18).

(18) a. **Da Vesna pročita ovu knjigu.*
DA Vesna read.3.SG.PRES this book
'Vesna should read this book.' [Vrzić 1996: 292: (2d)]
b. *Vesna treba pročitati ovu knjigu.*
Vesna should read.INF this book
'Vesna should read this book.' [Vrzić 1996: 292: (2e)]

The distribution of covert modality (which we assume is triggered by WOLL) can be derived from the assumption that WOLL must be identified (licensed) structurally by an irrealis element. Interrogative, exclamative, and imperative C have been analyzed as irrealis elements (Givón 1995: 119, Palmer 2001: 172–173, Mauri 2008: 175, Magni 2010: 243), and thus the difference between (17) and (18a), schematized in (19), follows.

(19) a. $C_{INTERROGATIVE}$ [IRR] $[_{TP/ModP}$ WOLL [F: ___]] (17)

b.*$C_{DECLARATIVE}$ $[_{TP/ModP}$ WOLL [F: ___]] (18a)

In our account, the feature combination of T/Mod in (17) is [+FINITE, WOLL], which again is only possible in irrealis contexts. As in *decide* complements, the visible present tense in (17) is not a semantic tense. Unlike BCS, English does not allow such configurations. As shown in (20a), finite questions cannot involve a modal interpretation (an overt modal would be necessary). We assume that this is due to a lexical gap — [+FINITE, WOLL] does not have a spell-out in English. Note, however, that covert modality is found in non-finite contexts: non-finite questions (20b), and infinitival relatives (20c), express exactly such a modal interpretation, which shows that, like in BCS, T can be specified as a covert WOLL, i.e., WOLL that is not licensed by tense but by an irrealis element.

(20) a. *Which book is John reading/does John read?* *WOLL
b. *John wonders which book to read.* ✓WOLL
Can mean: … *which book he should read*
c. … *a book (for John) to read.* ✓WOLL
Can mean: *a book John should/could read*
(Hackl and Nissenbaum 2012)

5. Da in different domains

In this section, we provide further motivation for the syntactic differences in the structure of the three types of complements as proposed in (7) as well as for the low positions of *da* in T/Mod or *v*. Sočanac (2011) notes that future complements and tenseless complements differ regarding whether adverbs (see below for a refinement) or topics can occur between *da* and the verb.

(21) a. *Hoćeš / *Možeš da brže dođeš?*
want.2.SG / *can.2.SG DA quicker come.2.SG
'Do you want to/ can you come quicker?'
[Based on Sočanac 2011: 64, (25a), (26a)]
b. *Hoću *Moraš da Ivana pozoveš.*
want.1.SG *must.2.SG DA Ivan.TOP invite.2.SG
'I want you to/You must invite Ivan.'
[Sočanac 2011: 64, (25b), (26b)]

Assuming a topic/focus position at the edge of the *v*P-domain (Stjepanović 1998, 1999, 2003), this distribution follows if *da* can either occur in T/Mod or in *v*. Topics or focalized adverbs can appear after *da* in future complements (e.g., complements of *hteti* in (21)) since *da* is in Mod, but not after *da* in tenseless complements (e.g., complements of *moći* and *morati* in (21)), which typically lack a TP/ModP (but see below for vacuous T/Mod projection) — thus *da* is in *v* in these cases as in (22b).

(22)

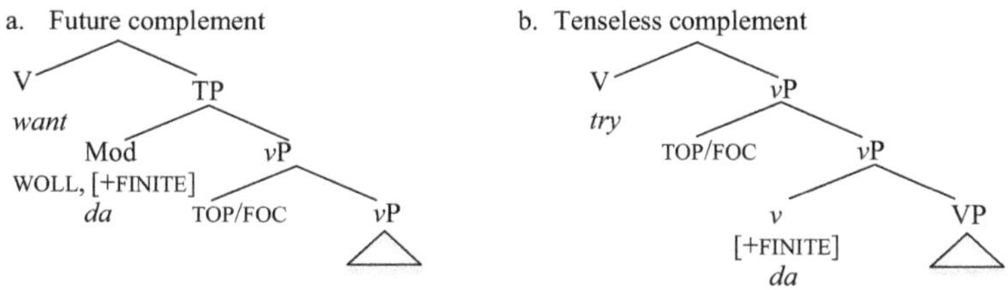

We treat *da* as a finiteness 'visualizer'. The modal WOLL (without accompanying tense) and *v* are not morphologically realized. If these heads are inserted with a [+FINITE] feature, *da* can be seen as the morphological spell-out of this feature (subject to certain restrictions, see below). We hypothesize that *da* spells out [+FINITE] on a clausal head (C, T, *v*), if no other feature of that head overtly expresses finiteness. For instance, if there is a semantic tense feature in T, the verb realizes that feature (either via lowering or V-movement) and [+FINITE] is made visible via the (true) tense feature; it would not be spelled out as *da* in addition. It is important again that the morphological present tense we see in future and tenseless infinitives in (22) is not the result of a semantic present tense feature, but the default spell-out of a verb selected by a [+FINITE] T or *v*. In other words, *da*/[+FINITE] T and *v* in (22) select a morphological present tense form, which is semantically vacuous.

Let us look in more detail at the distribution of (low) adverbs in the three types of complements. As shown in (23) for one variety of BCS, tenseless complements prefer the order adverb » *da*, future complements allow either order, and propositional complements only allow the order *da* » adverb.

(23) a. *Počeli* *su* {?**da*}[5] *brže* {✓*da*} *stižu.* Tenseless
started.PL.MASC are {?*DA} quicker {✓DA} arrive.3.PL.PRES.IMPFV
'They started to arrive quicker.'

b. *Odlučili* *su* {✓*da*} *brže* {✓*da*} *hodaju.* Future

5 The contrast is clearer in *i*-focus constructions such as i. The *da*—ADV order improves if the ADV is defocused, e.g., by focusing the verb, ii.(thanks to B. Arsenijević for pointing this and the examples below out to us):

decided.PL.MASC are {✓DA} quicker {✓DA} walk.PRES.3.PL.PFV
'They decided to walk quicker.'

c. *Kazali su {✓da} brže {*da} stižu.* Propositional
said.PL.MASC AUX {✓DA} quicker {*DA} arrive.3.PL.PRES.IMPFV
'They said they are coming quicker.'

The structure for tenseless complements deriving the low position of *da* was given in (22b). In future contexts, the embedded clause projects both *v* and T/Mod, and if *da* can be either in T/Mod or in *v*, as we suggest, the two options in (23b) are correctly derived. One question arising at this point is whether it is possible to have two *da*'s within one clause. We show below that this is indeed the case in propositional complements, but it is not possible in future complements—in (23b) only one *da* can be realized. We preliminarily suggest that there is a selectional restriction of *da*—every *da* has to occur with a (separate) finite verb afterwards. As shown in (24a), if T/Mod is [+FINITE] and realized as *da*, the lower *v*/V head needs to spell out as a finite verb. The same is the case for *da* in *v* in (24b), which again requires V to be finite. What is excluded, however, is spelling out an additional *da* in T/Mod in (24b), since that *da* would not 'select' a finite verb, but just another *da*, which we assume is impossible. The higher [+FINITE] feature is thus not spelled out as *da* in (24b), possibly because the feature is deleted at spell-out. We leave a further formalization of this selectional restriction of *da* open, since it requires a more in-depth commitment to how selection is implemented.

(24) a. Future complement #1 b. Future complement #2

---

i. *Mogli su {✓i brže} da {*i brže} stignu.*
could.3.PL AUX {FOC quicker} DA {*FOC quicker} arrive.3. PL.PRES.PFV
'They could have arrived even faster.' [B. Arsenijević, p.c.]

ii. *Mogli su da brže STIGNU.*
could.3.PL AUX da quicker arrive.3.PL.PRES.PFV
(*mesto što su iskoristili tu jednu kartu da brže odu u park*)
'They could have arrived faster (instead of using that one ticket to go to the park faster).'

We tentatively assume that in ii, the adverb is adjoined to VP (instead of *v*P), but the distribution of *i*-focus constructions in different embedding contexts requires further research.

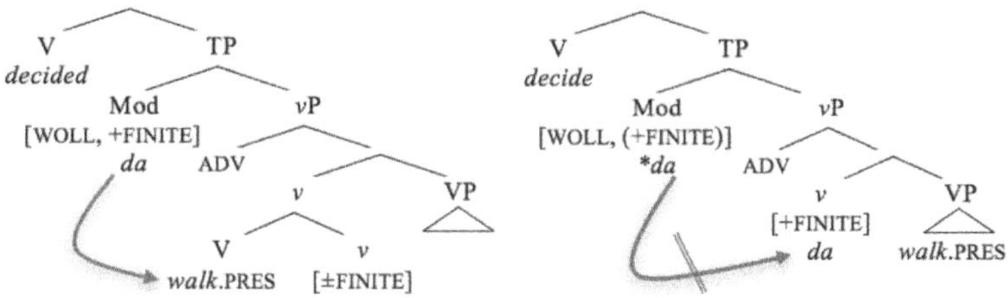

The selectional restriction of *da* predicts that two *da's* are possible, as long as each *da* is followed by a finite verb. This is exactly what we find in (25). Since in this case, the tense domain carries both a (true) tense feature and WOLL, the T/Mod head is spelled out as *će* 'will'. If C and *v* also include a [+FINITE] feature, both heads are spelled out as *da*, since each of them is followed by a finite verb.

(25) a. *Kaže da će da dođe.*
says DA will.3.SG DA come.3.SG.PRES
'He says he will come.' [Sočanac 2011: 55, (8)]

b.

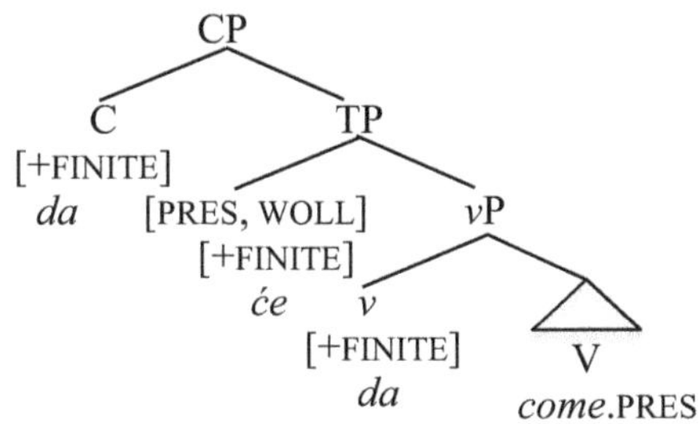

Finally, propositional complements as in (23c) (without a finite verb in T) only allow the higher *da*. The structure for (23c) is given in (26). Since T has a semantic tense feature, this feature is realized on the verb and no *da* is spelled out in T. There are several ways in which the relation between T and the verb can be established (lowering, head movement, feature valuation, morphological merger), and it is not essential for this paper which relation is adopted. The only concept we need is that there is a dependency between T and V and that this dependency cannot reach across spell-out domains. Thus for T to 'see' V, since *v*P is a phase and VP a spell-out domain, V has to move at least to *v*, as illustrated in (26). With V being in *v*, there is no need to spell-out *v* as *da*, since the now complex *v* head is already marked for finiteness through the verb. Lastly, C, which can only have the feature [+FINITE] in BCS, is spelled out as *da* since it selects a finite T+V (possibly the verb undergoes further movement to T) as required.

(26)

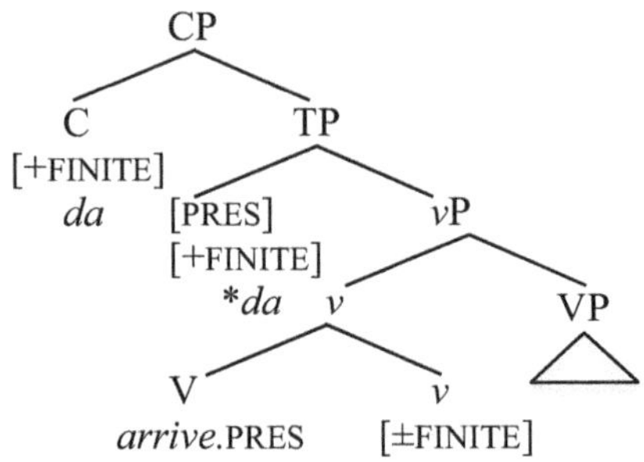

6. Towards a typology of finiteness

In section 3, we have seen that propositional complements must be finite in BCS. English represents the opposite case: all types of complements can be non-finite, however, tenseless complements typically resist being finite.

(27) a. ??*Leo tried that he would win.*
b. *Leo decided that he would leave.*
c. *Leo claimed that he left/will leave.*

Table 3: Distribution of finiteness

Complement	**Finite**		**Non-finite**		**Unexpected**		
	English	**BCS**	**English**	**BCS**	**Language X**	**Language Y**	**Language Z**
Try	✗	✓	✓	✓	[+FINITE]	[±FINITE]	any value
decide	✓	✓	✓	✓	[±FINITE]	[−FINITE]	[±FINITE]
Claim	✓	✓	✓	✗	any value	any value	[−FINITE]

The 'degree' of finiteness can differ across languages, however, there is a clear generalization: when *v* is finite (as diagnosed, e.g., by the availability of finite *try*-complements), T and C can be finite as well, but not vice versa. Similarly, if a language allows non-finite propositional complements, it also allows non-finite future and tenseless complements. This is indicated in the finiteness scale in (28), with BCS (as discussed so far) and English restricting the finiteness values at different ends of the scale. In what follows, we illustrate another variety of BCS which combines the special settings of English and BCS#1 as noted in (28c).

(28) [+FINITE] ⇠ C — T — *v* ⇢ [−FINITE]
a. [$_{CP}$ [+FINITE] [$_{TP}$ [±FINITE] [$_{vP}$ [±FINITE]]]] BCS#1
b. [$_{CP}$ [±FINITE] [$_{TP}$ [±FINITE] [$_{vP}$ [−FINITE]]]] English
c. [$_{CP}$ [+FINITE] [$_{TP}$ [±FINITE] [$_{vP}$ [−FINITE]]]] BCS#2

In some varieties (roughly Bosnian), speakers use infinitives more frequently and may prefer infinitives over *da* complements in tenseless and future complements. In our approach, this is implemented by the lack (or dispreference) of a [+FINITE] *v*P domain (due to extensive bilingualism within BCS and resulting possible dialectal code switching, judgments are not categorical but gradient). Interestingly, in these varieties, the low position of *da* with respect to adverbs is more marked and dispreferred (unless the adverb is focused in which case we assume that it moves to a higher position).

(29) a. *Odlučili su brže hodati.*
decided.PL.MASC AUX quicker walk.INF
'They decided to walk quicker.'
b. *Odlučili su {✓da} brže {✓$_F$/??da} hodaju.*
decided.PL.MASC AUX {✓DA} quicker {✓$_F$/??DA} walk.PRES.3.PL.PFV
'They decided to come quicker.' [A. Talić, p.c.]

Furthermore, in tenseless complements, too, if a *da* complement is used, which is dispreferred overall, the unmarked order is *da* adverb as shown in (30). Since finite *v* is not available/dispreferred in BCS#2, the only/best way to derive a *da* complement in tenseless contexts, is to project a vacuous TP, which has the effect that finite future and tenseless complements behave alike regarding adverb placement, but the latter are themselves marked.

(30) a. *Počeli su {✓da} brže {✓$_F$/?da} stižu.* BCS#2
started.PL.MASC AUX {✓DA} quicker {✓$_F$/?DA} arrive.3.PL.PRES.IMPFV
'They started to arrive quicker.' [A. Talić, p.c.]
b. *started* [$_{TP}$ Ø$_{T,\,[+FINITE]}$ → *da* [*v*P ADV … V.PRES]]

Finally, note that the structures in (24) find a parallel in English in the distribution of the infinitival marker. Assuming that negation marks the left edge of the *v*P, (31) shows that the infinitival marker can occur either to the left of negation in T or C, or the right of negation in *v* (since negation occurs before *have*, a constituent negation structure is unlikely for (31a)).

(31) a. *Leo claimed to not have eaten all the cookies.*
b. *Leo claimed not to have eaten all the cookies.*

This is expected if the morphological feature relevant in English is [−FINITE], whereas it is [+FINITE] in BCS, and if these features are distributed as in (28). Thus, languages can be divided into predominantly marking finiteness or non-finiteness.

References

Abusch, Dorit. 1985. "On verbs and time." PhD thesis, University of Massachusetts.

Abusch, Dorit. 1988. "Sequence of tense, intensionality, and scope." In *Proceedings of the 7th West Coast Conference on Formal Linguistics*. Stanford: CSLI Publications, 1–14.

Bošković, Željko. 1997. *The syntax of nonfinite complementation: An economy approach*. Cambridge: MIT Press.

Givón, Talmy. 1995. *Functionalism and grammar*. Benjamins.

Hackl, Martin and Jon Nissenbaum. 2012. "A modal ambiguity in for-infinitival relative clauses." *Natural language semantics* 20: 59–81.

Kratzer, Angelika. 1998. "More structural analogies between pronouns and tenses." In *Proceedings from Semantics and Linguistic Theory VIII*. Ithaca: CLC Publications, 92–110.

Magni, Elisabetta. 2010. "Mood and Modality." In *New perspectives on historical Latin syntax II*. Berlin: Mouton de Gruyter, 193–275.

Mauri, Caterina. 2008. *Coordination relations in the languages of Europe and beyond*. Walter de Gruyter.

Palmer, Frank R. 2001. *Mood and Modality*. Cambridge: Cambridge University Press.

Pesetsky, David. 1992. *Zero syntax II: An essay on infinitives*. Cambridge: MIT.

Progovac, Ljiljana. 1993a. "Locality and subjunctive-like complements in Serbo-Croatian." *Journal of Slavic Linguistics* 1: 116–144.

Progovac, Ljiljana. 1993b. "Subjunctive: the (mis)behavior of anaphora and negative polarity." *The Linguistic Review* 10: 37–59.

Progovac, Ljiljana. 1994. *Negative and positive polarity: A binding approach*. Cambridge University Press.

Progovac, Ljiljana. 1996. "Clitics in Serbian/Croatian: Comp as the second position." In *Approaching second: Second position clitics and related phenomena*, Aaron Halpern and Arnold Zwicky (eds.). Stanford: CSLI, 441–428.

Rizzi, Luigi. 1997. "The fine structure of the left periphery." In *Elements of grammar: Handbook of generative syntax*, Liliane Haegeman (ed.), Dordrecht: Kluwer, 281–337.

Sočanac, Tomislav. 2011. "Subjunctive in Serbian/Croatian." In *Geneva Generative Papers*, 49–70.

Stjepanović, Sandra. 1998. "Short distance movement of wh-phrases in Serbo-Croatian matrix clauses." Paper presented at the Workshop on Comparative Slavic Morphosyntax, Spencer.

Stjepanović, Sandra. 1999. "What do second position cliticization, scrambling, and multiple Wh-fronting have in common?" PhD thesis, University of Connecticut.

Stjepanović, Sandra. 2003. "Multiple wh-fronting in Serbo-Croatian matrix questions and the matrix sluicing construction." In *Multiple Wh-fronting*, Cedric Boeckx and Kleanthes K. Grohmann (eds.). Amsterdam: Benjamins, 255–284.

Stjepanović, Sandra. 2004. "Clitic climbing and restructuring with "finite clause" and infinitive complements." *Journal of Slavic Linguistics* 12: 173–212.

Stowell, Tim. 1982. "The tense of infinitives." *Linguistic Inquiry* 13: 561–570.

Todorović, Neda. 2015a. "Aspectual distribution in embedded contexts—Serbian and beyond." Talk given at the Workshop on Aspect, Cornell University.

Todorović, Neda. 2015b. "Tense and aspect (in)compatibility in Serbian matrix and subordinate clauses." *Lingua* 167: 82–111.

Todorović, Neda and Susi Wurmbrand. 2015. "(In)Finite possibilities of 'da': Restructuring the tense and aspect domains." Workshop on aspect in embedded clauses, ZAS, Berlin.

Vrzić, Zvjezdana. 1996. "Categorial status of the Serbo-Croatian "modal" da." In *Annual Workshop on Formal Approaches to Slavic Linguistics*. Ann Arbor, 291–312.

Wurmbrand, Susi. 2001. *Infinitives: Restructuring and clause structure*. Berlin: Mouton de Gruyter.

Wurmbrand, Susi. 2014a. "Restructuring across the world." In *Complex Visibles Out There. Proceedings of the Olomouc Linguistics Colloquium 2014*. Olomouc, 275–294.

Wurmbrand, Susi. 2014b. "Tense and aspect in English infinitives." *Linguistic Inquiry* 45: 403–447.

Wurmbrand, Susi. 2015a. *The cost of raising quantifiers*. Ms. University of Connecticut. Storrs.

Wurmbrand, Susi. 2015b. "Restructuring cross-linguistically." In *Proceedings of the North Eastern Linguistics Society Annual Meeting 45*. Amherst: GLSA, 227–240.

Joanna Błaszczak

The Puzzling FUTURE*

1. The issue

In the literature, there is a lot of controversial discussion as far as the status of future is concerned (see De Brabanter, Kissine, and Sharifzadeh 2014; Mucha 2015 for recent overviews). Many scholars doubt that future is a real tense category. In contrast to past and present tense, future eventualities cannot be located in the actual world for the simple reason that they have not occurred yet. In other words, 'any future event is potential rather than actual […]' (Chung and Timberlake 1985: 243) and it seems to be more a modal category than tense. The main goal of this short paper is to contribute to this general debate about the nature of future tense by pointing out some interesting observations from Slavic languages. Just like many other languages, Slavic languages also have different means of expressing future time reference. These means are different in different Slavic languages or groups of Slavic languages (see Whaley 2000). While in some Slavic languages the term 'future tense' is justified, in Polish – against the common belief or traditional grammar – there are in fact no future tense forms strictly speaking. Nevertheless, similar meanings can be realized in different Slavic languages, despite different means having been employed. If this is so, then the puzzling question is how future time reference is possible without future tense and why there is so much variance in the way future time reference is realized.

The paper is organized as follows. Section 2 gives a brief overview of arguments based on facts from neurolinguistics, language acquisition, and typology, which provide evidence for the marked status of future (as compared to past (or present) tense). The subsequent discussion in section 3 aims at shedding some light on the nature of future, in particular on the question of whether what is commonly referred to as 'future tense' is a tense category at all. With this background, we will return to Slavic data in section 4, where it will be briefly demonstrated how future time reference is realized especially in Polish, since

---

* This work was supported by the Foundation for Polish Science under Grant FOCUS number F5/09/P/2013 of January 27, 2014. I would like to thank Kristina Mihajlovic for proofreading the paper.

it is argued to lack future tense forms. The paper will conclude with some general observations regarding the nature of future tense in Slavic against a broader crosslinguistic background.

2. The marked status of future

There are several arguments pointing out that the future is indeed different from other tenses. For example, neurolinguistic evidence shows that 'there are specific areas in the frontal pole and medial temporal lobes that are more involved with the future than with the past' (Suddendorf and Corballis 2007: 302). Furthermore, even if both past and future thinking display similar characteristics (see Anderson et al. 2012), there is also experimental evidence suggesting that future event simulation might in fact be cognitively more demanding. In contrast to recalling a specific past event, which requires a mental search for a unique event, generating a hypothetical future event can involve an infinite combination of information from various episodic memories (see Crane, Lind, and Bowler 2012).

Additionally, evidence coming from language acquisition research seems to suggest a similar conclusion. According to findings that have been reported across languages, children usually acquire marking for future time reference after they use marking for past time reference (see, e.g., Bloom, Lifter and Hafitz 1980). However, with a closer look, it appears that overtly marked past or present tense forms do not necessarily have to precede overtly marked forms of future time reference in child language (see Swift 2003) and that the question of the time of acquisition of future forms cannot be considered without taking into account the aspectual values of the particular forms to be acquired (see Weist 2014 for a recent discussion). Despite this, the future might be regarded as being marked in yet another sense. As Weist et al. (1984: 362–3) point out, '[t]he heavy modal usage and the limited quality of anticipated future time references indicate that the deictic future is somewhat more difficult for children to represent than the deictic past.'

The marked status of future is also reflected in the fact that the future is 'practically always marked overtly by an auxiliary or affix' (Greenberg 1966: 47).[1] From a typological point of view, it is relatively rare for a language to totally lack any grammatical means for marking the future (see Dahl and Velupillai 2011).

1 As argued by Haspelmath (1998), cases of the present tense being formally more marked than the future can be explained diachronically.

Another striking fact is that languages usually possess more than one marker that can be used as future (see Bybee, Perkings, and Pagliuca 1994: 243).[2] And even more importantly, even in the so-called tenseless languages without obligatory morphological tense marking, the future must be overtly expressed. This is illustrated in (1) from St'át'imcets (Salish). Whereas superficially tenseless sentences may receive both present tense and past interpretations, as in (1a), they cannot receive a future interpretation. Even if a temporal adverbial with a clear future meaning is present in a sentence, as in (1b), this is not enough to express future time reference. An overt future marker must be used for this purpose, as shown in (1c) (Matthewson 2006: 676–8).

(1) a. sáy' sez'-lhkan (St'át'imcets)
play-1sg.subj
'I played.' / 'I am playing.'
b. *sáy'sez'-lhkan natcw / zánucwem
play-1sg.subj one.day.away / next.year
Intended: 'I will play tomorrow / next year.'
c. sáy'sez'-lhkán *kelh*
play-1sg.subj kelh
'*I played / *I am playing / I will play.'

The fact that future time reference must be overtly marked can be explained in terms of the Simplicity Constraint on Interpretation (Smith, Perkins, and Fernald 2003: 186). This constraint determines that for sentences appearing without direct temporal information, one should choose the interpretation that requires the least information added or inferred. Accordingly, by default, bounded events will be interpreted as being located in the past, while unbounded situations will be located in the present. However, neither of them will receive a future time interpretation by default. This is so because past and present tense are simpler than the future for they 'lack the element of uncertainty, the modal factor that is

2 For example, West Greenlandic has five different future markers, each of them having a specific interpretation or specific use: *-jumaar* 'vague future', *-ler* 'about to/near future', *-niar* 'intended/inevitable future', *-ssa* 'future/should', *-ssamaar* 'planned future' (Trondhjem 2014: 124). The question of what specific semantic distinctions underly the use of different future markers may be regulated differently in different languages. E.g., the English (*will/be going*) and the Indonasian (*akan/mau/pasti*) future markers are argued to be based on different aspectual operators (progressive-like and generic-like) (Copley 2010); the underlying distinction betwen the East Javanese future markers (*arep/bakal*) is that of intention vs. prediction (Vander Klok 2010).

always present in expressions of futurity' (Smith, Perkins and Fernald 2003: 186); see also section 3.

3. The nature of future tense

As Dahl (1985: 103) points out, '[...], when we talk about the future, we are either talking about someone's plans, intentions or obligations, or we are making a prediction or extrapolation from the present state of the world. As a direct consequence, a sentence that refers to the future will almost always differ modally from a sentence with non-future time reference' (ibid.). Similarily, Chung and Timberlake (1985: 243) note that future morphemes tend to have modal overtones because modality involves degrees of uncertainty, and 'situations in the future are inherently uncertain as to actuality'.[3] For this reason, future is often regarded as an irrealis category. If we agree with the assumption of Chung and Timberlake (1985: 241) that the realis/irrealis distinction is basically one of actual vs. non-actual events, then indeed there seems to be a link between future and irrealis, given that 'any future event is potential rather than actual' and '[i]n practice many languages do not distinguish morphologically between future tense and potential (irrealis) mood' (ibid., p. 243). However, it would be wrong to generally associate future with uncertainity. In fact, some future eventualities can be interpreted as being planned (see Copley 2002, 2014; Błaszczak and Klimek-Jankowska 2013b; see also footnote 2 and section 4.2). Equally, it would be wrong to generally subsume futures under the cover term 'irrealis'. For example, in St'át'imcets, as argued by Matthewson (2006), the future marker *kelh* is not possible in any irrealis contexts except future ones, which makes it implausible that it could be regarded as an irrealis marker. Furthermore, Winford (2000a) provides evidence that in creole languages future tense categories are distinguished from other categories expressing different types of irrealis meaning associated with mood and modality.

This short discussion reveals the main source of difficulty of analyzing the future: the fact that, unlike markers used for the reference to past and present states of affairs, those used for the reference to future states of affairs seem to convey not just future temporal reference but also modal meanings. But should this be taken to mean that future markers entail the modal meaning

---

3 According to Bybee, Perkins, and Pagliuca (1994), modality senses associated with future markers might be attributed to the specific lexical sources out of which such markers have developed.

they convey or whether they are merely compatible with it? Of course, this question cannot be answered generally, but controversial discussions in the literature show that in fact it is difficult to answer this question even for one particular future marker in one language, as the ongoing debate on the English *will* illustratively demonstrates (see, e.g., Sarkar 1998; Copley 2002; Kissine 2008; see van de Vate 2011; Mucha 2015 for a general discussion). Even if one denies that future tense encodes modality, still the question is whether it is a real tense. One could follow here – as Winford (2000a, 2000b) in his analysis of Sranan shows – Dahl's (1985) distinction between the dominant and secondary meanings (uses) of a category and assume that the dominant meaning of future markers is 'later time reference' and that the modal senses associated with such markers are in fact secondary meanings arising from implicatures inferred from the context. Following this line of reasoning, the future can be assigned to the domain of tense. This is in opposition to Bybee (1985: 157), for whom 'the future does not belong in the same grammatical category as the past', and Matthewson (2006), who suggests that the future is never itself a tense, but rather involves another element, which combines with tense. What is this other element? Here, Matthewson puts forward the idea that the element in question is a modal or temporal ordering predicate comparable to Abusch's (1985) WOLL. In English WOLL is a non-overt morpheme which combines with present or past and surfaces as *will* and *would* respectively. In contrast, in St'át'imcets the future marker *kehl* (recall ex. (1)) is taken to be the overt spell-out of the morpheme WOLL. This marker *kehl* combines with a covert tense morpheme which restricts the reference time to non-future values. Depending on which time reference is picked out (present or past), either an ordinary future reading (comparable with the English *will*) or a 'past future' reading (comparable with the English *would* form) are yielded (see Matthewson 2006 for details). This example reveals one important aspect of crosslinguistic variation: one of the two components of future meaning might be overt in some languages but covert in others. On the surface, the meaning components of the future can thus appear as being lexicalized in one morpheme in some languages, as is the case of the English future marker *will* or St'át'imcets *kehl*. However, the meaning components of future can be expressed by two independent grammatical markers from which the overall future meaning is compositionally derived. As Mucha and Zimmermann (2016: 20) point out, this is the case in Hausa, where – as they argue (cf. Mucha and Zimmermann 2016: 19) – future-oriented meanings consist of two components: a modal component, which is realized as *zaa*, and an aspectual component, expressed by so-called subjunctive aspect. Since the latter component shifts the time of eventuality to a time after the reference time it is reanalyzed by the authors, following Mucha (2015), as a marker of prospective aspect.[4,5]

Another important aspect of crosslinguistic variation concerns the question of whether future time reference is entailed or not by a given future marker (see Tonhauser 2011). While the St'át'imcets future marker *kehl* and the Guaraní future marker *-ta* obligatorily convey future time reference, this is not so in the case of *will* in English, as evidenced by the fact that *will* can realize present time reference with epistemic modality; see (2c) (Kissine 2008: 130).

(2)	a.	Mary will come.	*future/prediction*
	b.	Oil will float on water.	*generic*
	c.	Mary will be at the opera now.	*epistemic*
	d.	In winter, Mary will always wear a green coat.	*habitual/dispositional/ volitional*
	e.	You will leave tomorrow by the first train.	*deontic*

Crosslinguistically, future markers also differ with respect to the question of which modal meanings they are compatible with (or entail) (see Tonahauser 2011). While English *will* can have various modal uses (see (2b–e)), the Guaraní future marker *-ta* is only compatible with the modal meanings of intention and prediction/expectation, hence modal meanings which are intrinsically future-oriented, whereby the former (intention) has a circumstantial modal base and the latter (prediction) involves an epistemic modal base with stereotypical ordering source (see Tonhauser 2011: section 3.2).[6]

---

4 The usual assumption in the literature (see Klein 1994, inter alia) is that tense expresses the temporal relationship between the utterance time (UT) and the reference time (RT), while aspect is a relation between the reference time (RT) and the event time (ET). See also Tonhauser (2011), who in her analysis of the Paraguayan Guaraní future marker *-ta* also argues that it should be analyzed as a prospective aspect and not as future tense since it locates the eventuality time in the future of the reference time.

5 In Medumba, another African language analyzed by Mucha (2015: 229), future-oriented readings also involve a modal element which is claimed to always co-occur 'with a covert prospective time shifter or with overt prospective-time shifters that come with a remoteness specification'.

6 In Copley's (2002) account it is bouletic and inertial orderings that give rise to the future-oriented modal readings of intention and prediction. In a nutshell, bouletic ordering sources are based on the commitments of an animate entity, and inertial ordering sources are based on Dowty's (1979) concept of inertia worlds which can be roughly defined as a set of worlds in which things proceed normally. In the former case (intention), there must be an animate actor who is able to bring about the truth of a

Finally, let us note that also the question of whether epistemic readings are available for particular future markers or not can be subject to crosslinguistic variation. While English *will*, as has already been pointed out above, allows for a present epistemic reading (see (2c)), '*will* with the past appears to force future shifting' (Giannakidou and Mari 2016: 77). In contrast, future markers in other languages, e.g., in Greek and Italian, allow for epistemic readings with both past and non-past. Giannakidou and Mari (2016) call futures which appear to be equivalent to the universal epistemic modal MUST 'epistemic futures'.[7] Interestingly, FUT and MUST can even combine (which is treated as an instance of 'modal concord') and the reading remains the same; see (3a–c) (Giannakidou and Mari 2016: 77–8, 80).

(3) a. I Ariadne tha troi tora. (Greek)
the Ariadne FUT eat.npst.ipfv.3sg now
'Ariadne must be eating now.' *epistemic, now*
b. I Ariadne tha milise xthes.
the Ariadne FUT talk.pst.3sg yesterday
'Ariadne must have spoken yesterday.' *epistemic, past*
c. I Ariadne tha prepi na milise xthes
the Ariadne FUT must subj talk.pst.3sg yesterday.
'Ariadne must have spoken yesterday.'

Summing up and returning to the question we started with, namely, what the nature of future is, the discussion in this section has shown that while scholars agree that future eventualities are qualitatively different from the past and present tense ones and that future markers usually also have modal meanings, there is still no simple and uniform answer to the above question, though the view that perhaps there is universally no future tense seems to be a popular if not the prevelant opinion in the pertinent literature (see, among others, Enç 1996; Copley 2002; Matthewson 2006; Mucha 2015; Mucha and Zimmermann 2016; Giannakidou and Mari 2016 and the reference cited therein for discussion). Now that the general background has been provided, we can return to the puzzling question of the future in Slavic.

---

proposition in the future. In the latter case (prediction), the truth of the proposition depends on certain contingent facts about the world.

7 Giannakidou and Mari (2016: 111) take the fact that epistemic future is equivalent to the epistemic modal verb MUST as evidence 'that the grammatical category 'future' cannot be a purely temporal one'. They analyze the epistemic futures and MUST as 'biased modals'.

4. Slavic futures

In the following I will focus on three different Slavic languages, Bulgarian, Slovenian and Polish, which represent three different methods of expressing future time reference. It will be shown that despite their different etymologies (recall footnote 3) and clear syntactic differences, the constructions in question can express similar meanings.

4.1. Different origins, different syntax

The future tense in Bulgarian seems at first glance to provide direct evidence for the alleged connection between futurity and modality (but see section 4.2). It developed – just like in the other Balkan Slavic languages – from the Old Slavic modal verb *xotěti* 'will/want' plus infinitives structures.[8] As shown in Tomić (2004), individual Balkan Slavic languages represent different stages of the development in question, whereby Bulgarian and Macedonian are the languages with the most grammaticalized futures: a finite modal verb has reduced to a non-finite future marker and it is followed by a finite (present tense) lexical verb. Importantly, both perfective and imperfective complements are possible; see (4a) and (4b). In Macedonian the non-finite modal clitic can also take verbal complements in the past tense; cf. (4c) (Tomić 2004: 524).[9,10]

---

8 In this respect, future tenses in the Balkan Slavic languages are similar to future tenses in other Balkan languages (as Roberts and Roussou 2002: 37, 45 show, the origin of the future markers in Greek and Romanian is also the verb 'want': *thelo* and *velle*, respectively) and also to English future constructions with the auxliary *will*, which historically also derives from a modal verb, more specifically, from an Old English verb *willan* meaning 'wish' (see Lightfoot 2006: 37 f. and the references cited there).

9 Note that also future perfect is possible, constructed with the present perfect under FUT, as (i) demonstrates (Roumyana Pancheva, p.c.).

(i)	Azšte	sum	došla.	(Bulgarian)
	I FUT	be.prs.1sg	come.prf_ptcp.pfv.sg.f	
	'I will have come.'			

10 To account for these facts, Tomić (2004: 524) assumes that the modal clitic heads ModP (Modal Phrase), which subcategorises for MoodP with an empty Mood operator, is located to the left of T/AgrSP and VP, as indicated in (i).

(i) $[_{\text{ModP}}\ [_{\text{Mod}}\ \textit{šte}\ [_{\text{MoodP}}\ [_{\text{Mood}}\ [_{\text{T/AgrSP}}\ [_{\text{T/AgrS}}\ [_{\text{VP}}]]]]]]]$

(4) a. Ti *šte* dojdeš utre. (Bulgarian, Roumyana Pancheva, p.c.)
you FUT come.prs.pfv.2sg tomorrow
'You will arrive tomorrow.'

b. Az *šte* rabotja cjal den.
I FUT work.prs.ipfv.1sg whole day
'I will be working all day.'

c. Petar *ḱe* dojdeše. (Macedonian)
Petar FUT come.sbjv.pst.3sg
'Petar would have come.'

Given these facts, it seems that the Bulgarian future tense could in principle be analyzed in terms of a temporal or modal ordering predicate WOLL (cf. Abusch 1985). As mentioned in section 3, WOLL can be realized overtly, as in St'át'imcets, or non-overtly, as in English, and it can combine with the present or past and surface as 'will' and 'would' respectively. While in the mentioned languages, the ordering predicate and the tense are bundled together and lexicalized in one morpheme, Bulgarian, following this analysis, would represent another interesting case in which these two meaning components are expressed independently: in the form of a modal particle, being an instantiation of WOLL, and a perfective or imperfective lexical verb in the present (or past) tense form. In this respect, Bulgarian would in some sense resemble a situation observed in Hausa, where – as was pointed in section 3 – the overall future meaning is also compositionally derived from two meaning components which are independently lexicalized: a modal and an aspectual component.

Like Bulgarian, Slovenian also has a compound future tense. It is realized by means of a future auxiliary taking either perfective or imperfective complements. However, unlike Bulgarian, the lexical verb complement is not a finite verb but an *l*-participle and the future auxiliary is not a non-finite particle but a clitic inflected for person and number (see (5)).

(5) a. Janez ne *bo* pisal. (Slovenian, Frank Marušić, p.c.)
Janez NEG be.aux.3sg write.ptcp.ipfv.sg.m
'Janez will not write.' ('Janez will not be writing.')

b. Pismo *bomo* napisali v 3 ure.
letter be.aux.1pl write.ptcp.pfv.sg.m in 3 hours
'We will write the letter in three hours.'

Most importantly, the Slovenian future auxiliary has a completely different origin than that in Bulgarian, namely it can be traced back to the Common Slavic verb **byti* 'be(come)', or, more precisely, its perfective present forms (going back to the Common Slavic stem **bǫd-*) (see van Schooneveld 1951; Whaley 2000: 22). As argued in Whaley (2000: 145), the Common Slavic future perfect appears to be a very likely source of the Slovenian compound BE-future construction as it explains both the participial form of the verbal complement and the lack of the aspectual restriction: in the future perfect construction, the complement in the form of an *l*-participle could also be perfective or imperfective.

Now, given that in the Slovenian future tense there is no obvious modal element, the interesting question is how future meaning is obtained in such non-modal future constructions. Błaszczak and Klimek-Jankowska (2012, 2013a) analyze the Slovenian future auxiliary as a purely functional TP-related element (a 'higher auxiliary').[11,12] Given its high position it does not have any influence on the selection of the aspectual form of the *l*-participle: it can take both [+ipfv] and [+pfv] verbal complements. Just like other tense auxiliaries, the future auxiliary in Slovenian has just a temporal function (in this case that of locating the event time after speech time: $ST < ET$). The whole aspectual distinctions/interpretational differences in periphrastic future constructions in Slovenian are due to the aspectual marking on *l*-participle.[13] On the proposed analysis, the overall future meaning in Slovenian – just like in Hausa and Bulgarian – is thus compositionally derived from two meaning components, but this time the identified meaning

11 This assumption is additionally supported by the negation facts (cf. (5a)): on the standard assumption NegP precedes TP in Slovenian ($NegP > TP > VP$) (see Borsley and Rivero 1994). Note also that the future auxiliary in Slovenian is a second position clitic (Franks and Holloway King 2000).

12 That the future auxiliary in Slovenian is devoid of the lexical content is corroborated by the fact that it might co-occur with another BE (the lexical BE spelling out the lower VP-part of the tree), as shown in (i) (Frank Marušić, p.c.).

(i) a. *bom* (standard literary Slovenian)
be.1sg
'I will be.'

b. *bom* *bil* (dialects of Slovenian)
be.aux.1sg be.ptcp.sg.m
'I will be.'

13 In a nutshell, Błaszczak and Klimek-Jankowska (2013a: 24) assume, following Borik (2002), that perfective aspect requires that there cannot be any overlap between the speech time and the reference time and the event time must be included in the reference time $ST \cap RT = \emptyset \;\&\; ET \subseteq RT$. Given that, the combination of a future auxiliary, which requires that ST must precede ET, and perfective aspect, which requires that ET is included in RT and that ST and RT do not overlap, yields the meaning that the reference time must also be located after the speech time: $ST < RT \;\&\; ET \subseteq RT$, i.e., $ST < [_{RT}\ ET]$. In contrast, in the case of imperfective aspect (defined by Borik (2002)

components are: a temporal component (corresponding to the auxiliary) and an aspectual component (corresponding to the non-finite lexical verb in the form of an *l*-participle).

Polish represents the most intriguing case. Like in Bulgarian and Slovenian, Polish also uses perfective and imperfective futures but – unlike what we have observed in Bulgarian and Slovenian (recall ex. (4) and (5)) – these two futures are not realized in a uniform way. Whereas a perfective future corresponds to a perfective form of a present tense verb (there is no auxiliary involved), the imperfective future is composed of a BE-auxiliary, traditionally called "a future auxiliary," and an imperfective lexical verb, in the form of an *l*-participle or an infinitive (see (6)).

(6) a. On napisze list. (Polish)
he write.prs.pfv.3sg letter.acc
'He will write a letter.'

b. On nie *będzie* pisał / pisać listu.
he NEG be.aux.3sg write.ptcp.ipfv.sg.m / write.inf.ipfv letter.gen
'He will not write / be writing a letter.'

Even if superficially the construction with a participial complement in (6b) looks very much like its Slovenian counterpart in (5a), there are important differences between them. First of all, the compound BE-future in Polish only allows for imperfective complements, unlike that of Slovenian (see (5b)). Secondly, the compound BE-future in Polish has a different diachronic source, namely it most possibly arose as the result of the reinterpretation of the Common Slavic change-of-state verb **bǫd-* (perfective present forms of **byti* 'be(come)') as an inceptive verb, with the future implication becoming later the core meaning of the verb (see Whaley 2000: 137–40). Thirdly, the original compound future form in Polish was the infinitival future; the participial future is an innovative construction (see Whaley 2002; Błaszczak et al. 2014 for discussion). Fourthly, *będzie* in Polish is a VP-related element (a

as non-perfective, i.e., the external negation of the semantics of perfective aspect), it is just required that either ST and RT overlap or it is not the case that ET is included in RT. As Błaszczak and Klimek-Jankowska (2013a: 26–7) demonstrates, a combination of the first condition, i.e., the reference time overlaps with the speech time, $ST \cap RT \neq \emptyset$, with the semantics of the future auxiliary in Slovenian, $ST < ET$, yiels the meaning that the reference time overlaps with the speech time while the event time follows the speech time, i.e., $[_{RT}\ ST < ET]$.

'lower auxiliary').[14,15] Given its low position, it can directly select its verbal complement: it is compatible only with [+ipfv] complements. In this respect *będzie* shows a similar behavior to phase verbs like 'begin', which also only select imperfective VP-complements. To explain why *będzie* is compatible only with [+ipfv] verbal complements, Błaszczak and Klimek-Jankowska (2012, 2013a) assume that Polish *będzie*, unlike its Slovenian counterpart, is not completely devoid of the lexical content: it denotes a state BE.[16] Denoting a state, *będzie* is compatible only with [+durative] eventualities, hence only [+ipfv] VP-complements are possible.

Given that in the Polish perfective and imperfective future tense constructions, there is not only no obvious modal element but also no genuine tense auxiliary, the interesting question is how future meaning is obtained there and whether it is obtained in the same way in the simple perfective (6a) and the compound imperfective (6b) futures. Błaszczak et al. (2014) argue that there is one mechanism of obtaining future meaning in Polish, namely the combination of perfective aspect and present tense is what gives rise to the future time reference. More exactly, the role of the perfective aspect is to forward-shift the reference time and to locate it right after the speech time.[17] In the case of simple future realized as a present tense form of a perfective lexical verb these two components are

---

14 This assumption is additionally supported by the negation facts (cf. (6b)): on the standard assumption NegP follows TP in Polish (TP > NegP >VP) (see Borsley and Rivero 1994). See also footnote 11.

15 Błaszczak et al. (2014) assume that the auxiliary *będzie* belongs to the extended projection of the imperfective lexical verb and it occupies the Asp head.

16 Unlike in Slovenian (recall footnote 12), in Polish the future auxiliary cannot co-occur with another BE. Examples like (i) below are completey unacceptable.

(i) a.	**będę*	*był*	b.	**będę*	*być*	(Polish)
	be.aux.1.sg	be.ptcp.sg.m		be.aux.1.sg	be.inf	
	(intended: 'I will be')					

17 Independent evidence that the combination of present tense and perfective aspect (in periphrasitic constructions) is sufficient to trigger a future time reference comes from cases like those in (i) (see Błaszczak et al. 2014: 190–1 and the references cited there). In (i) the present tense modal verb is followed by an imperfective or a perfective infinitival complement. Note that only in the latter case we have a clear future reading.

(i) a.	Muszę	*myć*	tę	klatkę schodową	za karę.	(Polish)
	must.1sg	clean.inf.ipfv	this	staircase.acc	as punishment	
	'I have to clean this staircase as a punishment.'					
	('I am cleaning a staircase because I have to.')				*present reading*	

clearly identified. What about the imperfective compound future? In the latter case it is the auxiliary *będzie* that bears perfective present tense morphology (as was noticed above, it originates from the perfective present tense paradigm of the Old Church Slavonic verb *byti* 'to be' (van Schooneveld 1951)). What makes *będzie* different from perfective present lexical verbs is that *będzie* is a Kimian state (see Maienborn 2001 for discussion), i.e., it does not introduce a typical eventuality argument but rather a referential argument for a temporally bound property exemplification. Since perfective aspect on *będzie* does not have any lexical access to an eventuality argument, it cannot operate on it, i.e., it cannot establish a relation between the time of the event (ET) and the reference time (RT).[18] The perfective BE auxiliary in the Polish compound future is thus semantically deficient. The second component of the compound future, the imperfective complement, is also semantically deficient in the sense that it cannot by itself establish a temporal relation with the speech time ST (but unlike *będzie* it introduced an eventuality argument). Despite their deficiencies, as Błaszczak et al. (2014: 201) observe, the two elements of the compound future form in Polish are complementary to each other: 'the perfective aspect on *będzie* requires that there is no overlapping between the speech time (ST) and the reference time (RT), which – just as in the case of [simple future] – can only be fulfilled if the RT follows the ST; the imperfective aspect on the lexical complement of *będzie* establishes a relation between the event time (ET) and the reference time (RT) in such a way that the forward-shifted RT is properly included in the event time (ET)' (ibid.). The event time (ET) can (although it does not have to) coincide with the speech time (ST): ST > RT $\subseteq$ ET (ST < $[_{ET}$ RT]; see footnote 13).

To conclude, the case of the future tense constructions in Polish shows even if a language does not contain any modal or any genuine future auxiliary, future time reference can be alternatively derived from the combination of perfective aspect and present tense. It should be noted that the role of perfective aspect in

---

b. Muszę	*umyć*	tę	klatkę schodową	za karę.
must.1sg	clean.inf.pfv	this	staircase.acc	as punishment

'I have to clean this staircase as a punishment.'
('I will clean a staircase because I have to.') *future reading*

18 Recall that on Borik's (2002) analysis perfective aspect is defined as: ST $\cap$ RT = Ø $\wedge$ ET $\subseteq$ RT. Imperfective aspect is just the external negation of the semantics of pefective aspect: $\neg$ [ST $\cap$ RT = Ø $\wedge$ ET $\subseteq$ RT] = $\neg$ [ST $\cap$ RT = Ø] $\vee$ $\neg$[ET $\subseteq$ RT] (see also footnote 13). See Błaszczak and Klimek-Jankowska (2013a), Błaszczak et al. (2014) for details of the proposed analysis.

Polish as forward-shifting the reference time bears a resemblance to other 'time-shifters' assumed in the literature (recall footnotes 4 and 5).

4.2. Semantic similarities

In the previous section we have seen that Bulgarian, Slovenian and Polish futures have different origins and show clear syntactic differences. Whereas the future marker in Bulgarian is a modal clitic occupying a position to the left of TP, the Slovenian future marker is temporal auxiliary located in T^0. In the case of the Polish compound future, the auxiliary *będzie* belongs to the extended projection of the imperfective lexical verb and it occupies the Asp head. In the Polish simple (perfective) future there is no auxiliary element at all. Despite their syntactic differences and in spite of the quite different etymologies of the respective auxiliaries (WANT vs. BE(COME)) (see also footnote 3), futures in Bulgarian, Slovenian and Polish show a similar range of meanings or uses. In addition to their purely temporal readings, they can appear both in contexts expressing intention or willingness as well as contexts expressing a pure prediction, as illustrated in (7) and (8), respectively.[19]

(7) *Context:* intention/willingness ('I promise that .....')

a. *šte* ti pomogna utre. (Bulgarian)
FUT you.dat help.prs.pfv.1sg tomorrow

b. ti *bom* jutri pomagal. (Slovenian)
you.dat be.aux.3sg tomorrow help.ptcp.ipfv.sg.m

c. *będę* ci jutro pomagał. (Polish)
be.prs.pfv.1sg you.dat tomorrow help.ptcp.ipfv.sg.m
'I will help you tomorrow.'

(8) *Context:* prediction ('Look at his face.')

a. *šte* se razplače (vseki moment). (Bulgarian)
FUT REFL cry.prs.pfv.3sg (every moment)

b. Vsak hip *bo* zjokal. (Slovenian)
any moment be.aux.3sg cry.ptcp.pfv.sg.m

c. Zaraz się *rozpłacze.* (Polish)
immediately REFL burst-into-tears.prs.pfv.3sg
'He is going to cry/will start crying any moment now.'

---

19 The following Bulgarian examples are due to Roumyana Pancheva (p.c.) and the Slovenian ones are due to Frank Marusić (p.c.). The Polish examples are adopted from Błaszczak et al. (2014).

Interestingly, note that in epistemic contexts of the sort illustrated in (9) we also find future.

(9) a. *Context:* epistemic ('Try this wine! What sort of wine do you think is this?')

Tova	*šte*	e	Barolo.	(Bulgarian)
this	FUT	be.prs.3sg	Barolo.	

'This will be Barolo.'

a.'

Tova	*šte*	/ *trjabva*	da e	Barolo.
this	FUT	/ must	SBJV be.prs.3sg	Barolo.

'This will/must be Barolo.'

a."

Tova	*šte*	*trjabva*	da e	Barolo.
this	FUT	must	SBJV be.prs.3sg	Barolo

'This must be Barolo.

b.

To	*bo*	(gotovo)	Barolo.	(Slovenian)
this	be.prs.pfv.3sg	(for sure)	Barolo	

'This will be Barolo (for sure).'

b.'

To	*je*	(gotovo)	Barolo.
this	be.prs.ipfv.3sg	(for sure)	Barolo.

'This is Barolo (for sure).'

c.

To	*będzie*	Barolo.	(Polish)
this	be.prs.pfv.3sg	Barolo.	

'This will be Barolo.'

c.'

To	*musi*	być	Barolo.
this	must	be.inf	Barolo.

'This must be Barolo.'

c."

To	*będzie*	musiało	być	Barolo.
this	be.prs.pfv.3sg	must.ptcp	be.inf	Barolo

'This will have to be Barolo.'

As indicated in the translations, a purely epistemic reading, comparable to MUST, seems to be available. Roumyana Pancheva (p.c.) points out that in the contexts at hand a future form with a subjunctive *da*-clause is also possible.[20] This form is parallel to modal constructions with 'must' in Bulgarian, as shown in (9a'). It seems that in Bulgarian FUT and MUST can

20 According to Svetlana Petrova (p.c.), while a pure future form (without a subjunctive complement) is possible with stative predicates such as 'be at home', in other cases a future form with a subjunctive complement is preferred; cf. (i-a) vs. (i-b).

even co-occur (see (9a")),[21] which would make the Bulgarian future in such cases comparable to epistemic futures of the sort observed in Greek (recall ex. (3) in section 3).[22] In contrast, as indicated in (9c"), a combination of future and MUST in Polish results in a future (deontic) interpretation (the epistemic interpretation seems to be lost). In Polish there are also no epistemic readings with the past (unlike in Bulgarian, see footnote 22). It should also be noted that such epistemic uses of futures seem to be limited. Clear examples of epistemic uses always concern the future form (analyzed as perfective present form) of the verb 'be' in contexts such as those illustrated in (9a,b,c); see also footnotes 20 and 21. The intriguing question is why present time reference (on the epistemic interpretation) is possible in the first place.

(i) a. Marija *šte* e na rabota. (Bulgarian) *epistemic, now*
Mary FUT be.prs.3sg at work
'Mary will be at work now.'
b. Marija *šte* da se hrani v momenta.
Mary FUT SBJV REFL eat.prs.3sg at moment
'Mary will be eating at the moment.'

21 According to Svetlana Petrova (p.c.), while such 'modal concord' cases are fine with stative predicates such as 'be at home' (see (i)), with other predicates such as 'eat' they would be difficult to interpret as present epistemic: 'rather, the interpretation would be 'will have to' (necessity in the future)'. Compare also the Polish example in (9c").

(i) Marija *šte* *trjabva* da e v kašti. (Bulgarian) *epistemic, now*
Mary FUT must SBJV be.prs.3sg at home
'Mary must be at home.'

22 It should be noted that in Bulgarian, just like in Greek and Italian, epistemic futures with past are possible, also in a combination with MUST, as shown in (i) (due to Svetlana Petrova (p.c.)).

(i) a. Maria *šte* se e hranila včera. (Bulgarian) *epistemic, past*
Mary FUT REFL be.prs.3sg eat.prf_ptcp.sg.f yesterday
'Mary must have eaten yesterday.'
b. Marija *trjabva* da se e hranila včera.
Mary must SBJV REFL be.prs.3sg eat.prf_ptcp.sg.f yesterday
'Mary must have eaten yesterday.'
c. Marija *šte* *trjabva* da se e hranila včera.
Mary FUT must SBJV REFL be.prs.3sg eat.prf_ptcp.sg.f yesterday
'Mary must have eaten yesterday.'

Perfective present tense in Polish can otherwise only refer to future, only imperfective presents can be used for referring to ongoing situations.[23] One could follow here the suggestion put forward by Mucha (2015). To account for the behavior of the future maker á^{ʔ} (a modal element) in Medumba, which always co-occurs with a covert future-shifting element (see footnote 5) but at the same time is also used to express present-oriented modality, Mucha (2015: 180) adopts the idea that in the case of stative predicates the contrast between perfective and imperfective aspect is neutralized as statives require an overlap relation between reference time and eventuality time rather than an inclusion relation. More precisely, 'stative predicates are inherently unbounded in the strictest sense, i.e. every moment at which a state holds is preceded and followed by another moment at which the state holds, it is always true that, if a stative eventuality holds at the utterance time, it will also hold at some time after the utterance time' (ibid.). Note however that even this account would need to be further qualified since not all statives readily allow for a present-oriented epistemic interpretation, as (10) demonstrates. In (10c) only a future interpretation seems to be possible.

(10) a.

Ona	musi	być	chora	(dlatego	nie	przyszła)	(Polish)
she	must	be.inf	sick	(that's why	not	come.pst.3sg.f)	

'She must be sick (that's why she didn't come).'

b.

Ona	pewnie	jest	chora	(dlatego	nie	przyszła).
she	surely	be.prs.ipfv.3sg	sick	(that's why	not	come.pst.3sg.f)

'She is sick for sure (that's why she didn't come).'

c.

#Ona	będzie	chora	(dlatego	nie	przyszła).
she	be.prs.pfv.3sg	sick	(that's why	not	come.pst.3sg.f)

'She will be sick (that's why she didn't come).'

23 The perfective present form cannot be used in a context which implies that the eventuality is taking place at the moment of speaking or was taking place in the past; cf. (i) vs. (ii).

(i) *

Obserwuję / Obserwowałam,	jak	Ewa	zrobi	porządki.
observe.prs./pst.ipfv.1sg	how	Eve	do.prs.pfv.3.sg	cleaning

Lit.: '*I am / was observing how Eve will be cleaning.'

(ii)

Obserwuję / Obserwowałam,	jak	Ewa	robi	porządki.
observe.prs./pst.ipfv.1sg	how	Eve	do.prs.ipfv.3.sg	cleaning

Lit.: 'I am / was observing how Eve is cleaning.'

(11) *Context:* 'What do you think what she is doing now?'

a. Ona pewnie je teraz obiad.
   she surely eat.prs.ipfv.3sg now dinner
   'She is surely eating now dinner.'

b. Ona będzie teraz jeść obiad.
   she be.prs.pfv.3sg now eat.inf.ipfv dinner
   'She will now be eating dinner.'

Finally, note that in Polish in some contexts also futures with non-stative imperfective predicates can receive an 'epistemic now' interpretation, as shown in (11) (see also footnote 20). Interestingly, a similar situation is found in the already mentioned case of the Medumba future modal *áʔ*. As Mucha (2015: 177) points out, in addition to stative predicates, also eventive predicates with the future modal and a covert future shifter allow for present epistemic readings if they are also marked for imperfective, even though future imperfective (progressive) is the most natural interpretation. As Mucha (2015: 179) argues, this is so because the truth conditions of such imperfective sentences are compatible with a present epistemic reading. The truth conditions on the proposed analysis require that the event is ongoing at some future time interval. However, as Mucha (2015) explains, '[g]iven that time intervals can be as short as instantaneous moments, in any reasonably conceivable case in which an eventuality includes the utterance time [giving rise to the present epistemic interpretation in question], it will also be true that there is a time in the future, however short, which is included in the time of the [...] event' (p. 179). Note that given the analysis proposed for the Polish imperfective compound BE-future in section 4.1, the compositionally derived meaning is: $ST < RT \subseteq ET$. The event time follows the speech time and it contains the reference time but the boundaries of an event, understood here as a combination of the state BE and the event denoted by the imperfective complement of *będzie*, are open. Due to that, as was pointed out section 4.1, the event time (ET) can (although it does not have to) coincide with the speech time (ST) in the case of imperfective future. This very fact seems to facilitate the present epistemic interpretation of imperfective futures. The proposed compositionally derived semantics of the periphrastic imperfective future form also explains the observation by Błaszczak and Klimek-Jankowska (2012, 2013a) regarding an interesting distinction in the use of Polish and Slovenian perfective and imperfective futures, in addition to their usual semantic aspectual differences.[24] This

24 An informal questionnaire conducted with a few Bulgarian speakers shows that this observation holds for Bulgarian as well.

distinction has to do with the question of whether the future action is settled at the moment of speaking or not.[25] In a context in which the future situation can be understood as a natural continuation of a plan which holds at the moment of speaking – imperfective future is preferred. As Błaszczak and Klimek-Jankowska explain, this is so because in the semantics of imperfective future there is an option of not having a temporal gap between ET and ST, i.e., the event time (ET) can coincide with the speech time (ST). The shorter the gap is the less possible it is that such a pre-planned future eventuality will be changed or prevented. In contrast, in the semantics of perfective future it is possible to obtain compositionally a temporal gap between the moment of speaking (ST) and the begin of the future eventuality (ET). This makes such futures more compatible with contexts in which we want to prevent or to change a future event.

5. Concluding remarks

The discussion of the Bulgarian, Slovenian and Polish futures in section 4 has revealed that even closely related languages can employ different means of realizing

25 For example, in a 'being amazed' context only an imperfective future seems to be good; see (i). Surely one can only be amazed by something which is already presupposed to be true. In contrast, in a 'warning context', as in (ii), which implies that the hearer can still do something to prevent the action of falling, hence the action of falling is not pre-arranged or otherwise planned at the moment of speaking, only perfective future seems to be good. See Błaszczak and Klimek-Jankowska (2013a, 2013b) for further contexts and a formal analysis.

(i) [*Context:* Have you heard the latest news? The boss chose John to organize the biggest conference we have ever had.]
Jestem zaskoczony, ✓*imperfective* / # *perfective*
be.prs.1sg amazed
że najbardziej niezorganizowana osoba w naszej firmie
that most unorganized person in our company
będzie organizować tak ważną konferencję.
be.aux.3sg organize.inf.ipfv so important conference
'I am amazed that the most unorganized person in our company will be organizing such an important conference.'

(ii) [*Context:* We see a blind man walking towards a precipice. We see that he is just about to fall down. So we want to warn the man to prevent him from falling.]
Uwaga, spadniesz! ✓*perfective* / # *imperfective*
caution fall-down.prs.pfv.2sg
'Be careful. (If not) you are going to fall down!'

future time reference, thus confirming the view that there is a strong variation in this regard crosslinguistically. It is also the case that some general patterns as to how future meaning is derived can be established. In general, it seems that future time reference involves more than one meaning component which can be lexicalized into one marker or expressed as independent grammatical markers, whereby the assumed meaning ingredients can be overt or covert. Usually, it is modality, tense and aspect, in various combinations, that make future meaning possible. The case of Polish shows that future time reference can be established even if a language lacks a genuine future tense. As was argued above, it is a combination of present tense and perfective aspect which ensures this. In a genuinely tenseless language such as Hausa which does not possess any overt or covert tense marking (but recall the discussion in section 3 about a covert tense morpheme in St'át'imcets), future time interpretation is established by means of modal and aspectual markers (see Mucha 2015; Mucha and Zimmermann 2016).

Superficially, a dividing line between the three investigated Slavic languages in section 4 could be that of 'modal futures' vs. 'non-modal futures', with Bulgarian belonging to the first group and Slovenian and Polish being representatives of the second group. This distinction seems to correlate with the syntactic differences observed in section 4.1. A modal future of the Bulgarian sort can take finite complements (of either aspect), hence also complements in the past tense are in principle possible. Such a future marker can also be used to express epistemic readings with present and past, and it can co-occur with MUST. Non-modal futures, in contrast, cannot take finite complements, hence they do not allow for epistemic readings with the past. Neither do they allow for a co-occurrence with MUST. But they can co-occur with verbal complements marked for aspect, either unselectively, i.e., they can combine with complements of either aspect, as in Slovenian, or they can impose aspectual restrictions on their complements, as in Polish.

However, on closer inspection, this 'modal future' vs. 'non-modal future' division will have a hard time accounting for the facts observed in section 4.2, namely that futures in all three investigated Slavic languages show similar meanings/uses and in addition to temporal uses, that they can also be used to express intentional and predictive interpretations. But if 'the commonly observed interpretive effects of intention and prediction are triggered by bouletic or inertial ordering sources' (Mucha and Zimmermann 2016: 8) (see also footnote 6 and the discussion in section 3), then the question arises as to how to account for such effects in the case of 'non-modal' futures. One possibility would be to assume that future tense forms can be used to express the meanings of intention and prediction/expectation since such modal meanings are intrinsically future-oriented, hence future forms are simply compatible with such contexts. Problematic cases of present-oriented epistemic necessity contexts, pointed out in section 4.2., would require a special treatment, for example, along the line suggested by Błaszczak and Klimek-Jankowska (2012, 2013a, 2013b) in their analysis of the Polish and Slovenian future constructions, or similar to Mucha (2015) in her analysis of Medumba future. Another possibility would be to assume that also in the case of 'non-modal' futures in Slovenian and Polish there is a covert modal element whose core meaning consists simply in universal quantification over possible worlds. Interestingly, on such an analysis the proposed modal element for the Polish and Slovenian futures would in fact be a covert counterpart of the overt modal marker *á*ˀ in Medumba whose semantics is that 'of a very general universal modal with no temporal meaning components' (Mucha 2015: 175). In view of the observed similarities in section 4.2 between Polish and Medumba regarding the availability of present-oriented epistemic readings with futures, the envisaged account would in fact be desirable. Such an account would also fit well in frameworks that assume similar ingredients (overt or covert) to derive observed crosslinguistic patters (recall the discussion in section 3).[26]

References

Abusch, Dorit. 1985. "On verbs and time." PhD thesis, University of Massachusetts.

Anderson, Rachel J, Stephen A. Dewhurst and Richard A. Nash. 2012. "Shared cognitive processes underlying past and future episodic thinking: The impact of imagery and concurrent task demands on event specificity." *Journal of Experimental Psychology: Learning, Memory and Cognition* 38: 356–365.

Bloom, Lois, Karin Lifter and Jeremie Hafitz. 1980. "Semantics of verbs and the development of verb inflection in child language." *Language* 56: 386–412.

Błaszczak, Joanna, Patrycja Jabłońska, Dorota Klimek-Jankowska, and Krzysztof Migdalski. 2014. "The riddle of future tense in Polish: How much 'future' is there in 'future tense'?" In *Future Tense(s) / Future Time(s)*, Philippe De Brabanter, Mikhail Kissine and Saghie Sharifzadeh (eds.). Oxford: Oxford University Press, 165–204.

Błaszczak, Joanna and Dorota Klimek-Jankowska. 2012. "Futures in Polish and Slovenian from the perspective of a force-dynamic model." In *Proceedings of Sinn und Bedeutung 16: The Utrecht Meeting, 2011* (MIT Working Papers in

26 Note that also Kissine (2008) in his analysis of English *will* argues that the modal component of propositions containing this marker can be explained in terms of 'a restriction of the domain of quantification of a covert epistemic necessity' (p. 153).

Linguistics), Ana Aguilar-Guevara; Anna Chernilovskaya and Rick Nouwen (eds.). Cambridge: MIT Press, 85–98.

Błaszczak, Joanna and Dorota Klimek-Jankowska. 2013a. "Futures in Polish and Slovenian: 'A hole in a sock' theory." In *Formal Approaches to Slavic Linguistics (FASL 20): The Second MIT Meeting, 2011*, Alexander Podobryaev (ed.). Ann Arbor: Michigan Slavic Publications, 17–32.

Błaszczak, Joanna and Dorota Klimek-Jankowska. 2013b. "Futures, futurates, plans and forces." In *Formal Description of Slavic Languages: The Ninth Conference. Proceedings of FDSL 9, Göttingen 2011* (Linguistik International 28), Uwe Junghanns, Dorothee Fehrmann, Denisa Lenertová and Hagen Pitsch (eds.). Frankfurt am Main: Peter Lang, 9–35.

Borik, Olga. 2002. "Aspect and reference time." PhD thesis, Utrecht University. [Published 2006 by Oxford University Press].

Borsley, Robert D. and Maria-Luisa Rivero. 1994. "Clitic auxiliaries and incorporation in Polish." *Natural Language and Linguistic Theory* 12: 373–422.

Bybee, Joan L. 1985. *Morphology: A study of the relation between meaning and form*. Amsterdam and Philadelphia: John Benjamins.

Bybee, Joan, Revere Perkins, and William Pagliuca. 1994. *The evolution of grammar. Tense, aspect, and modality in the languages of the world*. Chicago: The University of Chicago Press.

Chung, S. and A. Timberlake. 1985. "Tense, aspect, and mood." In *Language Typology and Syntactic Description*, Vol. III, Timothy Shopen (ed.). Cambridge: Cambridge University Press, 202–258.

Copley, Bridget. 2002. "The semantics of the future." PhD thesis, MIT. [Published 2009 by Routledge].

Copley, Bridget. 2010. "Aspectualized futures in Indonasian and English." In *Layers of Aspect* (Studies in Constraint Based Lexicalism), Patricia Cabredo-Hofherr and Brenda Laca (eds.). Stanford: CSLI Publications, 101–124.

Copley, Bridget. 2014. "Causal chains for futurates." In *Future Tense(s) / Future Time(s)*, Philippe De Brabanter; Mikhail Kissine and Saghie Sharifzadeh (eds.). Oxford: Oxford University Press, 72–86.

Crane, Laura, Sophie E Lind, and Dermot M. Bowler. 2012. "Remembering the past and imagining the future in autism spectrum disorder." *Memory* 21(2): 157–166.

Dahl, Östen. 1985. *Tense and aspect systems*. Oxford: Blackwell.

Dahl, Östen and Viveka Velupillai. 2011. "Chapter 67: The future tense." In *The World Atlas of Language Structures (WALS) Online*, Matthew S. Dryer and Martin Haspelmath (eds.). Munich: Max Planck Digital Library.

De Brabanter, Philippe, Mikhail Kissine, and Saghie Sharifzadeh. 2014. "Future tense vs. future time: An introduction." In *Future Tense(s) / Future Time(s)*,

Philippe De Brabanter, Mikhail Kissine, and Saghie Sharifzadeh (eds.). Oxford: Oxford University Press, 1–25.

Dowty, David. 1979. *Word meaning in Montague grammar*. Dordrecht: Reidel.

Enç, Mürvet. 1996. "Tense and modality." In *The Handbook of Contemporary Semantic Theory*, Shalom Lappin (ed.). Oxford: Blackwell, 345–358.

Franks, Steven and Tracy Holloway King. 2000. *A handbook of Slavic clitics*. New York: Oxford University Press.

Giannakidou, Anastasia and Alda Mari. 2016. "Epistemic future and epistemic MUST: Non-veridicality, evidence, and partial knowledge." In *Mood, Aspect, Modality Revisited. New Answers to Old Questions*, Joanna Błaszczak, Anastasia Giannakidou, Dorota Klimek-Jankowska and Krzysztof Migdalski (eds.). Chicago: The University of Chicago Press, 75–117.

Greenberg, Joseph H. 1966. *Language universals, with special references to feature hierarchies*. (Janua Linguarum, Series Minor 59.) The Hague: Mouton.

Haspelmath, Martin. 1998. "The semantic development of old presents: New futures and subjunctives without grammaticalization." *Diachronica* 15(1): 29–62.

Kissine, Mikhail. 2008. "Why *will* is not a modal?" *Natural Language Semantics* 16: 129–155.

Klein, Wolfgang. 1994. *Time in language*. London, New York: Routledge.

Lightfoot, David. 2006. *How new languages emerge*. Cambridge: Cambridge University Press.

Maienborn, Claudia. 2001. "On the position and interpretation of locative modifiers." *Natural Language Semantics* 9: 191–240.

Matthewson, Lisa. 2006. "Temporal semantics in a supposedly tenseless language." *Linguistics and Philosophy* 29: 673–713.

Mucha, Anne. 2015. "Temporal interpretation and cross-linguistic variation. A formal semantic analysis of temporal and aspectual reference in Hausa and Medumba." PhD thesis, University of Potsdam.

Mucha, Anne and Malte Zimmermann. 2016. "TAM-coding and temporal interpretation in West African languages." In *Mood, Aspect, Modality Revisited. New Answers to Old Questions*, Joanna Błaszczak, Anastasia Giannakidou, Dorota Klimek-Jankowska and Krzysztof Migdalski (eds.). Chicago: The University of Chicago Press, 6–44.

Roberts, Ian and Anna Roussou. 2002. "The history of the future." In *Syntactic Effects of Morphological Change*, David W. Lightfoot (ed.). Oxford and New York: Oxford University Press, 23–56.

Sarkar, Anoop. 1998. "The conflict between future tense and modality: The case of *will* in English." *Penn Working Papers in Linguistics* 5: 91–117.

van Schooneveld, Cornelis H. 1951. "The aspect system of the Old Church Slavonic and Old Russian verbum finitum *byti*." *Word* 7(2): 96–103.

Smith, Carlota S., Ellavina Perkins, and Theodore Fernald. 2003. "Temporal interpretation in Navajo." In *The Proceedings of SULA 2, Vancouver, BC*, Jan Anderssen, Paula Menéndez-Benito and Adam Werle (eds.). GLSA, University of Massachusetts, Amherst, 175–192.

Suddendorf, Thomas and Michael C. Corballis. 2007. "The evolution of foresight: What is mental time travel, and is it unique to humans?" *Behavioral and Brain Sciences* 30: 299–351.

Swift, Mary. 2003. "Early time reference in Inuktitut child language: The role of event realization and aspectual interpretation." In *The Proceedings of SULA 2, Vancouver, BC.*, Jan Anderssen, Paula Menéndez-Benito and Adam Werle (eds.). GLSA, University of Massachusetts, Amherst, 193–202.

Tomić, Olga. 2004. "The syntax of the Balkan Slavic future tenses." *Lingua* 114: 51–542.

Tonhauser, Judith. 2011. "The Paraguayan Guaraní future marker *-ta*: Formal semantics and cross-linguistic comparison." In *Tense Across Languages*, Monika Rathert and Renate Musan (eds.). Tübingen: Niemeyer, 207–231.

Trondhjem, Naja F. 2014. "Markers of futurity and aspect in West Greenlandic." In *Future Tense(s) / Future Time(s)*, Philippe De Brabanter, Mikhail Kissine and Saghie Sharifzadeh (eds.). Oxford: Oxford University Press, 114–137.

Vander Klok, Jozina. 2010. "On the semantics of future markers in East Javanese." Paper presented at AFLA-17 (Austronesian Formal Linguistics Association XVII), Stony Brook University, May 7–9, 2010.

van de Vate, Marleen Susanne. 2011. "Tense, Aspect and Modality in a Radical Creole: The Case of Saamáka." PhD thesis, University of Tromsø.

Weist, Richard M. 2014. "Future temporal reference in child language." In *Future Tense(s) / Future Time(s)*, Philippe De Brabanter, Mikhail Kissine and Saghie Sharifzadeh (eds.). Oxford: Oxford University Press, 87–113.

Weist, Richard M., Hanna Wysocka, Katarzyna Witkowska-Stadnik, Ewa Buczkowska, and Emilia Konieczna. 1984. "The defective tense hypothesis: on the emergence of tense and aspect in child Polish." *Journal of Child Language* 11(2): 347–374.

Whaley, Marika L. 2000. "The evolution of the Slavic 'be(come)'-type compound future." Ph.D. thesis, The Ohio State University.

Winford, Donald. 2000a. "Irrealis in Sranan. Mood and modality in a radical creole." *Journal of Pidgin and Creole Languages* 15(1): 63–125.

Winford, Donald. 2000b. "Tense and aspect in Sranan and the creole prototype." In *Language Change and Language Contact in Pidgins and Creoles* (Creole Language Library 21), John McWhorter (ed.). Amsterdam/Philadelphia: John Benjamins Publishing Company, 383–442.

Julia Bacskai-Atkari

Equatives, Comparatives, and Polarity in Slavic*

1. Introduction

This article examines the role of polarity marking in overtness requirements on the left periphery of comparative subclauses, especially regarding the differences from equative subclauses. The phenomenon can be well observed in Slavic, where comparative complementisers tend to be transparent in terms of marking negative polarity.

Embedded degree clauses fall into two major types: AS-clauses (equatives) and THAN-clauses (comparatives). They are illustrated in (1) below: (1a) shows an equative clause, (1b) shows comparison to a lower degree, and (1c) shows comparison to a higher degree.

(1) a. Anthony is as tall **as** Mary is.
  b. Anthony is taller **than** Mary is.
  c. Anthony is less tall **than** Mary is.

Regarding degree semantics, the following can be established: AS-clauses encode degree equality (d=d') and THAN-clauses encode degree inequality (d≠d'). The relevant semantics of the examples in (1) can be schematised as follows:

(2) a. $\exists d \exists d'[\textsc{tall}\ (a,d)\ \&\ \textsc{tall}\ (m,d')\ \&\ (d=d')]$
  b. $\exists d \exists d'[\textsc{tall}\ (a,d)\ \&\ \textsc{tall}\ (m,d')\ \&\ (d>d')\ \&\ (d\neq d')]$
  c. $\exists d \exists d'[\textsc{tall}\ (a,d)\ \&\ \textsc{tall}\ (m,d')\ \&\ (d<d')\ \&\ (d\neq d')]$

The relation between the degrees is encoded by the matrix Deg (*as/-er/more/less*) and partially by the subclause. In AS-clauses, both encode degree equality. In THAN-clauses, the matrix Deg encodes superiority or inferiority, and the subclause encodes merely degree inequality (referred to as "degree negation"). Evidence for the lack of further specification by the subclause comes from the fact that while the matrix degree determines the choice between AS and THAN, there are no subtypes in comparative complements according to superiority/inferiority.

Degree negation in THAN-clause can also be reflected lower than the THAN-CP itself in the subclause. As shown already by Seuren (1973), comparative

* This research was funded by the DFG (BA 5201/1-1).

subclauses are negative polarity environments, and negative polarity items are licensed. Consider:

(3) She would rather die than **lift a finger** to help.

In (3) above, the element *lift a finger* is a negative polarity item that is licensed to appear only if there is a (covert or overt) negation element present in the structure.

In connection with the issue of negative polarity, the following questions arise. First, the question is whether negative polarity has a reflex in the CP-domain: it is expected that the licensor of negative polarity items, see (3), is located high in the clause. Second, it should be clarified whether and how C heads in AS-clauses and THAN-clauses differ: based on the semantics given in (2), they are expected to differ inasmuch as comparatives express inequality. Third, it should be investigated whether comparative operators suffice as overt markers instead of complementisers: as shown by Bacskai-Atkari (2016), operators suffice in equative clauses in various languages but this is apparently not the case in comparatives.

Using data from Czech, Polish, Serbo-Croatian and partially Russian, this paper proposes that Slavic languages provide explicit answers to these questions. Since degree operators are essential in this matter, section 2 examines the status of these operators in the respective languages, concentrating on degree questions, where operators are obligatory. Section 3 then discusses the availability of degree operators in equatives, showing that while ordinary degree operators indeed show up in these constructions, some languages show them either as grammaticalised complementisers or they allow only relative operators that are not tied to a degree interpretation. Finally, section 4 examines the same questions in comparatives, showing that operators in comparative subclauses do not suffice as overt markers, except in languages that allow them to be inserted directly into C. The findings presented in this paper are important for the theory because they show that the consistent differences between equatives and comparatives can be traced back to general requirements that follow from the semantic properties of the constructions. In addition, the study summarises a systematic investigation of degree constructions in the Slavic languages under scrutiny.

2. Degree operators

Equative and comparative subclauses contain relative operators as degree operators: these can be overt or covert (cf. Bacskai-Atkari 2014b). These often have their interrogative counterparts; the phenomenon is illustrated for English *how*, which is available in certain non-standard dialects in embedded degree clauses as well:[1]

(4) a. **How tall** is Mary?
b. % Anthony is as tall as **how tall** Mary is.
c. % Anthony is taller than **how tall** Mary is.

In interrogatives, the degree operator must be overt; movement targets a [Spec,CP] position. The theoretically possible configurations regarding the relative positions of the operator and the lexical AP are as follows (cf. Bacskai-Atkari 2014a, 2014b):

(5) a. OP AP …
b. OP … AP (…)
c. OP …

In (5a), the lexical AP moves together with the operator to the [Spec,CP] position. In (5b), the AP is stranded. Finally, in (5c) there is no lexical AP present: the operator is a proform. Similar variation can be observed in the case of lexical NPs as well. Note also that a single operator may allow for more than one configuration: in particular, stranding in (5b) is always optional and allows for the option in (5a), even though one may be preferred to the other.

Slavic languages demonstrate all of the following types. First, there are operators that always take an AP(/NP) to the [Spec,CP], resulting in the configuration given in (5a). Second, there are operators that may also strand the AP; hence, both (5a) and (5b) are possible. Third, there are proform operators that render the pattern in (5c).

---

1 The cross linguistic observation of Bacskai-Atkari (2014b: 98–123) is that languages or dialects that have overt comparative operators license these both in ordinary comparatives such as (4b) and in so-called subcomparatives such as (4c), and there is no significant difference between the judgements for the two. That is, constructions like (4b), where the gradable adjective is identical in the two clauses, and constructions like (4c), where the gradable adjective in the subclause is different from the one in the matrix clause (and therefore contrastive) are about equally grammatical. This holds for English, where speakers judged the sentences equally grammatical (Bacskai-Atkari 2014b: 109). Naturally, some speakers may find constructions like (4b) slightly marked due to redundancy, but it is equally possible for other speakers to perceive (4c) as slightly marked due to its relative conceptual complexity. However, this does not affect the overall claim that the constructions are both grammatical.

Polish *jak* shows no stranding (see also Borsley and Jaworska 1981: 81). Consider:

(6) **Jak wysoki** jest Karol? / ***Jak** jest Karol **wysoki**?
how tall is Charles how is Charles tall
'How tall is Charles?'

By contrast, stranding allowed with Czech *jak*, Polish *jako*, Serbo-Croatian *koliko*, and with Russian *naskol'ko*. The Czech data are illustrated in (7):

(7) **Jak vysoký** je Karel? / **Jak** je Karel **vysoký**?
how tall is Charles how is Charles tall
'How tall is Charles?'

The Polish data are given in (8) below (see Borsley and Jaworska 1981: 81):

(8) **Jaki wysoki** jest Karol? / **Jaki** jest Karol **wysoki**?
how tall is Charles how is Charles tall
'How tall is Charles?'

The Serbo-Croatian pattern is illustrated by (9):

(9) **Koliko visok** je Petar? / **Koliko** je Petar **visok**?
how tall is Peter how is Peter tall
'How tall is Peter?

Finally, the Russian data are given in (10):

(10) ? **Naskol'ko vysok** Piotr? / **Naskol'ko** Piotr **vysok**?
how tall Peter how Peter tall
'How tall is Peter?'

Apart from operators taking APs, there are proform operators in Slavic, such as Czech *jaký* (which is always a proform) and Polish *jako* (which is optionally a proform but may take an AP as well and then it is inflected, as in (8) above). An example from Czech is given in (11):

(11) **Jaký** je Karel?
how is Charles
'What is Charles like?'

The Polish pattern is illustrated in (12) below (cf. Borsley and Jaworska 1981: 92):

(12) **Jaki** jest Karol?
how is Charles
'What is Charles like?'

Naturally, the fronted *wh*-element in main clause interrogatives can only be interpreted as an operator. The question arises whether there is a potential ambiguity of head-sized relative operators in equative/comparative subclauses between an operator interpretation and a C head interpretation (cf. the analyses of Jäger 2010 and Bacskai-Atkari 2014a for similar instances in the historical development of German *wie*). The expectation is that ambiguity (between operator and C head) and reanalysis (from operator into C head) is possible if the operator takes no AP: this is possible in the stranding and in the proform patterns.

3. Equatives

Contrary to English, where the overt presence of the head *as* is obligatory, AS-clauses in Slavic languages may be introduced by operators, too. Evidence for the operator-status of these elements comes from the availability of a co-occurring AP(/NP).

Let us start with Czech. The examples in (13) show the difference between *jak* and *jako*:

(13) a. Ten stůl je stejně dlouhý, **jak široká** je ta kancelář
the table is same long how wide is the office
'The table is as long as the office is wide.'
b. Ten stůl je stejně dlouhý, **jak** je ta kancelář **široká**.
the table is same long how is the office wide
'The table is as long as the office is wide.'
c. *Ten stůl je stejně dlouhý **jako široká** je ta kancelář.
the table is same long how wide is the office
'The table is as long as the office is wide.'
d. Ten stůl je stejně dlouhý, **jako** je ta kancelář **široká**.
the table is same long how is the office wide
'The table is as long as the office is wide.'

Hence, *jak* behaves like an ordinary operator that may take the lexical AP to the [Spec,CP] position, though the AP may also be stranded. By contrast, *jako* cannot take the lexical AP to the [Spec,CP], as demonstrated by the ungrammaticality of (13c); since the presence of an overt AP is allowed, as in (13d), it should also be obvious that the ungrammaticality of (13c) cannot be attributed to *jako* obligatorily being a proform: instead, the pattern demonstrates that *jako* is a C head. Further evidence for the difference between *jak* and *jako* regarding their syntactic status comes from co-occurrence options with other operators. Consider:

(14) a. *Renault stojí stejně **jak** **(kolik)** stojí Dacia.
Renault costs same how how.much costs Dacia
'Renault costs as much as Dacia.'

b. ? Renault stojí stejně **jako** **(kolik)** stojí Dacia.
Renault costs same as how.much costs Dacia
'Renault costs as much as Dacia.'

The ungrammaticality of (14a) follows naturally if *jak* is an operator: only one degree operator is allowed in the subclause, and that is either *jak* or *kolik*. By contrast, the doubling pattern in (14b) is allowed, though slightly marked since the overt presence of the operator *koliko* is superfluous. The question is how this kind of doubling can be analysed formally.

I propose that there is a split in the overt marking of semantic/syntactic features. In equatives, there are two relevant properties, referred to as [rel] and [compr] in shorthand. The property [rel] stands for relative, and it refers to the encoding of the relative nature of the clause (see Chomsky 1977 on comparative clauses being relative clauses). The property [compr] stands for comparative, and it refers to the encoding of a comparison property (equative or comparative). The relevant structures involving *jak* and *jako* are schematised in (15):

(15)

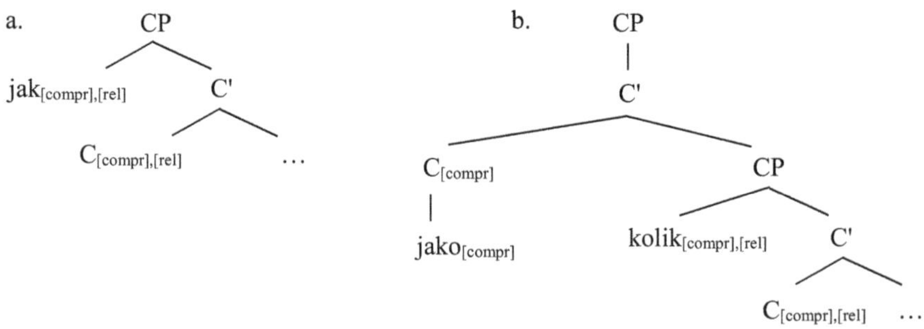

In (15a), the C head is specified as [compr] and [rel], and the element *jak* moving to the specifier carries both properties, hence the features are checked off. The same applies to (15b) as well, with the exception that the [compr] property is doubled on a second C head. Note that the feature [rel] cannot be doubled syntactically (that is, appearing on two separate C heads) as there can be only one relative operator present in the structure, while the comparison property is not unique to operators. In case the relative operator is zero, the complementiser may be inserted into the lower C head as well, in which case *jako* lexicalises the [compr] property on its own, as in (13d). The generation of the higher CP in (15b) is enabled by the matrix degree element, which selects a CP complement headed by particular C elements.

The availability of Serbo-Croatian *što* provides evidence for the lower CP marking [rel]:

(16) Pavao je visok **kao** **što** je visok Petar.
Paul is tall as what is tall Peter
'Paul is as tall as Peter is.'

The structure (regarding the overt elements) is given in (17); note that a covert comparative operator moves to the lower [Spec,CP] position:

(17)

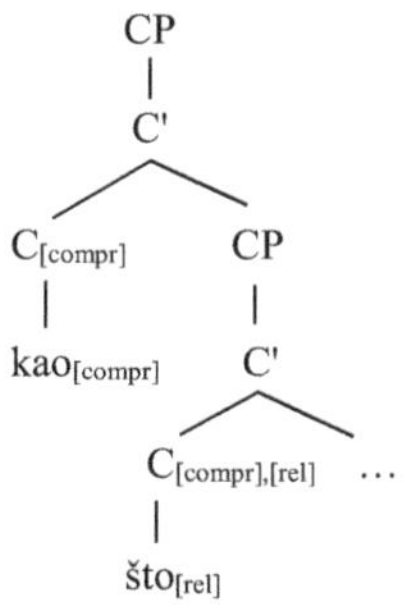

As can be seen, in this case the element *što*, which has no degree specification (but is an appropriate relativiser), appears lower than the comparative complementiser in the structure. The lower C head still carries the [compr] specification, which is checked off by the covert comparative operator, and [compr] is hence doubled, similarly to (15b). However, as opposed to (15b), doubling is not optional in (17) since *što*, unlike Czech *kolik*, does not mark the [compr] property overtly, and this function has to be taken over by the higher C head (*kao*).

Regarding overt encoding in equative clauses, then, the following points can be established. Overt encoding can be carried out both by C heads (complementisers) and by operators. In the case of C heads, while the C head is syntactically specified as both [compr] and [rel], the inserted lexical element does not necessarily carry both of these features. Complementisers specified as [rel] only, such as Serbo-Croatian *što*, occupy a lower C head. The higher C head (whenever there is a split CP) is specified for [compr] only and complementisers specified as only [compr] can be inserted into this position. On the other hand, operators are invariably specified as both [rel] and [compr]: the [compr] feature is required by degree semantics, and the [rel] feature ensures that the operator moves up to the [Spec,CP].

Operators can grammaticalise into complementisers in equatives because operators encode the relevant properties overtly and no further features need to be acquired. In addition, operators may stand alone in equatives, which facilitates their reinterpretation.

Consider the syntactic paradigm for Polish equatives (cf. Borsley and Jaworska 1981):

(18) a. Maria jest tak wysoka **jak** **wysoki** był Karol.
Mary is as tall how tall was Charles
'Mary is as tall as Charles was.'
b. Maria jest tak wysoka **jak** Karol był **wysoki**.
Mary is as tall how Charles is tall
'Mary is as tall as Charles was.'
c. Maria jest taka wysoka **jaki** **wysoki** był Karol.
Mary is as tall how tall was Charles
'Mary is as tall as Charles was.'
d. Maria jest taka wysoka **jaki** Karol był **wysoki**.
Mary is as tall how Charles is tall
'Mary is as tall as Charles was.'

Both *jak* and *jaki* can take the AP to the [Spec,CP] and both allow the stranding of the AP as well. The behaviour of *jako* is expected based on its behaviour as an interrogative operator, see (8); Polish *jako* is thus similar to Czech *jak*. On the other hand, the behaviour of Polish *jak* in (18b) is unexpected inasmuch as stranding is possible, contrary to what we saw in interrogatives. In addition, *jak* appears on its own (without the AP) in elliptical clauses:

(19) Maria jest tak wysoka **jak** Karol.
Mary is as tall how Charles
'Mary is as tall as Charles.'

Hence, *jak* demonstrates a first step towards reanalysis, but the process is not yet complete, as demonstrated by the availability of constructions like (18a).

By contrast, a complete reanalysis can be detected in the case of Czech *jako*, Serbo-Croatian *kao* and *koliko*, and Russian *kak* in AS-clauses. Regarding Serbo-Croatian *koliko*, note that *koliko* in AS-clauses is different from its interrogative operator counterpart with respect to its syntactic behaviour. Consider:

(20) a. Pavao je visok **koliko** je Petar **visok**.
Paul is tall as is Peter tall
'Paul is as tall as Peter.'

b. *Pavao je visok **koliko visok** je Petar.
Paul is tall as tall is Peter
'Paul is as tall as Peter.'

If *koliko* were an operator in AS-clauses, then (20b) should be possible; since, however, only (20a) is grammatical, *koliko* must be a complementiser.

Hence, operators show various stages with respect to reanalysis in Slavic.

4. Comparatives

Let us now turn to THAN-clauses, which have to express degree negation in addition to [rel] and [compr]; the property of degree negation will be abbreviated as [d-neg]. Crucially, the comparative operator cannot encode this property since it is not a negative operator: it is associated with the degree *d'* and cannot at the same time express that $d \neq d'$. There is ample cross-linguistic evidence that the [d-neg] property is marked by the C head above operator, hence double CPs are generated in THAN-clauses. Note that the C head encoding [d-neg] has to be overt since negative polarity/negation has to be marked morphologically (Dryer 2013). The comparative complementiser is often morphologically transparently negative: this applies to Czech *než*, Polish *niż*, and Serbo-Croatian *nego* and *no*.

In addition to the overt complementiser, an overt operator may appear in certain languages but not in others. In Polish, the presence of an overt operator is not allowed (cf. Bacskai-Atkari 2015); recall that there is no doubling in Polish equatives either. Consider:

(21) Maria jest wyższa **niż** (***jak wysoki** był) Karol.
Mary is taller than how tall was Charles
'Mary is taller than Charles.'

The combination of a C head and an operator is possible in Czech (cf. Bacskai-Atkari 2015):

(22) a. ? Ten stůl je delší, **než** **jak** **široká** je ta kancelář.
the table is longer than how wide is the office
'The table is longer than the office is wide.'

b. Ten stůl je delší, **než** **jak** je ta kancelář **široká**.
the table is longer than how is the office wide
'The table is longer than the office is wide.'

While doubling is possible, the presence of the overt operator does not substitute the overt presence of the complementiser: the presence of *než* is obligatory. Consider:

(23) a. *Ten stůl je delší, **jak** **široká** je ta kancelář.
the table is longer how wide is the office
'The table is longer than the office is wide.'

b. *Ten stůl je delší, **jak** je ta kancelář **široká**.
the table is longer how is the office wide
'The table is longer than the office is wide.'

Considering all factors, the Czech pattern is expected. On the one hand, the behaviour of *jak* is expected based on its behaviour in interrogatives and in AS-clauses. On the other hand, the behaviour of *než* is expected cross-linguistically: [d-neg] has to be encoded on the head overtly. The structure showing the positions of *než* and *jak* is shown in (24):

(24)

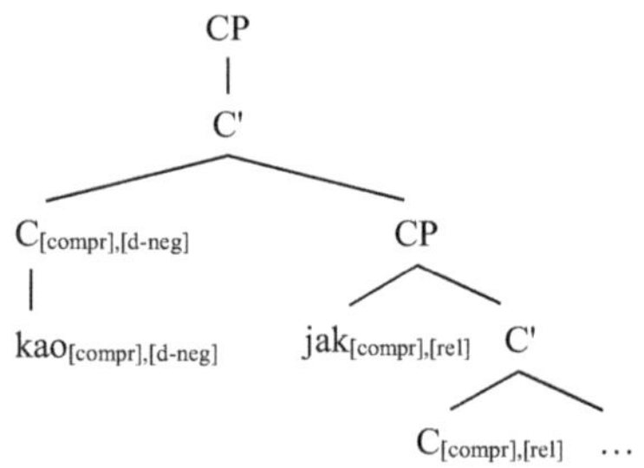

As can be seen, while the [compr] feature is again doubled, the marking of [rel] and [d-neg] is split: [rel] can be encoded only once and it is encoded on the lower C head so that the movement of the operator is as short as possible, and [d-neg] has to be encoded separately.

Again, it is possible, just like in equatives, that the lower C head lexicalises merely [rel] overtly on the head and the operator is silent. Evidence for this comes from Serbo-Croatian:

(25) Pavao je viši **nego/no** **što** je Petar.
Paul is taller than what is Peter
'Paul is taller than Peter.'

Note that while both *nego* and *no* are possible elements corresponding to *than*, the distribution of *no* seems to show considerable differences among Croatian and Serbian dialects; in the subsequent discussion, I will therefore only use *nego* but the behaviour of *no* would not differ. The structure regarding *nego* and *što* is given in (26):

(26)

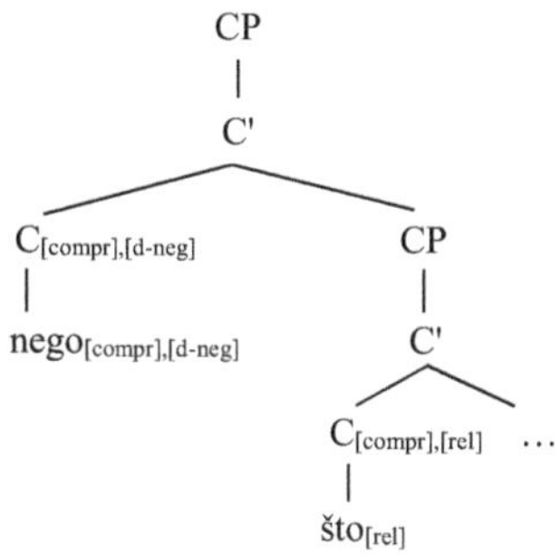

Two comparative C heads are also possible; Serbo-Croatian *koliko* may appear as a lower C:

(27) ? Pavao je viši **nego** **koliko** **(*visok)** je Petar.
Paul is taller than how tall is Peter
'Paul is taller than Peter.'s

The corresponding structure is given in (28) below:

(28)

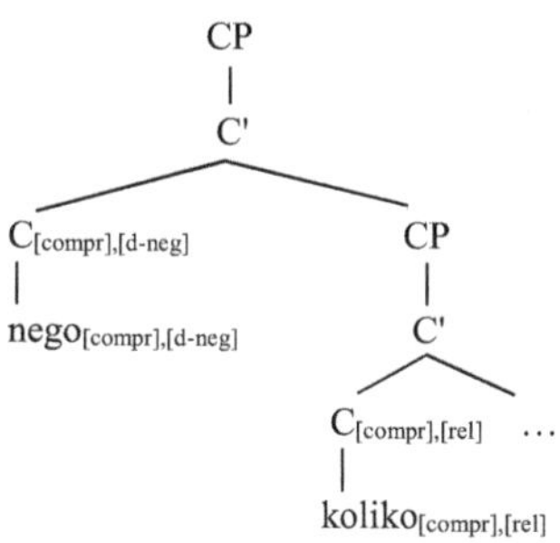

The difference between (26) and (28) lies in the feature specification of the complementiser inserted into the lower C head. In either case, the complementiser *nego* (or *no*) is obligatory.

The Serbo-Croatian pattern is again expected. On the one hand, the behaviour of *koliko* is expected based on its behaviour in AS-clauses, as opposed to interrogatives: in AS-clauses, it is already a grammaticalised C head and not an operator. On the other hand, the behaviour of *nego* (and *no*) is expected cross-linguistically since the encoding of [d-neg] has to be carried out by an overt element in the head.

Regarding overt marking, the following points can be established so far. In all the patterns, a comparative complementiser can be detected: examples include Polish *niż*, Russian *čem*, Czech *než*, and Serbo-Croatian *nego* and *no*. An operator may appear overtly in addition to the comparative complementiser, such as Czech *jak*. Moreover, a lower complementiser may appear in addition to the regular comparative complementiser, such as Serbo-Croatian *koliko* and *što*. However, a pattern where a comparative operator appears on its own (without the higher comparative complementiser) is excluded, unlike what we saw in equatives.

An apparent counter-example to this seems to be Czech *jak* in examples like (29) below:

(29) Marie je vyšší, **jak** (*je) Karel.
Mary is taller how is Charles
'Mary is taller than Charles.'

However, the appearance of a single *jak* is subject to restrictions. An AP is excluded, see (23), and the clause is always elliptical, as shown by the ungrammaticality of the copula in (29).

I propose that in examples like (29) only one CP is generated, and the operator moves to the C head and not to the [Spec,CP]. Ellipsis effectively eliminates the (feature) mismatch between the base-generation site and the landing site. The relevant structure is given in (30):

(30)

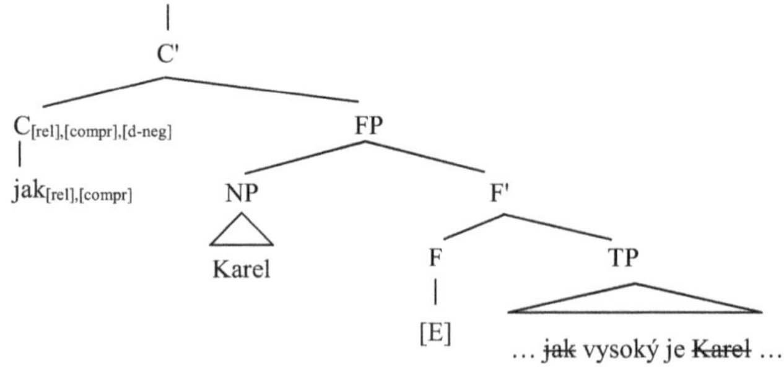

In line with Merchant (2001), I assume that the remnant (the NP *Karel*) moves to the specifier of a functional projection (FP), the head of which contains the ellipsis feature [E]. Regarding the issue of head-sized operators moving to C, the following points should be mentioned. The phenomenon is not restricted to Czech comparatives but can be detected in certain German dialects (such as Alemannic and Bavarian) in embedded interrogative clauses, too, as shown by Bayer and Brandner (2008). Bayer and Brandner (2008) argue that such a movement operation constitutes no violation of the Chain Uniformity of Chomsky (1995), as head-sized operators have a dual status anyway (they are heads and phrases at the same time); there is no feature mismatch either in interrogatives. In Czech, however, the comparative operator moving to the C head encoding [d-neg] causes a feature mismatch between the base-generation site and the landing site, because the operator cannot originate as [d-neg]. Ellipsis saves the construction by eliminating this mismatch, similarly to sluicing repairing island violation effects (see Merchant 2001).

Hence, a comparative operator taking over the complementiser function in THAN-clauses is not as straightforward as in AS-clauses. The behaviour of Czech *jak* is still consistent with the general theory that the property of [d-neg] is marked on C head.

Regarding overt marking, then, the conclusions have to be slightly modified. There are patterns involving a single comparative complementiser, such as Polish *niż*, Russian *čem*, Czech *než*, and Serbo-Croatian *nego* and *no*. An overt operator may appear in addition to the comparative complementiser, such as Czech *jak*. In addition, a lower complementiser may appear in addition to the regular comparative complementiser, such as Serbo-Croatian *koliko* and *što*. Finally, while comparative operators are normally not possible on their own, they may be licensed if they move to the C head; this is a language-specific option, and it can be detected with obligatory ellipsis in the case of Czech *jak*.

5. Conclusion

This paper examined some issues related to the syntax of degree operators and embedded degree clauses in Slavic. The major conclusions can be summarised as follows. Degree operators appear in the [Spec,CP] either with or without lexical XPs (the latter case is either the result of stranding the XP or the operator is a proform). In AS-clauses, clause typing is marked overtly either by complementisers or by operators, or by combinations (C+C, C+operator). In THAN-clauses, clause typing is marked overtly by a C head (lexicalised normally by a complementiser and in certain cases by a moved operator), or by combinations (C+C, C+operator). The minimal difference between AS-clauses and THAN-clauses is due to demands on the overt marking of [d-neg] in THAN-clauses, and hence the asymmetry can be accounted for in a principled way.

References

Bacskai-Atkari, Julia. 2014a. "Cyclical change in Hungarian comparatives." *Diachronica* 31(4): 465–505.

Bacskai-Atkari, Julia. 2014b. *The syntax of comparative constructions: Operators, ellipsis phenomena and functional left peripheries*. Potsdam: Universitätsverlag Potsdam.

Bacskai-Atkari, Julia. 2015. "Information structure and clausal comparatives in Czech and Polish." In *Slavic grammar from a formal perspective: The 10th anniversary FDSL conference, Leipzig, 2013*, Gerhild Zybatov et al. (eds.). Frankfurt am Main: Peter Lang, 27–42.

Bacskai-Atkari, Julia. 2016. "Towards a cross-linguistic typology of marking polarity in embedded degree clauses." *Acta Linguistica Hungarica* 63(4): 389–409.

Bayer, Josef and Ellen Brandner. 2008. "On wh-head-movement and the Doubly-Filled-Comp Filter." In *Proceedings of the 26th West Coast Conference on Formal Linguistics*, Charles B. Chang and Hannah J. Haynie (eds.). Somerville, MA: Cascadilla Proceedings Project, 87–95.

Borsley, Robert D. and Ewa Jaworska. 1981. "Some remarks on equatives and related phenomena." *Studia Anglica Posnaniensia* 13: 79–108.

Chomsky, Noam. 1977. "On WH-movement." In Peter Culicover et al. (eds.) *Formal syntax*. New York: Academic Press. 71–132.

Chomsky, Noam. 1995. *The Minimalist Program*. Cambridge, MA: MIT Press.

Dryer, Matthew S. 2013. "Negative morphemes." In *The world atlas of language structures online*, Matthew S. Dryer and Martin Haspelmath (eds.). Leipzig: Max Planck Institute for Evolutionary Anthropology. Available at http://wals.info/chapter/112 (last accessed: 14 May 2015).

Jäger, Agnes. 2010. "Der Komparativzyklus und die Position der Vergleichspartikeln." *Linguistische Berichte* 224: 467–493.

Merchant, Jason. 2001. *The syntax of silence: Sluicing, islands, and the theory of ellipsis*. Oxford: Oxford University Press.

Seuren, Pieter. 1973. "The comparative." In *Generative grammar in Europe*, Ferenc Kiefer and Nicolas Ruwet (eds.). Dordrecht: D. Reidel, 528–564.

Marcin Wągiel

Entities, Events, and Their Parts: The Semantics of Multipliers in Slavic*

1. Introduction

Since the early days of formal semantics (starting with Montague 1973) the meaning of quantificational expressions such as numerals has been constantly receiving a lot of attention. Over the last several decades, extensive and extremely important work has been done in this area leading to a number of influential theories of cardinals (cf. Barwise and Cooper 1981, Scha 1981, Landman 2004, and Ionin and Matushansky 2006 among many others). Nevertheless, it seems that there is still a vast territory left unchartered since natural languages exhibit multiple classes of numerical expressions that did not receive nearly as much recognition as cardinal numerals. An example of such a somewhat neglected class are multipliers such as English *double*. Though such expressions are common in natural languages, see (1), as for now their semantic properties are surprisingly understudied and I am not aware of any formal attempt to account for their behavior and meaning.

(1) a. *double*
b. *doppelt* (German)
c. *doppio* (Italian)
d. *dvojnoj* (Russian)
e. *dvigubas* (Lithuanian)
f. *dupla* (Hungarian)
g. *shuāng* (Mandarin)

* I would like to sincerely thank Pavel Caha, Jakub Dotlačil, and Viola Schmitt for their extremely helpful and insightful comments which improved the main idea behind this paper in a significant way. I am also grateful to Daniel Büring, Lisa Bylinina, Guglielmo Cinque, Mojmír Dočekal, Berit Gehrke, Nina Haslinger, Manfred Krifka, Marijana Marelj, Rick Nouwen, Susan Rothstein, Radek Šimík and the audiences at the FDSL 11, SinFonIJA 8, and CECIL'S 5 conferences as well as Leiden – Utrecht Semantic Happenings and 12th Event Semantics workshop for their puzzling questions and inspiring remarks. All errors are, of course, my own. I gratefully acknowledge that the research was supported by a Czech Science Foundation (GAČR) grant to the Department of Linguistics and Baltic Languages at the Masaryk University in Brno (GA17-16111S).

The fact that multipliers have been somewhat overlooked is even more striking given the fact that they exhibit a non-trivial quantificational behavior that differs from the one involved in cardinal numerals. For instance, consider examples such as those in (2). The noun phrase in (2a) simply denotes a set of singular entities having the property of being a crown. Interestingly, although the phrase in (2b) is true of a plurality of two entities, (2c) can be only interpreted as referring to a single individual similarly to (2a). There is, however, a crucial difference between the two expressions since (2c) seems to involve what I will refer to as SUBATOMIC QUANTIFICATION, i.e., quantification over elements within the inner structure of a denoted entity. In other words, the multiplier in (2c) restricts the denotation of the noun to only those crowns that have a particular complex form.

(2) a. *crown*
 b. *two crowns*
 c. *double crown*

In this paper, I will discuss the distribution and semantic properties of Slavic multipliers with a special focus on Polish. I will argue that such expressions are compositional and involve quantification over parts within mereological structures constituting atomic individuals. I will provide an analysis that accounts for a representative subset of data and point out some non-trivial consequences as well as possible extensions of the proposed account.

The paper is organized as follows. In Section 2, I present the data concerning the morphology and non-trivial quantificational behavior of multipliers in Polish, Czech, Russian, and Bosnian-Croatian-Serbian (BCS). In Section 3, I introduce the theoretical background for the analysis based on the theories of Krifka (1989, 1990, and 1995). In Section 4, I come up with an analysis that accounts for a subset of environments in which Slavic multipliers can occur. In Section 5, I provide additional contexts some of which seem to be problematic for the proposed approach and sketch possible extensions of the analysis. Section 6 concludes the paper.

2. Slavic multipliers

2.1. Morphology

Since it is widely recognized that the derivational morphology in Slavic languages is particularly rich, in recent years increasing attention has been drawn to the semantics of Slavic morphologically complex numerical expressions which lead to a number of insightful investigations concerning such constructions in Czech (Dočekal 2012 and 2013), Polish (Wągiel 2014 and 2015), and Russian (Khrizman 2015). While previous research focused mainly on the impact of numeral morphology on the collective/distributive alternation, in this paper I will examine the adjectival domain and present evidence of what appears to be subatomic quantification, i.e., quantification over cognitively salient parts of entities and events. To this end, I will focus on Polish, Czech, Russian, and BCS multipliers, which unlike their English counterparts exhibit a complex derivational structure. Such lexical items will be exemplified in the text by expressions derived from the numeral root *dw-/dv-* ('two'). Let us assume the following morphological make-up of the multipliers in question.[1]

(3) a. *po>dw-ój<n-y* (Polish)
circumfix>numeral_root-non_cardinal_stem<circumfix-inflectional_marker

b. *dv-oj-it-ý* (Czech)
numeral_root-non_cardinal_stem-derivational_suffix-inflectional_marker

c. *dv-oj-n-oj* (Russian)
numeral_root-non_cardinal_stem-derivational_suffix-inflectional_marker

d. *dv-o-struk-i* (BCS)
numeral_root-non_cardinal_stem-derivational_suffix-inflectional_marker

As can be witnessed in (3a)–(3d) all the multipliers in question consist of numeral roots and some additional morphology including the morphemes *po>...<n-/-it-/-n-/-struk-* and the suffixes *-ój-/-oj-/-o-* which mark a non-cardinal stem[2] as well as inflectional markers. In general, Slavic multipliers

1 In (3) masculine forms represent whole declensional paradigms. For BCS in (3d), the derivationally complex adjective *dvostruki* ('double') has been chosen for sake of exposition despite the fact that there is also another BCS multiplier, namely *dupli* ('double'). Although it seems that there is a difference in the distribution of the two forms, I assume that there is no relevant semantic distinction between them with respect to the phenomena discussed in this paper.

2 These morphemes appear in the multipliers derived from the numeral roots referring to the numbers 2–3. In the multipliers derived from the roots referring to the number 4, the suffix *-ór-/-er-/-oro-* occurs instead, e.g., Polish *po>czw-ór<n-y*, Czech *čtv-er-n-ý*, Russian *četv-er-n-oj*, and BCS *četv-oro-stuk-i* (all 'quadruple').

exhibit adjectival morphology and agree with modified nouns in case, number, and gender. I will refer to the derivational circumfix *po*〉…〈*n*- in Polish and the suffixes -*it*-, -*n*-, and -*struk*- in Czech, Russian, and BCS respectively as multiplicative morphemes. Moreover, in this paper I assume that inflectional markers and morphemes constituting non-cardinal stems have no contribution to the semantics of multipliers. Therefore, in the compositional analysis I will focus only on the interaction between numeral roots and multiplicative morphemes.

Such an approach might seem in fact a considerable simplification since affixes marking non-cardinal stems are attested not only in multipliers, but also in a variety of other numerical expressions. For instance, consider Polish denumeral group nouns such as *dwójka* ('(group of) two'), derived numerals presupposing that a plurality is heterogeneous with respect to the natural gender of referents such as *dwoje* ('two (one male and one female)')[3], taxonomic numerals like *dwojaki* or *dwoisty* (both 'twofold') as well as denumeral verbs such as *podwoić* ('to double').[4] Prima facie, it seems appealing to assume that the appearance of non-cardinal stem markers in all the above cases is non-coincidental from the semantic point of view. Therefore, an alternative approach could assign, e.g., Polish -*ój*-/-*oj*-/-*oi*- a meaning general enough to cover the whole variety of considered expressions, i.e., an underspecified operation on numbers different from the one employed in cardinals. Nevertheless, in this paper I will remain agnostic with respect to that possibility and I will assume that the discussed markers are semantically vacuous and that their sole function is purely structural, specifically they simply form stems. Similar, for sake of simplicity I will ignore all the intricacies related to the semantics of gender as well as its relationship with quantification (see, e.g., Arsenijević 2016 and Fassi Fehri 2016) and the role of inflectional markers in coding such an interaction.

2.2. Semantic behavior

Let us now consider phrases in which multipliers modify a noun. We will start with a set of examples in (4)[5] which are semantically analogous and equivalent to the English phrase in (2c). These examples will be considered as illustrative since

3 See Wągiel (2014, 2015) for a discussion and possible analysis of expressions such as *dwójka* and *dwoje*.

4 Notice that -*ój*-, -*oj*- and -*oi*- are allomorphs.

5 In the text, I will use the following abbreviations: cases: nom – Nominative, gen – Genitive, acc – Accusative, ins – Instrumental; numbers: sg – singular, pl – plural; genders: m – masculine, f – feminine, n – neuter, ia – inanimate.

they are all attested in representative text corpora such as the National Corpus of Polish, Czech National Corpus, Russian National Corpus, and Croatian National Corpus. Furthermore, the Polish noun *korona* ('crown') ranks at the 13th place on the list of collocation candidates within two-words collocations for the form *podwójna* ('double') in the balanced sample of the National Corpus of Polish whereas the Czech noun *koruna* ('crown') ranks at the 7th place for the form *dvojitá* ('double') in a corresponding Czech sample in the Czech National Corpus.

(4) a. *podwójna* *korona* (Polish)
double.nom.sg.f crown.nom.f
'double crown'
b. *dvojitá koruna* (Czech)
c. *dvojnajakorona* (Russian)
d. *dvostruka kruna* (BCS)

As has been mentioned in Section 1, noun phrases such as those in (4) denote sets of singular (and not plural) individuals despite numeral roots occurring in the morphological make-up of multipliers modifying a noun. Nevertheless, it is clear that in such examples quantification is involved albeit it is not quantification over individuals. To illustrate this claim, let us consider a historical example in (5).[6]

(5) a. *Pszent* *to* *podwójna* *korona.* (Polish)
Pschent.nom.m this double.nom.sg.f crown.nom.f
'The Pschent is a double crown.'
b. ⊨ *Pszent* *składa się* *z* *dwóch* *części.*
Pschent.nom.m consists.sg from two.gen.ia parts.gen.ia
'The Pschent consists of two parts.'

The sentence in (5a) indicates a complex inner structure of the Pschent and, hence, entails the sentence in (5b). If it is true of an object that it is a double crown, it has to be a crown and it has to consist of two elements. However, it is not sufficient that an object consists of any two elements (it is not the case that every crown consisting of two parts is a double crown), but rather of elements having a particular property, i.e., a property of a whole. In other words, a double crown consists of two parts which can be considered crowns themselves. For

6 In the following text, the discussed phenomena will be exemplified mainly by Polish examples, nevertheless the generalizations should hold for every language in question.

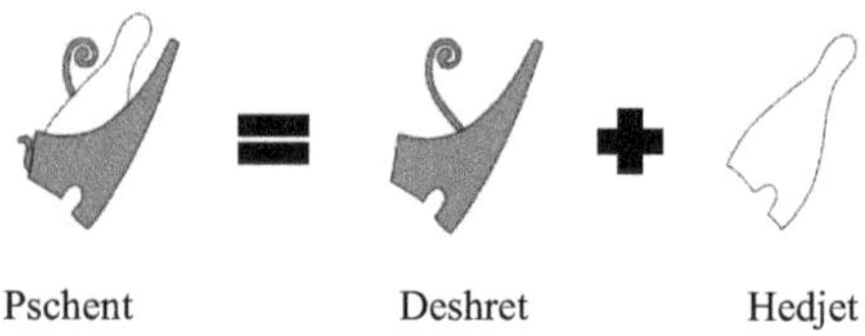

Figure 1: The design of the Ancient Egyptian Pschent. Source: The pictures in Figure 1 are based on the work by fi:Käyttäjä:kompak shared on Wikimedia Commons under the CC BY 2.5 license; URL: https://commons.wikimedia.org/wiki/File:Pschent2.svg, https://commons.wikimedia.org/wiki/File:Deshret.svg, and https://commons.wikimedia.org/wiki/File:Hedjet.svg.

instance, the reader familiar with ancient history will recognize the Pschent as a crown worn by rulers of Ancient Egypt. Historically, the Pschent combined two parts, i.e., the Red Deshret Crown of Lower Egypt and the White Hedjet Crown of Upper Egypt, as demonstrated in Figure 1, and represented the pharaoh's power over all of the unified kingdom. One could say it is a two-in-one crown.

Note that there is only one cut which divides the Pschent into the Deshret and Hedjet and this characteristic can be generalized to any hypothetical double crown. In other words, not every part of a double crown is a crown itself. On the contrary, in this and similar cases within the set of all the parts of a whole there are exactly two parts of which a property of the whole holds. Therefore, the semantics of Slavic predicates such as those in (4) and others corresponding to the English phrase *double crown* does not involve the property of divisivity which, among other things, differentiate them from mass nouns that sometimes are assumed to have divisive reference (Cheng 1973).[7]

Other examples of this sort include the phrases in (6) with nouns ranked relatively high as collocation candidates in the National Corpus of Polish.[8] A double garage referred to in (6a) is a building with two entrances leading to separate parking spaces. A double door from the example in (6b) is a door made of two independently moving leaves. Finally, a double layer in (6c) is a layer consisting of two layers merged together.

7 I will ignore the minimal-parts problem (e.g., Quine 1960) here and I will simply assume that linguistic representations are sensitive only to some level of granularity accessible for human perception. For instance, the fact that at the microscopic level a substance consists of particles is not encoded in the semantics of a particular mass term.

8 The noun *warstwa* ('layer') ranks at the 7th place for the form *podwójna* ('double') whereas *drzwi* ('door') ranks at the 23rd place for the form *podwójne* ('double').

(6) a. *podwójny* *garaż* (Polish)
double.nom.sg.m garage.nom.m
'double garage'
b. *podwójne* *drzwi*
double.nom.pl.ia door.nom.pl.ia
'double door'
c. *podwójna* *warstwa*
double.nom.sg.f layer.nom.f
'double layer'

Certainly, examples such as those in (4) and (6) do not exhaust the combinatorial potential of Slavic multipliers and some more problematic cases will be discussed subsequently in Section 5. Nevertheless, the data discussed above indicate that at least a subset of constructions involving multipliers implicates clear cases of subatomic quantification. Noun phrases such as those in (4) and (6) denote sets of singular atomic objects with a complex inner structure and multipliers quantify over particular parts of this structure, i.e., parts that have a property of the whole. I will refer to such elements as self-sufficient parts.

At this point, let us attempt to formulate a first generalization related to the behavior of Slavic multipliers.

(7) Generalization: If a multiplier α derived from a numeral root β denoting a number n modifies a noun phrase γ denoting a set A, then the resulting noun phrase δ denotes a subset B of A such that for every member of B holds that it has n self-sufficient parts.

Before we turn our attention to some less obvious examples in Section 5 and see how far the generalization in (7) can get us, let us now sketch a framework within which an analysis of phrases such as those in (4) and (6) will be proposed.

3. Framework

3.1. Background

In the analysis, I assume the lattice-theoretic approach in line with Link (1983) which allows for linguistic applications of mereology. Furthermore, I adopt the main concept behind a number of theories developed by Krifka (1989, 1990, and 1995) to account for measuring and counting in natural language. Though there are differences between particular analyses, the core of the system is based on the assumption that numerals refer to numbers, i.e., abstract objects of a primitive semantic type n (see Scha 1981), and counting involves special operations associating entities and numbers. Despite the fact that such a view contrasts with the standard Generalized Quantifier Theory (Barwise and Cooper 1983), it seems that it gains ground since a similar proposal have been postulated by Rothstein (2012 and 2013) who argues that number words name integers and are semantically analogous to proper names of singular individuals.

In the system of Krifka, counting is possible via different measure functions which directly relate individuals to numbers. Such measure functions are defined to be extensive. As such they are additive and have the Archimedean property which is guaranteed by the fact that counting relates to quantization, i.e., one can only count individuated entities. To account for quantification in both nominal and verbal domain, Krifka (1989) proposes the **NU** (for 'natural unit') operation. However, I will slightly simplify it using the # symbol instead. Such an operation for a property *P* would return a measure function yielding a number of objects of which *P* is predicated. For instance, for a property **student** a measure function #(**student**) counts particular students. In Krifka (1995), in order to differentiate between kind-level and object-level entities the **OU** (for 'object unit') and **KU** (for 'kind unit') operations are introduced. Since this paper does not deal with issues related to genericity, I will ignore the distinction. In principle, however, the analysis developed here is compatible with the approach developed in Krifka (1995).

Since space prohibits discussing the question whether there is a semantic distinction between singular and plural terms (e.g., Link 1983 and Landman 2000) or not (e.g., Krifka 1995), I will refrain from considering the problem here and I will assume that it plays no role with respect to the phenomena accounted for in this paper. Moreover, I will use a term 'counting expression' to refer to any expression involving numeral quantification, i.e., to both numeral phrases and noun phrases containing multipliers. I will also assume that both cardinals and multipliers belong to a broader category of expressions which I will address as 'number words'.

3.2. Counting expressions

Building on Krifka's approach, let us propose a general semantic structure for counting expressions as in Figure 2.

In the model presented in Figure 2 three elements constituting semantics of counting expressions are assumed, i.e., a property *P* and a number *n* associated with *P* via μ which stands for any operation that would yield an extensive measure function for *P*. Though the semantic structure in Figure 2 is proposed to be universal, different languages may vary with respect to the distribution of particular components, i.e., cross-linguistically (or perhaps even across different constructions in a particular language) given semantic objects may be assigned to different syntactic categories such as nouns, classifiers, measure words, and

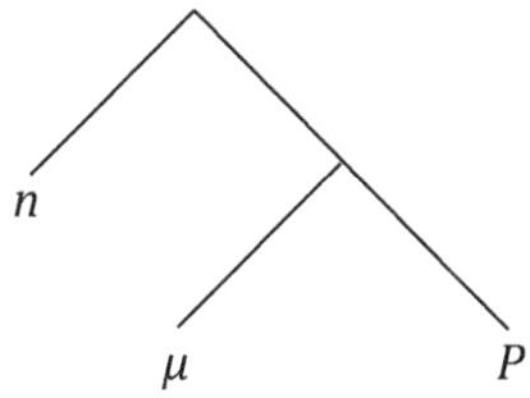

Figure 2: A semantic structure of counting expressions

numerals. For counting atomic objects in languages such as English (including Slavic), let us adopt the # operation which, when applied to a property, returns a measure function yielding a number of objects constituting a (complex) entity bearing that property. Furthermore, for the purposes of this paper let us assume that the measure function #(*P*) is introduced by numerals.[9] Based on the adopted approach, the numeral phrase translates as in (8), where **N** is a predicate associated with the noun phrase whereas **n** stands for a number associated with the numeral. In general, the numeral phrase is true of an *n*-number of entities having a property *P*, see (8a). For instance, (8b) is a function from entities to truth values such that it yields True for any collection of two individuals who are students.

(8) a. $[\![\text{NumeralP}]\!] = \lambda x[\mathbf{N}(x) \wedge \#(\mathbf{N})(x) = \mathbf{n}]$
b. $[\![\text{two students}]\!] = \lambda x[\mathbf{student}(x) \wedge \#(\mathbf{student})(x) = 2]$

With all the theoretical tools in place, let us now turn to the proposal of the semantics for examples such as (4) and (6) from Section 2.

4. Analysis

4.1. Components

The core of the proposal is as follows. I assume here that nouns merely refer to properties, whereas numeral roots simply denote numbers. Furthermore, I posit compositional semantics for Slavic counting expressions including numerals and multipliers. In both types of expressions, the role of the numeral root is to

9 This is in line with one of two possible analyses of English proposed by Krifka (1995); see also Bale and Coon (2014) for intriguing empirical basis of such an account. Another possibility is to attribute the introduction of measure functions to count nouns, e.g., via the **NU** operation (Krifka 1989; see also Rothstein 2010 for a similar proposal). Such an analysis may be considered advantageous in accounting for countability since it differentiates typally between mass and count nouns. For sake of simplicity, however, in this paper I will not pursue the second option.

define cardinality of counted objects with no specification with respect to the nature of those objects while various operators introduce specific restrictions on the domain of quantification defining the exact type of objects the number word counts. In particular, cardinals embody a measure function involving quantification over individuals whereas multipliers have an incorporated measure function involving subatomic quantification. In the numeral phrase, the cardinal maps atomic individuals onto numbers, whereas the noun provides a property that holds of entities involved in quantification. On the other hand, the noun phrase modified by the multiplier does not involve counting of entire entities, but rather the multiplicative morpheme introduces an operation that maps parts of an individual having a property denoted by the noun onto integers.

Having set up the general idea, let us now implement it in a compositional manner. Within the adopted view, count nouns undergo atomization but do not have a built-in means allowing for counting and simply refer to properties of individuals. Thus, the Polish count noun *korona* ('crown') from the example (4a) translates as (9) and denotes a set of entities having the property of being a crown. Furthermore, since I do not make a semantic distinction between singular and plural nominals, the very same meaning is also assigned to the plural form *korony* ('crowns').

(9) $[\![\text{korona}]\!] = \lambda x[\mathbf{crown}(x)]$

Next, I propose that Slavic numeral roots are merely names of numbers, i.e., expressions of type *n*, and denote integers which are assumed to be abstract objects constituting a domain in the ontology of the model. For instance, the semantics of the Polish morpheme *dw-* ('two') is simply the number 2, as introduced in (10a). In addition, I assume that number words are predicate modifiers, i.e., expressions of type $\langle\langle e, t\rangle, \langle e, t\rangle\rangle$. Hence, in order to derive the number word, the numeral root needs to combine with an element of type $\langle n, \langle\langle e, t\rangle, \langle e, t\rangle\rangle\rangle$. In case of cardinals, I will refrain here from speculation whether such an expression has a formal exponent and I will simply assume CARD to be a covert element introducing the # operation, see (10b), which combines with the numeral root. As a result, the integer denoted by the root saturates the number variable slot and we obtain the cardinal numeral *dwa* ('two')[10] which is a function from a property of individuals to a set of pairs of individuals having that property, as presented in (10c).

(10) a. $[\![\sqrt{\text{dw-}}]\!] = 2$
b. $[\![\textsc{card}]\!] = \lambda n \lambda P \lambda x[P(x) \wedge \#(P)(x) = n]$
c. $[\![\text{dwa}]\!] = \lambda P \lambda x[P(x) \wedge \#(P)(x) = 2]$

10 Since I ignore gender here, the whole paradigm including the feminine form *dwie* ('two') used in the examples (13a) and (13c) also translates as (10c).

Finally, to account for the semantic effects regarding multipliers and attributed to multiplicative morphemes as observed in (4) and (6) let us propose the self-sufficient parts-counting operation $\boxplus$.[11] For a property P, the $\boxplus$ operation yields a number of self-sufficient parts of an atomic entity of which P is predicated. Assuming a mereology for individuals, a self-sufficient part can be defined as follows.

(11) For an atomic entity x that has a property P, y is a self-sufficient part of x iff (i) y is a part of x and (ii) y itself has a property P.

The definition in (11) applies only to atomic entities and not to non-atomic masses or plural individuals. The conjunct (i) ensures the parthood relationship whereas the restriction (ii) accounts for the fact that a self-sufficient part resembles the individual it is a part of. The parthood relationship is necessary to capture the intuition that only objects within the part-whole structure of an atomic entity are regarded as self-sufficient parts. The moment they become disconnected from the whole, they can no longer be considered such elements. Notice also that the definition in (11) does not exclude the existence of other (non-self-sufficient) parts within the whole involving a self-sufficient part and I believe it is the way it should be. The reason is that the entity can have components that themselves do not resemble the whole yet are its parts, e.g., jewels, orbs, crosses, or *fleurs-de-lis* in case of crowns. In fact, even self-sufficient parts can consist of such elements. For instance, consider the make-up of the Pschent in Figure 1. The Red Deshret Crown of Lower Egypt includes the Uraeus, i.e., the stylized form of an Egyptian cobra, which itself does not have the property of being a crown.

I posit that similar to CARD Slavic multiplicative morphemes are expressions of type $\langle n, \langle\langle e, t\rangle, \langle e, t\rangle\rangle\rangle$. However, unlike CARD they introduce the $\boxplus$ operation. As an illustration, the semantics of the Polish multiplicative circumfix *po⟩…⟨n-* is postulated in (12). The morpheme denotes a function that maps self-sufficient parts of individuals having a property P onto a number n.

(12) $[\![\text{po}\rangle\ldots\langle\text{n-}]\!] = \lambda n \lambda P \lambda x[P(x) \wedge \boxplus(P)(x) = n]$

With all the ingredients in place, let us now examine how all the pieces fit together.

4.2. Composition

In this section, I will demonstrate how Polish noun phrases involving counting expressions such as those in (13a)–(13c) are derived in the trees in Figures 3–5

11 Here is a mnemonic. The $\boxplus$ symbol is a square constituted by four smaller squares each of which is both a part of the whole and has a property of the whole. Hence, $\boxplus$ stands for 'self-sufficient parts'.

and interpreted in the formulae (14)–(16) respectively. In general, I assume that in semantic composition names of numbers combine with expressions involving measure functions, i.e., with the CARD operator or the multiplicative morpheme, and nouns to form predicates of pluralities of individuals or their parts.

(13) a. *dwie* *korony* (Polish)
two.nom.ia crowns.nom.ia
'two crowns'
b. *podwójna* *korona*
double.nom.sg.f crown.nom.f
'double crown'
c. *dwie* *podwójne* *korony*
two.nom.ia double.nom.pl.ia crowns.nom.ia
'two double crowns'

Let us start with giving a structure and interpretation of the numeral phrase in (13a).

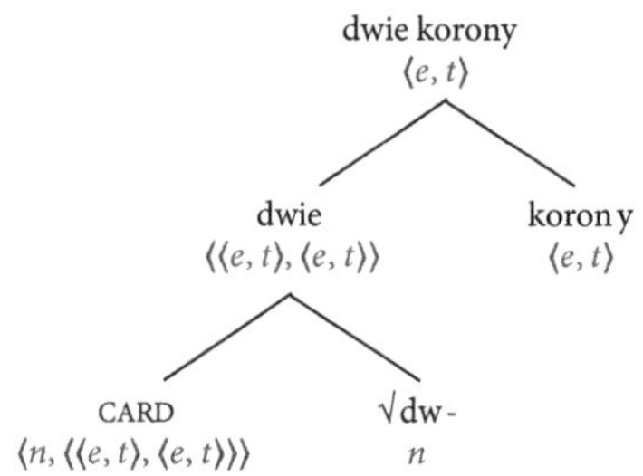

Figure 3: A semantic tree of (13a)

(14) Interpretation of (13a)

$[\![\textsc{card}]\!] = \lambda n \lambda P \lambda x[P(x) \wedge \#(P)(x) = n]$

$[\![\surd\text{dw-}]\!] = 2$

$[\![\text{dwie}]\!] = \lambda P \lambda x[P(x) \wedge \#(P)(x) = 2]$

$[\![\text{korony}]\!] = \lambda x[\mathbf{crown}(x)]$

$[\![\text{dwie korony}]\!] = \lambda x[\mathbf{crown}(x) \wedge \#(\mathbf{crown})(x) = 2]$

In Figure 3 and (14), the null CARD operator denotes a function from a property of individuals to a set of pluralities consisting of *n*-number entities having that property and requires composing with the numeral root, i.e., an expression of type *n*, in order to saturate the number argument. I assume here that the inflectional marker *-ie* is semantically vacuous and does not receive any interpretation. The resulting cardinal is a predicate modifier and, assuming standard Function Application, it combines with the plural noun *korony* ('crowns') to derive a counting expression denoting a set of pairs of crowns.

The composition of the counting expression in (13b) which involves a multiplier proceeds in a similar way.

(15) Interpretation of (13b)

⟦po⟩…⟨n-⟧ $= \lambda n \lambda P \lambda x[P(x) \wedge \boxplus(P)(x) = n]$

↳ ⟦√dw-⟧ $= 2$

⟦podwójna⟧ $= \lambda P \lambda x[P(x) \wedge \boxplus(P)(x) = 2]$

↳ ⟦korona⟧ $= \lambda x[\mathbf{crown}(x)]$

⟦podwójna korona⟧ $= \lambda x[\mathbf{crown}(x) \wedge \boxplus(\mathbf{crown})(x) = 2]$

In Figure 4 and (15), the derivation starts with the multiplicative circumfix *po⟩… ⟨n-* which can be considered semantically analogous to CARD since it comprises a built-in measure function in its semantics. In the first step, the

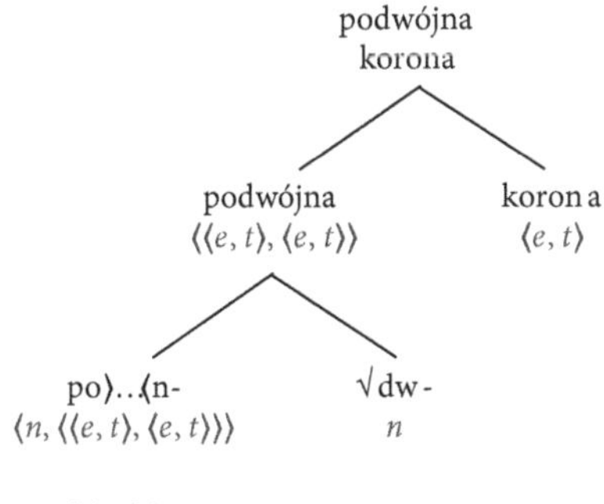

Figure 4: A semantic tree of (13b)

number variable needs to be saturated by the integer-denoting numeral root. As a result, we obtain a predicate modifier, i.e., the multiplier *podwójna* ('double'), which denotes a set of ordered pairs of a property and an individual whose internal structure consists of two self-sufficient parts. Again, I assume that morphemes *-ój-* and *-a* play no role in the semantic composition. Finally, in order to saturate the predicate variable the multiplier combines with the noun and the resulting expression denotes a function from complex individuals to truth values. In other words, (13b) refers to a set of crowns such that they consist of two sub-crowns, e.g., a set of Ancient Egyptian Pschents. The $\langle e, t\rangle$ type of the noun phrase allows for further modification including compatibility with cardinal numerals in order to further count such double crowns.

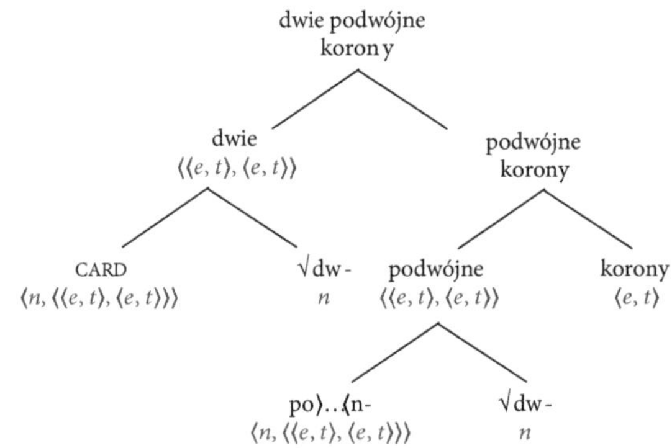

Figure 5: A semantic tree of (13c)

(16) Interpretation of (13c)

$[\![\textsc{card}]\!] = \lambda n \lambda P \lambda x[P(x) \wedge \#(P)(x) = n]$

$[\![\sqrt{}\text{dw-}]\!] = 2$

$[\![\text{dwie}]\!] = \lambda P \lambda x[P(x) \wedge \#(P)(x) = 2]$

$[\![\text{po}\rangle\ldots\langle\text{n-}]\!] = \lambda n \lambda P \lambda x[P(x) \wedge \boxplus(P)(x) = n]$

$[\![\sqrt{}\text{dw-}]\!] = 2$

$[\![\text{podwójne}]\!] = \lambda P \lambda x[P(x) \wedge \boxplus(P)(x) = 2]$

$[\![\text{korony}]\!] = \lambda x[\mathbf{crown}(x)]$

$[\![\text{podwójne korony}]\!] = \lambda x[\mathbf{crown}(x) \wedge \boxplus(\mathbf{crown})(x) = 2]$

$[\![\text{dwie podwójne korony}]\!] = \lambda x[\mathbf{crown}(x) \wedge \boxplus(\mathbf{crown})(x) = 2 \wedge \#(\mathbf{crown})(x) = 2]$

Finally, Figure 5 and (16) account for the fact that it is possible to quantify over entities denoted by counting expressions such as (13b), as demonstrated in (13c). Here, in the final step of the derivation the cardinal *dwie* ('two'), i.e., a predicate modifier of type $\langle\langle e, t\rangle, \langle e, t\rangle\rangle$, combines with the noun phrase *podwójna korona* ('double crown') denoting a set of double crowns. The resulting counting expression is a predicate and denotes a set of pairs of crowns consisting of two parts that can be considered crowns themselves.

5. Complications and extensions

5.1. Events

I believe that the analysis developed in Section 4 gives some intriguing insights into issues concerning plurality and quantification in the adjectival domain. The proposed account seems to work pretty well for a significant subset of constructions in which multipliers appear including examples such as those in (4) and (6). Nonetheless, Slavic multipliers co-occur also with nouns that at first sight appear to be problematic for the proposed analysis which at this point fails to elucidate all the data. In this section, I will discuss such cases and hypothesize about possible extensions of the approach.

We have already seen that the proposed analysis accounts for a number of noun phrases denoting properties of individuals. However, as indicated by examples such those in (17) Slavic multipliers combine as well with deverbal nouns which do not seem to involve reference to entities.

(17) a. *podwójne* *morderstwo* (Polish)
double.nom.sg.n murder.nom.n
'double murder'
b. *dvojnoje* *ubijstvo* (Russian)
c. *dvostruko* *ubistvo* (BCS)
d. *dvojitá* *vražda* (Czech)
double.nom.sg.f murder.nom.f

To account for phrases such as (17) I extend the system by adopting standard Neo-Davidsonian frameworks (e.g., Carlson 1984, Dowty 1989, and Parsons 1990). Therefore, in the ontology of the model I assume events which are spatiotemporal things, i.e., concrete particulars with a location and time (the claim dating back to Davidson 1967). Though events are of primitive type *v*, they can be associated with individuals via thematic relations which constitute subatomic semantics of event-denoting expressions. Furthermore, following Grimshaw

(2011) I assume that with the exception of participant and result nominals deverbal nominalizations denote properties of events. Finally, along the lines of Bach (1986) I assume that pluralities of events are obtained similar to pluralities of individuals.

A standard test for deverbal nominals (e.g., Grimshaw 1990) shows that a noun such as Polish *morderstwo* ('murder') refers to an event since it can be felicitously modified by event-modifying predicates such as *mieć miejsce* ('take place') and *być świadkiem* ('witness'), as indicated in (18).

(18) a. *Morderstwo miało miejsce w piątek.* (Polish)
murder.nom.n had.sg.n place.acc.n in Friday.acc.m
'The murder took place on Friday.'

b. *Jan był świadkiem morderstwa.*
Jan.nom.m was.m witness.ins.m murder.gen.n
'Jan witnessed the murder.'

It follows that, assuming the ⊞ operation can be applied to events, the analysis seems to be able to account for examples such as (17) in which the multiplier modifies a deverbal nominal. Let us then extend the definition of a self-sufficient part from (11) to include events, as introduced in (19).

(19) For an atomic entity or event *x* that has a property *P*, *y* is a self-sufficient part of *x* iff (i) *y* is a part of *x* and (ii) *y* itself has a property *P*.

An intuitive way to understand subatomic quantification within the structure of an event involves temporal characteristics. Within this view, a self-sufficient part of an event is a subevent of which the same property as of the whole event holds. For instance, in a murder scenario in which a maniac stabbed to death two victims with a knife one after another there would be two relevant parts of the whole murdering event, i.e., stabbing victim 1 and stabbing victim 2, and each of those subevents can be considered a murder as well, see Figure 6. In such a case the multiplier in, e.g., (17a) quantifies over self-sufficient parts of the murdering event, i.e., subevents that are murders themselves. Since there is no murder without a victim, the phrase infers that there were two individuals murdered during the complex murdering event which seems to be the expected result.

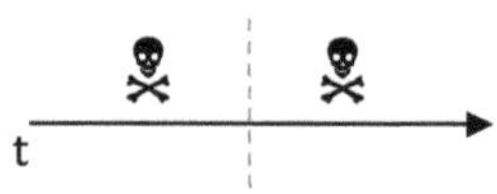

Figure 6: Parts of a double murder event in a knife-stabbing scenario

Nonetheless, one could object that such an approach cannot account for situations such as a bomb scenario in which an intended explosion affected two victims leading to a double murder. In such a case, quantification over temporally subsequent subevents is not possible since the explosion had an immediate effect and there was virtually no running time of the event. However, I believe there is no reason to assume that temporal chunks are the only possible parts that constitute an event. Since events are complex peculiarities involving not only times, but also locations, in a bomb scenario described above it is still possible to differentiate between parts of an event in spatial terms. Consider the situation depicted in Figure 7. Even with no temporally defined subevents it is quite straightforward that one could specify two areas within the space in which the explosion took place, as indicated by the dashed line. As a result, we obtain two parts of the murdering event each of which turns out to have the property of the whole and since individuals are in general assumed to occupy space, it should be possible to draw divisions like that with respect to any event.

An interesting problem for future research concerns what the restrictions on such subevents are. So far, both discussed scenarios involved an agent/theme asymmetry, i.e., a unique agent and two patients. In principle, however, it does not have to be that way. For instance, one can wonder whether an expression such as *podwójne morderstwo* ('double murder') can refer to an event in which two different murderers simultaneously killed one and the same person, e.g., by shooting. Though the scenario is somewhat implausible since there is usually one cause of death, according to my intuitions it would still fall into the denotation of the phrase. An approach similar to the one discussed in the bomb scenario would be necessary to account for such an example. In particular, quantification over parts of the event space would be required, but this time with the location divided with respected to agents rather than themes. As a result, each of the spatial chunks would include the victim and an agent and, hence, fulfill

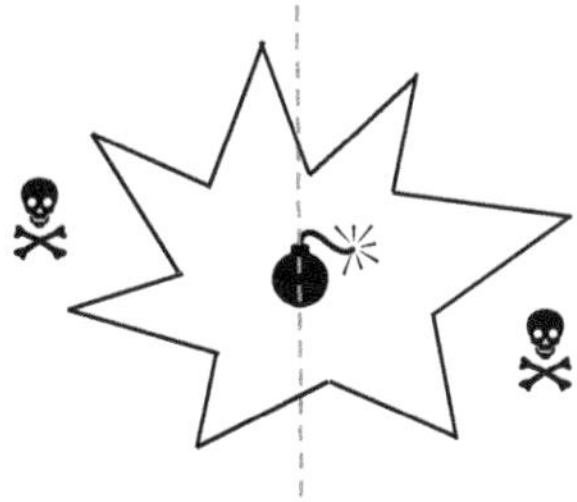

Figure 7: Parts of a double murder event in a bomb scenario

the requirement to be regarded as a murdering event. At this point, one should probably wonder how far the proposed extension could go. For instance, does a murdering event in which one agent performs the act of killing of one person using simultaneously two different instruments, say a hammer and a gun, qualify as a double murder? In this paper, I will remain agnostic with respect to this issue since it seems that in this case the intuition is sort of blurred. I find the discussion of potential restrictions on self-sufficient subevents to be an important topic, nonetheless since space prohibits, I will leave the detailed analysis of subatomic quantification in the domain of eventualities for future research.

5.2. Portions

In Section 2, we have discussed examples involving count nouns. Nonetheless, Slavic multipliers co-occur also with mass nouns which at first sight may appear to be problematic for the proposed account. For instance, it seems that the noun phrases in (20) do not refer to parts of coffee, but rather to a standard amount, i.e., a big cup of coffee, which consists of two standard amounts of coffee, i.e., equivalent two normal cups of coffee.

(20) a. *podwójna* *kawa* (Polish)
double.nom.sg.f coffee.nom.f
'double coffee'
b. *dvojitá káva* (Czech)
c. *dupla kahva/kava/kafa* (BCS)
d. *dvojnoj kofe* (Russian)
double.nom.sg.m coffee.nom.m

Prima facie, it may seem that there is no straightforward correlation between the proposed analysis and examples such as (20) given that the definitions in (11) and (19) make reference to atomicity. However, I believe the analysis can be saved when we involve an interaction between the self-sufficient parts-counting $\boxplus$ and some sort of a mass-count shift. For this purpose, I adopt the standard Universal Packager operation (see, e.g., Bach 1986, Jackendoff 1991, and Landman 1991) which yields quantized portions (or packages) of substance for a given mass entity.[12] Assuming that the mass noun *kawa* ('coffee') is shifted by the Universal Packager operation before it is modified by the multiplier (and

12 An alternative approach to be taken is to enrich the structure with a classifier. As suggested by Selkirk (1977) and subsequent work it is plausible to assume that possibly every natural language generally uses classifiers which are often null.

there are good reasons to presume that it is the case since only after the shift mass nouns combine with number words) the resulting count noun refers to a standard or contextually determined portion of coffee, specifically a cup of coffee. The multiplier then asserts that within the package there are two standard or contextually determined portions, i.e., two cups of coffee. As a result, we obtain a double coffee, i.e., a standard portion consisting of two smaller parts that have a property of being a standard portion of coffee as well which is actually analogous to the treatment of cases such as (4) and (6). Furthermore, note that in the discussed coffee scenario the portion of beverage is defined pragmatically and (at least to some extend) fixed. In other words, there are exactly two parts of the amount of coffee constituting double coffee that are standard portions. Smaller or bigger amounts are simply not standard with respect to coffee.[13]

Interestingly, it seems that there is a deep relationship between multipliers and packaging. One could easily imagine that multipliers would also interact with another mass-count shift, specifically with Universal Sorter (see, e.g., Bunt 1985) which converses the mass noun into a count denotation referring to quantized subkinds. However, it seems there is no such interaction since phrases such as those in (20) lack the relevant interpretation. In particular, (20a) is not true of substance consisting of two kinds of coffee, say a drink brewed from a mixture of *Coffea arabica* and *Coffea canephora* beans. This fact seems to suggest that multipliers operate only on mereologies involving object-level entities (tokens) and cannot count self-sufficient parts of kind-level individuals (types). If such a hypothesis could be validated empirically, explaining the restriction would be an interesting question to pursue.

5.3. Social roles

Another piece of data that appears to be problematic for the approach developed here is constituted by phrases with nouns referring to social roles in examples as in (21). Such phrases do not refer to an individual who consists of two parts, but rather they seem to involve a relationship between an individual and two other entities. To be an agent means to be an agent for some intelligence agency, i.e., one cannot be an agent without an employer for whom they spy. In this case, the multiplier seems to quantify over entities denoted by the argument of the noun which is not expected on the approach developed here.

13 Of course, the standard can differ with respect to other beverages. Note that counting expressions such as *double coffee* and *double martini* refer to different amounts of a substance.

(21) a. *podwójny* *agent* (Polish)
double.nom.sg.m agent.nom.m
'double agent'
b. *dvojitý agent* (Czech)
c. *dvojnoj agent* (Russian)
d. *dvostruki agent* (BCS)

At this stage, it is unclear how to integrate the ideas developed in this paper with the treatment of examples such as (21). A possible extension of the proposed analysis is to assume that nouns such as *agent* involve some kind of an abstract association to entities related to denoted individuals, e.g., an association between agents and intelligence agencies, and that such an association is subject to mereological relations. A promising perspective to pursue involves adopting the notion of roles into the presented semantic framework (see Sowa 1984, Steimann 2000, and Zobel 2016). Intuitively, roles are functions or capacities of individuals, i.e., social constructs independent of the individuals that bear them. Crucially for our purposes, for an individual to bear a particular role, it must stand in a certain relationship to other individuals. Following Zobel (2016), one could distinguish between class nouns such as *man* (properties of individuals of type $\langle e, t \rangle$) and role nouns such as *agent* by adding a new type r referring to roles and a shifting mechanism relating roles and individuals. Role nouns would then essentially denote properties of roles (type $\langle r, t \rangle$), although they could be shifted to refer to properties of entities. Within this view, multipliers would quantify over self-sufficient parts of roles rather than individuals and the whole phrase could then be shifted to refer to entities if required. This would account for the fact that expressions such as those in (21) denote individuals performing a complex role, i.e., individuals involved in activities and bearing responsibilities related to two distinct intelligence agencies. However, developing an explicit analysis of the interaction between subatomic quantification and roles is rather challenging and it goes beyond the scope of this paper to propose a precise implementation of the idea. Therefore, this topic is left for further research.

5.4. Structured parts

Finally, the last problematic case concerns phrases in which the multiplier does quantify over parts of an individual or event, see (22a) and (23a) respectively, but such parts are not self-sufficient.

(22) a. *podwójny* *hamburger* (Polish)
double.nom.sg.m hamburger.nom.m
'double hamburger'

b. *dvojitý hamburger* (Czech)
c. *dvojnoj gamburger* (Russian)
d. *dupli hamburger* (BCS)

(23) a. *podwójny* *axel* (Polish)
double.nom.sg.m axel.nom.m
'double axel'
b. *dvojitý axel* (Czech)
c. *dvojnoj aksel'* (Russian)
d. *dvostruki aksel* (BCS)

Consider the example in (22a). It is not the case that its referent consists of two parts that are hamburgers themselves, but rather that it consists of two patties in a bun. Similar, (23a) is not true of a figure skating element in which a skater jumps, spins in the air, lands and jumps, spins in the air, and lands again. On the contrary, it refers to one jump with two spins. This is something that cannot be captured by the ⊞ operation and it seems that the analysis developed in this paper fails to account for such data. Nevertheless, I would like to suggest that in fact it might be the case that counting self-sufficient parts is a particular instance of a more general subatomic quantification over particular parts constituting an inner structure of an entity or event.

The analysis can be extended to deal with the problematic examples such as those in (22) and (23) by assuming a mereology with what Champollion and Krifka (2016) call structured parthood to account for the status of significant or, in other words, perceptibly distinguished parts of a whole (for an overview and discussion of related philosophical issues see, e.g., Simons 1987 and Varzi 2010). The difference between structured and unstructured elements is that the former are cognitively salient parts of a whole whereas the latter are not. Furthermore, structured and unstructured parthood have different structural properties. Structured parthood is not transitive, whereas unstructured parthood is. Table 1 gives some examples of structured part relations.

For some time, it has been recognized that structured parthood plays an important role in organizing lexicons of natural languages, specifically via semantic relations such as meronymy and hyponymy (see, e.g., Cruse 1986). However, in contemporary mereological approaches to natural language semantics, the impact of structured part relations on compositional semantics seems to be somewhat neglected (e.g., Champollion 2012 and Champollion and Krifka 2016). However, it appears that there is unrelated evidence that cognitively salient

Table 1: Examples of structured parthood (Simons 1987: 10)

Whole	Part
a (certain) man	his head
a (certain) tree	its trunk
a house	its roof
a mountain	its summit
a battle	its opening shot
an insect's life	its larval stage
a novel	its first chapter

parts are not only linguistically relevant, but also form a hierarchy of some sort. Consider the contrasts between (24b), (25b) and (24c), (25c) respectively. In ordinary life situations, when talking about hamburgers it is perfectly normal to paraphrase (24a) as (24b), i.e., to define a hamburger as an object consisting of a bun with a patty. Similar, (25b) is a perfectly normal paraphrase of (25a), i.e., an axel jump is described as a jump with a spin. It is, however, odd to use (24c) and (25c) in such contexts.

(24) a. *hamburger*
b. *bun with a patty*
c. *#patty with a bun*

(25) a. *axel*
b. *jump with a spin*
c. *#spin with a jump*

I will hypothesize that the structure of entities such as hamburgers and events such as axel jumps is in fact linguistically encoded and that structured parts form hierarchies like those given in (26). In particular, a patty is a more salient part of a hamburger than a bun, as indicated in (26a), while a spin is more salient part of an axel than a jump, see (26b). The relevant elements are more salient in the sense that they constitute essential components differentiating a whole from other objects falling into the denotation of a relevant hypernym.

(26) a. *hamburger: patty > bun*
b. *axel: spin > jump*

With this in mind, I posit that some linguistic expressions are sensitive to hierarchical relations between parts. For instance, *with*-phrases in paraphrases described above, see (24) and (25), select for more salient parts within the mereological structure of an entity or event denoted by a paraphrased noun. This gives us a promising perspective to extend the approach developed in this paper to account for examples such as those in (22) and (23). In such a framework, self-sufficient parts would constitute a particular case within a class of structured parts, specifically a subclass of cognitively most salient elements.

6. Conclusion

In this paper, I have focused on topics concerning quantification in the adjectival domain. I have presented novel data concerning Slavic multipliers such as Polish *podwójny*, Czech *dvojitý*, Russian *dvojnoj*, and Bosnian-Croatian-Serbian *dvostruki* (all 'double') which suggest that multipliers are sensitive to the internal part-whole structure of objects denoted by nouns they modify and involve what I call subatomic quantification, i.e., quantification over cognitively salient parts of an entity or event. On the basis of morphological evidence, I have argued that Slavic multipliers are compositional. Building on the theories of counting developed by Krifka (1989, 1990, and 1995), I have proposed a unified system for numerals and adjectives. The analysis assumes a mereology of structured parts of entities and events and accounts for a representative subset of data. According to the proposal, Slavic numeral roots are names of numbers and hence denote integers whereas multiplicative morphemes introduce a specialized measure function, i.e., the self-sufficient parts-counting operation $\boxplus$ which returns a number of self-sufficient parts of an entity or event of which a property denoted by a noun is predicated. In other words, multipliers quantify over cognitively salient parts which, similarly to complex entities or events they constitute, have themselves a property of a modified noun.

References

Arsenijević, Boban. 2016. "Gender as a grammaticalized classifier system: The case of the Serbo-Croatian neuter". A manuscript available online on LingBuzz. URL: http://ling.auf.net/lingbuzz/002848.

Bach, Emmon. 1986. "The algebra of events". *Linguistics and Philosophy* 9: 5–16.

Bale, Alan and Jessica Coon. 2014. "Classifiers are for numerals, not for nouns: Consequences for the mass/count distinction". *Linguistic Inquiry* 45(4): 695–707.

Barwise, Jon and Robin Cooper. 1981. "Generalized quantifiers and natural language". *Philosophy, Language, and Artificial Intelligence* 4(2): 241–301.

Bunt, Harry. 1985. *Mass terms and model-theoretic semantics.* Cambridge: Cambridge University Press.

Carlson, Gregory. 1984. "Thematic roles and their role in semantic interpretation." *Linguistics* 22: 259–79.

Champollion, Lucas. 2012. "Linguistic applications of mereology". A script to the 24th European Summer School in Logic, Language and Information ESSLLI 2012 course. 13th–17th August 2012. Opole, Poland.

Champollion, Lucas and Manfred Krifka. 2016. "Mereology". In Maria Aloni and Paul Dekker (eds.), *The Cambridge handbook of formal semantics*. Cambridge University Press. 369–88.

Cheng, Chung-Ying. 1973. "Comments on Moravcsik's paper". In Jaakko Hintikka, Julius Moravcsik and Patrick Suppes (eds.), *Approaches to natural language*. Dordrecht: Reidel. 286–88.

Cruse, D. Alan. 1986. *Lexical semantics*. Cambridge: Cambridge University Press.

Davidson, Donald. 1967. "The logical form of action sentences". In Nicholas Resher (ed.), *The logic of decision and action*. Pittsburgh: University of Pittsburgh Press. 81–95.

Dočekal, Mojmír. 2012. "Atoms, groups and kinds in Czech". *Acta Liguistica Hungarica: An International Journal of Linguistics* 59: 109–26.

Dočekal, Mojmír. 2013. "What do we count with numerals? Semantic analysis of Czech group-denoting and kind-denoting NPs". In Uwe Junghanns, Dorothee Fehrmann, Denisa Lenertová and Hagen Pitsch (eds.), *Formal Description of Slavic Languages: The ninth conference. Proceedings of FDSL 9, Göttingen 2011*. Frankfurt am Main: Peter Lang. 87–105.

Dowty, David. 1989. "On the semantic content of the notion "thematic role"". In Gennaro Cherchia, Barbara H. Partee and Raymond Turner (eds.), *Properties, types, and meanings Vol II*. Kluwer. 69–130.

Fassi Fehri, Abdelkader. 2016. "Semantic gender diversity and its architecture in the grammar of Arabic". *Brill's Journal of Afroasiatic Languages and Linguistics* 8: 154–199.

Grimshaw, Jane. 1990. *Argument structure*. Cambridge, MA: MIT Press.

Grimshaw, Jane. 2011. "Deverbal nominalization". In Claudia Maienborn, Klaus von Heusinger and Paul Portner (eds.), *Semantics: An international handbook of the natural language meaning Vol. 2*. Berlin: de Gruyter Mouton. 1292–1313.

Ionin, Tania and Ora Matushansky. 2006. "The composition of complex cardinals". *Journal of Semantics* 23(4): 315–60.

Jackendoff, Ray. 1991. "Parts and boundaries". *Cognition* 41: 9–45.

Khrizman, Keren. 2015. "Cardinal/Collective alternation in Russian numerals". A paper presented at the 11th conference on Formal Description of Slavic Languages FDSL 11. 2nd–4th December 2015. University of Potsdam.

Krifka, Manfred. 1989. "Nominal reference, temporal constitution and quantification in Event Semantics". In Renate Bartsch, Johan van Benthem and Peter von Emde Boas (eds.), *Semantics and contextual expression*. Dordrecht: Foris Publication. 75–115.

Krifka, Manfred. 1990. "Four thousand ships passed through the lock: Object-induced measure functions on events". *Linguistics and Philosophy* 13: 487–520.

Krifka, Manfred. 1995. "Common nouns: A contrastive analysis of English and Chinese". In Gregory N. Carlson and Francis Jeffry Pelletier (eds.), *The generic book*. Chicago: University of Chicago Press. 398–411.

Landman, Fred. 1991. *Structures for semantics*. Dordrecht: Kluwer.

Landman, Fred. 2000. *Events and plurality: The Jerusalem lectures*. Dordrecht: Kluwer Academic Publishers.

Landman, Fred. 2004. *Indefiniteness and the type of sets*. Oxford: Blackwell.

Link, Godehard. 1983. "The logical analysis of plurals and mass terms: A lattice-theoretical approach". In Rainer Bäuerle, Christoph Schwarze and Arnim von Stechow (eds.), *Meaning, use and the interpretation of language*. Berlin: Walter de Gruyter. 303–23.

Montague, Richard. 1973. "The proper treatment of quantification in ordinary English". In Jaakko Hintikka, Julius Moravcsik and Patrick Suppes (eds.), *Approaches to natural language*. Dordrecht: Reidel. 221–42.

Parsons, Terence. 1990. *Events in the semantics of English: A study in Subatomic Semantics*. MIT Press.

Quine, Willard van Orman. 1960. *Word and object*. Cambridge, MA: MIT Press.

Rothstein, Susan. 2010. "Counting and the mass/count distinction". *Journal of Semantics* 27: 343–97.

Rothstein, Susan. 2012. "Numericals: Counting, measuring and classifying". In Ana Aguilar Guevara, Anna Chernilovskaya and Rick Nouwen (eds.), *Proceedings of Sinn und Bedeutung 16: Volume 2*. Cambridge, MA: MITWPL. 527–42.

Rothstein, Susan. 2013. "A Fregean semantics for number words". In M. Aloni, M. Franke & F. Roelofsen (eds.), *Proceedings of the 19th Amsterdam Colloquium*. URL: http://www.illc.uva.nl/AC/AC2013/uploaded_files/inlineitem/23_Rothstein.pdf. 179–86.

Scha, Remko. 1981. "Distributive, collective and cumulative quantification". In Jeroen Groenendijk, Theo M. V. Janssen and Martin Stokhof (eds.), *Formal methods in the study of language*. Amsterdam: Mathematisch Centrum. 483–512.

Selkirk, Elisabeth. 1977. "Some remarks on noun phrase structure". In Peter W. Culicover, Thomas Wasow and Adrian Akmajian (eds.), *Formal syntax*. New York: Academic Press. 285–316.

Simons, Peter. 1987. *Parts: A study in ontology*. Oxford: Clarendon Press.

Sowa, John F. 1984. *Conceptual structures: Information processing in mind and machine*. Reading, MA: Addison-Wesley.

Steimann, Friedrich. 2000. "On the representation of roles in object-oriented and conceptual modelling". *Data & Knowledge Engineering* 35: 83–106.

Varzi, Achille C. 2010. "Mereology". In Edward N. Zalta (ed.), *The Standford Encyclopedia of Philosophy*. Spring 2010. Stanford, CA. URL: http://plato.stanford.edu/archives/spr2010/entries/mereology/.

Wągiel, Marcin. 2014. "Boys, girls, and scissors: A semantic analysis of Polish NPs headed by the numeral *dwoje*". In Ludmila Veselovská and Markéta Janebová (eds.), *Nominal structures: All in complex DPs*. Olomouc: Palacký University. 69–84.

Wągiel, Marcin. 2015. "Sums, groups, genders, and Polish numerals". In Gerhild Zybatow, Petr Biskup, Marcel Guhl, Claudia Hurtig, Olav Mueller-Reichau and Maria Yastrebova (eds.), *Slavic grammar from a formal perspective. The 10th anniversary FDSL conference, Leipzig 2013*. Frankfurt am Main: Peter Lang. 495–513.

Zobel, Sarah. 2016. "On the notion of roles in formal semantics". A paper presented at the Linguistics Colloquium. 2nd November 2016. University of Göttingen.

Aida Talić

Affixal-Article Languages and Structural Parallelism in Slavic and Beyond*

1. Introduction

I examine the structural complexity in the domain of N and A, focusing on languages with affixal articles, including Bulgarian, Romanian, Danish, Icelandic, Norwegian, Swedish, and Standard Arabic. I discuss cross-linguistic variation regarding two parallel operations, left-branch extraction (LBE) in the domain of N ((*) EXPENSIVE, HE LIKES CARS.) and intensifying adverb extraction (AdvE) in the domain of A ((*) TERRIBLY, HE WAS TIRED.). Although many languages that disallow LBE also disallow AdvE and many languages that allow LBE also allow AdvE, the two operations are not always correlated. Crucially, while all languages with an affixal definite article pattern with languages with a non-affixal definite article in disallowing LBE (Bošković 2005), I show that Bulgarian, Romanian, and Icelandic pattern with languages without articles in allowing AdvE. I argue that this similarity between languages with affixal articles and languages without articles is due to a deep structural similarity between the two groups of languages that separates them from languages with non-affixal articles. Furthermore, I discuss several contexts where affixal article languages drop the definite article and where they pattern with languages without articles in the domain of N. When the article is dropped, affixal article languages behave like languages without articles with respect to the interpretations of superlatives, the interpretation of expressions with *most*, and PP-adjunct extraction from the nominal phrase.

I first discuss LBE and AdvE and different sources of functional structure in a domain in different languages in Section 2. In Section 3, I examine affixal article languages and why they pattern with articles-less languages regarding a number of phenomena in the domain of N and A.

* I am grateful to Željko Bošković, Nadira Aljović, Jonathan Bobaljik, Susi Wurmbrand, Vera Gribanova, and the audiences of FASL 24, SinFonIJA 8, and FDSL 11, and one anonymous reviewer for stimulating comments.

2. Structural parallelism in the extended domain of N and A

In this section, I discuss LBE in the domain of N and AdvE in the domain of A, as well as the structural complexity of the two domains in different languages, focusing on a particular proposal that domains of N and A tend to have the same amount of structure within a language, even though they may differ cross-linguistically (Talić 2015a).

It is well-known that languages differ in whether they allow LBE in the nominal domain, as in (1). Uriagereka (1988), Corver (1992), and Bošković (2005) establish a generalization that only languages without articles may allow LBE.

(1) a. *Expensive he saw cars.
    b. Skupa je vidio auta. (BCS)
       expensive is seen cars (Bošković 2012)

In Talić (2015a; 2015b), I discuss a parallel process in the adjectival domain, AdvE, and show that languages also differ in whether they allow it. While languages like English do not allow AdvE (2a), languages like Bosnian/Croatian/Serbian (BCS) do (2b).

(2) a. *Terribly he was tired.
    b. Strašno je bio umoran. (BCS)
       terribly is been tired

Dutch, German, Brazilian Portuguese, French, Italian, Spanish, Finnish, Hungarian, and Cypriot Greek pattern with English (2a), and Polish, Russian, and Slovenian pattern with BCS (2b). Thus, at first AdvE seems to make the same cut between languages as LBE:[1]

(3) a. Languages with a definite article disallow AdvE.
    b. Languages without a definite article may allow AdvE. (to be revised)

The similarity between the two processes and the overlap between languages that allow both LBE and AdvE give rise to the question whether there is some deep connection between LBE and AdvE.

LBE is one of a large number of syntactic/semantic properties separating languages with and without articles, based on which Bošković (2005, 2008,

---

1 I put aside affixal article languages for the moment, and turn to them in detail in the following section, where I show that LBE and AdvE are not always correlated.

2012 *et seq*) argues that languages that do not have a definite article also lack DP projection in the nominal domain, i.e. that over twenty phenomena distinguishing between languages with and without articles cannot be reduced to phonology (where D is overt or null) (see also Fukui 1988; Corver 1992; Zlatić 1997; Chierchia 1998; Baker 2003, among others). Regarding LBE, Bošković (2014) gives a phase-based account of the split in (1) under a contextual approach to phases. Phases are standardly assumed to define locality domains, where only the head and the edge of a phase are accessible for syntactic operations outside of the phase (*Phase Impenetrability Condition (PIC):* Chomsky 2000; 2001). While only vP and CP are phases for Chomsky (2000, 2001), it has been argued recently by a number of researchers that the phasehood of a category depends on its syntactic context (Bobaljik and Wurmbrand 2005; Bošković 2005, 2014, among others). In that respect, Bošković argues that every lexical category projects a phase and that the highest projection is a phase in the extended domain of a lexical category. Then, DP is the highest projection and a phase in the domain of N in languages with articles, but in languages without articles where DP is missing, NP is a phase. Bošković argues that the contrast in (1) follows from this structural difference in the nominal domain. First, given the PIC, phrasal movement must proceed via phasal edges. However, Bošković (1994, 2005) argues that a moving element needs to cross at least one maximal projection, i.e. movement steps cannot be too short either (a constraint often referred to as *anti-locality*; the name is due to Grohmann 2003). Thus, adopting the traditional assumption that AP is NP-adjoined, for an AP to move out of DP in English in (1a), the AP first needs to move to SpecDP due to the PIC. This step, however, crosses only a segment of NP, and violates anti-locality (4a). In BCS in (1b), the NP-adjoined AP is at the edge of a phase, and it is free to move out without violating any constraint (4b).

(4) a. $[_{DP}$ **D** $[_{NP}$ expensive $[_{NP}$ N]] (phase head is bolded)
b. $[_{NP}$ skupa $[_{NP}$**N**]

In Talić (2015a; 2015b), I argue that AdvE reflects a structural difference between languages in the adjectival domain, and propose that the extended projections of N and A are parallel (for a discussion about different extended projections, see also e.g. Abney 1987; Bošković 2004):

(5) *Structural Parallelism*
   a. If a language allows bare lexical structure without a functional layer in the domain of one lexical category, it may allow bare lexical structure in the domain of other lexical categories. (e.g. the language can have bare NP and bare AP).[2]
   b. If a language never allows bare lexical structure, i.e. it always requires a functional layer in the domain of one lexical category, it must have a functional layer in the domain of all lexical categories (e.g. bare NP or bare AP are never allowed).

Based on (5), languages like English always have a functional projection (XP) above AP, while languages like BCS can have a bare AP. Then, XP is a phase in English, as the highest projection in the domain of A, but AP is a phase in BCS. Assuming that intensifying adverbs are AP-adjoined, the account of (2) is parallel to the account of (1). A moving AdvP in languages like English first needs to move to SpecXP due to the PIC, but this violates anti-locality (6a). In languages like BCS, AdvP originates at the edge of the AP phase, so it can move freely (6b).

(6) a. [$_{XP}$ **X** [$_{AP}$ terribly [$_{AP}$ A]] (phase head is bolded)
   b. [$_{AP}$ strašno [$_{AP}$ **A**]

In sum, both LBE and AdvE are blocked in languages with non-affixal articles because of the presence of the functional layers in their respective domains, but they are allowed in languages without articles because those functional projections are missing.

It is worth noting here that the amount of structure in the extended domain of a lexical category can vary in different constructions in the same language. Regarding the nominal domain, Bošković (2014) shows that while BCS typically has a bare NP, it can have more structure in this domain (see Despić 2011 and Bošković 2014 for a discussion of binding and movement in the presence of a QP projected by a numeral or a quantifier in the domain of N in BCS). Similarly, in the presence of an additional affix on an adjective, the extended domain of A also contains functional structure. For instance, BCS has two forms of adjectives. The form given in (2) is the so-called "short form", which occurs both in the predicative and the attributive position. With this form, AdvE is possible in both (2) and (7a). In the "long form" given in (7b), which can only occur in the attributive

2 Note that this is a one-way correlation. I focus here on the categories N and A, putting aside V and P in this paper due to space limitations.

position, an affix that is added on top of the short-form morphology (see Aljović 2002; Talić 2015b for more details). With this form, AdvE is not possible (7b). The long-form affix is a realization of a functional head associated with specificity marking on adjectives, and this functional projection blocks AdvE, in the same way AdvE is blocked in languages that do not allow bare APs (2a).

(7) a. Izuzetno$_i$ su kupili [t_i skup] automobil. (BCS)
extremely are bought expensive.SF car
'They bought an *extremely* expensive car.'

b. *Izuzetno$_i$ su kupili [t_i skup**i**] automobil.
extremely are bought expensive.**LF** car

Crucially, functional structure in a domain can have two different sources in different languages. First, if we take the language split in (5) to be due to a parametric difference between languages (see Bošković 2008, 2012 for the NP/DP parameter), then in languages that never allow bare lexical projections (5b), functional structure is present for deep formal (syntactic) considerations (the setting of the relevant parameter in these languages). From this perspective, in languages like English, DP is always projected in the domain of N and an XP is also always projected in the domain of A. In contrast, in languages that may allow bare lexical projections (5a), functional structure is absent due to the parameter setting in basic cases. However, when there is additional semantic motivation and morphology realizing an additional functional head, then even in these languages functional structure can be projected. In languages like BCS, where NP and AP are typically bare, additional structure is present in the domain of N in the presence of functional heads like quantifiers (see Despić 2011 and Bošković 2014), as well as in the domain of A in the presence of a functional head realized by an additional affix, as in (7b).

Bearing this in mind, in the following section, I discuss several syntactic and semantic properties separating languages with and without articles (see Bošković 2005/2012) from the perspective of several affixal article languages (Bulgarian, Romanian, Icelandic, Danish, Norwegian, Swedish, and Arabic), and argue that at a deep level these languages resemble languages without articles, i.e. they belong the group of languages in (5a).

3. (Non-)Bare extended projections in affixal article languages

3.1. AdvE vs. LBE

So far, we have seen languages where both AdvE and LBE are blocked (languages with a non-affixal definite article) and languages where both AdvE and LBE are possible (languages without articles), which raises the question whether the two operations are always correlated. Affixal article languages show that they are not.

It turns out AdvE is possible in Bulgarian, Romanian, and Icelandic as illustrated with Bulgarian in (8) (see Talić 2015a), which leads to the generalization in (9).

(8) Užasno$_i$ bjah [t$_i$ umoren]. (Bulgarian)
terribly was tired
'I was *terribly* tired.'

(9) Languages without a definite article and languages with an affixal definite article may allow AdvE.

The generalization in (9) indicates that, just like languages without articles, languages with affixal articles allow bare APs, i.e. that they belong to the group of languages in (5b). However, Bošković (2005) shows that affixal article languages pattern with languages like English with respect to LBE. The example in (10) shows that LBE is not possible in Bulgarian. The same is true for Romanian (see Petroj 2014) and Icelandic (see Talić 2015a).

(10) *Kakva prodade Petko t kola. (Bulgarian)
what-kind-of sold Petko car
Intended: 'What kind of car did Petko sell? (Bošković 2005: 3)

This indicates that affixal article languages have functional structure above the lexical projection (NP) in the nominal domain in these cases, which blocks LBE (unlike in the extended domain of A in the examples in (8)). Does this contrast between the domain of N and the domain of A in affixal article languages show that the basic structural parallelism in (5) does not hold? Investigating further syntactic and semantic properties that correlate with the presence of a definite article in the nominal domain in Section 3.2, I will show that (5) holds in these languages as well.

Recall first that functional structure is present in the domain of N and A even in languages that allow bare lexical projections in the presence of additional morphological and semantic motivation, as shown for the domain of A in BCS in (7). Similar to this contrast in BCS, Icelandic has an adjectival form that can be found both in the predicative and attributive position (indefinite form), and a form reserved only for the attributive position (definite form). Interestingly, AdvE is possible with the former (8c)/(11a), but not with the latter (11b), parallel to BCS in (7).

(11) a. Rosalega$_i$ keypti hún [t_i fallega] úlpu. (Icelandic)
extremely bought she beautiful.ACC.F.INDEF jacket. ACC.F
'She bought an *extremely* beautiful jacket.'
b. *Rosalega$_i$ keypti hún [t_i falleg**u**] úlpu-**na.**
extremely bought she beautiful.ACC.F.**DEF** jacket. ACC.F-**the**

This also indicates that, in the presence of additional morphological motivation, functional structure is projected in the domain of A in Icelandic and blocks AdvE.

With this in mind, I suggest that although Bulgarian, Romanian, and Icelandic are languages that in principle allow bare NPs and APs based on (5), they do project functional structure under certain conditions. Particularly, Chierchia (1998) argues that the definite article in languages like English has the meaning of the *iota*-operator in semantics, changing expressions of type *<e,t>* to *e*, while in languages without articles this interpretation is achieved by pure type-shifting in semantics. Furthermore, Chierchia argues that covert type-shifting in a language for any type-shifting operation is not available if the language has an overt item contributing the same interpretation (*The Blocking Principle*). For example, type-shifting from <e,t> to e is not available in languages that have a definite article. Thus, what makes the nominal domain in languages without articles (where LBE is possible) and in affixal article languages (where LBE is blocked) different is the semantic and morphological motivation for functional structure in affixal article languages; i.e. although both groups of languages in principle allow bare lexical projections, the right semantic interpretation cannot be achieved in languages with affixal articles without projecting a DP. The existence of articles blocks covert type shifting. DP then blocks LBE in affixal article languages just like in languages that never allow bare NPs (1a)/(4).

If the presence of DP in affixal article languages is merely due to the interface considerations (semantics and overt manifestation), rather than due to a deeper formal requirement (5), there are a couple of interesting predictions: (i) when the semantic motivation for the presence of an article in the nominal domain is missing, we expect to find cases where the article is dropped; and (ii) when the article is dropped, these languages should exhibit some behavior of languages without articles. In the following section, I turn to several contexts of this sort.

3.2. Article dependent properties and article-drop

While the definite article typically contributes the definiteness interpretation (Chierchia 1998), there are also contexts where the definite article is present but the definiteness interpretation comes from a different element, or the expression is not interpreted as definite at all. Bulgarian, Romanian, Icelandic, Danish, Norwegian, Swedish, and Standard Arabic can drop the definite article in certain contexts of this sort, in which case they behave like languages without articles.

Starting with weak definites, the definite article in such DPs in English does not have a prototypical interpretation of uniqueness (see Aguilar-Guevara 2014). Interestingly, Bulgarian, Romanian, and Icelandic do not use an article in such contexts.

(12) a. (Toj) slusha radio. (Bulgarian)
(he) listens radio.
'He is listening to the radio.'

b. S-a dus la Pravalie. (Romanian)
REFL-has went to store.INDEF
'He went to the store.

c. Hann fór út í búð. (Icelandic)
he went out in store
'He went to the store.

Furthermore, superlatives represent another context where the definite article does not contribute the definiteness interpretation, which is visible from the lack of a definiteness effect. E.g., English allows extraction out of indefinite DPs as in (13a), but not out of definite DPs (13b).

(13) a. Who did you see pictures/a picture of t?
b. *Who did you see the/these pictures of t? (definiteness effect)

However, Szabolcsi (1986) shows that, despite the presence of the definite article in superlatives, there is no definiteness effect, i.e. extraction out of superlative DPs is possible as in (14).

(14) Who did you see the best picture of t? (no definiteness effect)

In superlatives uniqueness is standardly assumed to be achieved by the –est morpheme (see Sharvit and Stateva 2002). In fact, Heim (1999) shows that on certain readings, superlatives have indefinite interpretation, and treats the article *the* as a semantically vacuous element in this context (*the* in English is then present merely for formal reasons; it is essentially an expletive semantically.)

Interestingly, precisely in this context where the presence of the definite article is not motivated by semantics, affixal article languages can omit the article, which has consequences for the interpretation of superlative expressions. The interpretation of superlative expressions like (15a) depends on the comparison class relevant for their evaluation (see Szabolcsi 1986; Pancheva and Tomaszewicz 2012, a.o.). For the reading in (15b), the DP *the best albums by U2* determines the comparison class: a set of albums by U2 in a given context without considering who has them (absolute reading). In (15c) the comparison class is determined by *John,* an element *external* to the superlative: the albums whose quality is compared are albums owned by John and by other alternatives to John (relative reading with external focus (REF)). In (15d) the comparison class is determined by *by U2*, an element *internal* to the superlative DP: the albums whose quality is compared are albums by U2 and albums by other alternatives to U2 (relative reading with internal focus (RIF)). Crucially, Pancheva and Tomaszewicz (2012) show that the RIF reading is not available in languages like English.

(15)	a.	John has the best albums by U2	
	b.	'John has the best albums U2 has ever made.'	(absolute)
	c.	'John has better albums by U2 than anyone else does.'	(REF)
	d.	#'John has better albums by U2 than by any other band.'	(RIF)

Bulgarian can either use the definite article or drop it in superlatives. When the article is present, as in (16a), Bulgarian behaves like English, i.e. the sentence cannot have the RIF reading. However, when the article is absent (16b), both readings in (16c–d) are available, just like in Slavic languages without articles (Pancheva and Tomaszewicz 2012).[3]

(16)	a.	Ivan	ima	naj-dobri-**te**	albumi	ot	U2.	(Bulgarian)
		Ivan	has	superlative-good-**the**	albums	by	U2.	(P&T 2012: 296)
	b.	Ivan	ima	naj-dobri	albumi	ot	U2.	
		Ivan	has	superlative-good	albums	by	U2	(P&T 2012: 295)
	c.	'John has better albums by U2 than anyone else does.'						(REF)
	d.	'John has better albums by U2 than by any other band.'						(RIF)

We find a similar effect in other affixal article languages. In DPs with adjectives, Danish, Norwegian, and Swedish use a non-affixal article, in which case Danish omits, and Norwegian and Swedish keep, the affixal article. These languages can

3 It is also possible to omit the definite article in Icelandic superlatives in some contexts, although Bulgarian and Icelandic are not exactly the same in this respect.

omit the prenominal article, and Norwegian and Swedish also omit the affix, in superlatives of quantity, as illustrated for Swedish in (17a–b). When the article is present (17a), the sentence receives a proportional reading ('more than half of the albums U2 has ever made'), and it cannot get the RIF reading (parallel to English and Bulgarian with article). However, when the articles are absent (17b), the sentence receives both relative readings (17c–d).

(17) a. John har **de** flesta plattor**na** av U2. (Swedish)
John has **the** most albums by U2
'John has most of the albums by U2.' (proportional)
b. John har flest plattor av U2.
John has most albums by U2
c. 'John has more albums by U2 than anyone else does.' (REF)
d. 'John has more albums by U2 than by any other band.' (RIF)

In Standard Arabic, the definite article is a prefix. In superlatives, the article can be present on both the adjective and the noun, as in (18a), in which case the sentence gets an absolute reading as in (18b). When the article is dropped from the adjective (18c), the sentence receives the RIF reading (18d), parallel to Bulgarian in (16b) and Swedish in (17b). When both articles are dropped (18e), the sentence receives the REF reading (18f), which is available in English, in affixal article languages when the article is present or dropped, and in languages without articles.

(18) a. lada John **al**-albumaat **al**-afdhal li U2. (Standard Arabic)
owns John **the**-albums **the**-best for U2
'John has the best albums by U2.'
b. John has the best albums that U2 has ever made.
c. lada John afdhal **al**-albumaat li U2.
own John best **the**-albums for U2
'John owns the best albums by U2.'
d. John has better albums by U2 than by any other band. (RIF)
e. lada John afdhal albumaat U2.
own John best albums U2
'John owns the best albums by U2.'
f. John has better albums by U2 than anyone else does. (REF)

Another context where dropping an article leads to affixal article language behaving like languages without articles concerns the readings of *most*. Živanović (2007) and Bošković and Gajewski (2011) observe a cross-linguistic variation with respect to readings of sentences containing *most*, where only languages that have articles allow the majority reading of *most*. In such contexts in Bulgarian, Dubinsky and Tasseva-Kurktchieva (2014) observe a very interesting pattern: whether a sentence with *most* gets a majority reading or relative reading depends on whether *most* in Bulgarian occurs with a definite article or not. Crucially, when the article is dropped (19a), the majority reading (19b) is not available and the sentence gets the relative reading (19c) as in article-less languages; but when the article is present (19d), the sentence gets the majority reading (19e), the relative reading being unavailable (19f).[4]

(19) a. Poveče hora poznavat Ivan. (Bulgarian)
more people know Ivan
b. #'More than half of the people know Ivan.' (Majority reading)
c. 'More people know Ivan than know anyone else.' (Relative reading)
d. Poveče**to** hora poznavat Ivan.
the.more people know Ivan
e. 'More than half of the people know Ivan.' (Majority reading)
f. # 'More people know Ivan than know anyone else.' (Relative reading)
(D&T-K 2014)

Thus, when the article is dropped, Bulgarian behaves like a language without articles.

Moreover, Bošković (2008, 2012) establishes the generalization that only languages without articles may allow adjunct extraction out of nominal phrases (see (20a) vs. (20b)). However, Dubinsky and Tasseva-Kuktchieva (2014) observe that adjunct extraction is not possible when the article is present, but adjunct extraction is possible when the article is dropped (20c).

(20) a. Sa kojeg universiteta si upoznao nekoliko studenata? (BCS)
from which university are met several students
b. *Ot koj universitet sreštna-ha nyakolko-**to** studenti? (Bulgarian)
from which university met-they several-**the** students
c. Ot koj universitet sreštna-ha nyakolko studenti?
from which university met-they several students
'From which university did they meet several students?' (D&T-K 2014)

We have seen that the functional structure present in the nominal domain in affixal article languages due to them having an affix realizing definiteness can

4 Danish also patterns with Bulgarian with respect to the majority reading of *most*, i.e. this reading is possible when the definite article is present, but not when it is dropped.

be absent in several contexts, which supports them being in the same group as languages without articles with respect to (5).

3.3. No-AdvE affixal article languages

Not all affixal article languages allow AdvE. For instance, AdvE is not possible in Danish, Norwegian, Swedish, Standard Arabic, and Yemeni Arabic:

(21) a. *Ekstremt$_i$ er han [t_i klog]. (Danish)
extremely is he smart
Intended: 'He is *extremely* smart.'
b. *jidd-an$_i$ Aħmad THaki-un t_i[5] (Standard Arabic)
very-acc Ahmad smart-nom
Intended: 'Ahmad is *very* smart.'

This raises the question whether these languages are in the same group as languages like English or languages like BCS and Bulgarian with respect to (5). Note first that (9) is a one-way correlation, i.e. belonging to the group of languages that allow bare APs (languages without a definite article and those with affixal articles) is a necessary condition for AdvE, but AdvE can be blocked independently. In fact, this is parallel to Bošković's (2005) generalization about LBE, since, as Bošković points out, there are languages that lack articles and disallow LBE, like Mandarin Chinese. Thus, even though Danish, Norwegian, Swedish, and Standard Arabic, and Yemeni Arabic disallow AdvE, they may belong to languages that allow bare lexical projections. This is supported by their behavior in (17)–(18). We have seen that when the definite article is dropped in Swedish and Arabic, just like in Bulgarian, these languages behave like languages without articles. This suggests that even affixal article languages that disallow AdvE (Arabic, Danish, Norwegian, and Swedish) are grouped with languages without articles with respect to (5), i.e. they may allow bare lexical projections.

4. Conclusion

I have discussed phenomena that may serve as diagnostics for the amount of structure in the domain of N and A across languages, and argued that there are two sources for functional structure in an extended domain of a lexical category: (i) deep formal (syntactic) considerations (as in languages like English that never

5 A speaker of Arabic speaking the Levantine dialect (in addition to the Standard variant) finds AdvE acceptable.

allow bare lexical projections); and (ii) interface considerations/overt manifestation and semantics (as in languages like BCS that allow bare lexical projections). Focusing on affixal article languages, I have argued that these languages side with BCS and allow bare lexical projections both in the domain of N and the domain of A. While these languages project DP in the domain of N due to the presence of an article, I have shown that in the lack of semantic motivation for the presence of a definite article (definiteness), it is possible to drop the article in these languages. When the article is dropped, these languages sometimes behave like languages without articles, which suggests that they allow bare NP.

References

Aljović, Nadira. 2002. "Long adjectival inflection and specificity in Serbo-Croatian." *Recherches linguistiques de Vincennes* 31: 27–42.

Abney, Steven. 1987. "The English Noun Phrase in its sentential aspect." PhD thesis, Massachusetts Institute of Technology.

Aguilar-Guevara, Ana. 2014. *Weak definiteness: Semantics, Lexicon, and Pragmatics*. Utrecht: LOT.

Baker, Mark. 2003. *Lexical categories*. Cambridge: Cambridge University Press.

Bobaljik, Jonathan and Susi Wurmbrand. 2005. "The domain of agreement." *Natural Language and Linguistic theory* 23: 809–865.

Bošković, Željko and Jon Gajewski. 2011. "Semantic correlates of the NP/DP parameter." *North East Linguistic Society (NELS)* 39: 121–134.

Bošković, Željko. 1994. "D-structure, θ-criterion, and movement into θ-positions." *Linguistic Analysis* 24: 247–286.

Bošković, Željko. 2004. "Object shift and the clause/PP parallelism hypothesis." *West Coast Conference on Formal Lingusitics (WCCFL)* 23: 101–114.

Bošković, Željko. 2005. "On the locality of left branch extraction and the structure of NP." *Studia Linguistica* 59: 1–45.

Bošković, Željko. 2008. "What will you have, DP or NP?." *North East Linguistic Society (NELS)* 37: 101–114.

Bošković, Željko. 2012. "On NPs and clauses." In *Discourse and grammar: From sentence types to lexical categories*, Günther Grewendorf and Thomas Ede Zimmermann (ed.). Berlin: Mouton de Gruyter, 179–246.

Chierchia, Gennaro. 1998. "Reference to kinds across languages." *Natural Language Semantics* 6: 339–405.

Chomsky, Noam. 2000. "Minimalist inquiries." In *Step by step: Essays on minimalist syntax in honor of Howard Lasnik*, Roger Martin, David Michaels, and Juan Uriagereka (ed.). Cambridge, Mass.: MIT Press, 89–155.

Chomsky, Noam. 2001. "Derivation by phase." In *Ken Hale: A life in language*, Michael Kenstowicz (ed.). Cambridge, Mass.: MIT Press, 1–52.

Corver, Norbert. 1992. "On deriving certain left branch extraction asymmetries." *North East Linguistic Society (NELS)* 22: 67–84.

Despić, Miloje. 2011. "Syntax in the absence of determiner phrase." PhD thesis, University of Connecticut.

Dubinsky, Stanley and Mila Tasseva-Kurktchieva. 2014. "On the NP/DP languages frontier: Bulgarian as a transitional case." Poster presented at the 89th *Annual Meeting of the Linguistic Society of America*, Portland, OR.

Fukui, Naoki. 1988. "Deriving the differences between English and Japanese." *English Linguistics* 5: 249–270.

Grohmann, Kleanthes. 2003. *Prolific domains*. Amsterdam: John Benjamins.

Heim, Irene. 1999. "Notes on superlatives." Ms., Massachusetts Institute of Technology.

Pancheva, Roumyana and Barbara Tomaszewicz. 2012. "Cross-linguistic differences in superlative movement out of nominal phrases." *West Coast Conference on Formal Linguistics (WCCFL)* 30: 292–302.

Petroj, Vanessa. 2014. "On code-switching within the TNP." Ms., University of Connecticut.

Sharvit, Yael and Penka Stateva. 2002. "Superlative expressions, context, and focus." *Linguistics and Philosophy* 25: 453–505.

Szabolcsi, Anna. 1986. "Comparative superlatives." *MIT Working Papers in Linguistics* 8: 245–265.

Talić, Aida. 2015a. "Adverb extraction, specificity, and structural parallelism." *Canadian Journal of Linguistics* 60(3): 417–454.

Talić, Aida. 2015b. "Adverbial left-branch extraction and the structure of AP in Slavic." *Formal Approaches to Slavic Linguistics* 24: 399–418.

Uriagereka, Juan. 1988. "On government." PhD thesis, University of Connecticut.

Zlatić, Larisa. 1997. "The structure of the Serbian noun phrase." PhD thesis, University of Texas at Austin.

Živanović, Sašo. 2007. "Quantificational aspects of LF." PhD thesis, University of Ljubljana.

Andrew Murphy

A New Generalization about Left-Branch Extraction in Slavic

1. Introduction

In this paper, I propose the following novel generalization about Left-Branch Extraction (LBE) in Slavic:

(1) *Left-Branch Extraction Generalization:*
Left-Branch Extraction cannot be the second step of multiple wh-fronting.

This generalization, which I argue can be viewed as cumulative constraint violation, will allow us to obtain a unified explanation for two puzzling restrictions regarding the interaction of multiple *wh*-fronting and LBE in Slavic. The first puzzle is why Slavic languages that allow both multiple *wh*-fronting and LBE independently do not allow these processes to combine (Fernández-Salgueiro 2006; Grebenyova 2012). Furthermore, this constraint will also allow us to explain the unexpected emergence of Superiority effects with LBE in languages that otherwise do not obey Superiority in main clauses. Finally, a new subject/object asymmetry in cases of mixed multiple wh-fronting will be discussed and shown how this does not provide a challenge to the generalization in (1), given standard assumptions about successive-cyclic movement.

2. Multiple *wh*-fronting and Superiority

As discussed by Rudin (1988) and Bošković (2002), a number of Slavic languages (e.g. Russian, Polish, Bulgarian, Slovenian[1], Serbo-Croatian) exhibit the 'multiple *wh*-fronting' property that all *wh*-phrases in a multiple *wh*-question are required to appear in clause-initial position. Below are examples from Russian, Polish and Serbo-Croatian:

(2) Kto$_1$ kogo$_2$ t$_1$ priglasil t$_2$ na užin?
who whom invited to dinner
'Who invited whom to dinner?' (*Russian*; Grebenyova 2012:21)

1 However, Slovenian is argued to be an optional multiple wh-fronting language (see Mišmaš 2015).

(3) Koj$_1$ kakvo$_2$ e t$_1$ kupil t$_2$?
who what is bought
'Who bought what?' (*Bulgarian*; Bošković 2002:353)

(4) Kto$_1$ co$_2$ t$_1$ kupił t$_2$?
who what bought
'Who bought what?' (*Polish*; Bošković 2002:359)

(5) Ko$_1$ koga$_2$ t$_1$ vidi t$_2$?
who whom sees
'Who sees whom?' (*Serbo-Croatian*; Rudin 1988:449)

Multiple *wh*-fronting languages also differ with regard to Superiority, i.e. whether the closest wh-phrase (here, the subject) moves first or not. In Bulgarian, the base order of wh-phrases is maintained (in violation of Superiority) (6), whereas Serbo-Croatian does not show sensitivity to Superiority in main clauses (7).

(6) a. Koj$_1$ kakvo$_2$ t$_1$ pravi t$_2$?
who what does
b. *Kakvo$_2$ koj$_1$ t$_1$ pravi t$_2$?
what who does
'Who is doing what? (*Bulgarian*; Rudin 1988:481f.)

(7) a.. Ko koga t$_1$ voli t$_2$?
who whom loves
b. Koga ko t$_1$ voli t$_2$?
whom who loves
'Who loves whom?' (*Serbo-Croatian*; Bošković 2002:353)

3. Left-Branch Extraction

A subset of Slavic languages also allow for violations of what Ross (1967) called the *Left-Branch Condition*. Whereas it is ungrammatical to sub-extract a determiner or possessive pronoun from a noun phrase in English (8), this is perfectly grammatical in a number of Slavic languages.

(8) *Whose$_1$ did John see [$_{DP}$ t$_1$ friend]?

Below, I list examples of languages that allow Left-Branch Extraction in addition to multiple *wh*-fronting.[2]

(9) Čju$_1$ on kupil [$_{NP}$ t$_1$ mašinu]?[3]
whose he bought car
'Whose car did he buy?' (*Russian*; Grebenyova 2012:83)

(10) Jaki$_1$ Paweł kupił swojej żonie [$_{NP}$ t$_1$ samochód]?
what Pawel bought his wife car
'What car did Pavel buy for his wife?' (*Polish*; Wiland 2010:335)

(11) Čijeg$_1$ si vidio [$_{NP}$ t$_1$ oca]?
whose are seen father
'Whose father did you see?' (*Serbo-Croatian*; Bošković 2005:11)

4. Impossible Multiple Left-Branch Extraction

Intuitively, we would expect that if a language allows both for LBE and requires that both *wh*-phrases move to clause-initial position, then these processes should be permitted to combine. However, what we find is that this combination is ungrammatical in all Slavic languages that permit both processes independently as shown below (this is also true for Czech, Pavel Caha p.c.).

12) *Kakoj$_1$ čju$_2$ [$_{NP}$ t$_1$ aktër] kupil [$_{NP}$ t$_2$ mašinu]?
which whose actor bought car
'Which actor bought whose car?' (*Russian*; Grebenyova 2012:82)

(13) *Czyjej$_1$ jaki$_2$ kupił Paweł [$_{NP}$ t$_1$ żonie] [$_{NP}$ t$_2$ samochód]?
whose what bought Pawel wife car
'What car did Pavel buy for whose wife? (*Polish*; Wiland 2010:339)

(14) *Čiji$_1$ kavka$_2$ [$_{NP}$ t$_1$ otac] kupuje [$_{NP}$ t$_2$ kola]?
whose what.kind father buy car
'Whose father bought what kind of car?' (*Serbo-Croatian*; Fernández-Salgueiro 2006:134)

2 Czech also falls into this category, but I do not give examples here for reasons of space.

3 I follow Bošković (2008 *et seq.*) in assuming that Slavic languages, which lack determiners do not project a DP. Furthermore, it is exactly these languages that allow for LBE (see e.g. Bošković 2005).

From a theoretical point of view, this is entirely unexpected. For example, the standard analysis of LBE following Bošković 2005 is that LBE is the result of the interaction of anti-locality and the presence of a DP phase. Bošković argues that only languages with overt determiners project a DP phase. Thus, sub-extraction from DP requires that the wh-phrase first moves to the edge of DP. However, this movement step violates *anti-locality*, a constraint on movement being too short (e.g. Abels 2003; Grohmann 2003). Due to the presence of a DP phase, the *wh*-phrase must first move to the Spec-DP and it is this movement step in (15) that violates *anti-locality* since it does not cross a maximal projection other than NP. This is what rules out Left-Branch Extraction in DP languages.

(15) $[_{CP}\ C_{[wh]} \ldots [_{DP}\ wh_1\ D\ [_{NP}\ t_1\ ]]$

In a language that lacks determiners, and therefore a DP projection, this problem does not arise since there is no phase requiring an intermediate stop at Spec-DP. However, if an NP-language also allows multiple *wh*-fronting, then it there is nothing the theory of LBE that rules out the derivation of ungrammatical multiple LBE as in (16).

(16) $[_{CP}\ wh_1\ wh_2\ C_{[wh]} \ldots [_{NP}\ t_1\ ] \ldots [_{NP}\ t_2\ ]\ ]$

Consequently, additional stipuations must be added in order to rule this out. In the following section, I will show how the generalization in (1) can derive these, and other facts when viewed as the result of cumulative constraint violation.

5. Analysis

Recall that in the previous section, it was shown that languages which allow both LBE and multiple wh-fronting independently, do not allow for the two processes to be combined. On a descriptive level, this can be captured by the constraint proposed in (1), repeated below.

(17) *Left-Branch Extraction Generalization:*
Left-Branch Extraction cannot be the second step of multiple wh-fronting.

This constraint can be implemented as an instance of cumulative constraint violation (Haegeman et al. 2014). Cumulative constraint violation refers to a situation in which two grammatical constraints can be violated in isolation, but not simultaneously. Concretely, suppose that languages which allow LBE do so because they tolerate violations of Ross' (1967) *Left-Branch Condition*. Furthermore, let us assume that languages allowing multiple wh-fronting also do so at the expense of some constraint. What makes multiple wh-fronting special under a particular view is that it requires movement to multiple specifiers of the same C head.[4] Following Murphy (2017), we can call this constraint **Multiple Specifier*, (which I refer to as *MULT-SPEC, for convenience). Violations of this constraint are tolerated only by languages which allow multiple fronting of constituents. On this view then, the generalization in (17) can be derived by assuming that a single step of wh-movement can violate one, but not both of these constraints.

5.1. Deriving the ban on multiple LBE

To see, this consider the abstract derivations in (18). In (18a), the first step of multiple wh-fronting is permitted since it only violates *Left-Branch Condition* (LBC). It does not violate *MULT-SPEC, because it creates the first specifier. Furthermore, (18b) shows that the second step of multiple wh-fronting is also possible, if it does not involve movement of a left-branch. However, the derivation in (18c), which corresponds to the cases of impossible multiple LBE discussed in Section 4, is ruled out because both constraints are violated simultaneously.

(18)

a. $[_{CP}$ *wh*$_1$ $[_{C'}$ $C_{[wh]}$ … $[_{NP}$ t_1 NP$]$ … $[_{NP}$ *wh* NP$]$ … $]]$ (✓*MULT-SPEC & ✗LBC)

b. $[_{CP}$ *wh*$_2$ $[_{C'}$ *wh*$_1$ $[_{C'}$ $C_{[wh]}$ … t_1 … t_2… $]]]$ (✗*MULT-SPEC & ✓LBC)

c. *$[_{CP}$ *wh*$_2$ $[_{C'}$ *wh*$_1$ $[_{C'}$ $C_{[wh]}$ … $[_{NP}$ t_1 NP$]$ … $[_{NP}$ t_2 NP$]$ … $]]]$ (✗*MULT-SPEC & ✗LBC)

4 In what follows, I depart somewhat from Rudin's (1988) classic distinction between [+MWF] and [-MWF] languages and assume that multiple wh-fronting involves movement to multiple specifiers of the C domain even in languages such as Serbo-Croatian and Polish (see Bošković 2016:21). In fact, it has been shown that virtually all of Rudin's diagnostics for different landing sites of multiple see (e.g. Schütze 1994; Bošković 2002, 2003 *et seq*, also see Murphy 2017: § 4.2 for further discussion).

Thus, this analysis derives the descriptively adequate constraint that the second of multiple wh-fronting cannot involve LBE from the illicit cumulative interaction of independently required constraints. Of course, one also requires an explicit theory of cumulative interaction. While developing this goes beyond the scope of this paper, it seems clear that it requires that syntactic constraints are viewed as violable as in Optimality Theory, see Murphy (2017) for a proposal based in the framework of Harmonic Grammar.

5.2. Deriving the emergence of Superiority effects

The constraint in (17) also has welcome consequences in another area of the grammar. Aside from the ban on multiple LBE, there is another interesting difference between LBE and ordinary *wh*-movement. Whereas languages such as Polish and Serbo-Croatian do not show Superiority effects in main clauses, as we saw in (7), if we combine *wh*-movement with LBE, we see that an ordering restriction emerges:

(19) a. Kogo$_2$ czyja$_1$ spotkała [$_{NP}$ t$_1$ matka] t$_2$?
who.ACC whose.NOM met mother
b. *Czyja$_1$ kogo$_2$ spotkała [$_{NP}$ t$_1$ matka] t$_2$?
whose.NOM who.ACC met mother
'Whose mother met who?' (*Polish*)

(20) a. Šta$_2$ kakve$_1$ [$_{NP}$ dve [$_{NP}$ t$_1$ devojke]] često čitaju t$_2$?
what.ACC what.kind.NOM two girls often read
b. *Kakve$_1$ šta$_2$ [$_{NP}$ dve [$_{NP}$ t$_1$ devojke]] često čitaju t$_2$?
what.kind.NOM what.ACC two girls often read
'What do what kind of two girls read?' (*Serbo-Croatian*)

What we see in these examples is that only the '2 > 1' order of moved elements is possible. Assuming the order of elements in the left-periphery transparently reflects the order in which movement takes place, we observe the closer element (*wh*$_1$) must move first, respecting Superiority as defined by Chomsky (1973).

Interestingly, this restriction also follows from the constraint in (17). In a derivation involving the extraction of both a *wh*-left branch and non-left branch, if the *wh*-object moves first (in violation of derivational Superiority), then the next step of LBE simultaneously creates a second CP specifier, as ruled out by (17):

(21)

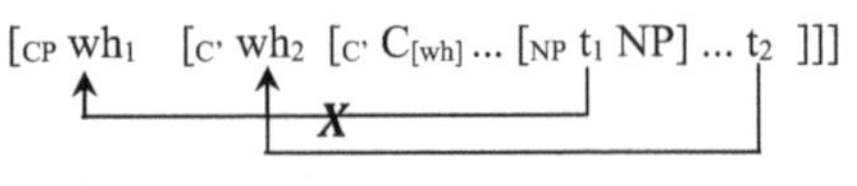

(*Superiority violating*)
(✘*MULT-SPEC & ✘LBC)

However, if LBE takes place first, then this does not violate the constraint in (17), since this step of LBE creates the first CP specifier. In language with multiple *wh*-fronting, there is no problem with the second step creating a second specifier by non-LBE:

(22)

$[_{CP}\ wh_2\ [_{C'}\ wh_1\ [_{C'}\ C_{[wh]} \ldots [_{NP}\ t_1\ NP] \ldots t_2\ ]]]$ (*Superiority respecting*)

(✗*MULT-SPEC & ✓LBC)

As a result, we derive the fact that Superiority restrictions unexpectedly emerge with LBE from exactly the same constraint that rules out multiple LBE. Namely, while both the constraints against multiple specifier creation and LBE can be violated in isolation, simultaneous violation leads to ungrammaticality.

5.3. On a subject/object asymmetry with multiple wh-fronting and LBE

The previous section showed that in cases of 'mixed' multiple wh-fronting where LBE only applies from the subject, an ordering restriction emerges such that LBE must be the first step of movement. Interestingly, the situation is different if LBE takes place solely from the object, with extraction of an ordinary wh-subject. As (23) and (24) show, either order of extraction is possible.

(23) a. Kto$_1$ czyją$_2$ spotkał t$_1$ [t$_2$ matkę]?
who.NOM whose.ACC met mother.ACC
b. Czyją$_2$ kto$_1$ t$_1$ spotkał [t$_2$ matkę]?
whose.ACC who.NOM met mother.ACC
'Who met whose mother?' (*Polish*)

(24) a. Ko$_1$ kakve$_2$ jasno t$_1$ vidi [(dve) [t$_2$ devojke]?
who what.kind clearly sees two girls
b. Kakve$_2$ ko$_1$ jasno t$_1$ vidi t$_1$ [(dve) [t$_2$ devojke]?
what.kind who clearly sees two girls
'Who sees what kind of (two) girls clearly?' (*Serbo-Croatian*)

While this may seem like a challenge for the generalization in (1), it can be shown to follow if we take standard considerations about phases and successive-cyclic movement into account. Following Chomsky (2000, 2001). *v*P and CP are assumed to constitute phases, and therefore movement out of the *v*P must make an intermediate stop at the edge of *v*P. Importantly, this leads to a fundamental difference between subject and object extraction – namely, that objects must first move to the edge of *v*P before then carrying on to Spec-CP, whereas subjects do not, since they are already base-generated at the phase edge. It is this basic structural difference that can be exploited to explain why the constraint in (17) does not hold for object extraction.

First, consider a case of extraction of a subject left-branch as the second step of multiple fronting. In the first step of (25), the wh-object moves to the edge of *v*P and is then extracted to Spec-CP. The second step, however, involves both Left-Branch Extraction and creation of a multiple specifier and is therefore ruled out.

(25)

$*[_{CP}\ wh_1\ [_{C'}\ wh_2\ [_{C'}\ C_{[wh]} \ldots [_{vP}\ [_{NP}\ t_1\ NP]\ [_{v'}\ t_2\ [_{v'} \ldots t_2 \ldots]]]]]]]$

(✗*MULT-SPEC & ✗LBC)

However, in the reverse situation in which sub-extraction proceeds from an object, then the left-branch first moves to the edge of *v*P, as in (26). From this position, it no longer counts as a left-branch for the purposes of movement to Spec-CP. This means that when wh_2 is extracted to Spec-CP from the edge of *v*P, the LBC constraint is not violated and the derivation is grammatical.

(26)

$[_{CP}\ wh_2\ [_{C'}\ wh_1\ [_{C'}\ C_{[wh]} \ldots [_{vP}\ t_1\ [_{v'}\ t_2\ [_{v'} \ldots [_{NP}\ t_2\ NP] \ldots]]]]]]]$

(✗*MULT-SPEC & ✓LBC)

Thus, under the view that only objects can 'lose' the property of being a left-branch by virtue of an intermediate movement to Spec-*v*P, we have a principled explanation for why the derivational constraint in (17) applies to subject, but not object LBE in cases of mixed multiple wh-fronting.

6. Conclusion

In this paper, I have shown that two problematic facts surrounding Left-Branch Extraction, namely the ban on multiple LBE and the emergence of Superiority effects, can be explained with the single generalization that a single step of Left-Branch Extraction cannot create an additional specifier. Whereas other approaches would have to postulate distinct stipulations for each problem, the present account allows for a unified explanation of the two phenomena as the result of a derivational restriction on the creation of multiple specifiers of

C. It was also demonstrated that an asymmetry between subjects and objects regarding the scope of this constraint can be shown to follow from independent assumptions about the nature of successive-cyclic movement. Furthermore, this constraint is actually more elegant than it may seem, as it can be viewed as the cumulative interaction of independently-required, violable syntactic constraints against LBE and multiple *wh*-fronting respectively. It is only when a movement step violates both these constraints simultaneously that ungrammaticality ensues.

References

Abels, Klaus. 2003. "Successive cyclicity, anti-locality and adposition stranding." PhD Thesis, University of Connecticut.

Bošković, Željko. 1999. "On multiple feature checking: Multiple wh-fronting and multiple head movement." In *Working Minimalism*, Samuel D. Epstein and Norbert Hornstein (eds.), Cambridge, MA: MIT Press, 159–187.

Bošković, Željko. 2002. "On Multiple Wh-Fronting." *Linguistic Inquiry* 3: 351–384.

Bošković, Željko. 2003. "On wh-islands and obligatory wh-movement contexts in South Slavic." In *Multiple Wh-Fronting*, Cedric Boeckx and Kleanthes K. Grohmann (eds.). Amsterdam: John Benjamins, 27–50.

Bošković, Željko. 2005. "On the Locality of Left-Branch Extraction and the Structure of NP." *Studia Linguistica* 59: 351–384.

Bošković, Željko. 2008. "What will you have DP or NP?" In *Proceedings of NELS 37*, Emily Elfner and Martin Walkow (eds.). Amherst: GLSA, 101–114.

Bošković, Željko. 2016. "Getting really edgy: On the edge of the edge." *Linguistic Inquiry* 47: 1–33.

Chomsky, Noam. 1973. "Conditions on Transformations." In *A Festschrift for Morris Halle*, Stephen R. Anderson and Paul Kiparsky (eds.). New York: Holt, Rinehart & Winston. 232–286.

Chomsky, Noam. 2000. "Minimalist Inquires: The Framework." In *Step by Step: Essays on Minimalist Syntax in Honor of Howard Lasnik*, Roger Martin, David Michaels, Juan Uriagereka and Samuel Jay Keyser (eds.). Cambridge, MA: MIT Press. 89–155.

Chomsky, Noam. 2001. "Derivation by Phase." In *Ken Hale: A Life in Language*, Michael Kenstowicz (ed.). Cambridge, MA: MIT Press. 1–52.

Fernández-Salgueiro, Gerardo. 2006. "On the Incompatibility of WH-movement with Left-Branch Extraction in Serbo-Croatian." In *Proceedings of FASL 14*,

James E. Lavine, Hana Filip, Steven Franks and Mila Tasseva-Kurktchieva (eds.). Ann Arbor: Michigan Slavic Publications, 157–171.

Grebenyova, Lydia. 2012. *Syntax, Semantics and Acquisition of Multiple Interrogatives: Who wants what?* Amsterdam: John Benjamins.

Grohmann, Kleanthes K. 2003. *Prolific Domains: On the Anti-Locality of Movement Dependencies.* Amsterdam: John Benjamins.

Haegeman, Liliane, Ángel L. Jiménez-Fernández and Andrew Radford. 2014. "Deconstructing the Subject Condition in terms of cumulative constraint violation." *The Linguistic Review* 31. 73–150.

Mišmaš, Petra. 2015. "On the Optionality of Wh-Fronting in a Multiple Wh-Fronting Language." PhD thesis, University of Nova Gorica.

Murphy, Andrew. (2017). "Cumulativity in Syntactic Derivations." PhD thesis, Universität Leipzig.

Richards, Norvin. 2001. *Movement in Language: Interactions and Architectures.* Oxford: OUP.

Rudin, Catherine. 1988. "On Multiple Questions and Multiple WH Fronting." *Natural Language and Linguistic Theory* 6: 455–501.

Ross, John R. 1967. "Constraints on variables in syntax." PhD thesis, MIT.

Schütze, Carson T. 1994. "Serbo-Croatian Second Position Clitic Placement and the Phonology-Syntax Interface." In *Papers on phonology and morphology (MIT Working Papers in Linguistics* 21), Andrew Carnie, Heidi Harley and Tony Bures (eds.). Cambridge, MA: MIT Press, 373–473.

Wiland, Bartosz. 2010. "Overt Evidence from Left-Branch Extraction in Polish for Punctuated Paths." *Linguistic Inquiry* 41. 335–347.

Susan Rothstein

Perfective is a V operator in Slavic, though not in English*

1. Introduction and background

In this paper I argue that the perfective is a V operator in Slavic, while it is a VP operator in English. This was originally proposed in Filip & Rothstein 2005, Filip 2008, who termed it 'the telicity parameter'. In Rothstein 2013, I showed that there is good evidence that the same contrast holds for imperfectivity in its progressive interpretation, suggesting that low V-scope is quite a general property of Slavic aspectual operators. In this paper, I return to the perfective operator, bringing new evidence that it has scope only over V and not over the internal arguments of V or over modifiers. Due to space constraints only a part of the data and summary of the analysis can be presented here, and more detailed argumentation will follow in Rothstein (in preparation). I begin with a brief introduction and review of Rothstein 2013, and then continue with the new data.

In English, perfective and progressive operators are clearly VP operators. Aspect may be shown by the auxiliary, which also selects the participial form (1a/b), or it may be unmarked (1c). In Slavic, the perfective/imperfective contrast is marked on the verb (2b/3b).

(1) a. John is building a house.
b. John has built a house
c. John built a house

(2) a. Ivan stroil dom
Ivan build$^{\text{IMPF PAST}}$ house
'Ivan was building a house.'

b. Ivan postroil dom
Ivan build$^{\text{PERF PAST}}$ house
'Ivan built a house'

* I should like to thank Hana Filip, Keren Khrizman and Maria Gepner for discussion of the data and the material in this paper, as well as audiences at FASL 22, FDSL 11, and the SFB colloquium at Düsseldorf University in November 2015. This work was partially supported by Israel Science Foundation Grants 850-10 and 1345-13.

(3) a. Maša kupila gazetu
Masha buy$^{\text{PERF PAST}}$ newspaper
'Masha bought a newspaper.'

b. Maša pokupala gazetu
Masha buy $^{\text{IMPF2 PAST}}$ newspaper
'Masha was buying a newspaper (when I met her).'

While the morphology suggests that the operator expressed by V-marking in (2) and (3) may have lower scope than the operator expressed by the auxiliary in (1), the evidence that this is the case is semantic. Rothstein 2013 argues that the progressive operator PROG licensed by the imperfective in (2a) indeed has scope only over the verb. Following Kagan 2010, imperfective root verbs are treated as plural predicates denoting sets of plural events, with singular events the borderline case of plurality. PROG, the progressive operator in both English and Slavic, is the default imperfective operator. It maps a set of events Σ onto a set of parts of event in Σ, with completed events included in the set of partial events (i.e. a superset of Σ consisting of all events in Σ and their parts). Assume that the verb *work* and its Russian counterpart *rabotat'* both denote a set of events of working, which we will call WORK. In the progressive *is working* and the Russian counterpart *rabotaet*^{IMFP}, PROG applies to the set of events in WORK, to yield a set of partial, possibly incomplete, events of working. With a simple sentence *he is working/on rabotaet*^{IMPF}, it makes no semantic difference if PROG has V or VP scope. However, in more complex sentences it does. In English, PROG is clearly a VP operator, and has scope over the complex consisting of V, its arguments and VP-internal modifiers. Adverbials within VP are under the scope of PROG, but higher adverbials are outside the VP. If, in Slavic, PROG has scope over V, both thematic arguments of V and adverbials must be outside the scope of the aspectual operator. We show here that this is the case for temporal adverbials and themes in Russian. For more extensive argumentation showing that the effect holds more widely, see Rothstein 2013.

In English the temporal adverbial *for two hours* naturally has scope under PROG. Suppose it is 1pm and you want to speak to John. I say (4a):

(4) a. John is working for two hours. He will finish work at 2pm.
b. John [PROG(work for two hours)]

This has the interpretation given by (4b): "At the reference time (here identical to the utterance time), there is an event in progress which is an event of working for two hours. It will be completed at 2pm". (4) is true if witnessed at the reference time by a partial event of *work-for-two-hours.* Crucially, *for two hours* modifies the completed event and is under the scope of PROG. In the context given, the partial event which makes (4) true has a duration of only one hour. The same holds for examples in the past tense. In contrast, this reading is not possible for the equivalent sentence in Russian. The only possible interpretation of (5a), which has the structure in (5b), is that there is/was an event going on which is a partial event of working, and this partial event had, at the reference time, been going on for two hours.

(5) a. Ivan rabotaet /rabotal (uže) dva časa
Ivan work$^{\text{IMPF PRES}}$ /work$^{\text{IMPF PAST}}$ already two hours
'Ivan has/ had already been working for two hours (at that moment).'
b. Ivan [[PROG(work)] for two hours]

This reading is predicted if the temporal adverbial *for two hours* is outside the scope of PROG, where it can only modify the partial event as in (5b). Contrasts in the interpretation of adverbials expressing the length of the path and in the distribution of thematic arguments discussed in Mehlig 2008 also follow from this difference in the scope of PROG. Mehlig, following Koševev 1996, argues that numericals are infelicitous in the scope of the progressive operator in Russian. In English, (6a) is felicitous, but (6b) is not:

(6) a. Mary is solving two problems for homework. She hasn't yet started on the second one.
b. Igor' rešaet dve zadački, kotoryje jemu dali
Igor solve^{IMPF} two problems which to him give^{PERF}
Vtoruju on ešče ne načal rešat.'
Second he yet not start^{PERF} solve^{IMPF}.
'Igor is solving two problems given to him.
He has not yet started solving the second one.'

This contrast is expected if the theme argument is under the scope of PROG in (6a), but outside it in (6b). (6a) makes an assertion about a partial event of solving two problems and leaves open what the theme of the partial event is. (6b) makes an assertion about a partial solving event, and, since the theme argument is outside the scope of PROG, asserts that two problems are the theme of the partial event.

2. Perfectivity

As Tatevosov (2011) writes, "... it is reasonable to assume as a null hypothesis that perfective and imperfective/progressive operators are derivationally symmetric." As we have shown that PROG, the default interpretation of imperfective aspect, is a V operator in Russian, there is a *prima facie* case for suggesting that perfective is also a V operator.[1] There is quite a lot of evidence to support this claim. First, as noted by many (Wierzbicka 1967, Forsyth 1970, Chvany 1983, Krifka 1992, Filip 2008, Filip and Rothstein 2005), in Slavic, the perfective verb forces a quasi-definite, maximal interpretation of a bare plural or mass direct object and a telic interpretation of the VP. (7), from Wierzbicka 1967, and (8) show the maximality effect on the theme argument, while (9), from Filip and Rothstein 2005 shows that a perfective verb with a bare plural object takes a telic modifier *za pět minut* 'in five minutes'.

(7) a. On zjadł^{PERF} oliwki
'He ate (up) all the olives.'
b. On jadł ^{IMPF} oliwki (Polish)
'He ate olives.'

(8) a. Ivan pil vino
Ivan drink$^{IMPF\ PAST}$ wine
'Ivan drank wine/?the wine.'
b. Ivan vypil vino (Russian)
Ivan drink$^{PERF\ PAST}$ wine
'Ivan drank the wine/*wine.'

(9) Za pět minut / #pět minut oblékl^{PERF} děti do zimních kabátů (Czech)
In five minutes /#five minutes dressed^{PERF} children$^{PL.ACC}$ in winter coats
'He dressed the children in winter coats in/??for five minutes.'

These data contrast with English, where a mass or bare plural theme argument usually forces an atelic interpretation of the VP, even when the head V is an accomplishment. Note in (12) that even the telic particle *up* does not force a telic reading if the direct object is a bare plural or mass.

(10) a. #John dressed children in coats in five minutes.
b. John dressed children in coats for five minutes. (Then someone else took over).
c. John dressed the children in coats in five minutes.
d. #John dressed the children in coats for five minutes.[2]

(11) a. Otto drank wine for two hours. Then he switched to beer.
b. Otto drank wine #in two hours.
c. Otto drank the wine in two hours/#?for two hours.

1 I will not discuss here whether the V-operator is syntactic or lexical.
2 (10d) has an acceptable, but irrelevant, reading where *for five minutes* modifies the result state.

(12) a. She ate (up) olives for hours/#in hours.
b. He ate (up) olives as if there was no tomorrow.
c. He ate up the olives in half an hour.

So while in English, the direct object determines whether the VP has a telic or non-telic interpretation, in Slavic, the perfective status of the V determines the interpretation of the direct object of the V forcing a maximal, quasi-definite interpretation. This is already good evidence that the perfective has scope only over the V, as discussed in Filip and Rothstein 2005. Note that, as Filip 2005 shows, this quasi-definite effect only holds when the direct object is an incremental theme, a fact we will come back to later.

The most obvious problem for the hypothesis that perfective has V scope is the claim that some so-called perfectivizing prefixes have high scope outside the VP and above the secondary imperfective. I shall briefly discuss three issues connected with this, showing that ultimately all three support a V-scope analysis.

Svenonius 2004 and others have argued that perfectivity is introduced by lexical prefixes and that these divide into two classes, lexical and superlexical prefixes, with each class having different syntactic scope. Lexical prefixes change the meaning of the verb stem, add or modify arguments, or add a result phrase. They have idiosyncratic interpretations and may 'change' the meaning of the verb. They also scope under the secondary imperfective, and Svenonius assigns these prefixes VP scope. Superlexical prefixes are considered to be aspectual modifiers filling a high position in the tree and are adjoined above VP. They include inceptive *za-*, delimitative/attentuative *po-*, cumulative *na-*, repetitive *pere-* as well as others. Superlexical prefixes have a systematic semantic contribution as modifiers, do not affect argument structures and scope over secondary imperfectives. Some prefixes may be ambiguous between lexical and superlexical prefixes, with a different interpretation in each case. Clearly, if superlexical prefixes are perfectivizers and have scope over the VP, then they are a problem for the claim that perfectivity is a V operator.

However, while there is evidence to support different semantic subclasses of prefixes, there are counterexamples to the arguments which assign superlexical prefixes high scope.

To start with, despite the characteristics just mentioned, the distinction between superlexical and lexical prefixes is very badly defined, and there is no agreement among linguists as to how to categorize many prefixes. Zinova (2016) shows that only inchoative *za-* is superlexical in all accounts. More seriously, prefixes assumed to be superlexical do in fact affect the argument structure of the verb, as Filip 2005 has shown for cumulative *na-*, widely agreed to be a superlexical prefix. *Na-* affects argument structure in a number of ways. It makes the V that it modifies transitive (13) and it changes the case-assigning properties of the verb, specifying that theme is marked genitive (14). Furthermore, it modifies only an incremental theme argument, as shown in (15) [(14) and (15) from Filip 2005]. Since *na-* interacts with argument structure in this way, it is more plausible that it is a lexical operator on V rather than an adverbial modifier in Aspect Phrase.

(13) a. Ivan ljubit gotovit' /***na**gotovit'
Ivan likes prepare$^{\text{IMPF INF}}$ / **na**-prepare $^{\text{PERF INF}}$
'Ivan likes to cook.'
b. Ivan ljubit **na**gotovit' edy na nedelju
Ivan likes na-cook $^{\text{PERF INF}}$ food ^{GEN} for week
'Ivan likes to prepare (a lot of food) for a whole week.'

(14) a. on varen'je varil
he jam $^{\text{ACC MASS}}$ cook $^{\text{IMPF PAST}}$
'He was cooking the/some jam.'
b. on kak-to varen'ja **na**-varil
he somehow jam $^{\text{GEN MASS}}$ na-cook $^{\text{PERF PAST}}$
'He made / cooked up a lot of jam.'

(15) moi rodstvenniki **na**-darili rebjatam xorošix kukol
My relatives na-give presents $^{\text{PERF PAST}}$ children good dolls $^{\text{GEN PL}}$
'My relatives gave the children a lot of nice dolls.'
NOT: 'A lot of my relatives gave the children some nice dolls.'
NOR: 'My relatives gave nice dolls to a lot of the children.'

Thirdly, prefixes usually assumed to be superlexical do, in fact, scope under the secondary imperfective. Zinova cites *zakurivat'* 'to be in the process of lighting up a cigarette', where secondary imperfective has scope over inceptive *za-*. Žaucer 2009 shows that in Slovenian, different scopal relations occur with a single prefix depending on the verbal stem:

(16) a. **na**-polnje-**va**-ti škatlo
na-fill^{IMPF} box
'be filling up the box'
b. **pre**-**na**-polnje-**va**-ti škatlo
over-on-fill^{IMPF} box
'be filling up the box too much, be over-filling the box'

(17) a. **pre**-ora-**va**-ti njivo
over-plow^{IMPF} field
'be plowing up the field'
b. **na**-**pre**-ora-**va**-ti se njive
on-over-plow self^{PERF} field
'get one's fill of plowing up the field'

(16–17) show that the position with relation to the secondary perfective is variable, suggesting that both operators apply at the same level, without the order being structurally determined:.

Superlexical prefixes, however, do often occur higher than the secondary imperfective, for example *po-* in *povydavat'* 'to hand out (something) for a while' (example from Mehlig 2008), which is constructed as in (18);

(18) vy-dat'^{PERF} → vy-da-va-t'$^{\text{IMPF2}}$ → po-vydavat'^{PERF}

If perfective is a V operator, then this implies that the secondary imperfective, which is lower than the perfectivizing prefix, must be a V operator too. While this is contrary to the general assumption that secondary imperfectivity has scope over VP (or is even higher), closer examination of the data suggests that secondary imperfectivity is also a V operator.

First, as we already saw in example (6), Mehlig 2008 shows that progressive interpretations of root imperfectives do not usually allow numerical incremental themes. Another example illustrating this is (19). Since PROG has V scope, the sentence can only mean 'there is a partial event of eating going on which has 100 grams of meat as its theme.' Thus *100 grams of meat* can only be the theme of the partial event, and as a consequence, (18) does not have the interpretation that Masha is gradually eating 100 grams of meat. It does have a felicitous interpretation where the whole 100 grams of meat are being eaten at the same time (for example, if Masha is a large lion.)

(19) #sejčas Maša est 100 grammov mjasa
now Masha eat $^{\text{IMPF PRES}}$ 100 grams meat
'Masha is eating 100 grams of meat now.'

Secondary imperfectives show the same restrictions on incremental theme on the progressive interpretation, as shown in (20). If the explanation for the infelicity of (19) applies to (20) too, then the incremental theme of the secondary imperfective verb is also outside the scope of PROG and thus PROG (and the secondary imperfective) must be a V operator:

(20) #on pjet /vypivaet dva s polovinoj litra vody sejčas
he drink$^{\text{IMPF PRES}}$ /drink$^{\text{IMPF2 PRES}}$ two with half liters water now
'He is drinking two and a half liters of water now.'

There is further, stronger evidence that secondary imperfectivization affects the interpretation of the direct object, and must thus have low scope over V. We saw in (6) and (7) that root imperfectives allow either maximal or indefinite interpretations of the incremental theme, while perfectives force a maximal quasi-definite interpretation. We argued, following Filip and Rothstein 2005, that this is because the distinction between imperfective and perfective is already determined at the V level. The contrasts between (6) and (7) are replicated when imperfective aspect is secondary imperfectivity. In (21), the verb *vydat'* is perfective, and the bare plural direct object has a definite or total interpretation. In contrast, in (22), the verb has undergone secondary imperfectivization, and the direct object has a non-specific, non-maximal interpretation. This is the case on both the progressive and the habitual interpretations, in (22) and (23) respectively.

(21) on vydal knigi i ušel domoj
he vy-give $^{\text{PERF PAST}}$ books and went home
'He gave out the books and went home.'

(22) What was he doing at 2.30?
a. on vydaval knigi
he vy-give $^{\text{IMPF2 PAST}}$ books
'He was giving out (the) books.'
b. on vydaval knigi v tečenije dvux časov
he vy-give $^{\text{IMPF2 PAST}}$ books in course two hours
'He was giving out books for two hours.'

(23) What was his job in the library?
On vydaval knigi
he vy-give $^{\text{IMPF2 PAST}}$ books
'He gave out books.'

If secondary imperfectivity is an aspectual operator with scope over the VP, we would expect it to operate on the interpretation of *on vydal knigi* in (22/23), and thus to preserve the quasi-definite, maximal interpretation of the direct object. This would force an interpretation for (22) "there was a partial event going on of his giving out the books". The fact that this interpretation is not obligatory strongly suggests that that the secondary imperfective dictates the choice of direct object interpretation and is thus a V operator.

There is thus good evidence that perfectivity and imperfectivity under its progressive interpretation are V operators. In Rothstein 2013, I showed how certain properties of imperfective interpretations follow if the progressive operator PROG is assigned V scope. In the rest of this paper, I will sketch an outline of a semantics for perfectivity which would explain why it forces quasi-definite, maximal interpretations on incremental themes.

3. A semantics for perfectivity

I will sketch a semantic account based on English and Russian. While I assume, based on the data in sections 1 and 2, that the theory will generalize to at least some other Slavic languages, I make no guarantees as to which languages, and I leave open the possibility that some languages in the Slavic family may differ in the implementation of aspectual semantics.

We will assume a neo-Davidsonian framework for verb semantics. Following much work on aspectual semantics (e.g. Parsons 1990; Krifka 1992, 1998; Landman 1992, 2000, 2008; Rothstein 2004), we assume that verbs denote sets of events at type <E, t>, and that thematic roles denote functions from events into their participants at type <d,<E,t>>. Expressions of the form λe. Ag(e) = a are added to verbal predicates as modifiers. Verbs, and all phrasal projections headed by verbs thus denote sets of events, and are expressions of type <E,t>. Bare verbs in English denote set of pluralities of events, i.e. singular and plural events (Landman 2000). We follow Kagan 2010 in assuming that in Russian, root imperfective verbs also denote sets of plural events, where plural includes singularities as the borderline case.

Aspectual operators are operations on sets of events, mapping sets of events into sets of events, and are expressions of type <<E,t>,<E,t>>. As such, it is possible for aspectual operators to attach to any verbal projection, V or VP and to any higher projection (if your theory includes Aspect Phrase) if that projection is also of type <E,t>. Rothstein 2013 shows that the semantic contrasts discussed in (6), as well as the infelicity of (19) and (20) can be accounted for under the assumption that the progressive operator attaches to VP in English, after thematic arguments and VP-internal adverbials are added, while in Russian it attaches to V before any modification by thematic arguments or adverbials. Simplified representations for (6a) and (6b) are given in (24) and (25) respectively, adopting an intentional semantics for the progressive which maps a set of events onto a set of partial events. DEVELOPS INTO(e', e) holds if e' is an initial part of e (i.e. e' is part of e and has the same starting point), but crucially, the complete e event may not exist in the actual world (Landman 1992).

(24) Mary is solving two problems.
= Mary [PROG [solve two problems]]

$= \exists e' \exists e[\text{SOLVE}(e) \wedge \text{Th}(e) = 2 \text{ PROBLEMS} \wedge \text{DEVELOPS INTO}(e',e) \wedge \text{Ag}(e') = \text{Mary}]$
= There is an event e' going on with Mary as agent which is a partial event of solving two problems.

(25) Igor rešaet dve zadački
=Igor[[PROG(solve)] [two problems]]
$= \exists e' \exists e[\text{SOLVE}(e) \wedge \text{DEVELOPS INTO}(e',e) \wedge \text{Theme}(e') = 2 \text{ PROBLEMS} \wedge \text{Ag}(e') = \text{Igor}$
= There is an event going on with Igor as agent which is a partial event of solving, and which has two problems as its theme.

This explains the intuition that (25) is acceptable only if the two relevant problems are being worked on simultaneously, since in Russian the thematic role is attached outside the PROG operator, and $\lambda e.\text{Theme}(e)=2$ PROBLEMS can only modify the partial event e'.

We now outline a semantics for the perfective operator PERF, which like PROG is a VP operator in English but a V operator in Russian. Perfective predicates denote sets of singular, maximal completed events (Filip and Rothstein 2005, Filip 2008). PERF is an operator which applies to an imperfective verb denotation and maps it into a perfective denotation. We assume, following Filip 2004 that verbal prefixes in Russian do not introduce PERF. Filip argues this at length, showing, crucially, that so-called perfectivizing prefixes can attach to perfective verbs as well as to root imperfectives, and in both cases can stack, as in (26) and (27). Filip shows that this means that they cannot denote functions from imperfective to perfective denotations.

(26) a. skazat' → **pere**-skazat' → **nedo-pere**-skazat'
say PERF INF — PREFIX-say PERF INF — NEG-PREFIX- PREFIX say PERF INF
'to say' — 'to retell' — 'to stop short of [re]telling the whole story'

b. prygat' → pryg-**nu**-t' → **ot**-pryg-**nu**-t'
jump IMPF INF — jump- SUFFIX-t' PERF INF — PREFIX- jump- SUFFIX-t' PERF INF
'to jump' — 'to jump once' — 'to jump away'

(27) rabotat' → **za**rabotat' → **pod-za**-rabotat'
work IMPF INF — PREFIX- work PERF INF — PREFIX-PREFIX- work PERF INF
'to work' — 'to earn' — 'to earn a little money'

I assume, following Filip and Rothstein 2005, Filip 2008 that the perfective operator is a morphologically null operator which applies to non-perfective V denotations after all morphological affixation has taken place. The perfective operator applies to a non-perfective predicate V which denotes a plural set, and picks out a subset of V, the set of maximal completed events in V. Maximal entities are (contextually) unique, thus the singular denotation follows. The perfective operator is defined in (28), adapted from Filip and Rothstein 2005, Filip 2008. It is a *maximalization operator* MAX_E, of type <<E,t>,<E,t>>.

(28) The perfective operator PERF = MAX_E, a monadic operator, such that
$MAX_E(\Sigma) \subseteq \Sigma$,
mapping a set of plural events Σ onto the set of maximal, completed events $MAX_E(\Sigma)$.

In English, MAX_E applies at the VP level, after thematic roles and VP modifiers have been added. The denotation of the perfective VP in *John drank wine* is given in (29). It denotes the set of completed maximal events of drinking wine:

(29) drank the wine = [PAST[PERF [DRINK WINE]]]
$= \lambda e.\ e \in MAX_E$ (DRINK WINE) $\wedge$ PAST(e)

In Russian, perfectivization applies at the V level. This gives (30), the set of events which are maximal completed events of drinking, which have some quantity of wine as theme.

(30) Ivan vypil vino
drank the wine = [PAST[[[PERF [DRINK]] WINE]
$= \lambda e.\ e \in MAX_E$ (DRINK) $\wedge$ Th(e) = WINE $\wedge$ PAST(e)

If perfectivization is not expressed as part of prefixation, but nonetheless follows the prefixation operation, then what is the relation between them? Answering this requires thinking about what it is to be a maximal or completed event. Maximality and completedness are relative to a parameter or dimension. As discussed in Krifka 1998, Rothstein 2004, 2008, events have properties only under a particular description. As Krifka 1998 points out, the same event can be described as a telic or maximal event using the predicate *run a mile* and as an atelic event using the description *run*. An event which satisfies an atelic description can satisfy one related telic description but not another, so that a running event which is a complete event in *run a mile* may not be in the denotation of *run to the store*. And an event in *run a mile* may only be part of an event in *run two miles*. Similarly, a building event can be a complete event of building a house in the denotation of *postroit' dom*, but fail to be a completed event of building a lot of houses in the denotation of *nastroit' domov*. A reading event can be a complete event of reading a book in the denotation of *pročitat' knigu*, but an incomplete event of reading a book to pieces in the denotation of *začitat' knigu*. Maximality or completedness are always with respect to a particular parameter (Filip and Rothstein 2005, Filip 2008).[3] So while *build* and *stroit'* denote sets of events of building, these building events may or may not be complete, depending on what parameter is chosen to evaluate them. As Rothstein 2008 suggests, in English, where the maximality operator operates at the VP level, lexical material incorporated into the VP may specify what counts as a maximal event. While *read* and *read books*, are atelic, *read the book/three books/200 pages, read for two hours, read herself asleep/read the book ragged* are all telic. In each case, the standard for determining what counts as a completed maximal event is different: in the first case, the extent of the incremental theme determines the end point of the event, in the second case the temporal adverbial *for two hours* determines the end point, and in the third case, the end point of the reading event is determined by a result state introduced by a resultative predicate. If the endpoint of the event is determined by the incremental theme, then this theme itself must have a determined quantity, and can be neither a bare plural nor a bare mass noun (Dowty 1979, Krifka 1992, Rothstein 2004 and many others).

In Russian, by contrast, perfectivity is a V operator. This predicts, correctly, that VP internal material outside the V does not contribute to perfectivity, and thus all material contributing to determining the criteria for determining what counts as a maximal event must be V-internal. There seem to be three mechanisms for determining criteria for maximality. First, there is the case of *bare perfective* verbs, of which Isačenko 1960 lists 43 examples. In these cases, the meaning of the verb itself expresses what counts as a maximal event. Achievements are the clearest examples of verbs which inherently denote maximal events. For example, *arrive* in English, *javit'sa*^{PERF} in Russian denote sets of change-of-state events where the change is from a situation or state of not being in a certain place to a state of being in that place. The termination point of the event – which defines what counts as a maximal event – is the beginning of the state of being in the new place. Bare perfectives in Russian are not restricted to classical achievements, but they are typically verbs denoting changes of state

3 Completedness and maximality are not identical, and neither are telicity and perfectivity, but an analysis of the differences is beyond the scope of this paper. See Rothstein in preparation for further discussion.

where the nature of the change determines the terminal point, for example verbs of transaction such as *kupit'*PERF 'buy', and *dat'*PERF 'give', as well as verbs of change of position such as *leč* 'lie down', *sest'* 'sit down'. Thus an event in the denotation of *kupit'* is complete only when the transaction has legally taken place while an event in the denotation of *leč* is complete when lying down position is reached by the subject.

Most verbs, however, do not lexically express an endpoint. However, prefixes, or the infix–*nu* add lexical information as to what the end point of the event is and this information determines the parameter with respect to which maximality is determined. For example, in *na-stroit'*, 'to build a lot', the prefix *na-* indicates that maximality is with respect to the quantity of the theme, while in *za-stroit'* 'to build up area', *za-* indicates that maximality is with respect to whether or not a particular area is filled up. In *do-stroit'* 'to finish building', the *do-* prefix indicates that the termination of the event is determined by the completedness of the state of the incremental theme and so on. The prefix *po-* indicates that maximality is with respect to the temporal parameter, as in a *guljat'*, 'to walk' in contrast to *po-guljat'*, 'to walk for a while'. The infix –*nu* is a semelfactive operator. While *prygat'* denotes a set of jumping events which we can call JUMP, *prygnut'* denotes the subset JUMP which consists of events of a single jump. Prefixes operate on *prygat'* in the normal way, so *po-prygat'* 'to jump for a while' denotes sets of jumping events which are maximal relative to the temporal parameter. Multiple prefixation, or prefixation together with –*nu* infixation constrains the end point of an event more tightly than a single prefix or infix does, as in the examples of verbs with stacked prefixes in (26) and (27) above. *Prygnut'* (in 26b) can be further constrained as in *ot-prygnut* (to jump away from), where the maximal event is a maximal event of jumping away from a specified source. *Rabotat'*, the imperfective form of 'work' is the basis for perfective *zarabotat'* 'to earn', and through a second prefixing operation to *pod-za-rabotat'*, 'to earn a little money'.

The third type of perfective verb is the so called 'paired perfective'. Here, the perfective form is also marked by prefixation, but unlike in the examples just discussed, the prefix seems to have no lexical content beyond enforcing completion. These paired perfectives occur with accomplishment verbs which take an incremental theme, as in the pairs *stroit'*IMPF- *postroit'*PERF 'to build', *čitat'*IMPF- *pročitat'*PERF 'to read', *pit'*IMPF -*vypit'*PERF 'to drink', and so on. In these cases, the prefix indicates that the parameter for maximalization is the incremental structure of the event denoted by the verb. Crucially, incrementality is built into the semantics of imperfective accomplishment verbs, as argued in Braginsky and Rothstein 2008 and Mehlig 2008, 2012. Incrementality is derived from the relation between an event and its theme, as expressed in (31a), which is a simplified form of the decomposed accomplishment template from Rothstein 2004 (30b).

(31) a. stroit': $\lambda e.\ \text{BUILD}(e) \wedge \forall x[\text{Th}(e,x) \rightarrow \text{Incrementally Affect}\ (e,x)]$

b. stroit': $\lambda e.\exists e_1,e_2[e = {}^S(e_1 \sqcup e_2)$
$\wedge\ \text{ACTIVITY}_{<X>}(e_1) \wedge \text{Ag}(e_1) = x \wedge \text{Th}(e_1) = y$
$\wedge\ \text{BECOME}_{<Y>}(e_2) \wedge \text{Arg}(e_2) = \text{Th}(e_1)$
$\wedge\ \text{INCR}(e_1, e_2, C(e_2))]$

Paired perfectives occur when maximalization is with respect to the incremental relation. The apparently empty prefix on a paired perfective verb has the semantic effect of indicating that this is the case. Since perfectivization, and thus maximalization occurs at the V level before the incremental theme argument is added, the interpretation of the perfective verbs *postroit'*^{PERF} and *vypit'*^{PERF} will be as in (32):

(32) a. postroit'^{PERF}: $\text{MAX}(\lambda e.\text{BUILD}(e) \wedge \forall x[\text{Th}(e,x) \rightarrow \text{Incrementally Affect}\ (e,x)])$
= the set of maximal completed incremental building events

b. vypit'^{PERF}: $\text{MAX}(\lambda e.\text{DRINK}(e) \wedge \forall x[\text{Th}(e,x) \rightarrow \text{Incrementally Affect}\ (e,x)])$
= the set of maximal completed incremental building events

The effect is that maximality is with respect to what happens to the incremental theme.

We are now in a position to explain the data in (7)–(9), which showed that in contrast to English, a bare plural or mass incremental theme of a perfective accomplishment in Slavic has a quasi-definite, maximal interpretation. This follows from the maximality operator introduced by the perfective. When the maximality operator applies to a set of (plural) incremental events, it yields a set of maximal incremental events. When incrementality is defined in terms of an affected theme as in (32), the maximal event is one which has reached the preset terminal point, the point where the theme argument is completely affected by the event. Thus the denotation of the theme must be maximal in the event. When the theme is a bare plural or mass noun, the fact that the direct object is maximal leads to the implication that it is uniquely identifiable in context, since, as Kadmon 1990 shows, there is one salient maximal quantity of N per context. Maximality and uniqueness lead to familiarity or definiteness, since definiteness follows from uniqueness. The effect in Russian is slightly weaker than in the cases Kadmon discusses, and thus 'quasi-definite', since the uniqueness is an implication derived from the semantics of incrementality and is not lexically specified by a determiner. This is illustrated in (33), where a complete incremental event of building houses requires a contextually salient group of houses to be the maximal theme of the event (33a), while a complete incremental event of drinking wine requires a unique contextually relevant maximal quantity to be totally consumed as in (33b):

(33) a. Ivan postroil doma
Ivan build$^{\text{PERF PAST}}$ houses
'There was a completed event of Ivan building the total salient quantity of houses.'

b. Ivan vypil vino
Ivan drink$^{\text{PERF PAST}}$ wine
'There was a completed event of Ivan drinking the total salient quantity of wine.'

This explains two important points, First, quasi-definiteness is only a constraint on interpreting bare NP complements, as shown in the contrast between (34a), where the bare plural is interpreted as quasi-definite, and (34b) where *kakie-to knigi* 'some books' in (34b) is indefinite:

(34) a. on vydal knigi i ušel domoj
he vy-give$^{\text{PERF PAST}}$ books and went home
'He gave out the/a specified quantity of books and went home.'

b. on vydal im kakie-to knigi i ušel domoj
he vy-give$^{\text{PERF PAST}}$ them some books and went home
'He gave then some books and went home.'

In (34a), there is no quantity specification on the bare predicate, and maximality is determined contextually with respect to the event. In (34b), the determiner constrains the interpretation lexically, and maximality is thus relative to the particular object witnessing the sentences. Secondly, quasi-definite effects are correctly predicted to occur only when the theme is incrementally affected by the event, since only in these cases is the terminal point of the event set to the point at which the theme is completely affected. Thus quasi-definite interpretation of the theme will occur either when the verb is a 'paired' perfective as in (33), or when the prefix lexically constrains the incremental theme, but does not change the incremental meaning of the verb. (35) illustrates the second case. In (35a) *pere-* does not change the incremental structure of the root verbs, and the direct object is interpreted as maximal and there is a definiteness implicature. In (35b), *na-* changes the parameter of maximality. The event is maximal with respect to the quantity of houses build rather than with respect to the incremental process of building incrementality, and the bare object is non-specific.

(35) a. rabočie perestroili komnaty
workers pere-build$^{PERF\ PAST}$ rooms
'Workers rebuilt (all) the rooms/ the rooms in the house.'
b. oni nastroili xruščevok /* xruščevki
they na-build $^{PERF\ PAST}$ xruschevka $^{GEN\ PL}$ / xruschevka $^{ACC\ PL}$
'They built a lot of xruscevka houses.'

5. Conclusions

This paper has argued that aspectual operators are V operators in Russian and other Slavic languages, while they are VP operators in English. Space constraints mean that the arguments and the analysis can only be given in an abbreviated form, but nonetheless, the data seem to support this account. One obvious issue which I have not discussed concerns the interpretation of secondary predication. If perfective is a V operator and the secondary imperfective can scope under so-called perfectivizing prefixes, as in *povydavat*^{PERF} in (18), the secondary imperfective must be a V operator too. This is semantically plausible though discussion of the analysis must be left for another paper. The outline of the analysis would be as follows: Assume that root imperfectives denote sets of plural events, while the perfective operator maps root imperfective denotations onto sets of singular events. The natural function of the secondary imperfective is then to map the singular set denoted by the perfective predicate back onto a plural set. The perfective predicate *vydat'*^{PERF} denotes MAX(λe.Give-out(e)), the set of maximal singular giving out events, but the secondary imperfective *vydavat'*^{IMP2} denotes the pluralization of this set, PLURAL(MAX(λe.Give-out(e))). Plurality here is naturally the plurality of iteration. Such a plural verb can come under the scope of a prefix and a second-level perfectivization operation, as in *po-vydavat'*^{PERF}, which denotes a set of maximal singular events consisting of iterations of giving out events, MAX_{TEMP}(PLURAL(MAX(λe.Give-out(e)))). But, further discussion must be left to another paper.

References

Braginsky, Pavel and Susan Rothstein, 2008. "Vendler Classes and the Russian Aspectual System." *Journal of Slavic Linguistics* 16.1.

Chvany, Catherine, 1983. "On 'Definiteness' in Bulgarian, English and Russian." In Michael Flier (ed.), *American Contributions to the 9th International Congress of Slavicists*, Kiev.

Dowty, David, 1979. *Word Meaning and Montague Grammar*. Berlin: Springer (Kluwer).

Filip, Hana. 2004. "Prefixes and the Delimitation of Events." *Journal of Slavic Linguistics* 12, 55–101.

Filip, Hana. 2005. "Measure and Indefinites." *Reference and Quantification: The Partee Effect*. Festschrift for Barbara Hall Partee, edited by Gregory N. Carlson and Francis Jeffry Pelletier. CSLI: Stanford, CA. 229–288.

Filip, Hana 2008. "Events and Maximalization." In *Theoretical and Crosslinguistic Approaches to the Semantics of Aspect*, Susan Rothstein (ed.). Amsterdam: John Benjamins, 217–256.

Filip, Hana and Susan Rothstein. 2005. "Telicity as a semantic parameter." In *Formal Approaches to Slavic Linguistics 15*, James Lavine, Steven Franks, Hana Filip and Mila Tasseva-Kurktchieva. Michigan Slavic Publications: Ann Arbor, 139–156.

Forsyth, James. 1970. *A Grammar of Aspect: Usage and Meaning in the Russian Verb*. Cambridge: Cambridge University Press.

Isačenko, Alexander. 1960. *Grammaticheskij Stroj Russkogo Jazyka v Sopostovlenii s Slovackim*. (Russian Grammar in Comparison to Slovak) Morfologia, pt.2. Bratislava.

Kadmon, Nirit. 1990. "Uniqueness." *Linguistics and Philosophy 13* (3):273–324.

Kagan, Olga. 2010. "Russian Aspect as Number in the Verbal Domain." In Brenda Laca and Patricia Hofherr (eds.), *Layers of Aspect*. Stanford: CSLI Publications: 91–112.

Koševel, Aleksandr D. 1996. "Referencial'nyj podxod k analizu jazykovyx značenij." *Moskovskij lingvističeskij al'manax 1*: 82–194.

Krifka, Manfred. 1992. "Thematic Relations as Links between Nominal Reference and Temporal Constitution." In *Lexical Matters*, edited by Ivan Sag and Anna Szabolsci. Stanford: CSLI, 29–53.

Krifka, Manfred. 1998. "The Origins of Telicity." In *Events and Grammar*, edited by Susan Rothstein. Berlin: Springer (Kluwer), 197–235.

Landman, Fred. 1992. "The progressive." *Natural Language Semantics* 1: 1–32.

Landman, Fred. 2000. *Events and Plurality*. Berlin: Springer (Kluwer).

Landman, Fred. 2008. "1066: On the differences between the tense-perspective-aspect systems of English and Dutch." In Susan Rothstein (ed.), *Theoretical and Cross-linguistic Approaches to the Semantics of Aspect*. Amsterdam: Benjamins, 107–166.

Mehlig, Hans Robert. 2008. "Aspect and bounded quantity complements in Russian." In Susan Rothstein (ed.), *Theoretical and Cross-linguistic Approaches to the Semantics of Aspect*. Amsterdam: Benjamins, 257–290.

Mehlig, Hans Robert. 2012. Hybrid predications in Russian, Journal of Slavic linguistics, vol. 20, 2, 171–227.

Parsons, Terry. 1990. *Events in the Semantics of English*. Cambridge, Mass: MIT Press.

Rothstein, Susan. 2004. *Structuring Events: A Study in the Semantics of Lexical Aspect*. Blackwell: Oxford.

Rothstein, Susan. 2008. "Telicity, atomicity and the Vendler classification of events." In Susan Rothstein (ed.), *Theoretical and Cross-linguistic Approaches to the Semantics of Aspect*. Amsterdam: Benjamins, 43–78.

Rothstein, Susan (ed). 2008. *Theoretical and Crosslingustic Approaches to the Semantics of Aspect*. Amsterdam: Benjamins.

Rothstein, Susan. 2013. "On the scope of aspectual operators." In Cassandra Chapman, Olena Kit, Ivona Kučerová, *Proceedings of Formal Approachs to Slavic Linguistics The McMaster Meeting 22*. Michigan Slavic Publications: Ann Arbor, 245–265.

Svenonius, Peter. 2004. "Slavic Prefixes inside and outside VP." *Nordlyd* 32 no. 2: 323–361.

Tatevosov, Sergei. 2011. "Severing Perfectivity from the Verb." *Scando-Slavica* 57:2, 216–244.

Wierzbicka, Anna. 1967. "On the semantics of verbal aspect in Polish." *To Honor Roman Jakobson*. Volume 3. Paris: Mouton, 2231–49.

Žaucer, Rok. 2009. "A VP-internal/Resultative Analysis of 4 "VP-External" Uses of Slavic Verbal Prefixes." Ph.D. dissertation, University of Ottawa.

Zinova, Yulia. 2016. "Russian verbal prefixation: A Frame Semantic Analysis." Ph. D. dissertation Heinrich-Heine-University, Düsseldorf.

Miloje Despić

On Negative Imperatives, Aspect and Agree

1. Introduction

The cross-linguistic availability of *Negative Imperatives* (NI) has been explored in great detail (e.g., Han 2000, Zeijlstra 2006 etc.) and it has been shown that some languages do not allow "true" NIs (Spanish, Modern Greek, Italian, Romanian, Portuguese, Catalan, etc.). For instance, as shown in (1) (Zeijlstra 2006: 406), in Spanish the imperative form of the verb (1b) is not possible with negation (e.g. (1c)). Instead, Spanish uses the subjunctive form (e.g., (1d)) to express the meaning of negative imperative:

(1) a. Tu no lees.
you.sg neg read-2sg
'You don't read.'

b. Lee!
Read-2sg-imp
'Read!'

c. *¡No lee! (*True NI)
Neg read-2sg-imp
'Don't read'

d. ¡No leas! (Subjunctive NI)
Neg read-2sg-subj
'Don't read!'

Languages like Dutch, German, Swedish, Norwegian, on the other hand, do allow NIs, as the Dutch example in (2c) illustrates (Zeijlstra 2006: 405–6):

(2) a. Jij slaapt niet.
you sleep neg
'You don't sleep.'

b. Slaap!
sleep
'Sleep!'

c. Slaap niet! (True NI)
sleep neg
'Don't sleep!'

Although in the majority of studies investigating the ban on NIs Slavic languages are categorized as not allowing NIs, this is in fact true only in part. As is relatively well-known (especially among Slavicists), whether or not NIs are allowed in these languages mainly depends on aspectual properties of the verb taking the imperative form. In particular, while NIs are possible with imperfective verbs, they are in general not compatible with perfective verbs. As Riđanović (2012: 327) points out: "There is an unusual constraint on the use of the negative imperative in all Slavic languages: apart from a few exceptions, it does not occur with perfective verbs. Instead, speakers of Slavic languages (including Bosnian) use the negative imperative form of the corresponding imperfective verb." (see also Ivić 1958). Thus, as shown in (3d) below, NIs are not possible with perfective verbs in Bosnian/Croatian/Serbian (BCS hereafter):

(3) a. Positive imperative with imperfective
✓Jedi tu jabuku!
eat-imperf-imp that apple
'Eat that apple!'

b. Positive imperative with perfective
✓Pojedi tu jabuku!
eat-perf-imp that apple
'Eat that apple!'

c. Negative imperative with imperfective
✓Ne jedi tu jabuku!
Neg eat-imperf-imp that apple
'Do not eat that apple!'

d. Negative imperative with perfective
*Ne pojedi tu jabuku!
Neg eat-perf-imp that apple
'Do not eat that apple!'

Due to space limitations I will mainly focus on BCS in this paper, but much of what I say may be extended to other Slavic languages. Now, there are certain exceptions to the ban on NIs with perfective verbs, which are quite systematic. First, in BCS, NIs are possible with perfective verbs in what I call *analytic imperatives*. In these constructions, the imperative inflection is displaced and shows up on the particle *moj*, which is located right after the negation (see also Kosta 1999). The verb itself, on the other hand, takes either the infinitive form (4a), or the default present tense form as part of the *da*-clause (4b).

(4) a. Nemoj pojesti tu jabuku!
Neg-imper eat-perf-inf that apple

b. Nemoj da pojedeš tu jabuku!
Neg-imper that eat-perf-pres-2.s that apple

Second, throughout Slavic, NIs are possible with perfective verbs which lack voluntary agency. As shown in Kučera (1985), perfectives are allowed in NIs in Czech only with verbs which lack volitionality, describing unintentional/accidental events (5). The perfective aspect may be used in negative commands when the focus is on avoiding the result, adducing the meaning of a warning not to proceed with an action that is imminent (see e.g., Rothstein 1993 for Polish, Bogusławski 1985 and Chaput 1985 (among others) for Russian.) This is also illustrated for Polish and Russian in (6) and (7), respectively.

(5) a. Nenachlaď te se!
Neg-catch cold-perf-imp
'Do not catch cold!'

b. Neztrať ten klíč!
Neg-lose-perf-imp that key
'Do not lose that key!'

c. Neutop se!
Neg-drown-perf-imp
'Do not drown!'

(Kučera 1985: 121)

(6) Nie zgub tego klucza!
Neg lose-perf-imp that key
'Don't lose that key!' (Rothstein 1993: 728)

(7) Smotri, ne podgad'!
Look neg mess up-perf-imp
'Watch you, don't mess up!' (Timberlake 1993: 861)

BCS is similar in this respect: perfective NIs are allowed only with certain verbs involving involuntary psychological actions, like *zaboraviti* 'forget' (see (7)), *iznenaditi se* 'get surprised', *propustiti priliku* 'miss a chance' etc.

(8) Ne zaboravite ključeve!
Not forget-perf-imp keys
'Do not forget the keys!'

As Iatridou and Pancheva (2012) observe, why would the perfective bring in a volitionality restriction and moreover, why only in the negative imperative?

This is a rather puzzling state of affairs, but I will argue in this paper that the seeming complexity of these facts is an effect of a special (but quite simple) alignment of a few essentially syntactic factors.

2. An overview of the proposal

In this section I will present a thumbnail sketch of my analysis, while in Section 3 I discuss its main components in more detail.

I argue that examples like BCS (9) below violate formal properties of some *syntactic* mechanism. That is, they are not a result of a purely semantic/interpretative constraint.

(9) *Ne pojedi tu jabuku!
Not eat-perf-imp that apple
'Do not eat that apple!'

The main evidence for this comes from the fact that negative perfective commands *can* easily be expressed with analytic imperatives given in (4). Such examples show that there isn't some interpretative incompatibility between NIs and the perfective aspect. My analysis is based on the following three hypotheses:

(i) Imperative inflection on the verb in (10b) has to be licensed through the operation *Agree* by the operator responsible for the imperative meaning/imperative clause type (I-OP), as shown in (10a).

(10)

AGREE

a. T(I-OP) … [… V …]

b. Pojedi tu jabuku.
Eat-perf-imp that apple
'Eat that apple!'

In simple positive imperatives, I-OP is located in T (e.g., Jensen 2003), not in C.[1] In other words, among different flavors of T, there is also T_{IMP}.

(ii) Following Han (2000) and Zeijlstra (2006) I assume that I-OP cannot be in the scope of negation in logical forms of sentences, an observation which goes back to Frege. Thus, when NegP is present I-OP is necessarily located in the next highest functional projection, namely C, on the assumption that NegP is projected above TP.[2]

(iii) The final assumption is that imperfective verbs are located above the external argument introducing head *v*, whereas perfective verbs are always located in the complement of *v* (e.g., Travis 2010, Svenonious 2005), as shown in (11).

(11) $[_{AspP1}$ ASP1 $_{(IMPERFECTIVE)}$ $[_{vP}$ *v* $[_{AspP2}$ ASP2 $_{(PERFECTIVE)}$]]]

This particular set of assumptions derives the ban on perfective NIs in the following way: at the point when C, in which I-OP is located in NIs, is merged, the complement of the *v* phase head, where the perfective verb is located, is spelled-out (Chomsky 2001). This is illustrated in (12b). There is no problem with imperfective verbs since they are located above the *v*P-phase domain, as shown in (12a).

(12)

a. $[_{CP}$ C(**I-OP**) $[_{NEGP}$ NEG $[_{TP}$ T $[_{AspP1}$ ASP1(<u>IMPERF</u>) $[_{vP}$ *v* $[_{AspP2}$ ASP2 $[_{VP}$]]]]]] SPELL-OUT

AGREE

b. $[_{CP}$ C(**I-OP**) $[_{NEGP}$ NEG $[_{TP}$ T $[_{vP}$ *v* $[_{AspP2}$ ASP2 $[_{VP}$]]]]]] SPELL-OUT

1 It could also be the case that I-OP is located in a special projection JussiveP as in Zanuttini 2008 in positive imperatives.

2 As noted in Zeiljstra (2006: 415, ft. 14), what is important is that I-OP, as an illocutionary force operator (or imperative clause type marker), is located in the highest given functional projection, taking scope over the whole propositional content: i.e., it cannot be located below other functional projections. Thus, I-OP does not have to be always located in C.

At the same time, we can directly explain the exceptions to the ban on perfective NIs. Consider first analytic imperatives in (4). Here, I-OP can from C license imperative inflection directly on T (instead on V), without violating any locality restriction:

(13) AGREE

[$_{\text{CP}}$C(I-OP)[$_{\text{NEGP}}$ NEG(NE) [$_{\text{TP}}$ T (MOJ) …]]]

In the case of verbs which lack voluntary agency (i.e., (5)–(8)), we can assume that they lack *v*P phase (or that they involve a 'weak' *v*P-phase in the sense of Chomsky 2001). I-OP can then enter *Agree* with the perfective verb since the external (agent) argument introducing *v*P phase is not present, i.e., there can be no locality violation in (12b) if the (strong) phase head *v* which triggers cyclic spell-out is not present.

3. Imperatives, Negation and Agree

The central idea of my proposal and the main contribution of this paper as I see it is that perfective NIs are disallowed in BCS (and other Slavic languages) due to a violation of *syntactic locality*. In this section I will present a particular way of implementing the general theory of syntactic locality to derive this ban, which is based on the notion of *Phase* and the operation *Agree*. But it is important to emphasize at the outset that other approaches to syntactic locality can in principle derive the facts discussed as well (i.e., analyses based on intervention, movement, upward *Agree* etc.), as long as they adopt a structure like (11) and the assumption that I-OP cannot stay in the scope of negation.

My analysis is based on Chomsky's (2001: 13) definition of the Phase Impenetrability Condition (PIC) in (14).

(14) PHASE IMPENETRABILITY CONDITON (Chomsky 2001: 13)
  a. [$_{\text{ZP}}$ Z … [$_{\text{HP}}$ α [H YP]]]
  b. The domain of H is not accessible to operations at ZP, but only H and its edge.

I will also follow the standard assumption that C and *v* are phase heads. According to (14) then, at the point when C is merged, the complement of *v*, namely VP, is spelled-out, i.e., it becomes inaccessible for syntactic operations from C:

I also follow Pesetsky and Torrego (2007) etc. in assuming a four-way feature typology given in (15):

(15) a. uninterpretable unvalued features (*u*F[])
b. interpretable valued features (*i*F[val])
c. interpretable unvalued features (*i*F[])
d. uninterpretable valued features (*u*F[val])

Pesetsky and Torrego (2007) argue that (15c–d) are particularly useful in explaining the distribution of tense inflection in English. It is independently known that English verbs do not move as high as T, even though they carry tense inflection. However, if tense is interpreted in T, the question is then how does T know that (16) should be interpreted as *past*, given that the past tense morphology is on the verb? According to Pesetsky and Torrego (2007) this happens via *Agree* (e.g., (17a)). In particular, T has an interpretable unvalued features (*i*T[]), which needs to be assigned a particular value in order for the whole sentence to have tense interpretation. This value is provided by the uninterpretable but valued feature (*u*T[past]), on the verb, as in (17b):

(16) I walked.

(17) a.

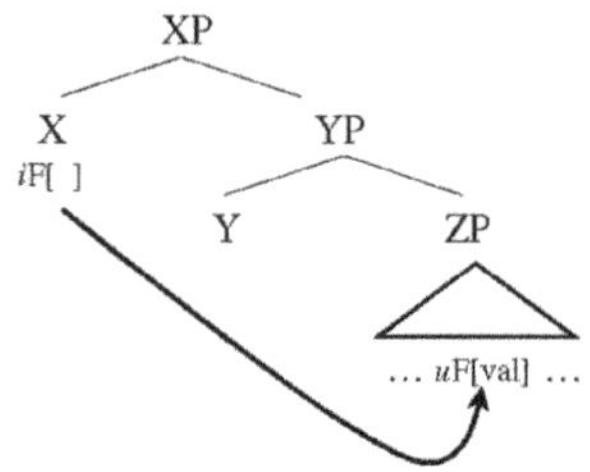

b.

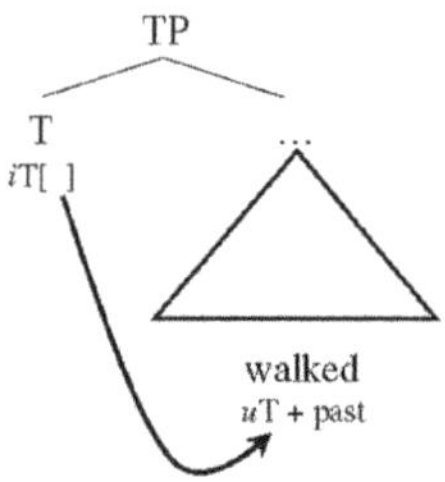

I assume that the position of T is BCS declaratives in (18) is occupied by the auxiliaries *će* 'will' and *je* 'is'.

(18) BCS declaratives:

a. Jovan će doći /dolaziti.
John will arrive-perf-inf /arrive-imperf-inf

b. Jovan će da dođe /dolazi.
John will that arrive-perf-pres / arrive-imperf-pres
'John will arrive.'

c. Jovan je došao /dolazio.
John is arrive-perf-past-prt / arrive-imperf-past-prt
'John arrived.'

Given that negation immediately precedes auxiliaries (e.g., (19)), I will assume that NegP is located higher than TP, as in (20).

(19) a. BCS declaratives:
Jovan *ne*-će doći /dolaziti.
John neg-will arrive-perf-inf /arrive-imperf-inf
b. Jovan *ne*-će da dođe /dolazi.
John neg-will that arrive-perf-pres / arrive-imperf-pres
'John will not arrive.'
c. Jovan *ni*-je došao /dolazio.
John neg- is arrive-perf-past-prt / arrive-imperf-past-prt
'John arrived.'

(20) [$_{NEGP}$ NEG(**ne**) [$_{TP}$ T (**će**) …]]]

In positive imperatives T has an interpretable but unvalued I-OP feature which is valued by an uninterpretable but valued I-OP feature on the verb, via *Agree*, as in (21). In other words, although the verb carries the imperative inflection (see (22)), the clause type (i.e., command) and its illocutionary force are determined in a higher position, namely T.

(21)
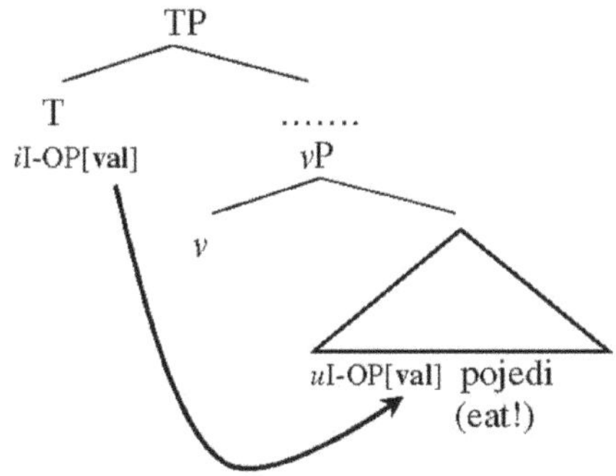

(22) *Imperative Inflection*:
a. poјed-*i* eat-2-sg-imper b. pojed-*ite* eat-2-pl-imper c. pojed-*imo* eat-1-pl-imper

Since I-OP cannot be in the scope of negation, when NegP is present, the interpretable unvalued I-OP feature must be located in next highest functional projection, namely C. However, since C is a phase head, it triggers cyclic spell-out when it is merged; i.e., the complement of the lower *v*-phase head in which the perfective verb is located is spelled out. In other words, the interpretable unvalued I-OP feature on C cannot be valued by the uninterpretable but valued I-OP feature on the perfective verb, because at the point when C is merged, the perfective verb is no longer available for syntactic operations. This locality problem does not arise with imperfective verbs, since they are located above *v*P, by assumption.

In the case of analytic imperatives in (4), the particle *moj* carries the uninterpretable but valued I-OP feature; i.e., it has imperative inflection (see (23)). Since *moj* shows up right after negation, it is reasonable to assume that it is located in T, just like regular auxiliaries in (19). Diachronically, *ne+moj* goes back to the negated imperative of the modal verb *moći* 'can, be able' (e.g., Szucsich 2010), but synchronically the *moj* part is "bleached out" of any semantic content. The only function of *moj* then is to supply the uninterpretable but *valued* I-OP feature which *i*I-OP [] on C can successfully probe in a syntactically licit configuration (e.g., (24)).

(23)	a.	ne-moj	b.	ne-mojte	c.	ne-mojmo
		neg-2-sg-imper		neg-2-pl-imper		neg-1-pl-imper

(24) AGREE

[$_{CP}$C(***i*I-OP[ ]**)[$_{NEGP}$ NEG(NE) [$_{TP}$ T (MOJ ***u*I-OP[val]**) ...]]]

Since the locality problem which the use of *moj* is meant to resolve is created by the presence of NegP it also follows that *moj* cannot be used to license positive imperatives, in which the locality problem in question never arises:

(25) a. *Moj pojesti tu jabuku!
eat-perf-inf that apple
'Eat up that apple!'
b. *Moj da pojedeš tu jabuku!
that eat-perf-pres that apple

Finally, recall that perfective NIs are allowed with certain verbs which lack volition/voluntary agency. This is not surprising on this kind of approach, since the obligatory lack of agency of the verbs in questions can be related to the 'deficiency' of their corresponding *v*Ps. That is, on the phase-based approaches little *v*, which defines a phase domain, also introduces the external argument/agent. These verbs then either do not have *v*P or their *v*P is deficient in the sense that it does not define a phase domain or trigger cyclic transfer (i.e., it is not a "strong phase"; Chomsky 2001). There is a clear pattern in (5)–(8) which calls for a unified account; it cannot be a mere accident that perfective verbs are allowed in (true) NIs exactly when the lack of agency is presupposed. The point of variation between different Slavic languages then comes down to the question of which verbs under which circumstances may be associated with this type of 'non-agentive', 'deficient' *v* head.

4. On the structural position of perfective and imperfective verbs

One of the crucial assumptions of my analysis is that imperfective verbs are located above *v*P, whereas perfective verbs are in the complement of *v*, as in (26) (similar structures have been proposed in Travis 2010, Svenonious 2005 etc.). There are many arguments in support of this structure, but I can present here only one due to space limitations (see Despić in preparation, for other arguments, based on nominalizations, idiomatic readings etc.)

(26) $[_{\text{AspP1}}$ ASP1 $_{\text{(IMPERFECTIVE)}}$ $[_{\text{vP}}$ v $[_{\text{AspP2}}$ ASP2 $_{\text{(PERFECTIVE)}}]]]$

The structure in (26) predicts that we should find structures in which the availability of the external argument depends exclusively on the aspectual properties of the verb. A well-known example of this sort comes from Russian *–sja* passives: in these constructions the nominal corresponding to the initial subject (external) argument may appear as an adjunct in the instrumental case *only* if the verb is imperfective (e.g., Babby 1975). A similar type of contrast can also be seen in BCS *se*-passives, when they are modified by agentive adverbs like *intentionally* or *voluntarily*.[3]

(27) a. Kolači su se (namerno) jeli u podne.
Cakes are refl intentionally eat-imperf-past-prt in noon
'Cakes were (intentionally) being eaten at noon.'
b. Kolači su se (*?namerno) pojeli u podne.
Cakes are refl intentionally eat-perf-past-prt in noon
'Cakes were intentionally eaten at noon.'

The adverb *intentionally* can be used felicitously only in (27a) where the verb takes the imperfective form. When the verb is perfective, as in (27b), the use of the adverb coerces the implausible, true reflexive reading (i.e., "cakes intentionally ate themselves"). This kind of contrast is exactly expected under the structure in (26), if *se*-passivization targets AspPs; i.e., in the case of perfective

3 In BCS the demoted subject is expressed with a prepositional 'by phrase' (i.e., 'od strane + genitive') which is preferably left out in general and often sounds unnatural.

verbs this process applies at the level which does not include *v*P, since by assumption perfective verbs are located lower than the *v* phase head (which introduces the external argument). The opposite holds for imperfective verbs, which are assumed to be higher than *v*.

5. Conclusion

I argued in this paper that the unusual ban on perfective NIs in BCS (and Slavic) is essentially a result of one cross-linguistic and one cross-Slavic phenomenon: (i) the imperative operator cannot be in the scope of negation in logical forms of sentences, and (ii) perfective verbs are in general located in the complement of *v*, in contrast to imperfectives which are located higher than *v*. The central proposal then is that perfective NIs are excluded because syntactic locality is violated; i.e., when NegP is present the imperative operator (located in C) is too far away from the perfective verb to enter successful *Agree* relationship with it. I presented an analysis based on phase theory and *Agree*, but other approaches to syntactic locality can in principle explain the same facts as long as they assume points (i) and (ii) above. For instance, in models which do not assume phases, it could be argued that the imperative operator always probes from C, and that the Neg+*v* complex counts as an intervener, but not Neg or *v* alone. Conversely, in approaches based on movement, it could be argued that the verb cannot cross the Neg+*v* complex on the way to C, but that it can cross just Neg (where the negative particle cliticizes to it) or just *v*. I leave exploration of these possibilities for future work (see Despić in preparation for a more detailed discussion).

References

Bogusławski, Andrej. 1985. "The problem of the negated imperative in perfective verbs revisited." *Russian Linguistics* 9: 225–239.

Babby, Leonard H. 1975. "A transformational analysis of transitive *–sja* verbs in Russian." *Lingua* 35: 297–332.

Chomsky, Noam. 2001. Derivation by phase. In *Ken Hale: A life in language*, ed. by Michael Kenstowicz, 1–50. Cambridge, Mass.: MIT Press.

Chaput, R. Patricia. 1985. "On the question of aspectual selection in denials." In *The Scope of Slavic Aspect*, Michael S. Flier and Alan Timberlake (eds.). Columbus Ohio: Slavica Publishers, 224–233.

Despić, Miloje. In preparation. "Negative imperatives and aspect: from locality to argument structure." Ms. Cornell.

Iatridou, Sabine and Roumyana Pancheva. 2012. "Negative imperatives." *Lecture notes. NYI 10, Cog Fest July 18*, St. Petersburg.

Ivić, Milka. 1958. "Upotreba vida u slovenskom imperativu s negacijom." *Славянская Филология II*: 108–111.

Han, Chung-hye. 2000. *The Structure and Interpretation of Imperatives: Mood and Force in Universal Grammar*. New York and London: Garland.

Jensen, Britta. 2003. "Syntax and semantics of imperative subjects". *Nordlyd* 31: 150–164.

Kosta, Peter. 1999. "Prohibitiv und Prventiv im Slavischen (Zur Grammatik, Semantik und Pragmatik des verneinten Imperativs unter besonderer Bercksichtigung des Russischen, Tschechischen und Sdslavischen)." *ARS PHILOLOGICA: Festschrift für Baldur Panzer zum 65. Geburtstag*, Karsten Grünberg und Wilfried Potthoff. Frankfurt am Main u.a.: Lang, 283–294.

Kučera, Milan. 1985. "Aspect in negative imperatives." In *The Scope of Slavic Aspect*, Michael S. Flier and Alan Timberlake (eds.). Columbus Ohio: Slavica Publishers, 118–128.

Pesetsky, David and Esther Torrego. 2007. "The syntax of valuation and the interpretability of features." In *Phrasal and Clausal Architecture*, Simin Karimi, Vida Samiian, and Wendy Wilkins (eds.). Amsterdam: John Benjamins, 262–294.

Riđanović, Midhat. 2012. *Bosnian for Foreigners (with a Copmprehensive Grammar)*. Sarajevo: Rabic.

Rothstein, Robert A. 1993. "Polish." In *The Slavonic Languages*, Bernard Comrie and Greville Corbett (eds.). London and New York: Routlege, 686–758.

Szucsich, Luka. 2010. "Mood in Bosnian/Croatian/Serbian." In *Mood in the Languages of Europe Vol. II: Slavic and other European languages*, Björn Rothstein and Rolf Thieroff (eds.). Tübingen: Niemeyer, 394–408.

Svenonius, Peter. 2004. "Slavic prefixes inside and outside the VP." *Nordlyd 32.2: Special Issue on Slavic Prefixes*: 205–253.

Timberlake, Alan. 1993. "Russian." In *The Slavonic Languages*, Bernard Comrie and Greville Corbett (eds.). London and New York: Routlege, 827–886.

Travis, Lisa. 2010. *Inner Aspect: The Articulation of VP*. Dordrecht: Springer.

Zanuttini, Raffaella. 2008. "Encoding the addressee in the syntax: evidence from English imperative subjects." *Natural Language and Linguistic Theory* 26:185–218.

Zeijlstra, Hedde. 2006. "The ban on true negative imperatives." *Empirical Issues in Syntax and Semantics* 6: 405–424.

Peter Kosta

On Extraction and Clitic Climbing out of Subject-/Object-Control Clauses and Causative Clauses in Romance and Czech*

1. Clitic Climbing and higher vs. lower Datives in causatives and control verbs in French, Italian and Czech

Kayne (2004:192)[1] has pointed to the fact that in French there is a peculiar asymmetry regarding the behavior of Clitic Climbing (CC) out of Control vs Causative Clauses. In my paper, I would like to take this descriptive generalization as a starting point showing that in Czech and Italian, both languages allowing in principle for CC, the same asymmetry holds. In order not only to describe but also explain this asymmetry, we will consider the following UG candidates, namely locality (external merge, minimal move and Minimal Link Condition, hereafter abbreviated as MLC), Phase Impenetrability Condition (hereafter abbreviated as PIC) and Phase-Hood (hereafter abbreviated as PH). The working hypothesis will follow from answering the following questions: (1) which Phrases in which language and in which construction are Phases? (2) Which extraction data confirm the viability of PIC, and, finally, (3) at which level of representation and when take these extractions place?

Firstly, a Causative requires a specific structure in which the subject of the transitive infinitive must be assigned Dative case. This can be seen on the fact that the subject of the embedded infinitive in a French causative with *faire* ('make', 'do') cannot precede the infinitive, contrary to the usual position of subjects, cf. the contrast in (1) vs. (2):

---

* The author would like to thank the participants of the FDSL 11 conference for their suggestions and improvements and the two anonymous reviewers for their comments on this paper. All remaining flaws and shortcomings go to the responsibility of the author.

1 This article has been published also as chapter 5 in Kayne (2005). In conclusion of Kayne's approach, the P of the Dative PP + internal Subject in French and Italian acts as a probe for internal Merge to a non-Argument position similarly to ECM and Raising constructions but contrary to Control constructions where the Infinitive can be preceded by any material independently of the surface structure of the Infinitive clause.

(1) *Jean a fait Paul manger la tarte.
*Jean has made Paul eat the cake t

(2) √ Jean a fait manger Paul.
Jean has made Paul eat.

But when the infinitive takes a direct object, the infinitival subject must be preceded by the preposition à. The same contrast can be observed in the b-sentences in Italian:

(3) a. *Jean a fait manger Paul la tarte.
*Jean has made eat Paul the pie.
b. *Gianni ha fatto mangiare Paolo la torta.

(4) a. *Jean a fait manger la tarte Paul.
*Jean has made eat the pie Paul.
b. *Gianni ha fatto mangiare la torta Paolo.

(5) a. Jean a fait manger la tarte à Paul.
Jean has made eat the pie to Paul.
b. Gianni ha fatto mangiare la torta a Paolo.

Secondly, the subject-related 'à DP' of causatives is similar to ordinary 'P DP' with respect to its position relative to a direct object:

Thus, (i) an extraction from within an adjunct is banned:

(6) ?? Le professeur que je me suis endormi après avoir écouté.
The professor that I me am fell asleep after have listened.

(7) *Le professeur à qui je me suis endormi après avoir parlé.
The professor to whom I me am fell asleep after have spoken (to).

(ii) The Subextraction of *en* or *combien* is only possible out of direct objects but not out of PPs:

(8) Le capitain **en** a fait ramper trois dans la boue.
the captain of-them has made crawl three in the mud

(9) *Le capitain **en** a fait manger de la boue à trois.
the captain of-them has made eat of the mud to three

(10) Combien a-t-elle fait manger d'enfants.
how many has she made eat of children

(11) *Combien a-t-elle fait manger cette tarte à d'enfants.
how many has she made eat this pie to of children

Thirdly, both, in French and in Italian, the causative construction is not an instance of control as can be shown on the following facts. In the absence of direct object of the infinitive, the embedded subject in the causative construction generally cannot be preceded by the Dative assigning preposition "à". In French, the order Dat > Acc is excluded even if the Dative is assigned by the PP, but in Italian, the order Dat > Acc is licensed but marked by a different Information Structure (IS), where the Acc > DP is the Focus domain and the Dative PP is extracted from the Focus Phrase, cf. (12a) vs (12b):

(12) a. *Jean a fait manger à Paul (la tarte).
* Jean has made eat to Paul (the pie)
b. #Gianni ha fatto mangiare [[a Paolo]$_t$ [$_{FocP}$ (la **TÓ**rta) t]]
#Gianni has made eat to Paul the pie.

Contrary to it, the object control clause with PRO allows for this option without any restriction for both Romance languages, cf.:

(13) a. Jean a dit à Paul [PRO de manger (une tarte)].
Jean has told to Paul [PRO to eat (a pie)].
b. Gianni ha detto a Paolo [PRO di mangiare (una torta)].
Gianni has told to Paul to eat (a pie).

In the following contribution, it will be shown that the same distribution as in the Romance languages French and Italian, can be observed in Czech with Clitic Pronominal Objects. Thus, In French, clitic climbing is allowed in causatives, but not in control constructions: this is exactly the same evidence in Czech which allows clitic climbing out of Causatives but not out of Subject and Object control constructions.

(14) a. Jean les a fait manger à Paul. (French)
b. *Jean les veut manger. (subject control)
c. *Jean les a dit à Paul de manger. (object control)

(15) a. Jan *je* CL$_{ACC.PL}$ dal jíst dětem (bonbóny). (Czech)
John them CL$_{ACC.PL}$ give eat children$_{DAT}$ (the sweets)
John made the children eat them (the candies).
b. Jan *je* CL$_{ACC.PL}$ chce jíst ~~je CLAcc.pl~~
John themCL$_{ACC.PL}$ wants to eat
John wants to eat them

c. *Jan je$_{\text{CLACC.PL}}$ řekl Pavlovi sníst ~~jeCLAcc.pl~~
*John them$_{\text{CLACC.PL}}$ told to Paul$_{\text{DAT}}$ to eat ~~them~~$_{\text{CLACC.PL}}$
John told to Paul to eat them (the candies).

d. *John them told Paul$_{\text{Dat}}$ to eat.
John told Paul to eat them

e. #Jan řekl Pavlovi *JE* sníst.
John told to Paul them to eat
(if *JE* is focused, the result is marginally accepted)

As opposed to French, in Czech, the sensitivity for Clitic Climbing seems to depend on the speech act class of the matrix verbs: thus, the directive speech act verbs with the illocution <to order> allow only marginally for clitic climbing out of object control clauses:

(16) a. Jan *poručil/nařídil/rozkázal* [lower Dative Phrase NP Pavlovi]
John ordered/directed/commanded [Lower Dative Phrase NP Paul]
[PRO sníst banány]]
[PRO eat bananas]]

b. *Jan *je$_i$* poručil/nařídil/rozkázal…
*John them$_{\text{CL_ACC}}$ ordered/directed/commanded
[lower Dative Phrase NP Pavlovi [PRO t_i sníst]]
[lower Dative Phrase NP to Paul [PRO t sníst]].

It seems that this contrast must be explained by both locality, phase-hood and PIC: The observation is that the direct object/Accusative Clitic pronoun cannot cross the lower indirect Object in Dative of the embedded clause because the lower Dative DP is presumably in the specApplP (the lower Applicative Phase) position into which the Accusative Clitic cannot move since the SpecAplP position is already filled by the base generated Dative Clitic. Because the Applicative Phrase is not a Phase, it does not license additional Spec-positions above like Phase-heads would do. So, even if there is a light *v*P position above the lower AplP, it is not visible as a Probe for the Accusative Clitic (due to PIC), which has been base generated in a lower lexical VP position where it also receives its Case Accusative. If the head of a lower Apl projection is not a phase head it cannot act as a probe for movement!

We first introduce the original version of the Phase Impenetrability Condition (PIC) and revise it following Kosta (in prep.):

(I) *Phase Impenetrability Condition* (PIC; Chomsky (2000; 2001)):The domain of a head X of a phase XP is not accessible to operations outside XP; only X and its edge are accessible to such operations.

(II) *Phase Impenetrability Condition* (PIC) (revised version from Kosta, in prep.)
A phase[2] (CP, *v*P, VP) is not accessible for further computation (internal or external merge) iff:
(i) a merged element α has not reached the edge of the phase,
(ii) the interfaces PF or LF cannot interpret the *EPP-/ phi-/wh*-features of α[φ] if α in a phase {α[φ] {b[•]}} has not reached an edge phase position.

We can see in (II) (ii) that in a merged SO situation, only α can be read off by the interfaces for a feature [φ] since it is at the edge of a phase, while b is internal to the merged phase and cannot be interpreted (we use a dot • for a non-interpretable feature in b[•]). In order to get a Label, the element b[•] has to move via internal merge to a higher position in order to be interpreted. This situation is typical for any kind of movement (be it wh-, NP- or head movement of a non-valued/interpretable lexical or functional category). We assume by stipulation that Clitic Climbing is an instance of NP-movement from an unlabeled Phase internal position with a non-interpretable feature in b[•]). to a higher labeled Edge Probe position of a phase where it can be valued and where it can get an interpretable feature.

However, this scenario is problematic for Clitical pronouns with respect to the fact that we have to define which kind of feature is the feature for Clitics. It cannot be Case which drives the movement since Chomsky (2000) and especially in Chomsky (2008) Case does not trigger Move (internal Merge) at all (as opposed to Minimalist Program Chomsky 1995 in which Case could serve as trigger e.g. in Raising constructions or in Control Infinitives). We assume, that this feature must be a EPP feature due to the fact that Clitics[3] must climb as high as possible at S-structure in CC languages (e.g. Italian, French and Czech but not in German or English).

---

2 An anonymous reviewer makes a different observation as to Spanish. He/she seems to make the following observation: When you say ‚a phase', do you mean the whole thing or the complement of the phase head? Assume that CPs are phases. Then, if the ‚phase' refers to CP, something in Spec-C should not be accessible either. But maybe something adjoined to CP would (I'm referring to Chomsky-adjunction here, not to daughter-adjunction. Maybe sister-adjunction as well?). I cannot really at present answer this problem, but I am concerned about it.

3 An anonymous reviewer makes the following observation: Not in Spanish (which also behaves differently from French and Italian in other respects in its auxiliary system, so I guess this falls into place). If you have a sequence of auxiliary verbs, intermediate positions are perfectly possible. Furthermore, the results have no semantic differences, making it one of the very truly optional rules of the grammar.

The direct object/Accusative -Clitic cannot cross the lower indirect Object in Dative of the embedded clause because the lower applicative Dative NP is presumably in a lower Applicative Phase position out of which it cannot move further up. If the lower Dative addressee theta-role NP is an applicative NP with the Theta-role benefactive or malefactive, the grammaticality upgrades to a marginal semantic acceptability (marked with #), cf. (16) c:

(16) c. #Jan *je* poručil/nařídil/rozkázal
*John them$_{CL_ACC}$ ordered/directed/commanded
[higher ethic Dative Phrase NP Pavlovi [PRO sníst]].
[higher Dative Phrase NP away from Paul [PRO t to eat]]

The explanation could be that the lower applicative phrase as a target of typical Argumental Dative constructions (often Addressee as Theta-role) serves as Barrier and is impenetrable for further computation of another Argumental (direct object) NP. Thus, it cannot even be crossed by an Argumental Clitic NP in Accusative (with the Theta-role Theme) because the outer specifier position of the Dative NP/DP is occupied by the argument and builds a barrier qua Relativized Minimality (Rizzi 1990, 1997ab), thus is not accessible for successive movement of the Accusative Clitic NP (following PIC).

In case of optional quasi-Argumental or pseudo-Argumental positions (such as those with Dativus ethicus, Benefactive or Malefactive Dative), the NP is not Argumental but rather an *adjunct* which does not project an Argumental NP but rather an adjunct. If adjunction is a post-syntactic late insertion (much in the sense of late adjunct insertion as formulated in Kosta & Krivochen 2012, Krivochen & Kosta 2013 and Kosta & Krivochen 2014), the marginal #- interpretation in (16) c. is not due to ungrammaticality, rather it is caused by processing short term memory problems caused by non-locality or distance (former notion of bounding nodes within the LGB Bounding Theory 1981, or later Theory of Barriers in Chomsky 1982). This fact is confirmed by subject control clauses which do not allow for an addressee interpretation of the Dative NP at all, cf.:

(16) d. #Jan je poručil/nařídil/rozkázal [higher applicative Phrase NP Pavlovi] [PRO sníst]].

Rather, they do allow for a benefactive or malefactive Theta-role interpretation of the Dative NP, which is assumed to stand higher in the tree, presumably in a higher applicative position:

(16) e. Pavel *je* chtěl [NP$_{\text{Dat higher applicative Phrase}}$ Petrovi] sníst (=*banány*).
Paul CL$_{ACC}$ them wanted (of) Peter eat (=bananas)

The data and contrasts are confirmed by another Romance Clitic Climbing language, namely Italian. In Italian, CL climbing out of object control verbs is banned (cf. 17a vs 17b):

(17) a. Giovanni ha ordinato a Paolo di mangiar*le* Giovanni
Aux commanded to Paul to eat themCL_{ACC}
b. *Giovanni *le* ha ordinato a Paolo di mangiare Giovanni
them CL_{ACC} AUX commanded eat

It is possible to use the verb ***ordinare*** in the sense of "to order", but then the clitic cluster must be topicalized, thus stands in CP:

(18) Giovanni gliele ha ordinate.
Giovanni him them has ordered

Similarly as in Czech, Clitic Climbing in Italian is allowed in Subject control clauses if the Dative Clitic has the Theta-role malefactive/benefactive and not addressee, i.e. is base generated in a high applicative phrase

(19) Paolo gliele voleva mangiare.
Paul of him$_{CL_DAT}$ them$_{CL_ACC}$ wanted eat

2. Clitic Climbing asymmetry of CL IO/DO in Control Constructions vs. Causatives in Czech

A peculiar asymmetry between Ditransitives and Causatives shows up in contexts with both Dative CL climbing and Accusative CL climbing in Czech:

(20) a. Petr$_{NOM}$ chtěl Pavlovil$_{DAT}$ darovat zesilovač$_{ACC}$
Peter$_{NOM}$ wanted (to) Paul$_{DAT}$ donate (an) amplifier$_{ACC}$
b. Petr *mu ho* chtěl darovat.
√ CLDAT > CLACC
c. Petr * *ho mu* chtěl darovat.
*CLACC > CLDAT

We should expect that the same asymmetry disappears when a causative verb instead of a subject control verb is chosen; and this is exactly what happens; thus, this prediction is born out, both word orders are allowed: *CLDAT > CLACC* in (21) b, *CLACC > CLDAT* in (21) c:

(21) a. Petr dal Pavlovi ušít oblek.
Paul gave Peter DAT a suitACC made
b. Petr *mu ho* dal ušít. √
CLDAT > CLACC
Petr him it gave made
c. Petr *ho mu* dal ušít. √
CLACC > CLDAT
Petr it him gave made[4]

3. The Analysis

3.1. Anti-Causatives, Causatives and Control Constructions[5]

Recall that Anti-Causatives and Unaccusatives have a very similar structure:

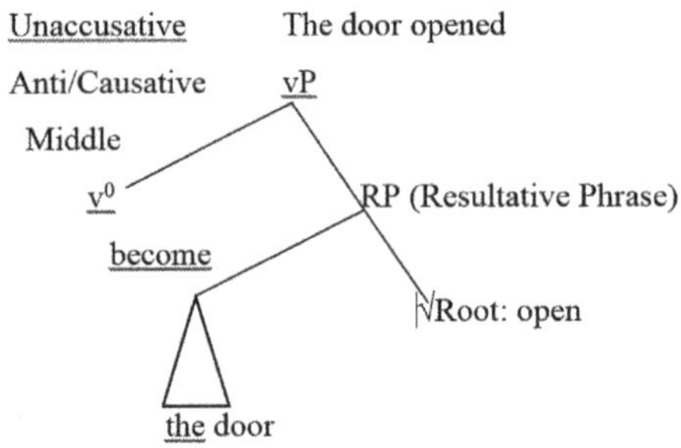

Unaccusatives and Anti-Causatives

4 In Franks (2018a) and (2018b), the ordering of Clitic Pronouns is treated from the perspective of so-called "Person Case Constraint" (PCC) effects. These are ordering restrictions on co-occurring clitic pronouns, where only certain person combinations are felicitous but the possibilities vary cross-linguistically. It is further argued that languages may differ in terms of how these two features are arranged, accounting for additional systems. Finally, speculations are offered on how feature spreading enlightens PCC violation repair strategies. Since Czech seems to belong to so-called strictly descending systems, it is predicted that in a combination in which all three persons appear, the first person has always to precede the second person and the second person has to precede the third person. Following Franks (2018b), the clitic ordering in Strictly Descending POC (Ultra-Strong) is as follows: In a combination of clitic pronouns, the argument with the "higher" person specification (where 1st » 2nd » 3rd) has to come first. In our examples, we consider only Dative and Accusative Clitics of the same (3rd) Person.

5 An anonymous reviewer suggests that with this analysis, „there may be some problems with the ‚resultative phrase', and that it that it obscures the fact that Romance languages

Contrary to that, the Causatives have the following structure (following Kosta 2004, 2015, 2016, Kosta in prep., and Harley 2006/2008):

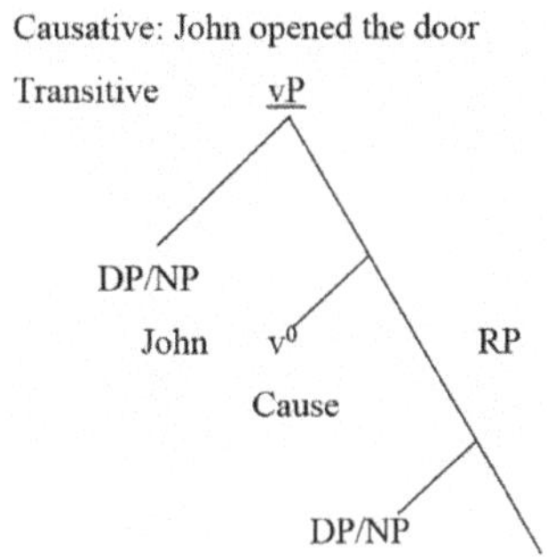

Causatives Harley (2006/2008)

The Explanation for the contrast between the ban on extraction out of Object Control constructions of Clitics (in the sense of Clitic Climbing = CC) vs licensing the CC out of Causatives may lie in the following analysis.

Following Pylkkännen (2008), the benefactive are typically in a higher Applicative position and they also are typical for causative constructions such as in (22a), as opposed to the addressee oriented double transitive construction in (22b):

(22) a. He let ***his wife*** eat the food.
b. I baked him a cake.

do not have resultative constructions. You cannot ‚burn the toast black' in Romance. Pylkkanen relegates the Romance facts to a footnote without explaining them, thus effectively forcing a contradiction. More concretely, my question is what in this analysis separates predicative complements (depictives, which are not islands) from true resultatives (which are)." I do not have much to say on this point so far, but I shall try to think about it in future analyses.

Introducing Arguments

by

Liina Pylkkänen MIT PhD diss. 2008

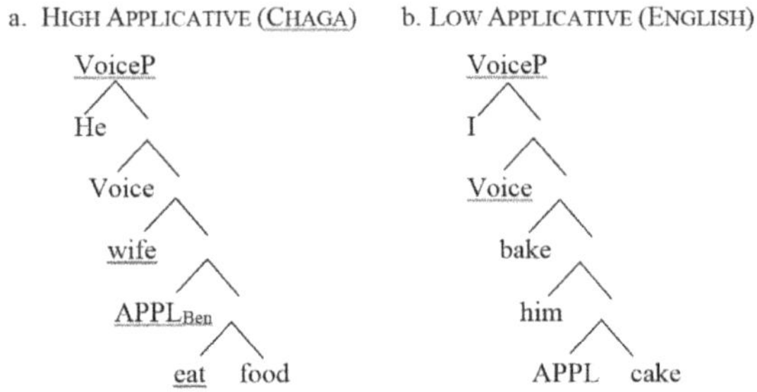

High vs Low Applicatives

Thus, in the case of Causatives and Higher Applicative, the extraction of Dative Clitic is possible over Accusative DPs/NPs because they form the same higher Applicative Phase and the features for Case can be read of at the Edge of the Phase Higher Applicative.Contrary to this situation, in Object Control constructions, the upper and the lower part of the Control Construction build three different Phrases, namely a VP with the lower Accusative NP/DP, a low Applicative Phrase with the Addressee Dative NP/DP and a higher VoicePhase which is not accessible for further computation since the Addressee Dative NP/DP is not an edge position of the lower Applicative.

3.2. Further evidence from German Dative/Accusative asymmetries

The situation with the asymmetry of case assignment of Dative and Accusative in object control constructions vs Causatives shows up in German even in clauses with full DPs (non-clitic), where the precedence of Dative over Accusative is evident:

(23) a. Paul befahl dem Peter das Kind abzuholen.
b. *Paul befahl das Kind dem Peter abzuholen.

Here we do not even get the malefactive interpretation under (23b).

We know that usually in German, midrange scrambling should allow for displacement and free scrambling between indirect and direct objects (cf. Haider 1993; Fanselow 1987; 1988; on comparison between Russian and German cf. Kosta 2002; and between Czech and German Kosta 2006):

(24) a. Paul gibt dem Professor das/ein Buch.
b. Paul gibt das Buch/ein Buch dem Professor.
c. Paul gibt es ihm /Paul gibt's ihm.
d. *Paul gibt ihm es. /* Paul gibt'm es.

Again, the situation with both full NPs and Clitics changes even in German, when we have causative constructions:

(25) a. Paul ließ den Peter das Kind abholen.
b. Paul ließ das Kind [FOK den PÉter] abholen.
c. Paul ließ es ihn abholen.
d. Paul ließ ihn es abholen.

The explanation for this complex scenario must lie within the grammar and especially within the ability or disability to transmit F-features to NPs in long distance environments in non- permeable Phase contexts which is e.g. the object control constructions due to a IP/TP phrase which in fact does not count as Phase under standard assumptions of the phase theory (only light *v*Ps and CPs and DPs are real phases). This would lead us to the conclusion that Causatives are in fact not two separate Phrases (one with the Causative verb and a lower one with the full verb in infinitive), but rather a subpart of the *v*P *Phase* and this fact allows for double case assignment in the sense we have already postulated for transitive and causative constructions.

3.3. Conclusion and problems

Causative Constructions (both the periphrastic type with a Causative light *v*P and the inflected synthetic type with Causative morphemes, cf. Kosta 2015) are subparts of atransitive light *v*P Phase which can be articulated in some languages as VoiceP (cf. Alexiadou, Borer & Schäfer 2014, Kosta 2015), in other languages as a special CausP. Since Causatives are in terms of phase-hood *v*Ps, they are licensed for feature inheritance and/or for feature transmission and are accessible for any further computation at the edges following PIC. As opposed to them, Control Infinitive Constructions being TPs are non-Phases[6], thus it follows that they are neither permissible for feature inheritance nor for feature

6 The fact that Infinitives are non-Phases follows also from the fact that if Infinitives are TPs rather than CPs in Control Constructions, Phase-hood is already outranked by the fact that TP in Infinitives is a defective functional category. This can be also deduced from independent further evidence.

transmission. The CC can be licensed only if there is a EPP feature triggering CC and the Case and Theta hierarchy of the S-Structure follows the hierarchy of the Base-generated (D-structure) with respect to Case assignment and Theta-role assignment (on this criterion cf. also Kosta 2015). This explains why the lower applicative NP/P is assigned Dative by the control verb why the Accusative is assigned by the lexical head of the VP (V^0). This Case/Theta-role hierarchy must be maintained until Spell-Out because this hierarchy of Case assignment is fixed at S- Structure already before internal Merge (Move) or CC to a higher position can take place. This fixed order of CC cannot be reordered by any other operation (e.g. Split-Extraction, Right- or Left Dislocation, Topicalization, Scrambling or Contrast Focus) before Spell-out. Rather, the complex of Clitics builds a block similar to Clitic Cluster at PF (cf. Kosta & Zimmerling 2013, Zimmerling & Kosta 2013, Uhlířová, Kosta & Veselovská 2018).

Since Causatives are *v*P Phases, they are licensed for feature inheritance and/or for feature transmission.

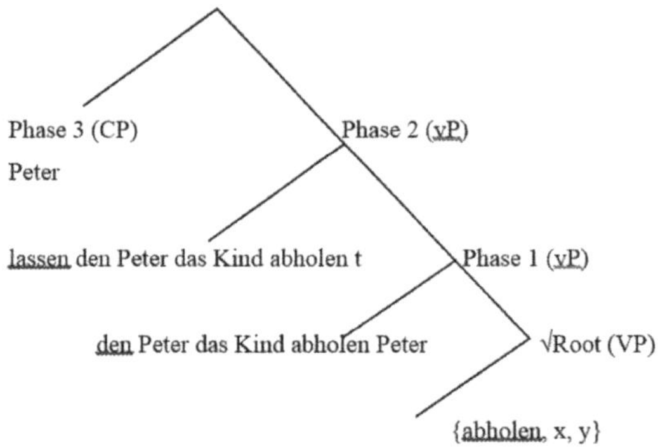

Causatives and Phasehood

In contrast, control constructions are not phases, so they are not licensed for feature transfer or feature inheritance. The contrast between the permission to inherit the case-characteristics of the clitic pronouns in both variants Dat > Acc and Acc > Dat in Causative Phases, and not to inherit them in control infinitives is therefore logically derived from the phase-like or non-phasal nature of both constructions.

To my mind, there is, so far, no alternative for this kind of analysis. There are problems if we take Case as the trigger for CC because Case is not a trigger for Movement at all since Chomsky (2000–2008), and we reject the kind of analysis established by Pesetsky and Torrego (2007) for independent reasons, too. There are some further perspectives in this take of Phase-hood parametrization. We believe that there is a good reason to argue that at least some problems of freezing effects (remnant movement, improper movement and long distance scrambling but also Topicalization, Wh-Movement and Scrambling, cf. Kosta, in prep.) can be explained by the theory of Phase hood and locality. If in a sentence an Operation of displacement has taken place, it cannot be moved out of this already moved phase once again because the Labels which triggered this movement are deleted after the new phase has been reached (and the information about this is canceled as soon as the Phase has been established). Alternatively, the Phrase out of which a movement should take place is not a Phase at all (thus establishing the structural context of so-called Islands for movement). The first scenario can be observed in case of freezing when a moved Phrase has reached a Phase and is thus not accessible for further computation due to (II) PIC. Consider the following examples: the first one in (26a) in which Topicalization of a VP out of a causative VoiceP is very bad, and second, a wh-Movement after VP Fronting out of causative VoiceP is ungrammatical.

(26) a. ? [VP den Peter abholen t]Top [VoiceP ließ Paul [VP den Peter abholen das Kind]]!
b. *Was/*Wen [VP den PÉter abholen t] Top Top [VoiceP ließ Paul [VP__ das Kind]]?

References

Alexiadou, Artemis, Hagit Borer and Florian Schäfer (eds.). 2014. *The Syntax of Roots and the Roots of Syntax*. Oxford: (Oxford Studies in Theoretical Linguistics 51).

Alexiadou, Artemis and Florian Schäfer. 2014. "Towards a Non-uniform Analysis of Naturally Reflexive Verbs." *Proceedings of WCCFL* 31, 1–10, ed. R. E. Santana-LaBarge.

Alexiadou, Artemis, Berit Gehrke, and Florian Schäfer. 2014. "The argument structure of adjectival participles revisited." In *Lingua* 149, 118–138.

Babby, Len. 2002. "Argument Suppression and Case in Russian Derived Nominals." In Kosta, Peter and Jens Frasek (eds.), *Current Approaches to Formal Slavic Linguistics. Contributions of the Second European Conference on Formal Description of Slavic Languages – FDSL II held at Potsdam University,* November 20–22. 1997. Frankfurt am Main etc.: Peter Lang (Linguistik Interational 9), 9–21.

Baker, Mark. 1985. "The Mirror Principle and morphosyntactic explanation." In *Linguistic Inquiry* 16, 373–415.

Baker, Marl. 1988. *Incorporation*. Chicago: Chicago University Press.

Baker, Mark. 2002. "Building and merging, not checking: the nonexistence of (Aux)-SVO languages." In *Linguistic Inquiry* 33, 321–328.

Baker, Mark C. 2008. *The Syntax of Agreement and Concord*. Cambridge: Cambridge University Press.

Baker, Mark, Kyle Johnson and Ian Roberts. 1989. "Passive Arguments Raised." In *Linguistic Inquiry* 20, 219–252. [cited as BJR 1989].

Belletti, Adriana and Luigi Rizzi. 1988. "Psych verbs and θ-theory." In *Natural Language and Linguistic Theory* 6, 291–352.

Bresnan, Joan and Sam Mchombo. 1995. "The lexical integrity principle: evidence from Bantu." In *Natural Language and Linguistic Theory*, 13, 181–254.

Cinque, Guglielmo. 1999. *Adverbs and Functional Heads*. Oxford: Oxford University Press.

Cinque, Guglielmo. 2006. *Restructuring and Functional heads. The Cartography of Syntactic Structure*. Vol. 4, Oxford: Oxford University Press.

Clark, Eve V. 2009. *First Language Acquisition*. Second Edition. Cambridge: Cambridge University Press.

Chierchia, Gennaro. 1989. "A Semantics for Unaccusatives and its Syntactic Consequences." Unpublished Ms. Cornell University, Ithaca, NY.

Chomsky, Noam. 1970. "Remarks on nominalisation." In Roderick A. Jacobs and Peter S. Rosenbaum (eds.), *Readings in English Transformational Grammar*. Waltham, MA: Ginn, 184–221.

Chomsky, Noam. 1981. *Lectures on Government and Binding. The Pisa Lectures*. Dordrecht – Holland: Foris Publications (Studies in Generative Grammar 9).

Chomsky, Noam. 2005. "Three factors in language design." In *Linguistic Inquiry*, 36 (1), 1–22.

Chomsky, Noam. 2000. "Minimalist Inquiries: The Framework." In Roger Martin, David Michaels and Juan Uriagereka (eds.), *Step by Step: Essays on Minimalism in Honor of Howard Lasnik*, Cambridge, MA, 89–155.

Chomsky, Noam. 2001. "Derivation by Phase." In: Kenstowicz, Michael J. (ed.), *Ken Hale. A Life in Language*. Cambridge, MA, 1–52.

Chomsky, Noam. 2004. "Beyond Explanatory Adequacy." In Adriana Belletti (ed.), *Structures and Beyond*, Oxford, OUP, 104–131.

Chomsky, Noam. 2005a. *On Phases*. Ms. MIT.

Chomsky, Noam. 2005b. "Three Factors in Language Design." In *Linguistic Inquiry*, Volume 36, Number 1, Winter 2005 1–22.

Chomsky, Noam. 2007. "Approaching UG from below." Ms. MIT.

Chomsky, Noam. 2009. "Opening Remarks." In Massimo Piattelli-Palmarini, Juan Uriagereka and Pello Salaburu (eds.), *Of Minds and Language: The Basque Country Encounter with Noam Chomsky*. Oxford: Oxford.

Chomsky, Noam. 1995. *The Minimalist Program*. Cambridge, MA University Press, 13–43.

Chomsky, Noam. 2020. "Minimal Computation and the Architecture of Language." In this volume Radeva-Bork, Teodora and Kosta, Peter (eds.), *Current Developments in Slavic Linguistics*. University of Potsdam, December 2nd–4th 2015. Frankfurt am Main: Peter Lang Edition 2020, 13–23.

Cinque, Guglielmo. 1990. *Types of Ā-Dependencies*. Cambridge, Mass.: The MIT Press (LIM 17.).

Cinque, Guglielmo 1999. *Adverbs and Functional Heads: A Crosslinguistic Perspective*. New York 1999 (Oxford studies in comparative syntax).

Collins, Guglielmo 2002. "Eliminating Labels." In Samuel D. Epstein and T. Daniel Seely (eds.). *Derivation and Explanation in the Minimalist Program*. Oxford: Blackwell, 65–89.

Croft, William. 1990. *Typology and Universals*. Cambridge: Cambridge University Press. (Cambridge Text books in Linguistics).

Di Sciullo, Anna Maria and Boeckx, Cedric (eds.). 2011. *The Biolinguistic Enterprise. New Perspectives on the Evolution and Nature of Human Language Faculty*. Oxford: Oxford University Press.

Epstein, Samuel David. 1999. "Un-Principled Syntax and the Derivation of Syntactic Relations." In Epstein, Samuel David and Norbert Hornstein (eds.), *Working Minimalism*. Cambridge, MA. MIT Press, 317–345.

Evans, Nicholas and Stephen C. Levinson. 2009. "The myth of language universals: Language diversity and its importance for cognitive science." In *Behavioral and Brain Sciences* 32, 429–492.

Fanselow, Gisbert. 1987. *Konfigurationalität. Untersuchungen zur Universalgrammatik am Beispiel des Deutschen*. Tübingen: Narr.

Fanselow, Gisbert. 1988. "German Word Order and Universal Grammar." In Reyle, Uwe and Christian Rohrer (eds.), *Natural Language Parsing and Linguistic Theories*. Dordrecht: Reidel, 317–355.

Folli, Raffaella and Harley, Heidi. 2006. "Benefactives aren't Goals in Italian." In *Romance Languages and Linguistic Theory 2004*, ed. by Jenny Doetjes and Paz Gonzales. Amsterdam: John Benjamins, 121–142.

Franks, Steven L. 2017. *Syntax and Spell-Out in Slavic*. Bloomington: Indiana University (Slavica Publishers).

Franks, Steven L. 2018. "Person Feature Geometry and Pronominal Clitic Ordering Preferences." *Zeitschrift für Slawistik*, 63(4): 627–661.

Haider, Hubert. 1993. *Deutsche Syntax-Generativ*. Tübingen: Narr.

Harley, Heidi. 2006. "On the Causative Construction." // *https://ling.auf.net/lingbuzz/000433=*

Harley, Heidi. 2008. "On the Causative Construction." In *The Oxford Handbook of Japanese Linguistics*, edited by Shigeru Miyagawa. Oxford, New York: Oxford University Press. Print Publication Date: Nov 2008.

Kayne, Richard S. 2004. "Prepositions as Probes." In Belletti, Adriana (ed.), *Structures and Beyond. The Cartography of Syntactic Structures*, Volume 3. Oxford University Press, New York, 192–222.

Kayne, Richard S. 2005. "Prepositions as Probes." In Kayne, Richard S. (2005), *Movement and Silence*. Oxford University Press, New York, 85–104.

Kosta, Peter. 2002. "Minimalism and Free Constituent Order (in Russian as Compared to German)." In Kosta, Peter and Jens Frasek (eds.), *Current Approaches to Formal Slavic Linguistics (Linguistik International. Band 9)*. Frankfurt am Main, Berlin, Bern, Bruxelles, New York, Oxford, Wien: Peter Lang, 253–272.

Kosta, Peter. 2006. "On free word order phenomena in Czech as compared to German: Is Clause Internal Scrambling A-movement, A-Bar-Movement or Is It Base Generated?" In *Zeitschrift für Slawistik* 51 (3), 306–321.

Kosta, Peter and Jens Frasek. 2004. "Neakuzativita (ergativita) vs. neergativita v češtině, polštině a jiných slovanských jazycích na rozhraní morfologie a syntaxe." In Hladká Zdeňka and Karlík Petr, *Čeština - univerzália a specifika 5*, Praha: Nakladatelství Lidové noviny, 172–194 [= Unaccusativity (Ergativity) vs. Unergativity in Czech, Polish and Some Other Slavic Languages at the Morpho-Syntactic Interface].

Kosta, Peter. 2010. "Causatives and Anti-Causatives, Unaccusatives and Unergatives: Or How Big is the Contribution of the Lexicon to Syntax." In Aleš Bičan, Jan Klaška, Petra Macurová, Jana Zmrzlíková (eds.), *Karlík a továrna na lingvistiku. Prof. Petru Karlíkovi k šedesátým narozeninám*. Brno: Masarykova univerzita, 230–273.

Kosta, Peter. 2011. "Causatives and Anti-Causatives, Unaccusatives and Unergatives: Or how big is the contribution of the lexicon to syntax?" In Kosta, Peter and Schürcks, Lilia (eds.), *Formalization of Grammar in Slavic Languages. Contributions of the Eighth International Conference on Formal Description of Slavic Languages-FDSL VIII 2009*. University of Potsdam, December 2–5, 2009. Frankfurt am Main etc.: Peter Lang (Potsdam Linguistic Investigations. Vol. /Bd. 6), 235–295.

Kosta, Peter and Diego Krivochen. 2012. "Some Thoughts on Language Diversity, UG and the Importance of Language Typology: Scrambling and Non-Monotonic Merge of Adjuncts and Specifiers in Czech and German." In *ZfSl* 57(4), 377–407.

Kosta, Peter and Anton Zimmerling. 2013. "Slavic Clitics Systems in a Typological Perspective." In Lilia Schürcks, Anastasia Giannakidou, Urtzi Etxeberria (eds.), *Nominal Constructions: Slavic and Beyond*. Berlin, New York: de Gruyter (Studies in generative grammar SGG 116), 439–486.

Kosta, Peter. 2015. "On the Causative/Anti-Causative Alternation as Principle of Affix Ordering in the Light of the Mirror Principle, the Lexical Integrity Principle and the Distributed Morphology." In *Zeitschrift für Slawistik* 60(4): 570–612.

Kosta, Peter. (In prep.). *The Syntax of Meaning and the Meaning of Syntax: Minimal Computations and Maximal Derivations in a Label-/Phase-Driven Generative Grammar of Radical Minimalism*. To appear in *Potsdam Linguistic Investigations*. 2020.

Krivochen, Diego and Peter Kosta. 2013. *Eliminating Empty Categories: A Radically Minimalist View on their Ontology and Justification*. Frankfurt am Main: Peter Lang (Potsdam Linguistic Investigations, Vol. 11).

Krivochen, Diego. 2014. "(Anti-)Causativity and the Morpho-Phonology-Semantics Tension." In *Semantics-Syntax Interface*, 1(2), 82–117.

Müller, Gereon. 2014. *Syntactic Buffers: A Local–Derivational Approach to Improper Movement, Remnant Movement, and Resumptive Movement*. Institut für Linguistik Universität Leipzig (LA 91).

Pylkkänen, Liina. 2002. "Introducing Arguments." MIT, Mass. PhD diss. = 2008.

Pesetsky, David and Esther Torrego. 2001. "T-to-C movement: causes and consequences." In Michael Kenstowicz (ed.), *Ken Hale: a life in language*. Cambridge, Mass.: MIT Press, 355–426.

Pesetsky, David and Esther Torrego. 2004. "Tense, case, and the nature of syntactic categories." In Jacqueline Gueron and Jacqueline Lecarme (eds.), *The syntax of time*. Cambridge, Mass.: MIT Press.

Pesetsky, David and Esther Torrego. 2007. "The Syntax of Valuation and the Interpretability of Features." In Simin Karimi, Vida Samiian and Wendy K. Wilkins (eds.), *Phrasal and clausal architecture*. Amsterdam: John Benjamins, 262–294.

Rizzi, Luigi. 1990. *Relativized Minimality*, MIT Press, Cambridge Mass, 147.

Rizzi, Luigi. 1997a. "The Fine Structure of the Left Periphery." In Liliane Haegeman (ed.), *Elements of Grammar*. Dordrecht: Kluwer, 281–337.

Rizzi, Luigi. 1997b. "A Parametric Approach to Comparative Syntax." In Lilliane Haegeman (ed.), *The New Comparative Syntax*. London: Longman, 95–124.

Uhlířová, Ludmila, Peter Kosta and Ludmila Veselovská. 2018. "Klitikon." In *Nový encyklopedický slovník češtiny online* (https://www.czechency.org/slovnik/KLITIKON).

Zimmerling, Anton and Peter Kosta. 2013. "Slavic clitics: a typology." In *STUF*, Akademie Verlag, 66 (2), 178–214.

Bulgarian

Elena Dimova, Christine Tellier

On Multiple Free Relatives that are not

1. Introduction

As is well known, Slavic languages display multiple Wh-fronting in interrogatives, as shown in (1) from Bulgarian:

(1) Koj kakvo može da vzeme?
who what can to take
'Who can take what?'

Given this, we are led to wonder whether these languages also allow multiple Wh relative clauses. Though this has never, to our knowledge, been attested in headed relatives, it has sometimes been claimed to occur in free relatives. One such example is given in (2), from Rudin (2007):

(2) Vzemajte koj kakvoto može.
take-imp. who what can
'Let everyone take what(ever) they can.'

It is not obvious, however, that such examples instantiate genuine multiple free relatives (MFRs). In keeping with the traditional view, we assume that free relatives (FRs) in general (as in English *I ate what you cooked*) have the following central characteristics. First, they contain a Wh-phrase in the initial position of the syntactic constituent following the verb (leaving aside for the time being the category of this constituent). Secondly, the fronted Wh-phrase satisfies the s/c-selectional requirements of both the main verb and the embedded verb, a property known as 'matching'. A MFR, then, would be defined as a relative containing two Wh-phrases, both of which satisfy the first condition in languages that allow multiple Wh-fronting, and the second condition in any language.[1]

In this paper, we argue that the bracketed constituent in (2) is indeed a FR in the sense just defined, but not a MFR. We call such constructions Pseudo

1 In our view, cases where a FR is embedded within another FR, such as (i) below, from Donati & Cecchetto (2011:545), are not multiple free relatives in the sense intended.

(i) I finally read [what you wrote about [what I claimed in that article]].

Multiple Free Relatives (PMFRs). We show that in apparent cases of multiple Wh free relatives in Bulgarian, the first Wh constituent in the linear sequence (call it Wh1) has topic-like properties. The second Wh constituent (Wh2) is invariably the one that fulfills the categorial, case-matching and selectional requirements of the main and the embedded verb. The facts adduced here bear on the long-debated issue of the categorial status (CP, DP, XP) of free relatives in general, and on the more recent question of labeling of such constructions. Another consequence of our analysis concerns the problem of non-local selection: why is the second Wh-phrase selected by the verb over the first one? We propose that the overt morphological properties of Wh-phrases in Bulgarian may constitute an important clue towards an answer to these questions.

2. Pseudo multiple free relatives

In this section, we examine the behavior of each Wh-phrase in PMFRs. We start by showing that the first Wh constituent in PMFRs has topic-like properties, while the second one (Wh2) does not. The arguments in favor of this claim rest on the interpretation of Wh1, on the possibility of resumption by a clitic and on restrictions on the type of Wh-constituents that can occupy the Wh1 position. Next, we show that the second Wh-constituent (Wh2) is the one that fulfills the categorial, selectional and Case requirements of both the main and the embedded verb.

2.1. Wh1 has topic-like properties

2.1.1. Interpretation

The idea that Wh-phrases can act as Topics is not new; this claim has been made for multiple Wh-interrogatives in Bulgarian (see, e.g. Jaeger 2004, Krapova & Cinque 2008, Dimova 2012). One relevant observation in this regard concerns the interpretation of the first Wh-phrase in multiple Wh-interrogatives. As Kiss (1993) has pointed out, the wider scope Wh-operator in multiple Wh-questions is interpreted as a "distributive universal quantifier, a synonym of *each*". In the Hungarian example (3), for instance, the target of the first Wh-phrase is a set of things known to the speaker, hence the interpretation given in parentheses:

(3) Mit kinek hozott János? (Kiss 1993: 98)
what-ACC who-DAT brought John
'For whom did John bring what?'
(For each thing, who did John bring it for?)

The same is true for multiple Wh-questions in Bulgarian. (4a) is possible when the set of things given is salient in the context or situation (for instance, we know that there are two presents) and the speaker wants the listener to specify to whom he/she will give each of these things. That is, the target of interrogation is the indirect object. Similarly, (4b) is only possible if the set of persons is salient and the speaker wants to know about each person what the listener will offer to him/her.

(4) a. Kakvo na kogo šte dadeš?
what-ACC who-DAT will give-2p.sg.
'To whom will you give what?'
(For each thing, who will you give it to?)
b. Na kogo kakvo šte dadeš?
who-DAT what-ACC will give-2p.sg.
'What will you give to whom?'
(For each person, what will you give to him?)

These observations relate to topicalizability in the following way. As Krifka (2001) has remarked, quantifiers based on *each* presuppose a set of discourse-salient entities, hence are naturally topical. Note that, as expected, quantified DPs with *each* can occur in Topic positions in Bulgarian, as shown in (5):

(5) Vsjaka statija sâm ja čela dva pâti.
each article aux. it-cl. read two times
'As for each article, I have read it twice.'

Turning now to PMFRs, we observe that the first Wh-constituent (*koj(to))* is also interpreted as a universally quantified expression. This is true in (2), and also in (6) below, as the translation indicates:

(6) Jam koj(to) kakvoto gotvi. (Dimova 2014)
eat-1sg. who what cook-3sg.
'I eat what each person/everyone cooks.'

2.1.2. *Resumption*

In Bulgarian, clitics can resume dislocated Topic constituents (Krapova 2002, Franks & Rudin 2005), see (7a), although resumption of topicalized constituents is not obligatory (cf. (7b)).

(7) a. [$_{TOP}$ Na Ivan] mu dadoh knigata. CLLD-Topic
to Ivan him-cl. gave-1sg. book-the
'As for (to) Ivan, I gave the book to him.'
b. [$_{TOP}$ Na Ivan] dadoh knigata. Clitic-less Topic
to Ivan gave-1sg. book-the
'As for (to) Ivan, I gave the book.'

Crucially, however, non-Topic constituents cannot be resumed by a clitic, cf. (8):

(8) [$_{FOC}$ NA IVAN] (*mu) dadoh knigata.
to Ivan him-cl. gave-1sg. book-the
'TO IVAN, I gave the book.' (not to Maria)

Now, in PMFRs, the first constituent (Wh1) can be resumed by a clitic, but the second one (Wh2) cannot be:

(9) a. Vojnicite otivat kogo(to) kâdeto go izpratjat.
soldiers go-3pl. whom where him send-3pl.
'The soldiers go where they send each of them.'
b. Pitaše kâde(to) kogoto (*go) vidi.
asked-3sg where whom him see
'He asked whoever in every place he saw (him).'

This suggests that Wh1 in these examples – and only Wh1 – has Topic-like properties.

2.1.3. Non-topicalizable constituents

As a rule, topicalization is restricted to constituents that are referential or that correspond to a salient entity in the discourse. Non-referential constituents such as *sto kilograma* 'one hundred kilograms' in (10) cannot be topicalized:

(10) *Mislja sto kilograma če Ivan teži.
think-1sg. one hundred kilograms that Ivan weighs
'I think, 100 kilos, Ivan weighs.'

As for Wh-phrases, those that are non-referential, like *kakto* 'how', can be fronted in both questions and relatives (including FRs, cf. (11a)). Strikingly, however, such Wh-phrases cannot occupy the Wh1 position, as shown in (11b):

(11) a. Jam sushi kâde(to) kakto go napravjat.
eat-1sg. sushi where how it-cl. make-3pl.
'I eat sushi at each place however they make it.'

b.	*Jam	sushi	kakto	kâdeto	go	napravjat.
	eat-1sg.	sushi	how	where	it-cl.	make-3pl.

This supports the view that the first Wh phrase in PMFRs indeed functions as a Topic.

2.2. Wh2 satisfies the Matching requirement

As pointed out in Dimova (2014), whenever a FR displays two fronted Wh constituents, it is systematically the second one that fulfills the categorial, case-matching and selectional requirements of both the main and the embedded predicate. This is shown in (12):

(12)	a.	Sâbrahme	na	kogo(to)	kakvoto	bjaha	izpratili.
		gathered-1pl.	to	whom	what	aux.	sent-3pl.
		'We gathered what they sent to everyone.'					
	b.	*Sâbrahme	kakvo(to) na	kogoto		bjaha	izpratili.
		gathered-1pl.	what to	whom		aux.	sent-3p.

The verb *sâbrahme* c-selects a DP complement. As (12b) illustrates, this DP cannot occupy the first position (Wh1) in the string of Wh-phrases. Note also that the particle *-to*, which occurs in Wh-relative clauses in Bulgarian, is obligatory only on Wh2. We return in section 4 to the role the particle *-to* plays in our analysis.

We thus conclude that the constructions under study are not MFRs. They are simple FRs, where the "head" of the free relative – the constituent selected by both the main and the embedded verb – is the second Wh-phrase, and where the first Wh phrase is acting as a Topic.

Before sketching an analysis of Bulgarian PMFRs, we must lay out the approach to FRs we will be adopting. This is the object of the next section.

3. The category of FRs

The dual properties of FRs have long been recognized and have stimulated a lively debate over the last four decades or so. Regarding their internal structure, FRs resemble interrogative CPs, as they involve Wh-movement. This is why, among other reasons, many scholars have treated them as bare CPs: see for instance Rooryck (1994), Jacobson (1995), van Riemsdijk (2006), Caponigro (2003), Šimík (2010). On the other hand, FRs differ from interrogative CPs in several ways, for instance they display matching effects that are unobserved in embedded interrogatives, and they have the distribution of DPs (or of other categories such as PPs or AdvPs). This has prompted a number of researchers to treat them as non-bare CPs, that is, as CPs modifying a "head". Variations of this analysis bear on the position of the Wh-constituent (outside CP or in Spec,CP) and the nature of the head (it is either the Wh-phrase itself or another head – for instance a null nominal): see Bresnan & Grimshaw (1978), Groos & van Riemsdijk (1981), Larson (1987), Citko & Gračanin-Yuksek (2016), among many others.

The crux of the matter is that internal merge of the Wh-constituent in FRs is very similar to that in Wh-questions, yet in FRs, the merged Wh determines the categorial and distributional properties of the syntactic object. In recent years, this has given rise to a number of proposals that we might loosely group under the "Move and Project" class (see, e.g. Iatridou, Anagnostopoulou & Izvorski 2001, Donati 2006, Citko 2008, Donati and Cecchetto 2011 and Ott 2011). In some of these proposals, the FR is a CP to start with, but upon internal merge of the Wh-constituent to CP, the Wh-constituent, is allowed to project, relabeling CP. The question is then the following: what allows (or rather, forces) the Wh-phrase to project in FRs, but prevents it in Wh-questions? For Donati (2006) and Donati and Cecchetto (2011), the difference lies in the nature of the fronted Wh: while it may be phrasal in interrogatives, it must be bare in FRs.[2] This is illustrated by the contrast in (13):

(13) a. I wonder what book you read.
b. *I read what book you read.
c. I read what you read.

One problem with this analysis, however, is that it does not carry over straightforwardly to Bulgarian, where the counterpart of (13b) is well-formed:[3]

(14) Četa kojato kniga četeš.
read-1sg which book read-2sg.
'I read the book that you read.'

One proposal consistent with the Bulgarian data is Ott's (2011) phase-based analysis, whereby a fronted Wh-phrase in FRs will project, irrespective of its

2 These authors conclude that in FRs, the merged Wh can only be a head. Under a labeling algorithm such as proposed by Chomsky (2008), the syntactic object formed by the merger of a head with a phrase receives the label of the head; this results in "relabeling" FRs like (13c) as DPs.

3 This is also true in examples like *I read whatever book you read*; however, Donati (2006), and Donati & Cecchetto (2011) assimilate cases with *-ever* to headed relatives.

makeup and category. Ott's analysis builds on the observation that the C head (C_{FR}) in FRs differs from the C in interrogatives; in particular, C_{FR} is not selected and does not have interpretable features (i.e. it lacks Force, or sentence type). Under this view, the difference between embedded interrogatives and FRs, both CPs at the point of internal merge of the Wh-phrase, is that C_{FR}, owing to its lack of interpretable features, must transfer (spell-out) along with TP. This is illustrated in (15a) for interrogatives and (16b,c) for FRs, transferred material greyed out:

(15) a. I [$_{vP}$ wonder [$_{CP}$ **what**$_i$ **C**$_Q$ [$_{TP}$ you T wrote t$_i$]]]
b. I [$_{vP}$ read [$_{CP}$ **what**$_i$ C$_{FR}$ [$_{TP}$ you T wrote t$_i$]]]
c. I [$_{vP}$ read [$_{DP}$ **what**$_i$ C$_{FR}$ [$_{TP}$ you T wrote t$_i$]]]

As C_{FR} is transferred in FRs (15b), the CP label is lost. On the next cycle, this leaves the nominal Wh-phrase in (15c) as the only visible element at the next phase. The matrix predicate selects the DP. This provides a natural explanation of the apparently conflicting nature of FRs, where the Wh-phrase appears to be "both internal to the FR […] and external to it […]: it is both, but at different derivational stages." (Ott 2011: 186)

Ott's analysis handles the fact that FRs are not limited to DPs; they can also have the distribution of AdvPs or PPs.[4] Whatever the category of the fronted Wh-phrase, it will determine that of the FR. However, Ott's account does not straightforwardly accommodate the Bulgarian PMFRs described at the outset of this paper. Indeed, at the point where C_{FR} is transferred, there remain two visible constituents at the next phase, as illustrated in (16):

(16) a. [$_{vP}$ sâbrahme [$_{CP}$ **na kogo(to)**$_k$ **kakvoto**$_i$ C$_{FR}$ [$_{TP}$ bjaha izpratili t$_i$ t$_k$]]]
b. *[$_{vP}$ sâbrahme [$_{CP}$ **kakvo(to)**$_k$ **na kogoto**$_i$ C$_{FR}$ [$_{TP}$ bjaha izpratili t$_k$ t$_i$]]]

Both constituents could in principle determine the category of the FR, yet invariably only the second one in the linear sequence does. This would suggest perhaps that timing is involved in such labeling, i.e. that a C_{FR}-headed object be labeled as soon as a Wh-phrase internally merges with it. Be that as it may, we will sketch a different analysis that does not rely on phases or on the transfer of C_{FR} along with TP, but that builds instead on c-selection and on the crucial role of the particle *-to* in Bulgarian.

---

4 See, e.g. Bresnan & Grimshaw 1978: 335–36, and *pace* Larson 1987, Donati & Cecchetto 2011.

4. The role of *–to*

One striking fact about Bulgarian concerns the occurrence of the particle *-to*, which can be affixed to Wh-words in certain contexts. This particle is precluded in Wh-questions, but it is obligatory in all relatives (headed, free, correlatives), as well as equatives and comparatives.[5] Historically, invariant *-to* originates from a demonstrative, just as the definite article does. It has been analyzed as a definiteness marker/article, a modal element, a relative complementizer or a nominalizer.[6] Here, we take the view that *-to* is affixed to a Wh-word in the lexicon and that it is not definite; rather, its function is to turn a Wh-word with interrogative content into a non-interrogative operator. Our contention is that Bulgarian overtly marks a property shared by relatives in other languages, namely that the Wh-phrase is non-interrogative.

Let us assume that *-to* in Bulgarian endows the Wh-word with a [REL] feature that must be checked with a C head bearing the same feature. The [REL] feature signals that the constituent must enter into a predicative relation with either a nominal head (for headed relatives) or a correlate (for correlatives). In other words, a constituent labeled REL can be a predicate, but cannot be selected as an argument. In accordance with Chomsky's (2013:45) labeling algorithm, the feature [REL] (prominent and shared) will be selected as the label of the syntactic object formed by merger of the Wh-*to* constituent and CP. At the point of Wh-merge, free and headed relatives are indistinguishable and are labeled REL, as (17) illustrates:

(17) Merge Wh: $[_{REL}$ Wh-to $[_{CP}$ $C_{REL}]]$

If, however, the constituent labeled REL is merged with V, the predication relation cannot obtain. This will force relabeling of the syntactic object in accordance with the c-selectional restrictions of the verb. The label of the constituent is then determined by the Wh-phrase bearing both the prominent [REL] feature and the categorial label consistent with the c-selectional requirements of the verb.

Let us now return to PMFRs, and see how labeling is effected in such cases.

---

5 The particle *-to* is optional on Wh-topics, where it appears to convey a distributional meaning. We leave this usage aside, concentrating on obligatory *-to*, which we take to be a distinct particle.

6 For an extensive discussion on *–to*, see Franks and Rudin (2015).

5. Labeling in PMFRs

Consider the derivation of a PMFR. First, a Wh-constituent merges with CP. As this constituent bears the feature [REL], which is prominent and shared with C_{REL}, it is the label of the syntactic object (18a,b). Next, another Wh (with topic-like properties) merges to the REL syntactic object, yielding the configuration in (18c,d):

(18) a. **kakvoto**$_i$ [C_{REL} bjaha izpratili t_i na kogo(to)]
b. [$_{REL}$ kakvoto$_i$ [C_{REL} bjaha izpratili t_i na kogo(to)]
c. **na kogo(to)**$_k$ [$_{REL}$ kakvoto$_i$ bjaha izpratili t_i t_k]
d. [$_\alpha$ na kogo(to)$_k$ [$_{REL}$ kakvoto$_i$ bjaha izpratili t_i t_k]]

Since there is no prominent feature shared by the Wh-phrase *na kogo(to)* and the REL constituent, the resulting syntactic object remains unlabeled, as signalled by the use of α in (18d). We may assume that unlabeled constituents are transparent for the purposes of c-selection: in effect, upon merger of V, the unlabeled constituent is invisible. Thus, V invariably c-selects the only visible constituent in the structure, which is the constituent labeled REL in (18d). This idea embodies the observation that adjuncts and topic constituents are transparent for the purposes of c-selection (see e.g. Shlonsky 2006, Hornstein 2009).

6. Conclusion

In this paper, we have argued that apparent cases of multiple free relatives in Bulgarian are in fact simple free relatives with one Wh-constituent acting as a Topic. Building on the morphological properties of Wh-constituents in relative clauses (specifically, the obligatory affixation of the particle *-to*), we have sketched an analysis of free relative formation and labeling, which also accounts for the fact that an intervening Topic Wh-constituent is transparent to the phenomenon of c-selection and matching.

References

Bresnan, Joan and Jane Grimshaw. 1978. "The Syntax of Free Relatives in English." *Linguistic Inquiry* 9, 331–391.

Caponigro, Ivano. 2003. "Free Not to Ask: On the Semantics of Free Relatives and Wh-Words Cross-linguistically." PhD thesis, University of California, Los Angeles.

Chomsky, Noam. 2008. "On phases." In *Foundational issues in linguistic theory: Essays in honor of Jean-Roger Vergnaud*, Robert Freidin, Carlos P. Otero and Maria Luisa Zubizarreta (eds.). Cambridge, MA: MIT Press, 133–166.

Chomsky, Noam. 2013. "Problems of projection." *Lingua* 130: 33–49.

Citko, Barbara. 2008. "Missing Labels." *Lingua* 118: 907–944.

Citko, Barbara and Martina Gračanin-Yuksek. 2016. "Multiple (coordinated) (free) relatives." *Natural Language and Linguistic Theory* 34:2, 393–427.

Dimova, Elena. 2012. "Bulgarian Multiple Wh-ordering, Specificity and Superiority." *Paper presented at the 7th Annual Meeting of Slavic Linguistics Society*, University of Kansas, Lawrence.

Dimova, Elena. 2014. "A New Look at Multiple Free Relatives: Evidence from Bulgarian." *Paper presented at the 9th annual meeting of the Slavic Linguistics Society*, University of Washington, Seattle.

Donati, Caterina. 2006. "On wh-head movement." In *Wh-movement: Moving on*, Lisa Lai-Shen Cheng and Norbert Corver (eds.), Cambridge, MA: MIT Press, 21–46.

Donati, Caterina and Carlo Cecchetto. 2011. "Relabeling Heads: A unified account for relativization." *Linguistic Inquiry* 42: 519–560.

Franks, Steven and Catherine Rudin. 2005. "Bulgarian clitics as K^0 Heads." In *Formal Approaches to Slavic Linguistics: The South Carolina Meeting*, Steven Franks, Frank Gladney and Mila Tasseva-Kurktchieva (eds.), Michigan Slavic Publications, Ann Arbor, 106–118.

Franks, Steven and Catherine Rudin. 2015. "Invariant –to in Bulgarian." In *Studies in Accentology and Slavic Linguistics in Honor of Ronald F. Feldstein*, Miriam Shager, Edna Andrews, George Fowler and Steven Franks (eds.), Bloomington, IN: Slavica Publishers, 99–136.

Groos, Anneke and Henk van Riemsdijk. 1981. "Matching Effects in Free Relatives: A Parameter of Core Grammar." In *Theory of Markedness in Generative Grammar*, Adriana Belletti, Luciana Brandi and Luigi Rizzi (eds.), Scuola Normale Superiore, Pisa, 171–216.

Hornstein, Norbert. 2009. *A Theory of Syntax*. Cambridge: CUP.

Iatridou, Sabine, Elena Anagnostopoulou and Roumyana Izvorski. 2001. "Observations about the Form and Meaning of the Perfect." In *Ken Hale: A Life in Language*, Michael Kenstowicz (eds.) Cambridge, MA: MIT Press, 189–238.

Jacobson, Pauline. 1995. "On the quantificational force of English free relatives." In *Quantification in Natural Languages*, Elke Bach, Eloise Jelinek, Angelika Kratzer and Barbara Partee (eds.), Dordrecht: Kluwer, 451–486.

Jaeger, Florian T. 2004. "Topicality and Superiority in Bulgarian wh-questions." In *Formal Approaches to Slavic Linguistics: The Ottawa Meeting. 2003*, Olga Arnaudova, Wayles Browne, Maria-Luisa Rivero and Danijela Stojanović (eds.), Ann Arbor, Mich.: Michigan Slavic Publications, 207–228.

Kiss, Katalin É. 1993. "Wh-movement and Specificity." *Natural Language and Linguistic Theory* 11: 85–120.

Krapova, Iliyana. 2002. "On the left periphery of the Bulgarian sentence." *University of Venice Working Papers in Linguistics* 12: 107–128.

Krapova, Iliyana and Guglielmo Cinque. 2008. "On the Order of Wh-Phrases in Bulgarian Multiple wh-Fronting." In *Formal Description of Slavic Languages: The Fifth Conference, Leipzig 2003*, Gerhild Zybatow, Luka Szucsich, Uwe Junghanns and Roland Meyer (eds.), Frankfurt am Mein, Peter Lang, 318–336.

Krifka, Manfred. 2001. "Quantifying into question acts." *Natural Language Semantics* 9, 1–40.

Larson, Richard K. 1987. ""Missing prepositions" and the analysis of English free relative clauses." *Linguistic Inquiry* 18: 239–266.

Ott, Dennis. 2011. "A note on Free Relative Clauses in the Theory of Phases." *Linguistic Inquiry* 42:1, 183–192.

Riemsdijk, Henk C. van. 2006. "Free Relatives." In *The Blackwell Companion to Syntax Vol. II*, Martin Everaert and Henk van Riemsdijk (eds.), Oxford: Blackwell, 338–382.

Rooryck, Johan. 1994. "Generalized Transformations and the Wh-Cycle: Free Relatives as Bare Wh-CPs." In *Minimalism and Kayne's Asymmetry Hypothesis*, Jan-Wouter Zwart (ed.), Groningen: Groningen University, 195–208.

Rudin, Catherine. 2007. "Multiple Wh relatives in Slavic." In *Formal approaches to Slavic Linguistics*, Richard Compton, Magdalena Goledzinowska and Ulyana Savchenko (eds.). Ann Arbor: Michigan Slavic Publications, 282–307.

Shlonsky, Ur. 2006. "Projection étendue et cartographie de SC." *Nouveaux cahiers de linguistique française* 27, 83–93.

Šimík, Radek. 2010. "Free relatives at the interface." In *Structure preserved: studies in syntax for Jan Koster*. Jan-Wouter Zwart and Mark De Vries (eds.), Amsterdam/Philadelphia: John Benjamins, 321–328.

Gergana Popova, Andrew Spencer

Stacked Periphrases

1. Introduction

Periphrases are syntactic (multiword) constructions that realize inflectional properties, such as the Russian imperfective future with BYT′ 'be' + infinitive: *budu* 'I.am' *vstavat′* 'to.stand.up' 'I will stand up' (vs the synthetic perfective future *vstanu*). While periphrases typically inherit the structural properties of related syntactic constructions, it has been argued that they also exhibit morphological properties, specifically that they fill in cells in otherwise inflectional paradigms (Börjars et al., 1997, Sadler and Spencer, 2001, Ackerman and Stump, 2004, Bonami, 2015 amongst others. For reviews of the issues involved see, for example, Brown et al., 2012 and Spencer and Popova, 2015). Another important argument in favour of a morphological approach is what Ackerman and Stump (2004) have dubbed 'the morphosyntactic non-compositionality' of periphrases: the periphrase as a whole expresses information (a morphosyntactic or morphosemantic feature or its value) which is not expressed by any of the elements that belong to the construction and may in fact be incompatible with the information expressed by those elements. For instance, the Bulgarian negated future tense consists of the present tense of the negative form of the verb IMAM 'have' and the inflected present tense form of the lexical verb, conjoined with the particle *da*. Thus, future tense is expressed by two present tense verbs.

The insight that periphrases have a role to play in morphology has led to a number of proposals for morphological accounts, many in the context of inferential-realizational morphology, including Ackerman and Stump (2004), Bonami and Samvelian (2009), Bonami and Webelhuth (2013). One of the most explicit accounts is that of Bonami (2015). Bonami proposes a formal approach within Paradigm Function Morphology (Stump 2001) and HPSG which treats periphrastic constructions as morphological entities, whilst at the same time accounting for their syntactic properties. Taking Bonami's approach as our point of departure we will focus on two related issues: information flow in syntactic representations, and the direction of stacking or nesting in embedded periphrases. We introduce Bulgarian nested periphrases in the next section. In section 3 we summarize some of the crucial features of Bonami's approach to periphrasis, which we then use as a springboard for the discussion of information flow and the direction of nesting in section 4.

2. Stacked inflectional periphrases in Bulgarian

We will focus here on the perfect, the future and the future perfect, reprising the discussion in Popova and Spencer (2013). The perfect tense periphrase is composed of an inflected present tense form of the auxiliary verb *săm* 'be' and the *l*-participle of the main verb (see 1a). The future tense periphrase is composed of the inflected present tense form of the main verb and the uninflecting particle *šte*, historically a form of *šta* 'want' (1b), here glossed ŠTE.[1]

(1) a. Perfect: Az săm čela knigata.
I(F) be.1SG.PRS read.L-PTCP.F.SG book.DEF
'I(F) have read the book'.

b. Future: Az šte četa knigata.
I(F) ŠTE read.1SG.PRS book.DEF
'I(F) will read the book'.

Both *săm* and *šte* exhibit clitic-like behaviour. *Săm* cannot occupy clause-initial position and enters the clitic cluster. *Šte* can be in clause initial position and can host the clitic cluster, but does not inflect and cannot bear main stress. The cluster linearizes as follows: AUX (except BE.PRS.3SG) » DAT » ACC » BE.PRS.3SG. It stays to the left of the verb, unless this will position clause-initially a clitic that requires a host to its left, in which case the cluster moves post-verbally.

Importantly, the future periphrasis can be formed with either of two alternative forms of SĂM, *săm* or *băda*, (2).

(2) Az šte săm/băda na rabota utre.
I ŠTE be.1SG at work tomorrow
'I will be at work tomorrow'.

This alternation applies only to BE in the future tense, it isn't possible with the present tense copula, or in the perfect tense, as illustrated by (3a, b).

(3) a. Az săm/*băda na rabota dnes.
I be.1SG at work today
'I am at work today'.

---

1 We employ the following abbreviations in addition to the standard Leipzig Glossing Conventions: ARG-STR – argument structure, AGR – agreement, AUX – auxiliary, CONT – CONTENT (feature), HPSG – Head Driven Phrase-Structure Grammar, LID – lexical index/identifier, PFV – perfective aspect, LPTCP – l-participle, PF – paradigm function, PFM – Paradigm Function Morphology.

b. Toj e/*băde čel tazi kniga.
He be.3SG read.LPTCP.M.SG this book
'He has read this book.'

Bulgarian also has a future perfect periphrasis, illustrated in (4), to which the *săm/băda* alternation applies.

(4) Future perfect: Toj šte e/băde čel knigata.
He ŠTE be.3SG.PRS read.LPTCP.M.SG book.DEF
'He will have read the book.'

We take this to mean that the correct interpretation of the future perfect is that the future periphrasis in fact applies to the BE auxiliary used in the perfect periphrasis, (5).

(5) READ{fut,prf} → BE{fut} ⊗ READ{lptcp} → [šte săm/băda] ⊗ čela
...where ⊗ stands for whatever morphosyntactic function delivers the appropriate combination of auxiliary verb/clitic + main verb

We return to the nesting properties of the periphrases after we have introduced some of the essential features of Bonami's (2015) recent formalisation, which places the paradigmatic non-compositional nature of periphrases at its centre.

3. Bonami's approach

Most of the recent discussions of periphrasis assume a word-and-paradigm approach to morphology (e.g. Sadler and Spencer, 2001, Ackerman and Stump, 2004, Brown et al., 2012). Bonami's work fits within this tradition. More specifically, he assumes a Paradigm Function approach to morphology (PFM), as formalized in Stump (2001). In PFM, morphological elements are exponents of morphosyntactic features. The word-forms of a given lexeme are determined by that lexeme's paradigm function (PF), which maps a pairing of ⟨Lexeme,features⟩ to a pairing of ⟨inflected wordform,features⟩:[2]

(6) Paradigm Function (PF) (Stump 2001: 43): $PF(\langle X, \sigma\rangle) =_{def} \langle Y, \sigma\rangle$

Central to Bonami's approach is the intuition that typical periphrases are like flexible semi-transparent idioms, in which the syntactic structure is represented

2 The PF is generally mediated as a set of Realization Rules, but since they play no crucial role in the discussion of periphrasis we ignore them here.

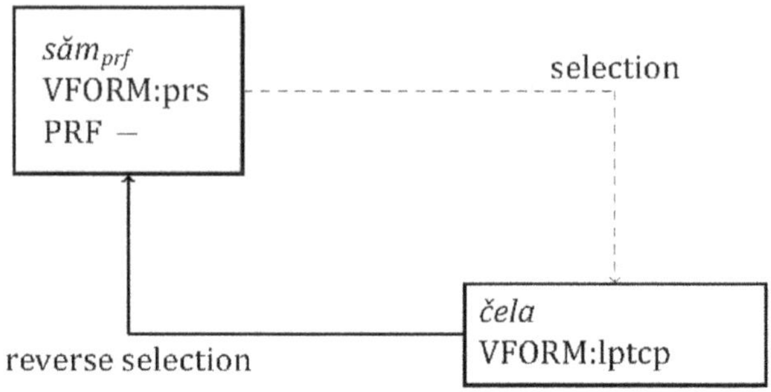

Figure 1: Reverse selection for *săm čela* '(I) have read (F)'

as normal, but where the elements that constitute the periphrase are restricted to collocate with each other. Periphrases, like idioms, are non-compositional. To model this situation, Bonami borrows from existing HPSG accounts of idioms the mechanism of reverse selection. A periphrase (idiom) has two parts: an ancillary element (e.g. an auxiliary verb) and a main element (e.g. lexical verb participle). The ancillary element selects the main element in the syntax (via, say, the head-complement relationship, or the head-adjunct relationship) but the main element, the syntactic dependent, also selects the ancillary element, the syntactic head, through reverse selection. The reverse selection requirement is governed by the morphology, i.e. it is introduced by the paradigm function. We illustrate the basic architecture in Figure 1.

Bonami's analysis aims to capture the morphological role of periphrases by locating the features expressed by the whole construction on the lexical head and then ensuring that that word form reverse selects the appropriate form of the ancillary. The two elements then conjointly express the content of the periphrase. A mechanism is then needed to link the construction as a whole with these features. To do this, Bonami exploits HPSG HEAD features together with a novel set of features he calls INFL(ectional).

HEAD features are those that the HEAD daughter shares with its mother and hence are associated with the phrase as a whole. The INFL features are the input (and output) of the morphological paradigm functions (Bonami 2015:99). The interface between the INFL features and the syntactic representation is constrained as follows: 'Every feature within INFL corresponds to some feature already present somewhere in the syntactic representation. For ordinary synthetic words, syntactic features and corresponding INFL features have matching values. In periphrases they typically differ, both on the ancillary and the main

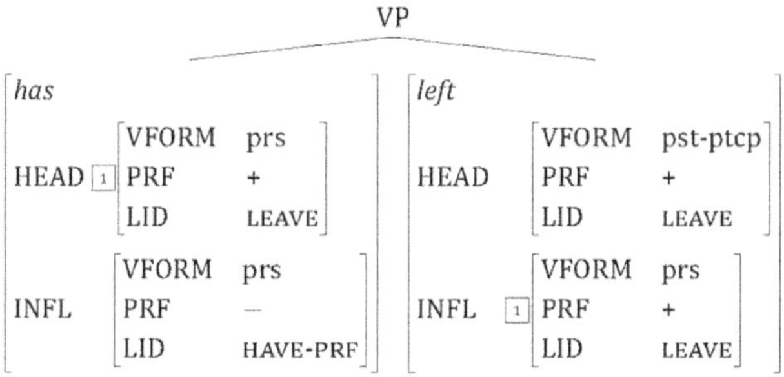

Figure 2: Structure for *has left* in Bonami's (2015) model (adapted from Bonami 2015:100)

element.' The INFL/HEAD distinction is meant to allow the right 'information flow' in periphrasis, as illustrated in Figure 2. The features expressed by the periphrase as a whole are encoded as INFL features of its main element. These are shared as HEAD features of the ancillary element, as shown by the [1] tags. Since the ancillary element is the HEAD daughter of the syntactic structure as a whole, its HEAD features are the ones percolated to the phrase level and so they become properties of the phrase as a whole.

We will argue that Bonami's analysis encounters difficulties when confronted with Bulgarian. First, the PF must stipulate that the auxiliary should carry the opposite value of whatever feature the periphrastic construction realizes. This doesn't follow from any observable properties of periphrasis but it is needed in the formalism to avoid illicit recursive application (e.g. *perfect of a perfect of a … perfect) and exclude forms like **have had … read*. This seems to commit us to saying that all periphrastic features are binary: if the periphrastically realized feature were set valued the PF would have to be defined over the negation of one of those values. For instance, suppose we had good reason for setting up a feature TENSE with values {prs, pst, fut}, and suppose that [TENSE:pst] and [TENSE:fut] were both expressed periphrastically (as is the case for imperfective verbs in, say, Czech). How would we specify the ancillary element realizing each of these features so as to ensure that we didn't obtain double past or double future periphrases?

In addition, there are a number of questions raised by the conceptualization of information flow shown in Fig. 2. The first concerns the INFL features of the main element. On the one hand, the main element is the exponent of the features associated with the periphrasis as a whole. On the other hand, however, the main element can itself be inflected for a somewhat different set of features, as in the case of the Bulgarian future tense, where the main element is itself an inflected verb. In the morphology, the PF that realizes the periphrasis refers to another PF that 'inflects' the main element. So the main element in a periphrase becomes associated with two sets of morphosyntactic features: one that reflects its own morphological form, as well as the set that belongs to the periphrastic construction as a whole. Both should be reflected as INFL features, as both of these sets 'feed' the morphological component. However, Bonami's formalism suggests that one of these potential INFL sets gets directly expressed as HEAD features of the main element.

The second question is this: the mechanism by which the features are passed from the components of the periphrase to the construction as a whole depends on the ancillary element being the head of the construction as a whole. So it won't work whenever the ancillary element is not the head.

Another set of questions arises when the inflectional paradigm of an ancillary element itself includes a periphrastic realization ('embedded, nested, stacked' periphrasis). Nested periphrases are modelled by the successive application of more than one PF. In the case of the Bulgarian nested periphrase illustrated in (4), we would expect the perfect PF to apply first and realize an *l*-participle of the main verb carrying the set of features associated with the construction as a whole, and reverse selecting for a future form of the auxiliary BE. The specification of future tense on the auxiliary will then trigger another PF, which will realize the form of BE inflected for the appropriate features, reverse selecting for the particle *šte*. However, it is hard to see how this mechanism can work if the ancillary element itself is periphrastically inflected, by means of a second ancillary. The HEAD features of that second ancillary should be shared with the INFL features of the first ancillary, not with the INFL features of the lexical head, but it is unclear how this is to be achieved in Bonami's framework.

Finally, it is unclear how to relate Bonami's INFL features to other types of feature deployed in PFM, particularly Stump's CONTENT features. We address that question directly in our own analysis.

4. Realizational-constructional model of periphrasis

FORM vs. CONTENT paradigms

A central pillar of Bonami's account is the factorizing of morphosyntactic properties or features into the HPSG HEAD features and a new class of features, INFL. A number of authors have noted the need for a bifurcation in the morphosyntactic feature sets in order to account for various mismatches which occur between the morphological form of an inflected word and its morphosyntactic function. A particularly clear instance of this is deponency, found when a lexeme inflects for one set of features but behaves syntactically as though it inflected for an incompatible feature set. The standard example is that of the deponent verbs of classical Indo-European languages (Latin, Greek, Sanskrit) as well as many modern languages, which are 'passive in form but active in meaning'. To describe such mismatches Stump (2002, 2016) introduces a distinction between two types of paradigm, the FORM and CONTENT paradigms. The FORM paradigms define morphological forms and their paradigmatic relations, while the CONTENT paradigms define the corresponding (abstract) pairings of a Lexical Index (LID) with the corresponding syntactically 'visible' morphosyntactic properties (the LID is an arbitrary index serving to individuate lexemes, including homonyms such as BANK1, BANK2). The CONTENT features feed semantic interpretation, by specifying those properties that (can) influence meaning, such as 'plural number' or 'past tense'. The two paradigms are co-defined by rules of Paradigm Linkage. In the default case Paradigm Linkage is the identity function and the two sets of features are isomorphic, but in cases of mismatch we have a more complex relationship. Some of the FORM properties are morphomic, i.e. purely morphological, and therefore have no CONTENT paradigm correspondent. This is true of inflectional class properties, for instance, but arguably is also true of semantically inert forms such as participles.

In periphrasis we also find a complex relationship between different sets of features. On the one hand, the periphrastic construction as a whole realizes a feature which may bear little resemblance to those expressed by its elements. Thus, although the verbal elements in the future negative construction in Bulgarian are both in the present tense, the construction as a whole expresses future tense. On the other hand, the features borne by the components of the periphrase must be visible to the syntax. This is necessary for agreement, for instance. It is also necessary for the linearization of the auxiliaries in the clitic cluster, where the 3SG present tense BE auxiliary is linearized separately from the other clitics. The syntax needs to know the identity and morphological properties of the uninflecting particle *šte*, which behaves differently from the past tense auxiliary form based on the same verbal root, and so on. In this sense, it is not sufficient to equate the inflectional features of the elements of the construction with FORM features and the features on the level of the construction itself with CONTENT features. Both sets of features need to be available to syntax, and to morphology. We propose to state this much more directly.

To do this, we introduce a distinction between what we will call two types of CONTENT features (features visible to syntax): CONT_{wd}, CONT_{ph}. The CONT_{wd} features relate just to the individual (synthetically) inflected word form. For nested periphrases we use the $\mathrm{CONT}_{wd/ph}$ distinction to reconceptualize the information flow for a 'simplex' periphrasis such as the Bulgarian perfect tense as in Fig. 3. We assume a principle which states that CONT_{ph} features are passed from the element that reverse selects to the element reverse selected for. An advantage of this is that CONT_{ph} can be passed between elements without relying on the HEAD feature mechanisms for percolation, which means that it is no longer a requirement for the ancillary element of a periphrase to be the head of the construction.

More interesting is the case where the auxiliary itself has to be inflected for (CONTENT) features, but those features are realized periphrastically, as in the future perfect. In such cases the auxiliary verb (e.g. *săm/băda*) is treated

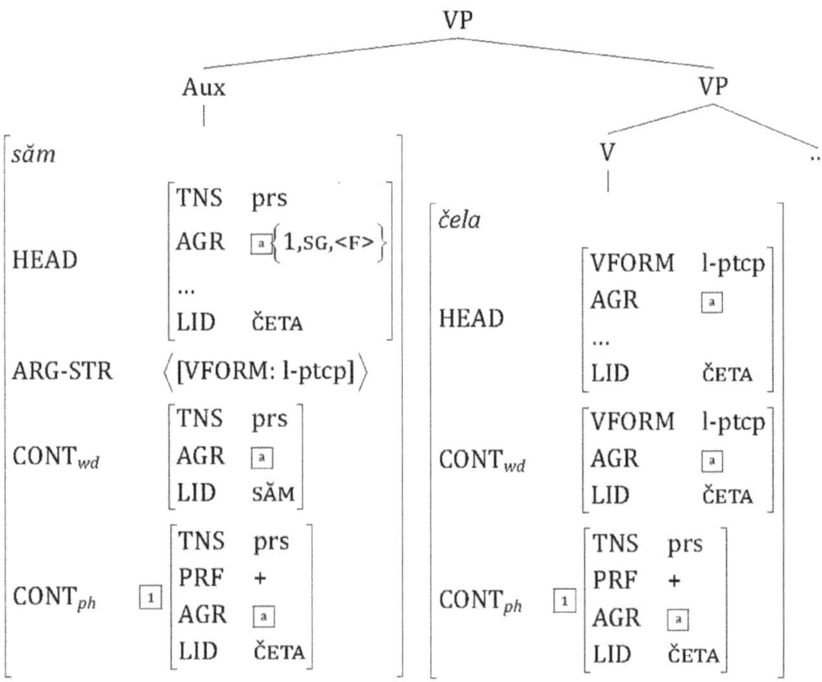

Figure 3: Simplex periphrasis: *(Az) săm čela* 'I(F) (have) read'

as an ordinary lexeme with respect to future inflection, i.e. it collocates with *šte*. This is a periphrase, so it licenses another splitting of $CONT_{ph}$ features. However, this new split applies to the ancillary lexeme SĂM/BĂDA, not to the main verb. Therefore, we have an 'inner layer' of $CONT_{ph}$ features, distinguished from the main verb's $CONT_{ph}$ features by its LID (amongst other features, possibly), as illustrated in Fig. 4 (simplifying for readability). To achieve this information flow, however, we need to allow the sets of features that serve as input to the PFs to map to (at least) two kinds of features in syntax, $CONT_{wd}$, $CONT_{ph}$. (This, in fact, brings our account closer to the model of Stump 2002, 2016.)

Bonami's system allowed him to constrain the direction of the nesting of periphrases. Thus, for the Bulgarian future perfect periphrase, the PF for perfect needs to apply first, to exclude forms like **(az) šam štjal četa* and to exclude recursion, so we don't have a form like **šte šta četa*. We need to propose an alternative account of the directionality of nesting and constraints on recursion.

Ancillary elements as inflectionally defective lexemes

To avoid recursion, we will adopt a solution originally proposed for the English auxiliary system by Pullum and Wilson (1977). We will argue that the ancillary elements (auxiliary verbs) are informationally defective, and are systematically uninflectable for certain properties, in the limit, being totally uninflectable particles. We reconfigure Bonami's feature negating device as a principle of systematic defectivity (we could motivate this on typological grounds, though without incorporating the typological observation directly into the formal machinery). To see how this works, we consider the Bulgarian future tense. (We continue to treat the future marker as a kind of auxiliary verb, even though its actual behaviour is that of a semi-grammaticalized clitic. See Popova and Spencer 2013 for full justification.) The future marker *šte* is uninflectable, i.e. it is maximally defective inflectionally, having the lexical representation shown in (7), from which we can see that it selects a complement marked [TNS:prs].

(7) $\textit{šte} = \begin{bmatrix} \text{HEAD} & [\ ] \\ \text{ARG-STR} & \langle \ldots, [\text{TNS: prs}] \rangle \\ \text{CONT} & \begin{bmatrix} \text{VFORM} & \text{šte} \\ \text{LID} & \text{ŠTE} \end{bmatrix} \end{bmatrix}$

By contrast, the lexeme BE can be associated directly (i.e. with its own LID) with one or more of at least the feature sets in (8).

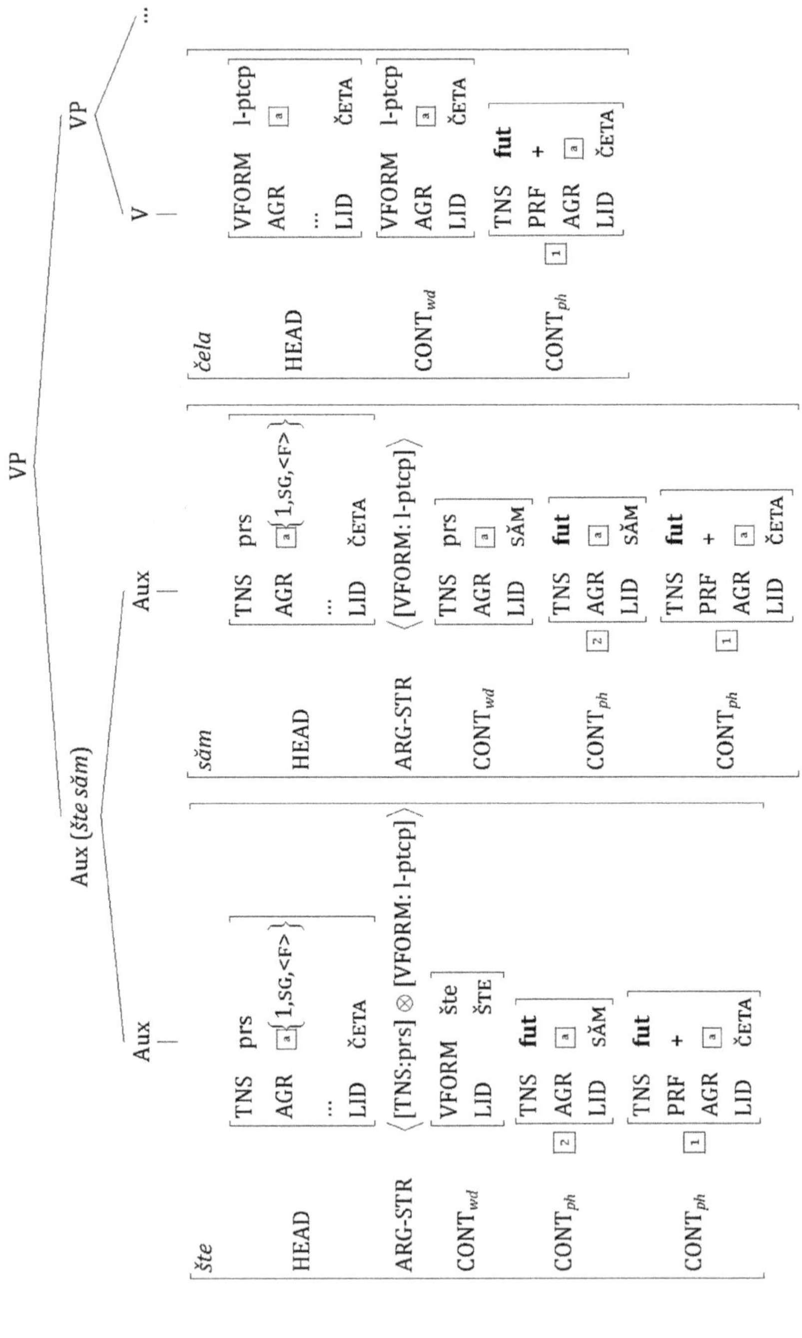

Figure 4: Stacked periphrasis : *(Az) šte săm čela 'I(F) will have read'*

(8) $$\textit{s\u{a}m} = \begin{bmatrix} \text{HEAD} & [\quad] \\ \text{ARG-STR} & \left\langle \ldots, [\text{VFORM: l-pfv}] \right\rangle \\ \text{CONT} & \begin{bmatrix} \text{TNS} & \text{prs} \\ \text{AGR} & \boxed{\text{a}} \\ \text{LID} & \text{BE-PRF} \end{bmatrix} \\ \textbf{OR} & \\ \text{CONT} & \begin{bmatrix} \text{TNS} & \text{fut} \\ \text{AGR} & \boxed{\text{a}} \\ \text{LID} & \text{BE-PRF} \end{bmatrix} \end{bmatrix}$$

On our analysis, then, recursion is ruled out because the ancillary elements are defective for precisely the features that would permit it. This approach suggests a formal way of treating the diachronic grammaticalization processes which give rise to such periphrases, but space considerations preclude further discussion.

5. Conclusions

Periphrases are syntactic constructions which realize cells in an inflectional (morphological) paradigm. However, periphrases are often featurally non-compositional. Bonami's (2015) HPSG/PFM account seeks to capture the non-compositionality as a form of idiomaticity coded by means of reverse selection. His analysis calls upon a distinction in syntactic representations between HEAD/INFL features. We have argued against reverse selection and offer a modification of Bonami's feature dichotomy. We generalize Stump's (2002, 2016) distinction between FORM and CONTENT paradigms. The content of the periphrase is encoded with an additional layer of CONTENT features. Where the ancillary itself can be inflected periphrastically ('stacked/nested' periphrasis) periphrasis gives rise to its own additional layer of CONTENT features, but relativized to the (LID of the) ancillary. This permits a straightforward account of information flow.

All models of periphrasis have to account for the paradigmatic organization of periphrases – like inflectional affixation, periphrasis is not generally recursive. We code this by assuming that the lexical representations of ancillaries are defective for certain features, specifically, the feature(s) expressed by the periphrase itself. The analysis retains the desirable morphology-syntax interface of Bonami's model without its technical and conceptual disadvantages and it permits us to apply the periphrastic functions in the right order in the case of stacking. In the limit, the ancillary becomes completely empty of content, i.e. a clitic/affix. We thus capture the notion of 'semantic bleaching' in grammaticalization.

References

Ackerman, Farrell and Gregory Stump. 2004. "Paradigms and periphrastic expressions." In Louisa Sadler and Andrew Spencer (eds.), *Projecting Morphology, Stanford Studies in Morphology and the Lexicon*. CSLI Publications, Stanford, California, 111–157.

Bonami, Olivier. 2015. "Periphrasis as collocation." *Morphology*, 25(1): 63–110.

Bonami, Olivier and Pollet Samvelian. 2009. "Inflectional periphrasis in Persian." In *Proceedings of the 16th International Conference on Head-Driven Phrase Structure Grammar*. University of Göttingen, CSLI Publications, 361–380.

Bonami, Olivier and Gert Webelhuth. 2013. "The phrase-structural diversity of periphrasis: a lexicalist account." In Marina Chumakina and Greville Corbett (eds.), *Periphrasis: The Role of Syntax and Morphology in Paradigms*. Oxford University Press, Oxford, 141–167.

Börjars, Kersti, Nigel Vincent and Carol Chapman. 1997. "Paradigms, periphrases and pronominal inflection." In Geert Booij and Jaap van Marle (eds.), *Yearbook of Morphology 1996*. Kluwer Academic Publishers, Dordrecht, 155–180.

Brown, Dunstan, Marina Chumakina, Greville Corbett, Gergana Popova and Andrew Spencer. 2012. "Defining 'periphrasis': key notions." *Morphology* 22: 233–275.

Popova, Gergana and Andrew Spencer. 2013. "Relatedness in periphrasis: a paradigm-based perspective." In Marina Chumakina and Greville Corbett (eds.), *Periphrasis: The Role of Syntax and Morphology in Paradigms*, volume 180 of Proceedings of the British Academy. Oxford University Press/British Academy, 191–225.

Pullum, Geoffrey. and Deidre Wilson. 1977. "Autonomous syntax and the analysis of auxiliaries." *Language* 53: 741–788.

Sadler, Louisa and Andrew Spencer. 2001. "Syntax as an exponent of morphological features." In Geert Booij and Jaap van Marle (eds.), *Yearbook of Morphology 2000*. Kluwer, Dordrecht, 71–96.

Spencer, Andrew and Gergana Popova. 2015. "Periphrasis and inflection." In Matthew Baerman (ed.), *The Oxford Handbook of Inflection*. Oxford University Press, Oxford, 197–230.

Stump, Gregory. 2001. *Paradigm Function Morphology. A Theory of Inflectional Form*. Cambridge University Press, Cambridge.

Stump, Gregory. 2002. "Morphological and syntactic paradigms: Arguments for a theory of paradigm linkage." In Geert Booij and Jaap van Marle (eds.), *Yearbook of Morphology 2001*. Kluwer Academic Publishers, 147–180.

Stump, Gregory. 2016. *Inflectional Paradigms. Content and Form at the Syntax-Morphology Interface*. Cambridge University Press, Cambridge.

Hagen Pitsch

Bulgarian *da* as a Non-Indicative Placeholder*

1. Introduction

This paper is concerned with the interpretation of Bulgarian *da*-constructions and the semantics of *da*. *Da*-constructions are (at least) made up of the uninflected element *da* and a verb phrase (VP) in an indicative (IND) tense form; cf. (1):[1]

(1) $[_{XP}$ ***da***$_{X}$ … $[_{VP}$ V$_{IND}$ (VP)]]

While the syntax of Bulgarian *da*-constructions seems thus rather simple (though more has to be said about XP), their meaning is less obvious, which is the reason to address it once again. There is a long-standing debate in the literature on whether or not *da*-constructions form the Bulgarian subjunctive mood.[2] Authors denying this view either (i) argue that Bulgarian lacks such a category altogether (e.g., Genadieva-Mutafčieva 1970, 1976), or (ii) suggest that *da*-constructions may function not only as subjunctives, but also as infinitivals (e.g., Popov 1968; Lempp 1981; Krapova 1998, 2001), or (iii) propose a varying number of homonymous *da*-constructions with diverse functions and meanings (e.g., Petkova Schick 1977; Maslov 1981; Tilkov et al. 1983; Ivanova 2014).

The goal of this paper is to account for the interpretation of Bulgarian *da*-constructions as well as to support the view that Bulgarian has not only

---

* Thanks are due to Andreas Blümel, Eva Csipak, Uwe Junghanns, Frank Sode, Viola Schmitt and Hedde Zeijlstra – for listening to my ideas and for valuable advice – and to the audience of FDSL 11 for a helpful discussion. I am also indebted to Krăstina Arbova-Georgieva for important suggestions and help with the data.

1 Indicative tenses report situations as (to be) realized. Among them, the present, present perfect, past perfect and (seldom) the imperfect occur in *da*-constructions, while the aorist, the future and future perfect do not (cf. Krapova 1998: 81). The past future and past future perfect are non-indicative tenses and resemble *da*-constructions in reporting situations as hypothetical/unrealized. But other than *da*-constructions, which often show a 'possible future' interpretation (Krapova 1998: 81–82), they relate to (a relative) past.

2 Among the authors holding this opinion are, e.g., Weigand (1907), Seliščev (1952), Maslov (1962), Bernštejn (1961), Kramer (1992), Smirnova (2010, 2012).

subjunctive, but also infinitival CPs.[3] I will argue that *da* marks the absence of the indicative with its characteristic supposition of *subject certainty* (Siegel 2009). Furthermore, I will assume that Bulgarian *da*-constructions form a semantic default used when more specific moods are blocked as they would cause a semantic failure in the given context (cf. Schlenker 2005). Importantly, this view still allows the distinction of subjunctive-like and infinitive-like *da*-constructions (cf. Popov 1968; Krapova 1997, 1998, 2001), since this distinction is not based on the (semantically vacuous) particle *da*, but rather on the properties of the Tense complex of the relevant *da*-construction. Consequently, *da* can unambiguously be identified with the category of mood and simultaneously be dissociated from the notion of finiteness.

The paper is structured as follows: Section 2.1 recapitulates Siegel's (2009) analysis on the semantics of Balkan subjunctives. In Section 2.2, I argue for a distinction of finite vs. non-finite *da*-constructions in Bulgarian (cf. Krapova 1998). In Section 2.3, the priorly introduced ingredients are combined into the proposal proper. Section 2.4 serves to illustrate my assumptions concentrating on *da*-complements. Section 3 will summarize the paper.

2. The proposal

2.1. Semantic default and subject certainty

In this section, I recapitulate Siegel's (2009) proposal on the semantics of mood in Balkan languages, among them Bulgarian, which will be the first ingredient of my proposal. Siegel argues that, 'while indicative morphology is specified as being [+realis], subjunctive morphology is underspecified for semantic content, and appears as a default when other, more specified, "moods" cannot appear.' (Siegel 2009: 1879) Assuming Bulgarian *da*-constructions to be subjunctives, this amounts to the claim that they do not contribute to sentence semantics. It follows that they represent the neutral choice within the Bulgarian mood system, a choice employed whenever the remaining moods are too specific.[4] As Siegel (2009) points out, 'treating subjunctive as a default in this way is appealing because subjunctive morphology appears in such a wide range of environments,

---

3 This paper thus adds to the discussion led in, a.o., Maslov (1962), Genadieva-Mutafčieva (1970), Petkova Schmidt (1977), Siegel (2009), Smirnova (2012).

4 See similar analyses by Quer (1998), Portner (1997), Schlenker (2005), Portner & Rubinstein (2013), a.o.

Table 1: Mood in Bulgarian (I).

∅	indicative	*subject certainty*
da	non-indicative	---

environments for which it has proved to be very difficult to provide any unified analysis.'[5] (Siegel 2009: 1879)

The second important insight of Siegel's analysis is that, 'in Balkan, indicative is correlated with a higher degree of certainty on the part of the subject than is subjunctive.' (Siegel 2009: 1879) Note that this does not mean that the subjunctive is associated with a 'weaker' indicative semantics, since the mentioned correlation is a relative one and based on the fact that the subjunctive is in opposition to the indicative. In fact, the subjunctive is void of semantic content.[6] From the discussed assumptions, it is possible to preliminarily outline the mood system of modern Bulgarian as in Table 1 (imperative omitted).

2.2. Finite and non-finite da-constructions;

The second ingredient of my proposal is the claim that *da*-constructions happen to occur in two varieties, namely finite and non-finite *da*-constructions. In her paper on subjunctive complements in Bulgarian, Krapova (1998) (see also Krapova 1997, 2001) makes the observation that Bulgarian has two types of S[ubjunctive]s (i.e. *da*-constructions) which she calls 'Type I Ss' and 'Type II Ss', respectively. This distinction is based on the differing semantic and syntactic properties of the involved null subjects (cf. Krapova 1998: 75). In short,

5 Smirnova (2012) is an attempt for such an analysis. Smirnova assumes the Bulgarian subjunctive to presuppose weaker epistemic commitment than the indicative. More precisely, it is claimed to presuppose that the domain with respect to which the relevant proposition is evaluated is non-homogenous, while the indicative presupposes a homogenous domain. Importantly, Smirnova assumes that both the indicative and the subjunctive are meaningful mood forms, while Siegel's (2009) account allows the latter to be a semantically vacuous default.

6 Two details of Siegel's analysis should be noted: First, the attitude holder is not necessarily the speaker but rather the subject of the relevant clause. Second, the supposition of *subject certainty* 'need not be old information [...] [which] means that it has some assertion-like properties in that it can be used to bring new information into the discourse.' (Siegel 2009: 1863) This proves to be of advantage when it comes to analyzing independently used *da*-clauses. Unfortunately, I cannot discuss this special group of *da*-constructions due to space limitations.

while the first type of *da*-constructions has a *pro* subject, the other one contains PRO. But Krapova adds that 'the relevant factor [responsible for this difference] is the referential (and morphological) content of embedded Tense.' More precisely, she assumes 'that Tense comes in two varieties – T_{nom} and T_{null}. The former corresponds to a [+T] specification and checks Nominative Case, while the latter corresponds to [-T], to indicate lack of temporal specification, and checks Null Case.' Finally, she argues 'that the control relation in Type II Ss is not imposed by the anaphoric properties of PRO, but follows from, or at least correlates with the specific temporal reference of the clause in which it is licensed.' (Krapova 1998: 80)

I will adopt Krapova's insight that Bulgarian features two varieties of *da*-constructions. In the next section, the hitherto discussed ingredients will be combined to arrive at an integrated proposal which leads to a more refined picture of the Bulgarian mood system, taking into account the important conclusion that *da*-constructions may either be subjunctive or infinitival expressions.

2.3. Combining both ingredients

The present proposal is a conjunction of Siegel (2009), according to whom the Balkan subjunctive is a semantic default correlated with decreased *subject certainty*, and of Krapova (1998) who claims that Bulgarian *da*-constructions may be tensed or untensed.

An important insight of this conjuction will be that *da*-constructions should be characterized as *subjunctives* – expressing no, little or relatively decreased certainty on the part of their subject referent – only when they are finite. On the contrary, non-finite *da*-constructions should be characterized as *infinitivals* as they represent the Bulgarian equivalent (substitute) of the synchronically missing (diachronically lost) infinitive.

But before going into details, I shall briefly sketch necessary assumptions about the syntax of Bulgarian *da*-constructions. In (1), I used XP which still calls for a category. Krapova (1998) assumes that T in (subjunctive) *da*-constructions is either [+T] or [-T]. On the other hand, she locates *da* in C/Fin, thus analyzing it as a complementizer.[7] Since I associate *da* with the category of mood, I will rather follow Rivero (1994, 2005) who locates *da* in the head of a Modal Phrase

7 The same view is hold by Penčev (1998). In her paper on the Bulgarian system of auxiliaries, Krapova (1999) proposes *da* to be in T, which however relates to *da* in periphrastic tenses, not in subjunctive clauses.

Table 2: Distribution of non-/finite Bulgarian *da*-constructions.

	complement	**adjunct**	**indepedent use**
finite	+	+	+
non-finite	+	+	–

(MP) above TP.[8] She adds that 'Bulgarian resembles other Balkan languages and lacks "restructuring"/clitic climbing, which is why clitic pronouns must remain in the embedded clause/phase without exception.' (Rivero 2005: 1086) Taking this for granted, *da*-constructions are always CPs.[9] With this said, (1) can now be completed, thus arriving at a more detailed clause structure of Bulgarian *da*-constructions (possible additional projections not excluded):

(1') [CP C [MP ***da***M [TP T[±T] [VP VIND (VP)]]]]

Now, given Krapova's distinction of finite and non-finite *da*-constructions, a question that arises is how these types are distributed. The data (a part of which is cited in this paper) suggest that their distribution is as in Table 2.

Due to space limitations, I have to confine myself to the class of *da*-complements.

2.4. Da-complements;

Da-complements are determined by the argument structure of the respective matrix predicate. As far as the complement position is occupied by a finite *da*-CP, the situation is clear: Since the *da*-CP is tensed, a Nominative subject is licensed. Moreover, the [+T] specification yields a 'possible future' (Krapova 1998: 81) interpretation of the situation denoted by the *da*-CP. Furthermore, as a rule such cases exhibit disjoint subject reference; cf. (2a):[10]

8 Rivero suggests that M is also the base position of the future particle *šte*, thus accounting for its complementary distribution with *da*. This receives additional semantic support assuming its modal origin (< present tense form of Old Bulgarian *xotěti* 'want'). Presumably owing to this origin, *šte*-clauses are always finite ([+T]).

9 This does not exclude Raising from, and Control into, *da*-constructions. As in many other languages, this seems to be related to the fact that they are non-indicatives which, in turn, makes them transparent for certain syntactic operations. A recent attempt to explain these transparency effects is made by Kanno & Nomura (2012).

10 The following glosses are used: ACC = accusative; AOR = aorist; DEF = definite article; NEG = negation marker; NOM = nominative; SG = singular. Many examples are (minimal) pairs, contrasting *da*-constructions with *če*-clauses. For the sake of consistency,

(2) a. Iskam [Marija DA pee]. (Smirnova 2012: 547)
want.1SG Maria v sing.3SG
'I want Maria to sing.'
b. *Iskam [če Marija pee].
want.1SG that Maria sing.3SG

The pair in (2) also shows that *iskam* 'want' is a predicate that is, as far as clausal complements are concerned, restricted to *da*-CPs. The reason is its semantic content: *Iskam* is a volitional verb, thus it goes well with unrealized (desired) propositions, but can by no means be sensibly combined with a complement about the truth or reality of which the subject is supposed to be certain.

Note, however, that *iskam*-sentences may also exhibit subject coreference as in (3):

(3) Iskaš [da peeš].
want.2SG DA sing.2SG
'You want to sing.'

Assuming the existence of non-finite *da*-CPs, it seems natural that the *da*-CP in (3) is non-finite.[11] Still, there are two possible analyses for *iskam*: It may either be a Raising or a Control predicate. In the former case, the subject of the *da*-CP moves into the matrix structure, leaving a trace in its base (and intermediate) position(s). In the latter case, the *da*-CP contains PRO which is controlled by the subject of *iskaš*. Both cases are schematized in (4):

(4) a. DP_i V $[_{CP}$ … t_i $\boldsymbol{da}_M$ $T_{[-T]}$ …] (Raising from a non-finite *da*-CP)
b. DP_i V $[_{CP}$ … PRO_i $\boldsymbol{da}_M$ $T_{[-T]}$ …] (Control into a non-finite *da*-CP)

I leave open the question which of these analyses is more adequate to capture (3). What is more important is that non-finite *da*-constructions may generally occur in these two environments, depending on the properties of their relevant matrix predicate. Thus, while *moga* 'can' behaves like a Raising predicate, *započvam* 'begin', *zabravjam* 'forget' and *znam* 'know <u>how</u>' behave like

the *da*-example is always given first. Sometimes, this required switching the original sequence.

11 An analysis arguing for finite-only complements in Bulgarian would have to propose that the *da*-CP in (3) contains a *pro* subject which is interpreted as being coreferent with the matrix *pro* subject.

Control predicates.[12] Noticeably, Rivero remarks that 'Bulgarian auxiliaries resemble Balkan raising/control verbs, so take full clauses as complements.' (Rivero 2005: 1090) This supports the above-mentioned claims, namely that non-finite *da*-constructions are CPs and that they may occur in Raising or Control structures. Importantly, it also means that the relevant matrix predicates either are auxiliaries or assume auxiliary-like properties when combined with non-finite *da*-constructions.

A Raising case is illustrated in (5). It features the modal verb *moga* 'can'. It is a Raising predicate as it provides an external argument position to which it does not assign a thematic role. As a consequence, the subject from within the non-finite *da*-CP can be raised into the matrix where the Nominative is licensed. Notice that the bracketting in (5) indicates that two distinctly realized subject DPs are ruled out (cf. Lempp 1981: 62), thus corroborating the view that the involved *da*-CP is non-finite:

(5)	{az}	moga	{az}	da	rabotja	(cf. Lempp 1981: 62)
	I	can.1SG	I	DA	work.1SG	

'I can work.'

The Control case is illustrated in (6). Since znam '*know* (*how*)' assigns a thematic role to its external argument position, the embedded subject cannot be raised. It follows that (6) must contain PRO. As noted by Krapova (1998: 75), the latter does not alternate with lexical DPs. Much like in (5), this means that two distinctly realized subject DPs are ruled out.

(6)	Znam	[da	peja].	(http://www.politika.bg/article?id=9778)
	want.1SG	DA	sing.1SG	

'I know how to sing.'

While *znam* in (6) shows a modal interpretation ('know how'; Krapova 1998: 74), it is interpreted veridically ('know') when combined with an indicative *če*-clause; cf. (7b):

(7) a.	*Znam	[Marija	da	pee	].	(Smirnova 2012: 547)
	know.1SG	Maria	DA	sing.3SG		

12 Krapova (1998: 74) subsumes these verbs under the term *control verbs*, i.e. verbs which take in any non-freely interpreted empty category (cf. Joseph 1992). She also mentions *opitvam se* 'try' and *uspjavam* 'succeed' and notes that some of these verbs show ambiguities in their behavior as Raising rather than Control predicates.

b. Znam [če Marija pee].
want.1SG that Maria sing.3SG
'I know that Maria sings.'

Under the desirable assumption that there is only one lexical entry for *znam*, its modal and veridical interpretations, respectively, should arise due to the properties of its complement. Accepting Siegel's (2009) subjunctive-as-default analysis, the veridical interpretation results from the amalgamation of *subject certainty* (indicative) with the lexical content KNOW. But why is *znam* restricted to occur with non-finite *da*-CPs as in (6), while it cannot be used with finite *da*-CPs as in (7a)? I suggest the following explanation: Due to their tense specification, finite *da*-CPs are interpreted as hypothetical/unrealized situations (cf. Krapova 1998: 82).[13] However, this kind of situation is completely incompatible with KNOW: Since knowing something clearly requires to be certain about it, finite *da*-CPs are ruled out. On the other hand, non-finite *da*-CPs are not necessarily interpreted as hypothetical/unrealized situations due to the fact that they are untensed. I suggest that they are interpreted as bare events instead,[14] and conclude that combining such a bare (abstract) event with KNOW yields the modal interpretation observable in (6).

Bare events also play a role in the interpretation of sentences featuring matrix verbs of perception; cf. (8):

(8) Vidjax (ja) [Mila da zatvarja prozoreca].
(cf. Werkmann 2007: 3)
see.AOR.1SG her.ACC Mila.ACC DA close.3SG window.DEF
'I saw Mila close the window.'

13 In Siegel's (2009) terms, they are correlated with *subject uncertainty* due to their semantic vacuity. At this point, it may seem that the interpretations suggested by Krapova (1998) and Siegel (2009) contradict each other. Note, however, that Siegel's notion of *subject (un)certainty* relates to the category of mood, while the interpretations suggested by Krapova follow from properties of embedded tense. Assuming that mood and tense interact, the contradiction turns into a plausible explanation: It is exactly due to the subjunctive – marking the absence of *subject certainty* – that the embedded tense receives a hypothetical, unrealized etc. interpretation.

14 Importantly, non-finite *da*-CPs are not restricted to denote bare events. They may also be interpreted as hypothetical, unrealized etc. situations (propositions) in appropriate contexts. On the contrary, finite *da*-CPs are restricted to exactly this kind of interpretation due to their tense specification.

Werkmann (2007) observes that (8) expresses a *direct perception report*. Note that the embedded subject *Mila* is in the Accusative, which is indicative of *Exceptional Case Marking* (ECM). Within the current proposal, these facts can be explained as follows: Higginbotham (1986) claims that direct perception amounts to perceiving bare events. Assuming that non-finite *da*-CPs may denote bare events, the fact that (8) is a *direct perception report* follows straightforwardly as the perception of bare events entails the perceived event to be included in the perceiving situation – it takes place before the eyes of the perceiver. As concerns ECM, the first thing to mention is that the Nominative on the embedded subject is not licensed due to [-T]. Furthermore, Raising is no option for the embedded subject to receive case as both argument positions of the matrix verb are already saturated. Control is no option either, since the *da*-CP occupies the direct object position of the verb of perception, so that *Ivo* cannot be claimed to occupy this matrix position from where it might control a potential PRO within the *da*-CP.[15] It follows that the only way of saving the structure – and of expressing a *direct perception report* in Bulgarian – is ECM: The embedded subject is exceptionally assigned the Accusative by the matrix predicate.

But Bulgarian verbs of perception may also combine with other types of complements:

(9) a. Viždam [Marija/tja da idva]. (Smirnova 2012: 553)
see-1.SG Maria/she.NOM DA come.3SG
'I see Maria coming.'

b. Viždam [če Marija idva].
see-1.SG that Maria.NOM come.3SG
'I see that Maria is coming.'

Following Smirnova, uttering (9a) is felicitous in a context where the perceiver sees a woman approaching, but is not entirely sure that it really is Maria. This interpretation differs crucially from the direct perception interpretation of (8). Rather, it is reminiscent of Siegel's claim that subjunctives express *subject uncertainty*. The semantic difference between (8) and (9a) can be accounted for assuming that these sentences differ in the finiteness of their *da*-CPs: While (8) contains a non-finite *da*-CP, the one in (9a) is finite. Hence,

15 Werkmann (2007) suggests a different analysis: The embedded subject is raised into the matrix object position where it receives a thematic role and the Accusative. Note that this implies the assignment of two thematic roles to one DP (and in fact also two matrix object positions), which is why I consider an ECM analysis more suitable.

the interpretation of (9a) arises on the grounds of *subject uncertainty*, while the interpretation of (8) follows from the fact that non-finite *da*-CPs have the potential of denoting bare events, thus enabling the expression of *direct perception reports* (Higginbotham 1983).

Finally, verbs of perception may also combine with indicative CPs as shown in (9b). Uttering (9b) is felicitous when 'the subject of perceptual experience is absolutely certain that the proposition *p* denoted by the embedded clause is true' (Smirnova 2012: 552). This description is nearly identical with Siegel's (2009) *subject certainty*. Therefore, it is legitimate to assume that the 'certainty interpretation' is due to the indicative. On the other hand, Werkmann (2007) notes that sentences like (9b) may be interpreted as *indirect perception reports*. This, in turn, is due to the fact that *če*-clauses denote propositions (independent situations), not bare events as non-finite *da*-CPs. I already mentioned that the perception of a bare event implies this event to be included in the perceiving situation. Such an inclusion is, however, not entailed in the case of perceiving an independent situation. In (9b), for example, it is absolutely possible to obtain a direct perception interpretation, but only if Ivo's smoking takes place in front of the perceiving individual. Importantly, however, it may also be the case that the perceiver merely infers that Ivo smokes based on certain details in the situation that he or she is actually perceiving (such as, e.g., smoke, ashes, a burning cigarette or the like).

I will finish my illustrations with the minimal pair cited in (10). It features the matrix verb *mislja* 'think'. This time, the relevant opposition is affirmative vs. negated:

(10) a. Mislja [{če / *da } Paulina e izjala tortata]. (Siegel 2009: 729)
think.1SG that DA Paulina be.3SG eaten cake.DEF
'I think that Paulina ate the cake.'

b. Ne mislja [{če / da } Paulina e izjala tortata
NEG think.1SG that DA Paulina be.3SG eaten cake.DEF
'I don't think that Paulina ate the cake.'

Interestingly, a *da*-complement is ruled out in the affirmative example (10a), but becomes available under sentential negation as in (10b). Since sentence polarity seems to be the factor determining the un-/availability of the finite *da*-construction, this case may be classified as an instance of so-called *polarity subjunctive*. Siegel 'argue[s] that indicative is associated with a greater degree of subject certainty. When applied to the negation cases, this means that indicative is associated with the meaning that the subject believes in the negation of the embedded clause. That is, indicative gets what has been called the Neg-Raising/

Table 3: Mood in Bulgarian (II).

M⁰	**finite**	**mood**	
∅	+	indicative *(subject certainty)*	
da	+	non-indicative	subjunctive
	–	(---)	infinitival

strengthening reading" (Siegel 2009: 1874) Hence again, the subject-as-default analysis works. Moreover, this is another example revealing that the form of a complement may affect the interpretation of a whole utterance. More specifically, the choice of one or another type of complement serves to disambiguate differing interpretations in Bulgarian.

3. Conclusion

The goal of this paper was to account for the interpretation of Bulgarian *da*-constructions, especially complements. In order to achieve this goal, I have combined two ingredients: First, I assumed Siegel's (2009) view according to which the indicative is associated with the supposition of *subject certainty*, while the subjunctive is a semantic default used whenever the indicative supposition is too specific. But as Bulgarian lacks a morphological infinitive, not all *da*-constructions are subjunctives correlated with *subject uncertainty*. What I tried to show is that *da*-CPs may also function as equivalents of infinitival structures in other language. I propose the term *non-indicative* to capture both functions of *da*-constructions. This said, Table 1 from above can be augmented as in Table 3.

In sum, it was shown that Bulgarian is likely to possess non-finite complements, namely non-finite *da*-CPs. Special evidence is supplied by the intricate class of verbs of perception, which may take three different types of complements, yielding three different interpretations. Furthermore, I argued *da* to be a modal (mood) particle not associated with the notion of finiteness. As a result, there is no need to assume more than one lexical entry for *da*. Moreover, *da* is semantically vacuous and, thus, a mere morphosyntactic placeholder marking what I call the Bulgarian *non-indicative*. Among other things, future work will have to examine whether the present assumptions apply to the whole range of relevant Bulgarian examples, and whether they extend to *da*-adjuncts as well as to independently used *da*-clauses.

References

Bernštejn, Samuil B. 1961. *Očerk sravniteľnoj grammatiki slavjanskich jazykov.* Moskva: AN SSSR.

Bresnan, Joan. 1972. "Theory of complementation in English syntax". Doctoral dissertation, MIT.

Büttner, Uwe. 2014. *Bulgarisch: Lehrbuch für Anfänger und Fortgeschrittene.* Leipzig: Universitätsbibliothek.

Genadieva-Mutafčieva, Zara. 1970. *Podčinitelnijat săjuz* da *v săvremennija bălgarski ezik*. Sofia: Bălgarska Akademija na Naukite.

Higginbotham, James. 1983. "The logic of perceptual reports: An extensional alternative to situation semantics." *The Journal of Philosophy* 80/2: 100–27.

Joseph, Brian. 1992. "Diachronic perspectives in control." In *Control and Grammar*, Richard Larson, Sabine Iatridou, Utpal Lahiri and James Higginbotham (eds.). Dordrecht: Kluwer, 195–223.

Kanno, Satoru and Tadao Nomura. 2012. "Syntactic finiteness of subjunctive clauses." In *Studies in English Linguistics and Literature* 22: 67–91.

Kramer, Christina E. 1992. "Analytic modality in Balkan Slavic." *Indiana Slavic Studies* 6: 113–22.

Krapova, Iliana. 1997. "On control in Bulgarian." In *Formale Slavistik*, Uwe Junghanns and Gerhild Zybatow (eds.). Frankfurt am Main: Vervuert, 93–107.

Krapova, Iliana. 1998. "Subjunctive complements, null subjects and case checking in Bulgarian." *University of Venice Working Papers in Linguistics* 8/2: 73–93.

Krapova, Iliana. 1999. "The system of auxiliaries in Bulgarian." In *Topics in South Slavic Syntax and Semantics*, Mila Dimitrova-Vulchanova and Lars Hellan (eds.). Amsterdam, Philadelphia: John Benjamins, 59–89.

Krapova, Iliana. 2001. Subjunctives in Bulgarian and modern Greek. *Comparative Syntax of Balkan Languages*, María Luisa Rivero and Angela Ralli (eds.). Oxford: Oxford University Press, 105–26.

Maslov, Jurij S. 1962. "K semantike bolgarskogo kon"junktiva." *Slavjanskoe jazykoznanie* 316/*Serija filologičeskich nauk* 64: 3–10.

Maslov, Jurij S. 1981. *Grammatika bolgarskogo jazyka: dlja studentov filologičeskich fakuľtetov universitetov*. Moskva: Vyssaja škola.

Lempp, Albrecht. 1981. *Das zusammengesetzte Verbalprädikat mit 'da' im Neubulgarischen*. München: Otto Sagner.

Penčev, Jordan. 1998. *Sintaksis na săvremennija bălgarski knižoven ezik*. Plovdiv.

Petkova Schick, Ivana. 1977. "Die bulgarischen 'da'-Konstruktionen als Träger spezifischer Modalitäten." *Linguistische Studien* A 43: 117–85.

Popov, Konstantin. 1968. "Za njakoi strukturni, semantični i stilistični osobenosti na prostite izrečenija v bălgarskija ezik." In *Otázky slovanské syntaxe II. Sborník symposia 'Strukturní typy slovanské věty a jejich vývoj', Brno 20.–22.10.1966*, Jaroslav Bauer (ed.). Brno: UJEP, 201–9.

Portner, Paul. 1997. "The semantics of mood, complementation, and conversational force." *Natural Language Semantics* 5: 167–212.

Portner, Paul and Aynat Rubinstein. 2013. "Mood and contextual commitment." In *Proceedings of SALT 22*, Anca Chereces (ed.). Chicago: CLC Publications 461–87.

Quer, Josep. 1998. *Mood at the Interface*. The Hague: Holland Academic Graphics.

Rivero, María Luisa. 1994. "Clause structure and V-movement in the languages of the Balkans." *Natural Language and Linguistic Theory* 12: 63–120.

Rivero, María Luisa. 2005. "Topics in Bulgarian morphology and syntax: A minimalist perspective." *Lingua* 115: 1083–128.

Schlenker, Philippe. 2005. "The lazy Frenchman's approach to the subjunctive: Speculations on reference to worlds and semantic defaults in the analysis of mood." In *Romance Languages and Linguistic Theory 2003: Selected Papers from 'Going Romance' 2003*, Twan Geerts, Ivo van Ginneken and Haike Jacobs (eds.). Amsterdam, Philadelphia: John Benjamins, 269–310.

Seliščev, Afanasij M. 1952. *Staroslavjanskij jazyk*. 2: *Teksty, slovar', očerki morfologii*. Moskva: Gosudarstvennoe učebno-pedagogičeskoe izdateľstvo Ministerstva prosveščenija RSFSR.

Siegel, Laura. 2009. "Mood selection in Romance and Balkan." *Lingua* 119: 1859–82.

Smirnova, Anastasia. 2010. "Cross-linguistic variation in the temporal domain: The meaning of the present tense in Albanian and Bulgarian." *Balkanistica* 23: 75–112.

Smirnova, Anastasia. 2012. "The semantics of mood in Bulgarian." *Proceedings from the Annual Meeting of the Chicago Linguistic Society* 48/1: 547–61.

Tilkov, Dimităr et al. (ed.). 1983. *Gramatika na săvremennija bălgarski knižoven ezik*. Tom 3: *Sintaksis*. Sofija: BAN.

Weigand, Gustav. 1907. *Bulgarische Grammatik*. Leipzig: Barth.

Werkmann, Valja. 2007. "Verbs of perception in Bulgarian." Abstract submitted to FDSL 7, Leipzig. http://www.uni-leipzig.de/~jungslav/fdsl/fdsl7/abstracts/Werkmann_FA.pdf

Margarita Dimitrova

Bulgarian Yes-No Questions – Clitic *li* and Polarity Items*[*]

1. Introduction

The paper deals with the distribution of the polarity items (PIs) in Bulgarian yes-no questions, particularly focusing on the occurrence of negation and the licensing of negative concord in these structures.

It has been long noticed (Ladd, 1981; Romero & Han, 2004; Büring & Gunlogson, 2000 a.o.) that negative yes-no questions are ambiguous structures, underlining the speaker's expectation for a positive value of the proposition. That is why negation in yes-no questions has often been considered expletive, i.e. semantically void of negative content (Brown & Franks, 1995, Espinal, 1997, 2000). Ladd (1981) makes the well-known distinction between Inner and Outer negation and moreover associates the expression of each one of these types with the distribution of the PIs. Therefore, it has been shown that Outer negation is only compatible with positive polarity items (PPIs), giving rise to positively biased yes-no questions (1a), while Inner negation can co-occur with negative polarity items (NPIs) expressing negative bias (1b):

(1) a. Isn't Jane coming, too?
    b. Isn't Jane coming, either?

In Holmberg (2013, 2016), it has been moreover shown that the position of the negation marker in Standard English contributes for the distinction between Inner and Outer negation. Hence, the "low", Pol(arity)P(hrase) internal, occurrence of the negation marker conveys Inner negation reading (2a), while Outer negation has been associated with the CP domain since it is structurally higher (2b). Or, to put it differently, Outer negation in Holmberg's terms is PolP external:

(2) a. Is this not the road to Lund?
    b. Isn't this the road to Lund? (Holmberg, 2016, ex. (77))

* This work has been developed under the PhD scholarship SFRH/BD/99302/2013 provided by *Fundação para a Ciência e a Tecnologia (FCT)* 'Foundation for the Science and the Technology'.

As for the pragmatics of negative yes-no question, Reese (2006, 2007) argues that these structures are akin to Tag-questions and claims that they are complex speech acts consisting in simultaneously *assertion* and *question*, much like in Ambar (2000, 2003) on wh-*in-situ* questions. Yoon (2011), on the other hand, suggests that the so called "expletive" negation is actually evaluative and, therefore, it contributes for the expression of the speaker's evaluations.

In what follows, I will concentrate on the distribution of the PIs in Bulgarian yes-no questions, showing that they not only favour the expression of bias but are moreover associated with distinct structural positions. What is more, the distribution of the PIs in negative yes-no questions appears to be strongly dependent from the occurrence of the interrogative clitic *li*: the element that licenses yes-no questions.

Thus, on one hand, I will discuss the syntactic structure of positively biased questions, i.e. the structures in which the negation marker co-occurs with the PPIs. On the other hand, I will observe the licensing of the NPIs which patterns with the licensing of focus phrases. Therefore, I will argue that the NPIs in Bulgarian yes-no questions undergo obligatory focus-movement: a result from the fact that they behave as wh-words (Haspelmath, 1997, Bhat, 2000; Bošković, 2008, 2009, Ambar, 2013).

The paper is organised as follows. In section 2, I illustrate the formation of Bulgarian yes-no questions, concentrating on the distribution of the clitic *li*. In section 3, I discuss negative yes-no questions, considering the crucial for the paper data concerning the licensing of negation and negative concord (subsection 3.2) and assuming a relation between the NPIs and focus movement (subsection 3.3). In section 4, I advance with the proposal for analysis, adopting recent studies on the syntax of yes-no questions (Holmberg, 2012, Ambar, 2013). Section 5 sets up the conclusion remarks.

2. The clitic *li*: question and focus

As pointed out above, the distribution of the PIs in Bulgarian yes-no questions is strongly connected with the distribution of the interrogative clitic *li*. As previously discussed in the literature (Rudin et al. 1999, Bošković, 2001, Izvorski, 1995 a.o), *li* is the element that enables the licensing of Bulgarian yes-no questions. Two *loci* for the clitic have been distinguished: (i) in enclisis to the verb, as in (2) and (ii) in enclisis to XPs different from the verb, as illustrated in (3):

(2) Ivan kupi li knigata?
John bought Q book.def
"Did John buy the book?"

(3) Ivan knigata li kupi?
John book.def Q bought
"Did John buy THE BOOK?"

The questions in (2) and (3) differ with respect to information structure. In (2), the enclisis of *li* into the inflected verb results in what has been defined as *neutral* yes-no question. In (3), on the other hand, the host of the clitic is obligatory associated with focus assignment, signalled by the capital letters in the translation. Thus, it has been generally assumed that whenever *li* encliticises into an element different from the verb, it assigns focus to its host, as in (3). Importantly, we can observe that licensing focus in Bulgarian yes-no questions is always associated with a pre-verbal position. As illustrated in (4) below, the post-verbal occurrence of the focalised constituent gives rise to odd sentences:

(4) ?Ivan kupi knigata li?[1]
John bought book.def Q
Intended: "Did John buy THE BOOK?"

What is more, the occurrence of the clitic is in the core of the focus-assignment. Observe that focalisation does not take place when *li* does not encliticise into the relevant host:

(5) *Ivan KNIGATA kupi li?
John book.def. bought Q
Intended: Did John buy THE BOOK?"

Therefore, considering (4) and (5), the two following requirements regarding the expression of focus in Bulgarian yes-no questions are formulated:

(i) the focalised constituent must move to a preverbal position;
(ii) the focalised constituent must host the clitic *li*;

As we will observe in what follows, the requirements in (i) and (ii) are crucial for the licensing of the NPIs in Bulgarian negative yes-no questions.

1 The example in (4) is felicitous when associated with a reading in which *li* scopes over the entire sentence. In these cases, a confirmation-like interpretation is confined to the structure.

3. Negation, polarity items and the clitic *li*

3.1. Negative concord

The present work will approach the distribution of the PIs in yes-no questions from the perspective of the licensing of negative concord. It is well known that the languages differ in allowing for negative concord. Bulgarian is *strict negative concord language*, in Giannakidou's (2000) lines, therefore the n-words (Laka, 1990) always co-occur with sentential negation. This co-occurrence applies for pre and post-verbal NPIs, as shown in (6) and (7) (differently from what has been observed on so called *non-strict negative concord languages*, Zanuttini, 1994, 1997, Matos, 1999, Zejlistra, 2004, a.o):

(6) Ivan *(ne) vidja ništo.
John not saw nothing
"John didn't see anything."

(7) Nikoj *(ne) vidja Ivan.
No one not saw John
"No one saw John."

Additionally, as the examples above illustrate, the obligatory co-occurrence between the n-words and the negation marker does not give rise to double negation reading: the negative elements take part of the same logical negation.

3.2. Negative yes-no questions and negative concord

However, even though Bulgarian is *strict negative concord language*, an unexpected blocking of negative concord occurs in yes-no questions. It appears that the NPIs cannot always felicitously co-occur with the negated verb. Thus, a sharp contrast between the PPIs and the NPIs can be observed in negative yes-no questions. Consider the examples in (8) and (9) below:

(8) *Ivan ne kupi li ništo?
John not bought Q nothing

(9) Ivan ne kupi li nešto?
John not bought Q something
"Didn't John buy something?"

The examples above draw an interesting asymmetry between the compatibility of the PIs with negation: while the NPI *ništo* "nothing" is infelicitous in (8), where it follows the neg.verb+*li* complex, the PPI *nešto* "something" is plausible. Returning to Ladd's distinction between Inner and Outer negation, discussed in section 1, the example in (9) reflects straightforwardly the latter type, in which the negation marker co-occurs with PPIs. Thus, the contrast between (8) and (9) gives rise to the assumption that whenever the clitic *li* follows the negated verb, only the Outer negation reading is available, since the negation marker does not license the NPIs, as in (8).

The above asymmetries regarding the compatibility between the PIs and the negation marker are not new to the literature. Similar data concerning other Slavic languages, namely Serbian-Croatian (10) and Russian (11), have been discussed:

(10) *Nije li Vera videla nikoga?
neg+AUX Q Vera see.PART.F.SG noone
"Didn't Vera see anyone?" (Milićević, 2006, ex. (9))

(11) Ljubit li Fedja kogo-nibud′ / *nikogo?
Likes Q Fedja who-any / *no-who
"Does Fedja like anybody?" (Brown & Franks, 1995, ex. (7))

Two types of analyses have been put forward: (i) analyses arguing that the NPIs are not licensed since negation is pleonastic (Brown & Franks, 1995) and (ii) analyses claiming that the negation in these structures does not license the NPIs since it is higher in the derivation (Milićević, 2006, Abels, 2002).

Let us now consider the behaviour of the PIs. While the blocking of negative concord has been object of previous discussions, the licensing of the NPIs in these structures has not received much attention. In Bulgarian it appears that the licensing of the NPIs in negative yes-no questions requires hosting the clitic *li*, as illustrated below:

(12) a. Ivan ništo li ne kupi?
John nothing Q not bought
"Didn't John buy anything?"

b. Nikoj li ne kupi knigata?
No one Q not bought book.def
"Didn't anybody bought the book?"

The licensing of both object and subject NPIs ((12a) and (12b), respectively) follows from raising and hosting *li*, which can be associated with the requirements for the expression of focus stipulated in (i) and (ii) of the preceding section 2. Thus, the data in (12) suggest that the NPIs in Bulgarian yes-no questions behave as focus phrases. The fact that they must obligatory move suggests that Bulgarian NPIs are inherently focalised.

What about the PPIs? As shown above, differently from their negative counterparts, the PPIs felicitously occur in a position following the neg.verb+*li* complex (ex. 9). However, they cannot host *li* in either positive (13a) or negative (13b) polar questions:

(13) a. *Ivan nešto li kupi?
John something Q bought
b. *Ivan nešto li ne kupi?
John something Q not Bought.

Thus, the behaviour of the PPIs sharply contrasts with that of the NPIs: the NPIs must host *li*, while the PPIs cannot provide a host for the clitic. The fact that the PPIs are infelicitous hosts for the clitic *li* moreover suggests that they cannot be focalised, a property already discussed in the literature (Tsimpli & Roussou, 1996 on Greek).

Additionally, we can observe that the PPIs cannot generally co-occur with sentential negation in declarative contexts (an exception is metalinguistic negation, Horn, 1989):

(14) *Ivan ne kupi nešto.
John not bought something

However, their co-occurrence is felicitous in yes-no questions, as in (9) above. The same holds for the NPIs, which are felicitously licensed pre and post-verbally in declaratives, as illustrated by the examples in (6) and (7). Thus, the data presented so far draws a contrast between declarative and interrogative structures for what concerns the behaviour the PIs. The trigger for this contrast seems to be a result from the occurrence of *li*.

Hence, returning to the blocking of negative concord, illustrated in (8) above, we can observe that when the clitic does not block the relation between the negation marker and the NPI, nothing goes wrong for licensing negative concord.

(15) Ivan li ne kupi ništo?
John Q not bought nothing
"Was it John the person who didn't buy anything?"

The example in (15) is focused question being the focalised element the subject Ivan which is the host of *li.*

However, although (15) contains negation, we can observe that it is not truly negative since the negative elements (the negation marker and the NPI *ništo* "nothing") take part of the so called "presupposed" information occurring on *li*'s right. The behaviour of the answering system confirms this assumption. Considering that Bulgarian has a polarity-based answering system (Holmberg, 2012), the minimal answers "yes" and "no" agree with the polarity of the question. The answers of the question in (15), however, refer to the element hosting the clitic *li,* as shown in (16) below:

(16) Q: Ivan li ne kupi ništo?
John Q not bought nothing
"Was it John the person who didn't buy anything?"
A1: Da.
Yes (It was John who didn't buy anything.)
A2: Ne.
No (It wasn't John who didn't buy anything.)

Importantly, the examples in (15) and (16) illustrate that the NPI *ništo* "nothing" can felicitously co-occur with the negation marker when another constituent is focalised.

Thus, it appears that the asymmetries illustrated above derive from the occurrence of *li*:

(17) Ivan ne kupi li *ništo?
John not bought Q *nothing
"Didn't John buy something?

(18) Ivan li ne kupi ništo?
John Q not bought nothing
"Was it John who didn't buy anything?"

Therefore, I suggest that positively biased questions (as in (9)) are not a result from the expletive nature of the negation marker but rather from the relation between the negated verb and the clitic, associated with the raising of the negated verb.

3.3. The NPIs and focus movement

In this subsection, I will discuss the licensing of the NPIs. The NPIs in Bulgarian yes-no questions obligatory undergo movement to pre-verbal position. What is more, they must host the clitic *li*:

(19) a. *Ništo ne kupi li Ivan?
nothing not bought Q John
Intended reading: "Didn't John buy anything?"
b. Ništo li ne kupi Ivan?
nothing Q not bought John

This behaviour of the NPIs can be readily associated with focus-movement. What is more, it has been previously argued in the literature that the NPIs in Serbian (Bošković, 2008, 2009) and Modern Greek (Tsimpli & Roussou, 1996) are inherently negative and focal. Thus, they bear focus stress and move overtly to a pre-verbal position. In Bošković, (2008, 2009), this is the Spec of FocP situated above NegP. This behaviour of the Serbian NPIs appears to be morphologically encoded, as shown in (20):

(20) *niko* "no one" = [n (neg) + i (focus ('even')) + ko (who)] Bošković (2008, ex. (21))

Returning to the behaviour of the NPIs in Bulgarian, it seems that they can be approached with respect to focus movement since their licensing in yes-no questions fully patterns with what has been observed on focus phrases. Previous works on the structure of Bulgarian yes-no questions and on the interrogative clitic *li* have suggested that what we are dealing with in XP-*li* questions are contrastively focalized XPs. The interpretation confined to these structures felicitously correlates with this assumption. We observe, however, that Bulgarian NPIs behave as focus phrases only in questions, since they are plausible pre and post-verbally in declaratives. Observe the contrast between the declarative in (21) and the questions in (22) below:

(21) a. Ne kupi NIŠTO.
not bought.3p.sg. NOTHING
b. NIŠTO ne kupi.
NOTHING not bought.3p.sg

(22) a. *Ne kupi li ništo?
not bought.3p.sg Q nothing
b. *Ne kupi ništo li?
not bought.3p.sg nothing Q
c. Ništo li ne kupi?
nothing Q not bought.3p.sg

What is more, the behaviour of the NPIs is not particularly associated with contrastive focus assignment, as in focused yes-no questions. Additionally, it has been previously observed in the literature (Rudin, 1986, a.o) that the clitic *li* appears in wh-questions, giving rise to dubitative wh-questions:

(23) Koj li kupi knigata?
who Q bought book.def
"(I am wondering) who bought the book?"

Importantly, the only plausible host for *li* in (23) is the wh-word which patterns with what we have observed with the licensing of the NPIs illustrated above.

Ambar (2013) moreover suggests that the PIs behave as wh-words in yes-no questions, observing that yes-no questions with PPIs (24) and wh-questions (25) pattern with respect to the way they are answered:

(24) Q: Quem vai contigo ao cinema?
"Who goes with you to the movies?"
A: Vai o Pedro.
goes Peter
Peter does

(25) Q: Alguém vai contigo ao cinema?
"Someone is going with you to the movies?"
A: Vai o Pedro.
goes Peter
Peter does (Ambar, 2013 ex. (33–34))

It appears that in both (24) and (25) above the answer identifies the value of the variable of the question.

Thus, considering Ambar's (2013) proposal and the fact that Bulgarian NPIs behave as focus phrases only in questions, I assume that the trigger for the NPIs behaviour is focus movement, which is not, however, associated with contrastive focus assignment but rather with the fact that the NPIs behave as wh-words.

4. Proposal

In this section, I will briefly refer to previous syntactic accounts of yes-no questions, focusing on the works of Holmberg (2012) and Ambar (2013): both considering the projection Pol(arity) P(hrase).

The projection PolP refers to the polarity intrinsically codified in yes-no questions, i.e. to the existence of the alternatives {p, ¬p} (Hamblin, 1973). In Holmberg (2012) it has been suggested that PolP has three possible values: affirmative, negative and open. In his lines, positive yes-no questions are open and valued affirmative or negative in the answer. What is more, Holmberg (2012) considers a focus projection situated above PolP which probes the polarity variable. Thus, the answers of yes-no questions consist in focus expressions, assigning value to the variable.

In Ambar (2013), PolP contains the values affirmative and negative. The interrogative operator originates in FocP and has the following representation: INT <Taff, neg>, <Faff, neg> in which T(rue) and F(alse) are valued in the answer, as in Holmberg (2012). Additionally, Int(errogative)P situated above FocP has been considered.

The data we have observed so far supports the view that Outer negation is structurally higher (Holmberg, 2013, 2016). As observed above, licensing NPIs and negative concord does not take place when the negated verb hosts *li*. Therefore, the proposal for an analysis that I assume below will not consider semantically void of negative content NegP. The structure in (26) follows:

(26) [TopP [Int(errogative)P [FocP [PolP [TP [NegP]]]]]]

For the time being, I suggest that the clitic *li* is generated in the head of IntP since it is the element responsible for the licensing of Bulgarian yes-no questions. In positively biased questions, where negative concord is blocked, the negated verb moves to Int° where it provides host for *li*:

(27) [TopP Ivan$_j$ [IntP [Int' ne kupi$_i$ li [FocP [Foc' ~~ne kupi~~$_i$ [PolP [Pol' ~~ne kupi~~$_i$
John not bought Q
[neg] [TP ~~Ivan~~$_j$ [T' ~~ne kupi~~$_i$ *ništo [Neg' ~~ne kupi~~$_i$]]]]]]
[NegP
*nothing

When, on the other hand, both the negative verb and the NPI remain within the TP domain, i.e. when a focalised XP raises to FocP and IntP and hosts *li*, negative concord is licensed:

(28) [TopP [IntP Ivan$_j$ [Int' li [FocP ~~Ivan~~$_j$ [PolP [uPol] [TP ~~Ivan~~$_j$ ne kupi$_i$ [NegP ~~ne~~ ~~kupi~~$_i$ ništo]]]]]]
John Q not bought nothing

The structure in (28) furthermore captures the fact that when negation is TP-internal PolP remains unvalued. Thus, it felicitously correlates with the behavior of the answering system discussed above.

As for the behavior of the NPIs, I propose a derivation in the sense of the one illustrated in (28) with the focalized subject Ivan: the NPI raises to FocP and IntP where it hosts the clitic.

(29) [TopP Ivan$_k$ [IntP ništo$_j$ [Int' li [FocP ~~ništoj~~ [PolP ~~ništo~~$_j$ [neg] [TP Ivan$_k$ [T' ne kupi$_i$ [NegP ~~ništo~~$_j$ [Neg' ne kupi$_i$]]]]]]]
John nothing Q not bought

5. Conclusion

Two problems have been pointed out in the present work: (i) one, related with the blocking of negative concord and (ii) another, related with the particular behaviour of Bulgarian NPIs which move overtly in Bulgarian negative yes-no questions.

The Bulgarian data and the asymmetries in the expression of Inner and Outer negation have encouraged the conclusion that the Outer negation reading is associated with the negated verb which is object of obligatory higher raising. Differently from previous accounts of negative yes-no questions, the current analysis has assumed that the expletive nature of the negation marker is not in the core of the expression of Outer negation.

As for the behaviour of Bulgarian NPIs, it has been assumed that the trigger for their movement is focus which surfaces as a consequence from the fact that they behave somewhat like wh-words, as previously noticed for the PPIs (Ambar, 2013).

Considering Ladd (1981) and more recent works, namely Reese (2006) and Yoon (2011) among others, I moreover suggest that the movement to Int(errogative)P(hrase) is followed by raising to higher domains accounting for the speaker's presupposition, evaluation and for the bias consistently present in negative polar questions. I leave this question for further research.

References

Abels, Klaus. 2002. "Expletive (!) Negation." In *Proceedings of FASL 10*, Toman Jindrich (eds.). Bloomington: Michigan Slavic Publications, 1–20.

Ambar, Manuela. 2013. "Yes-no questions, subjects, adverbs and left periphery – new evidence from Portuguese." In *Language Use and Linguistic Structure. Proceedings of the Olomouc Linguistics Colloquium 2013*, Joseph Emonds and Markéta Janebová (eds.). Olomouc: Palacký University, 15–32.

Bhat, D. N. Shankara. 2000. "The Indefinite-interrogative Puzzle." *Linguistic Typology 4*: 365–400.

Bošković, Željko 2009. "Licensing Negative Constituents and Negative Concord." In *Proceedings of the North East Linguistic Society 38*. GLSA, University of Massachusetts, Amherst, 125–139.

Bošković, Željko. 2001. "Li without PF movement." In *Formal Approaches to Slavic Linguistics: The Indiana Meeting* 2000, Steven Franks, Tracy Holloway King and Misha Yadroff (eds.). Ann Arbor: Michigan Slavic Publications, 57–75.

Bošković, Željko. 2008. "On two types of negative constituents and negative concord." In *Proceedings of FDSL 6.5*. Frankfurt am Main: Peter Lang, 9–35.

Brown, Sue and Franks, Steven. 1995. "Asymmetries in the scope of Russian Negation." *Journal of Slavic Linguistics 3*: 239–287.

Büring, Daniel and Gunlogson, Christine. 2000. *Aren't Positive and Negative Polar Questions the Same?* Ms. UCSC/UCLA. *Catalan working papers in linguistics 8*: 47–69.

Espinal, Maria Teresa. 2000. "Expletive negation, negative concord and feature checking." *Catalan Working Papers in Linguistics* 8: 47–69.

Giannakidou, Anastasia. 2000. "Negative…concord?" *Natural Language and Linguistic Theory* 18: 457–523.

Hamblin, Charles L. 1973. "Questions in Montague English." *Foundations of Language*, 10: 41–53.

Haspelmath, Martin. 1997. *Indefinite Pronouns*. Clarendon Press: Oxford.

Holmberg, Anders. 2012. "On the Syntax of Yes and No in English." In *Newcastle Working Papers in Linguistics 18*. CRILLS, Newcastle University, 52–72.

Holmberg, Anders. 2013. "The syntax of answers to polar questions in English and Swedish." *Lingua 128*: 31–50.

Holmberg, Anders. 2016. *The syntax of yes and no*. Oxford: Oxford University Press.

Horn, Laurence. 1989. *A natural history of negation*. Stanford: CSLI Publications.

Izvorski, Roumyana. 1995. "On Wh-Movement and Focus Movement in Bulgarian." *Paper presented at Console 2 University of Tubingen December 1993.*

Ladd, Robert. 1981. "A First Look at the Semantics and Pragmatics of Negative Questions and Tag Questions." In *Papers from the Seventeenth Regional Meeting of the Chicago Linguistic Society*, Chicago Linguistics Society, 164–171.

Laka, Itziar. 1990. "Negation in Syntax: On the Nature of Functional Categories and Projections." PhD thesis, MIT.

Matos, Gabriela. 1999. "Negative Concord and the Scope of Negation." *Catalan Working Papers in Linguistics* 7. Bellaterra: Universitat Autònoma de Barcelona, 175–190.

Milićević, Nataša. 2006. "On negation in yes/no questions in Serbo-Croatian." *UiL OTS Working Papers 2006*, Dotlačil, Jakub and Gehrke Berit (eds.), 29–47.

Reese, Brian. 2006. "The meaning and use of negative polar interrogatives." In *Empirical issues in syntax and semantics* 6, Olivier Bonami and Patricia Cabredo-Hofherr (eds.), 331–354.

Reese, Brian. 2007. "Bias in questions." PhD thesis, University of Texas, Austin.

Romero, Maribel and Han, Chung-Hye. 2004. "On Negative Yes/No Questions." *Linguistics and Philosophy 27*.5: 609–658

Rudin, Catherine, Kramer Christina, Billings Loren and Baerman Matthew. 1999. "Macedonian and Bulgarian li Questions: Beyond Syntax." *Natural language and Linguistic Theory* 17: 541–586.

Tsimpli, Ianthi-Maria and Roussou, Anna. 1996. "Negation and Polarity Items in Modern Greek." *Linguistic Review 13*.1: 1–33.

Yoon, Suwon. 2011. "Not in the Mood. The Syntax and Semantics of Evalautive Negation." PhD thesis, University of Chicago.

Zanuttini, Raffaela. 1997. *Negation and Clausal Structure — a Comparative Study of Romance Languages*. New York, Oxford: Oxford University Press.

Zanuttini, Raffaela., 1994. "Re-examining negative clauses." In *Paths towards Universal Grammar: Essays in Honor of Richard S. Kayne*, Guglielmo Cinque et al. (eds.). Washington: Georgetown University Press, 427–451.

Zeijlstra, Hedde. 2004. "Sentential Negation and Negative Concord." PhD thesis, University of Amsterdam.

Polish

Jacek Witkoś

On Accusative Numeral Subjects in Polish*

1. Introduction

This paper addresses the issue of higher Numeral Phrases used in the subject position in Polish (henceforth Accusative Numeral Subjects, ANS), where they show all the typical nominative subject properties (henceforth NOM) with two exceptions: they do not show full agreement for φ-features, nor do they occur in nominative. I argue that these properties result from a conspiracy of such factors as: a peculiar internal structure of these Numeral Phrases, their complex derivational history and their impoverished case paradigm. In this brief contribution I shall present compelling evidence that ANS behave like NOM and propose an eclectic account of some these facts, based on a combination of the phase theory (Chomsky 2000, 2001, 2008) as well as nano-syntax (Starke 2009, Caha 2009).

2. The empirical foundations

In Polish low quantifiers in the subject position behave in a regular manner, while high quantifiers (≥5, Q_H) require default agreement on T_{fin} (Babby 1987; Pesetsky 1982, 2014; Franks 1994, 1995, 2002; Przepiórkowski 1999, 2001; Baylin 2004; Bošković 2006; Pereltsvaig 2006; Przepiórkowski and Patejuk 2012; Willim 2015; Witkoś and Dziubała-Szrejbrowska 2016):

(1) a. Te trzy dziewczyny pracowały/*pracowało tam.
these-NOM three-NOM girls-NOM.PL worked -PL/SG there
'These three girls worked there.'

b. Te pięć dziewczyn *pracowały/pracowało tam.
these-ACC five-ACC girls-GEN.PL worked-PL/SG there
'These five girls worked there.'

Examples such as (2) constitute a challenge to Chomsky's (2000, 2001, 2008) theory of case valuation:

* This research was partly sponsored by the grant no. 2012/07/B/HS2/02308 issued by the Polish Science Centre.

(2) Te/tych pięć tancerek widziało maskaradę.
these-ACC/GEN five-ACC dancers-GEN.PL saw-3SG.N masquerade-F.ACC.SG
'These five girls saw the masquerade.'

We see here both an accusative subject and an accusative object in a configuration which is difficult to conceive of if structural case valuation were limited to a plain Agree relation between T and v probes and relevant nominal phrases.[1] The general scenario for the valuation of structural case must allow for such exceptions, at least in Polish.

The ANS shares five important properties with NOM: **(a)** only these two subject types require felicitous and rigorous binding of reflexive possessives, while other subject types allow for 'liberal' binding of reflexive possessives, **(b)** these two subject types can be coordinated, **(c)** they both participate in the Nom(Acc)/Gen alternation in the existential construction, **(d)** they can both follow the prepositions *niż* 'than' and *jak* 'as', which prototypically require nominal complements in NOM, and **(e)** they both show binding, control and referential properties of prototypical subjects (Franks 1994, 1995; Pereltsvaig 2006).

---

1 Przepiórkowski (1999, 2001) proposes that QHPs are marked for accusative in the subject position on the basis of the following comparison, among others:

(i) (tych/te) pięć kobiet stało.
these-F.GEN./these-F.NOM?/ACC five-F.NOM?/ACC women-F.GEN.PL stood-3SG.N
'These five women were standing.'

(ii) (tych/*ci) pięciu mężczyzn stało.
these-M.ACC /GEN//these-M.NOM? five-M.NOM?/ACC/GEN men-M.GEN.PL stood-3SG.N
'These five men were standing.'

The common case form of the demonstrative for both genders is accusative, on the assumption that its optional genitive reflects the placement of the demonstrative in the domain of the NP-complement and its subsequent raising to the domain of the numeral/quantifier. Franks (1994, 1995, 2002) develops a similar proposal. We can add one more argument for the accusative nature of ANS: Lavine and Franks (2008) discuss transitive adversity predicates which select for affected arguments in accusative. ANS can be coordinated with such accusative arguments, which confirms its accusative nature:

(iii) tych pięciu harcerzy i harcerkę zemdliło po śniadaniu.
these-M.ACC/GEN five-M.ACC boy scouts-M.GEN.PL and girl scout-F.ACC nauseated-3SG.N after breakfast.
'Five scouts and a scout girl felt nausea after breakfast.'

Polish has two types of anaphoric expressions: anaphoric (and reciprocal) pronoun *siebie* 'self' and a reflexive possessive *swój* 'self's'. Anaphoric binding in Polish is subject oriented to a large degree but the subject orientation shows specifically with the possessive reflexive:

(3) a. Chłopcy$_1$ zobaczyli swoich$_1$/ich$_{*1,2}$ braci.
boys-M.NOM.PL saw-3PL.M selves'/their brothers
'Boys saw their brothers.'

b. Pięciu chłopców$_1$ zobaczyło swoich$_1$/ich$_{*1,2}$ braci.
five-ACC boys-GEN.PL saw-3SG.N selves'/their brothers
'Five boys saw their brothers.'

c. Chłopcom$_1$ spodobały się swoje$_{?1}$/ich$_{1,2}$ zabawki.
boys-M.DAT.PL liked-3PL.F REFL selves'/their toys-F.NOM.PL
'The boys liked their toys.'

d. Chłopcom$_1$ było zimno w swoich$_{?1}$/ich$_{1,2}$ nowych kurtkach.
boys-M.DAT.PL was-3SG.N cold in selves'/their new jackets
'Boys were cold in their new jackets.'

Both the ANS and NOM require rigorous binding of the reflexive possessive, so a co-indexation between them and the pronominal possessive is either ungrammatical or strongly disfavored as a violation of Binding Condition B, cf. (3a–b). For comparison, the dative subject does not agree with the verb either but it binds a possessive element in a liberal manner by tolerating either the reflexive form or the pronominal one, cf. (3c–d). I assume that the 'liberal' binding results from meeting the EPP property of T and is partly a performance effect, while the 'rigorous' binding is a genuine core grammar property. If one follows a version of the binding theory where T is implicated as a target for anaphor (α) raising (see Chomsky 1986; Pica 1991) or a probe implicated in multiple Agree with both the antecedent and the anaphor (Rooryck and Wyngaerd 2011), it transpires that apart from the default agreement ANS behaves like a picture-perfect NOM, cf. (3b), unlike other non-nominative subjects.[2]

---

2 If binding holds of the LF branch of grammar, the contrast between examples such as (3b) vs. (3c–d) argues strongly against analyses of the ANS that reduce its case properties to late morphological expression of case features unvalued in narrow syntax, cf. (Willim 2015).

Both subject types can be coordinated; below an ANS and NOM (both singular and plural) can be successfully coordinated. Any other combination of cases within a coordinated subject is disallowed:

(4) a. Zosia i pięć harcerek poszły na spacer.
Zosia-F.NOM.SG and five-ACC girl.scouts-F.GEN.PL went-3PL.F for walk.
'Zosia and five girl-scouts went for a walk.'

b. Trzej harcerze i pięć harcerek wyszli.
three-NOM boy.scouts-M.NOM.PL and five-ACC girl.scouts-F.GEN.PL left-3PL.M
'Three boy scouts and five girl scouts left.'

It seems that both conjuncts share the status of structural cases, which sets them apart from all others. Both subject types alternate with Genitive under negation in the existential construction:

(5) a. Tancerki były na scenie.
dancers-F.NOM.PL were-3PL.NonVIR on stage
'Dancers were on the stage.'

b. Tancerek nie było na scenie.
dancers-F.GEN.PL not was-3SG.NEUT on stage
'Dancers were not on the stage.'

(6) a. Pięć tancerek było na scenie.
five-F.ACC dancers-F.GEN.PL was-3SG.NEUT on stage
'Five dancers were on the stage.'

b. Pięciu tancerek nie było na scenie.
five-F.GEN dancers-F.GEN.PL not was-3SG.NEUT on stage
'Five dancers were not on the stage.'

The shift from ACC to genitive and NOM to genitive in the existential construction is a test for the structural case status of a given nominal in Polish. The prepositions *niż* 'than' and *jak* 'as', used in comparative structures typically force their complements to appear in nominative, cf. (Kallas 1995) but ANS can also follow them in identical contexts:

(7) a. Zaanektowano krainę większą niż Wielka Brytania. (Kallas 1995: 99)
(was) annexed-3SG.NEUT a country-ACC larger than Great Britain-NOM
'A country larger than Great Britain was annexed.'

b. Jan zjadł więcej jabłek niż tych sześć studentek.
Jan ate more apples than these-GEN six-ACC students-FEM.ACC
'Jan ate more apples than these six students (did).'

Finally, Pesetsky (1982), Franks (1994, 1995) and Perelstvaig (2006), among others, claim that Russian numeral phrases are structurally ambiguous between QPs and DPs, which shows when they occupy the subject position in Russian, as QPs do not show nominative case and trigger default agreement:

(8) [DP/QP Pjat' ženščin] smotreli/smotrelo na Ivana.
five women-GEN.PL looked-PL/SG at Ivan
'Five women looked at Ivan.'

These authors provide a battery of tests supposed to additionally distinguish between NOM (DP) and QP subjects. Thus only in the agreeing pattern is the DP-subject able to bind an anaphoric pronoun, as well as control a PRO subject of the participial clause and a regular complement infinitive. On the other hand, only the QP subject triggering quirky agreement can be extracted from the embedded clause. The grammar of Polish does not show this (ANS/NOM) ambiguity and all equivalent Polish examples require the ANS with default agreement, though it shares all the functions of the NOM DP in Russian. The Polish ANS can successfully bind an anaphoric pronoun, control into a participial adjunct clause and control into an infinitival complement.[3] Furthermore, Pereltsvaig (2006) observes that the agreeing (DP) numeral subjects in Russian show the following properties: they allow for the individuated interpretation,

3 All Polish examples below correspond to the relevant ones in Russian in Franks (1994, 1995):

(i) Pięć kobiet patrzyło/*patrzyły na Jana.
five women-GEN.PL looked- SG/PL at Ivan
'Five women looked at Ivan.'

(ii) Pięć kobiet patrzyło/*patrzyły na siebie.
five women-GEN.PL looked- SG/PL at themselves
'Five women looked at themselves.'

(iii) PRO wracając do domu, pięciu chłopców weszło/*weszli do sklepu.
returning to home, five boys-GEN.PL dropped.in- SG/PL to store
'Returning home, five boys dropped in to the store.'

(iv) Pięć kobiet starało/*starały się PRO kupić tę książkę.
five women-GEN.PL tried- SG/PL REFL to.buy this book
'Five women tried to buy this book.'

(v) % Ilu ludzi, Jan myśli że, t przeczytało/ *przeczytali tę książkę?
how.many people-GEN.PL Jan thinks that read- SG/P this book
'How many people Ivan thinks that read this book?

specific interpretation, partitive interpretation and non-isomorphic wide scope.[4]

These interpretive correlations do not hold of Polish either, where the ANS must appear in all the relevant contexts and supports all relevant interpretations.[5] In a nutshell, the ANS in Polish is a spitting image of a regular NOM subject but for its case form and default agreement.

---

4 Pereltsvaig observes that the so-called individuate interpretation is possible only with NOM, while the ANS receives the group interpretation (cf. i); only NOM can receive a specific interpretation brought out by adjectives denoting specificity (cf. ii–iii); there is a correlation between NOM and a strongly partitive interpretation, that is referring to a subset of a previously mentioned set (cf. iv–vi); another correlation concerns a possibility of inverse scope readings with NOM and lack thereof with ANS (cf. vii–viii):

(i) Rol Dzejmsa Bonda ispolnjali/#ispolnjalo [pjat' izvestnyx aktërov].
role James Bond performed-PL/#performed-NEUT five famous actors
'Five famous actors performed the role of James Bond.'

(ii) V Mariinskom teatre tancevali [opredlënnye pjat' balerin].
in Mariinsky theater danced-PL certain five ballerinas
'A certain five ballerinas danced in the Mariinsky Theater.'

(iii) *V Mariinskom teatre tancevalo [opredlënnye pjat' balerin].
in Mariinsky theater danced-PL certain five ballerinas.
Intended: 'A certain five ballerinas danced in the Mariinsky Theater.'

(iv) U nas v gorod priexala gruppa balerin/ priexali baleriny iż Petersburga.
To our town came group ballerinas-GEN/came ballerinas from Petersburg
'A group of ballerinas from St. Petersburg came to our town.'

(v) … vo vcerasnem koncerte tancevali [pjatero iż nix].
in yesterday's concert danced-PL five of them
'five of them danced in yersterday's concert.'

(vi) *…vo vcerašnem koncerte tancevalo [pjatero iż nix].
in yesterday's concert danced-NEUT five of them
Intended: 'five of them danced in yesterday's concert.'

(vii) Každyj raz pjat' xirurgov operirovali Bonda.
every time five surgeons operated-PL Bond
'Every time five surgeons operated on Bond.'
ambiguous: (every >5 or 5 > every)

(viii) Každyj raz pjat' xirurgov operirovalo Bonda.
every time five surgeons operated-NEUT Bond
'Every time five surgeons operated on Bond.'
unambiguous: (every >5; #5 > every)

5 So, although NOM is completely unavailable in Polish and the ANS appears obligatorily, the individuated reading can be obtained nevertheless, (i); the specific interpretation brought out by adjectives denoting specificity is available, (ii); so is the strong partitive interpretation, referring to a subset of a previously mentioned set, (iii–iv),

3. The analysis

I assume that NPs are dominated by a functional sequence including a universal set of Case Projections, as stated in *Universal Case Contiguity* (Blake 1994, Caha 2009, 2010) and case suffixation follows from the raising of NP to a given case projection upon demand from an external case licensor, while the unused case projections become deleted:

(9)

$$[\,6\,[_{Com}\,F\,[\,5\,[_{Ins}\,E[\,4\,[_{Dat}\,D\,[\,3\,[_{Gen}\,C\,[\,2\,[_{Acc}\,B\,[\,1\,[_{Nom}\,[_{NP}\,A/Num_{H}\,N\ldots]]]]]]]$$

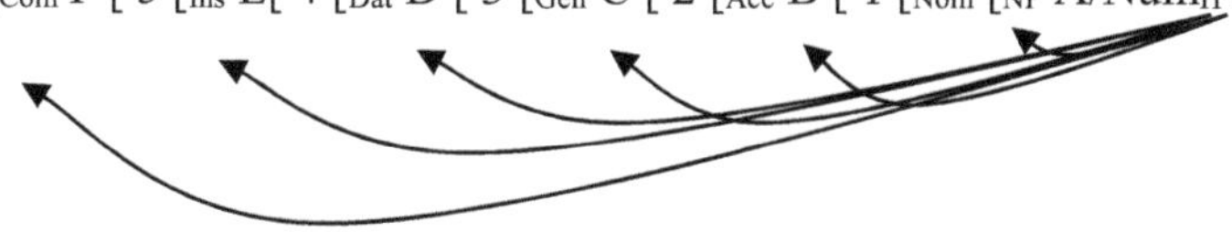

Polish numerals begin the derivation as members of the morpho-syntactic category adjective (A) but higher numerals (Q$_{H}$), which diachronically derive from nouns (cf. Rutkowski 2007, among others), show nominal properties (a full set of φ-features and need for case) in the context of the structural case licensing (cf. Babby 1987; Pesetsky 1982, 2014; Franks 1994, 1995, 2002; Przepiórkowski 1999, 2001; Baylin 2004; Bošković 2006; Pereltsvaig 2006; Przepiórkowski and Patejuk 2012; Willim 2015; Witkoś and Dziubała-Szrejbrowska 2016) and force an idiosyncratic derivation, whereby a single set of case projections needs to service both the case-greedy Num$_{H}$, as well as the original nominal N. As Num$_{H}$ occupies a superior position in (9) it values the structural case demanded by the

---

and it appears that both scope readings are available with the ANS in Polish, though the isomorphic scope reading is easier to access, (v):

(i)	Rolę	Jamesa	Bonda	*odegrali/odegrało	[pięciu	znanych	aktorów].
	role	James	Bond	*performed-PL/ performed-NEUT	five	famous	actors

'Five famous actors performed the role of James Bond.'

(ii)	W	Teatrze	Wielkim	*tańczyły/tańczyło	[pewne pięć	tancerek].
	in	Great	Theater	*danced-PL/danced-NEUT	certain five	dancers

'A certain five dancers danced in the Great Theater.'

(iii)	Do	naszego	miasta	przyjechała	grupa	tancerek/przyjechały	tancerki	z	Petersburga
	to	our	town	came	group	dancers-GEN/came	dancers-NOM	from	Petersburg

'A group of dancers from St. Petersburg came to our town.'

(iv)	…	podczas	wczorajszego	koncertu	*tańczyły/tańczyło	[pięć	z nich].
		in	yesterday's	concert	*danced-PL/ danced-NEUT	five	of them

'five of them danced in yesterday's concert.'

external case Probe.[6] Significantly, Num_H takes over the Case Projection sequence and forces its truncation, as it lacks the nominative form. In short, I assume that the relation between T_{fin} and the ANS to have the following relevant nature:[7]

(10) T_{fin}… ↔ … [… [$_{AccP}$ [$_{QP}$ [$_{NumP}$ te pięć] F_Q [$_{NP}$ dziewczyn]] …]]
[these five]-ACC girls-GEN

The Agree relation between T_{fin} and AccP is possible because of a specific internal feature make-up of the T_{fin} probe and a specific internal structure of the case feature on the nominal phrase. I assume that the head T_{fin} bears a dual two-pronged probe: one for φ-features and the other one for case. The case feature on T_{fin} is interpretable, although unvalued (cf. Pesetsky and Torrego 2007), so [case: structural]. The case feature on the nominal is internally structured in a way similar to how Bejar (2003) analyzes φ-features in Complex Subject Agreement languages,[8] with the lower elements of the feature hierarchy entailing the higher ones:

(11) a. nominative case: structural > nominative
b. accusative case: structural

In fact, the case feature on the nominal reflects the active projection in its Case Projection sequence.[9] I take structural case to mean accusative case by

---

(v) Za każdym razem pięciu chirurgów *operowali/operowało Bonda.
for every time five surgeons *operated-PL/ operated-NEUT Bond
'Every time five surgeons operated on Bond.'
ambiguous: (every > 5 or 5 > every)

6 See Witkoś and Dziubała-Szrejbrowska (2016) for a detailed account of this derivation and its consequences. I cannot discuss this crucial matter here for lack of space.

7 As argued in Witkoś and Dziubała-Szrejbrowska (2016) the structure of the Q_HP is slightly more complex due to a series of movements of [$_{NP}$ A/Q_H … N] within the case sequence:

(i) T_{fin}…↔ …[$_{GenP}$ [$_{AccP}$ te pięć dziewczyn] Gen]
[these five]-ACC girls-GEN

Yet, AccP is accessible to external probing by T_{fin} upon the definition of closeness in (Pesetsky and Torrego 2001), as neither GenP nor Gen c-command AccP.

8 Bejar (2003:65–66) proposes to capture complex subject agreement patterns through Probe/Goal relations involving structured φ-features, whereby a G(oal) values a P(robe) iff f(G) entails f(P), that is the content of G's feature set is at least as rich as that of P (or richer):

9 In this manner narrow syntax gains access to the case inflection paradigm of the nominal.

default. The feature internal composition in (11) means that nominative requires a more narrow licensing than accusative. I also assume that both the φ-features and the case feature are copied from the nominal onto the T_{fin} probe (Bejar 2003; Benmamoun et al. 2009; Marusić, et. al. 2015), so Agree is divided into two sub-operations: Agree-link and Agree-copy. In the standard case of NOM T_{fin} becomes involved in relation Agree with a regular NP:

(12) Cztery dziewczynki przyszły do szkoły.
four girls-NOM.PL.F came-NOM.PL.F to school
'Four girls came to school.'

(13) $T_{\{[_{\varphi}:][\text{case: structural}]\}} \ldots \leftrightarrow \ldots [_{vP} \ldots [_{NomP}\ NP_{\{[_{\varphi}\text{-features}][\text{case: } \ldots \text{ structural>nom}]\}}]$

The ensuing feature valuation involves copying of the value (content) of φ-features and the case feature onto T_{fin}:

(14) $T_{\{[_{\varphi}:\ _{\varphi}\text{-features}][\text{case: structural>nom}]\}} \ldots \leftrightarrow \ldots [_{vP} \ldots [_{NomP}\ NP_{\{[_{\varphi}\text{-features}][\text{case: } \ldots \text{structural>nom}]\}}]$

At this point, internally to head T_{fin}, the sub-components of the two-pronged probe are compared for the maximal effect of matching and valuation, in line with the following version of the Economy principle Maximize (Chomsky 2000, 2001):

(15) Maximize the matching effect, in that $[_{T}\ \{[\varphi + \text{val}] \leftrightarrow [\text{case: structural>nom}]\}]$

The formula in (15) is to be perceived as a positive correlation between full exposition of φ-features on T_{fin} only when its case probe sub-component bears the value [structural>nom].

The ANS violates Maximize in (15), as I assume that its case sequence is defective in that the bottom-most projection (Nominative Phrase) is truncated/defective ($[_{AccP}$ Acc $[Q_{H}P]$), so in this case the valuation of the features of the probe returns a different result:

(16) $T\{[\varphi:][\text{case:}]\} \ldots \leftrightarrow \ldots [_{QHP}\{[\varphi\text{-features}][\text{case: structural}]\}]$

The features of the goal are compatible with the ones of the probe and are copied onto it:

(17) $T\{[\varphi: \text{-val}][\text{case: structural}]\} \ldots \leftrightarrow \ldots [_{QHP}\{[\varphi\text{-features}][\text{case: structural}]\}]$

When the sub-components of the probe are now compared internally to head T_{fin}, the Economy principle Maximize of (15) is not met, as the case feature is only [case: structural] rather than [case: structural>nom]. This means that although they are compatible (so the derivation converges) the φ-features of T come out as default ([-val]). As a result, whenever nominative is an option within the case paradigm, it is always preferred over other case forms in the subject position.[10]

The special status of the accusative numeral subject is obtained through the fact that both the T_{fin} head and the ANS share the feature [case: structural], which sets it off from other non-nominative subjects, cf. (11). I assume that this partial non-distinctness of structural cases lies behind the binding pattern in (3a–b). In short: T_{fin} tolerates as its goal a NP bearing a structural case different from nominative (i.e. accusative) only if the given NP is defective and does not have an active NomP projection in its functional sequence. This type of subject is second best to the nominative one, nevertheless T_{fin} defaults to 3SG.NEUT.

This account does not overgenerate, as no other argument but the highest one in the thematic hierarchy can function as goal for T_{fin}:

(18)	a.	*Basię	czytało	książkę.
		Basia-F.ACC.SG	read-3SG.N	book-F.ACC.SG
	b.	Basia	czytała	*książka.
		Basia-F.NOM.SG	read-3SG.F	book-F.NOM.SG
	c.	Basia	czytała	książkę.
		Basia-F.NOM.SG	read-3SG.F	book-F.ACC.SG
		'Basia read a book.'		

In (18) the NP *Basia* and *książka* 'book' have the projection of NomP at the bottom of their functional sequences, so the economy principle of Maximize will force the copying of the [case: structural>nom] feature onto the [case: structural] probe of T and thus yield nominative and full agreement. At the same time, the NP *Basia* is closer to T than *książka* 'book'. Example (18b) is excluded as the Superset Condition of Starke (2009) prevents the nominative form (NomP) from representing a functional sequence (here AccP) which it does not contain.[11]

10 The attempted but failed φ-feature valuation resembles the proposal formulated in Preminger (2009):
You can fail but you must try: applying φ-agreement to a given structure is obligatory; but if the structure happens to be such that φ-agreement cannot culminate successfully, this is an acceptable outcome.

11 The Superset Principle (Starke 2009):
A lexical entry is inserted into a node if it contains that node.

4. Conclusions

ANS share many properties with Nom subjects but case and full φ-agreement with T_{fin}: **(a)** only these two subject types require felicitous and rigorous binding of reflexive possessives, **(b)** these two subject types can be coordinated, **(c)** they both participate in the Nom(Acc)/Gen alternation in the existential construction and **(d)** they both show binding, control and referential properties of prototypical subjects. This state of affairs results from two facts: one is a peculiar hybrid structure of the case sequence domain of QHPs (lexically-determined lack of NomP projection) and the other is a particular composition of the probe on T_{fin} and their interaction captured by Maximize in (15). T_{fin} includes an unvalued (though interpretable) undercalibrated liberal case probe and an unvalued uninterpretable φ-feature probe ($T_{\{[\varphi:][case:\ structural]\}}$), which means that on the one hand T_{fin} accepts ANS as a goal for structural case valuation as the case closest to NOM, while on the other Maximize prevents φ-agreement on T_{fin}.

The findings presented above have consequences beyond the grammar of Polish and contribute to a more universal view on case theory, specifically the question of the subjecthood diagnostics and status of non-nominative arguments in the subject position. The example of the ANS (and probably also of the widely discussed dative subject in Icelandic) shows that as long as the non-nominative subject becomes involved in an Agree relation with T_{fin} it does function like a fully-fledged subject despite the fact that the morphological outcome of this relation is imperfect due to independent reasons (here: default ϕ-agreement caused by lack of the nominative form). Other arguments fronted to the left periphery of the clause, possibly through interaction with the EPP property of T, also causing default agreement on the verb, like dative arguments in the subject position in Polish, do not become involved in Agree with T_{fin} for other features (case) and do not show such an extensive array of subjecthood properties.[12]

References

Babby, Leonard. 1987. "Case, prequantifiers, and discontinuous agreement in Russian." *Natural Language and Linguistic Theory* 5: 9–138.

12 See Witkoś et.al. (2018) for a discussion of many more subjecthood properties of the ANS, contrasted with dative arguments in the subject position.

Bailyn John F. 2004. "*The case of Q.*" In *Proceedings of Formal Approaches to Slavic Linguistics: The Ottawa Meeting 2003*, Olga Arnaudova (ed.). Ann Arbor: Michigan Slavic Publications, 1–36.

Bejar, Suzana. 2003. "Phi-syntax: A theory of agreement." Ph.D. thesis, University of Toronto.

Benmamoun Elabbas, Archna Bhatia and Maria Polinsky. 2009. "Closest conjunct agreement in head final languages." *Linguistic Variation Yearbook*: 9: 67–88.

Blake, Barry. 1994. *Case*. Cambridge: Cambridge University Press.

Bošković, Željko. 2006. "Case and agreement with genitive of quantification in Russian." In *Agreement Systems*, Cedric Boeckx (ed.). Amsterdam: John Benjamins, 99–120.

Caha, Pavel. 2009. "Nanosyntax of case." Ph.D. thesis, University of Tromso.

Chomsky, Noam. 1986. *Knowledge of language: Its nature, origin and use*. New York: Praeger.

Chomsky, Noam. 2000. "Minimalist inquiries." In *Step by step: Essays on minimalist syntax in honor of Howard Lasnik*, Roger Martin, David Michaels, Juan Uriagereka and Samuel J. Keyser (eds.). Cambridge, MA: The MIT Press, 89–156.

Chomsky, Noam. 2001. "Derivation by phase." In *Ken Hale: A life in language*, Michael Kenstowicz (ed.). Cambridge, MA: The MIT Press, 1–52.

Chomsky, Noam. 2008. "On Phases." In *Issues in linguistic theory: Essays in honor of Jean-Roger Vergnaud*, Robert Freidin, Carlos Peregrín Otero and Maria L. Zubizarreta (eds.). Cambridge, MA: The MIT Press, 133–166.

Franks, Steven. 1994. "Parametric properties of numeral phrases in Slavic." *Natural Language and Linguistic Theory* 12: 597–674.

Franks, Steven. 1995. *Parameters of Slavic morphosyntax*. New York: Oxford University Press.

Franks, Steven. 2002. "A Jakobsonian feature based analysis of the Slavic Numeric Quantifier Genitive." *Journal of Slavic Linguistics* 10: 141–181.

Kallas, Maria. 1995. „O konstrukcjach z przyimkiem *niż*." In *Wyrażenia funkcyjne w systemie i tekście*, Maciej Grochowski (ed.). Toruń: Wydawnictwo UMK 1995, 99–110.

Lavine, James and Steven Franks. 2008. "On accusative first." In *Proceedings to Formal Approaches to Slavic Linguistics: The Stony Brook Meeting 2007*, Andrei Antonenko, John Bailyn, and Christina Y. Bethin (eds.). Ann Arbor: Michigan Slavic Publications, 231–247.

Marušič, Franc L., Andrew Nevins and William Badecker. 2015. "The grammars of conjunction agreement in Slovenian." *Syntax* 18: 39–77.

Pereltsvaig, Asya. 2006. "Small nominals." *Natural Language and Linguistic Theory* 24: 433–500.

Pesetsky, David. 1982. "Paths and categories." Ph.D. thesis, MIT.

Pesetsky, David. 2014. *Russian case morphology and the syntactic categories*. Cambridge: The MIT Press.

Pesetsky, David and Esther Torrego. 2001. "T-to-C movement: Causes and consequences." In *Ken Hale, a Life in Language*, Michael Kenstowicz (ed.). Cambridge, MA: The MIT Press, 355–426.

Pesetsky, David and Esther Torrego. 2007. "The syntax of valuation and the interpretability of features." In *Phrasal and clausal architecture: Syntactic derivation and interpretation*, Simin Karimi, Vida Samiian and Wendy K. Wilkins (eds.). Amsterdam: Benjamins, 262–294.

Pica, Pierre. 1991. "On the interpretation between antecedent-Government and Binding: The case of long-distance reflexivization." In *Long-Distance Anaphora*, Jan Koster and Eric Reuland (eds.). Cambridge: Cambridge University Press, 119–136.

Preminger, Omer. 2009. "Failure to Agree is not a failure:φ-Agreement with post-verbal subjects in Hebrew." Manuscript, MIT/Harvard.

Przepiórkowski, Adam. 1999. "Case Assignment and the complement-adjunct dichotomy: A non-configurational constraint-based approach." Ph.D. thesis, Universität Tübingen.

Przepiórkowski, Adam. 2001. "Predicative case agreement with Quantifier Phrases in Polish." In *Generative Linguistics in Poland: Syntax and Morphosyntax*, Adam Przepiórkowski and Piotr Bański (eds.). Warsaw: Polish Academy of Sciences, 159–169.

Przepiórkowski, Adam and Agnieszka Patejuk. 2012. "The puzzle of case agreement between numeral phrases and predicative adjectives in Polish." In *The Proceedings of the LFG'12 Conference*, Miriam Butt and Tracy H. King (eds.). Stanford, CA: CSLI Publications, 490–502.

Rooryck, Johan and Guido V. Wyngaerd. 2011. *Dissolving Binding Theory*. Oxford: Oxford University Press.

Rutkowski, Paweł. 2007. „Hipoteza frazy przedimkowej jako narzędzie opisu składniowego polskich grup imiennych." Ph.D. thesis, University of Warsaw.

Starke, Michal. 2009. "Nanosyntax: A short primer to a new approach to language." *Nordlyd* 36(1): 1–6.

Willim, Ewa. 2015. "Case distribution and φ-agreement with Polish Genitive of Quantification in the feature sharing theory of *Agree*." *Poznań Studies in Contemporary Linguistics* 51(2): 315–357.

Witkoś, Jacek and Dominika Dziubała-Szrejbrowska. 2016. "Numeral Phrases as subjects and agreement with participles and predicative adjectives." *Journal of Slavic Linguistics* 24(1): 225–60.

Witkoś, Jacek, Piotr Cegłowski, Dominika Dziubała-Szrejbrowska and Paulina Łęska. (2018). *The syntax of Numeral Noun Constructios: a view from Polish.* To appear in 2017 in Peter Lang.

Olav Mueller-Reichau

On Concealed Properties in Polish Perfective Generics

1. Introduction

In two intriguing papers, Klimek-Jankowska (2008, 2012) has proposed an account of Polish generic sentences whose subject is a proper name and whose predicate is a present tense perfective verb form. (1) gives an example:

(1) *Janek przeżegna się przed kościołem (,ale na msze nie chodzi).*
Janek cross.PFV REFL before church but on mass not go.IPFV
'Janek makes the sign of the cross in front of a church, but he doesn't go to Mass.'

Generics like the one in (1) are analysed as forming a natural class with generics like the one in (2), which likewise have a perfective predicate, but which have a bare singular nominal as subject expression.

(2) *(Prawdziwy) katolik przeżegna się przed kościołem.*
true catholic cross.PFV REFL before church
'A (real) catholic makes the sign of the cross in front of a church.'

According to Klimek-Jankowska's theory, the common denominator between (1) and (2) is that both represent 'in virtue of'-generics in the sense of Greenberg (2002, 2003). The idea is, briefly put (more on that below), that the subject expression is in each case associated with a concealed property, which plays a crucial role in the interpretation of the sentences because it figures in a law-like structure present in the interlocutors' background knowledge and therefore licenses the predication of the explicit property (i.e. *przeżegna się przed kościołem* in the examples above).

That (1) and (2) are 'in virtue of'-generics sets them aside from another kind of genericity, i.e. descriptive generalizations over eventualities, manifesting themselves in Polish in the use of imperfective aspect:

(3)	*Janek*	*żegna*	*się*	*przed*	*kościołem.*
	Janek	cross.IPFV	REFL	before	church

'Janek makes the sign of the cross in front of a church.'

Henceforth, I will use the following terminological labels. Cases like (1) will be referred to as "dispositional generics", cases like (2) will be called "definitional generics", and for cases like (3) I will use the term "descriptive generics".

In this paper I agree that dispositional generics involve a concealed property in interpretation. I also agree that there is a close relationship between dispositional generics and definitional generics, which motivates the common use of perfective verb forms and which dissociates them from descriptive generics. I disagree, however, that the interpretation of sentences like (2) would involve a concealed property. Instead I will argue that a definitional generic is the *explication* of the law-like structure of background knowledge, the antecedent property of which constitutes the concealed property in dispositional generic statements. Moreover, I will argue with respect to dispositional generics, contra to Klimek-Jankowska, that the association between the proper name and the concealed property is not presupposed, but rather asserted content.

The paper is structured as follows. In section 2 I remind of how imperfective/descriptive generics are analyzed in the literature, viz. as generalizations over sufficiently many events. Section 3 describes the intuition, which is absent with imperfective generics, that the truth of a perfective generic has an underlying principled cause. Section 4 recapitulates, very briefly, Greenberg's (2002, 2003) theory of 'in virtue of'-generics, and section 5 shows how this theory is applied to Polish dispositional generics by Klimek-Jankowska. It is argued that the applied theory does not entirely fit the phenomenon. In section 6 I point to a potential problem that arises from this misfit. In section 7 I then address a real data problem that Klimek-Jankowska's theory faces, and in section 8 I discuss the solution that Klimek-Jankowska has offered to cope with this problem. In section 9 I propose a revision of Klimek-Jankowska's theory to overcome the problems discussed before. The section is divided into three subsections. First, I emphasize the involvement of background rules in the interpretation of perfective generics (9.1). Then I argue that definitional generics are direct expressions of background rules (9.2). Finally, I discuss the role that background rules play in dispositional generics (9.3). Section 10 shows that my account predicts there to be two kinds of contexts in which dispositional generics may reasonably be used, and that this provides a natural explanation for the apparent problem discussed before in section 7. Section 11 concludes the paper.

2. Imperfective generics express descriptive generalizations

The verbal predicate of a generic sentence in Polish may be coded by imperfective aspect as well as by perfective aspect. Klimek-Jankowska (2008, 2013) considers imperfective generics to express statistical generalizations, "made on the basis of a number of actual instances which allow us to conclude that there is some pattern or more specifically that the generalization is not limited to the actual instances only" (Klimek-Jankowska 2008:236).[1] Consider (3) above as an example. Accepting (3) as a true statement means taking it for real that Janek has on sufficiently many occasions made the sign of the cross in front of a church.

Since generics like (3) "make generalizations about patterns that appear in the world" (Krifka 2013:6), the term "descriptive generics" appears well-suited to designate this category. Another frequently used term is "inductive generics" (e.g. Carlson 1995, Cohen 1999, Gorishneva 2011).

Note that the statistical bias toward the expressed property (which renders the utterance true) need not be "principled" but may be caused by accidental circumstances.

(4) *Janek pije tanie wino (bo teraz nie ma pieniędzy na*
Janek drinks.IPFV cheap wine because now not has money on
dobre wino).
good wine
'Janek drinks cheap wine (because he has no money for good wine at the moment).'

It is in this respect that Polish imperfective (descriptive) generics differ from perfective generics, to which I turn now.

3. Perfective generics express "principled generalizations"

The generalizations perfective generics express are felt to be "principled". The following sentence, for instance, does not give a sound generic statement:

(5) ?*Janek wypije tanie wino.*
Janek drinks.PFV cheap wine
'Janek drinks cheap wine.'

---

1 This is reminiscent of Carlson's (1995: 225) wording who speaks of generalizations "where the base of the generalization is some observed set of instances; after 'enough' instances have accumulated, the generic form can be truly asserted".

We may assume that anybody (who drinks wine) will prefer good wine over bad wine if both options are available. Therefore, drinking cheap wine is nothing that we would expect a (normal) person to do for a principled reason. Since a principled reason is what perfective generics require, (5) sounds odd as a generic. Now consider (6), which is the negation of (5). For that sentence it *is* possible to determine a property that someone may have for a principled reason. There even is a certain latitude in the retrieval of the underlying reason. It may, for instance, be that someone does not drink cheap wine because he or she has courtly manners (cf. Klimek-Jankowska 2008: 328), or because he or she is a gourmet. Since there is a possible principled reason available, (6) is acceptable as a generic statement.

(6) *Janek nie wypije taniego wina.*
Janek not drinks.PFV cheap wine
'Janek does not drink cheap wine.'

To pin down these intuitions, Klimek-Jankowska (2008, 2013) proposes that the interpretation of a perfective generic sentence involves the processing of a concealed property besides the property which is explicitly expressed by the perfective verb form. The idea is that the availability of the concealed property is mandatory for the generic use of a perfective sentence as it is this property which supplies the "principled reason" for the overtly expressed generalization. With respect to (6), this approach suggests that Janek does not drink cheap wine (property 1) because he is, for instance, a gourmet (property 2). The proposal implies, accordingly, that there is a close tie between the truth of (6) and the truth of (7). The precise nature of the tie is the core topic of this paper.

(7) *Janek jest smakoszem.*
Janek is gourmet
'Janek is a gourmet.'

As noted in the beginning of this paper, Klimek-Jankowska (2008, 2012) proposes to identify concealed properties in Polish perfective generics with so-called 'in virtue of'-properties in the sense of Greenberg (2002, 2003). Therefore a brief recapitulation of Greenberg's theory is in order.

4. 'In virtue of'-generics

Greenberg's (2002, 2003) theory aims at accounting for the difference between indefinite singular generics and bare plural generics in English. (8) shows a minimal pair:

(8) a. *A boy does not cry.*
b. *Boys do not cry.*

The gist of Greenberg's (2002, 2003) proposal may be summarized as follows: Bare plural generics like (8b) may be used to express descriptive generalizations. In contrast to that, indefinite singular generics like (8a) lack the capacity to express descriptive generalizations. They only express 'in virtue of'-generalizations, which means that they can be truly asserted only if there is a relevant property in virtue of which the generalization is justified.[2] The question of how to calculate the relevant 'in virtue of'-property is answered by Greenberg along the following lines (cf. Oosterhof 2008:40):

(9) (i) "in virtue of" properties must be associated with another property denoted by the NP quantified over
(ii) A property P can only be "associated" with another property Q if it follows from our beliefs, norms and stereotypes about the actual world that every individual Q has the property P

As can be seen, determining the 'in virtue of'-property requires the existence of "another property", which is delivered "by the NP quantified over". In (8a), this "other property" is the property of being a boy, delivered by the NP *a boy*. A property that qualifies for serving as 'in virtue of'-property in that example would be, for instance, the property of being tough. We may depict the pieces of background knowledge that the interlocutors have to share for (8a) to be accepted by them as a true statement in the following way:

(10) Q: *boy* → P: *tough* → P′: *not-cry*

Simply speaking, the idea visualized in (10) is that the property of not crying can be truly predicated of any boy because it is known that the property of being a boy implies (is associated with) the property of being tough, which in turn implies (licenses the assignment of) the property of not crying.

Note that Greenberg's original approach is not designed to cope with dispositional generics, i.e. "principled generics" having a proper name (or other individual-referring) subject. We should therefore pay special attention to Klimek-Jankowska's way of applying the Greenbergian theory to dispositional generics.

2 Bare plural generics may also be used to express 'in virtue of'-generics.

5. Dispositional generics as 'in virtue of'-generics

Consider the dispositional generic in (11), which is Klimek-Jankowska's prime example.

(11) *Janek* *pomoże* *w* *potrzebie.*
J. help.PFV in need
'Janek will help you in need.'

Klimek-Jankowska analyzes (11) as involving the 'in virtue of'-property of having high empathy (cf. Klimek-Jankowska 2008:331). If this is correct, (11) should, on analogy to (10), be true in virtue of the existence of the "property chain" depicted in (12).

(12) Q: *Janek* → P: *have-high-empathy* → P': *help-you-in-need*

The implication from the 'in virtue of'-property P to P' constitutes the "background law-like evidence" that is identified by Klimek-Jankowska as a *conditio sine qua non* for Polish perfective generics:

> In uttering a perfective generalization, a speaker has in mind and a hearer needs to accommodate some background law-like evidence in virtue of which the generalization is true. (Klimek-Jankowska 2008: 327)

Accordingly, upon interpreting (11), the hearer successfully accommodates the required background rule (P → P'). Recall from (9) that, on Greenberg's original account, the retrieval of the background rule is warranted because the following conditions are met:

(13) (i) The property explicitly mentioned by the predicate expression matches the consequent property P' in a background rule, whereby
(ii) the antecedent property P of this rule is associated with property Q, where Q is the property explicitly mentioned by the subject expression.

Given this, notice an obstacle for retrieving the rule when the subject is a proper name: unlike common nouns, proper names have no lexical content. There therefore is no linguistically given relationship between the subject expression and P:

(14) (i) The property explicitly mentioned by the predicate expression matches the consequent property P' in a background rule, whereby
(ii) the antecedent property P of this rule is associated with property Q, where Q is a property implicitly associated with the individual explicitly mentioned by the subject expression.

Klimek-Jankowska's analysis of (11) is summarized in (15): What is asserted is the truth of the proposition ψ. This does not exhaust the meaning of the perfective generic, however, as the message necessarily also involves a presuppositional part, made up of the propositions φ and χ. The former is a "law-like" proposition, the latter is the "association" of Janek with the antecedent property of φ. Both φ and χ are presupposable, as the truth of each "follows from our beliefs, norms and stereotypes about the actual world" (see (9)). In case that proposition χ does not belong to the common ground, the addressee has to accommodate it.

(15) φ ∀x. have-high-empathy(x) → help-in-need(x) presupposition part
χ have-high-empathy(Janek)

ψ help-in-need(Janek) assertion part

6. A potential problem

Above we saw that the application of the 'in virtue of'-analysis to dispositional generics necessitates an adjustment of Greenberg's assumptions in order to maintain an associative tie between Q and P. Something along the lines of (14ii) has to hold. Now, in view of (14ii), it seems legitimate to assume that dispositional generics require contexts in which the hearer already knows that the given proper name is associated with property P (just like definitional generics require that the hearer already knows that the subject common noun is associated with P). This is not the case, however; a dispositional generic may be fully appropriate even in an introductory setting, where the hearer is for the first time acquainted with knowledge about the (bearer of the) proper name:

(16) A: *Kim jest ta Maria? Czy możesz mi coś o*
who.INS is this Maria PRT may.2SG me something about
niej powiedzieć?
her say
'Who is Maria? Can you tell me something about her?'
B: *Tak. Mogę ci powiedzieć na przykład, że Maria przed*
yes may.1SG you say for instance that Maria before
każdym kościołem się przeżegna.
every church REFL cross.PFV
'Yes. I can tell you, for instance, that Maria crosses herself in front of every church.'

Although A does not know anything about Maria, and although B knows that A does not know anything about Maria, B is in a situation to successfully utter a perfective generic to characterize Maria. Let us assume, for the sake of the argument and in analogy to (12), that the relevant "property chain" involved in (16) is Q: *Maria* → P: *strictly-religious* → P′: *make-the-sign-of-the-cross-in-front-of-a-church*. Does the fact that A has no background knowledge to ground the implicature Q → P run against (14ii)? Is this a problem for Klimek-Jankowska's analysis? Not really.[3]

The relevant common ground to which the proposition expressed by *Maria przed każdym kościołem się przeżegna* should be added is not the common ground as it was before the utterance. *That* common ground does indeed not contain the proposition that Maria is a strictly religious person. The relevant common ground for (16) is rather the common ground as it is changed by the utterance itself, thus taking into account the inferences drawn by A (von Fintel 2008: 11, see also Stalnaker 2002). All that Klimek-Jankowska would therefore need to claim to defend her approach is that A manages to adjust the common ground by drawing the relevant inference that Maria has the property of being strictly religious.

Although the above made argument is not conclusive, it should be noted that Greenberg's analysis is stretched beyond its limits when applied to dispositional generic sentences. To make it work properly, it is necessary to assume not only that the hearer has to determine a background rule as a precondition for letting the sentence update the common ground (this is still in line with Greenberg's original proposal). On top of that, it is necessary to also assume that the hearer has to determine a property of the bearer of the proper name *as a precondition for the fulfillment of the precondition* for letting the sentence update the common ground.

7. A real problem

We saw that, by treating dispositional generics as 'in virtue of'-generics, Klimek-Jankowska (2008, 2012) is committed to the assumptions that there is a presuppositional association between the bearer of the proper name and the concealed ('in virtue of'-) property and that, at least on some occasions, the hearer has to accommodate the respective proposition. So far I have only provided weak evidence against these assumptions. In this section I provide a more serious counter-argument. Compare (17) with (18):

---

3 Here I changed my mind on what I wrote in Mueller-Reichau (2017). Many thanks to an anonymous reviewer for convincing me to be more cautious on this point.

(17) *Nasza* *Balbina* *rozpłacze* *się* *przy* *drobnostkach.*
our Balbina cry.PFV REFL at trivialities
'Our Balbina starts crying for no apparent reason.'

(18) *Nasza* *beksa* *Balbina* *rozpłacze* *się* *przy* *drobnostkach.*
our cry-baby Balbina cry.PFV REFL at trivialities
'Our cry-baby Balbina will start crying for no apparent reason.'

The observation is that, while (17) gives a natural dispositional generic, (18) does not. The latter sentence only works as a non-generic statement about an anticipated future event. Within Klimek-Jankowska's analysis, the lack of the generic reading of (18) is unexpected and requires additional stipulations (see below). Consider (17) first. According to Klimek-Jankowska, the utterance presupposes (i) that there is a background rule saying that a cry-baby starts crying for no apparent reason and (ii) that Balbina is a cry-baby. To accept the sentence, the hearer has to first check for the respective propositions in her model of common ground, and to accommodate where necessary. But given this: Why should explicitly providing the information (ii), as in (18), be an obstacle for the interpretation as a dispositional generic? It should be rather the other way around, that is, (18) should more easily lend itself to a generic construal.

Klimek-Jankowska (2008: 332) addresses the problem just noted, her example being (19). Here, too, the observation is that the sentence is infelicitous as a generic statement.

(19) *Nasza* *kura* *Balbina* *zniesie* *jajka.*
our hen Balbina lay.PFV eggs
'Our hen Balbina lays eggs.'

It is plausible to assume a background rule saying that a hen lays eggs. By attributing *kura* to *Balbina*, (19) therefore directly provides an appropriate 'in virtue of'-property, appropriate in the sense that it identifies the antecedent property of a background rule whose consequent property matches the explicitly stated predicate. But why, then, is (19) bad as a dispositional generic?

8. Indirect inference?

Klimek-Jankowska (2008) proposes a solution to the problem raised by data such as (18) or (19). Here is how the solution goes (numbers adjusted):

> My claim is that perfective habituals serve as markers of an evidential mechanism of indirect inference. Habitual statements in (18) and (19) are statements of facts. They express propositions whose truth follows straightforwardly from the law-like evidence. [...] My explanation of the facts in (18) and (19) is that perfective habituals cannot be used to state obvious facts which follow directly from the definition of a subject. [...] In (18) and (19) we express a known fact which does not need to be inferred, hence the use of the perfective aspect would not serve its purpose of marking the evidential mechanism of indirect inference. (Klimek-Jankowska 2008: 332–333)

I totally agree that (18) and (19) express "facts which do not need to be inferred", and that this is what runs counter to the purpose of uttering a dispositional generic. The problem is that this does not go together well with the analysis that Klimek-Jankowska proposes for these utterances. According to her analysis, the fact (aka true proposition) that the hearer has to infer when confronted with a dispositional generic, in the case of (19) that Balbina is a hen, is of presuppositional nature. As such it is a precondition that needs to be satisfied before the assertively uttered sentence can serve its purpose to update the common ground. Now the question is: how plausible is a requirement of indirect inference if the goal of the inference is to set the stage for the real purpose of the utterance? I believe that the answer should be: very implausible. If the inference is a presupposition that the hearer is not aware of and, therefore, has to accommodate, nothing should stop the cooperative speaker from supporting the hearer by explicitly (directly) supplying the information to be accommodated.[4]

A related problem derives from the following Russian example, taken from Rassudova (1982: 84):

(20)	*On*	*očen'*	*dobryj*	*čelovek,*	*on*	*vam*	*vsegda*	*pomožet.*
	he	very	good	person	he	you	always	help.PFV

'He is a good person, he will always help you.'

The example may easily be replicated in Polish:

(21)	*Janek*	*jest*	*dobrym*	*chłopakiem,*	*on*	*ci*	*pomoże*	*w potrzebie.*
	Janek	is	good	fellow	he	you	help.PFV	in need

'Janek is a good fellow, he will help you in need.'

4 "Since communication is the point of the enterprise, everyone [i.e. every participant of the communication] will have a motive to try to keep the presuppositions [that each participant of the communication has] the same" (Stalnaker 1978/1999: 85; the square brackets are my additions).

The point is that in (21), the property that licenses the validity of the predicate is presented in no way indirectly; it is explicitly mentioned in the preceding sentence. This is unexpected given the strict constraint of indirect inference proposed by Klimek-Jankowska.

9. Alternative

9.1. Background rules

To overcome the above noted problems, I will now propose a slight but crucial modification of Klimek-Jankowska's theory. Specifically, I will propose that definitional generics do not involve a concealed property the way dispositional generics do, and that the concealed property of dispositional generic utterances does not belong to the presuppositional content (and, thus, is no 'in virtue of'-property), but rather to the assertive content. That examples like (18) and (19) do not lend themselves for a generic reading will immediately follow from this.

The basic idea is in harmony with Klimek-Jankowska's approach. I assume that, when uttering a dispositional generic like (22), the speaker is inviting the hearer to retrieve a law-like structure from background knowledge.

(22)	*Janek*	*pomoże*	*w*	*potrzebie.* (=(11))
	Janek	help.PFV	in	need
	'Janek will help you in need.'			

As before, I will call the "law-like structures" involved in the interpretation of perfective generics background rules. For a dispositional generic to be successfully uttered, there has to be at least one supporting background rule (nothing seems to exclude the possibility of there being more than one suitable rule available). With respect to (22), for instance, there is a rule available saying that a person who deserves being called your friend will help you in need. The rule may be spelled out in language, which gives us a definitional generic:

(23)	*(Prawdziwy)*	*przyjaciel*	*pomoże*	*w*	*potrzebie.*
	true	friend	help.PFV	in	need
	'A (true) friend will help you in need.'				

Note that I do not treat generic sentences like (23) to be 'in virtue of'-generics. Their interpretation does *not* involve implicit background information to be inferred, so here is where I depart from Klimek-Jankowska. Instead I take sentences like (23) to be definitional generics in the sense of Krifka (2012) (which is the up to now silent reason why I call them definitional generics throughout in this paper).

According to Krifka, definitional generics are special in that they do not talk about the world as it is, but about the language as it should be from the point of view of the speaker. What is meant by that will be explained in the next subsection.

9.2. Definitional generics

A *descriptive* generic sentence, which, as we saw above, is coded by imperfective aspect in Polish, is about the world, just like any non-generic sentence is. The speaker utters such sentences presupposing agreement on the intensions of the predicates in the language used. She wants to tell the hearer about a fact, in the case of descriptive generics about an empirically justified generalization (cf. section 2). If the hearer accepts the generalization as a true proposition, this will, as usual, update the common ground by excluding the set of those worlds incompatible with the accepted proposition (Stalnaker 1978/1999: 86. see also Irmer 2011: 57 ff.).

A *definitional* generic sentence is "fundamentally different" (Krifka). Here the speaker presupposes agreement with the hearer about the facts holding in the world, while the speaker's aim is to inform the hearer about the interpretation of a predicate in their shared language.[5] To be concrete, consider (24), which I repeat from the beginning of this paper:

(24)	*(Prawdziwy)*	*katolik*	*przeżegna*	*się*	*przed*	*kościołem.*
	real	catholic	cross.PFV	REFL	before	church

'A (true) catholic makes the sign of the cross in front of a church.'

This is a definitional generic, uttered by the speaker with the intention to introduce or remind of the fact that the extension of the predicate *katolik* is expected to only include individuals having the property of making the sign of the cross when coming across a church.

Definitional generics are normative in the sense of supplying a standard for evaluating individuals or actions in the world. If Janek points out that he is a catholic even though he does not make the sign of the cross in front of every church, he will, in the light of (24), (at best) qualify as a bad member of the category tied to the predicate *catholic*. The normative power of definitional generics is also the reason why the definiendum expression may well be accompanied by attributes like Polish *prawdziwy* or English *true* and the like.

5 Krifka (2012) conceives of the common ground as a pair <I,W>, whereby W is a set of possible worlds (the worlds compatible with the factual content of the common ground) and I is a set of appropriate interpretations (the interpretations that the interlocutors accept as reasonable).

Now, as already noted above, my claim is that definitional generics, i.e. perfective generics with a bare singular noun as subject, express rules, which are structures of background information stored in the form of rules and representing "our beliefs, norms and stereotypes" (recall (9)). Such a rule says, roughly speaking, that if an individual x is P, it is also P'. For ease of exposition I represent rules as in (25a), simply as universally quantified conditionals (see Cohen 2001 for a more appropriate logical treatment). Specifically, we may pin down the rule which is expressed by (24) as in (25b), and the one expressed in (23) as in (25c):

(25) a. $\forall$x. P(x) $\rightarrow$ P'(x)
b. $\forall$x. catholic(x) $\rightarrow$ make-the-sign-of-the-cross-in-front-of-a-church(x)
c. $\forall$x. friend(x) $\rightarrow$ help-in-need(x)

Definitional generics represent the direct way of referring to background rules. Dispositional generics, to which I turn now, represent an indirect way, so to speak. The common denominator is that, whenever a perfective verb form is used to state a generic in Polish, recourse is made to a background rule.

9.3. Dispositional generics

A *dispositional* generic likewise refers to a background rule. The speaker draws the hearer's attention to the consequent property of the rule, P', thereby expressing that P' is true of the subject individual. What is special about dispositional generics is that the hearer, understanding P' to be the consequent property of a familiar background rule, will be led to infer that the antecedent property of the rule, P, is true of the subject referent as well.

The question that arises at this point is: How does the speaker manage to "draw the hearer's attention" to the consequent property, as I just put it? The answer should be obvious: By using a perfective form instead of an imperfective form, which is the otherwise expected aspectual coding for generics (cf. section 2).

And so, following Klimek-Jankowska (2008, 2012), I take it that the concealed property involved in the interpretation of dispositional generics is the antecedent property of a rule given in the interlocutors' background knowledge. Where I differ from Klimek-Jankowska is that I analyze the association of the subject referent with the concealed property not as presuppositional meaning. By making this move, I avoid the troubles that I pointed at in section 6. Instead I propose that dispositional generics should be viewed as expressing double-assertions, so to speak. Let me again use (11) for illustration. The new proposal amounts to saying that the proposition χ does not belong to the presuppositional part of the utterance meaning, but to the assertion part; compare (15) and (26):

(26) φ $\forall$x. have-high-empathy(x) $\rightarrow$ help-in-need(x) presupposition part

---

ψ help-in-need(Janek) assertion part
χ have-high-empathy(Janek)

What is asserted by the dispositional generic (11) is the truth of the proposition ψ. In addition, the meaning involves the presupposition that φ is a true proposition. Besides the explicitly asserted proposition ψ, which can directly be read from the words of the sentence, the message includes the assertion of another, implicit proposition χ. The truth of χ is inferred from the truth of the explicitly asserted proposition ψ on account of the truth of the presupposed "law-like" proposition φ.

10. When the implicitly asserted proposition gets explicated

We may expect speakers of Polish to produce dispositional generics in a discourse where the implicitly asserted proposition gets explicated. There are two possibilities. The first case is when it is at issue whether the *antecedent* property of the presupposed rule is true or false of the subject referent. In that case, a dispositional generic will be used as an indirect way of answering the question of whether or not χ is true. The second case is when it is at issue whether the *consequent* property of the rule holds of the subject referent. Here a dispositional generic serves to answering the question of whether or not ψ is true. The background rule is exploited in two different ways in the two cases. Either the speaker makes use of the causal relation in (27a), or of the one in (27b). In the first case the speaker's communicative aim is to logically back up the assertion of χ, in the second case the aim is to back up the assertion of ψ:

(27) a. $\chi = 1$, because $\psi = 1$
b. $\psi = 1$, because $\chi = 1$

The case of (27a) is illustrated by (28), where the second sentence explicates the assertion implicitly conveyed by the first sentence (the dispositional generic). The case of (27b) is instantiated by (29) where the first sentence explicitly foreshadows the assertion that the second sentence (the dispositional generic) would otherwise implicitly express.[6]

---

6 I take the predicate *samarytanin* as denoting the property of having high empathy.

(28) *Janek pomoże w potrzebie. On jest naprawdę samarytaninem.*
Janek help.PFV in need he is really samaritan
'Janek will help you in need. He really is a samaritan.'

(29) *Janek jest samarytaninem. On ci na pewno pomoże w potrzebie.*
Janek is samaritan he you for sure help.PFV in need
'Janek is a samaritan. He will help you in need for sure.'

Packaging the antecedent predicate and the consequent predicate of the background rule together into one sentence about Janek will lead to a questionable result as a generic, because none of the two strategies in (27) can be made run:

(30) *?Samarytanin Janek pomoże w potrzebie.*
samarytanin Janek help.PFV in need
'Samaritan Janek will help in need.'

If the speaker wanted to follow strategy (27a), (30) would be inappropriate because the truth of the proposition χ that the speaker wants the hearer to infer from the explicit assertion of ψ is pre-given by the subject compound. Under the second possible strategy (27b), (30) likewise fails, for a similar reason: The speaker cannot base the truth of ψ on the explicit assertion of χ, because the information that Janek is a samaritan is presented as presupposed information. So this is how the revised approach to Polish perfective generics that I presented in this paper accounts for the apparent problem discussed in sections 7 and 8.

11. Conclusion

In this paper, I have addressed the issue of perfective and imperfective generics in Polish. While I had nothing to add to the common treatment of imperfective generics, I have argued for a modification of current analyses of perfective generics. I proposed that dispositional generics in Polish are special in that they express a second implicit assertion besides the explicit one (the one that can be directly read from the words). The successful inference of the silent assertion is warranted by a salient background rule. Perfective morphology is an overt indicator signaling that the explicit predicate which the speaker claims to be true of the subject referent matches the consequent property of a background rule. On the side of the hearer, this invites the inference that the antecedent property of the rule is true of the subject referent as well. I proposed that definitional generics are used to directly express background rules. I have argued against a treatment of perfective generics as 'in virtue of'-generics, thereby proposing a new relationship between dispositional generics and definitional generics.

References

Carlson, Gregory N. 1995. "Truth Conditions of Generic Sentences: Two Contrasting Views." In Gregory N. Carlson and Francis J. Pelletier (eds.), *The Generic Book*. Chicago: University of Chicago Press, 265–299.

Cohen, Ariel. 1999. *Think Generic! The Meaning and Use of Generic Sentences*. Stanford: CSLI.

Cohen, Ariel. 2001. "On the generic use of indefinite singulars." *Journal of Semantics* 18: 183–209.

Comrie, Bernard. 1976. *Aspect*. Cambridge: CUP.

Gorishneva, Elena. 2011. "Inductive vs. Non-Inductive Generics in Russian and Bulgarian." In Peter Kosta and Lilia Schürcks (eds.), *Formalization of Grammar in Slavic Languages*. Frankfurt a.M.: Peter Lang, 81–92.

Gorishneva, Elena. 2012. Aspekt und Generizität: Über die Rolle des (im) perfektiven Aspekts in generischen *Aussagen*. In: Luka Szucsich, Natalia Gagarina, Elena Gorishneva & Joanna Leszkowicz (Hgg.), *Linguistische Beiträge zur Slavistik XIX*. München: Sagner, 91–108.

Greenberg, Yael. 2002. "Two Types of Quantificational Modalized Genericity, and the Interpretation of Bare Plurals and Indefinite Singular NPs." In Brendan Jackson (ed.), *Proceedings of SALT 12*. CLC Publications, Cornell University.

Greenberg, Yael. 2003. *Manifestations of Genericity*. New York: Routledge.

Irmer, Matthias. 2011. *Bridging inferences. Constraining and resolving underspecification in discourse interpretation*. (= Language, Context, and Cognition 11). Berlin, Boston: de Gruyter.

Klimek-Jankowska, Dorota. 2008. "On an Analogy between English Nominal and Polish Aspectual Manifestations of Genericity." In Atle Gronn (ed.), *Proceedings of Sinn und Bedeutung 12*. Department of Literature, Area Studies and European Languages, University of Oslo, 318–336.

Klimek-Jankowska, Dorota. 2012. "Imperfective and perfective habituals in Polish: A bi-directional OT account of variation and ambiguity." *Journal of Logic, Language and Information* 21(1), 31–52.

Krifka, Manfred. 2012. "Definitional generics." In Alda Mari, Claire Beyssade and Fabio Del Prete (eds.), *Genericity*. Oxford: Oxford University Press, 372–389.

Mueller-Reichau, Olav. 2017. "Polish Perfective Generics." In Olav Mueller-Reichau and Marcel Guhl (eds.), *Aspects of Slavic Linguistics: Formal Grammar, Lexicon and Communication. Series Language, Context & Cognition 16*. Berlin, Boston: de Gruyter.

Oosterhof, Albert. 2008. *The semantics* of *generics in Dutch and related languages*. Amsterdam: John Benjamins.

Rassudova, Ol'ga P. 1982. *Upotreblenie vidov glagola v sovremennom russkom jazyke*. Moskva: Russkij jazyk.

Stalnaker, Robert. 1978. "Assertion." In Peter Cole (ed.), *Syntax and Semantics, Vol. 9: Pragmatics*. New York: Academic Press, 315–332; reprinted 1999 in R. Stalnaker, *Content and Context: Essays on Intentionality in Speech and Thought*, Oxford: Oxford University Press, 78–95 (page numbers refer to the latter).

Stalnaker, Robert. 2002. "Common ground." *Linguistics and Philosophy* 25(5–6): 701–721.

von Fintel, Kai. 2008. "What is presupposition accommodation, again?" *Philosophical Perspectives* 22(1): 137–170.

Anna Bondaruk

Is the Modal *dać* + *się* + Infinitive Structure in Polish Inchoative?

Introduction

The *dać* + *się* + infinitive structure has two basic functions in Polish. On the one hand, it expresses permissive causation, where the verb *dać* is associated with the meaning of 'let, allow'. On the other hand, it conveys dispositional modality, where *dać* acquires a modal interpretation.[1] It is the second use of this structure that is focused on in this paper. Since the modal *dać* + *się* + infinitive structure exhibits a transitivity alternation typical of inchoatives, an attempt is made in the paper to check whether the two structures are syntactically similar. The paper is composed of five sections. In section 2, the basic syntactic and semantic properties of the modal *dać* + *się* + infinitive structure are examined. Section 3 points out some characteristics typical of inchoatives in Polish. Section 4 compares the syntactic properties of the two structures under scrutiny. It is argued that these two constructions differ in the type of external argument they contain or imply. In the modal *dać* + *się* + infinitive structure, the external argument may be an agent or causer, while in inchoatives it is just an unintentional causer. This difference is accounted for in terms of feature composition of the Voice head associated with the two constructions (Alexiadou et al. 2006). Section 5 concludes the paper. The overall conclusion reached in the paper is that syntactically the modal *dać* + *się* + infinitive structure differs minimally from inchoatives.

---

1 The verb *dać* 'give' may also have a factive function (von Waldenfels 2012: 114), as in (i) below:

(i) Dałam naprawić zegar.
I-gave repair-inf clock-acc
'I have had the clock repaired.'

However, the factive function of *dać* 'give' is much less common in Polish than its permissive use (von Waldenfels 2012:117).

2. The syntactic and semantic properties of the modal *dać* + *się* + infinitive structure

The modal *dać* + *się* + infinitive structure comprises the verb *dać*, which usually serves as a ditransitive predicate meaning 'give'. However, in the structure under consideration the verb *dać* is deprived of this kind of meaning and acquires a modal interpretation, as can be seen in (1) below:

(1) Te problemy dają się rozwiązać.
these problems-3pl.nom dać[2]-3pl refl solve-inf[3]
'These problems can be solved.'

In (1), the verb *dać* is followed by the reflexive pronoun *się* and the infinitive, and it agrees in φ-features with the surface subject, which is typically inanimate.[4] The structural subject in (1) represents a Theme object of the embedded infinitive, and is co-referential with the reflexive. The structure in (1) is associated with the dispositional meaning, i.e. it ascribes a property to a subject that holds by virtue of inherent or implicit characteristics that the subject has (Lekakou 2005). In other words, the construction expresses the modal sense of possibility grounded in the properties of the subject (von Waldenfels 2012: 160).

The dispositional meaning found in the modal *dać* + *się* + infinitive structure is also typical of middles, like the one in (2):[5]

---

2 The verb *dać* used in the modal *dać* + *się* + infinitive structure is simply glossed as 'dać' throughout the paper.

3 The following abbreviations have been used in the paper: acc – accusative, dat – dative, inf – infinitive, instr – instrumental, nom – nominative, pl – plural, refl – reflexive, and sg – singular.

4 The *dać* + *się* + infinitive structure with an animate surface subject has usually a permissive causative interpretation. There exist some instances of the *dać* + *się* + infinitive structure that are ambiguous between the causative permissive and the modal interpretation with both animate and inanimate subjects.

5 A similar example, taken from the National Corpus of Polish (www.nkjp.wp), is given in (i) below:

(i) Sprawy trudne rozwiązują się łatwo.
matters-3pl.nom difficult solve-3pl refl easily
'Difficult matters are solved easily.'

The structure in (i) is an instance of the middle proper, as it contains an obligatory manner adverb, and it is associated with a generic interpretation.

(2) Te problemy rozwiązują się łatwo.
these problems-3pl.nom solve-3pl refl easily
'These problems are solved easily.'

When compared with (1), the middle in (2), lacks the verb *dać*, and contains only the verb *rozwiązywać* 'solve', which shows agreement in φ-features with the surface subject. Just like in sentence (1), the subject of (2) is a thematic object of the verb and it is co-referential with the reflexive. Finally, the manner adverb *łatwo* 'easily' is obligatorily present in (2).[6] The middle in (2) has a generic interpretation, and thus expresses a regularity, not a particular event.[7] A detailed comparison of the modal *dać* + *się* + infinitive structure with the middle construction is carried out in Bondaruk (2015). For the purpose of this paper, it is sufficient to observe that both the modal *dać* + *się* + infinitive structure and the middle share the same argument realization, with the thematic object surfacing in the structural subject position, and the reflexive *się* co-referential with it.

Actually, Bondaruk (2015) draws parallelism between the modal *dać* + *się* + infinitive structure and the so-called *lassen* middles in German, exemplified in (3), taken from Pitteroff (2014: 49) (cf. also Kosta 2010, who analyses German *lassen* middles and their Czech equivalents):

(3) Dieses Problem lässt sich (leicht) lösen.
this problem-nom lets refl easily solve-inf
'This problem can be solved (easily).'

The only significant difference between the German *lassen*-middle in (3) and the Polish modal structure like (1) lies in the choice of the main verb – in German it is *lassen* 'let', while in Polish it corresponds to *dać*.[8] The question whether the

6 When the manner adverb is removed in (2), the resulting structure, as in (4) below, has no longer a generic dispositional interpretation, typical of middles, but it expresses an ongoing action, and functions as an inchoative structure.

7 In Bondaruk (2015), it is argued that the modal *dać* + *się* + infinitive structure can be both generic and episodic.

8 The plural subject is used in the Polish example (1), instead of the singular one adopted in the German sentence in (3), because the sentence in (1) with the singular subject, as in (i), is ambiguous between the modal and the impersonal interpretation. This is so because masculine nouns in the singular are syncretic between the nominative and the accusative.

(i) Ten problem daje się rozwiązać.
this problem-3sg.nom/acc dać-3sg refl solve-inf
'This problem can be solved/One can solve this problem.'

surface similarities between the German *lassen*-middle and the Polish modal structure with *dać* reflect similarities in syntactic structure is addressed, to some extent, in section 4 (for details, cf. Bondaruk 2017).

3. Basic characteristics of inchoatives in Polish

Inchoative verbs (also called anticausatives) typically express a change of state of their grammatical subject without implying the participation of any agent or causer. In Polish there is a group of inchoative verbs which bears the reflexive marker *się*, as can be seen in (4):[9]

(4) Te problemy rozwiązują się.
these problems-3pl.nom solve-3pl refl
'These problems are being solved.'

The inchoative structure in (4) has the same argument realisation as the middle in (2) and the modal *dać* + *się* + infinitive structure in (1), namely the thematic object of the verb surfaces in the structural subject position and is co-referential with the reflexive. However, meaning-wise, the inchoative structure differs from both the middle and the modal construction, since it conveys the idea that a particular situation occurs spontaneously, and is not brought about by any intentional human agent (Ilić 2014: 165). This is confirmed by the fact that inchoatives can be modified by *by itself*, whose meaning corresponds to 'without outside help' (Alexiadou et al. 2006: 194). The relevant modifier that can be inserted within Polish inchoatives is the word *sam* 'by itself', as illustrated in (5):

(5) Te problemy rozwiązują się same.
these problems-3pl.nom solve-3pl refl by themselves
'These problems are being solved by themselves.'

Since the change of state expressed by inchoatives is not agent induced (cf. Kosta 2015: 580), it can never license an agentive *by*-phrase, as demonstrated in (6), where the agentive phrase is introduced by the preposition *przez* 'by':

9 It is not our objective to present a complete set of the properties of inchoatives in Polish (for a comprehensive presentation of the syntax and semantics of inchoatives in Polish, cf. Kibort 2004: chapter 3). We only focus here on those features of inchoatives that are relevant for their comparison with the modal *dać* + *się* + infinitive structure, undertaken in section 4.

(6)	*Te	problemy	rozwiązują	się	przez	młodych	ludzi
	these	problems-3pl.nom	solve-3pl	refl	by	young	people
	'These problems are being solved by young people.'						

Furthermore, agent oriented adverbs are disallowed in inchoative structures (for similar observations concerning Polish ichoatives, cf. Kosta 2015: 580, and for the relevant Czech structures, see Kosta 2010: 256), as can be seen in (7):

(7)	Te	problemy	rozwiązują	się	*celowo/przez przypadek.
	these	problems-3pl.nom	solve-3pl	refl	*on purpose/by accident
	'These problems are being solved on purpose/by accident.'				

Sentence (7) is grammatical only with the phrase *przez przypadek* 'by accident', which indicates that the change of state takes place in inchoatives unwillfully.

What is more, obligatorily agentive verbs are not normally found in inchoatives (cf. Alexiadou et al. 2006, Kosta 2010, 2015, inter alia), as confirmed by the ungrammaticality of (8b), the inchoative variant of (8a):

(8)	a.	Policja	wygoniła	nielegalnych	lokatorów.
		police-3sg.nom	chased-away-3sg	illegal	tenants
		'The police chased away illegal tenants.			
	b.	*Nielegalni	lokatorzy	wygonili	się.
		illegal	tenants-3pl	chased-3pl	refl
		'Illegal tenants got chased away.'			

In the literature, inchoative verbs as in (4) and (5) above are commonly treated as intransitive predicates without any implicit external argument (cf. Schäfer 2008, Martin and Schäfer 2014, among others). However, the possibility of having the causer introduced by *from* in English inchoatives like (9) and by its equivalent *od* in Polish inchoatives like (10) seems to cast doubt on this conclusion.

(9) The window cracked/broke from pressure. (Alexiadou et al. 2006: 194)

(10)	Okno	pękło/zbiło	się	od	podmuchu	wiatru.
	window-nom	cracked/broke	refl	from	blast	wind
	'The window cracked from the blast of wind.'					

Alexiadou et al. (2006) take the grammaticality of sentences like (9) and (10) to be indicative of the presence of an implicit unintentional causer in inchoatives (cf. also Kallulli 2007). Martin and Schäfer (2014: 213) argue that this hypothesis cannot be maintained as *by*-phrases in passives can take up an implicit agent and an implicit causer, as in (11), which is impossible in inchoatives, as shown in (12):

(11) The window was broken by the pressure/the explosion/John.

(12) *The window broke by John/by the explosion. (Martin and Schäfer 2014: 212)

Based on the grammaticality contrast between (11) and (12), Martin and Schäfer (2014) conclude that inchoatives lack an external argument of any kind. They propose that the *by itself* phrase actually means 'no particular cause', and its availability in inchoatives (cf. (5) above) testifies to the absence of any kind of external argument in this structure.

However, Martin and Schäfer's (2014) claim that inchoatives lack an external argument altogether turns out to be problematic when Polish inchoatives are taken into account. In contradistinction to English, Polish inchoatives can sometimes license causers or causing events introduced by *przez* 'by', as confirmed by the grammaticality of (13):

(13)	Liczba	turystów	zmniejszyła	się	przez	kryzys	o 10%.
	number-nom	tourists	diminished	refl	by	crisis	by 10%

'The number of tourists diminished by 10% because of crisis.'

The inchoative in (13) comprises an overt causer introduced by the preposition *przez* 'by'. Causative *przez*-phrases in inchoatives like (13) frequently contain an abstract causer.

Moreover, a causer argument in inchoatives may be realized as a dative case marked nominal, as shown in (14):

(14)	Młodym	ludziom	te	problemy	rozwiązują	się.
	young	people-dat	these	problems-3pl.nom	solve-3pl	refl

'These problems are solved for young people/Young people unintentionally solve these problems.'

The dative in (14) may be interpreted either as a beneficiary or unintentional causer (cf. Kibort 2004).

The grammaticality of (13) and (14) with an overt causer argument points towards the conclusion that Polish inchoatives without any overt causer like (4) above do have an implicit causer which triggers the change of state unintentionally. Since inchoatives have an implicit eternal argument, they resemble passives.

The difference between inchoatives and passives lies in that the former have an implicit external argument restricted to just an unintentional causer, while in the latter it corresponds to an agent or causer.

Finally, let us note that inchoatives normally have causative variants. For instance, the inchoative *rozwiązywać się* 'be solved' in (14) has a causative equivalent, *rozwiązywać* 'solve', as in (15):

(15)	Młodzi	ludzie	rozwiązują	te	problemy.
	young	people-3pl.nom	solve-3pl	these	problems-acc

'Young people solve these problems.'

In sentence (15), there is a nominative subject and an accusative object, and hence the verb it contains is undoubtedly transitive. The fact that intransitive inchoative verbs regularly alternate with causative transitive verbs is referred to in the literature as the causative alternation (cf. Levin and Rappaport Hovav 1995, Alexiadou et al. 2006, inter alia).

4. The modal *dać* + *się* + infinitive structure versus inchoatives

As has been noted in section 3, the same valency alternation that is observable in inchoatives, can be found both in middles and the modal *dać* + *się* + infinitive structure in Polish. In fact, Schäfer (2008) proposes that middles are syntactically inchoative, which leaves the question open whether the modal *dać* + *się* + infinitive structure can likewise be viewed as syntactically inchoative. Additionally, *lassen*-middles are analysed by Pitteroff (2014) as containing the matrix inchoative verb *sich lassen*.[10] Since the modal *dać* + *się* + infinitive structure is superficially similar to *lassen*-middles (cf. section 2), one may wonder whether the verb *dać*, along with *się*, in the structure under scrutiny can be regarded as inchoative, by analogy with Pitteroff's proposal advanced for German. Finally, cross-linguistically the reflexive is often viewed as a transitivity reduction marker, signaling that the internal argument is merged externally and the external argument is deleted

10 Due to space limitations, we do not dwell on Pitteroff's (2014) arguments in favour of treating *sich lassen* as inchoative in German (cf. Bondaruk 2017). Let us only note that Pitteroff observes that *sich* is not an argument of the embedded infinitive in German because it cannot be replaced with the dative, and it does not participate in case-copying (Kasuskongruenz, Fanselow 1991), the way German objects normally do. Pitteroff (2014) takes the surface subject to be the underlying complement of the infinitive, which subsequently, undergoes A-movement to the matrix clause.

(Lekakou 2005).[11] This might, in turn, point towards an analysis of *się* in the modal *dać* + *się* + infinitive structure as an inchoative marker. Taking all of the above mentioned observations into account, one might be inclined to analyse the Polish modal construction with *dać* as containing either an inchoative verb *dać się* or an inchoative embedded infinitive.

Let us first consider whether it is feasible to approach the verb *dać się* as inchoative in the structure analysed here. It appears that there are a number of arguments against treating *dać się* as inchoative. First of all, the reflexive does not form a unit with *dać*, but rather belongs to the infinitive, as can be seen in (16):

(16) Te problemy dają rozwiązać się bez trudu.
these problems-3pl.nom dać-3pl solve-inf refl without difficulty
'These problems can be solved without difficulty.'

In (16) the reflexive follows the infinitive, not *dać*, which argues against treating *się* as belonging to *dać*.

Secondly, if inchoatives are taken to represent unaccusatives (Levin and Rappaport Hovav 1995, Pitteroff 2014, among others) and hence to lack an external argument, then they are expected to preserve the meaning of idiomatic phrases. This, however, is not the case in the Polish modal structure with *dać*, as can be seen in (17) below (cf. Bondaruk 2017):

(17) Byk daje się wziąć za rogi.
bull-3sg.nom dać-3sg refl take-inf by horns
'The bull lets us take it by the horns.' not 'The bull can be taken by the horns.'

Sentence (17) contains an idiomatic phrase *wziąć byka za rogi* 'to take the bull by the horns', which in this case has only a literal meaning, i.e. the permissive causative interpretation.[12] The meaning of the idiom changes into the literal one in (17), which clearly points towards the conclusion that *dać* is not an inchoative verb, as it does assign an external theta role.

---

11 The reflexive is treated as participating in the detransitivisation process in those approaches that derive inchoatives from their transitive variants (cf. Levin and Rappaport Hovav 1995, Koontz-Garboden 2009, inter alia).

12 The idiomatic interpretation survives only in the impersonal structure like the one in (i) below:

(i) Byka daje się wziąć za rogi.
bull-3sg.acc lets refl take-inf by horns
'The bull can be taken by the horns.'

Finally, the reflexive *się* can sometimes be replaced with the instrumental case marked reflexive pronoun *sobą*, as can be seen in (18):

(18) Te łodzie dają sobą /się sterować.
these boats-3pl.nom dać-3pl refl-instr /refl-acc steer-inf
'These boats can be steered.'

The grammaticality of the instrumental reflexive undoubtedly shows that the reflexive depends for its case marking on the embedded infinitive, which can assign both the accusative and instrumental to its complement, as confirmed by the grammaticality of (19). This, in turn, presupposes that the reflexive does not belong to the matrix verb *dać*, and hence the two do not form an inchoative verb.

(19) Sterował łodziami /łodzie.
he-steered boats-3pl.instr/boats-3pl.acc
'He was steering boats.'

To sum up, three arguments have been provided against treating *dać się* in the modal *dać* + *się* + infinitive structure as inchoative. It has been shown that the reflexive does not form a unit with *dać*, but belongs to the infinitive, whose argument it represents and by which it is case marked. Moreover, idioms do not preserve their meaning within the modal structure with *dać się*, which additionally argues against its inchoative status.

Having dismissed the possibility of treating *dać* + *się* as an inchoative verb in the modal *dać* + *się* + infinitive structure in Polish, let us now check whether the embedded infinitive can instead be regarded as inchoative. In order to test whether the embedded infinitive is inchoative in the structure under scrutiny, let us first examine the range of modifiers it allows. It is worth noting that the agentive *przez* 'by'-phrase, banned from appearing in inchoatives (cf. sentence (6) above), is perfectly licit in the modal *dać* + *się* + infinitive structure. This is illustrated in (20) below:

(20) Te reformy dają się wprowadzić przez rząd.[13]
these reforms-3pl.nom dać-3pl refl introduce-inf by government
'These reforms can be introduced by the government.'

In (i), the phrase *byka* 'bull' is accusative case marked and serves as a complement of the infinitive. Hence, it does not trigger φ-feature agreement with the verb *dać*, which bears the default 3rd person singular feature.

13 Some native speakers of Polish find the modal *dać* + *się* + infinitive structure with agentive *przez*-phrase ungrammatical. Such sentences are, nonetheless, attested in the National Corpus of Polish (cf. von Waldenfels 2012: 164).

Furthermore, agent-oriented phrases such as *świadomie* 'deliberately' can occasionally be attested in the modal *dać* + *się* + infinitive structure, but are excluded with inchoatives (cf. (7) above). This is shown in (21):

(21) Te klątwy dają się zdjąć tylko świadomie.
these spells-3pl.nom dać-3pl refl remove-inf only deliberately
'These spells can be inactivated only deliberately.'

Sentence (21) is modeled on Pitteroff' example (50d) (cf. Piteroff 2014: 198), and its grammaticality improves if one imagines a world in which spells exist that can be inactivated by a magician only when he/she is forced to inactivate them.

The modifiers licit in inchoatives, such as *przez przypadek* 'by accident', and *sam* 'by itself', are incompatible with the modal *dać* + *się* + infinitive structure, as illustrated in (22):

(22) Te problemy dają się rozwiązać
these problems-3pl.nom dać-3pl refl solve-inf
*same /*przez przypadek.
*by themselves/*by accident
'These problems can be solved by themselves/by accident.'

The ungrammaticality of (22) with either of the two adverbials indicates that the change of state in the embedded clause does not happen spontaneously, as in the case of inchoatives (cf. (5) and (7) above), but is brought about willfully.

The data analysed so far have shown that the modal *dać* + *się* + infinitive structure differs from inchoatives as regards the type of an implied external argument. In the former it corresponds to an agent, while in the latter it refers to an unintentional causer. The modal *dać* + *się* + infinitive structure can also co-occur with an intentional or unintentional causer, introduced by *przez* 'by', as illustrated in (23):

(23) Te gałęzie dają się złamać przez wiatr/przez nacisk.
these branches-3pl.nom dać-3pl refl break-inf by wind/by pressure
'These branches can be broken by the wind/by pressure.'

The inchoative variant of (23), given in (24), contains the causative *od* 'from'-phrase.[14]

14 It is not possible to replace *przez* 'by'-phrase in (23) with the causer *od* 'from'-phrase (cf. (9) and (10) above), as demonstrated in (i) below:

(24)

Te	gałęzie	łamią	się	od wiatru/*przez wiatr.
these	branches-3pl.nom	break-3pl	refl	from wind/*by wind

'These branches break from the wind.'

Although *przez*-phrases with unintentional causers are possible in inchoatives (cf. (13) above), they are restricted to abstract causers, which explains the ungrammaticality of *przez*-phrase in (24).

However, the dative unintentional causer, frequently available in inchoatives such as (14) above, cannot be attested in the Polish modal structure under scrutiny, as shown in (25):

(25)

Te	problemy	dają	się	rozwiązać	młodym	ludziom
these	problems-3pl.nom	dać-3pl	refl	solve-inf	young	people-dat

'These problems can be solved by young people.' not ok
'These problems let themselves be solved by young people.' Ok

The sentence in (25) is ungrammatical with the modal interpretation. It allows only a permissive causative interpretation, in which the dative corresponds to the causer argument of the embedded verb. The incompatibility of the modal *dać* + *się* + infinitive structure with the dative causer indicates that this construction does not tolerate datives as unintentional causers, in contradistinction to inchoatives.

The overview of the differences between the modal *dać* + *się* + infinitive structure and inchoatives shows that the two differ only in the type of an external argument. Whereas the former allows agents or causers as explicit or implicit external arguments, the latter favours only one type of external argument, an overt or covert unintentional causer. The difference just mentioned is reflected in the distinct verb class restrictions that the two structures show. Compare the following data:

(26)

Policja	łamie	prawa	obywatelskie.
police-nom	break	laws-acc	civil

'The police break civil laws.'

(i)

*Te	gałęzie	dają	się	złamać	od	wiatru	/od
these	branches-3pl.nom	dać-3pl	refl	break-inf	from	wind	/from

nacisku.
pressure

'These branches can be broken from the wind/from pressure.'

(27)	*Prawa	obywatelskie	łamią się	(same).
	laws-nom	civil	break refl	(by themselves)
	'Civil laws are broken.'			

(28)	Prawa	obywatelskie	dają	się	łamać.
	laws-3pl.nom	civil	dać-3pl	refl	break-inf
	'Civil laws can be broken.'				

The verb *łamać* 'break' can be often found in inchoatives, as demonstrated in (29) below. The inchoative structure in (27) with the verb *łamać* 'break' is unacceptable, as by world-knowledge, the change of state expressed in (27) cannot be viewed as unintentionally caused, in contradistinction to the one in (29). (28), in turn, is perfectly licit, as an intentional causer or agent is allowed in this kind of structure.

(29)	Gałęzie	łamią	się.
	branches-3pl.nom	break-3pl	refl
	'Branches are broken.'		

It has been noted in section 3 that obligatorily agentive verbs do not form inchoatives (cf. (8b)). This restriction can be easily accounted for if one follows the analysis outlined above. Since an overt or covert external argument of inchoatives can only correspond to an unintentional causer, it is expected that it can never be realized as an agent.[15]

Actually, the reflexive marker present in the modal *dać* + *się* + infinitive structure, can be added to any transitive verb, whereby making it intransitive. The detransitivisation process also takes place in the case of reflexive inchoatives (cf. footnote 11, and Levin and Rappaport Hovav 1995, Koontz-Garboden 2009).[16] In the National Corpus of Polish, we can come across a lot of examples like (30), in which an inchoative variant of the transitive verb appears:

15 It is hard to test whether obligatorily agentive verbs are allowed in the modal *dać* + *się* + infinitive structure on account of the fact that obligatorily agentive verbs normally co-occur with an animate agent and an animate object (cf. (8a)), whereas in the structure analysed here the surface subject is always inanimate (cf. footnote 4).

16 However, the transitive source of inchoatives has been often questioned in the literature (cf. Alexiadou et al. 2006, Folli 2014, inter alia).

(30) Dobre biografie piszą się niemal same. (www.nkjp.pl)
good biographies-3pl.nom write-3pl refl almost by themselves
'Good biographies are written almost by themselves.'

An inchoative verb *pisać się* 'write' used in (30) can also be found in the modal *dać* + *się* + infinitive structure, as in (31):

(31) Dobre biografie dają się pisać.
good biograhpies-3pl.nom dać-3pl refl write-inf
'Good biographies can be written.'

The existence of a modal sentence in (31), equivalent to (30), shows that the modal structure with *dać* has a lot in common with inchoatives. The only difference between (30) and (31) lies in the nature of the causer of the writing event – in (30) it is an implied unintentional causer, while in (31) it is an agent.

The difference in the nature of an external argument present in the two structures analysed in this paper can be accounted for by appealing to the analysis of Alexiadou et al. (2006). Alexiadou et al. (2006) argue that agentivity and causation are associated with different heads, the former with Voice, which introduces external arguments, and the latter with CAUS, which is responsible for introducing a causal relation between the causing event and the resultant state. The presence of feature [+/- agentive] on Voice determines the type of an external argument found in a particular structure. Alexiadou et al. (2006) assume that [+agentive] Voice licenses agents, while [-agentive] Voice is found with causers. Alexiadou et al. (2006) propose that inchoatives with an implied causer project VoiceP with [-agentive] Voice on top of CAUSP. If this line of analysis is adopted to Polish, then inchoatives, which have been argued to host an implicit causer (or an explicit *przez*-phrase as in (13)), project VoiceP with [-agentive] Voice. Infinitival complements of the modal *dać* + *się* + infinitive, which contain an implicit agent, project VoiceP, whose Voice head is [+agentive], while those with an implicit causer project VoiceP with [-agentive] Voice. Consequently, the infinitival complement of the modal structure with *dać* has the same structure as inchoatives when it is associated with an implicit causer, but not when it contains an implicit agent.

5. Conclusions

The paper has shown that the modal *dać* + *się* + infinitive structure shares a number of similarities with inchoatives. It has been argued that inchoatives and the modal structure with *dać* only differ in one respect, namely the type of external argument they contain or imply. In the modal *dać* + *się* + infinitive structure, the implicit or explicit external argument corresponds to either an agent or causer, while in inchoatives the external argument, be it overt or covert, only refers to an unintentional causer. The claim that Polish inchoatives have an implicit external argument goes against Martin and Schäfer's (2014) account of English inchoatives, but falls in line with Alexiadou et al. (2006) and Kallulli (2007). Following Alexiadou et al. (2006), it has been suggested that inchoatives are projections of [-agentive] Voice, whereas the infinitival complement of the modal structure with *dać* is a projection of either [+agentive] or [-agentive] Voice. This makes the modal *dać* + *się* + infinitive structure only minimally distinct from inchoatives.

References

Alexiadou, Artemis, Elena Anagnostopoulou and Florian Schäfer. 2006. "The properties of anticausatives crosslinguistically." In *Phases of Interpretation*, Mara Frascarelli (ed.). Berlin and New York: Mouton de Gruyter, 187–211.

Bondaruk, Anna. 2015. "A comparison of the modal *dać się* structure with the dispositional middle in Polish." *Linguistics Beyond and Within* 1: 43–63. Online at: http://lingbaw.com/2015/Anna-Bondaruk.

Bondaruk, Anna. 2017. "Against a movement analysis of *dać* + *się* + infinitive structure in Polish." *Roczniki Humanistyczne* (5) LXIII: 7–31.

Fanselow, Gisbert. 1991. *Minimale Syntax*. Groningen: Rijksuniversiteit.

Folli, Raffaella. 2014. "Causatives and inchoatives in the lexicon and in the syntax." In *Causation and Grammatical Structure*, Bridget Copley and Fabienne Martin (eds.). Oxford: Oxford University Press, 351–371.

Ilić, Tatjana. 2014. "Modality and causation. Two sides of the same coin." In *Causation and Grammatical Structure*, Bridget Copley and Fabienne Martin (eds.). Oxford: Oxford University Press, 152–175.

Kallulli, Dalina. 2007. "Rethinking the passive/anticausative distinction." *Linguistic Inquiry* 38(4): 770–780.

Kibort, Anna. 2004. "Passive and passive-like constructions in English and Polish." PhD thesis, University of Cambridge.

Koontz-Garboden, Andrew. 2009. "Anticausativisation." *Natural Language and Linguistic Theory* 27: 77–138.

Kosta, Peter. 2010. "Causatives and anti-causatives, unaccusatives and unergatives: or how big is the contribution of the Lexicon to syntax." In *Karlik a továrna na lingvistiku. Prof. Petru Kalikovi k šedesátým narozeninám*, Aleš Bičan, Jan Klaška, Petra Macurová, and Jana Zmrzlíková (eds.). Brno: Masarykova Univerzita, 230–273.

Kosta, Peter. 2015. "On the causative/anti-causative alternation as principle of affix ordering in the light of the Mirror Principle, the Lexical Integrity Principle and the Distributed Morphology." *Zeitschrift für Slawistik* 60(4): 570–612.

Lekakou, Maria. 2005. "In the middle, somewhat elevated. The semantics of middles and its crosslinguistic realization." PhD thesis, University College London.

Levin, Beth and Rappaport Hovav, Malka. 1995. *Unaccusativity. At the syntax-lexical semantics interface*. Cambridge, Mass.: MIT Press.

Martin, Fabienne and Schäfer, Florian. 2014. "Causation at the syntax-semantics interface." In *Causation and Grammatical Structure*, Bridget Copley and Fabienne Martin (eds.). Oxford: Oxford University Press, 209–244.

Pitteroff, Marcel. 2014. "Non-canonical *lassen*-middles." PhD thesis, University of Stuttgart.

Schäfer, Florian. 2008. *The syntax of (anti-)causatives. External arguments in change-of-state contexts*. Amsterdam and Philadelphia: John Benjamins.

von Waldenfels, Ruprecht. 2012. *The grammaticalization of 'give' + infinitive. A Comparative study of Russian, Polish, and Czech*. Berlin: Mouton de Gruyter.

Russian

Egor Tsedryk

(Cor)relativization as a By-Product of *Wh*-Probing: The Case of Russian*

1. Introduction

Compared to correlatives in other languages (e.g., Hindi, Hungarian), correlatives in Russian, as in (1a), have received much less attention in the generative framework. Nevertheless, a recent discussion in Mitrenina (2010) and a seminal study in Inkova (2014) (though from a different theoretical perspective) have brought Russian into the spotlight. In this paper, I further the study of Russian correlatives, analyzing them in relation to light-headed relatives (1b), free relatives (1c), conditionals (1d) and *wh*-questions (1e).[1]

(1) a. [Kto pridët pervym], tot polučit bilet besplatno.
who.NOM will.come first that.NOM will.receive ticket for.free
[Lit.: 'Who'll come first, that person will receive a ticket for free.']

b. Tot, [kto pridët pervym], polučit bilet besplatno.
that.NOM who.NOM will.come first will.receive ticket for.free
[Lit.: 'That person who comes first will receive a ticket for free.']

c. [Kto pridët pervym] polučit bilet besplatno.
who.NOM will.come first will.receive ticket for.free
'Who comes first will receive a ticket for free.'

d. [Esli kto pridët pervym], tot polučit bilet besplatno.
if who.NOM will.come first that.NOM will.receive ticket for.free
'If anybody comes first, that person will receive a ticket for free.'

* I thank the anonymous reviewer for her/his insightful comments.

1 The term 'correlative' refers to the whole structure in (1a); 'correlative CP' will be used to refer to a subordinate clause within this structure. '(Cor)relative' is a shorthand for the structures in (1a–c). The term 'light-headed relative', applied to the structures like (1b), is borrowed from Citko 2004. For Inkova (2014), (1b) is one of the correlativization strategies available in Russian. (1c) could have a correlative structure with a null pronoun (*pro*) in the subject position of the main clause (see Izvorsky 1997). Whether or not there is *pro* in (1c) is irrelevant for my analysis.

e. [Kto pridët pervym]?
who.NOM will.come first
'Who'll come first?'

I claim that the bracketed CPs in (1), except the conditional in (1d), form a natural class of syntactic objects, defined in terms of a probing *wh*-feature. Correlative and conditional CPs follow the same subordination pattern (they are adjoined to the main clause), but they have a different quantificational feature in C. In (1d), this feature ranges over a closed domain of propositional alternatives. In (1a–c) and (1e), it ranges over an open discursive domain of persons. The following sections are organized as follows. Section 2 investigates the overall structure of correlatives. Section 3 examines correlatives in relation to conditionals. Finally, section 4 proposes a unified analysis of *wh*-questions, correlatives, light-headed relatives and free relatives, using the probe-goal model (Chomsky 2000 et seq.).

2. Probing the structure of correlatives in Russian

One of the questions surrounding correlatives concerns their possible derivational connection to headed relatives. In the case of Russian, the basic relevant structure would be a light-headed relative, as in (1b). Is (1a) derived from (1b)? According to Bhatt's (2003) analysis of correlatives in Hindi, there are three possible options: (i) low adjunction (correlative CP is attached to the demonstrative phrase); (ii) low adjunction, followed by high adjunction (correlative CP is attached to IP, moving from its low adjunction position); (iii) high adjunction without movement (correlative CP is attached directly to IP). To draw a parallel with Russian, options (i) and (ii) would correspond to (1b) and (1a), respectively, while option (iii) would apply to multi-head correlatives, as in (2), which clearly cannot be derived by movement.[2]

(2) [Kto kogo vstretit], tot togo i priglasit v teatr.
who.NOM who.ACC will.meet that.NOM that.ACC EMPH will.invite to theatre
[Lit.: 'Who'll meet whom, that (person) will invite that (other person) to the theatre.']

2 The emphatic particle *i* in (2) underlines the topic-comment partition of the main clause.

It is possible that CP movement in correlatives is a language-specific property, but the literature is far from being conclusive on this issue. Srivastav (1991) and Dayal (1996), for example, claim that all correlatives in Hindi, single- and multi-head, are base-generated structures: CP is adjoined to IP, functioning as a generalized quantifier that binds a variable (i.e., the demonstrative). As for other languages, Lipták (2012) argues that correlatives in Hungarian are not derived by movement, and Mitrenina (2010) also presents evidence against movement in Russian, even though some of her data (to which I return shortly) seem to imply the opposite.

The main argument against movement comes from the absence of reconstruction effects (i.e., interpretation of a lower copy that is supposedly left after movement). For example, the minimal pair in (3) shows that the fronted CP in (3a) does not reconstruct into the same position as in (3b), where Condition C is violated. Is it sufficient to conclude that the bracketed CP does not form a constituent with the demonstrative in (3a)?

(3) a. [Kogo Maša$_i$ vstretit pervym], tomu ona$_i$ otdast bilet besplatno.
who.ACC Maša will.meet first that.DAT she will.give ticket for.free
[Lit. 'Whom Maša$_i$ will meet first, to that (person) she$_i$ will offer a ticket for free.']

b. *Ona$_i$ otdast bilet besplatno tomu [kogo Maša$_i$ vtretit pervym].
she will.give ticket for.free that.DAT who.ACC Maša will.meet first
[Lit.: 'She$_i$ will a ticket for free to that (person) whom Maša$_i$ will meet first.']

Let us scrutinize the derivational steps needed to derive (3a) from (3b). One of such steps is topicalization of the demonstrative (Lipták 2012). Thus, if the CP forms a constituent with the demonstrative, it would be pied-piped by topicalization; the second step is movement of this CP out of the demonstrative phrase, as shown in (4).[3] In a non-cartographic perspective, I assume that topics are adjoined to TP. CP movement in (4) could be another case of TP-adjunction

3 It is possible that the dative demonstrative phrase undergoes a heavy NP shift in (3b), whereas its original position corresponds to the copy in (4). I use '*t*' as a notational convention for a copy left after movement.

(Dayal 1996, Bhatt 2003), or it could be a case of CP-adjunction, as proposed for comparative correlatives by Den Dikken (2005) (see also Citko 2009: 51–2 for discussion). I will clarify the nature of XP shortly.

(4) $[_{XP}$ CP$_j$ $[_{TP}$ [tomu t_j]$_i$ $[_{TP}$ ona otdast bilet t_i besplatno]]]

It is possible that the reconstruction site is not low enough to induce a violation of Condition C in (3a). That is, the fronted CP is reconstructed back to the demonstrative in a TP-adjoined position (i.e., its lower copy is interpreted in a sisterhood relationship with the demonstrative), but the whole demonstrative phrase does not reconstruct into a VP internal position (where only *tomu* might be sufficient for interpretation in a thematic position). Copies interpreted at LF would be distributed as follows.[4]

(5) $[_{TP}$ [tomu CP] $[_{TP}$ [ona otdast [tomu] besplatno]]

With this scenario, the lack of Condition C violation in (3a) is not an argument against a movement analysis, under which a correlative CP and the demonstrative form a constituent before topicalization reorders them at the left periphery.[5]

Interestingly, Mitrenina (2010) provides data that seem to indicate reconstruction to a lower position. For example, the pronoun contained in the correlative CP in (6) (Mitrenina's (17a)) receives a bound variable reading, which

4 We would have the same representation in (i), where the CP does not raise overtly. Note that in (i) there is no Condition C effect either.

(i) Tomu, [kogo Maša$_i$ vstretit pervym], ona$_i$ otdast bilet besplatno.
that.DAT who.ACC Maša will.meet first she will.give ticket for.free
[Lit. 'To that (person) whom Maša$_i$ will meet first she$_i$ will offer a ticket for free.']

5 The anonymous reviewer points out that the lack of reconstruction in (3a) can even be used as an argument against a base-generation account: if the fronted CP is a generalized quantifier, its movement in (4) creates a new bound variable reading that precludes reconstruction due to economy principles operating at LF (e.g., economy of variable binding in Fox (2000)). Elaborating this argument is beyond the scope of this paper; I will just mention Fox's *Condition C and scope reconstruction correlation*: "In the structural configuration in [(i) below], an element that contains the r-expression cannot undergo scope reconstruction." (Fox 2000:8; see also ch. 5).

(i) $[_{XP}$ … r-expression$_i$ …]$_j$ … pronoun$_i$ … t_j

is only possible within the scope of the quantified subject (*každyj* 'each') in the main clause.

(6) [Kakuju tarelku pered nim$_i$ postavjat], iz takoj každyj$_i$ i est.
which plate before him put.3PL from such each EMPH eats
[Lit.: 'Which plate is put in front of him$_i$, from such a plate everyone$_i$ eats.']

Under a movement analysis, derivation of (6) would involve three steps (see (7)): topicalization of the PP (containing the demonstrative phrase and the correlative CP), CP fronting, and noun ellipsis.[6] At LF, the whole PP is reconstructed into its base position, corresponding to t_j in (7).

(7) [$_{XP}$ [$_{CP}$ kakuju tarelku pered nim$_i$ postavjat]$_k$ [$_{TP}$ [$_{PP}$ iz takoj ~~tarelki~~ t_k]$_j$ [$_{TP}$ každyj$_i$ i est t_j]]]

However, reconstruction is not the only possible way to derive the bound variable reading in (6). The latter can also be a result of quantifier raising (QR). In (8), it is shown that correlativization is not a root phenomenon: the CP can be attached to an embedded clause, following the complementizer *čto* 'that'.

(8) Pravilo takoe, čto, [kakuju tarelku pered nim$_i$ postavjat], iz takoj
rule such that which plate before him put.3PL from such
každyj$_i$ i est.
each EMPH eats
'The rule is such that everyone eats from a plate that is put in front of him.'

That is, the correlative CP should be adjoined to TP, not to CP, of the main clause. Therefore, if *každyj* in (6) undergoes QR to the main Spec,CP, it takes scope over the pronoun contained in the correlative CP, as shown in (9). In this case, the CP is base-generated in a TP-adjoined position of the main clause (after the PP *iz takoj ~~tarelki~~* is topicalized – this step is not shown in (9)), and the quantifier *každyj* raises across the correlative CP.[7]

(9) [$_{CP (main)}$ každyj$_i$ [$_{TP}$ [$_{CP (correlative)}$ kakuju tarelku pered nim$_i$ postavjat] [$_{TP}$ iz takoj [$_{TP}$ t_i i est]]]]

6 There is a case mismatch between the deleted noun (genitive) and its antecedent (accusative); the genitive case, assigned by the preposition *iz* 'from', can be recovered from the demonstrative.

7 There is no weak crossover effect in (9) because the bound pronoun is deeply embedded in the correlative CP (see Fox 2000: 37, fn. 23). I thank the anonymous reviewer for bringing this point to my attention.

If the QR analysis of (6) is on the right track, the bound variable reading in (6) cannot be used as evidence in favour of a low adjunction of the correlative CP followed by its movement. A direct TP-adjunction is equally possible.

As we can see from the above discussion, the data in (3) and (6) are compatible with both movement and base-generation. Everything else being equal, multi-head correlatives (2) are arguably derived by direct TP-adjunction. For the sake of a unified analysis of correlatives, I will assume that the same derivational mechanism applies to single-head correlatives. However, nothing hinges on this assumption, and movement remains a viable option for single-head correlatives in Russian. I assume the following structure:

(10) $[_{\text{CP (main)}}\ [_{\text{TP}}\ [_{\text{CP (correlative)}}\ \text{Wh}_i\ (\text{Wh}_j)\ \ldots]\ [_{\text{TP}}\ \text{Dem}_i\ (\text{Dem}_j)\ \ldots]]]$

The correlative CP in (10) is merged right after the (last) demonstrative (Dem) is topicalized. I will now focus on the internal structure of the adjoined CP and the link between a *wh*-phrase (Wh) and Dem. The next section compares correlatives with conditionals.

3. Correlative and conditional CPs

Correlatives and conditionals are often analyzed as two closely related constructions. For example, *then* in (11) can be analyzed on a par with the demonstrative in correlatives (Izvorsky 1997, Bhatt and Pancheva 2006). The difference is that *then* is associated with the whole subordinate clause and not with a constituent within that clause. Bittner (2001) claims that both constructions involve 'topical maximization', which is individual-centered in correlatives and possibility-centered in conditionals.

(11) [If you come first]$_i$, then$_i$ you'll receive a ticket for free.

Based on data from Serbo-Croatian, Arsenijević (2009) proposes that correlative CPs are basically conditional CPs with topicalized (non-interrogative) *wh*-pronouns.[8] Russian seems to support this proposal; *esli* 'if' in Russian can license a non-interrogative *wh*-pronoun:

(12) a. [Esli kto pridët pervym], zovi menja. (cf. 1a)
if who.NOM will.come first call me
'If anyone comes first, call me.'

8 Arsenijević (2009) defines *wh*-pronouns as polarity sensitive (extreme non-specific) items with a 'weak existential commitment'.

b. [Esli kto kogo vstretit], my budem rady. (cf. 2)
if who.NOM who.ACC will.meet we will.be happy
'If anyone meets anybody, we'll be happy.'

According to Yanovich (2005), the *wh*-pronouns in (12) are Hamblin pronouns, which by definition have to be licensed by an alternative quantifier (e.g., *esli* 'if'). Therefore, we could hypothesize that a correlative CP is in fact a concealed *if*-clause (*if* is not lexicalized) with a topicalized Hamblin *wh*-pronoun, which undergoes the same type of movement as Dem in the main clause.

(13) $[_{\text{CP (main)}} [_{\text{TP}} [_{\text{CP (correlative)}}$ C-*if* $[_{\text{TP}}$ Wh_i (Wh_j) …]] $[_{\text{TP}}$ Dem_i (Dem_j) …]]]

This analysis implies that Wh is associated with Dem via pronominal coreference, not variable binding (see Belyaev and Haug 2014 for this type of association in Ossetic correlatives). Thus, what was referred to as a 'free relative' in (1c) could be an *if*-clause whose *wh*-pronoun is linked to a null pronoun (*pro*) in the main clause by coreference:

(14) [(Esli) kto$_i$ pridët pervym] *pro*$_i$ polučit bilet
if who.NOM will.come first *he/she* will.receive.3SG ticket
besplatno.
for.free
'(If) anyone comes first (that person) will receive a ticket for free.'

The so-called 'demonstrative requirement' (Lipták 2009) (and probably correlatives themselves) would be epiphenomenal: the demonstrative is just one of the pronominal realizations, and what we call 'correlatives' are exactly those cases when a pronominal is realized as a demonstrative in the main clause. However, this analysis runs into an empirical problem. It predicts that correlative CPs (those without an overt *if*) and conditional CPs (those with an overt *if*) should pattern alike with regard to pronominal coreference, but this is clearly not the case, as shown in (15).

(15) a. [Esli ty kogo$_i$ uvidiš'], skaži *pro*$_i$ čtoby *pro*$_{arb}$ zašli ko
if you who.ACC will.see tell him/her that.SUBJ they came.PL to
mne.
me
[Lit.: 'If you see anyone, tell (that one) that (they) come to me.']

b. *[Kogo$_i$ ty uvidiš'], skaži *pro*$_i$ čtoby *pro*$_{arb}$ zašli ko mne.
who.ACC you will.see tell him/her that.SUBJ they came.PL to me
[Lit.: 'Whom you will see, tell (that one) that (they) come to me.']

The *wh*-pronoun in (15a) is an antecedent for the null object in the main clause, which also embeds a subjunctive clause containing an arbitrary *pro* (recognized by the plural subject agreement on the verb). This type of coreference is not allowed in (15b), which suggests that we should have a different type of relationship between the adjoined CP and the main clause. Based on the minimal pair in (15), I discard the conditional analysis of correlatives presented in (13). The next section argues that Wh and Dem in Russian correlatives are linked by an operator-variable relation. I suggest that this relation is mediated by a probing feature in C.

4. *Wh*-probing

Srivastav (1991: 655) notes: 'The demonstrative requirement follows from the fact that a base-generated relative clause, being a quantifier, must bind a variable, and the demonstrative provides this variable.' However, Dem does not just provide a variable; being a variable, it requires an operator. In (16), Dem is a free variable that cannot be properly interpreted.

(16)	a.	*Tot	polučit	bilet	besplatno.	(cf. 1a–b)	
		that.NOM	will.receive	ticket	for.free		
		Intended: 'That one will receive a ticket for free.'					
	b.	*Tot	togo	i	priglasit	v	teatr. (cf. 2)
		that.NOM	that.ACC	EMPH	will.invite	to	theatre
		Intended: 'That person will (indeed) invite that other person to the theatre.'					

Moreover, Russian (and other Slavic languages; e.g., Polish, Bulgarian) does not use a generic relativizer in its correlatives and light-headed relatives. For each ontological category, there is a corresponding Wh-Dem pair, as shown in (17) (see Citko 2009: 55 for a similar paradigm in Polish). That is, there is a clear paradigmatic relationship between Wh and Dem. In correlatives and light-headed relatives, this relationship should also exist at the syntagmatic level.

(17)	PERSON	*kto* 'who'	*tot* 'that (person)'
	THING	*čto* 'what'	*to* 'that (thing)'
	PLACE	*gde* 'where'	*tam* 'there'
	TIME	*kogda* 'when'	*togda* 'then'
	MANNER	*kak* 'how'	*tak* 'that (way)'
	PROPERTY	*kakoj* 'which' + N	*takoj* 'such' + N

DEGREE	*čem* 'by what' + A (comparative)	*tem* 'by that' + A (comparative)
AMOUNT	*naskol'ko* 'by how much'	*nastol'ko* 'by that much'

Finally, as we have seen in (1), (cor)relative CPs in Russian are formally identical to *wh*-questions, except that the latter are not linked to Dem in a larger structure (compare, e.g., (18b) with (2); (18a) repeats (1e)).

(18) a. Kto pridët pervym?
who.NOM will.come first
'Who'll come first?'

b. Kto kogo vstretit?
who.NOM who.ACC will.meet
'Who'll meet whom?'

All in all, the Wh-Dem dependency in correlatives and light-headed relatives can be viewed as a two-way requirement: Dem, being a variable, needs to be bound and Wh has to bind Dem to avoid an interrogative reading at the interface. As a matter of fact, *wh*-pronouns in Russian are not predefined in the lexicon as interrogative and their actual interpretation depends on the syntactic context. Thus, in (19) we have the same *wh*-pronouns as in (18), but they have an indefinite reading, being part of a yes/no question.

(19) a. Pridët li kto pervym?
will.come Q who.NOM first
'Will anyone come first?'

b. Vstretit li kto kogo?
will.meet Q who.NOM who.ACC
'Will anyone meet anybody?'

Within the probe-goal model (Chomsky 2000 et seq.), the difference between (18) and (19) reduces to a probe-goal relationship between C and a *wh*-pronoun. That is, C has a probing feature in (18), but not in (19). More precisely, I assume that C in (19) has a quantificational feature, or simply [Q], that ranges over a set of alternative propositions, {p, ~p}. C in (18), on the other hand, has a probing *wh*-feature. I take the latter to be another kind of quantificational feature, [$_{wh}$ Q], that ranges over a specific domain corresponding to ontological categories in (17). [$_{wh}$ Q] itself does not have an ontological value (PERSON, THING, PLACE, etc.); this value is provided by a *wh*-pronoun as a bundle of its morpho-syntactic features, which are shared with (or copied to) [$_{wh}$ Q] in a probe-goal relationship.

A *wh*-pronoun in its turn has an unvalued polarity feature, which can have an interrogative, indefinite or definite value/reading. When a *wh*-pronoun falls under the scope of [Q] (no probing is involved), its polarity feature has an indefinite reading, as in (19). When a *wh*-pronoun is probed by [$_{wh}$ Q] in a root structure, its polarity feature has an interrogative value, as in (18). However, if CP is part of a larger syntactic structure, where it is associated with Dem or enters into a thematic relationship with a matrix predicate (i.e., receives a θ-role), we have a definite description. This is the case of light-headed relatives, correlatives and free relatives. I focus on these three constructions in the remainder of this section.

As a result of a probe-goal relationship, the *wh*-pronoun shares its features with the probe, and C ends up bearing what I call a 'featural image' of the goal. This is a set of morpho-syntactic features belonging to the *wh*-pronoun. I present it as {wh_i} with the same index as the goal (Wh_i) that moves to Spec,CP. In other words, the set of features belonging to the specifier is part of the CP label, as shown in (20) (the X-bar notation is used for illustration only).[9]

(20)

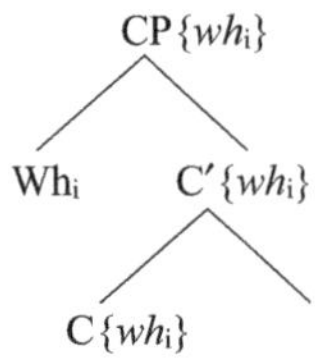

A CP like (20) can have interrogative or non-interrogative reading, depending on further selection and binding. In light-headed relatives, (21a), this CP is selected by Dem. In free relatives, (21b), it is selected by a verb assigning a θ-role.[10] In correlatives, (21c), it is adjoined to a structure that immediately contains a topicalized Dem. In all these cases, it is the featural image of *čto*, not

9 There is a question about the necessity to have a specifier in (20). If C bears the same set of features as a *wh*-pronoun, it is probably sufficient to assume that C{wh_i} itself is realized as a single *wh*-word, like *kto* 'who', *čto* 'what', *gde* 'where', *kogda* 'when', *kak* 'how' (pied-piping would only be required for PROPERTY, DEGREE and AMOUNT in (17), when categorial N and A features are not shared with C and the whole phrase has to move to take a wide scope). The idea to dispense with specifiers goes back to Strake (2001).

10 Another possible way of looking at free relatives is a relabeling analysis, under which Wh itself relabels CP into a DP (see Cecchetto and Donati 2015 and references therein). Under my proposal, there is no 'relabeling' in a strict sense: C has a *wh*-feature from the very beginning, but it is underspecified for categorial information. The fact that CP has a *wh*-pronoun's label in free relatives independently follows from the mechanics of the

čto itself, that is associated with the larger structure via binding or via selection by a head, Dem or V.[11]

(21) a. Ja kuplju to [CP{čto} čto ty zaxočeš'].
I will.buy that.ACC what.ACC you will.want
[Lit.: 'I'll buy that (thing), what you want.']

b. Ja kuplju [CP{čto} čto ty zaxočeš'].
I will.buy what.ACC you will.want
'I'll buy what you want.'

c. [CP{čto} čto ty zaxočeš'], to ja i kuplju.
what.ACC you will.want that.ACC I EMPH will.buy
[Lit.: 'What you want, that (thing) I'll buy.']

---

wh-probing without additional assumptions required for a relabeling analysis (e.g., the assumption that Wh has to be a word, not a phrase). A *wh*-probing approach allows a unified analysis of free relatives and correlatives in Russian, while a relabeling analysis would exclude correlatives, since the *wh*-fronting can be phrasal in correlatives (just like in *wh*-questions). I do not see any particular reason why the subordinate clauses in light-headed relatives, free relatives and correlatives would not form a natural class of CPs in Russian.

11 The anonymous reviewer points out a parallel between (21c) and (i), suggesting that correlative CPs could involve covert universal quantification and bringing up a possibility of analysis in terms of QR (along the lines of antecedent contained deletion).

(i) Vsë, čto ty zaxočeš', to ja i kuplju.
all what.ACC you will.want that.ACC I EMPH will.buy
[Lit.: 'What you want, that (thing) I'll buy.']

However, the reviewer's example in (i) appears to be an argument against CP movement in terms of universal QR. If (i) is to be derived by moving *vsë, čto ty zaxočeš'* from Dem, we expect this string of words to be a constituent at the base contrary to fact: the quantifier has to precede Dem, as shown in (ii) (vs. (iii)). If there is some kind of movement, *vsë* and *čto ty zaxočeš'* would move independently from each other.

(ii) Ja kuplju **vsë** **to,** čto ty zaxočeš'.
I will.buy all.ACC that.ACC what.ACC you will.want
[Lit.: 'I'll buy all that (things) what you want.']

(iii) *Ja kuplju **to vsë**, čto ty zaxočeš'.

In the case of multiple *wh*-fronting, I assume that C has more than one *wh*-feature. Suppose there are two such features. The first probe-goal relationship would be established with the highest *wh*-pronoun. As soon as a *wh*-feature finds its goal, it cannot probe anymore. The other *wh*-feature probes the next available *wh*-pronoun (a lower one), ignoring the higher one (that has already been probed). Due to the hierarchical structure that was built by Merge, the probe-goal relationships are established in the order that is a function of the structural relationship between the probed *wh*-pronouns. That is, from an unordered set of unvalued *wh*-features, we obtain an ordered set of the *wh*-featural images, as presented in (22a) (an index means that a *wh*-feature is linked to a goal; index *i* belongs to a structurally higher goal). *Wh*-movement creates a multi-Spec structure, as in (22b).[12]

(22) a. C{*wh*, *wh*} → C⟨wh_i, wh_j⟩

b.

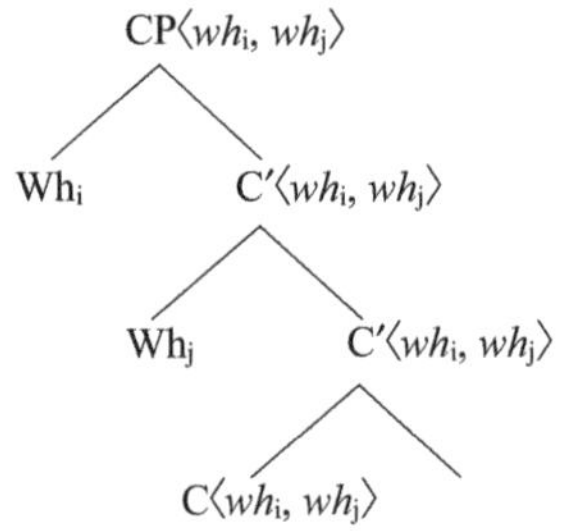

A CP with an ordered set of *wh*-featural images is combinatorially more restricted. Thus, it cannot be selected by Dem, which requires a one-to-one (operator-variable) relation. Dem can only be merged with a CP that has a single *wh*-feature. The binary nature of Merge does not allow more than one Dem to be merged with a single CP. Therefore, if Dem were merged with the CP in (22b), it would be associated only with one of the *wh*-featural images, while the remaining

12 The order of specifiers is irrelevant here; Wh_j could precede Wh_i in (22b) (Russian is known for its violations of superiority). Even if Wh_j preceded Wh_i, the ordered pair in C would still be the same, ⟨wh_i, wh_j⟩. The order of specifiers in (22b) reflects a maximal correspondence between the syntactic input (an ordered pair of feature sets) and the PF output (linear order). An optimality-theoretic constraint, operating at the sensory-motor interface, could be at work here. I leave this discussion aside for lack of space.

wh-featural image would be left without a variable to bind. As was noted above, if a *wh*-pronoun is not linked to Dem (via its featural image in C), it receives an interrogative interpretation, leading to a conflict at the conceptual/intentional interface: a CP cannot be interpreted as a question and a definite description at the same time. As for free relatives, the syntactic object in (22b) can be selected by a verb, as shown in (23a). Crucially, the verb selects an ordered pair of featural images, ⟨*kto*, *čto*⟩, not a single *wh*-pronoun, *kto* or *čto*. The sentence in (23a) has a pair-list reading. Finally in correlatives, each featural image binds a Dem in the matrix clause (see (23b)).

(23) a. Ja kuplju [$_{\text{CP}\langle\text{kto, čto}\rangle}$ kto čto zaxočet].
I will.buy who.NOM what.ACC will.want
'I'll buy to everyone what she/he wants.' (pair-list reading)

b. [$_{\text{CP}\langle\text{kto, čto}\rangle}$Kto čto zaxočet], to tomu ja i kuplju.
who.NOM what.ACC will.want that.ACC that.DAT I EMPH will.buy
[Lit.: 'Who wants what, that (thing) to that (person) I will buy.']

A unified analysis of *wh*-questions and (cor)relative CPs in Russian does not exclude their possible differences. Citko (2009) has pointed out that, in Polish, correlative CPs and *wh*-questions are quite similar, whereas free relatives do show differences with regard to multiple *wh*-pronouns, left branch extraction and reconstruction. I do not have space to discuss Citko's diagnostics here, but I would like to emphasize that some restrictions are indeed expected under the current analysis. For example, as was noted above, Dem can be merged with CP{wh_i}, but not with CP⟨wh_i, wh_j⟩, excluding light-headed relatives with multiple *wh*-pronouns. But this is a selectional restriction, which has nothing to do with the derivational cycle within CP itself.

5. Conclusion

The goal of this paper was to provide a unified analysis of correlatives, light-headed relatives, free relatives and *wh*-questions. It was shown that movement and base-generation are both plausible analytical options for single-head correlatives in Russian. I adopted a base-generation account for the sake of a unified analysis of single-head and multi-head correlatives. Correlative CPs are analyzed as TP-adjoined syntactic objects that bind a variable (topicalized demonstrative) in the main clause. The essence of my proposal is that (cor)relative CPs (including light-headed and free relatives) have a featural image of a *wh*-pronoun in C (and CP). This image results from a probe-goal relationship in syntax, and it makes CP available for association with a larger structure via theta or operator-variable dependency. In the absence of such a dependency, CP is construed as a *wh*-question. Finally, I excluded the hypothesis that correlative CPs in Russian are concealed *if*-clauses. *If*-clauses (just like yes/no questions) do not involve *wh*-probing and they cannot saturate Dem via an operator-variable relation (Dem can only be saturated by a pronominal coreference). However, I admit that some languages might use a conditional structure for their correlatives. After all, the difference is reduced to the type of the quantificational feature in C, which may or may not range over an ontological domain, [$_{wh}$ Q] vs. bare [Q].

References

Arsenijević, Boban. 2009. "{Relative{conditional{correlative clauses}}}." In *Correlatives cross-linguistically*, Anikó Lipták (ed.). Amsterdam: John Benjamins, 131–156.

Belyaev, Oleg and Dag Haug. 2014. "Pronominal coreference in Ossetic correlatives and the syntax-semantics interface." In *Proceedings of LFG 14*, Miriam Butt and Tracy Holloway King (eds.). Stanford, CA: CSLI Publications, 89–109.

Bhatt, Rajesh. 2003. "Locality in correlatives." *Natural Language and Linguistic Theory* 21: 485–541.

Bhatt, Rajesh and Roumyana Pancheva. 2006. "Conditionals." In *The Blackwell Companion to Syntax I*, Martin, Everaert, Henk van Riemsdijk, Rob Goedemans and Bart Hollebrandse (eds.). Oxford: Blackwell, 638–687.

Bittner, Maria. 2001. "Topical referents for individuals and possibilities." In *Proceedings of SALT XI*, Rachel Hastings, Brendan Jackson and Zsófia Zvolenszky (eds.). Ithaca, NY: Cornell University, 36–55.

Cecchetto, Carlo and Caterina Donati. 2015. *(Re)labeling*. Cambridge, MA: MIT Press.

Chomsky, Noam. 2000. "Minimalist inquiries: the framework." In *Step by step: essays on minimalist syntax in honor of Howard Lasnik*, Roger Martin, David Michaels and Juan Uriagereka (eds.). Cambridge: MIT Press, 89–155.

Citko, Barbara. 2004. "On headed, headless, and light-headed relatives." *Natural Language and Linguistic Theory* 22: 95–126.

Citko, Barbara. 2009. "What don't wh-questions, free relatives, and correlatives have in common?" In *Correlatives cross-linguistically*, Anikó Lipták (ed.). Amsterdam: John Benjamins, 49–79.

Dayal, Veneeta. 1996. *Locality in WH quantification: questions and relative clauses in Hindi*. Boston: Kluwer.

Dikken, Marcel den. 2005. "Comparative correlatives comparatively." *Linguistic Inquiry* 36: 497–532.

Fox, Danny. 2000. *Economy and semantic interpretation*. Cambridge, MA: MIT Press.

Inkova, Olga. 2014. *La corrélation en russe: structures et interprétations*. Frankfurt am Main: Peter Lang.

Izvorski, Roumyana. 1996. "The syntax and semantics of correlative proforms." In *Proceedings of NELS 26*, Kiyomi Kusumoto (ed.). Amherst: GLSA Publications, 133–47.

Izvorsky, Roumyana. 1997. "Subject free relatives in null-subject languages: Evidence from Slavic." In *Proceedings of FASL 4*, Wayles Browne, Ewa Dornisch, Natalia Kondrashova and Draga Zec (eds.). Michigan Slavic Publications, Ann Arbor, 267–288.

Lipták, Anikó. 2012. "Correlative topicalization." *Acta Linguistica Hungarica* 59: 245–302.

Lipták, Anikó. 2009. "The landscape of correlatives: an empirical and analytical survey." In *Correlatives cross-linguistically*, Anikó Lipták (ed.). Amsterdam: John Benjamins, 2–46.

Mitrenina, Olga. 2010. "Correlatives: evidence from Russian." In *Proceedings of FDSL 7.5*, Gerhild Zybatow et al. (eds.). Frankfurt am Main: Peter Lang, 135–151.

Srivastav, Veneeta. 1991. "The syntax and semantics of correlatives." *Natural Language and Linguistic Theory* 9: 637–686.

Starke, Michal. 2001. "Move dissolves into Merge: a theory of locality." PhD thesis. University of Geneva.

Yanovich, Igor. 2005. "Choice-functional series of indefinite pronouns and Hamblin semantics." In *Proceedings of SALT XV*, Efthymia Georgala and Jonathan Howell (eds.). Ithaca, NY: Cornell University, 309–326.

Keren Khrizman

The Cardinal/Collective Alternation in Russian Numerals*

1. Introduction

The paper offers the semantic interpretation of two types of numerals in Russian: 'cardinal' numerals (e.g. *pjat'* 'five') and 'collective' numerals (e.g. *pjatero* 'five individuals/a group of five individuals) (Vinogradov 1960).

The term 'collective' reflects the common assumption that such numerals are used to refer to a certain number of entities as a totality (Vinogradov 1960). Mel'čuk (1985) notes that NPs headed by such numerals often favor collective readings (1a) whereas their cardinal counterparts may be interpreted either distributively or collectively (1b).

(1) a. včera ko mne prixodili četvero neznakomyx mne studentov
yesterday to me came four^{COL} unknown$^{\text{GEN PL}}$ me student$^{\text{GEN PL}}$
'Yesterday a group of four students whom I didn't know came to see me.'

b. včera ko mne prixodili četyre neznakomyx mne studenta
yesterday to me came four^{CAR} unknown$^{\text{GEN PL}}$ me student$^{\text{GEN SG}}$
'Yesterday four students whom I didn't know came to see me. (together or separately)'

(Mel'čuk 1985:394)

In this paper I show that collective numerals do not denote groups. The two forms have a different semantics but the interpretational contrast in (1) does not directly reflect this. I propose that: (i) cardinal numerals in (1b) are predicate modifiers of plural nouns in the sense of Landman (2003/04); (ii) collective numeral NPs have properties of classifier constructions and, therefore, collective numerals as in (1a) are best analyzed as semantically complex predicates involving a lexically concealed classifier.

* The work on this project was supported by a Presidential Fellowship for Outstanding Doctoral Students from Bar Ilan University, a Rotenstreich Scholarship for Ph.D. Students from the Council for Higher Education of Israel, and Israel Science Foundation grant # 1345/13 to Susan Rothstein.

2. Cardinal and collective numerals are different

i. Interpretation and distribution

As mentioned, collective numerals are often associated with collective readings. However, such collective effects are not stable. As shown in (2) collective numerals may be used interchangeably with cardinals in unambiguously distributive contexts.

(2) a.

dvoe	molodyx	l'udej	polučili	**po**	odnomu	godu	kolonii	každyj
two^{COL}	young	people$^{GEN\ SG}$	received^{PL}	DIS	one	year	prison	each

'Two young men were sentenced to one year in prison each.'
[http://saratovdaily.ru/news/2016/07/29/27579:dvoe_parnej_poluchili_po_godu_kolonii_za_izbienie_muzhchini_i_krazhu_ego_telefonov.html]

b.

dva	molodyx	čeloveka	polučili	**po**	odnomu	godu	kolonii	každyj
two^{CAR}	young	person$^{GEN\ SG}$	received^{PL}	DIS	one	year	prison	each

'Two young men were sentenced to one year in prison each.'

In contrast, there is another interpretational difference between the two forms which is systematic. Cardinals are used in two ways. Either with count nouns to count entities (3a) or bare to refer to numbers as abstract objects (3b) (Vinogradov 1960).

(3) a.

dva	kotenka/	pjat'	kotjat
two^{CAR}	kitten$^{GEN\ SG}$	/five^{CAR}	kitten$^{GEN\ PL}$

'two kittens/five kittens'

b.

dva	plus	pjat'	ravno	sem'
two^{CAR}	plus	five^{CAR}	equal	seven^{CAR}

'Two plus five equals seven.'

Collective numerals, on the other hand, are only used to count individuals. Even bare occurrences of collective numerals make reference to a certain number of individuals and not to numbers as individuals in their own right. (4) can never have the meaning of (3b).

(4)

dvoe	plus	pjatero	èto	uže	semero
two^{COL}	plus	five^{COL}	COP	already	seven^{COL}

'Two people plus five people make seven people.'

ii. Lexical and morphological restrictions

Cardinals can modify any count noun. The collective form is restricted to masculine nouns denoting humans or young animals (5) (Vinogradov 1960, Melčuk 1985).

(5) a. pjatero studentov / #studentok
five^{COL} student^{MS} /student^{FM}
'five students'

b. pjatero kotjat / #kotov
five^{COL} kitten^{MS} /cat^{MS}
'five kittens'

c. # pjatero stolov / mašin
five^{COL} table$^{INAM\ MS}$ /car$^{INAM\ FM}$
'five tables/cars'

Melčuk (1985) suggests that these restrictions are lexical rather than morpho-syntactic. I argue that only the restriction to animacy is lexical. The data in (5) and (6) show that collective numerals as modifiers and in the bare form are systematically restricted to animate entities. All felicitous examples with collectives involve animate entities (5a,b) and (6a,b). This form can never be used to count inanimate individuals (5c) and (6c). Other restrictions ([+masculine, +young animal]) are not stable and show up only when nominal complements are involved (5a,b) vs. (6a,b). Moreover, Melčuk (1985) notes that some speakers may use feminine complements (e.g. *dvoe*^{COL} *doček*$^{FM\ PL}$ 'two daughters' (from 'Three sisters' by Chekhov)[1].This further supports the claim that the gender restriction is not part of the lexical meaning.

(6) a. Context: I had to take care of my friend's **dog** and **cat.**
èti **dvoe** menja prosto zamučili
these two^{COL} me simply tortured
'These two have simply killed me!'

b. v avirii postradali **četvero.** požiloj **mužčina**, **ženščina** i dvoe
in accident injured four^{COL} elderly man womam and two^{COL}
malen'kix detej
small children$^{GEN\ PL}$
'Four people were injured in the accident. An elderly man, a woman and two young kids.'

---

1 Many speakers however do not accept such examples noting that in the presence of explicit complements masculine agreement is obligatory and that examples with feminine nouns instantiate low register speech.

c. my kupili tri **motocikla.** #vse **troe** slomalis'
we bought three^{CAR} motorcycle$^{GEN\ SG}$ all three^{COL} broke
'We bought three motorcycles. All three have broken down.'

I thus conclude that the animacy requirement is part of the lexical meaning of collective numerals, whereas the restriction to masculine nouns denoting humans/young animals follows from morphosyntactic agreement properties of numerals of this type.

iii. Plural/Singular complements

Cardinal numerals from 2 to 4 (paucals) take singular complements (*dva*^{CAR} *studenta*^{SG}/**studentov*^{PL} 'two students'), higher cardinals require plural complements (*pjat'*^{CAR} *studentov*^{PL}/**studenta*^{SG} 'five students) (cf. Babby 1987, Franks 1995 and others). Collective numerals always take plural complements[2] (*dvoe*^{COL} *studentov*^{PL}/* *studenta*^{SG} 'two students', *pjatero*^{COL} *studentov*^{PL}/**studenta*^{SG} 'five students).

iv. (Non)-Obligatory complements

As we saw earlier, both cardinal and collective numerals can appear in the prenominal position. However nominal complements of cardinal numerals cannot be omitted (7a) (Mel'čuk 1985). Collective numerals, on the other hand, do not require nominal complements in the same constructions[3] (7b) (Mel'čuk 1985).

(7) a. stolik na **dve** *(persony)
table on two^{CAR} person^{PAUC}
'A table for two people'

b. stolik na **dvoix**
table for two^{COL}
'A table for two people'

v. Approximative Inversion (AI)

Cardinal numerals can invert with their complements. This non-canonical word order results into an approximative interpretation (8a) (cf. Mel'čuk 1985, Franks 1995). Collective numerals cannot undergo approximative inversion (8b) (Mel'čuk 1985).

2 With pluralia tantum paucals require the collective form (cf. Vinogradov 1960, Mel'čuk 1985)

3 Mel'čuk treats bare numerals in (7b) as 'nominal counterparts' of cardinal numerals.

(8) a. professor zavalil studentov pjat'
professor failed student$^{GEN\ PL}$ five^{CAR}

b. #professor zavalil studentov pjateryx
professor failed student$^{GEN\ PL}$ five^{COL}

'The professor failed about five students.'

The conclusion then is that the two forms have very different properties and thus ought to have a different semantics. In the following two sections I will offer a semantic interpretation of each form.

3. Russian cardinal numerals

Unlike in Russian, English numerals have received much attention in the literature. There has been much debate to as how numerals in different positions should be interpreted. Earlier accounts (e.g. Barwise and Cooper 1983) treated numerals in the prenominal position as in *three cats* as quantificational determiners. Landman (2003/04) showed that numerals are not determiners but adjectival predicates assigning cardinal properties to pluralities. Following Link (1983), Landman assumes that plural predicates denote sets of sums of atoms derived via applying the operation of closure under sum (*) to sets of atoms (9a–b). *Three* is an adjective denoting the set of sums of atoms (pluralities) each containing 3 elements (9c). It applies intersectively to the plural *cats* resulting in a plural predicate denoting the set of sums of atomic cats each containing three atoms (9d).

(9) a. $||\text{cat}||_{<e,t>} = \text{CAT} = \{a,b,c\}$
b. $||\text{cats}||_{<e,t>} = {}^*\text{CAT} = \{a,b,c, a\sqcup b, a\sqcup c, b\sqcup c, a\sqcup b\sqcup c\}$, equivalently $\lambda x.\ {}^*\text{CAT}(x)$
c. $||\text{three}||_{<e,t>} = \lambda x.\ |x|=3$
d. $||\text{three cats}\ ||_{<e,t>} = \lambda x.\ {}^*\text{CAT}(x) \wedge |x|=3$

Bare numerals can also be used as arguments (e.g. *Two plus five is seven*). Hofweber (2005) and Ionin & Matushansky (2006) have argued that numerals on apparent argument uses involve elliptical complements and therefore have the same semantics as numerals in the prenominal position. In contrast, Rothstein (2013, 2017) has argued that numerals on such uses are genuine arguments which refer to numbers. She provides a unified account for the two uses in the framework of property theory (Chierchia & Turner 1988) arguing that numerals are property expressions which shift between the property denotation at type <e,t>, $||\textit{three}|| = \lambda x.\ |x|=3$ and the individual correlate of the property, $||\textit{three}|| = 3$, at type n.

In the example (3) we saw that Russian cardinals also have two uses. Now I will bring evidence that Russian cardinals in the prenominal position as in (3a) are adjectival predicates and not determiners and that the bare cardinals in (3b) are genuine arguments.

i. Russian cardinals as adjectival predicates

Firstly, cardinals can appear in predicate positions where quantified expressions are infelicitous (10) (cf. Landman 2003/04).

(10) a. ego druzja èto dva soseda i tri odnoklassnika
his friends COP two neighbor$^{GEN\ SG}$ and three classmate$^{GEN\ SG}$
'His friends are two neighbors and three classmates.'
b. ego druzja èto # každyj sosed i každyj odnoklassnik
his friends COP every neighbor and every classmate
'His friends are every neighbor and every classmate.'

Secondly, noun phrases headed by cardinal numerals occur in the scope of determiners such as *every* (11). This indicates that cardinal numerals and NPs headed by them are predicates (cf. Rothstein 2017).

(11) každye dva goroda soedinjaet tol'ko odna doroga
every two^{CAR} city$^{GEN\ SG}$ connect only one road
'Every two cities are joined/connected by only one road.'
[http://znanija.com/task/2191185]

Thirdly, cardinal numerals in some cases allow accusative/genitive case alternation (12). Partee & Borschev (2004), Kagan (2005), Borschev et al. (2008) show that genitive complements of verbs are predicates at type <e,t> whereas the accusative alternates are genuine arguments at type e. The predicate interpretation of the numeral NP *dvux stranic* in (12a) can be derived only if the numeral is interpreted as a predicate modifier.

(12) ja ne pročital dvux stranic
I not read two$^{CAR\ GEN}$ page$^{GEN\ PL}$
'I didn't read (even) two pages.'

b. ja ne pročital dve stranicy
I not read two$^{CAR\ ACC}$ page^{PAUC}
'I didn't read the two pages.'
(Borschev et al. 2008: 5)

Given these arguments we conclude that Russian cardinals in the prenominal position are predicate modifiers and not determiners and that cardinal numeral NPs are plural count predicates and not generalized quantifier expressions.

ii. Russian cardinals as nominal arguments

Contra Hofweber (2005) and with Rothstein (2013, 2017) I argue that numerals in (3b) do not involve null complements. The claims is supported by the following two observations. Firstly, we have already seen in (7a) that Russian numerals do not allow elliptical complements *(*stolik na dva* 'a table for two'). If ellipsis is not possible in (7a) why would it occur in (3b)? Secondly, bare numerals occur in constructions where nominal complements are not allowed in the first place (13) (cf. Rothstein 2013, 2017).

(13)	#dve	vešči	umnožit'	na	dve	vešči	b. doščitat'	do	dvux	*veščej
	two^{CAR}	things	multiply	on	two^{CAR}	things	count	to	two^{CAR}	things

The conclusion is then that bare uses of cardinals as in (3b) cannot involve elliptical complements. Thus Russian cardinals, like English cardinals, are analyzable as property expressions used in two ways: in the prenominal position as predicate modifiers of pluralities at type <e,t> [4]and as a bare nominal arguments at type n.[5]

4. Collective numerals/numeral NPs in Russian are not collective predicates

Landman (1989/95, 2004) showed that the collective/distributive contrast in numeral constructions boils down to the notions of semantic singularity/plurality. On distributive interpretations numeral NPs denote plural predicates (sets of sums), whereas on the collective reading numeral NPs are singular predicates denoting atomic groups. Singular interpretations are derived from plural via a group operator ↑ first defined by Link (1984), which applies to pluralities and maps them onto singular groups.

One would naturally hypothesize that collective numeral NPs are collective predicates and that the collective morphology encodes the group operator. This is not the case.

Firstly, collective numerals and NPs headed by them are plural and not singular predicates. We have already seen this in (2a) where the collective numeral

---

4 Ionin & Matushansky argue that numerals crossliguistically are generated at type <<e,t>,<e,t>>. For objections see Rothstein (2013, 2017)

5 There has been much debate on whether numerals in Russian are adjectives or nouns and as to how case assignment occurs in numerals NPs (see Yadroff 1999, Ionin and Matushansky 2006). In this paper I do not undertake to explain how case is assigned. However, I bring evidence that semantically, cardinal numerals are adjectives which may shift to nominal interpretations when used as arguments.

NPs is modified by the distributive *–po* marker. The example is (14) shows that collectives can be modified by reciprocals. Both *–po* and reciprocals require count plural antecedents.

(14) èti troe (studentov) posmotreli **drug na druga** i požali plečami
these three^{COL} (student$^{GEN\ PL}$) looked each on other and shrugged shoulders
'The three (students) looked at each other and shrugged.

Secondly, collective numerals do not always have a collective interpretation. Collective and cardinal numerals can be used interchangeably in distributive contexts such as in (15a) where explicit collective (singular) expressions are not possible (15b).

(15) a. v **dvux** avarijax na dorogax baškirii pogibli **pjat'**
in two accidents on roads Bashkiria were killed five^{CAR}
čelovek, postradali **semero**
person$^{GEN\ PL}$ injured seven^{COL}
' Five people died and seven were injured in two different accidents in Bashkiria.'

[http://m.kp.ru/online/news/703770/]

b. #v dvux avarijax na dorogax baškirii pogibla **gruppa iz semi čelovek**
in two accidents on roads Bashkiria was killed group from seven^{CAR} person $^{GEN\ PL}$

Furthermore, if collectives had a collective semantics, we would expect *dvux*^{CAR} and *dvoix*^{COL} *in* (16) to show the same contrast as in Mel'čuk's data in (1). But they don't.

(16) a. rodila **dvux** synovej 1 janvarja
gave birth two^{CAR} son^{PL} first January
'She gave birth to two sons on the 1st of January.'

[https://m.ok.ru/profile/334132086264]

b. a potom rodila uže **dvoix** synovej, bez boli i bez krovi, tak legko
and then gave birth already two^{COL} son^{PL} without pain and without blood so easily
'And then I gave birth to two sons. With no pain, no blood. So easily.'

[http://enigma-project.ru/sonnik/rodit-rebenka]

c. rodila **dvux** synovej pogodok v 31 i v 32
gave birth two^{CAR} son^{PL} po-year in 31 and in 32
'I gave birth to two sons. One when I was 31 and the other one when I was 32.'
[http://forum.ykt.ru/mviewtopic.jsp?id=1857385]

d. my prožili 8,5 let. ja rodila **dvoix** synovej
we lived 8,5 year^{PL} i gave birth two^{COL} son^{PL}
'We lived together for 8.5 years. I gave birth to two sons.'
[http://likuniya.ru/nenavizhu-muzha-chto-delat.html]

Thus the term collective is a misnomer and collective numeral NPs are not collective predicates, but plural predicates.

5. Collective numeral NPs are classifier numeral expressions

We saw that collective numerals, even in the absence of nominal complements, make reference to n number of individuals as if a complement were involved, see (17).

(17) a. stolik na dvoix
table for two^{COL}
'a table for two (people)'

b. v komnatu vošli dvoe
into room went two^{COL}
'Two people entered the room.'

I argue that this characteristic has been incorrectly taken as an indication of the collective interpretation. Instead, this property indicates that collective numerals have a more complex internal structure. In particular, *troe (N)* is equivalent to *three animate entities (of N)*. While cardinals denote sets of sums of atomic individuals (pluralities), collective numerals denote sets of sums constructed out of animate individuals. This additional content is contributed by a concealed classifier, *three*^{COL} *(N)* → *three* $Cl_{animate}$ *(of N)*. The analysis predicts correctly the properties discussed in section 2.

i. Lexical and morphosyntactic restrictions

It is well known that classifiers impose lexical restrictions (including the animacy restriction) on their complements (Sussex 1976, Rothstein 2017). In Russian we observe this in optional classifiers *štuka, čelovek* and *golova*. *Štuka* selects inanimate nouns (18a), *čelovek* is used with nouns which denote humans (18b) and *golova* occurs with nouns referring to farm animals (18c)[6] (Sussex 1976).

6 Sussex (1976) points out that *štuka* may be used with animate nouns in colloquial informal speech. It also should be noted that the resulting interpretation in such cases is often ironic.

(18) a. na stole ležalo pjat' štuk/ #golov/ #čelovek ogromnyx jablok
on table lay five item$^{\text{GEN PL}}$/head$^{\text{GEN PL}}$/ person$^{\text{GEN PL}}$ huge apple$^{\text{GEN PL}}$
'There were five huge apples on the table.'

b. oni nanjali 20 čelovek/ #štuk/ #golov stroitelej
they hired 20 person$^{\text{GEN PL}}$ /item$^{\text{GEN PL}}$ /head$^{\text{GEN PL}}$ builder$^{\text{GEN PL}}$
'They hired 20 builders.'

c. fermer zakupil 20 golov/ #štuk/ #čelovek korov
farmer purchased 20 head$^{\text{GEN PL}}$ /item$^{\text{GEN PL}}$ /person$^{\text{GEN PL}}$ cow$^{\text{GEN PL}}$
'The/a farmer bought twenty cows.'

These restrictions are presuppositional and not truth-conditional. If the preposition is not satisfied the sentence in which it is used is infelicitous and not false (18) (for more discussion see Khrizman 2016). The restriction to animate entities associated with collective numerals is also presuppositional. Given that there were three apples on the table, the sentence in (19) is infelicitous but not false[7].

(19) # na stole ležalo troe jablok
on table lay three^{COL} apple$^{\text{GEN INANIM PL}}$
'There were three apples on the table.'

Furthermore, this concealed classifier can introduce certain morphosyntactic restrictions on nominal complements (e.g. default masculine agreement) which explains the agreement pattern illustrated in (5a,b).

ii. Plural complements

Collective numerals, unlike cardinals, take plural NP complements. Numeral classifier NPs also take plural arguments, even if they involve paucals (20) (Yadroff 1999).

(20) a. tri **jajca**/ pjat' **jaic**
three^{CAR} egg^{SG}/ five^{CAR} egg^{PL}
'three/five eggs'

b. pjat' štuk / tri štuki **jaic**
five^{CAR} item^{PL}/ three^{CAR} item^{SG} egg^{PL}
'three/five eggs'

7 I do not claim that the concealed classifier is semantically analogous to the above-mentioned optional classifiers (for a detailed analysis of the latter see Khrizman 2016). However, these data show that it is not unusual for Russian classifiers to impose lexical restrictions on their complements.

iii. Optionality of nominal complements

The optionality of NP complements follows, since the numeral already has a classifier as a complement. The analysis predicts correctly that, as we have already seen in (7a), a collective numeral without a complement can be replaced by a cardinal with a nominal, but not by a bare cardinal.

iv. Approximative Inversion

The observation that collective numeral NPs cannot undergo approximative inversion is also predicted. Khrizman & Rothstein (2015) show that AI inverts the numeral and classifier within a classifier phrase as in (21). If collective numerals are themselves [Num + Cl] and not bare numerals, they are not expected to undergo AI and invert with a noun.

<table>
<tr><td>(21)</td><td>a.</td><td>tri</td><td>litra</td><td>moloka</td><td>b.</td><td>litra</td><td>tri</td><td>moloka</td></tr>
<tr><td></td><td></td><td>three^{CAR}</td><td>liter^{SG}</td><td>milk^{SG}</td><td></td><td>liter^{SG}</td><td>three^{CAR}</td><td>milk^{SG}</td></tr>
<tr><td></td><td></td><td colspan="3">'three liters of milk'</td><td></td><td colspan="3">'about three liters of milk'</td></tr>
<tr><td></td><td>c.</td><td># moloka</td><td>tri</td><td>litra</td><td></td><td></td><td></td><td></td></tr>
<tr><td></td><td></td><td>milk^{SG}</td><td>three^{CAR}</td><td>liter^{SG}</td><td></td><td></td><td></td><td></td></tr>
</table>

We have now seen that the "puzzling" properties in (i)–(iv) which distinguish collective numerals from cardinals follow rather naturally from the classifier analysis.

5.1. Compositional interpretation of collective numerals

I argued that collective numeral NPs are plural count classifier expressions in which the classifier is built in the structure of the numeral. The function of the classifier is to introduce a presupposition restricting the domain of counting to animate entities. Now I will show how the construction is interpreted compositionally.

There are two potential ways to interpret this classifier. One option is to follow Krifka (1995) and assume that collective numerals involve a concealed measure classifier which applies to mass denotations and measures them is terms of OBJECT UNITS. Thus *three* ^{COL} *student* is semantically equivalent to *three object units of student* ^{MASS}. The problem with this analysis is that it derives collective numerals/collective numeral NPs as measure predicates analogous to *three kilos of meat* and not as count plural predicates such as *three boys*. Measure and count plural predicates have different properties. For example, measure predicates do not allow individuation whereas count plural predicates do (22) (cf. Landman 2004, Rothstein 2009/ 2017).

(22) a. # tri kilogramma mjasa ležali **drug na druge**

# tri	kilogramma	mjasa	ležali	**drug**	**na**	**druge**
three	kilo$^{GEN\ SG}$	meat^{MASS}	lay	each	on	other

b.

tri	studenta	posmotreli	**drug**	**na**	**druga**	i	požali	plečami
three^{CAR}	student$^{GEN\ SG}$	looked	each	on	other	and	shrugged	shoulders

'(The) three students looked at each other and shrugged.'

I have already shown in section 4 that collective numerals and NPs headed by them have properties of count plural predicates. Therefore I will not adopt Krifka's account. Instead, I will analyze collective numerals as involving a count classifier at type <n,<e,t>> which takes an n argument and produces a count predicate which expresses cardinal properties. This classifier also introduces a presupposition which restricts the domain of counting to animate entities (23a). As a result the derived numeral is a predicate denoting the set of pluralities constructed out of animate individuals (23b). When the collective applies to an animate plural noun such as *studentov*, the presupposition is satisfied and the resulting expression is another predicate denoting the set of pluralities of students each of which contains exactly three elements (23c).

(23) $||troe||_{<e,t>} = ||Cl||(3)$

a. $||Cl||_{<n,<e,t>>} = \lambda n \lambda x.\ |x|= n$, presupposition $x \in \{x\text{: x is animate}\}$

b. $||troe||_{<e,t>} = \lambda x.\ |x|= 3$, presupposition $x \in \{x\text{: x is animate}\}$
'The set of sums of animate individuals such that each sum has three atomic parts'

c. $||troe\ studentov||_{<e,t>} = \lambda x.\ {}^{*}STUDENT(x) \wedge |x|= 3$
The set of sums of students such that each sum has three atomic parts'

6. Conclusion

We explored the semantics of cardinal and collective numerals in Russian and argued that: (i) cardinals are property expressions ambiguous between predicates denoting sets of atomic sums with n atoms, $\lambda x.\ |x|= n$, and arguments denoting numbers; (ii) collective numerals are complex predicates which denote sets of sums of animate atomic entities, $\lambda x.\ |x|= n,\ x \in \{x\text{: x is animate}\}$. The restriction to animate entities is introduced by a lexically concealed count classifier.

References

Babby, Leonard. 1987. "Case, Prequantifiers, and Discontinuous Agreement in Russian." *NLLT* 5,1: 91–138.

Barwise, Jonh and Robin Cooper. 1983. "Generalized quantifiers and natural language." *Linguistics and Philosophy* 4, 2: 159–219.

Borschev, Vladimir, Elena V. Paducheva, Barbara H. Partee, Yakov G. Testelets and Igor Yanovich. 2008. "Russian genitives, non-referentiality, and the property-type hypothesis." In *Formal Approaches to Slavic Linguistics: The Stony Brook Meeting 2007*, Andrei Antonenko, John F. Bailyn, Christina Y. Bethin (eds.). Ann Arbor: Michigan Slavic Publications, 48–67.

Chierchia, Gennaro, and Ray Turner. 1988. "Semantics and Property Theory." *Linguistics and Philosophy* 11,3: 261–302.

Franks, Steven. 1995. *Parameters of Slavic Morphosyntax*. Oxford: Oxford University Press.

Ionin, Tania and Ora Matushansky. 2006. "The composition of complex cardinals." *Journal of Semantics* 2: 315–60.

Kagan, Olga. 2005. "Genitive case: a modal account." In *Proceedings of the Israel Association for Theoretical Linguistics, 21*, 1–21.

Khrizman, Keren. 2016. "Functional unit classifiers in (non)-classifier Russian." In *The Baltic International Yearbook of Cognition, Logic and Communication Volume 11: Number: Cognitive Semantics and Crosslinguistic Approaches,* Susan Rothstein and Jurģis Šķilters (eds.). Manhattan, KS: New Prairy Press.

Khrizman, Keren and Susan Rothstein. 2015. "Russian approximative inversion as a measure Construction." In *Slavic Grammar from a Formal Perspective. The 10th Anniversary FDSL Conference, Leipzig 2013*, Gerhild Zybatow, Petr Biskup, Marcel Guhl, Claudia Hurtig, Olav Mueller-Reichau and Maria Yastrebova (eds.). Frankfurt. am Main: Peter Lang Edition, 259–72.

Krifka, Manfred. 1995. "Common nouns: a contrastive analysis of English and Chinese." In *The Generic Book*, Gregory N. Carlson and Francis Jeffry Pelletier (eds.). Chicago: Chicago University Press, 398–411.

Landman, Fred. 1995. "Plurality." In *Handbook of Contemporary Semantics (1st Edition)*, Shalom Lappin (ed.). London: Wiley-Blackwell, 425–57.

Landman, Fred. 2003. "Predicate-argument mismatches and the adjectival theory of indefinites." In *From NP to DP: Volume 1*, Martine Coene and Yves D'hulst (eds.). Amsterdam: John Benjamins, 211–37.

Landman, Fred. 2004. *Indefinites and the Type of Sets*. Oxford: Wiley-Blackwell.

Link, Godehard. 1983. "The logical analysis of plurals and mass terms: a lattice-theoretical Approach." In *Meaning, Use and the Interpretation of Language*,

Arnim von Stechow, Christoph Schwarze and Rainer Bäuerle (eds.). Berlin: Mouton de Gruyter, 302 –23.

Link, Godehard. 1984. "Hydras. On the logic of relative clause constructions with multiple heads." In *Varieties of Formal Semantics*, Fred Landman and Frank Veltman (eds.). Dordrecht: Foris, 245–57.

Mel'čuk, Igor. 1985. *Poverxnostnyj Sintaksis Russkix Čislovyx Vyraženij*, *Wiener Slawistischer Almanach. Sonderband* 16. Vienna: Institut für Slawistik der Universität Wien.

Partee, Barbara H. and Vladimir Borschev. 2004. "The semantics of Russian Genitive of Negation: The nature and role of Perspectival Structure." In *Proceedings of Semantics and Linguistic Theory (SALT)*, 14, Kazuha Watanabe and Robert B. Young (eds.). Ithaca, NY: CLC Publications, 212–34.

Rothstein, Susan. 2009. "Individuating and measure readings of classifier constructions: Evidence from Modern Hebrew." *Brill's Annual of Afroasiatic Languages and Linguistics* 1: 106–45.

Rothstein, Susan. 2013. "A Fregean semantics for number words." In *Proceedings of the 19th Amsterdam Colloquium*, Maria Aloni, Michael Franke and Floris Roelofsen (eds.), 179–186.

Rothstein, Susan. 2017. *Semantics for Counting and Measuring*. Cambridge University Press.

Sussex, Roland. 1976. "The numeral classifiers of Russian." *Russian Linguistics* 3:145–55.

Vinogradov, Viktor. 1960. *Grammatika Russkogo Jazyka*. Akademija Nauk SSSR.

Yadroff, Michael. 1999. "Formal properties of functional categories: The minimalist syntax of Russian nominal and prepositional expressions." Ph.D. Thesis, Indiana University.

Serbo-Croatian, Slovenian

Boban Arsenijević

Referential Properties of Subordinate Clauses in Serbo-Croatian

1. Introduction

Serbo-Croatian (S-C) words *da* and *što*, used to introduce embedded clauses, often can occur in the same context, contributing different semantics to the aggregate expression. This is typically pointed out for their use in complement clauses as in (1).

(1) a. Jesam ti rekao **da** je Marija otišla na odmor?
aux1Sg you.Dat told *da* aux3Sg M gone on vacation
'Did I tell you that Marija went on vacation?' (I might have lied)
b. Jesam ti rekao **što** je Marija otišla na odmor?
aux1Sg you.Dat told *što* aux3Sg M gone on vacation
'Did I tell you that Marija went on vacation?' (it is a fact that she did)

As discussed in Arsenijević (2006, 2009, 2015), these two items also introduce relative clauses, illustrated in (2).

(2) a. Tražim kutiju **da** ima providan poklopac.
search.1Sg box *da* has transparent cover
'I'm looking for a box such that it has a transparent cover.'
b. Dodaj mi kutiju **što** ima providan poklopac.
pass.Imp2Sg me box *što* has transparent cover
'Pass me the box that has a transparent cover.'

Arsenijević (2015) shows that the use of *što* involves familiarity: the situation or the proposition of the embedded clause, be it a complement clause or a relative clause, must be familiar to the speaker, and in the prototypical case also to the hearer(s).

As is typically the case with referential familiarity, it also projects. For instance, it survives in non-veridical contexts as in (3). In spite of the non-veridicality of the conditional clause in which it embeds and an intentional verb which directly embeds it: having a transparent cover in this example must be familiar not just to the speaker, but (possibly for independent pragmatic reasons) also to the hearer.

(3) Ako nađeš kutiju **što** ima providan poklopac, daj mi je.
if find.2Sg box *što* has transparent cover give.2Sg me it
'If you find the/*a box which has a transparent cover, give it to me.'

These two items, *da* and *što*, can introduce not only complement and relative clauses as in (1) and (2) above, but they may be embedded under prepositions (and adverbs), in which case they become part of an adverbial clause. A particular type of semantic asymmetry between the two introducers remains across these contexts and uses, yielding surface effects which vary depending on the interaction of their semantics and the context.

The aim of this paper is to test the applicability of the previously proposed theoretical accounts of the asymmetry between these two items in the domain of adverbial clauses. Due to the limited space, the primary focus of the paper is on the empirical facts and the theoretical aspects are given in a rather sketchy fashion.

The paper is organized as follows. Section 2 outlines two analyses proposed for the asymmetry manifested by the opposition between *da* and *što* as embedded clause introducers. Section 3 overviews eight different clause types in this perspective. Section 4 is the conclusion.

2. Commitment of the subject, familiarity, and/or being part of the actual world?

While there is rich literature dealing with the semantics of the indicative vs. subjunctive expressions, very few of these works address the type of asymmetry in S-C illustrated in (1) and (2), which is characteristic of S-C and a few other Balkan languages. One recent analysis which addresses this asymmetry is Siegel (2009). She follows the earlier established association of the clause type instantiated by *da*-clauses with the category subjunctive, i.e. of *što*-clauses with the indicative, and argues that while the indicative in Romance languages specifies the commitment of the speaker to the truth of the clause, in Balkan languages it expresses the same kind of certainty, but on the part of the subject of the clause. Assuming with Topolinska (1995), Mišeska-Tomić (2004), Janić (2012) that the opposition between *da* and *što* can plausibly be seen as the opposition between subjunctive and indicative, her analysis implies that *što* marks the commitment of the subject of the matrix clause to the truth of the clause introduced by *što*, and *da* does not have this type of semantic contribution.

Arsenijević (2015) argues that a *što*-clause specifies the restriction of a referential expression in the matrix clause, such that it directly accessible in the discourse. The direct accessibility pertains to the restriction being a situation that is part of the actual world (more precisely, of the world to which the situation in the matrix clause belongs, the matrix world), or being a subdomain of the actual discourse: of the set of referents involved in a proposition that has explicitly been contributed to the discourse. In other words, *što* obviates modal embedding, and keeps the restriction situation that it introduces within the world in which the sentence is epistemically evaluated. *Da* always involves modal embedding, i.e. the content of the clause it introduces is always evaluated on the background of a plurality of possible worlds.

Arsenijević also argues that *što* involves a presupposition of familiarity similar to that of the familiarity accounts of nominal definiteness. More precisely, the situation or the predicate over situations contributed by the *što*-clause must be familiar to the speaker. Here, this approach comes close to Siegel's, but actually to her account for the non-Balkan, rather than Balkan type of opposition among embedded clauses.

In this paper, I provide an overview of the types of adverbial embedded clauses in S-C which involve the use of *da* or *što*, in order to test the applicability of the two analyses above. The overview is relatively shallow, and the analyses of the particular clause types that are outlined are not entirely formalized, partly due to restricted size of the article, and partly due to the fact that the research is still in progress.

Let me also note that the two analyses tested were not tailored to capture adverbial clauses: Siegel (2009) targets only complement clauses, and Arsenijević (2015) additionally considers relative clauses. Siegel, moreover, does not focus on the S-C *da* and *što*, but more on other similar oppositions in Balkan languages. Moreover Siegel (2009) does not discuss S-C, but focuses on a distinction in Bulgarian, which goes along similar lines, but displays also some important differences (see Janić 2012 for a detailed comparison). Hence, I am only testing the degree to which the two analyses can be extended to also cover S-C adverbial clauses, and not the degree to which they account for the empirical domain they have been developed for. Still, as the overview shows that the analysis from Arsenijević (2015) captures the adverbial clauses without substantial modification, its broader empirical coverage and ability to explain why the same items occur not just in complement and relative clauses, but also in a whole range of adverbial clauses, must count as a significant advantage.

3. *Da* and *što* in adverbial clauses: an empirical overview

Probably more than 90% of adverbial clauses in S-C are introduced by expressions which include either *da* or *što*, and never both together. Some of those expressions may introduce more than one clause types, while most are specialized for only one. In this section I give an overview of clause types introduced by such expressions, and of the expressions themselves, looking at the degree to which they fit the analyses sketched in section 2.

Since Siegel's (2009) analysis aims at complement clauses, mostly of attitude verbs and other predicates requiring sentient subjects, it is incompatible with at least certain adverbial clauses even without a more detailed overview. The reason is that her analysis is formulated in terms of the commitment of an interlocutor or an argument of the sentence to the content of the embedded clause. In case it is the subject, its sentience, and hence ability to act as the subject of evaluation, is guaranteed by the requirement of the selecting predicate for a sentient subject. No such requirement figures regarding adverbial clauses. Hence, they can occur in sentences without a single sentient referent, where the only available subjects of evaluation are the interlocutors and the topical sentient referents in the discourse.

(4) Sneg je pao pre nego **što** je svanulo.
snow Aux fallen before than *što* Aux dawned
'The snow fell before the dawn.'

In such cases her distinction between the two types of subjunctives, in Romance and in Balkan languages, can no longer obtain. The analysis in terms of the commitment of the subject of the clause becomes untenable. Either adverbial clauses in S-C, a Balkan language, behave like complement clauses in Romance, in having their indicative-subjunctive distinction deriving from the commitment of the speaker, or this type of analysis simply cannot account for the adverbial clauses. It will therefore suffice to inquire to what extent we can maintain that the indicative-subjunctive asymmetry in adverbial clauses can be captured in terms of the certainty on the part of the speaker of their truth.

The remaining part of this section provides an overview of the relevant clause types in S-C.

3.1. Similative and differentiative clauses

Serbo-Croatian words *kao* 'like' and *nego* 'than' establish comparison between constituents of a diverse set of categories, including clauses. The comparison typically targets the degree of a property, the polarity of the clause, or an explicitly introduced manner or property. The word *kao* 'like' compares by similarity and the word *nego* 'than' by a difference. They combine with both *da*- and *što*-clauses.

In favor of the analysis in terms of familiarity, when the second argument of either of these words is clausal, and it is introduced by *što*, it is presupposed to be true even if it occurs in modal or conditional contexts and the targeted dimension: degree, manner, property – is familiar to the interlocutors. In the example in (5), though it occurs within a conditional clause, there is a presupposition that the subject indeed occasionally, habitually or episodically saws wood.

(5) Ako svira gitaru kao **što** reže drva...
if plays guitar like *što* saws wood
'If she plays guitar the (familiar!) way she saws wood...'

If the comparison clause is introduced by *da*, a counterfactual interpretation emerges. The situation of the subject of the clause sawing wood is implicated to not intersect with any situation of the subject playing the guitar.

(6) Ako svira gitaru kao **da** reže drva...
if plays guitar like *da* saws wood
'If she plays guitar as if she were sawing wood...'

Interestingly for the analysis in terms of familiarity, if the adverbial clause with *što* has a subjunctively marked predicate, either by a subjunctive verb form, or by a perfective verb used in the present tense, as in (7), familiarity disappears: it is not familiar to any of the interlocutors how the wood will be sawn (note that the effect is not due to the future reference alone, as with a future verb familiarity still projects).

(7) Ako odsvira gitaru kao **što** prereže drva...
if plays.Perf guitar like *što* saws.Perf wood
'If she completes the/a guitar playing event the way she completes the/a wood-sawing event...'

Unless embedded in non-veridical contexts, subjunctive predicates cannot be used in regular complement and relative clauses – compare (8) with the counterparts in (1) and (2).[1]

---

1 This restriction holds only for bare complement and relative clauses. Subjunctive predicates in complement and relative clauses can be licensed by certain kinds of adverbial clauses, as in (i).

(i) Jesam ti rekao **što** Marija otputuje na odmor kad god padne sneg?
Aux1Sg you.Dat told *što* M travel.Perf on vacation when ever falls snow
'Did I tell you about it that Marija goes on vacation every time it snows?'

(8) a. *Jesam ti rekao **što** Marija otputuje na odmor?
Aux1Sg you.Dat told *što* M travel.Perf on vacation
b. *Dodaj mi kutiju **što** dobije providan poklopac.
pass.Imp2Sg me box *što* gets.Perf transparent cover

The non-veridical context of the conditional in (7) licenses the subjunctive morphology, which in turn cancels the familiarity contribution. This only means that familiarity is not asserted but rather part of a cancellable presupposition of *što* which projects through non-veridical contexts, but can get cancelled by explicit subjunctive morphology. The reason may be that the subjunctive morphology of the verb and the indicative contribution of *što* target the same category, and hence the one with a higher scope can cancel the other. As long as there is a presupposition of familiarity, this is in line with Arsenijević (2015).

It turns out to be crucial that the WOLL operator which induces the subjunctive interpretation, involved in the semantics of a perfective verb used in the present tense form, scopes higher than *što* – also for the generalization that the embedded clause is epistemically evaluated within the same time-pace as the matrix clause. As the (licensor of the) WOLL operator scopes over both the *što*-clause and the conditional which embeds it, both the *što*-clause and its embedder clause are evaluated against the same non-veridical context, under the restriction of evaluation against the same world.

In scalar differentiative clauses, a symptomatic asymmetry obtains between *što* and *da*. The combination of *nego* 'than' with *što* is used when the difference is between a degree in the embedded clause and a degree in the matrix clause, as in (9).

(9) Marija trči brže nego **što/*da** Petar vozi bicikl.
M runs faster than *što/da* Petar rides bicycle
'Marija is running faster than Petar is riding a/the bike'

(10) Marija više voli **da/??što** joj Petar peva nego
M more likes *da/što* her P sings than
da/??što je Marko izmasira.
da/što her M massages
'Marija prefers Peter singing for her to Marko giving her massage.'

This supports the view that *što* introduces situations which are part of the matrix world (the world of epistemic evaluation of the matrix clause), and *da*-clauses involve modal embedding.

3.2. Temporal adverbial clauses

The combination of *nego* 'than' with *da* and *što* occurs as a complement to the preposition pre 'before' in order to introduce temproal clauses for anteriority (the situation in the matrix clause preceedes that in the temporal adverbial clause).[2]

(11) Pre nego **što** je izašao, on joj je poslao poljubac.
before than *što* Aux3Sg leave he her Aux3Sg sent kiss
'…before he left, he sent her a kiss.'

(12) Pre nego **da** je izašao, on joj je poslao poljubac.
before than *da* Aux3Sg leave he her Aux3Sg sent kiss
'…when he was about to leave, he sent her a kiss.'

With *da*, the matrix clause can deny that the situation in the temporal adverbial clause has taken place, while with što this yields a semantic violation. This is exactly as expected if *što* marks that the embedded situation is part of the same world as the matrix situation (hence negating it in the matrix clause gives a contradiction), and *da* involves modal embedding.

(13) Pre nego **da** je izašao, odustao je i ostao kući.
before nego *da* Aux left.MSg gave_up Aux and stayed home
'When he was about to leave, he changed his mind and stayed home.'

(14) Pre nego **što** je izašao, #odustao je i ostao kući.
before nego *što* Aux left.MSg he gave up and stayed home
'Earlier than he left, he changed his mind and stayed home.'

As a final asymmetry, unlike the *što*-clauses, *da*-clauses combined with *pre nego* 'before' can be used to denote a modal comparison (von Fintel and Kratzer 2014).

(15) Emocije su deo kognicije, pre nego **da/*što** su to
emotions are part cognition before than *da/što* are that
dva odvojena procesa.
two separate processes
'Emotions are part of cognition, rather than the two separate processes.'

2 The sentence in (33b), with *da*, is more natural with the verb in the present form. This fully complies with the subjunctive kind of modal embedding attributed to *da* in this paper, but due to limited space, I do not dwell on this issue.

This fully complies with the view that *da* establishes, while *što* obviates modal embedding.

Temporal adverbial clauses (TAC) for posteriority are built in a similar, yet not identical way. One major difference is that they do not involve the item *nego* 'than', but rather directly combine the preposition *po* 'over' or nakon 'after' and the clausal embedder. The other is that they only accept *što*, and yield ungrammaticality with *da*: *po/nakon + što*, vs. **po/nakon + da*.

(16) Prodao je knjigu po-**što** je položio ispit.
sold Aux book *po-što* Aux passed exam
'He sold the book after/because he (had) passed the exam.'

The unavailability of *da* in anteriority TACs fits the analysis in terms of belongng to the matrix world. A TAC for posteriority introduces a situation which is temporally ordered after the matrix situation, and hence at the time of the matrix situation it cannot be epistemically evaluated. Therefore, depending on whether the epistemic evaluation takes place at the time of the matrix situation, or at some later time, the TAC can bear both the *da*- and the *što*-semantics, respectively. A TAC for anteriority introduces a situation which takes place before the matrix clause situation. Therefore, whether the epistemic evaluation time is at the time of the matrix situation, or at some later time, it needs to have already taken place in the same world in order for the temporal ordering to obtain, and hence they cannot be modally embedded.

As a further confirmation that the relevant notion is the one of being part of the matrix world, consider the non-veridical context in (17) combined with a subjunctive verba predicate of the type already discussed regarding the example in (7), where the što-situation is not even presupposed to be part of the actual world. Yet, due to the temporal ordering relation, in all the worlds containing the matrix situation, the embedded situation is contained as well – or in other words it shares the epistemic destiny of the matrix clause.

(17) Ako proda knjigu po-**što** položi ispit…
sold Aux book *po-što* passes exam
'If he sells the book after he passes the exam.' i.e. 'If [[sell book]$_1$ & [pass exam]$_2$ & 2<1]'

In both posteriority and anteriority TACs, the certainty of the truth of the embedded clause introduced by *što* or its absence with those introduced by *da*, can be the interlocutors', the speaker's, or by a prominent sentient referent in the discourse. This is in line with Siegel's (2009) view that it need not be the speaker, but not with her argument that it is the subject of the clause. The same holds for all other clause types discussed in the remaining part of this overview section.

3.3. Causal adverbial clauses

The combination of the preposition *po* 'over' with *što* (just like in TACs, incompatible with *da*) is also used to express the meaning of cause. Additionally, causal adverbial clauses are introduced by the combination of the prepositions *za* 'for' or *zbog* 'because', the default weak demonstrative *to* 'that' in the appropriate case form, and *što*: *za-to što, zbog toga što*.

(18)	Ne	dolazim	po-**što**/za-to **što**/zbog toga **što**	nemam	vremena.
	Neg	come.1Sg	over-*što*/for-that.Acc *što*/ because that.Gen *što*	Neg-have1Sg	time

'I'm not coming because I haven't got the time.'

This is also exactly as expected, considering that the cause situation is necessarily part of the same world as the caused situation. To further prove the point, *da* can be used with *zato* 'for that' and *zbog toga* 'because of that', but it introduces a purpose, rather than a cause clause.

3.4. Purpose clauses

Clauses involving the combination of *za* 'for' or *zbog* 'because', the default weak demonstrative *to* 'that' in the appropriate case form, and *da: za-to da*, *zbog toga da* introduce purpose clauses. As obvious in comparison with the causal combinations, purpose clauses and cause clauses from section 3.3 make minimal pairs different only in the use of *što* (cause) vs. *da* (purpose). This bears an interesting implication, that purpose is conceptualized as the cause which is in the modal/subjunctive domain.

(19)	Ljudi	biraju	deputate	(zato)	**da**	bi	radili.
	people	elect	representatives	for_that	*da*	would	worked

'People elect representatives in order to work.'

In all or almost all purpose clauses, the component consisting of a preposition and a demonstrative can, and preferably is dropped.

The clause introduced by *da* cannot be in the past or future tense – it can only be in the present, or in the subjunctive form (in the traditional literature referred to as the potential). This is again expected because the purpose is necessarily futurate, and the modal embedding imposed by *da* prevents another kind of interpretation.

(20)

*Ljudi	biraju	deputate	(zato)	**da**	su	radili.
people	elect	representatives	for_that	*da*	Aux.Pl	worked

near English counterpart: '*People elect representatives in order that they have worked.'

The causal combinations *zato što* 'for that *što*' and *zbog toga što* 'because of that *što*' can be combined with a clause headed by a subjunctive verb form, in which case only the reason clauses interpretation is available (because a materially instantiated cause cannot be subjunctive – but a subjunctive event can be part of a cause mediated by a sentient subjects reasoning: a purpose).

(21)

Ljudi	biraju	deputate	zato	**što**	inače	ne
people	elect	representatives	for_that	*što*	otherwise	Neg
bi	bili	zastupljeni.				
would	been	represented				

'People elect representatives because otherwise they wouldn't be represented.'

As is well known, reason clauses, just like cause clauses, presuppose truth (Karttunen 1971, a.o.). In spite of their subjunctive verbal predicate, they involve an epistemic attitude which holds in the matrix world: hence the use of the item *što*.

The asymmetry between purpose and reason adverbial clauses is illustrated in (22).

(22)

Ako	pozovem	zato	**što**	bih	zakazao	sastanak…
if	call.^{Perf}1Sg	for_that	*što*	would	schedule	meeting

'If the fact that I want to make an appointment be the reason of my call…'

(23)

Ako	pozovem	zato	**da**	bih	zakazao	sastanak…
if	call.^{Perf}1Sg	for_that	*što*	would	schedule	meeting

'If I call in order to schedule a meeting…'

In (22), the speaker's desire, or intention, to schedule an appointment is an established fact, while in (23), no such meaning obtains – it is only part of a possible future scenario.

3.5. Effect and means: *tako što/da* 'so that'

Adverbial pronoun *tako* 'so, in such/that way' combines both with *da* and with *što*, yielding the interpretations of effect and means (as a controlled, intentionally induced cause), respectively.

(24) Marija peva tako **da** staklo puca.
M sings so *da* glass breaks
'Marija sings in such a way that the glass breaks'

(25) Marija razbija staklo tako **što** peva.
M breaks glass so *što* sings
'Marija breaks glass by singing / uses singing to break glass.'

In the relevant respects, the parallel is the same as that between the cause and the purpose clauses, except that there, e.g. in (24), no intention of the agent is involved. The similarity extends to the fitting of the analysis in terms of belonging to the matrix world and the familiarity of the situational or propositional content of the embedded clause.

3.6. Constructions with *samo* 'only' + *da/što*, tek 'only' + *da/što*

Clauses with the particles *tek* 'just' and *samo* 'only' are closely related to the adverbial clauses with the meanings of temporal, causal and purpose interpretation. With *da*, they derive exhaustive, focal purpose clauses. With *što*, the derived interpretation is immediate temporal precedence of the subordinate clause situation with respect to the situation in the matrix clause (hence all the same as *po-što* clauses in the relevant respects).

(26) Zovu ga tek **da/što** izađe iz kuće.
call him only *da/što* leaves from house
da: 'They call him only for him to leave his house.'
što: 'They call him as soon as he leaves his house.'

The asymmetry again fits the view that the situation in the *što*-clause must be part of the matrix world, while *da* involves a degree of modal (subjunctive) embedding.

3.7. Exception clauses

These clauses are introduced by the combination of the preposition *osim* 'except' and either *da* or *što*. Similar to differential clauses, with *da*, exception is with respect to a set introduced by another *da*-clause, while with *što*, it is with respect to the content of the matrix clause. As expected, with *što*, in every world in which the matrix clause is true, the embedded clause must be true as well, while with *da* a subjunctive effect obtains: neither the *osim da* clause, nor of the one with respect to which the exception is established are presupposed to be true – both have a subjunctive type of interpretation.

(27)

Jovan	ne	zna	ništa	**da**	radi,	osim	**da**	plete.
J	not	knows	nothing	*da*	do	except	*da*	knits

'Jovan can't do anything, except to knit.

(28)

Jovan	ništa	ne	radi,	osim	**što**	plete.
J	nothing	not	do	except	*što*	knits

'Jovan doesn't do anything, except that he knits.'

3.8. Without-clauses

These clauses, characterized by the combination of the preposition *bez* 'without' and a complementizer, specify that no situation satisfying the predicade specified by the embedded clause took place. As they assert that no situation from a particular set was part of the matrix world, they are expected to be incompatible with *što*, and to only combine with *da*. This prediction is borne out.

(29)

Otvorio	sam	vrata	bez	**da/*što**	sam	ih	dotakao.
opened.MSg	Aux1Sg	door	without	*da/što*	Aux1Sg	it	touched.MSg

'I opened the door without touching it.'

4. Conclusion

The overview of the eight S-C clause types in which the opposition between *da* and *što* plays a role showed a uniform behavior regarding the central notions of the two analyses of the opposition considered: Siegel (2009) and Arsenijević (2015). In each of the considered clause types, contra Siegel (2009), the commitment involved by the semantics of *što* could be on the part of the speaker, of all the interlocutors, or of some discourse-prominent referent, possibly the subject of the sentence. And in each of the types, the *što* versions introduced clauses whose content was part of the same world as the matrix clause, joined by a familiarity effect which projected through non-veridical contexts, but could be canceled by a subjunctive verb form. The findings are compatible with the view that *što*-clauses introduce the resource situations for one of the referential expressions in the matrix clause (Arsenijević 2015), which is further compatible with the operator-movement analysis designed for strong factives by Haegeman and Urogdi (2010a,b). A more detailed investigation is necessary to develop a full-fledged formal analysis overarching all the clause types involving at least one of the two items *da* and *što*.

References

Arsenijević, Boban. 2015. "Individual- and situation-relatives: enriching descriptions, restricting reference and feeding incorporation." *Semantikzirkel.* Zentrum für Allgemeine Sprachwissenschaft (ZAS), May 27th 2015.

Arsenijević, Boban. 2009. "Clausal complementation as relativization." *Lingua* 119/2009: 39–50.

Arsenijević, Boban. 2006. "Dosledno semantički pristup relativnim rečenicama i kategoriji zavisnosti." *Srpski jezik* 11: 487–500.

Haegeman, Liliane and Urogdi, Barbara. 2010a. "Referential CPs: an operator movement account." *Theoretical Linguistics* 36 (2): 111–152.

Haegeman, Liliane and Urogdi, Barbara. 2010b. "Operator movement, referentiality and intervention." *Theoretical Linguistics* 36 (2): 233–246.

Janić, Aleksandra. 2012. "Kategorija subjunktiva u srpskom i bugarskom – uporedno proučavanje." MA thesis, University of Niš.

Karttunen, Lauri. 1971. "Implicative verbs." *Language*, 47: 340–358.

Siegel, Laura. 2009. "Mood selection in Romance and Balkan." *Lingua* 119(12): 1859–1882.

Topolinjska, Zuzanna. 1995. "Convergent Evolution, Creolization and Referentiality." In *Prague Linguistic Circle Papers*, Eva Hajičova, Miroslav Červenka, Oldřich Leška and Peter Sgall (eds.). Amsterdam: John Benjamins, 239–247.

Tomić, Olga Mišeska. 2004. "The Balkan Sprachbund properties: Introduction." In *Balkan Syntax and Semantics*, Olga Mišeska Tomić (ed.). Amsterdam: John Benjamins, 1–57.

von Fintel, Kai and Angelika Kratzer. 2014. "Modal Comparisons: Two Dilletantes in Search of an Expert." In *The Art and Craft of Semantics: A Festschrift for Irene Heim*, vol. 1, Luka Crnič and Uli Sauerland (eds.). Cambridge, MA: MIT Press, 175–179.

Marijana Marelj

A Seemingly Impossible Subset of Cognate Objects at the Interfaces

1. The allure of cognate objects

Cognate objects (henceforth: COs) have proved to be a prolific domain for probing into the workings of different modules and their interfaces (see, for instance, Kayser and Roeper, 1984; Jones, 1988; Moltmann 1989; Hale and Kayser, 1993 et seq.; Nakajima, 2006)

I start my pursuit by focusing on the existence of the COs of unaccusative verbs – a seemingly impossible subset of COs – that will inevitably spill over to the interplay between different modules of grammar and lead me to discuss the ontology of verbs and challenge the Implicit Object Conjecture (see, for instance Hale & Keyser, 1993; Uribe-Etxebarria, 1989).

The paper is organized as follows. Section 2 discusses different logical possibilities for the problem of the lack of syntactic space with the unaccusative COs and section 3 discusses the solution to it. While section 4 moves beyond the syntax and into the semantics-pragmatics interface pertaining to the unaccusative COs and offers the solution for the noted, but unresolved, mystery of the obligatory modification of the COs of unaccusative verbs, section 5 goes beyond the unaccusative-based COs and discusses the syntax and the semantics of the unergative-based COs. The crucial point of section 5 is that the ontology of verbs must include unergatives as a "primitive" category. Section 6 concludes the paper.

2. How to solve the puzzle of complements taking complements

Going back to, at least, Kayser and Roeper (1984), the generalization about the verbs found in the CO construction is that they are unergative. An "shy" example of the verb *die* as in (2a) has cropped up, though the fact that *die* is standardly argued to be an unaccusative, rather than an unergative verb has not attracted much attention. On its own, this should not be surprising. Since the lexicon is the repository of quirks and idiosyncrasies, the existence of a lone example can always be relegated as such. However, as it has been recognized recently, the empirical facts are different; a number of unaccusative verbs partake in this construction. Serbo-Croatian (1a)–(1b) and English ((1c) & (1d), from Kuno and Takami 2004:116) illustrate this:

(1) a. On je umro *prirodnom* *smrću.*[SC]
he $_{AUX.3SG}$ die.$_{PRT.M.SG}$ natural death.$_{INSTR}$
'He died a natural death.'

b. On raste *rastom* *Božijim.*
He grow.$_{3SG}$ growth.$_{INSTR}$ god.$_{GEN}$
'Grows as God causes it to grow.' (Colossians 2:19)

c. The stock market dropped *its largest drop* in three years today.

d. The apples fell just *a short fall* to the lower deck, and so were not too badly bruised.

The existence of (1) is surprising from the point of view of syntax. Namely, verbal predicates in (1) are syntactically unaccusative, which means that the surface subjects in the above examples are the complements of the relevant predicates, thus leaving no syntactic space for another complement – be it cognate or otherwise! So, the question that arises is the following: *how do the italicized phrases in (1) enter the syntactic structure (2) to start with*?

(2)

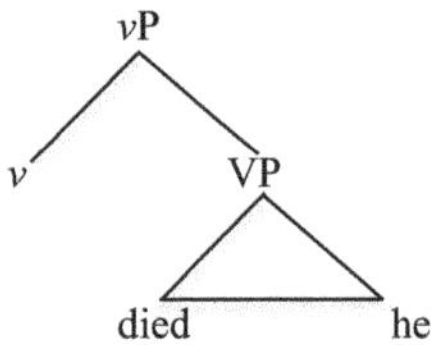

2.1. Challenge their unaccusative syntax

The first logical possibility is to hypothesize that these verbs, rather than being unaccusative, are garden-variety unergatives. In exploring their syntactic status, rather than looking at one-place verbs in isolation, I will look at these verbs in the context of transitive verbs and take that the parallel behavior of the direct object of a transitive verb and a sole argument of a one-place verb is sufficient for one to conclude that the sole syntactic argument of a one-place verb is base-generated as its object, i.e., that the verb is unaccusative. Knowing that there is no such thing as "bullet-proof" unaccusativity diagnostics, such methodology is necessary.

Bearing this methodological note in mind, look at the examples in (3). The relevant test here (see Zaenen 1993 a.o) pertains to the fact that the past participial can only be used attributively with verbs that have internal arguments. Both (3a) and (3b) illustrate this with *razbiti* (break) – a canonical transitive verb. Note that an example like (3a) is only acceptable if *man* functions as the internal argument of *break*, i.e., if the interpretation is that the man was broken. This leads me to conclude that a past participle in SC can modify internal arguments only. The grammaticality of (3c) and (3d) indicates that the sole syntactic arguments of *umreti* (die) and *pasti* (fall) are internal arguments. Consequently, these verbs are unaccusative. Not all verbs with a sole syntactic argument behave like this. Enforcing a past participle (be it an active *-l* participle or a passive *-n* participle) as in (3e) and (3 f), results in an ungrammatical output and the conclusion is that the sole syntactic arguments of *džogirati* (jog) and *hrkati* (snore) are not their internal arguments.

(3) a. Razbije-n-i čovek (*if the intended reading: *the man who broke something*)
broke.$_{\text{PRT.PASS.M.SG}}$ man.$_{\text{NOM}}$
'a broken man'

b. razbije-n-o ogledalo
broke.$_{\text{PRT.PASS.N.SG}}$ mirror.$_{\text{NOM}}$
'a broken mirror'

c. umr-l-o dete
die$_{\text{.PRT.PASS.N.SG}}$ child$_{\text{.NOM}}$
'a died child'

d. pa-l-I andjeo
fall$_{\text{.PRT.PASS.M.SG}}$ angel$_{\text{.NOM}}$
'a fallen angel'

e. *džogira-l-i/ *džogira-n-i čovek
jog$_{\text{.PRT.PASS.M.SG}}$ man.$_{\text{NOM}}$

f. *hrka-l-o/ *hrka-n-o dete
snore$_{\text{.PRT.PASS.M.SG}}$ child$_{\text{.NOM}}$

Importantly for our discussing, we can conclude that the sole-syntactic argument of verbs like *die* and *fall* do not behave like external argument of transitive verb, but rather like direct objects – internal arguments of such verbs.

2.2. Ramp up the machinery in syntax

If these verbs are unaccusatives that occasionally need to "accommodate" two internal arguments, we could increase the power of narrow syntax by allowing the computational system to create more syntactic space by obliterating the content of the traces left by the moved elements, thus allowing another element to merge into a previously occupied position. I will not embrace this solution, but it is important to mention it since a proposal along these lines – 'the conflation analysis' – was formulated by Hale and Kayser in their 1999 book to deal exactly with the cognate object construction. Specifically, they argue that cognate objects are the result of 'reinsertion' into the trace position created by conflation.

The proposal is clearly incompatible with our basic theoretical assumptions, a point that Hale and Kayser later also recognize; '[t]his is an impossible notion, not only for general theoretical reasons...... In fact, any serious consideration of cognate and hyponymous arguments leads directly to the conclusion that matters would be greatly simplified if conflation did not exist in any of the forms so far suggested' (2002: 88).

2.3. Argue that the cognate argument is not an argument

The first option we discussed focused on the syntactic status of the predicate and had to be rejected on empirical grounds. The second option zoomed in on the workings of the CS and had to be rejected on theoretical grounds, though, clearly, the consequences of reinserting elements into previously occupied positions is also empirical problematic for phenomena other than COs. The third logical option is to focus on the cognate element itself.

Based on a barrage of syntactic and semantic tests, Marelj (2016a) shows that the so-called cognate objects of unaccusative predicates in SC behave like typical predicates. The following pieces of data from SC (pertaining to the pronominalization as a test) underscore the point:

(4) a. Postao je matematičar/*on [Primary predicate]
become$_{.PRT.M.SG}$ $_{AUX}$ matematician$_{.NOM}$/he$_{.NOM}$
'He became a mathematician/*he.'

b. Smatraju Mariju lepoticom/*njome [Secondary predicate]
consider$_{.PRT.M.PL}$ Marija$_{.ACC}$ beauty$_{.INSTR}$/she$_{.INSTR}$
'They consider Maria a beauty/*her.'

c. Umro je prirodnom smrću/*njome [Cognate predicate]
die$_{.PRT.M.SG}$ $_{AUX}$ natural$_{.INSTR}$ death$_{.INSTR}$/it$_{.INSTR}$
'He died a natural death/*it.'

Since the pronoun *on* (he) above has an individual as its denotation, the impossibility of primary and secondary predicates (4a) and (4b), respectively, to be pronominalized is expected. As evident from (4c), COs of unaccusative verbs behave completely on a par with the canonical predicates. Unlike these

INSTR-predicates, genuine INSTR-arguments pronominalize without any difficulty (5):

(5) Ona gospodari svima u porodici/ ✓njima [Argument]
She rule$_{3SG}$ everyone$_{INSTR}$ in family$_{LOC}$/ they$_{INSTR}$
'She rules over everyone in the family/over them

The known caveat about the pronominalization as a semantic test does not affect the validity of the argument here. Namely, it has long been established that the denotation of some pronouns is a property (Kuno, 1972; Williams, 1983, i.a). Unlike the pronouns whose denotation is a propertly, it is only the pronouns whose denotation is an individual that cannot find themselves in predicative positions (6).

(6) a. On je postao muzičar.
he $_{AUX}$ become.$_{3SG}$ musician$_{.NOM}$
'He became a musician.'
b. Postao je to/*on.
Become $_{AUX}$ it.$_{NOM}$/he$_{.NOM}$
'He became it/*he'

Accordingly, since the complement of the verb *postati* (become) is a predicate, the pronoun used for +human entities ([+human] entities being the clearest cases of individuals) cannot be used. So, *on* (he) is out. Note, however, that *to* (it) can be used.

(7) a. Šta/*ko je on po profesiji? Muzičar
*What/*who is he by profession? A musician.*
b. Ko/*šta je postao muzičar? Miroslav.
*Who/*what became a musician?*

The contrast between (7a) and (7b) can be explained in the same way. Unlike *ko* (who) whose use is restricted to questioning arguments, the pronoun *šta* (what) can be used to question predicates. Again the relevant feature is [+human] (but see Marelj and Matushansky 2015 for discussion of the phenomena and the differences between South and East Slavic in this respect).

The right *wh*-word in the case of unaccusative COs is, however, not *šta* (what), but rather *kako* (how).

(8) Kako je umro? Užasnom smrću.
How $_{AUX}$ died.$_{PRT.M.SG}$ horrible death.$_{INSTR}$
How did he die? A horrible death.

This tells us that, interpretatively, the unaccusative COs are comparable to manner adverbs and manner adverbs are best analyzed as event predicates (see Davidson 1967; Parsons 1990, a.o). My proposal is to extend this analysis to the unaccusative COs, as the one in (9a):[1]

(9) a. Tristram je umro užasnom smrću.
b. ∃e [die (e, T) & horrible death (e)][2]

As indicated in (9b) *smrt* (death) is an event predicate that modifies the event variable directly.

3. The problem of the scarcity of syntactic space solved

Note now that the status of these nominals as modifiers – first order predicates of events – resolves the problem of the unaccusative syntax of the verbs under consideration here.

Regardless of whether we think of adjuncts as introduced into the structure via Chomsky adjunction, as a sister of V' that is under direct dominance of VP and whose linearization is different from that of arguments (Chomsky 1995) or if we think about them as creatures that involve a different plane altogether (Chomsky 2004), the crucial point here is that they will be ADJOINED. In semantic terms, the adjunction analysis is exactly the way these elements need to be integrated into the structure since they modify the event variable directly.[3]

(10)

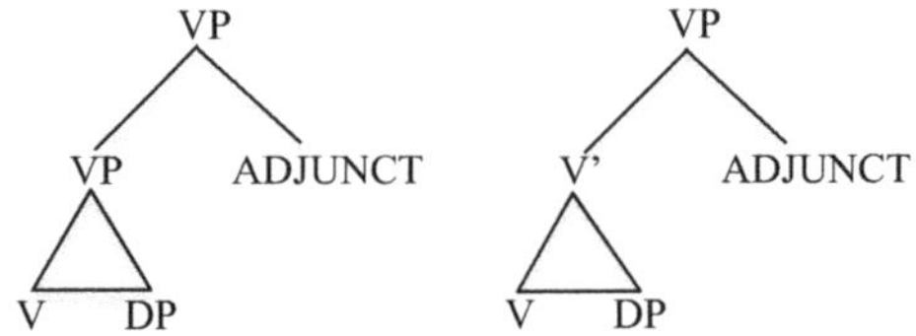

1 See also Moltmann (1989) for the same conclusion regarding parallel English and German data.

2 For ease of exposition, I drop the temporal information from the semantic formulae throughout.

3 Among the possible implementations, we find the original GB *Chomsky adjunction*, rendered in minimalism as a pair merge operations (see Chomsky 2000, 2001). And of course, there is a whole spectrum of the so-called cartographic approaches (see Cinque, 1999 et seq.) that are typically characterized by the treatment of adjuncts as specifiers. For the purposes of our discussion, (10) is sufficient.

4. Beyond the syntax and semantics of Unaccusative COs

The analysis I propose here also allows me to explain the noted, but not accounted for, obligatory presence of a modifier of the italicized nominals in examples like (11). I argue that the requirement is not a question of grammaticality. Rather, it a question of pragmatic infelicity Allow me to explain.

(11) a. #Umro je *smrću*
die.$_{\text{PRT.M.3SG}}$ $_{\text{AUX.3SG}}$ death$_{\text{.INSTR}}$

On its own, the fact that a nominal phrase is 'cognate' or not with respect to the main predicate is an idiosyncratic piece of information (see also Pereltsvaig 1999), without any relevance to grammar as such. However, I argue that when a SEMANTIC 'cognate' nominal is found in the role of a predicate, its 'cognatehood' becomes relevant from the point of view of pragmatics, whose requirement for informativeness – the Gricean Maxim of Quantity – will require it to be modified. These cognate predicates modify the event argument directly and this is the reason why they must be modified.

(12) a. #Tristram died a death
a'. Tristram died a *horrible* death.

(13) a. #Tristram je umro smrću
a'. ∃e [die (e, T) & death(e)]
b. Tristram je umro *užasnom* smrću.
b'. ∃e [die (e, T) & *horrible* death (e)]

Above I introduced the notion 'semantic cognate'. A semantic cognate differs from what we typically find in the literature discussed as a cognate in that it is related to the verb with respect to its meaning, but not necessarily in morphology. What I mean here with the notion *semantic cognates* is *something that is presupposed by the main predicate*. An element whose semantic contribution is *vacuous*. For instance, the meaning of *opomenuti* (warn) apparently presupposes *glas* (a voice) (compare (14) with (15a)), but it does not presuppose *prst* (a finger) (see (15b)). Note than neither *glas* nor *prst* are morphologically related to the relevant verb.

(14) Opomenuo ju je *tihim glasom.*
warn.$_{\text{PRT.M.SG}}$ she$_{\text{.ACC.CL}}$ $_{\text{AUX.3SG}}$ low$_{\text{.INSTR}}$ voice$_{\text{.INSTR}}$
'He warned her soto voce/in a low voice.'

(15) a. # Opomenuo ju je glasom.
warn.$_{PRT.M.SG}$ she$_{.ACC.CL}$ $_{AUX.3SG}$ voice$_{.INSTR}$
b. Opomenuo ju je *prstom*.
warn.$_{PRT.M.SG}$ she$_{.ACC.CL}$ $_{AUX.3SG}$ finger$_{.INSTR}$
'He warned her with his finger/waving his finger.'

5. Beyond the phenomenon of Unaccusative Cognate Objects

5.1. A closer look at the Unergative-based COs

As well known, a much bigger set of COs are based on what is traditionally referred to as unergative verbs – verbs that have external arguments (Kayser & Roeper 1984; Hale & Kayser 2002). Some examples in SC are given in (16).

(16) a. Sanja san. [SC]
dreams.$_{3SGPRES}$ dream.$_{ACC}$
'He dreams a dream.'
b. Živi život.
lives$_{.3SGPRES}$ life$_{.ACC}$
'He lives a life.'

Note now that if unergatives are treated as denominal verbs, where bare nouns (e.g., *dream*) are generated in the complement position of the semantically empty *DO* into which they subsequently incorporate (see Hale and Kayser, 1993 *et seq.*) (17), the puzzling scarcity of syntactic space arises again!

(17)

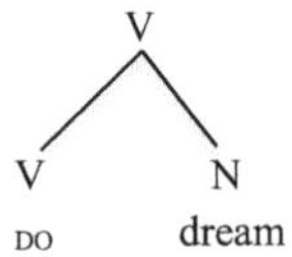

It is the lack of syntactic space that a structure in (17) imposes that originally motivated Hale and Kayser (1999) to propose the notion of 'conflation'. Since the notion 'conflation' is problematic (recall the discussion in 2.2), we still end up facing the same problem of the sparsity of syntactic space with started the discussion of the unaccusative-based COs!

Logically, the first step is to check if it is possible to implement the kind of solution I proposed for the underscored phrases in (1). After all, both types share the feature of being optional – a rule of thumb for diagnosing adjuncts.

This hypothesis is easily refuted on empirical grounds. Unlike the cognate objects of verbs in (1), the cognate object here pass the tests any run-of-the-mill (internal) argument does (see Marelj 2016a, 2016b for an elaborate discussion of diagnostics and the relevant literature). The SC examples in (18) present only two pieces of evidence to support this claim.[4]

(18) a. Sanjao je *svaki* san (koji je ikada postojao)
dream.$_{PRT.M.3SG}$ $_{AUX.3SG}$ every dream$_{.ACC}$ (that every existed)
'He dreamt *every* dream (that every existed).'

b. Svake noći *ga* je sanjao.
every night $_{CL.ACC.M}$ $_{AUX.3SG}$ dreamt.$_{PRT.M.3SG}$
'Every night he dreamt *it*.'

Perhaps it is their 'cognatehood' that is relevant to the computational system? This is, indeed, the line of reasoning that was pursued by Hale and Kayser (2002). Namely, what they propose is to split the group of cognate objects into those that are *zero-related* to the relevant verbs (like *dance a dance*) and those that do not share the root with the relevant verb like *dance a Mazurka* and argue that the former, but crucially not the latter, are the results of their incorporation mechanism.

But empirically, there does not seem to be a difference between these two types of objects since examples like (19) and (20) behave completely on a par with respect to the relevant tests!

(19) a. She danced a dance./She dreamt a dream.
b. A dance was danced./A dream was dreamt.
c. What did she dance?/What did she dream?
d. She danced a (fast) dance. /She dreamt a (beautiful) dream.
e. She danced every dance. /He dreamt every dream that night.

(20) a. She danced a Mazurka./She dreamt a nightmare.
b. A Mazurka was danced./A nightmare was dreamt.
c. What did she dance?/What did she dream?
d. She danced a (fast) Kolo./She dreamt a (horrible) nightmare.
e. She danced every Kolo./She dreamt every nightmare.

4 Space prevents us from discussion another important difference between the two types of COs here – obligatory vs. Optional presence of modification (see Marelj 2016b for a detailed account).

It is only the cognate objects of the verbs like *die* and *sleep* in *die a horrible death* & *sleep the sleep of the just* that behave as if they are not run-of-the-mill arguments.[5]

If the noun incorporation is not on the right track, we are left with two alternatives: a run-of-the-mill transitive syntax (21a) and (21b) a run-of-the-mill 'traditional' unergative structure.

(21) a.

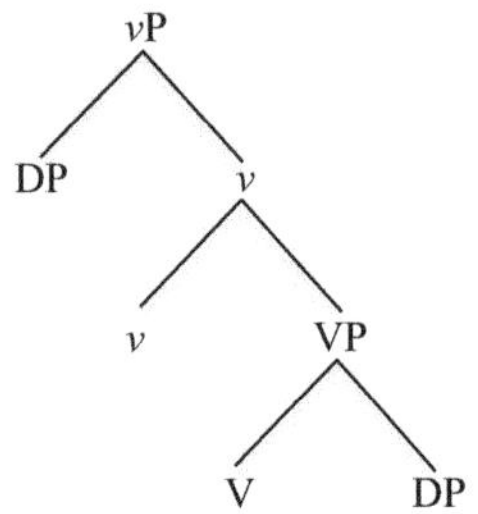

b.

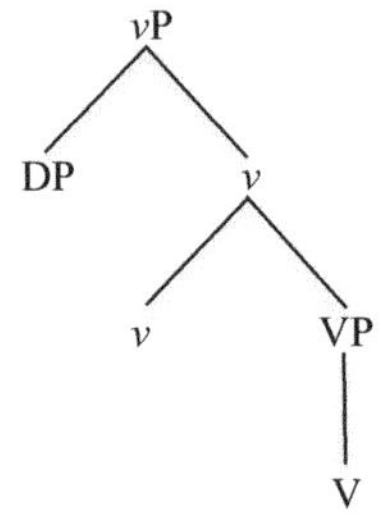

Indeed, the treatment of unergative verbs as hidden transitive is widely popular account of their structure and the Implicit Object Conjecture – the assumption all unergative verbs have direct objects – has been indorsed in many a work (Hale & Keyser 1993 i.a). Pereltsvaig (1999) and Nakayama (2006) argue for the regular transitive syntax for the unergative-based CO verbs. Such an account reduces the ontology of verbs types to transitives and unaccusatives.

Whereas I agree with the literature that a subset of what were labelled as traditional unergative verbs are indeed transitive verbs with a phonologically unrealized object, I will argue against the Implicit Object Conjecture for the entire set of unergative verbs on empirical grounds. In what follows, I will show that there are unergative verbs that simply cannot be analysed as a "primitive" class of transitive verbs. The upshot of my discussion is that the ontology of verbs needs to include three, rather than two, "primitive" types.

Again, I will employ the same methodology I used earlier. First, I establish the baseline by looking at the uncontroversial instances and only then compare their behaviour to the behaviour of the less transparent cases. Quite like in the previous discussion, we will start our exploration by zooming in on the cases of canonical transitive verb.

5 A careful reader might have noticed that so far, it looks as if it is only the unaccusative verbs occur with predicate cognates whereas that unike *die*, *sleep* is no unaccusative verbs. I will return to this 'puzzle' directly.

5.2. Invisible arguments & visible entailments

It has long been noted in the literature (Fodor and Fodor 1980 i.a.) for English, but the behavior is truly crosslinguistic, that the so-called unspecified objects are licensed with what seem to be run-of-the-mill transitive verbs like *pisati* (write), *jesti* (eat), and *piti* (drink). Such arguments are typically considered to be present, at least, semantically.

(22) a. Jeo je
eat.PRT.M.SG AUX.3SG
'He ate.'

b. Pisao je.
write.PRT.M.SG AUX.3SG
'He wrote.'

c. Pio je.
drink.PRT.M.SG AUX.3SG
'He drank.'

(23) a. Jeo je proso.
eat.PRT.M.SG AUX porrige.ACC
'He ate porridge.'

b. Pisao je pismo.
write.PRT.M.SG AUX letter.ACC
'He wrote a letter.'

c. Pio je vino/piće.
drink.PRT.M.SG AUX wine/drink
'He drank some wine/a drink.'

What makes the examples like (22) and (23) on a par is that when the unexpressed objects are missing from sentences, the sentences still make an *existence claim* with respect to the unfilled predicate slot. Hence, the equivalence in (24).

(24) a. Jeo je.⇔ Jeo je *nešto.*
He ate. ⇔ He ate *something.*

b. Pio je.⇔ Pio je *nešto.*
He drank.⇔ He drank *something.*

c. Pisao je ⇔ Pisao je *nešto.*
He wrote⇔ He wrote *something.*

Bearing this in mind, it is very natural to interpret the existence claim as to indicate the presence of a phonologically unrealized, but semantically active argument.[6]

So far, we established what the behavior of the uncontroversial transitive verbs look like. But how do we know that that the existence claim tells us something relevant about the argument structure of the predicate, rather then, for instance, telling us something about what is *implied*? Well, this is where the data on the absence of the existence claim will help us. Note first, as also noted by Fodor and Fodor (1980), the entailment/the existence claim holds not *only* if the covert semantic argument corresponds to the direct object position in the syntax, but for all cases of the so-called suppressed arguments as in passives (25a) or those cases of covert semantic arguments corresponding to oblique objects in syntax (25b).

(25) a. Tristram was killed ⇒ John was killed *by someone.*
b. Tristram is engaged/married ⇒ John is engaged *with someone/married to.*

Importantly, note now that the entailment does not exist in the case of unaccusatives! So, whereas *someone broke the window* entails *the window broke*, crucially, *the window broke* doesn't entail *someone broke the window.*

(26) a. The window broke.
b. The ship sank. No existence claim!
c. The ice melted.

How can this be explained? If the unaccusative/inhoative alternation lacks the external role in syntax as well as in semantics (see Reinhart 2016 i.a.) the lack of the existence claim follows. Hence, I conclude that the existence claim is minimally present when there is a covert semantic argument present. The lack of entailment here is also consistent with other tests typically used to argue that unaccusatives have no implicit argument whatsoever. Examples (27) and (28) illustrate two such tests (see Marelj 2004 for discussion and references):

(27) a. The ship was sunk by Bill
b. *The ship sunk by Bill

6 Some of the implicit arguments might also be syntactically active. I gloss over it here, since it is the semantic presence – which is uncontroversial – that is important for our discussion.

(28) a. The ice was deliberately melted.
b. #The ice melted deliberately.

Having established the behaviour of the transitive verbs and the behaviour of the unaccusative verbs, let us now move and explore how the unergative verbs behave.

5.3. Hidden objects

Some of the examples of the unergative verbs are given in (29). Even though there are no overtly realized objects, the existence claim about the unexpressed object holds in (29).

(29) a. Luka je pevao. ⇔ Luka je pevao *nešto.*
Luka sang. ⇔ Luka sang *something.*
b. Luka je sanjao.⇔ Luka je sanjao *nešto.*
Luka dreamt ⇔ Luka dreamt *something.*

If the existence claim is the right test, the only thing that makes this 'underlyingly' transitive verbs different from the run-of-the-mill example of a transitive verb like *break* or *open* is the fact that they can allow their complement to be phonologically unrealized. This is, indeed, the desirable conclusion. Recall that just like in the cases of regular transitive verbs, both the so-called zero-related cognate and the non-morphologically related complements of such verbs behave completely on a par (recall examples (19) and (20))! And these are exactly the cases for which I concur with Pereltsvaig and Nakayama in their analysis of their structure as simple transitive verbs and against the analysis proposed for a subset of these in Hale and Kayser (2002)

Unlike Pereltsvaig and Nakayama, I argue that not all the unergatives can be subsumed under the heading of transitives. In the following section, we will see that not all unergatives are hidden transitives. Moreover, their primitive status as unergative will be flashed out even more by the type of cognate object they can licence.

5.4. Unergatives as a primitive category

Some of the most frequent verbs that I argue belong to the primitively unergative class are given in (30).

(30) hodati (walk), šetati (wander), džogirati (jog), spavati (sleep)

The reason the sentences in (31) make no existential claim with respect to some unfilled predicate slot is simply because there is none! If there is no object, then these must be unergative. It is easy to verify that SC is not exotic in this respect. In English, for instance, *he walked* and *he slept* do not entail *he walked something* or *he slept something*, respectively.

(31)	a.	Hodao	je.	
		walk$_{.PRT.M.SG}$	AUX.3SG	
		'He walked.		No existence claim!
	b.	Spavao	je.	
		sleep$_{.PRT.M.SG.}$	AUX.3SG	
		'He slept.'		

But if this is true – if the existence claim is the litmus test for the presence/absence of an implicit argument, and consequently their underlyingly unergative syntax, how can we explain the fact that verbs license COs, as evident from (32)?

(32)	a.	Hodam	*hodom*	*lokalnog*	*alkića.*
		walk$_{.1SG}$	walk$_{.INSTR}$	local	alcoholic$_{.GEN}$
		'I walk the way a local alcoholic walks.'			
	b.	Spavam	*mirnim snom/*	*snom*	*pravednika.*
		sleep$_{.1SG}$	restfull$_{.INSTR}$ sleep.$_{INSTR}$	sleep.$_{INSTR}$	just.$_{GEN}$
	c.	He sleeps *the sleep of the just.*[7]			

Rather than being a problem, the fact that they license the kind of CO that they do is predicted under my account. The underscored phrases in (32) and are cognate predicates of the type that arise with unaccusative verbs as well. Since these are adjuncts, no problem of the lack of syntactic space arises here.

The second group that I would like to explore here is class of the Verbs of Emission (to use the terminology proposed in Levin 1993). Quite like the ones in (30) – these verbs do not make an existence claim either (33)–(34).

(33) zvoniti (ring), as a verb of emission: *Zvono zvoni* (*The bell is ringing*), zviždati (whistle), pištati (whistle), hrkati (snore)

---

7 The idiomatic *talk the talk and walk the walk* is the only example that I am aware of where modification is not necessary. Considering the meaning here is truly idiomatic – *to perform actions consistent with one's claims*, the lack of modification should not come as a surprise.

(34) a. Zvono je zvonilo.
bell$_{\text{.NOM}}$ AUX.3SG ring$_{\text{.PRT.N.SG}}$
'A/the bell was ringing.'
b. On je hrkao.
He$_{\text{.NOM}}$ AUX.3SG snore.$_{\text{PRT.M.SG}}$
'He was snoring.'

Again, as predicted under my account, these verbs can license only the event modifier phrases-adjuncts. They cannot licence cognate arguments.

(35) a. Zvono zvoni *neprijatnim* *zvukom.*
bell$_{\text{.NOM}}$ ring$_{\text{.3SG}}$ unpleasant.$_{\text{INSTR}}$ sound.$_{\text{INSTR}}$
'A/The bell make an unpleasant noise/produces an unpleasant sound.'
b. Hrče *najglasnijim* *hrkom* na svijetu.
snore$_{\text{.3SG}}$ loudest$_{\text{.INST}}$ snore$_{\text{.INSTR}}$ on world
'He snores the loudest in the word.'
(A story about *Medvjedić Hrkalo* – Google search)

Again, the adjunction analysis provides the right way for these event modifiers to be integrated into the structure since they modify the event variable directly.

6. Conclusion

The upshot of the analysis is that there are two groups of cognate nominals: i) 'cognate' arguments, which are complements of the relevant verbs, and ii) 'cognate' predicates – event modifiers. Whereas the modifier cognate object modifies the event variable directly, an argument modifies this variable indirectly, via the thematic role. MORPHOLOGICAL 'cognatehood' is idiosyncratic and of no relevance to grammar. Instead, I introduce the notion of SEMANTIC 'cognatehood', which becomes relevant in the case of the cognate predicates whose modification is required on pragmatic grounds. Syntactically, the status of cognate predicates as adjuncts makes it unproblematic for the unaccusatives to license them in syntax. As for the verbs that 'license' cognate arguments, I argue that whereas a subset of them is syntactically transitive, others are truly unergative.

References

Chomsky, Noam. 2000. "Minimalist inquiries: the framework." In *Step by step: Essays in honor of Howard Lasnik*, Roger Martin, David Michaels and Juan Uriagereka (eds.). MIT Press.

Chomsky, Noam. 2001. "Beyond explanatory adequacy." In *MIT occasional papers in linguistics 20*. MITWPL.

Cinque, Guglielmo. 1999. *Adverbs and functional heads: A cross-linguistic perspective*. Oxford University Press.

Davidson, Donald. "Truth and Meaning." *Inquiries into Truth and Interpretation*, Donald Davidson (eds.). Oxford: Claredon Press. 17–36.

Grice, Paul. 1975. "Logic and conversation". In *Syntax and semantics 3: Speech acts*, Peter Cole and Jerry L. Morgan. New York: Academic Press. pp. 41–58.

Hale, Kenneth and Samuel Jay Keyser. 1993. "On argument structure and lexical expression of syntactic relations." In *The view from building 20: Essays in Linguistics in honor of Sylvain Brombert*, Ken Hale and Samuel Jay Keyser. Cambridge, MA: MIT Press, 53–110.

Hale, Ken and Samuel Jay Keyser. 1997. "On the complex nature of simple predicators." In *Complex Predicates*, Alex Alsina, Joan Bresnan, and Peter Sells (eds.). Standford: CSLI Publications, 29–66.

Hale, Ken and Samuel Jay Keyser. 2002. *Prolegomenon to a theory of argument structure*. Cambridge, MA.: MIT Press.

Jones, Michael-Allen. 1988. "Cognate objects and the Case-Filter." *Journal of Linguistics* 24: 89–110.

Kuno, Susumu. 1972. "Some properties of non-referential noun phrases." In Roman Jakobson and Shigeo Kawamoto (eds.), *Studies in General and Oriental Linguistics. Presented to S. Hattori on Occasion of his Sixtieth Birthday*. Tokyo: TEC, 348–372.

Kuno, Susumu and Ken-ichi Takami. 2004. *Functional constraints in Grammar: On the unergative-unaccusative distinction*. Amsterdam: John Benjamins.

Levin, Beth. 1993. *English Verb Classes and Alternations: A Preliminary Investigation*. Chicago: The University of Chicago Press.

Marelj, Marijana. 2002. "Rules that Regulate the Co-occurrence of Feature Clusters in the Theta System." *Theoretical Linguistics* 28: 257–375.

Marelj, Marijana. 2004. "Middles and Argument Structure across Languages." PhD thesis. Utrecht: LOT.

Marelj, Marijana. 2011. "Bound-Variable Anahora and Left Branch Condition." *Syntax* 14: 205–229.

Marelj, Marijana. 2013. "Experiencing Linking – Psych Verbs at the Interface." In Elly van Gelderen, Michela Cennamo and Jóhanna Barðdal (eds.), *Argument Structure in Flux*. Amsterdam: Benjamins.

Marelj, Marijana. and Ora Matushansky. 2015. "Mistaking for: Testing the theory of Mediated Predication." *Linguistic Inquiry* 46/1, 43–76.

Marelj, Marijana. 2016a. "Tautološki objekt u srpskom jeziku." *Srpski jezik u savremenoj lingvistickoj teoriji*: 141–175. Niš: University of Niš.

Marelj, Marijana. 2016b. "In the South Slavonic Garden: Landscaping the landscape of arguments and non-arguments." *Linguistica* 56 (1): 193–209.

Marelj, Marijana. 2016c. "Theta Meets Case: An Extension." In *Concepts, Syntax, and Their Interface*, Martin Everaert, Marijana Marelj and Eric Reuland (eds.). Linguistic Inquiry Monographs. Cambridge, MASS: MIT Press.

Moltmann, Frederieke. 1989. "Nominal and Clausal event predicates." In *Papers from the 25th Annual Reginal Meetings of the Chicago Linguistic Society.* University of Chicago, 300–314.

Parsons, Terence. 1990. *Events in the Semantics of English: A study in Sub-Atomic Semantics. Current Studies in Linguistics Series* 21. Cambridge, Mass.: MIT Press.

Pereltsvaig, Asya. 1999. "Cognate Objects in Russian: Is the notion 'Cognate' relevant for Syntax?" *Canadian Journal of Linguistics* 44(3): 267–291.

Reinhart, Tanya. 2016. "Theta System: Syntactic Realization of Verbal Concepts." In *Concepts, Syntax and Their Interface*, Martin Everaert, Marijana Marelj, and Eric Reuland (eds.). Linguistic Inquiry Monographs. Cambridge, MASS: MIT Press.

Williams, Edwin. 1983. "Semantic vs. syntactic categories." *Linguistics and Philosophy* 6: 423–446.

Zaenen, Anni. 1993. "Unaccusativity in Dutch: Integrating Syntax and Lexical Semantics." In James Pustejovsky (ed.), *Semantics and the Lexicon*. Dordrecht: Kluwer, 129–161.

Neda Todorović

A Different Aspect of Tenses and Temporal Interpretation in Serbian

1. Introduction

It is a matter of an ongoing debate whether Tense is a universal category. Languages that have temporal morphology are standardly assumed to have TP; the question then arises for languages that lack temporal morphology. This question has been raised due to the syntactic and semantic properties that languages lacking overt temporal morphology observe. Namely, in a number of such languages, there is evidence for the lack of certain syntactic properties standardly associated with the presence of TP in the structure, e.g. the absence of certain subject-object asymmetries is Serbian and Korean (Bošković 2012). Regarding semantics, in languages which lack overt temporal morphology, e.g. seemingly complementary "Tense" markers (past-oriented and non-past) can co-occur in a clause (Halkomelem Salish (Wiltschko 2003), Japanese (Sawada 2015)).

The idea of the correlation between the absence of temporal morphology and the absence of TP has been advocated for some individual languages, such as Yucatec Maya (Bohnemeyer 2002), Halkomelem Salish (Wiltschko 2003), Chinese (Lin 2006), Guaraní (Tonhauser 2011), Slovene, Czech, Slovak, Polish, Serbian (Migdalski 2013), Korean (Kang 2014), *i.a.*; cf. Matthewson (2006) for Lillooet Salish; see also Bošković (2012) for a broader cross-linguistic claim (see also Ritter and Wiltschko 2014). Importantly, since all these studies deal with only individual languages or smaller groups of related languages, the claims that these authors make regarding the presence or absence of TP are confined to those languages, without broader cross-linguistic predictions, i.e. none of these authors gives an analysis that would make a prediction for any given language whether it will, or will not, have TP.

Todorović (2016) makes a broad cross-linguistic claim that TP is not universally projected – TP is projected only in languages with temporal morphology; languages without temporal morphology lack TP. This parametric difference, I argue, captures various syntactic and semantic properties of genetically unrelated languages. In this paper, I focus on semantic properties, in particular, on the difference between Serbian and Bulgarian in the distribution of aspect in so-called aspectual tenses, Aorist and Imperfectum. I argue that these differences can systematically be captured by resorting to the presence/absence of TP in a language – TP is present in Bulgarian, but absent in Serbian. Moreover, on the example of Serbian, I show that, even in the absence of TP, temporal interpretation can still be derived with aspectual and modal components. I also argue that, under a no TP-analysis of Serbian, we can account for a range of non-deictic interpretations of periphrastic past, Aorist and future forms, which are otherwise puzzling under the analysis which posits TP in the language.[1] Finally, I discuss the semantic distribution of various verbal forms, showing that the traditional labels are often misleading and need to be re-examined.

2. Absence of temporal morphology cross-linguistically

Serbian is a language with rich verbal morphology. However, despite this richness, no morphemes are temporal markers. Instead, traditionally labelled tense morphology denotes agreement and aspectual markers. In Table 1, with morphological present tense forms, there is no systematic temporal affix – agreement markers are added directly to the stem. With Aorist and Imperfect, the suffixes are agreement and aspectual markers (see Todorović 2016 for details).

While temporal marking is lacking, there is rich aspectual morphology in Serbian. In fact, aspect is obligatorily specified on the root, as in (1). In addition, Serbian derives perfective (2), (3) and imperfective interpretations (4) with an array of affixes (see also Todorović 2016).

(1)	a.	bac**i**ti	b.	bac**a**ti
		throw-**pf**.inf		throw-**impf**.inf

(2)	**Pre**-skočio	je	potok.
	over-jumped.**pf**.3.m.sg.	is	stream.
	'He jumped over the stream.'		

(3)	**Iz**- **po**- **iz**- bacivao	je	sve	knjige	sa	polica.
	cmpl-dstr-out-thrown-3.m.sg.**pf**.	is	all	books	from	shelves
	'He threw out all of the books from the shelves.'					

(4)	a.	iz-baci-ti	b.	iz-baci-**va**-ti
		out-throw-**pf**.inf		*out*-throw-**impf**-inf

---

1 The term 'periphrastic past' is used for the ease of exposition. I do not assume semantic past tense in the structure of these forms (section 3.2), as confirmed by the possibility of their non-past interpretation (section 3.4).

Table 1: Inflectional paradigm of verbs in Serbian

	Present tense *uraditi* **'to do' (pf.)**	**Aorist** *uraditi* **'to do' (pf.)**	**Imperfect** *orati* **'to plow' (impf.)**
1sg	uradi-m	uradi-h	ora-h
2sg	uradi-š	uradi-ø	ora-š-e
3sg	uradi-ø	uradi-ø	ora-š-e
1pl	uradi-mo	uradi-s-mo	ora-s-mo
2pl	uradi-te	uradi-s-te	ora-s-te
3pl	urad-e	uradi-š-e	ora-h-u

In that sense, despite its rich verbal morphology, Serbian actually patterns with languages that lack overt temporal morphology, e.g. Chinese. As is well known, Chinese has an array of aspectual markers, but it crucially lacks Tense markers. *Le* and *guo* in (5) refer to perfective (or perhaps Perfect) aspect interpretation, and *zhe* and *zai* in (6) to the imperfective, progressive or durative.[2] Crucially, (5) and (6) show that, even in the absence of temporal morphology, temporal interpretation can still be successfully derived.

(5) a. Ta da **le** majiang.
she play le mahjong.
'She played/has played mahjong.'
(Smith and Erbaugh 2005: 721)

b. Zhangsan chu-**guo** guo.
Zhangsan leave-guo country
'Zhangsan has been to other countries.'
(Klein, Li and Hendriks 2000: 760)

(6) a. Lisi **zai** chuan yi-jian qunzi.
Lisi zai put-on one-CL skirt
'Lisi is putting on a skirt.'
(Klein, Li and Hendriks 2000: 727)

b. Lisi chuan-**zhe** yi-jian quinzi.
Lisi wear-zhe one-cl skirt
'Lisi wears a skirt.'
(Klein, Li and Hendriks 2000: 727)

Unifying languages as genetically diverse as Chinese and Serbian, Todorović (2016) puts forward a broad cross-linguistic claim: in the absence of temporal morphology, TP is also absent in a language. Such a two-way division (TP vs.

2 There is no consensus on the nature of these morphemes (see e.g. Klein, Li and Hendriks (2000)).

no-TP) provides a systematic account of various syntactic and semantic properties in genetically unrelated languages, as discussed in section 3.[3]

3. The effects of the presence/absence of TP

This paper focuses on semantic properties which follow from the presence/absence of TP in a language; yet, a brief note is in order regarding syntactic evidence. Todorović (2015, 2016) shows that, with respect to VP-ellipsis, there is a systematic split between languages that have a TP and those that lack a TP: finiteness mismatches between the antecedent and the target are disallowed in TP languages and allowed in no-TP languages. I argue that finiteness mismatches in TP languages are not tolerated due to a mismatch in the T feature, thus violating the feature identity requirement for ellipsis. Finiteness mismatches in VP-ellipsis are disallowed in European and Brazilian Portuguese, Bulgarian, Danish and Hungarian, which are independently classified as TP languages (by having temporal morphology; they are also DP-languages). Serbian, Russian, Slovenian, Polish allow finiteness mismatches in VP-ellipsis; these languages lack temporal morphology and are thus no-TP languages (they also lack DP) (for details, see Todorović 2016).

In terms of semantics, I focus on the following two properties. First, in the absence of Tense in Serbian, Aorist and Imperfect observe aspectual restrictions. They, however, observe no aspectual restrictions in Bulgarian. I argue that these differences follow from the presence/absence of the TP-layer, i.e. TP is present in Bulgarian, but absent in Serbian. The second property is temporal interpretation in the absence of TP. On the example of Serbian, I show that aspectual and modal components can determine temporal interpretation. Furthermore, I show that what has traditionally been analyzed as tenses in Serbian receive a range of interpretations which are otherwise puzzling if Tense is present in the structure of these forms.

3 Additional motivation for a parametric division between languages comes from the parallelism with the nominal domain. I.e., it has been argued that DP can be projected in a language only if definite articles are morphologically realized in the language (see Bošković 2008, 2012 for a general cross-linguistic perspective; for individual languages, see e.g. Corver 1992, Chierchia 1998, Despić 2011, 2013). The parallelism between the nominal and the clausal domain can then be seen as an abstract link in terms of morphological realization of these projections – the absence of definite articles/temporal morphology is the reflex of the absence of DP and TP, respectively. Furthermore, Todorović (2016) shows that correlating the presence of DP and of TP in a language provides the right cut regarding finiteness mismatches in VP-ellipsis and aspectual tenses.

3.1. Aspectual tenses in Serbian and Bulgarian

In Serbian, past interpretations are most typically obtained via the Auxiliary *biti* 'be' and a participle (7). These forms allow for both the imperfective (7a), and the perfective (7b).

(7) a. Jovan je radio domaći.
Jovan is done-$_{\text{impf.}}$ homework
'Jovan was doing his homework.'

b. Jovan je uradio domaći.
Jovan is done-$_{\text{pf.}}$ homework
'Jovan finished his homework.'

Serbian also makes use of Aorist and Imperfect. Aorist typically denotes punctual and/or completed events, and Imperfect describes incompleted, long-lasting or repetitive events. Imperfect is archaic, but Aorist is still used, e.g. in vivid narration. Unlike periphrastic past, Aorist occurs only with the perfective (8a), while Imperfect occurs only with the imperfective (8b).

(8) a. Stiže / *stiza Jovan!
arrive-$_{\text{pf.AOR}}$ / *arrive-$_{\text{impf.AOR}}$ Jovan
'Jovan arrived!'/*'Jovan was arriving!'

b. Oni pecijahu *ispecijahu hleb.
they bake-$_{\text{impf.IM}}$ / bake-$_{\text{pf.IM}}$ bread
'They used to bake bread.'/*'They used to finish baking bread.'

Unlike Serbian, Bulgarian has temporal morphology (Scatton 1984, Todorović 2016). It also makes use of Aorist and Imperfect. However, both Aorist (9) and Imperfect (10) can occur with either imperfective or perfective aspect. The difference in meaning between the two forms in (9) and (10), respectively, is crucially contributed by aspect, e.g. whether the emphasis is placed on the completion, or the lack thereof (Scatton 1984).

9) a. Včera pročetoh edna kniga.
yesterday read-$_{\text{pf.AOR.1sg}}$ one book
'Yesterday I read a book (and finished it).'

b. Včera četoh edna kniga.
yesterday read-$_{\text{impf.AOR.1.sg}}$ one book
'Yesterday I was reading a book.'

(10) a. Sedeše na čardaka.
sit-$_{\text{impf.IM.1.sg}}$ on veranda
'He was sitting/ he used to sit on the veranda'

b. Večer sedneše na čardaka.
evening sit-$_{\text{pf.IM.1.sg}}$ on veranda
'In the evening he would sit down on the veranda.'

I propose that the difference between Serbian and Bulgarian stems from the presence/absence of TP. Based on the presence of true temporal morphology in finite forms in Bulgarian (which is also a DP language), but not in Serbian, Todorović (2016) argues that Bulgarian projects TP, while Serbian lacks it. The lack of restrictions in Bulgarian follows, I propose, from the following assumptions. First, the major contribution of the perfective and imperfective in (9) and (10) is aspectual, i.e. lexical (telicity) and viewpoint aspect (boundedness) (Scatton 1984), while the major contribution of Aorist and Imperfect is to locate the event in the past. This fits well with the difference between the forms in (9) and (10): the events are in the past, the difference between (a) and (b) being their boundedness. Second, the temporal component is computed in TP in Bulgarian, and the aspectual one in AspP. If such a division of labor is right, then Aorist and Imperfect should in principle combine with either aspect. The prediction is borne out.

When it comes to Serbian, I argue that it is precisely the absence of Tense that prohibits the co-occurrence of Aorist and Imperfect with both aspects. In particular, I propose that, due to the absence of Tense, Aorist and Imperfect are aspectualized in Serbian, i.e. they highlight certain aspectual, rather than temporal properties (to be specified immediately), these properties being responsible for the observed aspectual restrictions. Importantly, although Aorist and Imperfect have traditionally been classified as tenses in both Serbian and Bulgarian, their semantic properties show that such labels are misleading. Traditional labels of verbal forms should thus be re-examined by using the relevant semantic criteria (see also sections 4). In section 3.1.1, 3.1.2 and 3.2, I show how we obtain a past flavor of Aorist, Imperfect and periphrastic past in the absence of Tense. Importantly, in section 3.4, I show that this is not their only available interpretation.

3.1.1. Aorist in Serbian

Regarding Serbian Aorist, I propose that it highlights the aspectual component of the event, i.e. its completeness (11a) / punctuality (11b). Thus, unlike Bulgarian Aorist, which marks the past interpretation of the event, Serbian Aorist emphasizes certain aspectual properties of the event.

(11) a. (Konačno) napisah domaći!
finally write-1sg.**aor**. homework
'I finally finished my homework!'

b. U tom trenu ga odalami tako jako…
in that moment him-cl slam-3.sg.**aor** that strong
'And then (s)he slammed him with such a force…'

When it comes to the compatibility of Aorist only with perfectives, I propose that this follows from the aspectual component it conveys. Since it denotes completeness or punctuality, it is predicted to combine only with perfectives in Serbian, since only those mark the end-point of the event and only those occur with instantaneous events.

Regarding its past interpretation, I argue that the absence of TP is only an apparent issue; Aorist can be structurally represented as a two-tiered aspectual system (Smith 1991, Pancheva 2003). One tier is *viewpoint aspect*, which carries the information about the boundedness of the event. Perfective viewpoint aspect denotes the event which is contained within a given reference time interval (12) (the RTI). Imperfective denotes the event which contains the RTI (13). With Aorist, this tier is specified for the perfective. The second aspectual tier is *Perfect*, a time span generalizing over time intervals and extending backwards from the contextually salient RTI, as in (14). The default RTI is the Utterance Time (UT). The past interpretation of Aorist results from the *Perfect* tier, which extends backwards from the UT in this case, as in (15).

(12) Perfective: $\lambda P.\lambda t.\lambda w.\exists e\ [time(e) \subseteq t\ \&\ P(w)(e)]$ (Kratzer 1998)

(13) Imperfective: $\lambda P.\lambda t.\lambda w.\exists e\ (t \subseteq \tau(e)\ \&\ P(e)=1)$ (Kratzer 1998)

(14) $[PERFECT] = \lambda P.\lambda t.\lambda w.\exists t'\ [PTS(t', t)\ \&\ P(t')(w)]$ (à la Iatridou et al. 2001, Pancheva 2003)
PTS (t', t) iff t is a final subinterval of t'

(15) $\lambda w.\exists t'\ [PTS\ (t',t_c) \wedge \exists e\ [\tau\ (e) \subseteq t' \wedge K\ (w)(e)]]$

$\wedge$

UT $\lambda t.\lambda w.\exists t'\ [PTS\ (t',t) \wedge \exists e\ [\tau\ (e) \subseteq t' \wedge K\ (w)(e)]]$

$\wedge$

Perf: $\lambda K.\lambda t.\lambda w.\exists t'[PTS\ (t',t) \wedge K\ (t)(w)]$ AspP: $\lambda t.\lambda w.\exists e\ [\tau\ (e) \subseteq t \wedge K\ (w)(e)]$

3.1.2. Imperfect in Serbian

Imperfect denotes continuity, as in (16). Ongoingness or the lack of completion is compatible only with imperfectives, hence only those are expected to be felicitous in these environments.

(16) Prizor je bio divan: pod planinskim vrhovima **prostirahu se**
sight is been gorgeous under mountain peaks spread-$_{IM}$ SE
tamne šume borova…
dark forests pine-pl.
'The view was amazing: endless forests of pine trees were spreading out below the mountain peaks…' (Stanojčić and Popović 1992:384)

Regarding its temporal interpretation, I propose that Imperfect, similarly to Aorist, has two tiers of aspect; the viewpoint aspect is imperfective, as in (17). Like in the case of Aorist, the past interpretation results from the *Perfect* tier, which extends backwards from the UT in this case.

(17) $\lambda w.\exists t' [PTS (t',t_c) \wedge \exists e [t' \subseteq \tau (e) \wedge K (w)(e)]]$

$\wedge$

UT $\quad \lambda t.\lambda w.\exists t' [PTS (t',t) \wedge \exists e [t' \subseteq \tau (e) \wedge K (w)(e)]]$

$\wedge$

Perf: $\lambda P.\lambda t.\lambda w.\exists t'[PTS (t',t) \wedge P (t')(w)]$ AspP: $\lambda t.\lambda w.\exists e [t \subseteq \tau (e) \wedge K (w)(e)]$

In the next section, I discuss the interpretation of the traditionally labeled periphrastic past.

3.2. Periphrastic past

I propose that, in the absence of TP, structures as in (15) and (17), respectively, also refer to periphrastic past, with the past interpretation resulting from the *Perfect* tier. Thus, in terms of temporal interpretation, periphrastic past and Aorist are not substantially different. Rather, Aorist has more connotations, e.g. expressive meaning in sentence-initial position (Halupka-Rešetar & Todorović 2015) or the 'Hot news' Perfect connotations (cf. McCowley 1971), as in (18), which is not necessarily associated with a temporal component (Portner 2003).

(18) Pobediše ovi naši!
win-3.pl.aor these ours
'Our team has won!'

In section 3.3, I propose how to derive the interpretation of future forms when Tense is lacking.

3.3. Future interpretations

Future forms in Serbian are most typically obtained via the auxiliary *hteti* 'will' and infinitive:

(19) a. Ja ću pisati tezu.
I will-1.sg write-**impf**.inf thesis
'I will be writing my thesis.'
b. Ja ću u nekom trenu napisati tezu.
I will-1.sg. in some moment write-**pf**.inf. thesis
'I will have finished my thesis by some point.'

I propose that *hteti* in (19) is the overt realization of the modal *woll* component which introduces a time interval following a contextually salient RTI (20) (cf. backwards-shifting Perfect (14)) (for definitions of *woll*, see Abusch 1985 et seq., Copley 2002, *i.a.*). Combining the *woll* component with the aspectual component, we derive future perfectives (19b) as in (21); the event is included within the time interval following the UT. Future imperfectives (19a) are computed in the same manner, differing only in the viewpoint aspect value.

(20) $[\text{WOLL}]_{MB} = \lambda P.\lambda w.\lambda t.\ \forall w'[w \in' MB(w,t) \rightarrow AT([t,\_),w',P)]$ (Condoravdi 2002)

(21) $\lambda w.\ \forall w'\ [w' \in MB\ (w,t_c) \rightarrow \exists e\ [\tau\ (e) \subseteq [t_c, \_) \wedge K\ (w')(e)]$

$\wedge$

UT $\lambda t.\ \lambda w.\ \forall w'\ [w' \in MB\ (w,t) \rightarrow \exists e\ [\tau\ (e) \subseteq [t, \_) \wedge K(w')(e)]$

$\wedge$

$\text{woll}_{MB}: \lambda P.\lambda t.\lambda w.\ \forall w'[w' \in MB(w,t) \rightarrow P([t, \_)\ (w')]]$ AspP: $\lambda t''.\lambda w''.\exists e\ [\tau(e) \subseteq t'' \wedge K\ (w'')(e)]$

Note that the observed interpretations of traditional past and future forms in Serbian can also be captured under the TP-analysis of Serbian. However, the following section shows that there is a range of interpretations of these forms which are predicted and easily captured under a no-TP analysis, but which are puzzling under the analysis which posits Tense in the language.

3.4. Relative interpretations of Perfect and woll

By pursuing the no-TP analysis of Serbian, we are making the following prediction regarding the availability of interpretations: if Perfect and *woll* are, unlike Tense, non-deictic components, i.e. not strictly extending backwards/forward from the UT, then forms containing them should also allow for non-past or non-future interpretation, respectively. This prediction is borne out.

Consider first future forms. In addition to future interpretation, they can receive past interpretation in certain embedded clauses, as in (22).

(22) Jovan je onomad rekao da će doći u julu. Sad je avgust, a
Jovan is back.then said that will come in July now is August and
njega niod korova.
him not.even from weed
'Jovan said back then that he would come in July. It's August and he's nowhere to be found.'

Next, periphrastic past, which contains Perfect, can receive future interpretation, e.g. in matrix clauses:

(23) Ako nas uhvate, nastradali smo. (Riđanović 2012: 309)
if us.cl catch-3.pl.pres. suffered are
'If they catch us, we've had it.'

If Aorist also contains Perfect, we expect it to be able to receive non-past interpretation. Indeed, it can be used to denote future (24a) or habitual interpretation (24b).

(24) a. Nema nam spasa, pomrijesmo od gladi!
not.have-3.sg. we-acc. salvation die-**aor**.1.pl from hunger
'We can't be saved – we will starve to death.'
(Riđanović 2012: 317)
b. Ne diraj mi kompjuter ti pokvari svešto dotakneš.
not touch I-dat. computer you break-**aor**.2.sg all that touch-pres.2.sg.
'Don't touch my computer, you break everything you handle!'
(Riđanović 2012: 316)

The available interpretations in (22)–(24) are exactly what is expected under the no-TP analysis – unlike Tense, which is necessarily anchored to the UT, *Perfect* and *woll* introduce an interval which extends backwards/forward from a point which does not have to be the UT. In other words, atypical interpretations of these forms follow from the structure which contains these components and lacks Tense, and are otherwise puzzling under the analysis which posits Tense in the structure.

4. Re-examining traditional labels: Participles in Slavic

As shown by the semantic distribution of Aorist and Imperfect in Serbian and Bulgarian, traditionally labeled tenses show temporal properties in Bulgarian, but not in Serbian. Unlike Bulgarian and Serbian (to some extent), Slovenian, Polish and Russian do not use Aorist and Imperfect. Instead, for obtaining past interpretations, these languages make use of participles (all these languages lack TP (Todorović 2016)), as in Slovenian in (25a). Crucially, participles in Slovenian are also used for obtaining future interpretations (25b). Migdalski (2013) takes this as an indication that participles are not specified for past tense in Slovenian (and more generally in Slavic).

(25) a. Miha je udaril Ano.
Miha is hit-part. Ana
'Miha hit Ana.'

b. Vsi bodo dosegli svoj cilj.
Everyone be.pfv.1sg reach.part.pl self's goal
'Everyone will reach his/her goal.'
(Franks & King 2000: 33)

Similar non-past uses of participles are observed in Russian (antecedents of conditionals, regardless of their temporal orientation) and Polish (future-interpretations). Todorović (2016) argues that these forms also contain the *Perfect* component which introduces the interval extending backwards from the contextually salient RTI. Crucially, given that the *Perfect* is a non-deictic component, it does not necessarily have to span backwards from the UT. This is what I propose also captures future interpretation of these forms in Slavic. Furthermore, the lack of obligatory past-orientation of traditional past participles in Slavic, and the different semantic properties of Aorist and Imperfect in Serbian and Bulgarian call for re-examination of traditional verbal labels (for an elaborate discussion and additional evidence from Romance, see Todorović (2016)).

5. Conclusion

Taking as the initial point the parametric variation in the presence/absence of TP, I argued that such a two-partite division can account for semantic cross-linguistic differences. I focused on the aspectual distribution in Aorist and Imperfect in Serbian and Bulgarian, showing that these forms are unconstrained only in Bulgarian. I argued that the distribution follows from Bulgarian being a TP language and Serbian being a no-TP language. Furthermore, I explored how temporal interpretation is obtained in the absence of TP in Serbian, and showed that it can be derived by means of aspectual and modal components. I also showed that the absence of Tense in Serbian captures a range of available non-deictic interpretations, which are otherwise puzzling under the analysis which posits Tense in the language. Finally, semantic properties of Aorist and Imperfectum and participles in Slavic indicate that very often traditional labels should be re-examined.

References

Abusch, Dorit. 1985. "On verbs and time." PhD thesis, University of Massachusetts.

Bohnemeyer, Jürgen. 2002. *The Grammar of Time Reference in Yucatec Maya*. Lincom Europa.

Bošković, Željko. 2008. "What Will You Have, DP or NP?" In *Proceedings of the North East Linguistic Society* 37. Amherst, MA: GLSA, University of Massachusetts, 101–114.

Bošković, Željko. 2012. "On NPs and Clauses." In *Discourse and grammar: From sentence types to lexical categories* [= Studies in Generative Grammar 112], Gunther Grewendorf and Thomas Ede Zimmermann (eds.). Berlin: Walter de Gruyter, 179–242.

Chierchia, Gennaro. 1998. "Reference to kinds across languages." *Natural Language Semantics* 6: 339–405.

Condoravdi, Cleo. 2002. "Temporal Interpretation of Modals: Modals for the Present and the Past". In *The Construction of Meaning*, David I. Beaver, Luis D. Casillas Martinez, Brady Z. Clark, Stefan Kaufmann (eds.). CSLI Publications, 59–288.

Copley, Bridget. 2002. "The semantics of the future." PhD thesis. MIT.

Corver, Norbert. 1992. "On Deriving Left Branch Extraction Asymmetries." In *Proceedings of North East Linguistic Society* 22. Amherst, MA: GLSA, University of Massachusetts, 67–84.

Despić, Miloje. 2011. "Syntax in the Absence of Determiner Phrase." PhD thesis, University of Connecticut.

Despić, Miloje. 2013. "Binding and the Structure of NP in Serbo-Croatian." *Linguistic Inquiry* 44: 239–270.

Franks, Steven and Tracy Holloway King. 2000. *A Handbook of Slavic Clitics*. New York: OUP.

Giorgi, Alessandra and Fabio Pianesi. 1997. *Tense and Aspect: From Semantics to Morphosyntax*. Oxford: OUP.

Halupka-Rešetar, Sabina and Neda Todorović. 2015. "Serbian verbs and nouns front to be expressive." In *Grazer Linguistische Studien 83*, Remus Gergel and Andreas Blümel (eds.). Karl-Franzens-Universität Graz, 139–148.

Iatridou, Sabine, Elena Anagnostopoulou and Roumyana Izvorski. 2001. "Observations about the Form and Meaning of the Perfect." In *Ken Hale: A Life in Language*, Michael J. Kenstowicz (ed.), 189–238. Cambridge: MIT Press.

Kang, Jungmin. 2014. "On the Absence of TP and Its Consequences: Evidence from Korean." PhD thesis, University of Connecticut.

Klein, Wolfgang. 1994. *Time in language*. London and New York: Routledge.

Klein, Wolfgang, Ping Li and Hemriette Hendriks. 2000. "Aspect and assertion in Mandarin Chinese." *Natural Language and Linguistic Theory* 18: 723–770.

Kratzer, Angelika. 1998. "More Structural Analogies between Pronouns and Tenses." In *Proceedings from Semantics and Linguistic Theory* 8: 92–110.

Lin, Jo-Wang. 2006. "Time in a Language without Tense: The Case of Chinese." *Journal of Semantics* 23: 1–53.

Matthewson, Lisa. 2006. "Temporal Semantics in a Superficially Tenseless language." *Linguistics and Philosophy* 29: 673–713.

Migdalski, Krzysztof. 2013. "Diachronic Source of two cliticization patterns in Slavic." In *Challenging Clitics*, Christine Meklenborg Salvesen and Hans Petter Helland (eds.). John Benjamins Publishing, 135–158.

Pancheva, Roumyana. 2003. "The Aspectual Makeup of Perfect Participles and the Interpretations of the Perfect." In *Perfect Explorations*, Artemis Alexiadou, Monika Rathert, Arnim von Stechow (eds.). Mouton de Gruyter, 277–306.

Portner, Paul. 2003. "The (temporal) semantics and (modal) pragmatics of the perfect." *Linguistics and Philosophy* 26: 459–510.

Riđanović, Midhat. 2012. *Bosnian for Foreigners – with a comprehensive grammar*. Sarajevo: Rabic.

Ritter, Elizabeth and Martina Wiltschko. 2014. "The composition of INFL. An exploration of tense, tenseless languages, and tenseless constructions." *Natural Language and Linguistic Theory*, 32: 1331–1386.

Sawada, Tsuyoshi. 2015. "Pleonastic Merger." PhD Thesis. University of Connecticut, Storrs.

Scatton, Eric. 1984. *A Reference grammar of modern Bulgarian*. Cambridge, Mass.: Slavica Publishers.

Smith, Carlota. 1991. *The Parameter of Aspect*. Dordrecht: Kluwer.

Smith, Carlota and Mary S. Erbaugh. 2005. "Temporal interpretation in Mandarin Chinese." *Linguistics* 42: 713–756.

Stanojčić, Živorad and Ljubomir Popović. 1992. *Gramatika sprskog jezika*. Zavod za udžbenike i nastavna sredstva. Beograd.

Tonhauser, Judith. 2011. "Temporal Reference in Paraguayan Guaraní." *Linguistics and Philosophy* 34: 257–303.

Todorović, Neda. 2016. "On the Presence/Absence of TP: Syntactic properties and temporal interpretation." PhD thesis, University of Connecticut.

Wiltschko, Martina. 2003. "On the Interpretability of Tense on D and its Consequences for Case Theory." *Lingua* 113: 659–696.

Ana Werkmann Horvat

On Modal Strength in Croatian: A Judge Parameter Analysis

1. Introduction*

This paper aims to explore the modal strength relationship between necessity and possibility modals in Croatian. In English, the difference in modal strength manifests itself in the relationship between necessity modals, e.g. *must* and *ought* (Rubinstein 2012). Croatian data shows, on the other hand, that the modal strength effect can be found in possibility modals as well. This data offers further insight into some of the questions raised by Rubinstein (2012) about the existence of strong and weak possibility modals in natural languages.

The central question of this paper deals with contextual features that determine the strength of modal auxiliaries. My analysis explores the strength relationship between Croatian necessity and possibility modals (*morati* 'must, have to', *smjeti* 'may, to be allowed', *trebati* 'ought to, should', and *moći* 'may, can'), showing that modals rely on the nature of authority in the context in question. This analysis is grounded in Stephenson's work (2008) on epistemic modals, which is based on a judge parameter that acts as a contextual parameter. Crucially, it also shows that there are more similarities between non-epistemics and epistemics than initially suggested in the previous literature. The novelty of this approach lies in the fact that it can account for differences in strength by rejecting the domain restriction approach, which yields wrong results, while still maintaining Kratzer's (1981, 1991, 2012) notion of ordering sources.

* This paper is mainly based on parts of my master's thesis (Werkmann 2014). I would like to thank my master's thesis supervisor Dr Ana Arregui for invaluable advice and discussion, and Dr María Luisa Rivero, the reader of my thesis, for all of her informative feedback. I would also like to thank my informants for their help and patience in providing data and grammaticality judgements. Of course, any errors herein are my own. This project was funded by an Admission Scholarship from the University of Ottawa.

2. The puzzle

The primary goal of this proposal is to account for differences in modal strength between necessity modals (*morati* and *trebati*), as well as between possibility modals (*smjeti* and *moći)*. The test that is usually employed to demonstrate the modal strength differences are structures such as (1) and (2) (Rubinstein 2012, von Fintel & Iatridou 2008):

(1) You *ought* to open the door, in fact, you *must*.

(2) ?You *must* open the door, in fact, you *ought to*.

In sentences like (1) and (2), one order is acceptable, i.e. weak – strong (as in (1)), while the opposite order, i.e. strong – weak (as in (2)), does not yield an acceptable structure. Modal scalarity, which depends on modal strength, is tightly connected to the notion of scalar implicatures; that is, when ordered according to their strength, modals behave similarly to other language elements that trigger scalar implicatures (Horn 1972, 1989, Levinson 2000). This means that modals that are higher on the scale directly entail the truth of the lower element as well. Further, according to Gricean reasoning (Grice 1975), a cooperative speaker would commit to the stronger element if they could. The weaker propositions must come first; otherwise, the Gricean maxim *Be informative* is violated. In other words, the proposition expressed by the second clause must not be entailed by the first one.

This type of contrast has been used repeatedly in the literature to demonstrate the scalar position of modals and quantifiers (Copley 2006, von Fintel and Iatridou 2008, Rubinstein 2012). The same relationship exists between Croatian necessity modals:

(3)	*Trebaš*	oprati	ruke,	ustvari,	*moraš*.
	ought.PRS.2SG	wash.INF	hands	in-fact	must.PRS.2SG

'You ought to wash your hands, in fact, you have to.'

(4)	?*Moraš*	oprati	ruke,	ustvari,	*trebaš*.
	must.PRS.2SG	wash.INF	hands	in-fact	ought.PRS.2SG

'You have to wash your hands, in fact, you ought to.'

This is in line with native speaker judgements, who judge *morati* to be stronger, or more binding, than *trebati*.

On the other hand, if the same test is applied to possibility modals in Croatian, neither order works.

(5) ?*Moraš* oprati ruke, ustvari, *smiješ*.
may.PRS.2SG wash.INF hands in-fact may.PRS.2SG
'You may wash your hands, in fact, you are allowed to.'

(6) ?*Smiješ* oprati ruke, ustvari, *možeš*.
may.PRS.2SG wash.INF hands in-fact may.PRS.2SG
'You are to allowed wash your hands, in fact, you may.'

The puzzle lies in the fact that native speaker intuitions confirm that there is a strength relationship between possibility modals that cannot be captured by the above mentioned test (in (1) and (2)). If the test worked for (5) and (6), example (5) should be acceptable since native speakers consistently judge *smjeti* to be stronger. These intuitions are exemplified in 7 (a) and (b) and 8 (a) and (b).[1]

(7) Context: Your friend does not like if people start eating before everyone is sitting. Once everyone is seated, she says:
a. Sada *možete* jesti.
now may.PRS.2PL eat.INF
'You may now eat.'
b. ?Sada *smijete* jesti.
now may.PRS.2PL eat.INF
'You are now allowed to eat.'

(8) Context: The head commander in an army base never lets anyone eat before all soldiers are seated. Once everybody is seated, he says:
a. Sada *smijete* jesti.
now may.PRS.2PL eat.INF
'You are now allowed to eat.'
b. ?Sada *smijete* jesti.
now may.PRS.2PL eat.INF
'You may now eat.'

Akin to judgments for *morati*, native speakers report that *smjeti* carries the same sense of authority that is based on rules, regulations and consequences. These strength differences cannot be captured in an approach that is based on domain restriction, as shown in (5) and (6) since the entailments do not behave in the predicted manner.

1 My claim here is not that 7(b) and 8(b) are not acceptable at all, but rather that they are less acceptable in these contexts than the 7(a) and 8(a), mainly due to semantic-pragmatic reasons which will be discussed shortly.

3. Current proposals

Building on Kratzer's theory of modality,[2] von Fintel & Iatridou (2008) explore the idea that the semantics of weak necessity modals should include the distinction between the favoured worlds and the worlds among them who are the very best worlds of the most favoured worlds. The semantics of weak necessity modals such as *ought* would then include what is best, while the semantics of strong necessity modals would include what is required (von Fintel & Iatridou 2008). To achieve this distinction, they propose that weak necessity modals use an additional secondary ordering source that the strong modals do not use, to pick out and rank only the best of the already ordered worlds by the first ordering source. This means that weak epistemic modals would be sensitive, not just to hard evidence, but also to a set of propositions defining normalcy (the secondary ordering source), while weak deontic[3] modals would be sensitive to a less 'coercive' (von Fintel and Iatridou 2008: 119) set of rules in the secondary ordering source, in addition to the laws and regulations from the primary ordering source. Note that this account only suggests a solution for necessity modals – it does not offer tools to distinguish between possibility modals such as *smjeti* and *moći*.

As a critique of von Fintel and Iatridou's approach, Rubinstein (2012) raises the issue of the account's capability to determine which propositions go to the primary ordering source, and which to the secondary. One can intuitively determine which rules matter more and which less. However, that is not enough. There ought to be a clearer way to differentiate between propositions that belong to different ordering sources. Without a strict criterion for determining the differences between the ordering sources, this approach is not able to capture the differences between *ought* and *must* (Rubinstein 2012). However, even if it is possible to distinguish between propositions that belong to primary ordering

---

2 According to Kratzer (1981, 1991, 2012), modals quantify either universally or existentially over a set of possible worlds. The set of possible worlds over which the modal is quantifying is calculated from a modal base and an ordering source which ranks possible worlds from the modal base, while different modal flavours arise from the interaction of the modal base and the ordering source. The modal base takes into account relevant circumstances that hold in this world. An ordering source maps worlds to sets of propositions. It orders or ranks the worlds in which these rules are respected from the best to worst resulting in the set of only the most favoured worlds.

3 While the term *deontic* appears often in the literature, in this paper I will be using the term *priority modality* (Portner 2008; Werkmann Horvat 2017), to refer to a modal flavour category that includes flavours that are sometimes called *deontic, bouletic* and *teleological* flavour (Kratzer 2012; von Fintel 2006).

sources versus the ones that belong to secondary ones, there remains the intuition that weak necessity modals are, in fact, only sensitive to what can be found in secondary ordering sources, and not to the coercive set of rules from the primary ordering source.

Furthermore, for Rubinstein, the main concern lies in determining which properties of any conversational background are most relevant when deciding on the appropriate necessity modal in a given context. That is, what semantic features of weak and strong necessity modals make speakers select one over the other (Rubinstein 2012)? To answer these questions, Rubinstein proposes an analysis in which a presupposition about collective commitment plays a crucial role in determining the selection of modals. When a speaker uses a strong necessity modal, they presuppose a collective commitment to what is being said, whereas if a speaker were to use a weak necessity modal, they presuppose that the secondary priorities are still up for discussion, i.e. strong necessity modals rely on priorities that are presupposed to be collectively committed to in a given context, whereas weak necessity modals take into account priorities that are presupposed not to be collectively committed to (Rubinstein 2012).

Rubinstein's proposal uses a modal base and an ordering source, but it also includes priority slates, defined as 'individual records of the priorities that the participants in context are publicly committed to' (Rubinstein 2012: 78). She also adds that every proposition *p* in the ordering source need to be collectively committed to. Although Rubinstein uses the same tools for ordering the most favoured set of worlds as von Fintel and Iatridou (2008), she rejects their notion of secondary ordering sources and introduces the notion of secondary priorities restricting the domain to get the weak meaning in a necessity modal. As opposed to primary ordering sources, secondary priorities are not 'allotted a designated slot in the discourse context' (Rubinstein 2012: 80). Example (9) is the final lexical entry Rubinstein proposes for weak necessity modals:

(9) [[**ought to**]] $=\lambda q_{<s,t>}. \lambda w. \forall w': w' \in Fav(w) \cap C$ and b is a pertinent b.q (w'), where b is a secondary priority in answer to QUD[C4]

For Croatian data, this analysis implies that *morati* relies only on the primary ordering sources. On the other hand, *trebati* (lexical entry in (9)) considers what is good, recommended, and will lead to the best outcome, therefore, relying on secondary priorities. In other words, strong necessity modals take into account

---

4 Due to the page limit, I can not elaborate on Question Under Discussion (QUD) and Pertinent Answer. For more on that see Rubinstein's thesis from 2012, pp. 82.

primary ordering sources which rely on what is non-negotiable, while weak necessity modals rely on what is negotiable. This means that Rubinstein's analysis predicts weak necessity modals to take into account both non-negotiable and negotiable norms. However, Croatian data suggests that weak necessity modals do not respond to non-negotiable priorities at all. This is exemplified by the following data in (10) and (11).

(10) Context: There has been a diplomatic scandal between Croatia and Cuba. The Cuban diplomat is still in Croatia, but a lot of people think that the best thing to do is for him to go back to Cuba until the things calm down. A couple of co-workers discuss this after listening to the news.
Diplomat *treba/?mora* napustiti Hrvatsku.
diplomat ought.PRS.3SG/must.PRS.3SG leave.INF Croatia
'The diplomat ought to/?must leave Croatia.'

Since there is no collective commitment to what these colleagues are discussing among themselves, meaning that for the Cuban diplomat, this is a negotiable norm, I propose that there is no primary priority involved in the Cuban diplomat's leaving Croatia. In other words, no strict laws or regulations apply here; the only thing *trebati* is sensitive to are secondary priorities which, in turn, ensures the best outcome. However, they are not and cannot be bound by obligations and consequences if the propositions are not executed in the end. Thus, I suggest that a weak necessity modal is not, in fact, sensitive to non-negotiable norms at all, as predicted by Rubinstein's domain restriction account. Rather, a strong necessity modal is felicitous (and obliges participants to certain actions) in a different scenario:

(11) Context: There has been a diplomatic scandal between Croatia and Cuba. The Cuban diplomat is still in Croatia, but the Prime Minister of Croatia has decided that he must leave the country, for the two countries to preserve their good relationship. He issues an official statement.
Diplomat *mora/?treba* napustiti Hrvatsku.
diplomat must.PRS.3SG/ought.PRS.3SG leave.INF Croatia
'The diplomat must/?ought to leave Croatia.'

It seems that although the same priority is in question here, it has switched its status. The same priority, namely, to preserve the peace between the two countries, has now changed its status, from a secondary to a primary priority, and there is a different collective commitment, as all the participants are collectively committed to this priority. Therefore, strong necessity modals are sensitive to non-negotiable priorities, while weak necessity modals are sensitive to what is still negotiable and/or up for discussion.

4. Judge dependency in Croatian priority modals

4.1. Necessity modals

Stephenson (2007) suggests that the semantics of epistemic modals do not only rely on quantificational force and the nature of the modal base, but also on the person whose knowledge is relevant. Many scholars have tried to answer whose knowledge matters when the modal acquires the epistemic flavour (DeRose 1991, Egan, Hawthorne and Weatherson 2005, von Fintel and Gillies 2011). To account for the *knowers'* dependency of epistemic modals, Stephenson (2007) introduces the judge parameter which has previously been used by Lasersohn (2005) for predicates of personal taste. This is Stephenson's final proposal:

(12) $[[\textbf{might}]]^{c;w,t,j} = [\lambda.p_{<s,<i,et>>.}\ \exists<w',t',x>\in \text{Epist}_{w,t,j}: p(w')(t')(x) = 1]$

(13) $[[\textbf{must}]]^{c;w,t,j} = [\lambda.p_{<s,<i,et>>.}\ \forall<w',t',x>\ \text{Epist}_{w,t,j}: p(w')(t')(x) = 1]$

This approach employs the judge parameter in the semantics of epistemic modals by making the judge the person whose knowledge is relevant. The judge dependency is built directly into the meaning of the modals, 'so that … given a world-time-judge triple <w,t,j>, might p is true iff p is compatible with what j knows in w at t' (Stephenson 2007: 32). One of the questions Stephenson (2007) raises is whether analyses of other expressions, apart from predicates of personal taste and epistemic modals, could use the judge parameter as well. Following accounts such as Kratzer's (1981, 1991, 2012), which assume a unified account for epistemic and non-epistemic modals, I explore the idea that perspectival dependence plays a role in the semantics of priority modals as well.[5]

My proposal explores the way the judge parameter could be utilized to account for differences in strength in priority modals. I also show that, though it is not the matter of knowledge in the priority flavour, but rather the matter of authority that determines the rules and regulations in the modal base, the judge parameter can still be used to account for differences in modal strength. Consider the following two contexts.

5 However, note that there exists Croatian modal data which shows that epistemic and non-epistemic modals are structurally different and therefore a truly unified account might be difficult to achieve. For more on that, see Werkmann Horvat (2017).

(14) Context: Ivan is 10 years old. His mom comes to his room.

Moraš	pospremiti	sobu.
must.PRES.2SG	clean.INF	room

'You must clean the room.'

(15) Context: Ivan is 30 years old. His mom comes to visit him in his apartment.

Trebaš	pospremiti	sobu.
ought.PRES.2SG	clean.INF	room

'You ought to clean the room.'

There is a difference in the nature of authority in (14) and (15). The authority in (14) relies on non-negotiable norms, thus if Ivan rejects (14), the mother has the authority to impose certain consequences. In other words, the mother's level of authority is higher than that of Ivan's which is why she has the *privilege* to use a strong necessity modal. On the other hand, a pragmatically felicitous response to (15) would be Ivan's rejection of the propositions, or the unwillingness to take heed of the suggestion. In that case, the mother would respect the answer and accept it as a felicitous answer since the strength of her authority is not high enough. To differentiate between the two different types of authority, I suggest a division between a *dominant* and a *non-dominant authority*. The dominant authority proposes non-negotiable norms, while a non-dominant authority proposes negotiable norms. Thus, in a context where a weak necessity modal is used, the participants are non-dominant, while in a context where a strong necessity modal is used, the speaker using the strong necessity modal is a dominant authority over the other participant(s) in the conversational context. This suggests that while both necessity modals are universal quantifiers, they are sensitive to other contextual features, such as the properties of conversational participants, namely the level of dominance they carry in this conversation. The dominance of the authority also determines the level of obligation to the proposition. Propositions of a dominant authority are collectively committed to, whereas the ones that are proposed by a non-dominant authority are not collectively committed to. This is supported by the fact that the conversational participant can reject propositions made by a non-dominant authority, while they do not retain the same right if the proposition is made by a dominant authority.

Therefore, based on these assumptions, the lexical entries I suggest for the priority modals *morati* and *trebati* are:

(16) $[[\textbf{morati}]]^{c,g,f,j} = \lambda p.\lambda w.\forall w' \in max_g^{\,j}(w)\,(\cap f(w)):p(w')=1$

(17) $[[\textbf{trebati}]]^{c,g,f} = \lambda p.\lambda w.\forall w' \in max_g(w)\ (\cap f(w)):p(w')=1$

Lexical entries in (16) and (17) are based on Kratzer's approach (2012), which uses ordering sources. Both modals are still considered to be universal quantifiers, however, their ordering sources are different; that is, the crucial difference between the denotation proposed for *morati* as opposed to *trebati* is the existence of the notion of judge in (16) (based on Stephenson (2008)), which is added to the index and is of type *e*. This combination of Kratzter's and Stephenson's accounts considers context, modal base, ordering source and the judge parameter as contextual parameters.[6] The judge parameter influences the ordering source, i.e. modifies max_g. What differentiates the regular max_g from max_g^j is the influence the judge parameter has on the ordering of the worlds (the *g(w)* is determined by *j)*. In addition to the ordering source, which is a part of both denotations, in (16) the possible worlds from the modal base are ordered from the perspective of the judge, that is, the ordering source is *judge-sanctioned.* In the case of *morati* and *trebati*, the modal base and the ordering source interact to delimit the domain of quantification, but in the case of *morati*, the judge parameter determines the ordering. Additionally, for *morati*, the judge responds to the pragmatically dominant authority. Since the dominant authority has influence over consequences of not respecting propositions, it influences the ordering of the worlds in the modal base according to the rules proposed by the judge. A judge here has the *power* to determine the priorities in the ordering source. In other words, the judge can impose a certain ordering and has the *power* to enforce consequences if it happens that the actual world does not end up being one of the ideal worlds. On the other hand, *trebati* does not depend on the judge parameter. Contexts with *trebati* do not include a dominant authority, the ordering of the worlds depends on what is the best or recommended, without the influence of a non-dominant authority. In other words, the ordering source is not influenced by a judge, but only by which world is the best according to contextually determined parameters, just like any other ordering source in previously discussed approaches.

It might be claimed that the judge parameter is not necessary, and that the difference between modals lies in the type of rules. For example, *morati* is used in contexts in which the rules are stronger, law-like and the breaking of these rules

6 For a different view on whether modal base and the ordering source are to be considered contextual parameters or arguments of the modal, see Werkmann Horvat (2017). Note, however, that Werkmann Horvat (2017) is not concerned with the modal strength differences between different modals.

is somehow punishable, while *trebati* relies on softer rules. Even if we put aside the difficulty of differentiating between these rules (using formal and/or cognitive tools), which Rubinstein (2012) also identifies, the nature of the rules still does not capture the strength differences. Recall examples (14) and (15), here repeated as (18) and (19):

(18) Context: Ivan is 10 years old. His mom comes to his room.
Moraš pospremiti sobu.
ought.PRES.2SG clean.INF room
'You must clean the room.'

(19) Context: Ivan is 30 years old. His mom comes to visit him in his apartment.
Trebaš pospremiti sobu.
ought.PRES.2SG clean.INF room
'You ought to clean the room.'

The rules that these two examples rely on are basically the same. If we try to identify them, we would probably be able to come up with something like: *One keeps his/her room clean when guests are coming, One leaves good impression on relatives* etc. Clearly, these laws are not very strong or law-like; still, it is felicitous to use a strong necessity modal. The crucial difference lies in who is pragmatically *allowed* to use a strong necessity modal. This supports the idea that the difference in use of strong versus weak necessity modals does not only depend on the nature and strength of the rules but also on the nature of the speaker. An approach that only relies on the rules in a given context could not account for these differences.

Therefore, the main strength of this approach is its ability to capture the fact that weak necessity modals do not rely on the same non-negotiable facts as strong necessity modals. Proposals by von Fintel and Iatridou (2008) and Rubinstein (2012), which are based on domain restriction, assume that the same rules that count for strong necessity modals remain true for weak necessity modals. This also implies that there is a strict version of a modal scale in which strong modals fully entail weak modals which follows from any domain restriction approach. I argue that weak necessity modals are not sensitive to the same ordering source as strong necessity modals, and avoid this issue by avoiding a domain restriction analysis.

Furthermore, the judge parameter borrowed from Stephenson (2008) offers an intuitive way of capturing the relevant distinctions in modal strength. What makes this idea even more appealing is the fact that this type of analysis would build on Kratzer's notion of ordering source while at the same time allowing us to draw parallels between non-epistemics and epistemics. However, in the non-epistemic priority flavour, it is not the relevant *knowers* that we care about, but rather the relevant *authorities*.

4.2. Possibility modals

Von Fintel and Iatridou (2008) and Rubinstein (2012) mainly focus on necessity modals, but the latter briefly acknowledges the need to account for possibility modals as well. Usually, differences in strength are reported between different necessity modals (*must* stronger than *ought*), or between necessity and possibility modals (*must* stronger than *may*). While Croatian possibility modals *smjeti* and *moći* also seem to exhibit modal strength differences, they are not positioned on a scale as neatly as necessity modals. In other words, entailments which are true for necessity modals do not work in the same manner for possibility modals.

Recall examples 7(a–b) and 8(a–b). Native speakers report that *smjeti* carries a notion of stronger authority which can impose consequences if not respected. On the other hand, *moći* is reported to be weaker, relating to what is recommended, but not obligatory. This is similar to the intuitions reported for necessity modals. Since the quantificational strength of both modals is existential, I propose that the difference again lies in the presence of a judge parameter:

(20) $[[\textbf{smjeti}]]^{c,g,f,j} = \lambda p.\lambda w.\exists w' \in max_{g}^{\,j}(w)(\cap f(w)):p(w')=1$

(21) $[[\textbf{moći}]]^{c,g,f} = \lambda p.\lambda w.\exists w' \in max_{g}(w)(\cap f(w)):p(w')=1$

These lexical entries are similar to lexical entries for *morati* and *trebati*, except that they assume existential quantification. Like necessity modals, *smjeti*'s ordering source is judge-sanctioned, while the same is not true for *moći*.

This approach is advantageous to a regular domain restriction approach for the following reasons. Domain restriction approaches use the tests from examples (1) and (2) to predict entailment based on the size of the domain. For example, if lexical items are positioned on a scale, *morati* automatically entails *trebati*, and in addition to *trebati*, it also entails *moći* and *smjeti*. Though the entailments are clear when two necessity modals are compared, or necessity modals to possibility modals, the same relationship cannot be established between the two possibility modals, *smjeti* and *moći* (recall (5) and (6)).

Since *smjeti* is stronger, according to any domain restriction approach, it should have a wider domain over which it is quantifying than the *weaker* possibility modal, *moći*. Moreover, if we assume a smaller domain for *moći* and claim that this is how the weakening occurs, then we are also assuming felicity of the order in which *moći* comes first. However, this order is reported as infelicitous by native speakers. Therefore, this data suggest that the domain restriction approach should be rejected. The judge-parameter analysis correctly predicts that these two are not positioned on a scale but have a different type of relationship since the analysis is not based on domain restriction, but rather on a contextual parameter, which is why it does not follow directly from the analysis that what is stronger must entail what is weaker. Thus, it seems that languages such as Croatian, which are usually classified as systems of modals with scales, cannot be classified so uniformly. While generally Croatian is a system in which scales exist, not all modals can be placed neatly on a scale even when there is a reported intuitive difference in strength. My analysis, in a way, leaves more room for modals, and more options: modals that do or do not have scale-like relations in the same language system.

5. Conclusion

This paper explored modal strength differences in Croatian necessity and possibility priority modals. I suggested a novel analysis for both necessity and possibility modals based on a contextual judge parameter, in line with Stephenson's proposal (2008) for epistemic modals. I proposed that the difference in modal strength does not lie in the strength or size of modal quantification. Rather, modal strength is deeply dependent on the context and the authority which is present and which influences the modal meaning. It has been shown that this analysis is able to account for some intuitive differences native speakers report and previously problematic data. The proposed analysis is not based on quantificational force, as many analyses before suggested, but rather on the notion of judge applied to the ordering source of strong modals *morati* and *smjeti*.

Importantly, Croatian data also shows that possibility modals cannot be positioned on a scale as neatly as necessity modals can. Moreover, the peculiarity of the relationship between the two possibility modals in Croatian offers valuable data to contemporary research of modality and modal strength, as it shows that there is a modal strength relationship between *smjeti* and *moći*. It is not, however, as straightforward as one would expect for such a system as Croatian. The relationship between *smjeti* and *moći* leaves room for further research on the strength relationship between these two modals, and should be explored in future scholarship.

References

Copley, Bridget. 2006. "What should 'should' mean?" In *Ms of a paper given at the Workshop "Language under Uncertainty: Modals, Evidentials, and Conditionals"*, Kyoto University, January 2005.

DeRose, Keith. 1991. "Epistemic possibilities." *Philosophical Review 100*(4): 581–605.

Egan, Andy, John Hawthorne and Brian Weatherson. 2005. "Epistemic modals in context." *Contextualism in philosophy*: 131–168.

von Fintel, Kai. 2006. "Modality and language." In Donald M. Borchert (ed.), *Encyclopedia of philosophy, second edition*. Detroit: MacMillan Reference USA.

von Fintel, Kai and Anthony S. Gillies. 2011 "Might made right." In Andy Egan and Brian Weatherson (eds.), *Epistemic Modality*. Oxford: Oxford University Press, 108–130.

von Fintel, Kai and Sabine Iatridou. 2008. "How to say ought in foreign: The composition of weak necessity modals." In *Time and modality*, Jacqueline Guéron and Jacqueline Lecarme (eds.). Berlin: Springer, 115–141.

Grice, P. Herbert. 1975. "Logic and conversation." *Syntax and semantics 3*: 41–58.

Horn, Lawrence. 1972. "On the semantic properties of logical operators in English." PhD thesis, UCLA.

Horn, Lawrence. 1989. *A natural history of negation*. Chicago: University of Chicago Press.

Knežević, Božana and Irena Brdar. 2011. "Modals and modality in translation: a case study based approach." *Jezikoslovlje 12*(2): 117–145.

Kratzer, Angelika. 1981. "The notional category of modality." *Words, worlds, and contexts*: 38–74.

Kratzer, Angelika. 1991. "Modality." *Semantics: An international handbook of contemporary research*, Arnim von Stechow and Dieter Wunderlich (eds.), 639–650 .

Kratzer, Angelika. 2012. *Modals and conditionals: New and revised perspectives*. Oxford: Oxford University Press.

Lasersohn, Peter. 2005. "Context Dependence, Disagreement, and Predicates of Personal Taste." *Linguistics and philosophy 28*(6): 643–686.

Levinson, Stephen C. 2000. *Presumptive meanings: The theory of generalized conversational implicature*. Cambridge: MIT Press.

Portner, Paul. 2009. *Modality*. Oxford University Press.

Rubinstein, Aynat. 2012. "Roots of modality." PhD thesis, University of Massachusetts Amherst.

Stephenson, Tamina. 2007. "Judge dependence, epistemic modals, and predicates of personal taste." *Linguistics and Philosophy* 30(4): 487–525.

Werkmann, Ana. 2014. "On Modal Strength in Croatian." Unpublished master's thesis, University of Ottawa.

Werkmann Horvat, Ana. 2017. "Layers of Modality." DPhil thesis, University of Oxford.

Jelena Runić

Strong Pronouns in Slavic and Japanese

1. Introduction

Runić (2013) shows that there is a dichotomy between article and article-less languages with regard to clitic interpretation, such that sloppy interpretation of clitics is available only in the latter. This is illustrated in (1b) by Serbo-Croatian (SC), a language without articles, and in (1c) by its genetically similar yet quite different language with respect to the presence (or more precisely, absence) of articles – Macedonian. An appropriate context for both (1b) and (1c) is provided in (1a):[1]

(1) a. The context for sloppy reading:
Nikola and Danilo are best friends. They have many interests in common except their taste in movies is completely different. Specifically, Nikola likes comedies, whereas Danilo likes horror movies. In their town, a movie festival of all film genres takes place every summer. A comedy and a horror movie played at the same time in two different buildings. Given their very different tastes, Nikola and Danilo saw two different movies.

b. Nikola je video film, a video ga je i Danilo.
Nikola AUX.3SG saw film and saw it.CL.ACC AUX.3SG and Danilo
'Nikola saw a movie and Danilo saw it/one too.'
(SC, Runić 2013: 277)

c. Nikola vide (eden) film, a i Danilo go vide.
Nikola saw one film and Danilo it.CL.ACC saw
'Nikola saw a movie and Danilo saw it/*one too.'
(Macedonian, Runić 2013: 277)

In SC (1b), the clitic *ga* in the second conjunct can have a strict reading, referring to its antecedent, *film* (in other words, Nikola and Danilo saw the same film).[2] The English counterpart under such reading is the pronoun *it*. Interestingly, however, the clitic *ga* in the second conjunct can obtain a sloppy reading as well (in other words, the reference does not have to be its antecedent, *film*, from the

---

1 Franks (2013) first noted that the sloppy reading of clitics is possible in Croatian and Slovenian with some speakers.

2 Naturally, for such (strict) interpretation, the context in (1a) is redundant.

first conjunct, but any other such entity (hence, Nikola and Danilo may have seen two different movies). In English, the sloppy reading is typically obtained through the pronoun *one*, since this pronoun does not have referential features. On the contrary, such semantic freedom of clitics is banned in Macedonian (1c), where the pronoun *go* can only obtain a strict interpretation, on a par with the English pronoun *it*. In brief, SC and Macedonian display a strikingly dissimilar behavior with respect to clitic interpretation.[3]

Nonetheless, what was not noted in Runić (2013) is that such semantic flexibility in SC, as well as in other Slavic languages, is disallowed with a strong/full pronoun, as (2c) below demonstrates, in which the strong pronoun *njega* can have only the strict interpretation and thus must refer to the same clown, irrespective of the context in (2a). The contrast between the clitic *ga* and the full pronoun *njega* is straightforward from (2b) and (2c) respectively:

(2) a. The context for sloppy reading:
Nikola and Danilo are cousins who live in two different cities in Serbia. Specifically, Nikola lives in Belgrade, while Danilo lives in Niš. They are both five years old and their parents take them to circus performances whenever a circus is in town. A circus is in both Belgrade and Niš at the same time. Both Nikola and Danilo saw an interesting clown in the circus, albeit not the same one.

b. Nikola je video zanimljivog klovna, a video ga
Nikola AUX.3SG saw interesting clown and saw it.CL.ACC
je i Danilo.
AUX.3SG and Danilo
'Nikola saw an interesting clown and Danilo saw him/one too.'

c. Nikola je video zanimljivog klovna, a njega je
Nikola AUX.3SG saw interesting clown and him.ACC AUX.3SG
video i Danilo.
saw and Danilo
'Nikola saw an interesting clown, and Danilo saw him/*one too.'

Furthermore, the aforementioned pronominal asymmetry between (2b) and (2c) greatly resembles the interpretation of Japanese overt pronouns, which

---

3 Based on the data from other clitic languages, Runić (2013) concludes that there is a principled cross-linguistic variation, and that sloppy reading of clitics is possible only in languages without articles. This finding in turn supports Bošković's (2008, 2012) DP/NP Parameter, according to which languages differ syntactically and semantically depending on the presence/absence of articles in a language.

also seem to be semantically frozen. Thus, Şener and Takahashi (2010), among many others, observe that given an antecedent sentence in (3a), Japanese null arguments in (3b) can have both strict and sloppy interpretation, while overt pronouns (in 3c) can only have a strict interpretation. Consider the following examples (examples (3a) and (3b) are from Şener and Takahashi (2010: 79)):

(3) a. Taro-wa zibun-no hahaoya-o aisiteiru. (Japanese)
Taro-NOM self-GEN mother-ACC love
'lit. Taro loves self's mother.'

b. Hanako-wa ***e*** nikundeiru
Hanako-TOP hates
'Hanako hates *e*.'
(✓Hanako hates her (her = Taro's mother))
(✓Hanako hates her own mother (her = Hanako's mother))

c. Hanako-wa kanojo-o nikundeiru
Hanako-TOP her-ACC hates
'Hanako hates her.'
(✓Hanako hates her (her = Taro's mother))
(✓ Hanako hates her own mother (her = Hanako's mother))

Given the antecedent sentence in (3a), the null object *e* in (3b) can mean that Hanako hates Taro's mother (strict interpretation). Interestingly, the null object in (3b) can also mean that Hanako hates her own mother (sloppy interpretation), on a par with clitics in article-less languages (cf. (1b) and (2b)). Crucially, however, the replacement of the null pronoun with the overt pronoun *kanojo* blocks the semantic flexibility. (3c) thus can only have a strict interpretation, meaning that Hanako hates Taro's mother. Unlike (3b), (3c) cannot mean that Hanako hates her own (Hanako's) mother. Therefore, in terms of semantic freedom, the behavior of overt pronouns in Japanese is identical to the one of strong pronouns in Slavic, showing that the presence of strong/overt pronouns somehow blocks the sloppy interpretation.[4]

In sum, there is close parallelism between overt pronouns in Japanese and full pronouns in SC, showing that phonologically strong pronouns are very different from their null and clitic counterparts. In the remainder of this paper,

4 Similarly, there is close parallelism between clitic pronouns in article-less Slavic languages and null pronouns in Japanese. This state of affairs led Runić (2014) to argue against the prominent Argument Ellipsis Analysis (cf. Saito (2007), *i.a.*), according to which null arguments in Japanese are derived via ellipsis. Instead, Runić (2014) proposes a unified pronominal theory of null elements and clitics.

the distribution of strong/overt pronouns and clitic/null pronouns in SC and Japanese is discussed. In Section 2, I present several situations that have been used as a diagnostic tool for differentiating between strong and deficient pronouns in SC. In Section 3, I test Japanese pronouns to verify whether there is a parallel behavior between Japanese overt and SC strong pronouns. The tests in Section 2 and 3 involve a prominent discourse referent, the Overt Pronoun Constraint (Montalbetti 1984), and backwards pronominalization. After presenting the data, the role of focus is questioned in Section 3. Finally, Section 4 brings concluding remarks.

2. Strong vs. deficient pronouns

Cardinaletti and Starke (1999) posit typological differences between full pronouns and what they label as 'deficient pronouns.'[5] Specifically, they present a number of asymmetries between strong and deficient pronouns, as reflected in syntax, morphology, semantics, and prosody. One of the differences relevant for the discussion at stake involves so-called 'ostension' situations, which involve prominent discourse referents.[6] To illustrate, if a new referent is introduced in the discourse (e.g., by pointing to a person in a group), a strong pronoun is used, while the deficient one can be used only if there is a linguistic antecedent. Despić (2011:241) shows that SC patterns with other languages obeying this rule, French being just one out of many examples, as illustrated in (4a), followed by SC translation in (4b) (the symbol ☞ marks an ostention situation; DEF = deficient; STR = strong).

(4) a. J(e) {*☞**la**} ai aide {✓☞**elle**}. (French)
I her.$_{DEF}$ have helped her.$_{STR}$
b. Pomogao sam {*☞**joj**} /{✓☞**njoj**} (SC)
helped am her.$_{DEF}$ her.$_{STR}$
'I helped ☞her.'

Another diagnostics used for establishing the difference between strong and deficient pronouns is a well-known constraint on full pronouns, as put forth by Montalbetti (1984). Based on a distributional asymmetry between strong and

5 Cardinaletti and Starke (1999) actually propose a theory of tripartite typology of pronouns: strong, weak, and clitics.

6 Other differences include restrictions with respect to coordination and reference to (non)human entity, Θ-/base and peripheral positions, and c-modification. For details, see Cardinaletti and Starke 1999.

deficient pronouns with respect to the bound variable interpretation in Spanish, Montalbetti (1984) formulates the following principle:

(5) *Overt Pronoun Constraint* (OPC) (Montalbetti 1984: 94)
Overt pronouns cannot link to formal variables iff the alternation overt/empty obtains.[7]

How this principle operates can be illustrated with the opposition between Spanish, a language with the "overt/empty"pronominal contrast, and English, which lacks such an alternation. Thus, Spanish cannot use subject overt pronouns as bound variables, as illustrated in (6a), the reason being the availability of *pro* in the Spanish pronominal repertoire (cf. (6b)). English, on the other hand, lacks this pronominal alternation, overt pronouns thus can then function as bound variables, as the translations of (6) confirms: (The Spanish examples are from Montalbetti 1984: 82.)

(6) a. Muchos estudantes$_i$ creen que **ellos**$_{*i/j}$ son inteligentes. (Spanish)
many students believe that they are intelligent
b. Muchos estudantes$_i$ creen que ***pro***$_{i/j}$ son inteligentes.
many students believe that they are intelligent
'Many$_i$ students believe that they$_i$ are intelligent.'

Furthermore, Montalbetti (1984) shows that clitic pronouns, similarly to *pro*, are not subject to the OPC. For example, whereas clitics can be used for the bound-variable interpretation in (7a), the strong pronoun in (7b) cannot fulfill this task.[8] Again, English (7b) is grammatical. This is all illustrated in the following examples: (The Spanish examples are from Montalbetti 1984: 139.)

(7) a. Muchos estudiantes$_i$ creen que Juan los vio [e]$_i$. (Spanish)
many students believe that John them.CL saw
b. *Muchos estudiantes$_i$ creen que Juan los vio [a ellos]$_i$.
many students believe that John them.CL saw them
'Many$_i$ students believe that John saw them$_i$.'

Despić (2011) shows that SC behaves just like Spanish in the relevant respect, as the following example from Despić (2011: 243) demonstrates:

7 What is meant by 'overt/empty' is '*pro* and its overt counterpart' (Montalbetti 1984: 74)
8 Strong object pronouns in Spanish must be doubled, hence the presence of the doubled clitic *los* in (7b).

(8) a. Svaki predsednik misli da ga_i/??$njega_i$ svi vole. (SC)
every president thinks that him.CLITIC/him.STRONG everyone loves
'Every $president_i$ thinks that everybody loves him_i.'
b. Svaki $predsednik_i$ misli da je pro_i/??on najpametniji.
every president thinks that is *pro*/he smartest
'Every $president_i$ thinks that everybody loves him_i.'

Finally, Despić (2011: 273) also shows that, in contrast to English, the backwards anaphora reading in SC is excluded with a strong pronoun; only deficient pronouns can license a backwards anaphora reading. Strong pronouns can only have disjoint reference. This is illustrated with a minimal pair sentence contrast in (9). The examples are taken from Despić 2011: 273).

(9) a. Kada je pro_i ušao u sobu, $Jovan_i$ je počeo plakati. (SC)
when is.AUX *pro* entered in room, Jovan is.AUX started crying
b. Kada je $on_{*i/j}$ ušao u sobu, $Jovan_i$ je počeo plakati.
when is.AUX *pro* entered in room, Jovan is.AUX started crying
'When he entered the room, John started crying.'

It is well-know that if a language has two types of pronouns, deficient and strong, the backwards anaphora reading is possible only with a deficient pronoun. Thus, Larson and Luján (1984), among others, shows that there is a difference in interpretative effects between Spanish overt and null pronouns. Conversely, English lacks these effects due to the absence of the relevant pronominal differences. The difference between Spanish and English is illustrated in (10):[9]

(10) Cuando pro_i/*$él_i$ trabaja, $Juan_i$ no bebe. (Spanish, Larson and Luján 1984:1)
when pro/he works Juan NEG drinks
'When he_i works, $John_i$ doesn't drink.'

In sum, not only are SC strong pronouns unable to obtain a sloppy interpretation, but also they cannot obtain bound-variable and backwards-anaphora

---

9 Note, however, that focalized pronouns in English (which mandatorily bear emphatic stress) cannot co-refer in this context, as illustrated in (i). For discusson, see Akmajian and Jackendoff (1970), among others.
(i) '*When HE_i entered the room, $John_i$ started crying.'

readings. Conversely, only strong pronouns are permitted under ostension circumstances, when a new referent is introduced into the discourse. Before providing an account why such distributional properties occur between strong and deficient pronouns, let us explore whether Japanese overt pronouns pattern with SC strong pronouns. If the distribution of Japanese overt and null pronouns resembles SC strong and deficient pronouns, a unified analysis can then be in order.

3. Strong and deficient pronouns in Japanese and the role of Focus

First of all, in ostension situations, that is, when a new referent is introduced into the discourse, only overt pronouns can be used in Japanese, just like strong pronouns in SC. Thus, an asymmetry between a *pro*/deficient and an overt/strong pronoun is illustrated in (11), showing that only the strong pronoun *kanozy* is allowed in an ostension context:

(11) Watasi-wa {*☞*pro*}/ {✓☞ kanozy-o } tasuke-ta. (Japanese)
I-TOP *pro* she-ACC help-PAST
'I helped ☞her.'

Second, just like SC strong pronouns, Japanese strong pronouns are subject to the Overt Pronoun Constraint (Montalbetti 1984), as illustrated in (12) from Montalbetti (1984: 183):

(12) a. Daremo-ga$_i$ kare-ga$_{*i/j}$ atama-ga ii to omotte iru. (Japanese)
everyone-NOM he-NOM be-smart COMP think
b. Daremo-ga$_i$ $e_{i/j}$ atama-ga ii to omotte iru
everyone-NOM be-smart COMP think
'Everyone thinks that he is smart.'

In (12a), if the overt pronoun *kare* is bound by the quantifier *daremo*, the sentence is ungrammatical. (12b), on the other hand, contains an empty pronoun that can be bound by the quantifier expression *daremo*.

Finally, and again similarly to SC, Japanese overt pronouns are strongly dispreferred in backwards pronominalization contexts, while such reading is perfectly acceptable with *pro*:

(13) a. ??[**Kare-ga**$_{*i/j}$ heya-ni haitta toki] **John-wa**$_{*i/j}$ nakihajimeta. (Japanese)
he-NOM room-DAT entered when John- TOP cry.started

b. [$e_{i/j}$ heya-ni haitta toki] John-wa nakihajimeta
room-DAT entered when John- TOP cry.started
'When he entered the room, John started crying.'

In sum, Japanese overt/strong pronouns behave identically to the SC ones, in that they disallow bound-variable and backwards anaphora readings, while being required in ostension situations. Given the parallelism between the two, I argue that SC and Japanese strong pronouns should be analyzed under the same umbrella.

As mentioned above, the differences between strong and deficient pronouns have reflexes in the grammar across the board – in the syntax, semantics, morphology, and prosody. It has been widely discussed in the literature that strong and other emphatic pronouns are related to focus (Larson and Lujàn 1984, *i.a*). Likewise, clitics in SC have been argued extensively not to be related to focus (Browne 1974; Bošković 2001; Godjevac 2000, *i.a.*).

Based on the above tests, which reveal identical results with respect to the distribution and interpretation of SC and Japanese pronouns, I argue that, not only deficient but also strong pronouns in these languages should follow a unified analysis. The aforementioned situations have been argued to be related to focus. Thus, the ostention situation exhibits a prominent referent, newly introduced into the discourse which is the reflection of information focus. Focus typically cannot interfere with bound variable interpretation.[10] Finally, the backwards anaphora interpretation also requires the lack of focus. Evidence for this comes from English. Normally, English pronouns can act as bound variables because English does not have the morphological difference between strong and deficient pronouns, as illustrated in (14a). Note, however, that when the pronoun is focalized (with the use of stress in English), the sentence automatically becomes ungrammatical, as (14b) reveals:

(14) a. When he works, John doesn't drink. (Larson and Luján 1984: 2)
b. *When HE works, John doesn't drink.

10 See Larson and Luján (1984) and references therein on how these effects disappear when the strong/emphatic pronouns is more deeply embedded or when backwards anaphora is used just as an instance of anaphora (when the adverbial clause is not preposed). See also Despić (2011) for the discussion of focus operator.

Focalized pronouns refer to a unique referent, which thus cannot obtain the sloppy interpretation, but only the strict interpretation. This explains why strong pronouns in SC and Japanese do not have semantic freedom, as the deficient one.[11]

4. Conclusion

In this paper, I have shown that there is a great similarity between strong pronouns in Slavic and overt pronouns in Japanese. Specifically, unlike deficient (null and clitic) pronouns, strong pronouns do not show semantic flexibility and can have only a strict interpretation. In addition, I have run several tests involving a prominent discourse referent, the Overt Pronoun Constraint (Montalbetti 1984), and backwards pronominalization. The present tests have confirmed that Slavic strong pronouns and Japanese overt pronouns behave identically. Finally, I have linked strong pronouns to claims made in relation to emphatic pronouns involving focus.

References

Akmajian, Adrian and Ray Jackendoff. 1970. "Coreferentiality and stress." *Linguistic Inquiry 1*: 124–6.

Bošković, Željko. 2001. *On the Nature of the Syntax-Phonology Interface: Cliticization and Related Phenomena*. Amsterdam: Elsevier.

Bošković, Željko. 2008. "What will you have, DP or NP?" In *North East Linguistic Society (NELS) 37*, Emily Elfner and Martin Walkow (eds.). Amherst, MA: Graduate Linguistic Student Association of the University of Massachusetts at Amherst, 101–14.

11 This means that focus implies interpretation as a type <e> expression. This claim however may be too strong: Non-type <e> expressions can participate in contrastive focus, for example. In such a case, a type distinction between strong and weak pronouns as an independent stipulation would be needed. Another option is the possibility that the focus requirement and anaphoricity of the strong pronouns in the "sloppy" scenarios might be incompatible. Specifically, the pronoun would be anaphoric to the previous noun but also focused to contrast with it. A final option would be to link the contrast to the OPC. On this view, we would treat the sloppy readings as involving true sloppy readings with bound variables rather than as covert indefinites. Then the lack of sloppy readings could derive from the OPC. I leave all the possibilitiesopen.

Bošković, Željko. 2012. "On NPs and Clauses." In *Discourse and Grammar: From Sentence Types to Lexical Categories*, Günther Grewendorf and Thomas Ede Zimmermann (eds.). Boston: Walter de Gruyter, 179–246.

Browne, Wayles. 1974. "On the problem of enclitic placement in Serbo-Croatian." In *Slavic Transformational Syntax*, Richard Domenick Brecht and Catherine V. Chvany (eds.). University of Michigan: Michigan Slavic Publications, 36–52.

Cardinaletti, Anna and Michal Starke. 1999. "The typology of structural deficiency: A case study of the three classes of pronouns." In *Clitics in the Languages of Europe*, Henk van Riemsdijk (ed.). Berlin: Mouton de Gruyter, 145–233.

Despić, Miloje. 2011. "Syntax in the absence of Determiner Phrase." PhD thesis, University of Connecticut.

Franks, Steven. 2013. "The Slovenian orphan accusative, empty pronouns and noun phrase structure." In *The Nominal Structure in Slavic and Beyond*, Lilia Schürcks, Anastasia Giannakidou and Urtzi Etxeberria (eds.). Berlin: Walter de Gruyter, 129–82.

Godjevac, Svetlana. 2000. "Intonation, word order and focus projection in Serbo-Croatian." PhD thesis, Ohio State University.

Larson, Richard and Marta Lujàn. 1984. "Emphatic pronouns." Ms. [First distributed as "Focused pronouns" MIT, 1984.]

Montalbetti, Mario. 1984. "After binding: On the interpretation of pronouns." PhD thesis, MIT.

Runić, Jelena. 2013. "A new look at clitics: Evidence from Slavic." In *Formal Approaches to Slavic Linguistics (FASL) 21*, Steven Franks, Markus Dickinson, George Fowler, Melissa Witcombe and Ksenia Zanon (eds.). Ann Arbor, MI: Michigan Slavic Publications, 275–88.

Runić, Jelena. 2014. "A new look at Argument Ellipsis: Evidence from Slavic." In *NELS 43: Proceedings of the North East Linguistic Society*, Hsin-Lun Huang, Ethan Poole and Amanda Rysling (eds.). Amherst, MA: Graduate Linguistic Student Association of the University of Massachusetts at Amherst, 91–102.

Saito, Mamoru. 2007. "Notes on East Asian Argument Ellipsis." *Language Research* 43: 203–27.

Şener, Serkan and Daiko Takahashi. 2010. "Ellipsis of arguments in Japanese and Turkish." *Nanzan Linguistics* 6: 79–99.

Adrian Stegovec

Stating the Obvious: Unifying Restrictions on Subjects of Imperatives and Subjunctives

1. Introduction

Subject obviation is a phenomenon typically associated with subjunctive mood, and is often analyzed as directly following from some special property of subjunctive verbs. In this paper I look at data from Slovenian concerning imperatives and directive subjunctives, which pattern the same with respect to subject obviation. This can be observed in Slovenian, and not many other languages, due to the possibility of embedded imperatives. I propose that subject obviation can be tied to another phenomenon, the absence of exclusive first person subjects in all matrix directive clauses – imperatives and subjunctives used in directive speech acts. This generalization was in previous work on other languages exactly because of the impossibility of imperative embedding. The two restrictions appeared unrelated to each other because imperatives could never be compared to subjunctives in both matrix and embedded contexts.

1.1. Embedded imperatives

There is a long standing tradition in linguistics to assume that true imperative verbs cannot be embedded (see, among others, Sadock and Zwicky 1985, Han 2000). However, this view has been empirically challenged in the last 10–15 years. Some notable examples of languages that allow imperative embedding are: Korean (Portner 2007, Pak et al. 2008), Japanese (Oshima 2006, Schwager 2006), Old Scandinavian (Rögnvaldsson 1998), Colloquial German (Schwager 2006, Kaufmann and Poschmann 2013), Ancient Greek (Medeiros 2013), Mbyá (Thomas 2012), and (although controversial) even English (Crnič and Trinh 2009).

In Slovenian, embedded imperatives have been shown to occur as restrictive relative clauses and speech reports, illustrated in (1a) and (1b) respectively. In addition, they can also occur as argument clauses, and adnominal complement clauses (Sheppard and Golden 2002).

(1) a. To je film, ki si ga ogle-j čimprej. (Slovenian)
this $_{AUX.3.SG}$ film which self.$_{DAT}$ it.$_{ACC}$ see-$_{IMP.(2.SG)}$ a.s.a.p
'This is a/the film which you should see as soon as possible.'

b. Rekel je, da dela-j bolje.
said.$_{SG.M}$ $_{AUX3.SG}$ that work-$_{IMP.(2.SG)}$ better
'He said that you must work better.' (Sheppard and Golden 2002: 251)

Due to limited space, I cannot discuss the evidence showing that embedded imperatives in Slovenian involve true embedding (as opposed to direct quotation) and true imperatives (as opposed to surrogate verbal forms). For that, I direct the reader to the numerous works that deal with this question in more detail and, in my opinion, conclusively show that embedded imperatives are attested in Slovenian (see Sheppard and Golden 2002, Dvořák 2005, Rus 2005, Dvořák and Zimmermann 2008, Stegovec and Kaufmann 2015, and Stegovec 2016).

1.2. Subject obviation

In many languages, when a verb in the subjunctive mood is embedded under a volitional or directive verb, a ban on co-reference between the embedded and matrix subject is observed. This is illustrated with the Spanish example in (2).[1] If the two subjects are co-referential, the construction is ungrammatical (2a), while if they are not, it is perfectly grammatical (2b).

(2) a. *Queremos$_i$ [que ganemos$_i$]. b. Queremos$_i$ [que ganen$_k$]. (Spanish)
want.$_{1.PL}$ that win.$_{SUB.PRES.1.PL}$ want.$_{1.PL}$ that win.$_{SUB.PRES.3.PL}$
int.: 'We want to win. 'We want them to win.' (Quer 2006: 662)

This phenomenon is standardly called *subject obviation*, capturing the fact that the co-reference restriction applies only between the two subjects. As seen in (3), if the matrix object and the subject of an embedded subjunctive co-refer, the sentence is grammatical.

1 As a convention for marking reference in *pro*-drop languages, indices are put on person marking elements whenever the subject is dropped. This convention is not adopted to reflect the absence of a subject in the syntax, but merely to make glosses less cumbersome by avoiding the use of silent pronouns in the gloss.

(3) a. Les$_i$ pidió$_k$ [que se calleran$_i$]. (Spanish)
to.them ask.$_{PAST.3.SG}$ that$_{REFL}$ be.quiet.$_{SUB.PAST.3.PL}$
'S/he asked them to be quiet.' (Quer 2006: 662)

b. Elisa$_i$ forzó al niño$_k$ a [que tomara$_k$ la medicina]
Elisa forced.$_{3.SG}$ to.the child to that take.$_{SUB.PRES.3.SG}$ the medicine
'Elisa forced the child to take the medicine.' (Kempchinsky 2009: 1791)

Interestingly, although subject obviation is typically associated with subjunctives, the restriction is observed in Slovenian with embedded imperatives. As first noted in Stegovec and Kaufmann (2015), when an imperative is embedded under an attitude verb in Slovenian, its subject cannot be co-referential with the subject of the embedding matrix verb. As seen in (4a), if the matrix subject is 2nd person and the embedded subject is also 2nd person, and thus co-referential, the sentence is ungrammatical. Crucially, this only holds for subjects. As (4b) shows, when a matrix dative object is co-referential with the embedded subject, the same construction is grammatical (cf. (3)). This shows the restriction is indeed subject obviation.

(4) a. *Rekel si$_i$, da si pomaga-j$_i$ sam!
said$_{.SG.M}$ $_{AUX.2.SG}$ that self.$_{DAT}$ help-$_{IMP.(2.SG)}$ alone.$_{SG.M}$
int.: 'You said that you should help yourself on your own!'

b. Rekel (ti$_i$) jek, da mu$_{k,l}$ pomaga-j$_i$ sam!
said.$_{SG.M}$ (you.$_{DAT}$) $_{AUX.3.SG}$ that him.$_{DAT}$ help-$_{IMP.(2.SG)}$ alone.$_{SG.M}$
'He$_k$ said (to you$_i$) that you$_i$ should help him$_{k,l}$ on your own!'

Imperatives are not the only case where subject obviation is observed in Slovenian. *Directive subjunctives,*[2] which (much like subjunctives in Romance) are used with a directive function when no suitable imperative form is available, also pattern the same way. A directive subjunctive in Slovenian consists of a present indicative verb and the modal particle *'naj'*. Its use as a directive speech act is illustrated in (5), where a 3rd person subject is being directed (the addressee or someone else is expected to convey the direction). The directive subjunctive is used here because Slovenian lacks a 3rd person imperative form (see Section 2 for details).

2 Such clauses actually do have limited non-directive uses, which are discussed in Stegovec (2016). However, such non-directive readings are unavailable in embedded contexts, where subject obviation is observed.

(5) (Marko) **naj** <u>naredi</u> to sam!
(Marko.$_{NOM}$) $_{LET}$ do.$_{3.SG}$ this alone.$_{SG.M}$
roughly: 'Marko/he should do it himself.'

The subject obviation pattern is illustrated in (6). In the grammatical (6a), the directive subjunctive has a 1st person subject while the matrix subject is 3rd person (a distinct referent). Crucially, if both subjects are 1st person, as in (6b), the construction is not grammatical.

(6) a. Rekla je$_i$, da naj si pomagam$_k$ sam!
said.$_{SG.F}$ $_{AUX.3.SG}$ that $_{LET}$ self.$_{DAT}$ help$_{-1.SG}$ alone.$_{SG.M}$
'She said that I should help myself on my own!'
b. *Rekel sem$_i$, da naj si pomaga-m$_i$ sam!
said.$_{SG.M}$ $_{AUX.1.SG}$ that $_{LET}$ self.$_{DAT}$ help$_{-1.SG}$ alone.$_{SG.M}$
int.: 'I said that I should help myself on my own!'

The co-reference ban is not restricted to directive subjunctives with 1st person subjects. As seen in (7), 3rd person subjects of embedded directive subjunctives must be interpreted as non co-referential if the matrix subject is also 3rd person, which is a subject obviation pattern.

(7) Rekel je$_i$, da naj si pomaga$_{k,*i}$ sam!
said.$_{SG.M}$ $_{AUX.3.SG}$ that $_{LET}$ self.$_{DAT}$ help.$_{3.SG}$ alone.$_{SG.M}$
'he$_{k,*i}$ said that he$_{k,*i}$ should help himself on his own!'

We will see in the following section that a different restriction on subjects applies with imperatives and directive subjunctives in matrix environments, where crucially the restriction only becomes apparent if the two are analyzed as manifestations of the same construction.

2. Slovenian directive clauses in matrix environments

Most traditional definitions of directive speech acts (directives for short), like the one adopted by Searle (1976), restrict directives only to 2nd person imperatives, But as we have seen in (5), it is possible to perform a directive speech act with clauses where the subject is not 2nd person.[3] I propose directive speech acts are not so restricted and should be defined as in (8).

---

3 See also Stegovec (2016) for more examples and a longer discussion of why (5) is a true directive clause.

Table 1: A comparison of imperative and indicative verbal inflection

	IMPERATIVE		INDICATIVE	
	1P+2P	**2P**	**1P(+2P)**	**2P**
SG.		pomaga-**j**	pomaga-m	pomaga-š
PL.	pomaga-**j**-mo	pomaga-**j**-te	pomaga-mo	pomaga-te
DU.	pomaga-**j**-va	pomaga-**j**-ta	pomaga-va	pomaga-ta

(8) *Directive Speech Act.* A speech act where the speaker of a context *c* attempts to make an individual or group ensure the utterance's propositional content is realized.

The definition in (8) extends the list of potential directive clauses to constructions with 3rd and exclusive 1st person subjects. I will refer to clauses with the canonical function of a directive speech act as *directive clauses.* We will see below that the unification of imperatives and directive subjunctives into a common clause type not only simplifies the discussion of the two constructions, but also makes sense theoretically, as it allows for a straightforward derivation of both subject obviation and the subject restrictions discussed in this section.

2.1. Paradigm gaps in matrix directive clauses

In Slovenian, the imperative paradigm is restricted to 2nd and 1st person (2P and 1P) subjects. The imperative verb agrees in number and, in plural and dual (PL and DU) forms, also in person. In (9), we see 2P imperatives for all number values, which illustrates the presence of both the imperative morpheme *-j-* and the indicative agreement suffix (see also Table 1).[4]

(9) a. Pomaga-j si sam(-a)![5]
help-$_{\text{IMP.(2.SG)}}$ self.$_{\text{DAT}}$ alone.$_{\text{SG.M/-SG.F}}$
'Help yourself on your own!'

4 The examples also show the syntactic presence of a subject through the licensing of the subject oriented anaphor, and the inflected adverb which co-varies with the gender of the subject.

5 This is the only example where the full number paradigm is provided. Unless it is relevant for the discussion, parts of the paradigm will be left out in following examples in

b. Pomaga-j-te si sam-i/-e!
help-$_{\text{IMP-2.PL}}$ self.$_{\text{DAT}}$ alone-$_{\text{PL.M/-PL.F}}$
'Help yourselves on your own!'

c. Pomaga-j-ta si sam-a/-i!
help-$_{\text{IMP-2.DL}}$ self.$_{\text{DAT}}$ alone-$_{\text{DL.M/-DL.F}}$
'Help yourselves(*dual*) on your own!'

Although the paradigm extends to 1P subjects, 1P subjects are restricted to inclusive interpretations, as shown in (10): the 1P.PL subject must be interpreted as including both the speaker (1P) and the addressee (2P). Inclusive interpretations are only possible with non-singular subjects, so there are no 1P.SG imperatives. This is why I refer to the ban on 1P.SG and exclusive 1P.PL/DU subjects in imperatives jointly as the ban on exclusive 1P subjects.

(10) Pomaga-j-ta si sam-a/-i!
help-$_{\text{IMP-1.DU}}$ self.$_{\text{DAT}}$ alone-$_{\text{DU.M/-DU.F}}$
'Let's help ourselves(*dual*) on our own!'

By taking inclusivity to literally reflect the presence of both 1P and 2P features, we can generalize that Slovenian imperatives require a subject with at least 2P features. This can be extended to also explain the lack of 3P imperatives, where the paradigm gap, crucially, does not mean directive clauses in general are restricted to 2P(+1P) subjects. Recall that directive subjunctives are used when an imperative form is unavailable. In directive subjunctives, like (11), the indicative verb inflects for number and person, and the modal particle is invariable.

(11) Naj si pomaga sam(-a)!
$_{\text{LET}}$ self.$_{\text{DAT}}$ help.$_{\text{3.SG}}$ alone.$_{\text{SG.M/-SG.F}}$
'He should help himself on his own!' / 'She must help herself on her own!'

order to save space. Crucially, PL and DU always behave the same and the distinction between SG and PL/DU does not have an effect outside 1P cases.

Table 2: The full paradigm of matrix directive constructions in Slovenian

pomagati (help)	SINGULAR	DUAL	PLURAL
1+2P (imp.)		pomaga-**j**-va	pomaga-**j**-mo
2P (imp.)	pomaga-**j**	pomaga-**j**-ta	pomaga-**j**-te
3P (dir sub.)	**naj** pomaga	**naj** pomaga-ta	**naj** pomaga-jo

The existence of an imperative form for a particular person value blocks the use of directive subjunctives with that person value. Thus, in (12), directive subjunctives are banned with 2P subjects (12a) and 1P.PL/DU subjects (12b) despite the availability of 2P/1P forms.

(12) a. *Naj si pomaga-š sam(-a)!
LET self.$_{DAT}$ help$_{-2.SG}$ alone.$_{SG.M/-SG.F}$ int.:
'Help yourself on your own!'
b. *Naj si pomaga-va sam-a/-i!
LET self.$_{DAT}$ help$_{-1.DL}$ alone.$_{DL.M/-DL.F}$ int.:
'Let's help ourselves(*dual*) on our own!'

Interestingly, although imperatives are restricted to inclusive 1P subjects, (12b) is bad also with an exclusive reading. Thus, while imperatives and directive subjunctives do have a complementary distribution, exclusive 1P subjects are excluded with both imperatives and directive subjunctives. This is further shown in (13), where the banned subject is 1P.SG.

(13) *Naj si pomaga-m sam!
LET self.$_{DAT}$ help$_{-1.SG}$ alone.$_{SG.M}$ int.:
'I should help myself on my own!'

The two kinds of directive clauses have a complementary distribution (summarized in Table 2) with one crucial exception: the exclusive 1P subject ban applies with both. I will argue below that the latter is best analyzed together with subject obviation as part of a more general restriction. In contrast, the complementary distribution of imperatives and directive subjunctives should be analyzed as language specific morpho-syntactic competition.

3. Analysis

We saw in Section 1.2 that in Slovenian, subject obviation is active with both embedded imperatives and directive subjunctives; the subjects of matrix and embedded clauses cannot co-refer. This is illustrated for imperatives with (14) and directive subjunctives with (15).

(14) a. *$[_{CP1}$ **SU**$_i$ **said** $[_{CP2}$ **that SU**$_i$ **V**$_{IMP}$]]
b. $[_{CP1}$ SU$_i$ said $[_{CP2}$ that SU$_k$ V$_{IMP}$]]

(15) a. *$[_{CP1}$ **SU**$_i$ **said** $[_{CP2}$ **that** ***naj***$_{SUB}$ **SU**$_i$ **V**$_{IND}$]]
b. $[_{CP1}$ SU$_i$ said $[_{CP2}$ that *naj*$_{SUB}$ SU$_k$ V$_{IND}$]]

Comparing this to the restrictions in matrix directive clauses illustrated in (16) (for expository purposes the inclusive/exclusive distinction is left out), we see that there is only one gap. Looking at imperatives and directive subjunctives together as one construction, there is only one part of the paradigm with a consistent gap – exclusive 1P subjects (16a, d).

(16) a. *$[_{CP}$ **SU**$_{[1P]}$ **V**$_{IMP}]$ b. $[_{CP}$ SU$_{[2P]}$ V$_{IMP}]$ c. *$[_{CP}$ SU$_{[3P]}$ V$_{IMP}]$
d. *$[_{CP}$ ***naj***$_{SUB}$ **SU**$_{[1P]}$ **V**$_{IND}]$ e. *$[_{CP}$ *naj*$_{SUB}$ SU$_{[2P]}$ V$_{IND}]$ f. $[_{CP}$ *naj*$_{SUB}$ SU$_{[3P]}$ V$_{IND}]$

I will argue below that even though the two restrictions appear to be different on the surface, they are both in fact co-reference restrictions. Note that with embedded directives the matrix subject is the speaker in relation to the reported proposition, so for both (14,15) and the restriction is that the subject cannot also be the person (originally) uttering the proposition. In matrix contexts, an exclusive 1P directive clause means the speaker is both the attitude holder and the subject, and in an embedded context the banned configuration is one where the matrix subject (attitude holder) is the same individual as the embedded subject.

3.1. Binding violations with imperative operators

There are reasons to believe that the meaning of subjunctives can be ate least partly tied to an operator in MoodP (Kempchinsky 1986, 2009, Bianchi 2001), which is positioned between TP and CP. Similar proposals have also been made for imperatives (Schwager 2006, Kaufmann 2012). Following this intuition, I propose all directive clauses, whether surfacing as imperatives or directive subjunctives, have the underlying structure in (17).

(17) $[_{CP}$ C $[_{MoodP}$ OP$_{dir}$ $[_{TP}$ T $[_{vP}$ SU *v* $[_{ApplP}$ (IO) Appl $[_{VP}$ V (DO)]]]]]]

Let us stipulate that this kind operator may be considered a binder for Condition B,[6] and that it is itself bound by the matrix subject (attitude holder) in embedded directive clauses (18a), and by the speaker in matrix directive clauses (cf. also Kempchinsky 1986) (18b). Note that the speaker is actually syntactically represented here as SPEAKER, following Speas and Tenny (2003), but as I argue in Stegovec (2016), it is also possible to derive the binding of OP^{dir} as a parallel to control by extending the system of Pearson (2013).

(18) a. $[_{vP}$ SU_i v $[_{VP}$ V_{att} $[_{CP}$ C $[_{MoodP}$ OP_i $[_{TP}$ T $[_{vP}$ SU v […]]]]]]]

b. $[_{SAP}$ $SPEAKER_i$ SA $[_{CP}$ C $[_{MoodP}$ OP_i $[_{TP}$ T $[_{vP}$ SU v […]]]]]]

Condition B is a domain restricted binding condition, in that it is restricted to roughly the arguments of one clause, and I suggest the domain should be characterized in terms of phases (Chomsky 2000, 2001). Under this view, the subject and OP^{dir} are part of the same binding domain, but also the subject and any internal argument are part of the same binding domain to the exclusion of OP_{dir}. As CP and *v*P are phases (Chomsky 2000, 2001), both are separately the domains for Condition B. The subject, introduced in Spec, vP (the phase edge) is therefore in a unique position that is part of both binding domains, as illustrated in (19).

(19)

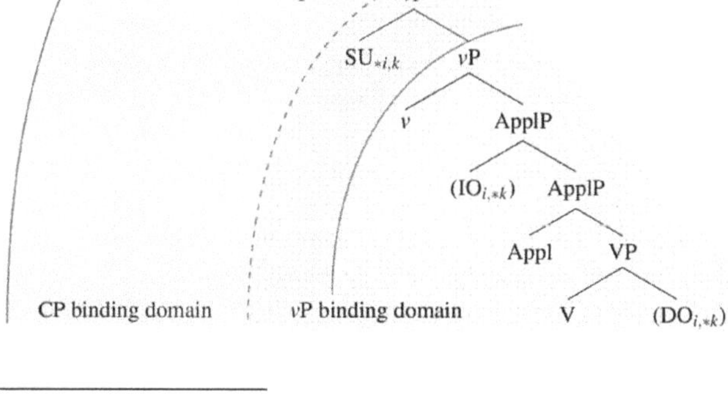

6 This stipulation, also made by Kempchinsky (1986), can actually be derived semantically. I argue in Stegovec (2016) that the relevant element is in fact a "perspectival PRO" that merges with MoodP due to the operator's semantic requirements. I simply adopt the stipulation here for reasons of space.

The position of the subject (SU) means that internal arguments (IO, DO) will trigger a Condition B violation when co-referential with SU, as they are within the *v*P binding domain.

Likewise, SU will violate Condition B when co-referential with OP^{dir}. Because OP^{dir} is bound by the speaker in matrix contexts and the matrix subject in embedded contexts, both subject restrictions are now derived. Crucially, if OP^{dir} is co-referential only with an internal argument, which is beyond the *v*P phase edge no Condition B violation should arise.[7]

3.2. Morphological blocking

Recall that, setting aside the exclusive 1P subject ban, imperatives and directive subjunctives are in a complete complementary distribution. Specifically, imperatives must be used whenever the addressee is interpreted as part of the subject (i.e. 2P features are present), while the directive subjunctive must be used in all other cases. I propose that what lies behind this is that although imperatives and directive subjunctives share the same base syntactic structure (see Section 3.1) and semantics (see Stegovec 2016), they differ in terms of the presence or absence of head movement of the verbal complex to OP^{dir}.[8]

I argue that OP^{dir} in fact has an over realization in both imperatives and directive subjunctives. Namely, it realizes as the imperative morpheme *-j-* in the former and the modal particle *naj* in the latter. This is captured within a late

---

7 There is a potential issue here, as any IO/DO can in principle move at least as high as Spec,*v*P and become accessible to OPdir. One way to explain why IO or DO are never included in the CP binding domain despite this option is to assume such movement is always focus-related. It is known that focus ameliorates subject obviation violations (Quer 2006), which can be tied to the fact that focus can void certain binding violations (see Eckardt 2002; Despić 2011). However, this analysis cannot be extended to IO/DO clitics, which under most analyses must move at least as high as Spec,*v*P and typically cannot be focused. Another option is an alternative definition for binding domains which also singles out SU as inherently present in two binding domains. At this point, I have to leave this question open to be resolved in future work.

8 This is not an entirely new idea (see Rivero and Terzi 1995; Han 2000). However, previous approaches of this kind place an interpretable 'imperative' feature on V (associated with imperative morphology), so that V must move to an imperative operator or C^0 to check its uninterpretable 'imperative' feature. Crucially, I argue that it is in fact the OP_{dir} which must bear the interpretable feature (associated with directive semantics, see Stegovec (2016) for details), but also that it is the OP_{dir} itself is potentially realized as imperative morphology.

insertion Distributive Morphology model (Halle and Marantz 1993, i.a.) with the vocabulary insertion rules in (20).

(20) I. OP ⇔ {-j-} / [[T]] II. OP ⇔ { naj } / elsewhere

Note that what conditions the realization of OP^{dir} is whether it is local to T (20-I) within a head complex or not (the elsewhere case, (20-II)). In other words, rule (20-I) can apply only if T or a head complex containing T first head-moves to OP^{dir}. Evidence for this can be found in Slovenian with the existence of suppletive imperative forms: *greste* "go.2P.PL" / *pejte* "go.IMP.2P.PL". As shown by Bobaljik (2012), suppletion is only sensitive to features within the same maximal projection, but not those outside a maximal projection boundary.

The two realizations of directive clauses can then be illustrated as in (21).[9] An imperative realization involves V head-moving to T and the resulting {V + T} head complex moving to OP^{dir} (21a). A directive subjunctive derivation conversely does not involve the last step (21b), so the OP^{dir} must realize as the modal particle *naj* as per the elsewhere rule (20-II).

(21) a. [$_{AGR}$ [$_{Mood}$ [$_{T}$ [$_{v}$ √HELP *v*] T{2P,PL}] OP] AGR] (imperative)
[[[**pomaga-**] **-j-**] **-te**]
b. [OP] . . . [$_{AGR}$ [$_{T}$ [$_{v}$ √HELP *v*] T{3P,PL}] AGR] (directive subjunctive)
[**naj**]. . . [[**pomaga-**] **jo**]

What is missing in the analysis is the actual trigger of head-movement to OP^{dir}, which I argue is the source of the complimentary distribution. I propose that OP^{dir} attracts {V + T} based only on the value of the person feature on T (acquired from the subject via Agree). This is reflected cross-linguistically with possible imperative paradigms, as they seem to always be restricted with respect to person value (all three persons, (inclusive) 1P and 2P, only 2P, or no imperative paradigm – cf. Jary and Kissine (2014)). Furthermore, even when imperatives and subjunctives share the same verbal morphology (see Schlenker 2005 for French), there is still a difference in the height of verb movement, which indicates that the morphological realization of imperative/subjunctive morphology should not be tied to the presence or absence of verb movement to C^0/ $Mood^0$. In the current approach this can be captured, because the rule responsible for imperative/subjunctive morphology (20) is entirely separate from verb

9 I assume, following among others Embick (2010), that the AGR head is inserted post-syntactically.

movement. The movement itself is triggered directly by a diacritic on OP^{dir} which is specified for a different person value in different languages: in Slovenian this means a diacritic which attracts T when it has 2P or 1P+2P features. At this stage, the link between person and verb movement is only a necessary stipulation given the cross-linguistics data. I have to leave it to future research to identify a deeper explanation of this link.

4. Conclusion

In Slovenian subject obviation and the ban on exclusive 1P subjects occur in both imperatives and directive subjunctives. I argued that the two phenomena are really a single binding restriction that arises between a directive operator and the subject of a directive clause. The two constructions thus share the same syntactic structure. This has implications for the study of both subjunctives and imperatives, as well as the nature of imperative embedding.

References

Bianchi, Valentina. 2001. *On person Agreement.* Ms. Scuola Normale Superiore, Pisa.

Bianchi, Valentina. 2003. "On Finiteness as Logophoric Anchoring." In Jacqueline Guéron and Liliane Tasmovski (eds.), *Temps at Point de Vue.* Nanterre: Université Paris X, 213–246.

Bobaljik, Jonathan. 2012. *Universals in Comparative Morphology.* Cambridge: MIT Press.

Chomsky, Noam. 2000. "Minimalist inquiries." In Roger Martin, David Michaels, and Juan Uriagereka (eds.), *Step by step.* Cambridge: MIT Press, 89–155.

Chomsky, Noam. 2001. "Derivation by phase." In Michael Kenstowicz (ed.), *Ken Hale: A life in language.* Cambridge: MIT Press, 1–52.

Crnič, Luka and Tue Trinh. 2009. "Embedding Imperatives." In Suzi Lima, Kevin Mullin and Brian Smith (eds.), *Proceedings of NELS 39*, 227–239.

Despić, Miloje. 2011. "Syntax in the Absence of Determiner Phrase." Ph. D. thesis, UConn.

Dvořák, Boštjan. 2005. "Slowenische Imperative und ihre Einbettung." *Philologie im Netz 33*: 36–73.

Dvořák, Boštjan and Ilse Zimmermann. 2008. "Imperative Subordination in Slovenian." In Anastasia Smirnova and Matthew Curtis (eds.), *Issues in Slavic Syntax and Semantics*, Volume 6. Newcastle: Cambridge Scholars Publishing, 14–34.

Eckardt, Regine. 2002. "Reanalyzing Selbst." *Natural Language Semantics 9*: 371–412.

Embick, David. 2010. *Localism versus Globalism in Morphology and Phonology*. Cambridge: MIT Press.

Halle, Morris and Alec Marantz (1993). "Distributed Morphology and the Pieces of Inflection." In Ken Hale and Samuel J. Keyser (eds.), *The View from Building 20*. Cambridge: MIT Press, 111–176.

Han, Chung-hye. 2000. *The structure and interpretation of imperatives: Mood and Force in universal grammar*. Outstanding Dissertations in Linguistics. New York: Garland.

Jary, Mark and Mikhail Kissine. 2014. *Imperatives*. Cambridge: Cambridge University Press.

Kaufmann, Magdalena. 2012. *Interpreting Imperatives*. Berlin: Springer.

Kaufmann, Magdalena and Claudia Poschmann. 2013. "Embedded imperatives – Empirical evidence from Colloquial German." *Language 89*: 619–637.

Kempchinsky, Paula. 1986. "Romance Subjunctive Clauses and Logical Form." Ph. D. thesis, UCLA.

Kempchinsky, Paula. 2009. "What can the subjunctive disjoint reference effect tell us about the subjunctive?" *Lingua 119*: 1788–1810.

Medeiros, David J. 2013. "Formal Approaches to the Syntax and Semantics of Imperatives." Ph. D. thesis, University of Michigan.

Oshima, David 2006. "Perspectives in Reported Discourse." Ph. D. thesis, Stanford University.

Pak, Miok, Paul Portner, and Rafaella Zanuttini. 2008. "Agreement in Promissive, Imperative, and Exhortative Clauses." *Korean Linguistics 14*: 157–175.

Pearson, Hazel. 2012. "The Sense of Self." Ph. D. thesis, Harvard.

Portner, Paul. 2007. "Imperatives and modals." *Natural Language Semantics 15*: 351–383.

Quer, Josep. 2006. "Subjunctives." In Martin Evaraert and Henk van Riemsdijk (eds.), *The Blackwell Companion to Syntax*. Oxford: Blackwell, 660–684.

Rivero, Maria-Luisa and Arontho Terzi. 1995. "Imperatives, V-movement and logical mood." *Journal of Linguistics 31*: 301–332.

Rögnvaldsson, Eiríkur. 1998. *The Syntax of the Imperative in Old Scandinavian*. Ms. University of Iceland.

Rus, Dominik. 2005. "Embedded imperatives in Slovenian." *Georgetown University Working Papers in Linguistics 4*: 153–183.

Sadock, Jerrold M. and Arnold M. Zwicky. 1985. "Speech act distinctions in syntax." In Timothy Shopen (Ed.), *Language Typology and Syntactic Description*, Volume 1. Cambridge: Cambridge University Press, 155–196.

Schlenker, Phillipe. 2005. "The Lazy Frenchman's Approach to the Subjunctive." In Twan Geerts, Ivo van Ginneken and Haike Jacobs (eds.), *Romance Languages and Linguistic Theory 2003*. Amsterdam: John Benjamins, 269–310.

Schwager, Magdalena. 2006. "Interpreting Imperatives." Ph. D. thesis, University of Frankfurt.

Searle, John R. 1976. "A classification of illocutionary acts." *Language in Society* 5: 1–23.

Sheppard, Milena Milojević and Marija Golden. 2002. "(Negative) Imperatives in Slovene." In Sjef Barbiers, Frits Beukema and Wim van der Wurff (eds.), *Modality and its Interaction with the Verbal System*. Amsterdam: John Benjamins, 245–260.

Speas, Peggy and Carol Tenny. 2003. "Configurational properties of point of view roles." In Anna Maria Di Sciulo (ed.), *Asymmetry in Grammar*. Amsterdam: John Benjamins, 315–343.

Stegovec, Adrian and Magdalena Kaufmann. 2015. "Slovenian imperatives: You can't always embed what you want!" In Eva Csipak and Hedde Zeijlstra (eds.), *Proceedings of Sinn und Bedeutung 19*. Göttingen: LinG, 621–638.

Stegovec, Adrian. 2016. *Obvia et Impera!* Ms. UConn. (http://ling.auf.net/lingbuzz/003078).

Thomas, Guillaume. 2012. "Embedded imperatives in Mbyá." In Hsin-Lun Huang, Ethan Poole and Amanda Rysling (eds.), *Proceedings of NELS 43*, 181–194.

Experimental Research

Irina A. Sekerina

The Attachment Preference of Relative Clauses: Is Russian a Truly High-Attaching Language?*

1. Introduction

Global structural ambiguity happens when more than one syntactic analysis is possible for a particular sentence, and each leads to a different semantic interpretation. The global structural ambiguity illustrated in (1) is referred to in the literature as *relative clause (RC) attachment ambiguity* because it contains a complex NP1-of-NP2-RC string, in which the RC (e.g., *who was on the balcony*) could structurally attach to either of the two NPs. When the RC modifies the NP1, the sentence means that the maid was standing on the balcony (high attachment); when it modifies the NP2, it is the actress who was on the balcony (low attachment) (Cuetos & Mitchell, 1988).

(1) Someone shot the maid of the actress who was standing on the balcony.

The RC attachment ambiguity enjoys special attention in psycholinguistics because it is the only phenomenon that allows for cross-linguistic variation in otherwise universal principle of Late Closure of the Garden Path theory of sentence processing (Frazier & Fodor, 1978). The Late Closure principle states that new constituents should be attached into the clause (or phrase) that is currently being processed. For sentences with the RC attachment ambiguity, the Late Closure Principle favors low attachment preference. Indeed, English exhibits a consistent preference for low attachment; around 60% of responses demonstrated this preference, as assessed in offline, pencil-and-paper questionnaires. Spanish and several other languages, however, exhibit high attachment preference (around 60%) using the same methodology (Gilboy et al., 1995). In a large cross-linguistic survey of attachment preferences in more than 20 languages, Grillo &

* I wish to thank Antje Sauermann for her help in data analysis and Lauren Sprandlin for her comments on the earlier version of this article. I am especially grateful to the anonymous reviewer whose really insightful comments on the contents have pushed me to re-think and improve on the ideas presented here.

Costa (2014) listed Romanian, Basque, and Chinese as low-attaching languages, and Dutch, Italian, and Greek as high-attaching ones (158–159: Tables 1 and 2).

There is no lack of theoretical explanation as to why languages differ with respect to RC attachment preferences (see Fernández, 2003, for an overview). The most recent linguistic explanation was one proposed by Grillo and Costa (2014) who attribute these cross-linguistic differences to the specific grammar options available in languages. Some languages (e.g., Spanish), but not others (e.g., English), allow for a *pseudo relative* (PR) construction that looks like the standard RC, and the availability of PRs correlates with high attachment.

Grillo and Costa's (2014) correlation between availability of the PR construction and high attachment preference in a language, however, does not seem to hold for Bulgarian and Russian, two Slavic languages: both are mostly high-attaching, but do not have PRs. Earlier research on Russian (Sekerina, 2003) and Bulgarian (Sekerina et al., 2004) established that both Russian and Bulgarian were high attachment languages (59–70%) based on the results of a traditional paper-and-pencil offline questionnaire, as illustrated in (2) for Russian (similar to Example in (1)). However, a follow-up, meticulous and systematic investigation of the RC attachment ambiguity in Russian by Fedorova and colleagues (see Fedorova, 2008, for an overview) that consisted of 14 experiments with 800 participants revealed that the linguistic properties of the materials (e.g., length of RC, NP1, and NP2; grammatical features of animacy, gender, and case) could reverse preference from high to low attachment.

(2) Николай знал сына полковника, который погиб
в автомобильной катастрофе.
Nikolaj knew the son of the colonel that died
in a car accident.'

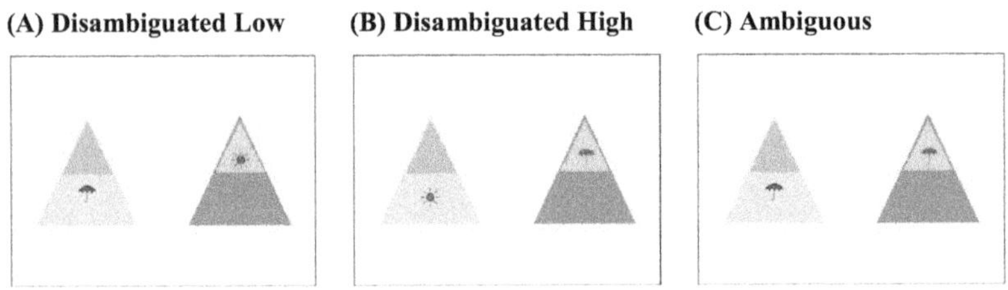

Figure 1: (A) Disambiguated Low attachment, (B) Disambiguated high attachment, and (C) ambiguous (Fernández and Sekerina, 2015: 235, Fig. 1). The left triangle is yellow and its tip is green; the right triangle is pink and its tip is light blue; the umbrella is navy; the sun is red.

In an attempt to isolate whether the lexico-semantic characteristics of the experimental sentences were responsible for changes in attachment preferences, we created a novel 'shapes' paradigm that employs semantically shallow materials, i.e., geometric shapes such as triangles and stars, presented visually and paired with ambiguous spoken sentences (Fernández & Sekerina, 2015). In the present study, the experimental question with the RC attachment ambiguity (3c) was preceded by a preamble (3a–b), illustrated below for Bulgarian:

(3) a. Ето един розов триъгълник и един жълт
This is a pink triangle and a yellow
триъгълник.
triangle.

b. Върховете им са различно оцветени
Their tips are of different colors.

c. Какъв цвят е върхът на триъгълника, в който е нарисуван
What color is the tip of the triangle in which is drawn
чадър?
umbrella
'What color is the tip of the triangle that has an umbrealla drawn in the middle?'

The novelty of this design was the fact that the experimental question in (3c) was always linguistically ambiguous, but the visual context could be manipulated to disambiguate it. As participants were listening to the preamble (3a–b), they were watching an animated PowerPoint presentation in which the shapes appeared in three steps until they were fully assembled. By the time the participants heard (3c), the visual display with the geometric shapes was completed in one of three ways (Fig. 1).

The task was to answer the experimental question in (3c) by naming the color of one shape: the correct answer in Fig. 1A was *green*, i.e., the color of the tip of the left triangle, in Fig. 1B, it was *blue*, i.e., the color of the tip of the right triangle, and either tip could be named in Fig. 1C. The choice of the color here allowed us to determine which attachment the participants preferred in the condition where the spoken question (3c) and the visual context (Fig. 1C) were both ambiguous. Unexpectedly, and in contrast to the results of the previous paper-and-pencil questionnaire, the Bulgarian participants chose low attachment in 63% of cases, that is, that the preferred answer corresponding to Fig. 1C was *green*.

We hypothesized that a possible explanation for this unexpected switch from high to low attachment preference within the same language and with the participants sampled from the same population could be individual differences among the participants (e.g., working memory capacity). Swets and colleagues (2007) demonstrated that low capacity English-speaking participants broke up long sentences with relative clauses in such a way that it led to high attachment. Similarly, Fedorova and Yanovich (2006; Fedorova, 2008) found that the language-specific high attachment preference in Russian could change to low in high working memory capacity participants. Thus, the language-specific preference can be unstable and change under the influence of both linguistic and individual differences factors.

Although we did not measure the working memory capacity of our Bulgarian participants, one particular finding from the 'shapes' experiment made us think that the individual differences in working memory capacity could not be the entire story in explaining the switch from high to low attachment preference. In the Disambiguated High visual context (Fig. 1B), participants' accuracy was very low (63.5%), in contrast to their ceiling performance in the Disambiguated Low visual context (98%) (Sekerina et al., 2004). The most frequent mistake that they made was to name the color of the entire triangle (e.g., *pink*) instead of the color of the tip (e.g., *blue*). We dubbed this 'whole-object' error. This prevalence of the 'whole-object' errors regardless of participants' working memory capacity suggests that in addition to various linguistic and individual differences factors, there may be other, domain-general factors that should be considered in the RC ambiguity resolution. Identification of all of the factors that can change preferences in a particular language and their relative weight should remain in the center of current psycholinguistic debate regarding the universality of sentence processing strategies. Without this, the entire discussion of general attachment preferences in different languages may lose its purpose.

In the present study, I propose an additional factor, *processing load*, that can change language-specific high attachment preference to low one, and thus should be taken into account when explaining cross-linguistic differences in RC attachment ambiguity. The fact that the high occurrence of the 'whole-object' error has already been found in two languages (Bulgarian, Sekerina et al., 2004; English, Fernández & Sekerina, 2015), and additionally now in Russian (this article), provides empirical support to the following hypothesis. Language processing is embedded in a general architecture of cognition. RC attachment ambiguity resolution is a complex linguistic phenomenon that induces high processing load because its successful processing requires simultaneous and rapid integration of linguistic information (i.e., ambiguous spoken sentences) with the visual representation from the cognitive domains of geometry and color. Processing of such complex phenomena overloads limited domain-general resources, such as working memory, and participants resort to low attachment in both Ambiguous and Disambiguated High sentences, resulting in a low attachment preference in the former case and errors in the latter. The experiment described below provides additional empirical evidence for the processing load hypothesis in an additional language, Russian.

2. Method

2.1. Participants

Monolingual Russian-speaking young adults (*N*=33, 7 men, M_{age} = 22 years), students at Moscow State University participated in the study in exchange for a small reimbursement equivalent to €3 (200 Russian rubles). This study was carried out in accordance with the ethical principles of psychologists and code of conduct of the American Psychological Association and was approved by the local Institutional Review Board. All participants signed the written informed consent in Russian in accordance with the Declaration of Helsinki.

2.2. Design and Materials

The experiment was comprised of nine experimental and 21 filler items. Each item consisted of a picture with two identical geometric shapes presented side-by-side (see Fig. 1). The number of the experimental items, nine, was small because it was difficult to create many diverse pictures with two parts that could be referred to using the NP1-NP2 format. Each pair of pictures was described with the following $NP1_{NOM}$-$NP2_{GEN}$ phrases:

#5 *рамка звёздочки* 'the frame of the star'
#7 *фундамент месяца* 'the foundation of the moon'
#9 *кончик треугольника* 'the tip of the triangle' (see Example 4)
#11 *контур прямоугольника* 'the contour of the rectangle'
#13, 19 *головка стрелочки* 'the head of the arrow'
#15 *контур ромба* 'the contour of the rhombus'
#17 *основание солнышка* 'the base of the sun'
#21 *хвостик ромба* 'the tail of the rhombus'

The pairs of pictures were presented together with two spoken preamble sentences (4a–b) and one experimental question (4c), identical to the Bulgarian ones in (3).

(4) a. Это розовый треугольник и жёлтый треугольник.
This is a pink triangle and a yellow triangle.

b. Их кончики различного цвета.
Their tips are of different colors.

c. Какого цвета кончик треугольника, на котором
What color is the tip of the triangle in which
нарисован зонтик?
is drawn an umbrella
'What color is the tip of the triangle that has an umbrealla drawn in the middle?'

The experimental question (4c) was always linguistically ambiguous in terms of the RC attachment, but the picture was manipulated in such a way as to create a visual context that either disambiguated the RC attachment (Fig. 1A–B) or maintained the ambiguity (Fig. 1C). There were three items in each of the three conditions for the Visual Display manipulation: three Disambiguated Low, three Disambiguated High, and three Ambiguous ones that were identical with the previous Bulgarian (Sekerina et al., 2004) and English studies (Fernández and Sekerina, 2015). Filler items also used the geometric shapes and were structured to resemble the experimental ones, but the sentences they were paired with did not contain the relative clause attachment ambiguity. The participants thought that their task was to identify the correct picture by naming the color similar to the experimental items.

The spoken materials were recorded by a trained linguist who is a native speaker of Russian (the author of this article) and were pronounced with natural prosody. There were two systematic pauses in each experimental question (4c): a short one after the *wh*-NP *какого цвета* 'which color' and a longer one after the comma that followed the NP2 *треугольника* 'triangle'. A third additional short pause was included after the NP1 *кончик* 'the tip' in the disambiguated low questions and half of the ambiguous ones. The disambiguated high questions did not require any additional pauses. Similar prosodic pausation was used for the 21 filler items as well.

Three versions of the experiment rotated the nine experimental items through the three Visual Display conditions in a Latin square design. Eleven participants were randomly assigned to one of the three versions.

2.3. Procedure

Participants were seated in front of a 17-inch Dell laptop (resolution of 1024 x 768 pixels) at a viewing distance of approximately 60 cm. In each trial, the shapes gradually appeared in three steps until the final picture with two identical shapes (i.e., triangles in Fig. 1) in different colors (yellow vs. pink) were completely assembled. Each step was animated using the built-in appear animation effect in PowerPoint and was accompanied by the spoken preamble sentence 1 (4a), followed by the preamble sentence 2 (4b), and completed with the experimental question (4c). The spoken materials were delivered over the external speakers attached to the laptop delivering the stimuli. In order to perform the task, participants had to name one color; their answers were recorded both by the digital VCR and on paper. In addition to collecting accuracy in voice responses and speed of color naming, we also recorded participants' eye movements. However, eye movement data are not reported in this article because of length constraints. The experiment lasted on average 12 minutes.

3. Results

3.1. Accuracy and attachment preferences

Disambiguated Trials. Participants' responses were coded as "correct" when they named the color of the correct tip (i.e., *green* for the Disambiguated Low, *blue* for the Disambiguated High condition, Fig. 1A–B), "error" when they named the color of the wrong triangle or the object inside (i.e., *navy* for the umbrella), and 'whole object' when they named the color of the correct whole picture instead of its part (i.e., the triangle *yellow* or *pink*, respectively).

Figure 2A presents the mean accuracy of naming colors in the Disambiguated Low and High trials. Mixed-effects logistic regression analysis in R (the *lme4* package) was used to examine the effect of Visual Display on accuracy of naming colors. The logistic part allows for modeling the nonlinear nature of the dependent variable bounded by 0 and 1; this approach is superior to an analysis of variance approach on transformed data (Jaeger, 2008).

The participants were significantly less correct in the Disambiguated High (77.2%) than in the Disambiguated Low conditions (96.9%) ($\beta = 31.18$, $SE = .86$, $z = 3.675$, $p < .001$): they made 8.9% 'whole-object' errors in the Disambiguated High condition, but none in the Disambiguated Low one ($\beta = -1.04$, $SE = .46$, $z = 2.269$, $p = .0233$).

Ambiguous Trials. Accuracy of responses to the experimental questions (Fig. 2A) in the Disambiguated trials served as control; the main point of interest was to establish preference of the RC attachment in the Ambiguous trials (Fig. 2B). A *Chi*-square test of independence compared the frequency of the two types of attachment preferences in the Ambiguous trials. The participants

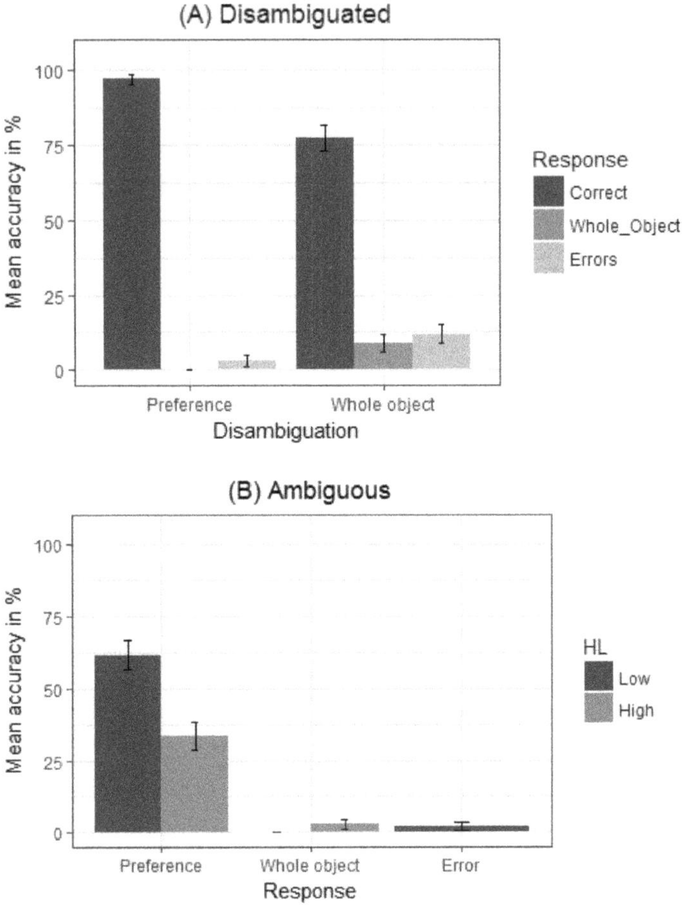

Figure 2: (A) Accuracy in the Disambiguated Low and High conditions. (B) Low and high attachment preferences in the Ambiguous condition (%). (Error bars represent SD.)

preferred low attachment significantly more (61.6%) than high attachment (33.3%), $\chi^2(1) = 7.6818$, $p < 0.01$. There were also 3% 'whole-object' errors. Thus, despite the fact that Russian previously has been argued to be a high-attaching language (offline paper-and-pencil questionnaires with written semantically deep materials in null context), the high attachment preference changed to low when the materials were semantically shallow, orally presented, and modulated by visual context.

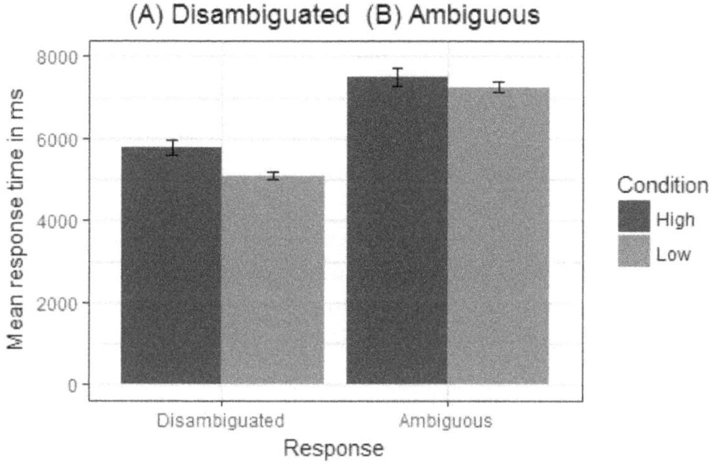

Figure 3: Naming times: (A) Disambiguated Low and High conditions. (B) Ambiguous condition. Correct trials only. (Error bars represent standard errors.)

3.2. Naming times

Participants' verbal responses naming colors as a response to the experimental question containing the ambiguous RC were measured in ms and were extracted from the video recording of the experiment. Only the times for the correctly answered questions were entered into the analysis (Figure 3).

Figure 3 presents the mean naming times in the Disambiguated High and Low (left panel) and in the Ambiguous trials (right panel). Recall that for the latter condition, the chosen color indicates participants' preference for the RC attachment site.

Naming times were log-transformed (because the raw data were not normally distributed) and analyzed using linear mixed-effects regression in R (*lme4* package). Results show that participants were faster in naming colors in the Disambiguated conditions (5394 ms) that in the Ambiguous ones (7372 ms). This 2-s difference was highly significant ($\beta = 0.159$, $SE = .012$, $t = 13.6$, $p < .001$) indicating that additional processing time was necessary for ambiguity resolution. Additionally, participants were significantly faster in naming colors in the Low attachment trails, both Disambiguated and Ambiguous (6186 ms), than in the High attachment ones (6580 ms) ($\beta = 0.042$, $SE = .0132$, $t = 3.2$, $p < .05$). There was no interaction between the ambiguity and visual context factors, which suggests that these two factors exerted an additive effect on naming times, with the Disambiguated Low condition being the fastest and the Ambiguous High being the slowest.

4. Discussion

Establishing a full list of factors—linguistic, individual differences, and domain-general—that explain both cross-linguistic differences in attachment preferences (i.e., high- vs. low-attaching languages) and language-specific instability of high attachment preference is an important empirical question in the ongoing psycholinguistic debate regarding the universality of parsing principles such as the Late Closure Principle. The results of the current study of processing of RC attachment ambiguity by Russian-speaking adults reveal that the language-specific high attachment preference in Russian established in the previous questionnaire studies (Fedorova & Yanovich, 2006; Sekerina, 2003) is unstable when using in a different experimental paradigm and can change to a low attachment preference.

The critical difference between the previous questionnaire studies and the current one is that we employed the 'shapes' paradigm developed in our earlier Bulgarian (Sekerina et al., 2004) and English (Fernández and Sekerina, 2015) experiments, which paired semantically shallow spoken sentences with the visual context of geometric shapes of different colors. Surprisingly, Russian participants consistently made 22.8% errors, including 'whole-object' ones, in the Disambiguated High condition. When they made 'whole-object' errors, they named the color of the low NP2 (triangle; low attachment) instead of the high NP1 (tip; high attachment). Similarly, the Ambiguous trials also revealed an unexpected Low attachment preference (61.6%). The results of naming times were parallel to the accuracy data, with Low attachment conditions taking less time to name the correct color than High attachment ones.

Note the striking parallelism between the current findings for Russian and our previous results for the Bulgarian 'shapes' experiment (Sekerina et al., 2004): Bulgarian participants made 20.5% errors in the Disambiguated High condition and showed 74.8% low attachment preference in the Ambiguous condition. English, which is a low attachment language to begin with, was also tested as a control case (Fernández and Sekerina, 2015), and the naming times were also faster in the Disambiguated Low condition. Thus, cross-linguistic evidence clearly supports an overwhelming preference for low attachment when spoken sentences are complex and interact with visual context, regardless of the language-specific attachment preference, low in English, or high in Bulgarian and Russian.

We propose that processing of the complex experimental materials in the 'shapes' paradigm creates a high processing load that overwhelms participants' domain-general resources in the form of working memory and causes an unexpected switch from high to low attachment preference. But how do we explain the difference in the processing load (i.e., high) in the 'shapes' paradigm, but not in the questionnaire studies (i.e., low)? We suggest that three properties of the 'shapes' paradigm are critical in causing high processing load. First, successful interpretation of the 'shapes' materials required simultaneous and rapid integration of linguistic information (i.e., ambiguous sentences) with the visual representation from the cognitive domains of geometry and color. Second, the sentences were presented orally, and the timing in spoken modality (i.e., listening) cannot be self-paced the way it is in visual modality (i.e., reading). Finally, the color-naming task of the 'shapes' paradigm requires judgments that are more online in nature than the choice of interpretation in offline questionnaires where participants are in a more "ideal" untimed situation of answering a written question to indicate their preferred interpretation.

Lewis and Phillips (2015) argue that properties of experimental materials such as in the 'shapes' paradigm lead to "misalignments" between linguistic representations and non-verbal visual context, initial interpretation and its reanalysis, and offline and online judgments. In dealing with the three misalignments in the 'shapes' paradigm under time constraints, the Bulgarian and Russian participants strained their limited domain-general resources, i.e., working memory, and produced less resource-demanding low-attaching interpretations that resulted in the unnoticed errors for the Disambiguated High items and the unexpected low attachment preference in the Ambiguous items. Independent evidence that sentences that do not obey the Late Closure Principle can lead to interpretation errors comes from the 'good enough' processing of garden-path sentences like *While Anna dressed the baby played in the crib* in English, in which participants often mistakenly answered the question *Did Anna dress the baby*? with *Yes* (Ferreira et al., 2002).

The hypothesis of the high processing load that strains domain-general resources needs to be tested further. The anonymous reviewer suggested a more direct manipulation in which the exact same experimental materials are made either 'high-load' or 'low-load'. If the combination of the linguistic and visual information from the 'shapes' paradigm is to be kept as is, one way to decrease the processing load of the Disambiguated High items is to manipulate the modality and present the spoken materials in (3–4) in the written form, similar to the way it is usually done in the questionnaire studies. We do have the data that speak to this point, but only for Bulgarian. Experiment 3 in Sekerina et al. (2004) was the replication of Experiment 2, in which with the spoken sentences were written on the screen above the shapes. The participants made 12% fewer errors in the Disambiguated High items in a written modality compared to a spoken one, a statistically significant reduction. However, there was no modality effect in terms of decreasing low attachment preference in the Ambiguous items. Future research in Russian should test the effect of the modality manipulation as well as exploring other methodological options to manipulate processing load (e.g., increasing the number of experimental items, exploring different configurations of the NP1-NP2, and changing the task to make it more salient such as presenting participants with black-and-white shapes and asking them to color different parts: *Use red to color the tip of the triangle that has an umbrella in the middle.*)

In sum, the change from high to low attachment preference in the Ambiguous items, combined with the robustly attested 'whole-object' errors in the Disambiguated High items in all three languages provides empirical evidence that high attachment can be computationally more complex and result in high processing load. When experimental materials combine linguistic and visual information and sentences are presented orally, keeping track of possible attachment sites and selecting the high attachment site requires working memory resources, and the low attachment site as the most recent one wins. Thus, we argue that processing load should be added to linguistic and individual differences factors that have been identified so far as having the power to tip attachment preference in high-attaching languages from high to low. Contribution of domain-general factors must be taken into account before the psycholinguistic debate about exceptions to universal parsing principles is settled.

References

Cuetos, Fernando and Mitchell, Don C. 1988. "Cross-linguistic differences in parsing: Restrictions on the use of the late closure strategy in Spanish." *Cognition 30*: 73–105.

Frazier, Lyn and Fodor, Janet D. 1978. "The sausage machine: A new two-stage parsing model." *Cognition* 6: 291–325.

Cuetos, Fernando, Don Mitchell and Martin Corley. 1996. "Parsing in different languages." In *Language Processing in Spanish*, Manuel Carreiras, Jose García-Albéa, and Nuria Sebastian- Gallés (eds.). Hillsdale: Erlbaum, 145–187.

Fedorova, Olga V. 2008. "К вопросу о валидности и надежности психолингвистических экспериментов." (in Russian). In *Когнитивные исследования*, Vladimir D. Solov'ev and Tatyana V. Chernigovskaya (eds.). Moscow: Institute of Psychology, 231–262.

Fedorova, Olga V. and Yanovich, Igor S. 2006. "Early preferences in relative clause attachment in Russian: The effect of working memory differences." In *The Proceedings of 14th FASL Workshop. The Princeton Meeting 2005*, James E. Levine et al. (eds.). Ann Arbor: Michigan Slavic Publications, 113–128.

Fernández, Eva M. 2003. *Bilingual sentence processing. Relative clause attachment in English and Spanish*. Amsterdam/Philadelphia: John Benjamins Publishing Company.

Fernández, Eva M. and Sekerina, Irina A. 2015. "The interplay of visual and prosodic information in the attachment preferences of semantically shallow relative clauses." In *Explicit and Implicit Prosody in Sentence Processing*, Lyn Frazier and Edward Gibson (eds.). Heidelberg: Springer, 241–262.

Ferreira, Fernanda, Karl G. D. Bailey and Vittoria Ferraro. 2002. Good-enough representations in language comprehension. *Current Directions in Psychological Science 11.1*: 11–15.

Gilboy, Elizabeth, Joseph-Maria Sopena, Charles Clifton Jr. and Lyn Franzier. 1995. "Argument structure and preferences in the processing of Spanish and English complex NPs." *Cognition 54*: 131–167.

Grillo, Nino and Costa, João A. 2014. "Novel argument for the universality of parsing principles." *Cognition 13.1*: 156–187.

Jaeger, Florian T. 2008. "Categorical data analysis: Away from ANOVAs (transformation or not) and towards logit mixed models." *Journal of Memory and Language 59*.4: 434–446.

Lewis, Shevaun and Phillips, Colin. 2015. "Aligning grammatical theories and language processing models." *Journal of Psycholinguistic Research 44*: 27–46.

Sekerina, Irina A. 2003. "The Late Closure Principle vs. the Balance Principle: Evidence from on-line processing of ambiguous Russian sentences." In *Current Approaches to Formal Slavic Linguistics. Contributions of the 2nd European Conference on Formal Description of Slavic Languages. Potsdam Meeting 199*, Peter Costa and Joseph Frasek (eds.). Frankfurt: Peter Lang, 205–217.

Sekerina, Irina A., Eva M. Fernández and Krassimira A. Petrova 2004. "Relative clause attachment in Bulgarian." In *The Proceedings of the 12th FASL Workshop. The Ottawa Meeting 2003*, Olga Arnaudova et al. (eds.). Ann Arbor: Michigan Publications, 375–394.

Swets, Benjamin, Timothy Desmet, David Z. Hambrick and Fernanda Ferreira. 2007. "The role of working memory in syntactic ambiguity resolution: A psychometric approach." *Journal of Experimental Psychology: General 136.1*: 64–81.

Stoyneshka, Iglika, Janet D. Fodor and Eva M. Fernández. 2010. "Phoneme restoration methods for investigating prosodic influences on syntactic processing." *Language and Cognitive Processes*, *25.7*: 1265–1293.

Traxler, Matthew J., Martin J. Pickering and Charles Clifton Jr. 1998. "Adjunct attachment is not a form of lexical ambiguity resolution." *Journal of Memory and Language 39.4*: 558–592.

Boban Arsenijević, Franc Lanko Marušič, Jana Willer Gold

Experimenting with Highest Conjunct Agreement under Left Branch Extraction

1. Introduction

A debate has developed in the recent theoretical and experimental linguistic literature on the status and the locus of conjunct agreement in South Slavic (SS; Marušič et al. 2007, Bošković 2009, Franks & Willer Gold 2014, Murphy & Puškar 2015; Marušič et al. 2015 and Willer Gold et al. 2016). One of the pertinent issues of the debate is the status of Highest Conjunct Agreement – agreement with the hierarchically highest conjunct (NP1) – in sentences with a preverbal subject. The question around which the debate revolves is a basic one: Is there Highest Conjunct Agreement (HCA) in Bosnian/Croatian/Serbian (BCS), and how is it blocked, or derived, respectively?

A standard view is that agreement emerges in syntax, when an unvalued Probe searches in its local domain for a Goal matching in features (Chomsky 2004). As the Probe only sees c-commanded Goals, a hierarchical locality of the Goal is one of the crucial prerequisites for agreement to obtain. Therefore, assuming an asymmetrical structure for a coordination phrase, agreement with a hierarchically highest conjunct is theoretically predicted to be a prominent agreement option (Benmamoun 1992, Munn 1999, Bošković 2013; Zeijlstra 2012; Preminger 2014; den Dikken 2014).

HCA has been argued to surface in Slovenian (Slo) and BCS when a coordinated subject is in the postverbal position, but only in Slovenian when it is preverbal (Marušič et al. 2015, Bošković 2009). Blocking of preverbal HCA in BCS has been argued to arise from the interaction of Move and Agree Probe in Left Branch Extraction (LBE) fertile environments (Bošković 2009). Since BCS is a strong LBE language, and Slovenian a weak LBE language (Fanselow and Féry 2013), this difference between Slo and BCS is expected.

Here we ask whether the reported variation in HCA is empirically robust, and if so – whether LBE is its true cause, by providing contrasted experimental evidence for the status of HCA under LBE between BCS and Slo, based on the following predictions:

(i) If LBE is really what blocks HCA for BCS but not for Slo, we should observe a difference in acceptability of HCA between Slo and BCS. Concretely, HCA should be judged better/more common in Slo than in BCS.

(ii) If LBE is really what derives LCA via the same mechanism that blocks HCA, we should observe a difference in acceptability of LCA between Slo and BCS. Concretely, LCA should be judged better/more common in BCS than in Slo.
(iii) If the two South Slavic (SS) varieties behave alike with respect to HCA, the difference in the acceptability of HCA under LBE should be related to the different level of acceptability of LBE between the two varieties.

Relevant for this debate is a recent large scale EMSS network comparative experimental production study of BCS and Slo that has provided evidence that HCA is a legitimate agreement strategy across all investigated varieties (Willer Gold et al. 2016). To further explore (i) and (ii), we present and discuss the results of an Acceptability judgment task over HCA-under-LBE uniformly designed and tested on native speakers of Zagreb variety of Croatian, Niš variety of Serbian, and Slovenian.

2. Theoretical grounding: Does LBE facilitate HCA?

2.1. Left-Branch Extraction in South Slavic languages

Large part of research on LBE phenomena comes from a long tradition of work on Slavic languages (Franks & Progovac 1994, Bošković 2005, Stjepanović 1998, 2014, a.o.). Although optional, LBE in BCS is a highly productive phenomenon. The example in (1) accentuates the flexibility of LBE by demonstrating the extraction of the highest element(s) of the (remnant) nominal constituent across the agreement Goal and Probe. The resulting structure is a highly discontinuous object. In Slo LBE is much more restricted. Examples like (1) are unacceptable in Slo.

(1) <u>Lijepe</u> je mladić <u>plave</u> imao <u>oči</u>. BCS
nice aux kid blue had eyes.
'The kid had nice blue eyes.'

To account for LBE in BCS, Franks & Progovac (1994) adopt Abney's (1987) AP-over-NP structure of DP – where NP is a complement of the A head. They argue the NP complement scrambles out of the DP and right-adjoins to IP. This is followed by fronting of the remnant DP containing the adjective to Spec-CP. Contrary to their approach, Bošković (2005) argues against Abney's DP and for the NP-over-AP structure for BCS. He defines LBE as constituent movement of an adjunct AP out of NP.

A similar operation of extraction of the initial XP from coordinated subjects is attested in strong LBE languages (Ross' (1967) Coordinate Structure Constraint Violation, CSCV), as illustrated in (2a) (Franks 2007; Fanselow & Féry 2013).

(2) a. Sestra će mi ga i njen muž pokloniti. (BCS, Franks 2007, p.107, ex. (7b))
sister will me it and her husband give
'It is SISTER and her husband who will give it to me.'
b. *Sestra mi ga bosta in njen mož podarila. (Slo)
sister me it will and her husband give
'Sister and her husband will give it to me.'

Stjepanović (1998, 2015), building her argument on the parallelism in the extraction possibilities for LBE and CSCV examples in BCS, extends the mechanics of LBE to both. Adopting Progovac's (1998a,b) structure for &P,[1] she argues that it is precisely this potential to extract the leftwards-most AP/&P that is responsible for CSCV (for her LBE from coordinated structures) in these languages. Stjepanović follows Bošković's (2013, 2014) assuming only the hierarchically highest Specifier/Adjunct counts as a phase edge. This explains the restrictions in multiple conjunct extraction possibilities to only hierarchically highest conjunct, i.e. the initial conjunct in our CSCV cases. Finally, movement of a lower adjective/conjunct in multiple adjectives/conjuncts examples, as in (1a), is only available once the initial/hierarchically highest adjunct/conjunct has undergone movement re-identifying the phase edge and freeing up the lower adjective/conjunct for extraction (which sounds counter-cyclic).

2.2. Highest Conjunct Agreement

In his work on Conjunct Agreement with Coordinated Subjects in BCS, Bošković (2009) attributes the lack of HCA in (3) to LBE. In short, Bošković argues that due to the availability of LBE, movement can target the structurally highest conjunct in parallel to the equidistant &P, whereby the emerging ambiguity blocks valuation and, hence, agreement with the highest conjunct in the subject position, (3).

(3) *Sva sela i sve varošice su juče uništena. (Bošković 2009)
All villages and all small-towns aux yesterday destroyed

1 $[_{\&P1}\ [_{\&P2}\ \&\ NP]\ [_{\&P1}\ \text{and}\ NP]]$

'All villages and small towns were destroyed yesterday.'

In more detail, the lexical verb may or may not be endowed with the EPP feature. When it is not, the highest conjunct, being the most local, valuates gender of the verb (number is valued by the ConjP), resulting in closest conjunct agreement with a postverbal subject. When the verb has an EPP feature, then, as the constituent that valuates the verb's gender and/or number must also be the constituent that satisfies the EPP, an ambiguity arises due to the availability of LBE/initial constituent CSCV in BCS. The probe finds both the initial constituent (NP1) and the entire coordinated subject as potential goals. Probing fails, and repeats until a constituent is reached which cannot move. Because this conjunct, i.e. the most deeply embedded conjunct, cannot move, there is no ambiguity and the entire &P needs to be Pied-pipped. As a result, preverbal subjects only have last conjunct agreement (LCA) as a (single conjunct) agreement option.

Assuming that the first conjunct extracts after the EPP triggered movement to the preverbal position, Bošković's account predicts no variation in acceptability of HCA and HCA under LBE for BCS. Whenever LBE is possible, it should also have the same effect on HCA. It also predicts that HCA will not be blocked in a language that does not allow LBE for subject constituents. In fact, Bošković predicts weak LBE languages that do not allow extraction of the first conjunct only have HCA as LCA cannot be derived. We turn next to one such weak LBE language – Slovenian.

In their study on Conjunct agreement in native speakers of Slovenian, Marušič et al. (2015) provide experimental evidence that a structurally highest element does act as an agreement Goal in preverbal position, see (4).

(4) Radirke in peresa so se prodajal**e** najbolje. (Marušič et al. 2015)
erasers$_{F.PL}$ and pens$_{N.PL}$ aux refl sold$_{F.PL}$ the best
'Erasers and pens sold the best.'

Couching their theoretical account in a multi-component framework, Marušič et al. assume a 2 Step Agree: Agree-Link and Agree-Copy, where Agree-Copy can operate before or after linearization yielding different outcomes under syntactic (HCA) or linear locality (LCA) for preverbal subjects.

Their theory has nothing to say about HCA under LBE in Slo. Quite independent of agreement such examples are expected to be less acceptable if not fully ungrammatical given that Slo, unlike BCS, does not allow CSC violations. While in strong LBE languages, extraction of Conj1 before Agree-Copy would impede

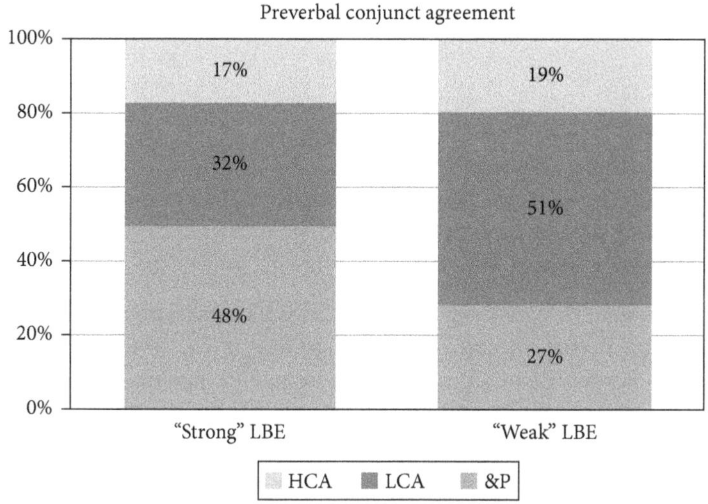

Figure 1: Shows mean values for agreement options in non-masculine mixed gender NF condition. Strong LBE language data represents the sample of BCS - NI, NS, SA, ZD, and ZG and weak LBE language Slo - NG.

the latter in finding Conj1's gender feature in order to Copy its value, consequently blocking HCA.

Building on the existing debate, a recent large scale comparative experimental study on conjunct agreement in native speakers of BCS and Slo (Willer Gold et al. 2016) has provided experimental evidence against Bošković's native speaker intuitions, showing that HCA is available in both Slo and BCS. Figure 1 shows that while strong and weak LBE languages might vary with respect to the ratio of LCA and &P agreement, HCA ratios are comparable across the two language types.

This encourages the extension of Marušič et al.'s theoretical account to BCS. In this perspective, it becomes relevant to investigate the acceptability of HCA under LBE by comparing experimental data form a strong and a weak LBE language. Such research can show us to what extent the LBE parameter really influences the availability of HCA, and thus offer a way to compare the models by Marušič et al. and by Bošković. As shown in (5a) and (5b) we are looking at split coordinated subjects with two plural conjuncts. As Slovenian is a weak LBE language, it does not allow any CSC violations, so all instances of LBE of the first conjunct are predicted to be bad even in cases when the two conjuncts are of the same gender and where there is no conflict in determining agreement.

(5) a. Olovke su i knjige prodane. BCS
pencils$_{F.PL}$ aux and books$_{F.PL}$ sold$_{F.PL}$
'Pencils and books are sold.'

b. *Radirke so in knjige prodane. Slo
erasers$_{F.PL}$ aux and books$_{F.PL}$ sold$_{F.PL}$
'Erasers and books are sold.'

To summarize, Bošković argues that HCA is blocked with preverbal subjects. Marušič et al. provide evidence for HCA and have a way of deriving it. On both views, since Slo has been argued to be a weak LBE language, acceptability of HCA under LBE in Slo is predicted to be low. However, considering that neither of the two theories directly explore the question of HCA under LBE in BCS, some room in determining the precise predictions of the two theories will need to be filled by speculation. In case Agree precedes LBE, the theories predict the acceptability of HCA under LBE to be related to the acceptability of HCA in non-LBE environments and to the acceptability of LBE. If LBE takes place prior to agreement and the first conjunct moves to Spec.TP, the two theories predict similar outcomes: they both predict HCA to be the best strategy. Depending on the location of the remnant ConjP, the two theories diverge. For Bošković, LBE means that the EPP feature is satisfied by the initial constituent within the conjoined subject. This is something that should be blocked by his ambiguity of goals, but if the ambiguity is resolved in some other way, it should result in HCA as the best strategy. For Marušič et al., the extraction of Conj1 prior to agreement would either force agreement with Conj1 if the remnant is in some position invisible to the probe or else impede agreement with this conjunct, so that no HCA would be expected.

3. Experimental investigation of HCA under LBE

The aim of this section is to bring experimental insight into the processing of LBE in the domain of Coordination; in particular, to shed more light on *(i) the acceptability of single conjunct agreement – HCA and (ii) the acceptability of HCA under LBE, in order to draw conclusions about LBE's potential to facilitate or block HCA*. To that aim we report on the results from an Acceptability judgement study with native speakers of BCS and Slo. The study included an identical experimental design implemented at six different locations included in the EMSS Network. Here we report on the data from three sites – Niš, Zagreb and

Nova Gorica/Ljubljana. Other sites within the BCS area gave very similar results to those from Zagreb and Niš.

3.1. Experimental materials and design

An Acceptability judgment task (1 to 5 scale) with a unified experimental design was carried out on native speakers of BCS and Slo at 3 experimental sites – Zagreb, Niš and Nova Gorica/Ljubljana. Participants were first year university students who were neither students of languages under investigation nor of psychology, and were educated in the local area and speaking the local variant (n=30*3). The design was crossed to include four two-level factors: NP1-position (continuous subjects, LBE), Agreement (HCA, *NSg),[2] NP1-gender value (F, N) and NP2-gender value (M, non-M), creating a 2x2x2x2 factorial design with 1 or 2 items per condition (n=20). Neuter singular was used in creation of ungrammatical items (*). Fillers of different structure and (mis)matching in agreement and case were used as distractors (n=24). Examples illustrating four critical conditions are presented in (6).

(6) Sample of material per condition used in Acceptability judgment task

HCA+NF:	Ogledala	i	slike	su	dostavljena	kamionom	
	mirror.NPl	and	painting.FPl	AuxPl	delivered.NPl	truck.Inst	
	'(The) mirrors and (the) paintings were delivered by truck.'						
*HCA+NF:	Ogledala	i	slike	su	dostavljeno	kamionom.	
	mirror.NPl	and	painting.FPl	AuxPl	delivered.NSg	truck.Inst	
	'(The) mirrors and (the) paintings was delivered by truck.'						
HCA+LBE+FN:	Knjige	su	i	pomagala	korištene	u	nastavi.
	book.FPl	AuxPl	and	accessory.NPl	used.FPl	in	lecturing
	'(The) books and (the) accessories were used in the lectures.'						
*HCA+LBE+FN:	Noge	su	i	stopala	ozlijeđeno	u	sudaru.
	leg.FPl	AuxPl	and	foot.NPl	injured.NSg	in	crash
	'(The) legs and (the) feet was seriously injured in the crash.'						

The experiment was implemented using IbexFarm experimental on-line platform (Drummond 2011). The experiment was administered in a single 30 min session, individually or in parallel to a group of 5 to 10 participants in a computer room under controlled conditions. The participants were asked to rate the sentences based on 'familiarity to their local variety', on a scale from 1 to 5 where 1 is bad and 5 is good.

2 NSg was the agreement value that was taken as one that is always ungrammatical, independent of all other factors.

3.3. Results and discussion

To assess and compare the status of HCA with and without LBE, we conducted a two-way ANOVA (Scheffe Test) with Site (ZG, NI, NG) and Cond (HCA, *HCA, HCA+LBE, *HCA+LBE) as fixed factors. The results for main conditions across three varieties are summarized (Mean) in Figure 2 and p-values are provided for statistically significant results. Three main results follow form the Acceptability judgment task.

Comparison of HCA across three varieties shows that HCA is available to a more or less equal degree across all three varieties as p-values (ANOVA and t-test) show no significant differences (HCA Mean: ZG=2.48, NI=2.56, NG=2.66), see Figure 2.

Comparison of HCA+LBE condition across three varieties shows a predicted split with respect to strong and weak LBE languages with this condition being rated lower in NG than in NI and ZG (HCA+LBE Mean: ZG=1.66, NI=1.57, NG=1.38, see Figure 2), even though due to a low number of items per condition, the differences do not reach statistical significance (p=.14). However, looking at the ratio of acceptability of the two main conditions – HCA vs HCA+LBE, in each of the three varieties, p-vales do show statistically significant results of different degrees. The two conditions differ in their acceptability the least in ZG (p<.01), somewhat more in NI (p<.001) and most significantly in NG (p<.00001) (as marked in Figure 1). This confirms the above observed results

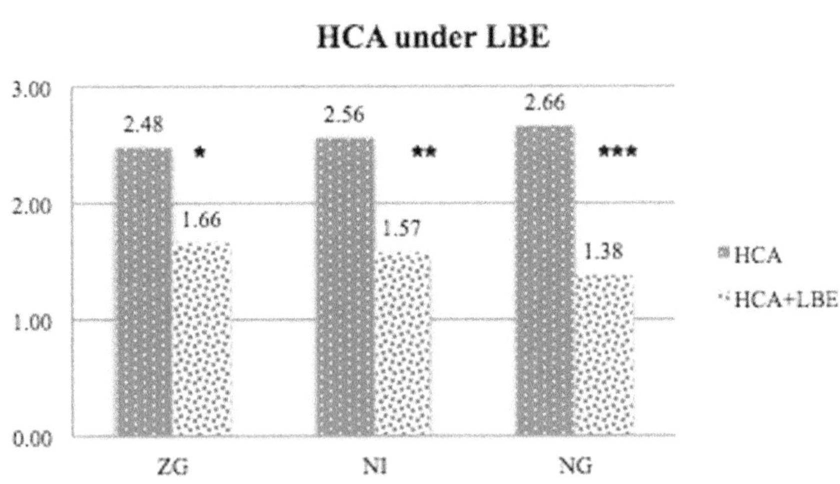

Figure 2:

indicating a split between BSC and Slo regarding LBE. It is also interesting to trace the p-values calculated by two-way ANOVA comparing HCA condition to HCA+LBE and to *HCA+LBE, which are the same for NG (both p<.00001), but not for NI (p<.001 and p<.00001, respectively) and ZG (p<.01 and p<.00001, respectively). Moreover, t-test over the comparison between HCA+LBE and *HCA+LBE condition for each of the three varieties, shows a statistically significant difference between the two conditions for ZG and NI (p<0.05) but not for NG (p=.81), confirming that the degradation in weak, but not in strong LBE languages comes from LBE, see Figure 3.

Because of lack of space, we do not discuss the variables M vs. non-M in Conj2 and the N vs. F in Conj1. For a more detailed discussion on effects of different gender values and conjunct combinations as agreement Goals, we refer the reader to Willer Gold et al. (2016), Marušič et al. (2015), Arsenijević et al. (in prep.), and Bošković (2009).

The results presented in this and the previous section show that HCA is equally available across all of the (here investigated) SS varieties, and that its acceptability diminishes with LBE. In weak LBE languages (namely Slovenian), both LBE conditions were judged equally unacceptable.

These results support the empirical reports of Marušič et al. (2015) and Willer Gold et al. (2016) regarding the availability of HCA as an agreement strategy in Slo and BCS HCA is a legitimate agreement strategy for preverbal conjoined

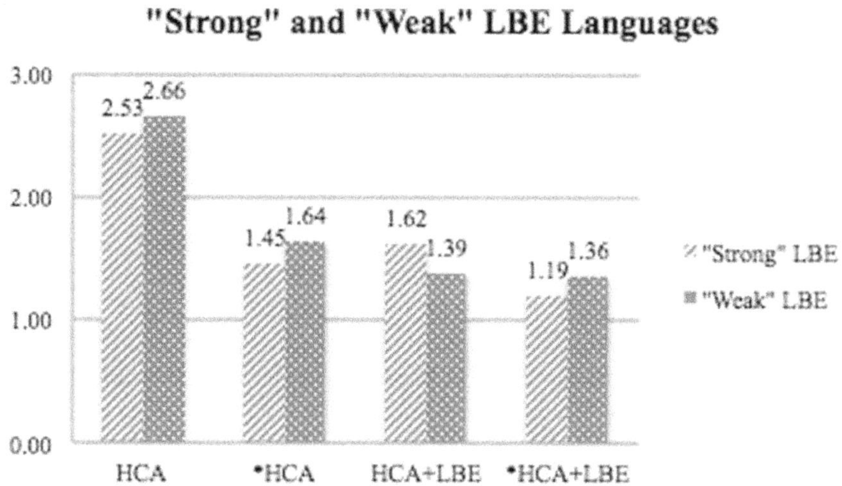

Figure 3:

subjects in BCS, contra Bošković (2009). The effects of LBE: a general degrading effect on HCA suggests that LBE degrades rather than improves HCA.

Our predictions stated above thus turned out to be all wrong:

(i) If LBE is really what blocks HCA for BCS but not for Slo, we should observe a difference in acceptability of HCA between Slo and BCS. Concretely, HCA should be judged better/more common in Slo than in BCS.
(ii) If LBE is really what derives LCA via the same mechanism that blocks HCA, we should observe a difference in acceptability of LCA between Slo and BCS. Concretely, LCA should be judged better/more common in BCS than in Slo.
(iii) If the two SS varieties behave alike with respect to HCA, the difference in the acceptability of HCA under LBE should be related to the different level of acceptability of LBE between the two varieties.

Add. (i): There was no difference between Slo and BCS in HCA.
Add (ii): LCA is actually judged better in Slo than in BCS.
Add (iii): HCA under LBE is judged in both varieties as ungrammatical, yet we know there is a difference in the acceptability of LBE in the two varieties. There is a difference in the ungrammaticality of HCA under LBE in BCS, but we are not sure we should give this difference any theoretical significance.

5. Conclusion

Bošković (2009) and Marušič et al. (2015) are not the only two theories of conjunct agreement, but we lack the space to discuss them all. We take these two as representative of two approaches to agreement (agreement in syntax proper vs. agreement (partly) in PF). Further, there are obviously many possible ways to derive CSC violations in BCS. The reader is referred to Arsenijević et al. (in prep.) for a full discussion of various options.

The presented results are more in line with Marušič et al. (2015) theoretical account of agreement than Bošković's; favouring the suggestion for the former account to be extended to BCS. There probably are ways to save Bošković's (2009) proposal and/or to further fine-tune the proposal by Marušič et al. (2015) to get a better match with what is predicted to be good and what should be underivable, but we need to leave this for another article.

All in all, looking at the instances of HCA in conjunction with a split coordinated subject, the theoretical proposal made in Marušič et al. (2015) is superior to Bošković (2009).

References

Abney, Steven Paul. 1987. "The English noun phrase in its sentential aspect." Doctoral dissertation, MIT, Cambridge, Mass.

Arsenijević, Boban, Franc Lanko Marušič and Jana Willer Gold. In prep. "On Conjunct Agreement with Split Conjunctions in South Slavic." Ms., University of Graz, University of Nova Gorica, University College London.

Bošković, Željko. 2005. "On the Locality of Left Branch Extraction and the Structure of NP." *Studia Linguistica* 59(1): 1–45.

Bošković, Željko. 2009. "Unifying first and last conjunct agreement." *Natural Language and Linguistic Theory* 27: 455–496.

Bošković, Željko. 2013. "Getting really edgy: On the edge of the edge." Ms., University of Connecticut Storrs.

Bošković, Željko. 2014. "More on the edge of edge." In *Formal approaches to Slavic linguistics: The McMaster Meeting 2013* (FASL 22), Cassandra Chapman, Olena Kit and Ivona Kučerova (eds.). Michigan, MI: Michigan Slavic Publications, 44–66.

Benmamoun, Elabbas. 1992. "Structural conditions on agreement." *Proceedings of NELS*. Vol. 22.

Chomsky, Noam. 2004. "Beyond explanatory adequacy." In *Structures and Beyond. The cartography of syntactic structures, Volume* 3, Adriana Belletti (ed.). Oxford: Oxford University Press. 104–131.

den Dikken, Marcel. 2014. "On feature interpretability and inheritance." In *Minimalism and beyond: Radicalizing the interfaces*, Peter Kosta, Steven Franks, Teodora Radeva-Bork, and Lilia Schürcks (eds.). Amsterdam: John Benjamins. 37–55.

Drummond, Alex. 2011. "IbexFarm." Version 0.2.7. Available at *http://spellout.net/ibexfarm/*.

Fanselow, Gisbert and Caroline Fry. 2013. "A comparative perspective on intervention effects on left branch extractions in Slavic." In *Non Progredi Est Regredi. Festschrift fr Alla Paslwaska*, Wolodymyr Sulym, Mychajlo Smolij and Chrystyna Djakiw (eds.). Lwiw: Pais, 266–295.

Franks, Steven. 2008. "Deriving discontinuity." In *Studies in Formal Slavic Linguistics*, Franc Marušič and Rok Žaucer (eds.). Frankfurt am Main: Peter Lang, 103–120.

Franks, Steven and Ljiljana Progovac. 1994. "On the placement of Serbo-Croatian clitics." *Indiana Linguistic Studies* 7: 69–78.

Franks, Steven and Jana Willer Gold. 2014. "Agreement strategies with conjoined subjects in Croatian." In *New insights into Slavic linguistics*, Sylwester Jaworski and Jacek Witkoś (eds.). Frankfurt am Main: Peter Lang, 91–115.

Marušič, Franc, Andrew Nevins and Amanda Saksida. 2007. "Linear Agreement in Slovene Conjuncts." In Formal Approaches to Slavic Linguistics 15: The Toronto Meeting, Richard Compton, Magda Goledzinowska and Ulyana Savchenko (eds.). Ann Arbor: Michigan Slavic Publications, 210–227.

Marušič, Franc, Andrew Nevins and William Badecker. 2015. "The grammars of conjunction agreement in Slovenian." *Syntax* 18 (1): 39–77.

Munn, Alan. 1999. "First-conjunct agreement: Against a clausal analysis." *Linguistic inquiry* 30(4): 643–68.

Murphy, Andrew and Zorica Puškar. 2018. "Closest conjunct agreement is an illusion." *Natural Language and Linguistic Theory* 36: 1207–1261.

Preminger, Omer. 2014. *Agreement and its failures*. Cambridge, MA: MIT Press.

Progovac, Ljiljana 1998a. "Structure for coordination (part I)." *GLOT International* 3(7): 3–6.

Progovac, Ljiljana 1998b. "Structure for coordination (part II)." *GLOT International* 3(8): 3–9.

Ross, John Robert. 1967. "Constraints on variables in syntax." PhD Dissertation. Cambridge, MA: MIT.

Stjepanović, Sandra. 1998. "Scrambling in Serbo-Croatian." Ms., University of Connecticut.

Stjepanović, Sandra. 2014. "Left Branch Extraction and the Coordinate Structure Constraint." In *NELS 44: Proceedings of the 44th Meeting of the North East Linguistic Society*, Volume 2, Jyoti Iyer and Leland Kusmer (eds.). Amherst, MA: GLSA, University of Massachusetts, 157–171.

Willer Gold, Jana, Boban Arsenijević, Mia Batinić, Nermina Čordalija, Marijana Kresić, Nedžad Leko, Franc Marušič, Tanja Milićev, Nataša Milićević, Ivana Mitić, Andrew Nevins, Anita Peti-Stantić, Branimir Stanković, Tina Šuligoj and Jelena Tušek. 2016. "Conjunct agreement and gender in South Slavic: From theory to experiments to theory." *Journal of Slavic Linguistics* 24: 187–224.

Zeijlstra, Hedde. 2012. "There is only one way to agree." *The linguistic Review* 29: 491–539.

Nikola Paillereau, Radek Skarnitzl

An Acoustic-Perceptual Study on Czech Monophthongs

1. Introduction

For more than a century, vowel formants have served for describing vowels. Although the first two formants are traditionally regarded as sufficient when characterizing vowel quality, higher formants were shown to be important for the acoustic description of certain vowels (Vaissière 2007). F3 is the main acoustic cue of contrasts based on labiality, but it also distinguishes among front unrounded vowels. While [i]-like vowels are realized with an F3 converging either with F2 (for mid-palatal [i] as in British English) or with F4 (for pre-palatal [i] as in Swedish or French), F3 of [e]-like vowels lies halfway between F2 and F4.

The incorporation of higher formants into the description of vowels is supported by perceptual integration, whereby formants separated by a critical distance of 3.5 Bark form only one perceptual peak (as proposed by Chistovich and Lublinskaja 1979 for F1-F2, and further extended to F2-F3-F4 by Schwartz and Escudier 1987). A strong convergence of two formants, F1/F2 in back vowels and [a̠], and F2/F3 or F3/F4 in front vowels, also characterize "focal vowels" (Badin et al. 1990). However, there does not seem to be a given distance between two converging formants, which would distinguish between front vowels that are focal (such as [i]) and non-focal (such as [ɛ]). In cross-linguistic studies, vowels produced with converging formants are thus generally interpreted as being more or less focal (Schwartz et al. 2005; Gendrot and Adda-Decker 2007).

1.1. Vowels of Czech

Czech is traditionally described as having five short and five long monophthongs, /ɪ iː, ɛ ɛː, a aː, o oː, u uː/, and three diphthongs, /o͡u a͡u ɛ͡u/ (Skarnitzl, Šturm & Volín, 2016). Hála (1941) was among the first to study acoustic properties of Czech vowels. The short–long pairs were reported to be identical in terms of quality, with small exceptions in the close front region, and the duration of long vowels was reported to be about twice that of the corresponding short vowels. Most recently, Skarnitzl and Volín (2012; further abbreviated as SV) examined F1 and F2 of Czech monophthongs in continuous read speech. The data point to a clear difference in high-vowel pairs. On average, the difference in F1 between [iː]

and [ɪ] exceeds 30%, and the difference in F2 slightly exceeds 5%, which confirms a previously described opening of [ɪ]. In addition, SV also pointed to a formant difference in the [u u:] pair, which exceeds 10% both in F1 and F2 (however, a tendency for a more peripheral tongue position of [u:] was already noted by Trávníček, 1932). The Czech vocalic system thus seems to be tending to a more symmetrical arrangement in the high region. As for the non-high vowels, [ɛ ɛ:], [a a:], and [o o:], the study doesn't indicate any qualitative difference between the short and long members. The mean formant differences are below 5%, the *just noticeable difference* in vowel formants (Kewley-Port and Zheng 1999). In contrast to the older studies, however, SV showed asymmetrical locations of the mid vowels, with the front [ɛ ɛ:] having higher F1 than the back [o o:].

The qualitative differences between short–long vowel pairs are supported by temporal differences: while the non-high long vowels are between 1.7 and 1.8 times longer than their short counterparts, [i:] is only 1.3 times longer than [ɪ], and [u:] is 1.6 times longer than [u] (Skarnitzl 2012). This quality–quantity cue trading is also corroborated by perceptual data, which show that Czech listeners exploit both spectral and temporal information for discrimination between the pairs, with the spectrum cuing the [ɪ/i:] difference more than the [u/u:] difference, and with Bohemian Czech listeners more sensitive to spectral changes than Moravian Czech listeners (Podlipský, Chládková and Šimáčková 2012).

1.2. Aim of the present study

As mentioned above, Czech vowels have been mainly described in terms of F1 and F2. We thus aim to provide values of the higher formants and examine how these contribute to the acoustic description of front vowels, especially [ɪ] and [i:]. In this perspective, we also examine the vowels' focal character. The second aim is to contribute to the recent attempts at disentangling the role of durational and spectral cues in the identification of Czech vowels. Our objective is to find to what extent the formant differences between members of high vowel pairs [ɪ/i:] and [u/u:] are perceived not only by native Czech listeners, but also by French listeners, whose native vowel system is based on four degrees of aperture without contrastive length.

The production and perceptual experiments are based on vowels uttered in isolation, i.e., surrounded by short pauses. According to Miller (1981), isolated vowels, which are produced without formant transitions due to coarticulatory effects, define the vowel target. Moreover, studying isolated vowels is a valid approach (Meunier, 2001). To our knowledge, the acoustic characteristics of Czech vowels in isolation have not yet been analyzed, apart from one comparative study of Czech monophthong vowels and French oral vowels (Paillereau 2016).

2. Experiment 1: Production

In the first experiment, we describe the acoustic realization of Czech isolated vowels and extend the results of Paillereau (2016). First we describe formant values and compare F1 and F2 with those reported by SV, then we address formant focalization.

2.1. Method

20 female native speakers from the Bohemian region, aged between 24 and 38 years (mean age = 27) produced ten Czech monophthong vowels in isolation [ɪ i:, ɛ ɛ:, a a:, o o:, u u:], embedded in carrier sentences such as: "Jana, říkám <a> jako ve slově Jana." ("*Jana, I say* <a> *as in the word Jana.*"). None of the speakers reported hearing or speaking difficulties. Before the recording session, each speaker was presented with the ten sentences and underwent a training session. All the sentences were mixed and repeated 4 times so that two identical sentences never succeeded one another. Recordings were obtained in a quiet room with a headband microphone AKG C520 and a sound card Edirol UA25, connected to a MacBook Pro, with a sampling frequency of 44.1 kHz and 16-bit quantization.

The target vowels were segmented and labelled manually in Praat (Boersma and Weenink 2015), with boundary placement being guided by the presence of full formant structure (i.e., F1 and F2, as well as F3 and F4 in front vowels). Initial glottal stops and final *voice decay time* were not considered to be part of the vowel. Vowels were analyzed in terms of vowel formants and duration. Vowel formants were measured in a semi-automatic way using a Burg-algorithm-based script, which allows the user to specify the precise position in the speech signal, with no phonation abnormalities. Formants were extracted at approximately the midpoint of each vowel, with the analysis window of 25 ms, in the 0–5,500 Hz range; however, the maximum frequency was either lowered or increased in cases of false detection.

In total, we worked with 800 vowels (20 speakers ′ 10 vowels ′ 4 repetitions), but as it was impossible to extract formant values from 7 vowels, the analyses are based on 793 items.

2.2. Results

Mean and variance values of vowel formants and duration are summarized in Table 1. Intrinsic duration is vowel dependent: the average duration of short vowels lies between 182 ms and 194.7 ms, whereas that of long vowels is between

Table 1: Mean duration (ms) and formant (Hz) values of Czech monophthongs; standard deviations are given in parentheses.

	F1	F2	F3	F4	duration
ɪ	401 *(52)*	2565 *(132)*	3112 *(152)*	4197 *(242)*	182.0
i:	256 *(39)*	2725 *(191)*	3626 *(197)*	4285 *(244)*	298.2
ɛ	698 *(52)*	2040 *(138)*	2920 *(128)*	4222 *(238)*	191.5
ɛ:	690 *(64)*	2098 *(137)*	2951 *(145)*	4274 *(253)*	325.9
a	834 *(91)*	1305 *(102)*	2750 *(195)*		188.0
a:	898 *(94)*	1417 *(129)*	2754 *(158)*		312.4
o	492 *(88)*	915 *(100)*	2753 *(231)*		194.7
o:	466 *(86)*	891 *(86)*	2743 *(260)*		313.1
u	340 *(52)*	683 *(111)*	2730 *(275)*		183.8
u:	291 *(43)*	630 *(96)*	2630 *(268)*		320.7

298.2 ms and 325.9 ms. Duration ratios are quite similar to each other, between 1.61 for [o/o:] and 1.74 for [u/u:], and do not correspond to those reported for continuous speech (Skarnitzl 2012; *cf.* section 1.1). Average formant values show that the pair [ɪ/i:] differs not only in F1 (401 Hz and 256 Hz respectively) and F2 (2565 Hz and 2725 Hz), as indicated by SV, but also in F3 (3112 Hz and 3626 Hz) and F4 (4197 Hz and 4285 Hz). In contrast to SV's data, isolated [a:] (= 1417 Hz) is produced with a higher F2 than [a] (= 1305 Hz), probably due to the speakers' Pilsner dialect.

These data, superimposed on those of SV, are depicted in the F1–F2 vowel quadrilateral in Figure 2. Isolated vowels, which are expected to be hyper-articulated, were indeed pronounced as more peripheral than those extracted from connected read speech, affected by coarticulation. As in SV's study, the high region is rather symmetrical, with short vowels being produced with a higher F1 than their long counterparts, and the mid region rather asymmetrical, with front vowels having a higher F1 than back ones.

Formant convergence in Czech vowels is illustrated in Figure 3, which shows the relative positions of individual formants. The plots indicate that the focal character of [i:] results from the convergence of F3 and F4, which are separated by 0.968 Bark. This distance is much lower than that reported by Gendrot and Adda-Decker (2007) for tense [i] (sometimes transcribed as long [i:]) in eight other languages (albeit in connected speech): the lowest value of 1.2 Bark is reported for French. The short, more open [ɪ] is focal due to the convergence of F2 and F3, which are separated by 1.13 Bark. In [ɛ ɛ:], no formant convergence is

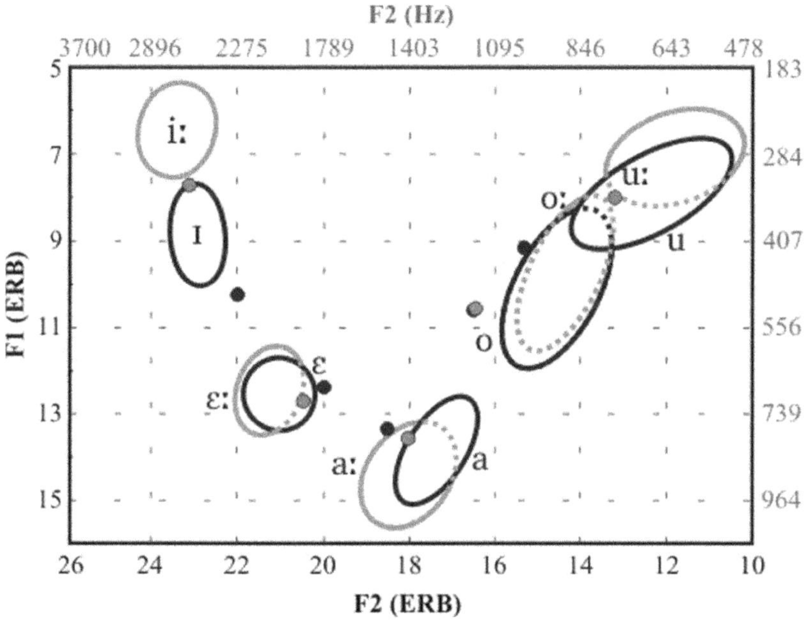

Figure 2: F1–F2 quadrilateral of Czech. The ellipses indicate 67% of the formant values. The dots show mean formant values taken from Skarnitzl and Volín (2012). Black ellipses and dots correspond to short vowels, grey ellipses and dots to long vowels.

observed, with the F2–F3 and F3–F4 distance being about 2.2 Bark. On the other hand, in back vowels and in [a a:], the first two formants converge. On average, the F1–F2 distance is smallest in [a a:] (2.7 Bark), followed by [u u:] (2.92 Bark), and it is biggest in [o o:] (3.12 Bark).

3. Experiment 2: Perception (identification)

The main purpose of this experiment is to determine to what extent Czech listeners from the Bohemian region are dependent on vowel duration in categorizing Czech vowels as either short or long.

3.1. Method

The second experiment consists of three series of identification tests, administered to 27 monolingual Czech secondary school students from Pilsen, aged

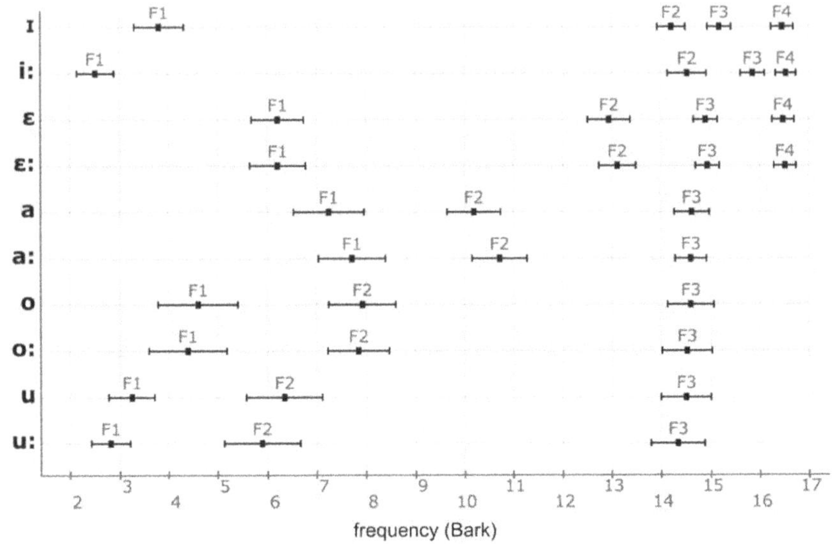

Figure 3: Relative position of formants in Czech vowels; the dot corresponds to the mean, the whiskers to 1 standard deviation from the mean.

between 11–12. First, listeners identified 40 Czech isolated vowels (10 vowels ′ 4 repetitions read by 4 of the female speakers from Experiment 1). 10 stimuli were part of a training phase, omitted from the analysis. This result serves as reference (REF). Next, the listeners identified 15 isolated phonologically long vowels (5 vowels ′ 3 repetitions) shortened to one half of the original duration (Sx2 condition), as well as 15 isolated phonologically long vowels shortened to 100 ms each, which corresponds, depending on the vowel and speaking rate, to about one third of the initial duration (S-100 condition). Finally the listeners identified 15 isolated phonologically short vowels lengthened to twice the original duration (Lx2 condition). In the S-100 and Sx2 conditions, the stimuli consisted of the central part of the signal. The perceptual tests were performed in two sessions, about 40 minutes each, in a classroom equipped with a high-quality sound system. Instructions were given in writing. A short pause was made every 10 minutes. Listeners indicated their responses on an answer sheet by choosing one of the ten written vowels (orthographic and phonetic transcriptions correspond in Czech, and the <y> grapheme was not used) and by giving a goodness score on a 5-point scale (1= completely sure, 5 = not sure at all about my choice).

Table 2: Proportion of Identification (PI), Goodness Ratings (GR) and Fit Index value (FI) of Czech isolated vowels in REF, Sx2, S-100 and Lx2 conditions. 81 responses per vowel in each category: 27 listeners ´ 3 repetitions.

	REF	Sx2	S-100	Lx2
	PI/GR/FI	**PI/GR/FI**	**PI/GR/FI**	**PI/GR/FI**
ɪ	0.96/4.8/4.6	0.21/4.1/0.9	0.8/4.9/3.9	0.35/4.4/1.5
i:	1/4.8/4.8	0.79/4.7/3.7	0.2/4.6/0.9	0.55/4.6/2.5
ɛ	0.98/4.6/4.5	0.98/4.7/4.6	0.98/5/4.9	
ɛ:	0.99/4.8/4.8			0.9/4.7/4.2
a	0.79/4.6/3.6	0.9/4.7/4.2	0.99/4.9/4.9	
a:	0.98/4.6/4.5			0.93/4.8/4.5
o	0.93/4.6/4.3	0.91/4.7/4.3	0.99/4.9/4.9	
o:	0.88/4.5/4			0.91/4.7/4.3
u	1/4.7/4.7	0.85/4.5/3.8	0.95/4.9/4.7	0.15/4.3/0.7
u:	0.99/4.6/4.6	0.15/4.1/0.6		0.85/4.5/3.8

3.2. Results

The results are expressed in terms of a *Fit Index* (FI) value (Guion et al. 2000), obtained by multiplying the identification score by the goodness rating, with a maximum of 5. Table 2 indicates the Proportion of Identification (PI), Goodness Ratings (GR) and Fit Index (FI) for all ten vowels identified in terms of intended categories in the REF condition, for [i: ɛ: a: o: u:] in the Sx2 and S-100 conditions, and for [ɪ ɛ a o u] in the Lx2 condition. Only identifications at more than 30% are included in the REF condition and at more than 10% in the other conditions.

It is apparent from Table 2 that Czech isolated vowels are identified in terms of intended categories with high goodness ratings, with long /i:/ and /ɛ:/ being the most well identified vowels (FI at 4.8) and with short /a/ being the least well identified vowel (FI at 3.6). On average, long vowels, undoubtedly because of their important absolute duration, are less often confused with their short counterparts than vice versa; this is most obvious in the case of the /a a:/ pair. The best-identified pair is /ɪ i:/, identified with an FI at 4.6 and 4.8 respectively, followed by /u u:/, identified with an FI at 4.7 and 4.6 respectively. This can be explained by the spectral differences of the two members within each pair (see sections 1.1 and 2).

In the Sx2 condition, stimuli are mostly categorized as short vowels, except for the [i]-like stimuli, which were categorized as long /i:/ in 79% of the responses (FI at 3.7). The [a]-like stimuli were identified as short /a/ with a higher FI than the original short /a/ (4.2 versus 3.6), which can be explained by the smaller absolute duration of short vowels in the Sx2 condition than in the REF condition. On the other hand, the [u]-like sounds were identified as short /u/ with an FI lower than the original short vowel (3.8 versus 4.7), which can be explained by the larger acoustic difference. In the S-100 condition, all vowels were mostly categorized as short vowels. In contrast to the Sx2 condition, in which vowels are longer, the [i]-like stimuli are in 80% of the responses identified as short /ɪ/ (FI at 3.9). This shows that duration is an important acoustic cue for Czech listeners and if vowels become too short, members of all vowel pairs are categorized as phonologically short, regardless of possible formant differences. In the Sx2 condition, stimuli are identified as phonologically short with a higher FI than in the previous conditions, which is again due to their short duration. The [u]-like vowel is categorized as short /u/ with the same FI as in the REF condition (at 4.7). Finally, the Lx2 condition shows that if short vowels are lengthened to twice their original duration, they are mostly categorized as phonologically long. However, the identification of high and non-high vowel stimuli again differs. The [i]-like stimuli are identified as /iː/ in only 55% of the responses (FI at 2.5); they are also categorized as /ɪ/ in 35% (FI at 1.5) and as /ɛː/ in 10% of the responses. The [u]-like stimuli are categorized as /uː/ in 85% (FI at 3.8) and as /u/ in 15% (FI at 0.7). The other stimuli are identified in at least 90% of the responses as phonologically long vowels.

4. Experiment 3: Perception (interlingual assimilation)

The aim of the third experiment was to examine the perceived relationship between the Czech vowel system, based on three degrees of aperture, and standard non-southern French vowel system, opposing mid-open and mid-close vowels.

4.1. Method

The perceptual test, administered to ten non-southern French listeners (M age = 39), comprised two sets of stimuli which were intermingled. In the first set, listeners identified ten French isolated vowels [i, e, ɛ, a, u, o, ɔ, y, ø, œ], recorded by three native Parisian female speakers. In the other set, the same listeners assimilated ten Czech isolated vowels [ɪ iː, ɛ ɛː, a aː, o oː, u uː], recorded by three of the native Czech female speakers from Pilsen used in the previous experiments, to the ten French vowel phonemes presented above. The listeners were not told they were identifying vowels from different languages. Stimuli were rated for goodness on a rating scale from 1 to 5, where 1 corresponded to "very badly pronounced" and 5 to "very well pronounced". The test, composed of 63 stimuli (3 stimuli presented in a training phase), took about 10 minutes.

4.2. Results

Results of both tests are interpreted in terms of a Fit Index (FI). Results of the first part of the test show that French focal vowels /i/ (FI at 4.6) and /u, a, y/ (FI at 4.5), as well as the front mid-high vowels /e/ (FI at 4.6) and /o/ (FI at 4.4), are more often identified in terms of the intended category and/or have a higher goodness rating than the other French mid vowels. Indeed, the vowels [ɛ, ɔ, ø, œ] were identified with an FI at 4, 3.9, 3.8 and 3.7, respectively. The standard deviation of the global mean FI is at 0.36. These results serve as a reference for the interpretation of the interlingual assimilation.

In the second part, Czech vowels assimilated to French vowels with an FI within 1 standard deviation from the mean FI for French vowels are considered as "good" exemplars, those within 2 standard deviations as "fair" exemplars, and those beyond 2 standard deviations as "poor" exemplars. This classification is taken from Guion et al. (2000). Table 3 indicates again the PI, GR and FI values of Czech vowels assimilated by French listeners. Vowels are listed according to their perceptual distance from the closest French vowel (expressed by a number of s.d.), from the smallest – indicating the biggest perceived difference – to the largest. Only identifications at more than 30% are included.

Table 3 shows that none of the Czech monophthong vowels is, according to our criteria mentioned above, a good exemplar of any French oral vowel. On the other hand, most Czech vowels are fair exemplars of French vowels. The best examples are the Czech short [ɪ] and long [a:], assimilated respectively to French /e/ and /a/ with an FI at 1.1 s.d. from the reference. Also assimilated fairly well are Czech short [u] and [o] to French /o/ and /ɔ/, respectively (FI at 1.38 s.d. from the reference). Finally, long [ɛ:] and [o:] are fair exemplars of French /ɛ/ and /ɔ/ respectively (FI at 1.66 and 1.94 s.d. from the reference). On the other hand, the corner vowels [a], [i:], [u:], along with the mid vowel [ɛ], can be considered as bad exemplars of the French vowels /a/, /i/, /u/, and /ɛ/, respectively, with an FI at 2.11, 3.33, 4.72, and 4.36 s.d. from the reference. Lastly, no Czech vowel stimulus was assimilated to any French rounded vowel at more than 30%.

Table 3: Proportion of Identification (PI), Goodness Rating (GR) and Fit Index value (FI) of Czech isolated vowels (CZ) to French categories (FR) (30 responses per vowel: 10 listeners ′ 3 repetitions).

CZ	FR	PI	GR	FI	Number of s.d
ɪ	e	1	4.2	4.2	1.11
a:	a	1	4.1	4.1	1.11
u	o	0.96	4.1	3.9	1.38
o	ɔ	1	3.4	3.4	1.38
ɛ:	ɛ	1	3.4	3.4	1.66
o:	ɔ	1	3.2	3.2	1.94
a	a	0.97	3.9	3.7	2.11
i:	i	1	3.4	3.4	3.33
ɛ	ɛ	0.81	3	2.4	4.36
u:	u	0.84	3.3	2.8	4.72

5. Discussion and conclusion

Experiment 1 shows that higher formants do participate in the acoustic definition of Czech vowels. By examining the positioning of F3 compared to F2 and F4 in front vowels and the perceptual distance of the converging formants, we showed that the short [ɪ] is a focal vowel of the F2/F3 type, and the long [i:] is a focal vowel of the F3/F4 type, whereas the mid [ɛ ɛ:] are, as expected, non-focal because their F3 lies approximately midway between F2 and F4. As demonstrated by Fant (1973) and Vaissière (2007), front high and mid-high vowels can actually share the same F1 and F2 values, and differ in higher formants. It would thus be interesting to examine whether there is a difference in the higher formants of [ɪ i:] in Moravian Czech, where these vowels have about the same F1 and F2 (Podlipský et al. 2012). Our data further show that [ɪ] and especially [i:] are very strongly focal, realized with even greater formant convergence than French [i] (Gendrot and Adda-Decker 2007). It must be kept in mind, however, that isolated vowels are typically realized with more extreme acoustic values than those obtained from continuous speech (*cf.* also SV and section 2.2. herein). The focal character of Czech vowels uttered in context should thus be examined in further studies.

Experiment 2 makes it clear that the best identified pairs of short/long vowels are high vowels. That may be either due to the general high perceptual salience of focal vowels (Schwartz et al. 2005) or to the fact that the vowels within these short/long pairs differ not only in duration but also in spectral characteristics, or to a combination of both factors. Experiment 2 also shows that Czech listeners perceive the spectral difference that exists between [ɪ i:] and only to a limited extent the one between [u u:]. Indeed, when [i:] is shortened to one half of its original duration, it is still most of the time identified as long [i:], which is not the case for [u:]. Nevertheless, when shortened to about one third of its original duration, the shortened [i:] is categorized as short /ɪ/. It therefore seems that all Czech vowels must maintain a certain duration to be interpreted as phonologically long by Czech listeners.

Experiment 3 shows that French listeners, whose native vocalic system operates with four degrees of aperture, perceive the spectral differences in the pairs of Czech high front vowels. Whereas vowels within each pair [a a:], [ɛ ɛ:] and [o o:] are assimilated to the same French vowel, that is, respectively, /a/, /ɛ/ and /ɔ/, vowels within the pairs [ɪ i:] and [u u:] correspond to different French timbres, i.e. /e i/ and /o u/, respectively, with the Czech short vowels being fair exemplars and long vowels bad exemplars of the French categories. To understand why long vowels are generally bad exemplars of French vowels, even if they are strongly focal as in French, vowel inherent spectral change should be examined in further studies. Indeed, French is known to have only pure monophthongs, produced with high muscle tension (Delattre 1953), whereas the Czech system also includes diphthongs. In languages with diphthongization, long (tense) vowels are generally produced with larger inherent formant movements than their short (lax) counterparts (Steinlen 2005).

Acknowledgements

The first author was supported by the Charles University PRIMUS project HUM/19. The second author was supported from European Regional Development Fund-Project "Creativity and Adaptability as Conditions of the Success of Europe in an Interrelated World" (No. CZ.02.1.01/0.0/0.0/16_019/000 0734). We thank Mgr. Milena Deglová and the pupils from Církevní gymnázium in Pilsen for participating in the perceptual tests.

References

Badin, Pierre, Pascal Perrier, Louis-Jean Bo and Christian Abry. 1990. "Vocalic nomograms: Acoustic and articulatory considerations upon formant convergences." *JASA* 78: 1290–1300.

Boersma, Paul and Weenink, David. 2015. "Praat: doing phonetics by computer." Version 6.0. Retrieved from *www.praat.org*.

Chistovich, Ludmilla A. and Lublinskaya, Valentina V. 1979. "The 'Center of gravity' effect in vowel spectra and critical distance between the formants: Psychoacoustical study of the perception of vowel-like stimuli." *Hearing Research* 1: 185–195.

Delattre, Pierre. 1953. "The phonetic modes of French." *The French Review* 27(1): 59–63. [in French]

Fant, Gunnar. 1973. *Speech Sounds and Features*. Cambridge: MIT Press.

Gendrot, Cédric and Adda-Decker, Martine. 2007. "Impact of duration and vowel inventory size on formant values of oral vowels: an automated formant analysis from eight languages." In *Proceedings of 16th ICPhS*, 1417–1420.

Guion, Susan G., James E. Flege, Reiko Akahane-Yamada and Jessica S. Pruitt. 2000. "An investigation of current models of second language speech perception: the case of Japonese adult's perception of English consonants." *JASA* 107: 2711–2724.

Hála, Bohuslav. 1941. *Acoustic Nature of Vowels*. Praha: Czech Academy of Sciences and Arts. [in Czech]

Kewley-Port, Diane and Zheng, Yijian. 1999. "Vowel formant discrimination: Towards more ordinary listening conditions." *JASA* 106: 2945–2958.

Meunier, Christine. 2001. "Le traitement de la variabilité dans la parole. Aspects théoriques et méthodologiques." *Travaux Interdisciplinaires du Laboratoire Parole et Langage d'Aix-en- Provence* 20: 69–90.

Miller, Joanne L. 1981. "Effects of speaking rate on segmental distinctions." In *Perspectives on the Study of Speech*, Peter D. Eimas and Joanne L. Miller (eds.). Hillsdale, NJ: Erlbaum, 39–73.

Paillereau, Nikola. 2016. "'Identical' vowels in L1 and L2? Criteria and implications for L2 phonetic teaching and learning." In *EUROSLA Yearbook 2016*, Sarah Ann Liszka, Pascale Leclercq, Marion Tellier and Georges Daniel Véronique (eds.). Amsterdam: John Benjamins, 144–178.

Podlipský, Václav J., Kateřina Chládková and Šárka Šimáčková 2012. "Length or height? Front-back symmetry in the Czech vowel system." Presented at *LabPhon13*, Stuttgart.

Schwartz, Jean-Luc and Escudier, Pierre. 1987. "Does the human auditory system include large scale spectral integration?". In *The Psychophysics of Speech Perception*, Marten E. Schouten (ed.). Dordrecht: Martinus Nijhoff Publishers, 284–292.

Schwartz, Jean-Luc, Christian Abry, Louis-Jean Boë, Lucie Ménard and Nathalie Vallée. 2005. "Asymmetries in vowel perception, in the context of the Dispersion–Focalisation Theory." *Speech Communication* 45: 425–434.

Skarnitzl, Radek. 2012. "Two kinds of *i* in the pronunciation of Czech." *Naše řeč* 95: 141–153. [in Czech]

Skarnitzl, Radek, Pavel Šturm and Jan Volín. *Sound Basis of Speech Communication: Phonetic and Phonological Description of Speech*. Praha: Karolinum. [in Czech]

Skarnitzl, Radek and Volín, Jan. 2012. "Reference values of vowel formants for young adult speakers of Standard Czech." *Akustické listy* 18: 7–11. [in Czech]

Steinlen, Anne. 2005. *The Influence of Consonants on Native and Non-native Vowel Production*. Tübingen: Gunter Narr Verlag.

Trávníček, František. 1932. *Introduction into Czech Phonetics*. Praha: Česká grafická unie. [in Czech]

Vaissière, Jacqueline. 2007. "Area functions and articulatory modelling as a tool for investigating the articulatory, acoustic and perceptual properties of the contrast between the sounds in a language." In *Experimental Approaches to Phonology*, Solé, Maria-Josep, Patrice Speeter Beddor, Manjari Ohala (eds.). Oxford: Oxford University Press, 54–72.

Mojmír Dočekal

On the Non-(Exhaustive and Contrastively Focused) Constituent Negation in Slavic*

1. Data and the issue

1.1. Introduction to the problem

The goal of this article is to develop a formal semantic account for Czech constituent negation. To accomplish this task, I will discuss the most frequent sub-types of phrases modified by a constituent negation (CN). One type of such a construction is exemplified in (1). Descriptively speaking, it is the constituent negation of a comparative (involving numerals) contained in an NP. I will not discuss complex issues concerning the syntactic and semantic nature of the comparative itself since the main topic of this article concerns the interpretation of the numeral's cardinality denotation and its semantic interaction with the constituent negation. Intuitively, the interpretation of (1) is close to a paraphrase such as 'At most/maximally two people testified truthfully'. The sentence comes from the SYN2010 corpus, which is the biggest and most representative corpus of contemporary Czech, and the context of the sentence corroborates the proposed intuitive meaning. The goal of my article is to derive the intuitive meaning of (1) in a compositional way and to compare the derivation to a different meaning which this type of constructions/sentences yields in English.

(1) Ne více než dva lidé vypovídali pravdivě.
no more than two people testified truthfully
'No more than two people testified truthfully.'

* This article benefited from conversations with many people which I would like to thank. First, of course, the audience at the FDSL conference, specifically Boban Arsenijević, Jakub Dotlačil, and many others. Next, I would like to thank Rick Nouwen in Utrecht as well as linguists from Brno, Pavel Caha, Markéta Ziková, and Hana Strachoňová among others. The final version of this article was improved by many comments and questions raised by an anonymous reviewer, whom I would like to thank as well. Especially I would like to thank Marcin Wągiel for help with the final version of the article. All errors are, of course, only mine. The research was supported by a Czech Science Foundation (GAČR) grant to the Department of Linguistics and Baltic Languages at the Masaryk University in Brno (GA17-16111S).

For Czech native speakers the intuitive meaning is straightforwardly compositional: if the meaning of the comparative in (1) can be captured by adopting the mathematical relation >, the meaning of the numeral is simply the number 2, and the meaning of the negation involves the reversal of the mathematical relation, then the meaning of the Czech phrase [no more than two people] is '≤ 2 people' which then interacts with the meaning of the VP in an entirely compositional manner. And if we were to describe only the Czech (or generally, as we will see, Slavic) data, the article could end here. However, the meaning described intuitively in this paragraph, appears to be surprising from the cross-linguistic perspective, as we will discuss immediately.

Speakers of Germanic languages interpret similar constructions in a very different way. This fact was reflected in Nouwen (2008), where the examples such as (2) are discussed at length. Nouwen claims that the most salient interpretation of negated comparatives with numerically modified NPs is upper bounded which means that the intuitive interpretation of (2) is exact (as opposed to the interval reading in Czech) and close to the paraphrase 'Exactly 30 people showed up'.[1] Nouwen (2008) observes that such a reading is both intuitively and theoretically surprising since following the same compositional steps as we did for (1), we would expect the interval reading for English as well.

(2) No more than 30 people showed up.

In this article, I will focus on the discussed type of CN in Slavic and, in some respects, I will compare it to sentential negation. Nevertheless, the main contribution of the article concerns the analysis of constituent negation. In Slavic languages it is easy to descriptively distinguish between constituent and sentential (verbal) negation, i.e., the first one does not license n-words whereas the latter does. Compare the ungrammaticality of (3-a) containing constituent negation with the grammaticality of (3-b) containing sentential negation. The ungrammaticality of (3-a) stems from the un-licensed n-word in object position.

(3) a. *Ne více než dva lidé navštívili nikoho.
No more than two people visited no-one
Intended: 'No more than two people visited no one.'

1 There is a pragmatic implicature on top of the exact interpretation which suggests that the number of people is surprisingly lower than expected. Nevertheless, the implicature seems not to interact with the whole semantic composition, so I will ignore it in the further part of the analysis.

b. Více než dva lidé nenavštívili nikoho
more than two people neg-visited no-one
'No more than two people didn't visit anyone.'

This paper is organized as follows. In Section 1.2 I introduce the formal machinery employed by Nouwen (2008) to account for the exact (upper-bounded) reading of English *no more*. Section 1.3 provides further comparative data from Czech and English and summarizes the basic pattern. In Section 2.1 I start with an observation concerning the focus-oriented behavior of Czech negation. Section 2.2 develops a formal semantic treatment of Czech constituent negation whereas in sections 2.3, 2.4 and 2.5 the proposed analysis is applied to the core types of Czech constructions involving constituent negation.

1.2. Compositional semantics of *no more*

The intuitive semantic composition discussed above is exactly mirrored by standard assumptions concerning the meaning of parts and their composition in (2), i.e., the meaning of a phrase *more than* α *P* is formalized as a quantifier over 2 arguments: a number α (denotation of the numeral) and a property P (denotation of the NP). For instance, the predicative use in (4) (simpler to treat than (2)) would be composed step-by-step in the following way. (4-a) is the set of sets with cardinalities > 3 (the meaning of *more than three*) and has to raise due to type reasons since the clausal subject is of type e whereas the comparative needs a property (P), i.e., (4-b) where the trace after the movement is λ-bound and the $\leq$-abstraction creates the required property of the $\langle e,t \rangle$ type. (4-c) is the result of functional application of the raised comparative to the property resulting from the λ-abstraction and it represents the intuitive meaning of (4), i.e., the maximal number of guests was more than 3.

(4) The number of guests was more than three.
  a. $[\lambda\alpha\lambda P.max_d(P(d))>\alpha](3)$
  b. $[\lambda P.max_d(P(d))>3](\lambda n[\text{the number of guests was } n])$
  c. $max_d(\lambda d.\text{the number of guests was } d) > 3$

Adding negation (in form of a negative determiner) is not expected to change anything in the composition and in the result, except, of course, reversing the relation from > to ≤. Therefore, the expected reading of (5) is (5-a), i.e., an interval reading, but as already mentioned, English negated comparatives do not get an interval interpretation but rather an exact cardinality reading, e.g., the 'exactly 3' reading for (5). The exact interpretation is the most salient interpretation of (5) and it is formalized in (5-b).

(5) The number of guests was no more than three.
   a. $max_d(\lambda$ d. the number of guests was $d) \leq 3$
   b. $max_d(\lambda$ d. the number of guests was $d) = 3$

In an example such as (6) where the negated comparative numeral is used in argument position the same unexpected exact meaning appears again. The composition is similar to (5) but for type reasons (the distinction between predicate and argument position) it is required to insert Hackl's counting quantifier *m*-many with semantics $\lambda A \lambda B.\exists x[\#x{=}m \wedge A(x) \wedge B(x)]$. The cardinality ($\#x$) comes from the numeral, the denotation of *A* is the meaning of its NP argument, and the denotation of *B* is the meaning of the VP argument. The English sentence in (2) repeated below as (6) has the truth conditions in (6-a) (the interval semantics) which again is strengthened to the equality reading formalized in (6-b) – exactly the same unpredicted reading as in (5).

(6) No more than 30 people showed up.
   a. $\max_d(\lambda y \exists x[\#x{=}y \wedge people(x) \wedge showed\_up(x)]) \leq 30$
   b. $\max_d(\lambda y \exists x[\#x{=}y \wedge people(x) \wedge showed\_up(x)]) = 30$

In general, the problem can be formulated in the following way: English numerical comparative negated with *no* has a surprisingly strengthened equative reading while the same construction in Czech yields just a theoretically and intuitively expected interval reading.[2] Nouwen's explanation of the English data pattern is as follows: he assumes that non-strict comparison (relations such as ≤ and ≥ which correspond to English negated comparatives like *no more than* and *no less than*) yields sensible implicatures which are then exhaustified through the

2 As the reviewer of this article correctly remarks, the English interpretation strategy for *no more* makes a lot of sense pragmatically, and thus the Czech interpretation can be viewed as surprising as well. I agree to some extent but it seems to me that we observe here a more general pattern, i.e., in many cases negation in natural languages has very weak literal truth-conditions. For example, the predicate logic formalization $\neg\exists x[book(x) \wedge read(\text{John},x)]$ of a sentence like *John didn't read a book* (with the wide scope of a negation) would be true in all models with a non-empty set of books and no intersection between this set and the set of things read by John. Though there are infinitely many such models the English sentence would be pragmatically coherently used only in a particular subset of such models, e.g., those where John read something different than a book. Therefore, it seems that natural languages somehow compensate the weak truth conditions of negated sentences but it is not granted a priori whether such strengthening happens through scalar implicatures, as in English, or through a focus strategy, as in Czech.

usual pragmatic strengthening, i.e., via negation of logically stronger alternatives/implicatures of the asserted sentence. According to Nouwen, (2) has the truth-conditions/at-issue meaning in (7-a) but in addition it has the scalar implicature in (7-b) which is negated because under negation 29 is logically stronger than 30. Consequently, the strengthened truth-conditions in (7-c) explain the equative reading of negated English comparatives.

(7) a. at issue: $\max_d(\lambda y \exists x[\#x{=}y \wedge people(x) \wedge showed\_up(x)]) \leq 30$
b. SI: $\neg\max_d(\lambda y \exists x[\#x{=}y \wedge people(x) \wedge showed\_up(x)]) \leq 29$
c. $\max_d(\lambda y \exists x[\#x{=}y \wedge people(x) \wedge showed\_up(x)]) = 30$

Nouwen further claims that the non-strict comparison differs from the strict comparison, i.e., relations such as > and < denoted by English comparatives *more than, less than*, which does not lead to the pragmatic strengthening/meaning enrichment (as discussed in the literature, e.g., Krifka (1999), Schulz and Van Rooij (2006), and Fox and Hackl (2006)). This is illustrated in (8) which has only the interval reading.

(8) More than 30 people came.
a. at issue: $\max_d(\lambda y \exists x[\#x{=}y \wedge people(x) \wedge came(x)]) > 30$
b. no SI

1.3. More data and the summary of the puzzle

To verify my intuitions, I conducted a small corpus study. I extracted all occurrences of negated comparative constructions from SYN2010 which is the most representative corpus of contemporary Czech. The corpus contained approximately 200 instances of the *no more than* and *no less than* type and one of the most frequent examples is, e.g., the negation of a time denoting comparative such as *ne více než dvě hodiny* 'no more than two hours'. The results of the study show that almost all of the occurrences of the construction yield the interval reading I have already discussed.[3] Next, I confronted the translation of (1) into Polish, Bulgarian, and Russian with native speakers of those languages and again all of them confirmed that the most salient reading they get is the interval one.

3 Some of the examples from the corpus are further discussed in Section 2, where I apply the proposed formalization to the core cases of Czech constituent negation. I went through the surrounding contexts of the excerpted sentences and in 95% of cases the context supported the interval rather than not the upper-bounded interpretation. The remaining 5% constituted the usual corpus mess, e.g., eliptical sentences and non-classifiable occurrences.

Therefore, it seems safe to claim that negated comparative numerals do have the interval semantics in Czech and it is highly probable that this empirical generalization holds for the whole Slavic language family as well.

The existence of the discussed distinction between English and Czech with respect to possible interpretations is surprising from Nouwen's perspective since his mechanism of obtaining the equality reading is supposed to be universal. Nonetheless, before we move to the explanation of the difference, let us look at more data which bring in evidence for the general nature of the difference.

1.2.1. Equality readings

Nouwen points out that examples such as (9-a) and (9-b) yield the equality readings as well. The ingredients are structurally similar, i.e., the comparative negated by *no,* but this time it is not a numeral what is compared but rather a degree to which some property holds. For instance, (9-a) is true iff the size of Holland equates to a very big city whereas (9-b) is true iff the extent to which a whale is a fish equates to the extent to which a horse is a fish.

(9) a. Holland is no more than a very big city.
  b. A whale is no more a fish than a horse.

The Czech translation of (9-a) is provided in (10). Again, it has only the interval reading, i.e., (10) would be true iff Holland's size is smaller or equal to the size of a very big city. Nevertheless, Czech is able to express the equality reading as well – in order to do so the ordinary prefixal verbal negation (on a lexical verb or on an auxiliary, depending on the tense, mood etc.) has to be used, as demonstrated in (11-a) and in (11-b). The first sentence equates the size of Holland to one big city and the second sentence is true iff exactly 2 people testified truthfully. Unlike constituent negation, Czech verbal negation has the equality reading as its primary meaning.[4]

(10) Holandsko je ne víc než jedno velké město.
  Holland is no more than one big city
  'Holland is no more than a very big city.'

(11) a. Holandsko není víc než jedno velké město.
  Holland neg-AUX more than one big city
  'Holland isn't more than a very big city.'

---

4 (11-a)/(11-b) can have the interval meaning as well but it is not the most salient interpretation.

b. Pravdivě nevypovídali víc než dva lidé.
truthfully neg-testify more than two people
'More than two people didn't testify truthfully.'

Furthermore, Nouwen claims that English *not* in examples such as (12-a) yields the interval reading, as observed in Czech. In other words, (12-b) states that the emperor remained at Rome exactly three months whereas (12-a) is true if the emperor remained there less than three months. Nouwen claims that *not* in the cases like (12-a) is used as a denial of the strict comparison and because of that it does not yield the strengthened equality reading.

(12) a. The victorious emperor remained at Rome not more than three months. '< 3 months'
b. The victorious emperor remained at Rome no more than three months. '= 3 months'

Let us summarize the empirical findings. It seems that English *no* in comparatives leads to the exhaustification unlike *not* which (probably due to its denial nature according to Nouwen) has just the interval (≤) reading. In Czech the readings are disambiguated with either pre-verbal *ne-* whose exhaustified reading is the most salient one while the constituent negation *ne* does not lead to exhaustification and gets an interval reading.

2. Solution

My solution to the discussed difference between Czech and English constituent negation (CN) will start in Section 2.1 where I summarize the data pointing at the focus particle behaviour of Czech CN. Next, in Section 2.2, I will propose a semantic formalization of Czech CN which reflects its focus sensitivite nature. In the following Sections 2.3 and 2.4 the semantics will be applied to most types of phrases which are modified by Czech CN to test the proposed formalization. Finally, in the Section 2.5 we will return to the original puzzle concerning the differencc bctween the availability of interpretations of negated comparatives with numerically modified NPs in Czech and English.

2.1. Syntactical behaviour of Czech CN

It is well known (see Jasinskaja (2012) a.o.) that Slavic focus particles (FP) have to c-command their associated F-marked expression, see (13), and in most cases (unlike English FPs) they have to be adjacent to the F-marked constituent, see (14).[5] CN behaves similar to all other FPs, as exemplified in (14) with a prototypical FP *pouze* 'only'.

(13) a. Já se choval [seriózně]$_F$ *ne/pouze.
I SE behaved seriously not/only
'I behaved only seriously.'

(14) a. I behave only [seriously]$_F$.
b. I only behave [seriously]$_F$.
c. Já *pouze/*ne jsem se choval [seriózně]$_F$.
d. Já jsem se choval pouze/ne [seriózně]$_F$.

However, in some environments, namely if the F-marked constituent is an NP embedded in another NP ([NP [NP]$_F$]) or if the F-marked NP is embedded in a PP ([P [NP]$_F$]), Czech FPs allow for non-adjacency and even in most cases such sentences sound distinctly odd if the FP are adjacent to their F-marked expression, see the contrast in (15) and (16). Again, in this respect Czech CN behaves like a prototypical Czech FP *pouze* 'only'. In general, Czech FPs (including CN) are reminiscent of German FPs such as *sogar* or *nur* (for the original observation of German facts see Büring and Hartmann (2001) and Reis (2005)).

(15) a. Pozval jsem pouze/ne [majitele [pivovarů]$_F$].
invited-I AUX only/not owners breweries-GN .
'I invited only/not owners of breweries.'
b. Pozval jsem [majitele *pouze/ne [pivovarů]$_F$].
invited-I AUX owners only/not breweries-GN

(16) a. Došli jsme pouze/ne [k [mostu]$_F$].
came-we AUX only/not to bridge.
'We came only/not to the bridge.'
b. Došli jsme [k *pouze/ne [mostu]$_F$].
came-we AUX to only/not bridge

5 As the anonymous reviewer correctly points out, the adjacency observation leaves a possibility of right adjacency as an alternative explanation. I believe that this unattested pattern (Czech focus particles generally cannot be right adjacent to their F-marked expressions) follows simply from the general c-command requirement; right adjacency would reverse the c-commanding dependency (in the usual left-branching scenario, of course).

On the basis of these observations I will further assume that Czech CN is a focus particle associated with an F-marked expression. If we look at an intuitive meaning of Czech CN, exemplified in (17-a), it seems to be best paraphrased in English by a negated cleft such as (17-b). In other words, indicating a further formalization, Czech CN seems to negate the truth-conditions of its clause (an ordinary semantic value in Rooth's terms) but it presupposes that at least one of the alternatives to its clause (where alternatives are computed from the focus point of view) has to be true. For instance, (17-a-b) is true if the speaker didn't invite owners of breweries but rather owners of something other than breweries, e.g., candy stores or coffeehouses, instead.

(17) a. Pozval jsem ne majitele [pivovarů]$_F$.
invited-I AUX not owners breweries-GEN
'I invited not the owners of breweries.'.
b. ≈ It were not owners of breweries, whom I invited.

Notice that Czech verbal negation is different from CN since it allows association with F-marked expression at distance, see (18-a), and it even allows for the F-marked expression c-commanding the negated verb, i.e., the opposite behaviour compared to FPs/CN. As for non-adjacency as in (17), the non-adjacency is a norm for verbal negation, unlike its exceptional behavior with CNs/FPs.

(18) a. Petr neprozradil Karlovi [to tajemství]$_F$.
Petr neg-revealed to-Karel the secret.
'Petr didn't reveal the secret to Karel.'
b. [To tajemství]$_F$ Petr Karlovi neprozradil.
the secret Petr to-Karel neg-revealed.
'To Karel Petr didn't reveal the secret.'

2.2. Formalization

In this section, I will formalize the intuition introduced above. Building on the semantics for FPs developed in Büring and Hartmann (2001), let us assume that Czech CN combines with a set denoting expression, i.e., a set of entities, a set of sets etc. It negates the its meaning (which results in the complement of the original set) – this complement output of negating the set formalizes the truth-condition effect at the ordinary semantic level. In addition, Czech CN asserts (or alternatively presupposes) that at least one of the sortally suitable focus alternatives to the negated F-marked expression fulfills the meaning of the predicate/rest of the sentence. The formalization of this reasoning is proposed in (19).

As we will see, the flexible type $\langle\alpha,t\rangle$ is exactly what we observe in various types of constituents modified by CN.

(19) If A is of type $\langle\alpha,t\rangle$, *ne A* is also of type $\langle\alpha,t\rangle$ and $[\![ne\ A]\!]$ is the set of all B such that B does not have the property $[\![A]\!]$ (i.e., $B \notin [\![A]\!]$) but it has a property (P) that is an alternative to A (i.e., in $[\![A]\!]^f$/ALT(A)).

Let me now illustrate how (19) works on a simple example where CN associates with a predicate F-marked NP as in (20). The formalization of (20) is given in (21) where *office_seeker(x)* represents the *A* (of type $\langle e,t\rangle$) from (19); it gets negated (the complement of the set of office seekers) and one of the alternatives (again of the $\langle e,t\rangle$ type), probably corresponding to social roles, professions etc., is supplied directly by the linguistic context introduced in (20), namely the property of being Christian, see (21)

(20) Snažím se být křesťanem, ne hledačem funkcí
want-I SE BE Christian not seeker office-GEN
'I want to be Christian, not office seeker.'

(21) a. $[\![not\ office\_seeker]\!] =$
$\lambda x[\neg office\_seeker(x) \wedge \exists P[P \in ALT(office\_seeker) \wedge P(x)]]$

2.3. Corpus verification

In this section, I will demonstrate how corpus data support my analysis of Czech CN as FP with semantics in (19). I selected 300 random sentences containing Czech CN from SYN2010 which is the largest corpus of contemporary Czech (100 million tokens) and classified the sentences according to (mostly) syntactic types of F-marked expressions negated by CN. Particular types with corresponding frequencies are listed in Table 1.

The most frequent contexts involve various degree/measure phrases (Nouwen's example belongs to this category), various PPs to some extent similar to the example (16), whole CPs, and finally NPs like in the example (20). In the remaining part of this section I will briefly discuss various types from the list and demonstrate that the proposed semantics can be applied without problems to the contexts in question giving raise to the intuitively appropriate truth conditions.

2.4. The most important types of constituents modified by CN

The most frequent type of construction from the corpus search is CN of degree/measure phrase exemplified by (22). In (22), the measure word *dost* 'enough' is

Table 1: Particular types with corresponding frequencies.

Measure phrases	PPs	CPs	NPs	Universal NPs	Another FOP	NumPs	APs	AdvPs	denial
22%	20%	16%	14%	14%	7%	5%	3%	1%	1%

part of the AdvP which is itself part of the conjoined AdvP in predicative position. To account for this type of construction I generally assume that location adverbs such as *blízko* 'close' are predicates of events (of type $\langle v,t\rangle$) whereas measure words like *dost* 'enough' are their modifiers (consequently of the $\langle\langle v,t\rangle,\langle v,t\rangle\rangle$ type). The formal semantics for (22) is then given in (23) which corresponds to a set of events which are not close enough and the subject of the sentence, i.e., *mrak* 'cloud', is the theme of those events. The value for the variable P is supplied by the context as *vábivě* 'temptingly'

(22) Mrak byl vábivě blízko, ale ne dost blízko.
cloud was temptingly close but not enough close
'The cloud was temptingly close but not close enough.'

(23) $[\![\textit{not enough close}]\!]=\lambda e[\neg enough(close(e))\wedge\exists P[P\in ALT(enough)\wedge P(close(e))]]$

The second most frequent type of constituent negated by CN involves PPs such as *(ať radši umřou tady) a ne v nějakém zapadákově* '(let them die here) and not in some dump'. Their composition with CN is similar to NPs in (20), so for the lack of space I will not deal with them in detail.

The third most frequent type of construction modified by CN comprises whole CPs, as exemplified in (24). What seems to be going on in such cases is that the CN in fact targets only one sub-constituent of the whole CP. In this example (and in the majority of other CN modified CPs) it targets the modal (or, in another, cases an auxiliary, phase verb etc.…). Thus, an accurate paraphrase of (24) would be: 'I don't desire to be a nursing father but I will have to be/… one'. In other words, the CN is focus associated at distance with the modal verb and the speaker presupposes some alternative propositional attitude to the proposition. Assuming that modal verbs are quantifiers over propositions (of the $\langle\langle s,t\rangle,t\rangle$ type), the semantics for (24) would look like (25), i.e., a set of such propositions which are not in the modality of *want* with respect to the speaker but in some alternative propositional modality. The proposition p in (25) is the set of all possible worlds where the speaker is a nursing father.

(24) ne že bych toužil být kojícím otcem
not that would-I desire BE nursing father
'Not that I desire for being nursing father.'

(25) $\lambda p[\neg want(I,p) \wedge \exists P[P \in ALT(want) \wedge P(p)]]$

Another construction which appears with CN quite often is the negation of the universal quantifier, as exemplified in (26). I assume that the type of the universal quantifier is a standard set of sets of entities ($\langle\langle e,t\rangle,t\rangle$), its force is universal as in the case of the modal verb in (24) (universal quantifier over propositions). In case of (26), the alternative to ∀ is the only one, namely ∃, and the accurate paraphrase of (26) is the following one: 'There are some Praguers who are satisfied with leatherette seats but it's not the case for all Praguers.' Formally, the meaning of (26) is represented in (27): it is a set of sets but not the set of sets containing the set of all Praguers (the meaning of ∀) but the set of sets having an intersection with the set of Praguers (the formal meaning of ∃) which intersects with the set of people who are satisfied with leatherette seats.

(26) Ne všem Pražanům ale koženkové sedačky vyhovují.
not all Praguers but leatherette seats fit
'Leatherette seats fit not all Praguers.'

(27) $[\![not\ all]\!] = \lambda Q[\neg all(Q) \wedge \exists P[P \in ALT(all) \wedge P(Q)]]$

Other types of constructions which can be found in the corpus, i.e., CN of focus particles, NumP, APs, and AdvPs as well as the denial subtype of CN, are also very interesting but for space reasons I have to skip their treatment and instead in the following section I will focus just on two mentioned constructions, namely on NumPs and denial interpretation of CN. In general, the aim of this section was to demonstrate that the proposed semantics for CN does capture all three types of CN which can be found in Czech (and which go far beyond what is usually discussed w.r.t. CN in the literature). Moreover, the proposed semantics captures one frequent feature of CN very well, i.e., CN is in most cases used contrastively: schematically *Predicate CN A but B* where *B* supplies the positive saturation of *Predicate* and *A* is negated by CN. The formalization encodes this property via the existential closure of the *P* variable which ranges over the alternatives of the negated constituents. It seems plausible to hypothesize that such a variable needs to have its value set by the context which corresponds to the positive counterpart to the negated constituent.

2.5. The FP solution for CN of comparative NumPs

Let us repeat the example which we started with as (28). We observed in Section 1 that unlike English, Czech allows and even prefers the interval reading for such sentences. Now we are ready to explain this interpretational difference between the languages. For (28) the ordinary semantic value is given in (28-a) where the numeral moves because of type requirements which semantically outputs the interval reading. But pragmatically CN requires at least one alternative of the focus marked phrase (*více* 'more' in this sentence) to be true. Nevertheless, we will see that the focus alternative computation in (19) will not cancel the literal interval reading in (28-b). I assume that comparative in numeral phrases is interpreted as a set of sets (⟨⟨*e*,*t*⟩,*t*⟩), specifically such sets which have cardinality specified by the number word of the NumP. In this case the *P(Q)* – the presupposed focus alternative to > – from (28-b) can be either = or ≤. Let's focus on each option:

1. Option 1: the presupposed focus alternative to > would be interpreted as the equality alternative to the F-marked > operator (*P*={=}); the meaning of the comparative would be a set of sets with cardinality exactly 2, e.g., one such set can look like {{*a*,*b*},{1,2},{3,4},…}.
2. Option 2: the presupposed focus alternative to > would be interpreted as the less or equal alternative to > (*P*={≤}); the meaning of the comparative would be a set of sets with cardinalities 2, 1, and 0, e.g., one such possible set can look like {{*a*,*b*},{1,2},{3,4},{*a*},{*b*},{∅}}.

There are two appropriate candidates for alternatives to >, i.e., the mentioned = relation (option 1) and ≤ (option 2). The existential closure in the CN meaning in (28-b) does not distinguish between them since it requires one of them to be satisfied but does not specify which one. This correctly predicts slight uncertainty of Czech speakers with respect to the interpretation of (28). In any case, majority of speakers agree with the primacy of the interval reading though some of them allow for the equality reading as the second one. I speculate that concurrence is in play here: since Czech CN is designed for the interval reading, if CN is not used, the otherwise ambiguous verbal negation is ceteris paribus interpreted as signalizing the equality reading. Crucially, unlike in English, the strengthening to the equality reading (which would mean that majority of speakers would allow only for the equality reading) with Czech CN does not happen.

(28) Ne [více než dva]$_F$ lidé vypovídali pravdivě.
no more than two people testified truthfully
'No more than two people testified truthfully.'
a. $\neg max_d(\lambda y \exists x[\#x{=}y \wedge people(x) \wedge truthful\_witness(x)])>2$
b. $\lambda Q[\neg more\_than\_two(Q) \wedge \exists P[P \in ALT(more\_than\_two) \wedge P(Q)]]$

The difference between Czech and English then comes from the fact that unlike English *no* Czech CN is a focus particle. According to Nouwen (2008), the equality reading in English arises through the implicature calculation. He assumes that English *no more than two* has implicatures based on the non-strict comparison ≤ ordering (0, 1, 2 in this case) which is strengthened via the standard negation of logically stronger implicatures (0,1 in this case). Under negation the scales reverse and 0 and 1 become logically stronger than 2, as was discussed for another example already in the section 1.1. For details see Nouwen (2008), but the core distinction between English and Czech is clear: in both languages the negated comparative gives raise to alternatives but they behave like classical scalar implicatures in English (and consequently they are strengthened to the equality reading) unlike in Czech where CN operates on the focus alternatives. In the case of negated comparative the hearer is not able to distinguish between two possible relations being presupposed (= and ≤); the fact which is formalized as the existential closure of the alternatives in (30-b). It follows that Czech negated comparative cannot be strengthened to the equality reading and we observe the interval reading.

In the corpus, I also found one example of CN interpreted as metalinguistic negation (or denial, to use terminology of Geurts (1998)), see (29). The example is different form the other discussed cases since the negation seems to target both the form and the interpretation. Thus, the correct paraphrase of (29) would be: Eliot doesn't call Kipling's work "poetry" (it's not true for Eliot that Kipling wrote poetry and Eliot doesn't want to call it poetry).[6] I agree with Geurts (1998) that the denial interpretation is not just the negation of form but that it is negation of meaning as well, i.e., it operates both on the use and the mention dimension. Therefore, (29) is different from the previous discussed types of CN where negation targets the meaning dimension only.

6 As the anonymous reviewer of my article correctly remarks, one example from the corpus points at marginality of metalinguistic negation. I agree completely but it is important to emphasize that such a construction does exist, it is totally productive, and behaves very differently from the other cases of Czech constituent negation.

(29) Eliot nazývá Kiplingovo metrické dílo "verši", ne "poezií".
Eliot calls Kipling's versical work "verses" not "poetry"
'Eliot calls Kipling's versical work "verses", not "poetry".'

The denial interpretation of English *not* is mentioned by Nouwen (2008) as well when he discusses examples such as (12) observed already by Jepsersen. As Nouwen explains, it seems that English *not* (unlike *no*) does have the interval reading we observed in Czech examples like (1). Nouwen (2008) blames the lack of the exhaustified/equality reading in cases such as (12) on the denial interpretation of *not*. He claims that *not* in such constructions is interpreted as denial and consequently the meaning is not strengthened because there are no scalar implicatures which would be exhaustified (at most there are alternatives in the form/mention dimension). I think Nouwen's solution works well for English where *not* in examples such as (12) is more marked than *no* and consequently more readily interpreted as denial since a more marked expression of negation is a signal that negation can or should be interpreted as denial because denial interpretation usually requires special signals such as, e.g., intonation. However, it would be in-adequate for the Czech examples of CN with the exception of clear denial cases such as (29). In Czech examples of CN there is no signal of formal markedness. So it seems that even if both languages allow for the interval reading with CN, they both arrive at them via different strategies, i.e., English through the denial interpretation of *not* whereas Czech through the computation of focus alternatives.

3. Summary

This article discussed CN in Czech and in some cases it contrasted its behaviour with English negation of the non-verbal type signaled with *no/not*. There were two perspectives pursued. The first one was broad, aiming at a descriptively adequate formal semantics for all cases of Czech CN. I consider the goal for finding a proper semantics for Czech CN reached since we arrived at a satisfactory formalization which explains semantic behavior of various sub-types of CN. The second perspective was more narrow and deeper: I compared Czech and English negated comparative numerals and demonstrated how their different interpretations follow from the proposed semantics for CN and particularly from the fact that Czech CN operates on focus alternatives of the F-marked phrase (unlike English *no*). Finally, we considered an alternative explanation of the interval/exact difference between Czech and English, namely the denial explanation of Nouwen (2008), and we discarded it as empirically in-adequate at least for Czech CN.

References

Büring, Daniel and Katharina Hartmann. 2001. "V3 or Not V3–An Investigation of German Focus Particles." *Natural Language and Linguistic Theory* 19: 229–81.

Corver, Norbert and Joost Zwarts. 2006. "Prepositional Numerals." *Lingua* 116 (6): 811–35.

Fox, Danny and Martin Hackl. 2006. "The Universal Density of Measurement." *Linguistics and Philosophy* 29 (5): 537–86.

Geurts, Bart. 1998. "The Mechanisms of Denial." *Language* 74(2): 274–307.

Jasinskaja, Katja. 2016. "Information Structure in Slavic." In Caroline Féry and Shinichiro Ishihara (eds.), *The Oxford handbook of Information Structure.* Oxford: Oxford University Press, 709–732.

Krifka, Manfred. 1999. "At Least Some Determiners Aren't Determiners." *The Semantics/Pragmatics Interface from Different Points of View* 1: 257–91.

Nouwen, Rick. 2008. "Upper-Bounded No More: The Exhaustive Interpretation of Non-Strict Comparison." *Natural Language Semantics* 16 (4): 271–95.

Reis, Marga. 2005. "On The Syntax Of So-Called Focus Particles In German – A Reply To Büring And Hartmann 2001." *Natural Language and Linguistic Theory* 23 (2): 459–83.

Schulz, Katrin and Robert Van Rooij. 2006. "Pragmatic Meaning and Non-Monotonic Reasoning." *Linguistics and Philosophy* 29 (2): 205–50.

Irina Stenger, Klára Jágrová, Andrea Fischer and Tania Avgustinova

"Reading Polish with Czech Eyes" or "How Russian can a Bulgarian Text be?" – Orthographic Differences as an Experimental Variable in Slavic Intercomprehension*

1. Introduction

Human language processing shows remarkable robustness, tolerating different kinds of imperfect linguistic signal. In particular, it is unclear how exactly a message encoded in one system is being processed and successfully decoded by a person used to a different system. Our goal is to gain insights about human performance at retrieving information available in unfamiliar encoding through intercomprehension, a mode of language use, also known as receptive multilingualism, which highlights an essential human ability to understand a language without having learned or acquired it. This is particularly apparent in the Slavic language family, where similarities between languages allow speakers of one Slavic language to effectively understand another Slavic language even if they are unable to use it for speaking or writing (Mel'ničuk 1986). Recognizable similarities and systematic differences of genetically related language varieties are due to the common origin in combination with a slow but steady development from unity to diversity (Carlton 1991, Mel'ničuk 1986). The expectation of mutual intelligibility is thus supported by the fact that modern Slavic languages as descendants of a single ancestor, traditionally referred to as Proto-Slavic or Common Slavic, whose characteristics can be reconstructed by comparing attested language varieties (Comrie and Corbett 1993, Carlton 1991). However, Townsend and Janda (1996: 25) point out that '[m]ost Slavs speak of understanding each other without much difficulty, but this is usually exaggerated and applies mostly to a simple concrete level.' Indeed, the degree of intelligibility of an unknown but closely related language depends on various linguistic as well as

* The presented study is supported by the German Science Foundation DFG within the project INCOMSLAV "Mutual Intelligibility and Surprisal in Slavic Intercomprehension" in the framework of the Collaborative Research Centre SFB 1102 "Information Density and Linguistic Encoding" (http://www.sfb1102.uni-saarland.de).

extra-linguistic factors (Gooskens 2013). We approach the challenge of mutual intelligibility from an information-theoretic perspective, taking into consideration the way information is encoded and decoded at different linguistic levels. Our methodology combines analyses of parallel corpora, information-theoretic modeling and a variety of experiments.

Our study focuses on reading intercomprehension, where orthography is the primary linguistic interface for extracting information from unknown encodings. When comparing different orthographic systems, special attention must be paid to the influence of the various descriptive levels (phonetics/phonology, graphemics/graphotactics, morphology/morphosyntax, semantics) as well as to historical, etymological and sociolinguistic factors (e.g., spelling reforms) (Sgall 2006, Penzl 1987). The question is: To what extent can a speaker of one Slavic language L1 understand a text written in another Slavic language L2? As the Slavic languages use two different scripts, we here investigate two language pairs: Czech and Polish (Latin script) vs. Bulgarian and Russian (Cyrillic script). Realistic scenarios could involve a Czech native speaker attempting to read a Polish newspaper or a Russian native speaker being confronted with a job announcement in Bulgarian.

The inter-Slavic orthographic correspondences established in (Fischer et al. 2015) take into consideration historically conditioned cross-linguistic variation between sound sequences. They were tested for applicability in a computational transformation experiment on parallel sets of formal cognates. Based on these orthographic correspondences, we can now investigate the effect of regular and irregular orthographic variation on readers' ability to comprehend a text in a related language. To this end, we are currently preparing a number of web-based experiments, including word translation tasks, multiple choice of isolated words, and recognition of cognate words in context.

That differences in orthography affect intelligibility is obvious, but which differences cause problems for readers, and which do not? Is the frequency of letters or the frequency of words more relevant in cognate recognition? What is the correlation between Levenshtein distance and the reader's ability to comprehend a related language? Could information-theoretic notions of conditional entropy and surprisal help us determine and predict human performance at reading intercomprehension? To what degree are all of these measures correlated? To identify which combination of factors we may expect to yield the best results, we here discuss various potential predictors that should help us to anticipate, analyze and evaluate the results of our web-based experiments with native Slavic speakers.

2. Preparatory work

We started with gathering diachronically motivated and synchronically attested inter-Slavic orthographic correlates in order to establish the linguistic basis of mutual intelligibility in the respective language pairs (Czech-Polish and Bulgarian-Russian). Historically conditioned analyses of cross-linguistic variation between sound sequences which allow for establishing the orthographic correlates were collected primarily from Bidwell (1963), Žuravlev et al. (1974–2012) and Vasmer (1973). In the process, we also attempted to account for the main lines of sound system evolution with regard to (i) the development of vowels and consonants, (ii) the development of specific sound combinations, and in particular (iii) the metathesis of liquids. This resulted in a compilation of diachronically-based orthographic correspondences: 103 unique correlates for Czech-Polish and 77 for Bulgarian-Russian, including one-to-one (matching) correspondences and mismatches which consist of single characters or of string of characters (e.g., CS-PL: *a:a, á:ią, ě:ię, z:dz, hv:gw, lou:łu, o:o, m:m, ou:ą, ů:ró, ří:rze, šť:szcz, c:c* etc.; BG-RU: *б:б, г:г, к:к, п:п, т:ть, б:бл, в:вл, ж:жд, м:мл, п:пл, а:а, е:е, ъ:у, и:ы, я:е, ла:оло* etc.). Only the correspondences which represented orthographic mismatches were automatically tested for their applicability on parallel cognate sets and the results of this orthographic transformation experiment are described in (Fischer et al. 2015). The hand-crafted parallel cognate sets were compiled on the basis of Pan-Slavic and internationalisms lists from the EuroComSlav project as well as standard Swadesh lists from the Wiktionary by carefully correcting the errors contained in the EuroComSlav sources and manually filtering the Swadesh lists for cognate pairs.[1] Eventually, all three lists were slightly modified, focusing exclusively on the form of the lexical units contained in them. Formal non-cognates (i.e. CS-PL *mnoho–wiele* '*many/much*'; BG-RU *ние–мы* '*we*') were removed. Formal cognates, if existing, were added to the lists where the pairs consisted of non-cognates (i.e., *mężczyzna* '*man*' was substituted by *mąż* '*husband*' in CS-PL *muž–mąż*; *звяр* '*beast*' was added to its Russian formal cognate *зверь* '*animal, beast*' for the BG-RU pair *звяр–зверь*). All this explains the variation in the amount of items in Table 1 for each list in the respective language pair. The linguistic items in these lists belong to different parts of speech, mainly nouns, adjectives and verbs. For the most part,

1 Pan-Slavic list: http://www.eurocomslav.de/kurs/pwslav.htm; http://www.eurocomslav.de/kurs/iwslav.htm; Swadesh-list: http://en.wiktionary.org/wiki/Appendix:Swadesh_lists_for_Slavic_languages.

Table 1: Number of cognate pairs

Word sets	Total number of items	
	CS-PL	BG-RU
Swadesh list	212	227
Pan-Slavic list	455	447
Internationalism list	262	261

the obtained automatic transformations could be seen as satisfactory for both language pairs (cf. Fischer et al. 2015).

With regard to identical and correctly transformed items, the best rates are 56.60% for CS-PL (in the Swadesh list) and 67.82% for BG-RU (in the internationalism list). In the results, there is a significantly higher rate of orthographically identical items for Bulgarian and Russian if compared to Czech and Polish (max. 87/262 items for CS-PL vs. 163/261 items for BG-RU, both in the internationalism lists). Furthermore the proportion of successfully transformed words differs in the respective pairs: (i) max. 204/455 items for CS-PL vs. 103/447 items for BG-RU, both for the Pan-Slavic lists, and (ii) min. 54/262 items for CS-PL vs. 14/261 items for BG-RU, both for the internationalism lists. Apparently, the set of correspondences works more successfully for CS-PL, while there is a high rate of identical items for BG-RU – for more details see (Fischer et al. 2015). It is the share of correctly transformed items from this computational transformation that will be used as test stimuli in our web-based experiments.

What can be seen as average orthographic distance in a given language pair is approximated by means of the Levenshtein algorithm. *Levenshtein distance* as a string similarity measure is equal to the number of operations needed to transform one string of characters into another through insertions, deletions and substitutions. For each character, we distinguish between base and diacritic. In terms of transformation cost, we assign a substitution cost of 1 to differences in the base. If two characters have the same base but different diacritics, we assign them a substitution cost of 0.5. For example, in order to transform the Russian word '*рыба*' (*ryba*) into the Bulgarian '*риба*' (*riba*) '*fish*' we must replace *ы* with *и*. This operation costs one point and thus non-normalized Levenshtein distance is 1.0. We considered non-normalized as well as normalized Levenshtein distances in our analysis. The normalized Levenshtein distance is obtained by dividing the non-normalized distance by the total length of the alignment that gave the minimum costs (cf. Beijering 2008). In our example we have 4 alignment slots and thus the normalized Levenshtein distance is 1/4=0.25 or 25%.

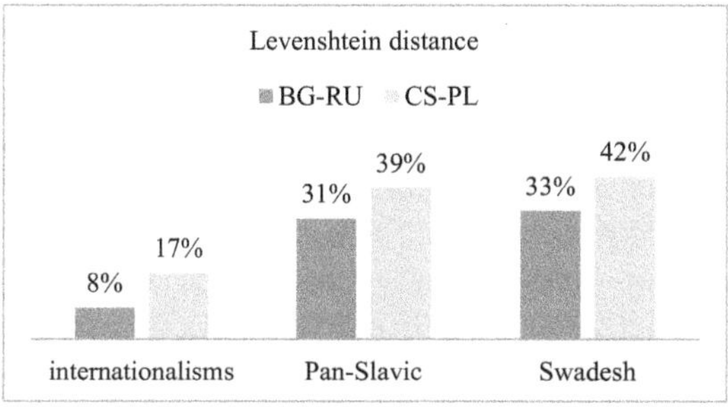

Diagram 2: Average orthographic distance by means of normalized Levenshtein distance

Furthermore, in order to obtain distances which are based on linguistically motivated alignments, the algorithm is adapted so that in the alignment a representation of vowels may only correspond to a representation of vowels and a representation of consonants only to a representation of consonants. Using the Levenshtein algorithm, we found that the average orthographic distance between Bulgarian and Russian is smaller than that between Czech and Polish throughout all lists (see diagram 2). We assume that the higher the distance, the more difficult it is to comprehend a given word in a translation task (cf. Gooskens 2005, 2007, Vanhove 2015), meaning that average Levenshtein distance would lead us to assume that Czech and Polish are less orthographically intelligible to each other than Bulgarian and Russian are.

In addition to our statistical word transformation experiment, we calculated the frequency of orthographic correspondences for the successfully transformed words (cf. Fischer et al. 2015). For example, the 204 transformable linguistic items for the Czech-Polish language pair from the Pan-Slavic list employ 71 orthographic correspondences, of which 21 are matching one-to-one correspondences (e.g., *a:a* (74), *o:o* (52), *s:s* (45)) and 50 mismatched orthographic correspondences (e.g., *ý:y* (45), *v:w* (42), *t:ć* (37)).[2] For Bulgarian and Russian, the Pan-Slavic list yielded 103 transformable items that employ 48 orthographic correspondences which can be divided into 25 matching (e.g., *c:c* (26), *o:o* (26), *a:a* (25)) and 23 mismatched orthographic correspondences (e.g., *я:е* (17), *ъ:у* (10), *и:ы* (10)).

2 Frequencies of orthographic correspondences given in round brackets.

3. Orthography as primary linguistic interface in reading intercomprehension

For detailed modeling of Slavic reading intercomprehension, we need an accurate and full description of what type of information is provided by the orthographic structure of the respective languages. The way information is encoded in a word is influenced by the phonetic/phonological space of the language as well as its morphological structure (cf. Frost 2012). In different Slavic languages the development of structured orthographies followed different paths at different times, and the established writing systems can be seen as a result of both linguistic and sociolinguistic factors (Sgall 2006, Kučera 2009). Most, if not all, Slavic orthographies that are based on the phonemic (phonological) principle of grapheme-to-phoneme correspondence (cf. Kučera 2009) use other orthographic principles as well, such as phonetic, morphological and historical/etymological. Such interaction provides the respective languages with a number of general patterns, but it is the prevailing combination of phonemic/phonetic and morphological principles in the Slavic orthographies that provides additional information, 'which makes the reading in highly inflectional languages like Slavic easier than if the orthographies were purely phonological transcriptions' (Kučera 2009: 73).

Since very little is known about the specific contribution of orthography to mutual intelligibility, we want to pinpoint exactly which of the occurring orthographic correspondences cause larger problems in intercomprehension and which ones are easily understood by speakers of related languages. We are particularly interested in the effect of mismatched orthographic correspondences on the readers' ability to comprehend a text in a related language. We also assume that languages with a smaller number of regular orthographic correspondences which cover a large portion of orthographic distance will be easier to understand than languages which need a larger number of correspondences to cover the same portion of distance (cf. Gooskens 2005). In order to assess the effect of each correspondence, we are preparing a series of web-based intercomprehension experiments, the results of which we will use for statistical analysis of orthographic intelligibility. Sometimes, the aim of such analyses is to assess the contribution of single linguistic factors to intelligibility (cf. Gooskens 2013). However, as various correlated factors may be at play, a comprehensive analysis must take all potential explaining factors into account.

4. Factors considered for prediction and explanation of orthographic intelligibility

In this section, we discuss the factors we consider as potential explanations for observed orthographic intelligibility. Our focus is on the already-established linguistic orthographic correspondences, which we assume to either facilitate or hinder intercomprehension. However, additional factors, such as word length, word frequency and, equally important, neighborhood density may independently explain and predict intercomprehension performance and thus skew an analysis that considers only correspondences. Some of the factors we discuss here are known to perform well as predictors of mutual intelligibility in speech semi-communication in related language varieties (cf. Gooskens 2007, Kürschner et al. 2008).

4.1. Nature, position and number of orthographic correspondences

We expect the nature, position, frequency and complexity of orthographic correspondences to influence the intelligibility of a written stimulus in an unknown language variety. The nature of correspondences may contribute to the degree of intelligibility (cf. Gooskens 2005). As mentioned in section 2, we distinguish between matching and mismatched correspondences. We hypothesize that matching orthographic correspondences positively affect intelligibility, and that mismatched correspondences affect it negatively. However, the mismatched correspondences may be more or less transparent and more or less regular. For example, it is likely easier for a Russian reader to guess that the Bulgarian grapheme <e> corresponds to <ë> in his or her own language, while guessing the other regular correspondences of the same Bulgarian grapheme to Russian <o> or <я> would be not as straightforward. Similarly, for some Czech-Polish orthographic correspondences, such as *á:a* and *l:ł*, it may be assumed that they will not pose a problem in reading intercomprehension as diacritics could be ignored.

In order to test what kind of correspondences differ in transparency, we furthermore distinguish between grapheme representations of vowels and grapheme representations of consonants. For example, Gooskens (2005: 5) points out Elert's (1981) prediction 'that […] consonants are more important than vowels, and that consonants at the beginning of words are more important than consonants in the middle or at the end of words.' At the same time, Vanhove and Berthele (2015) found – in an experiment on reading of individual cognates in the Germanic languages – that the position of different characters in cognates played a significant role: differences in word onset characters caused more confusion than differences in vowels or consonants at other positions in the words presented. Thus, we also consider the position of orthographic correspondences in the cognates used as test material.

Moreover, the number of mismatched correspondences in a word may itself influence the success of cognate recognition. We expect that the more mismatched correspondences there are between cognate words, the less transparent the cognates are and the more difficult it is to intercomprehend them. For example, 108 of our Bulgarian-Russian cognate pairs require exactly one orthographic correspondence to be transformed (e.g., *и:ы* in *бик – бык* '*bull*'), 18 Bulgarian-Russian cognate pairs have two different mismatched correspondences (e.g., *ъ:е* and *т:ть* in the word pair *смърт – смерть* '*death*'), and only 2 pairs require three different mismatched correspondences (e.g., *ла:ло, ъ:о* and *т:ть* in *лакът – локоть* '*elbow*'). Nevertheless, the nature and/or position of these correspondences is different and we may expect varying performance in a word translation task.

4.2. Levenshtein distance, word length and word frequency

Levenshtein distance as a measure for the orthographic distance of cognate pairs is considered a fairly good predictor of overall intelligibility (cf. Beijering et al. 2008, Gooskens 2007, Vanhove and Berthele 2015). Analyzing the influence of 11 linguistic factors on the intelligibility of Swedish words among Danes, Kürschner et al. (2008) calculated collinearity diagnostics which revealed that there is strong collinearity between word length, phonetic Levenshtein distance and lexical tones. They speculate that the reason for the collinearity between word length and Levenshtein distance may be explained by the fact that Levenshtein distance increases with longer words (cf. Kürschner et al. 2008: 96).

Word length influences normalized Levenshtein distance (see section 2), so that there is a natural correlation between these two values. In our case, however, diagram 3 shows that the calculated orthographic Levenshtein distance of the 128 Russian items to their Bulgarian cognates does not increase with the length of the Russian items.[3] The longer the word, the higher the number of alignment slots. This naturally decreases the value of the normalized Levenshtein distance, since the number of alignment slots is the divisor in the formula. We assume that longer words with a small Levenshtein distance are easier to recognize. The mean Levenshtein distance of our test material is 26% for BG-RU and 32% for CS-PL (compare with Levenshtein distance separated by lists in diagram 2).

Word length and word frequency are also correlated: shorter words tend to be more frequent than longer ones. The bubble size in diagram 3 represents the frequency of the stimuli. As Mahowald et al. (2013) pointed out, according to Zipf (1949) the reason for this relationship lies in that it maximizes communication efficiency by giving frequently used communication items shorter code

3 The 128 Russian items are the correctly transformed items through all three lists excluding doublets (see section 2).

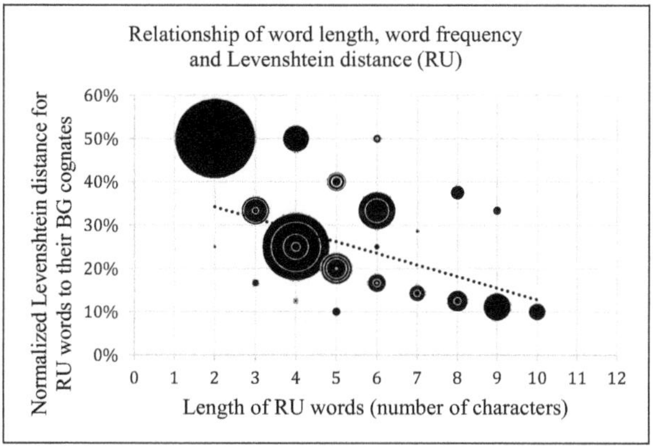

Diagram 3: Correlation between word length, word frequency and Levenshtein distance for the Russian stimuli

words – which take less effort to produce – than rare ones. Luce and Pisoni (1998) argued that highly frequent words have a permanent advantage in the recognition process. Vanhove and Berthele (2015) showed that the frequency of the word in question in the reader's language is a reliable predictor for intelligibility. However, Kürschner et al. (2008) revealed that log frequency as a separate variable has a low correlation with the intelligibility results, but it is nonetheless identified as a relevant factor in the prediction of word intelligibility in a combined model. Thus, the exact influence of word frequency on cognate recognition remains to be determined.

4.3. Word length, neighbourhood density and word frequency

As mentioned in the previous paragraph, word length was proved to influence intelligibility of individual words (cf. Kürschner et al. 2008). For example, Kürschner et al. (2008) find that longer words are more easily recognized than shorter words. This can be explained by the fact that longer words have fewer neighbours than shorter words (cf. Vitevitch and Rodriguez 2005). Kürschner et al. (2008: 90) define neighbours linguistically as 'word forms that are very similar to the stimulus'. Thus, neighbourhood density is the amount of similar words that might interfere in the process of cognate identification. Gooskens (2013) points out that words with a high neighbourhood density are often more difficult to recognize than those with few competitors. However, not only the quantitative effect of the neighbourhood density may influence the word recognition, but also the qualitative characteristics of the neighbours (cf. Kürschner et al. 2008) and their frequency (see section 4.4) may be relevant for word identification. We assume that the possible advantage of short words being more frequent than long words (see section 4.2), might be compensated by their higher neigbourhood density (cf. Kürschner et al. 2008) and also by the influence of the nature and position of mismatched orthographic correspondences.

We analyzed word lengths in terms of numbers of characters for our successfully transformable Czech, Polish, Bulgarian and Russian cognates. The mean word length (in characters) of the selected stimuli is: CS: 4.90, PL: 5.30, BG: 4.58, RU: 5.04. The longest word in Russian is *автомобиль* '*car*' and consists of 10 characters – accordingly, its Bulgarian cognate *автомобил* has 9 characters and is also the longest among the Bulgarian words. The two shortest word pairs in both of the languages (with both words consisting of 2 characters) are the personal pronoun '*you*': *ты* in Russian, *ти* in Bulgarian, and the noun '*hedgehog*': *ёж* in Russian, *еж* in Bulgarian. In general, the selected Czech items are shorter than the Polish, and the Bulgarian items are shorter than the Russian ones. In the Czech-Polish cognate list, the shortest word pair is *v* – *w* '*in*' and the longest word pair is *ministerstvo* – *ministerstwo* '*ministry*' (12 characters).

4.4. Word frequency and letter frequency

We assume that the frequency of words may influence the correct understanding of cognates, since readers are exposed more often to frequent words (cf. Kürschner et al. 2008). Word frequencies for our test material in Czech, Polish, Bulgarian and Russian are based on the frequency lists from the respective national corpora. The five most frequent stimuli in the Russian test material are: *ты* '*you*', *один* '*one*', *день* '*day*', *рука* '*hand/arm*' *голова* '*head*' and in the Bulgarian: *един* '*one*', *път* '*way*', *ден* '*day*', *ръка* '*hand/arm*', *име* '*name*'. However, we are interested not only in the frequency of the actual words, but also in the frequency of their neighbours as well as in the frequency of letters in the mismatched orthographic correspondences. For example, considering the Russian and Bulgarian cognates *рука* – *ръка* '*hand/arm*', we found that both words belong to the 100 most frequent nouns in their national corpora (cf. Jágrová et al. 2017). However, in another previous small-scale reading intercomprehension experiment of cognate words which was conducted in Moscow in 2015 with 16 Russian native speaker participants the Bulgarian stimulus *ръка* '*hand/arm*' was not correctly recognized at all – all 16 Russian readers translated it as *река* '*river*'. While the word *река* '*river*' is less frequent in Russian than the word *рука* '*hand/arm*' (cf. Ljaševskaja and Šarov 2009), the letter *е* is more frequent than the letter *у* in

Russian (cf. Ljaševskaja and Šarov 2009) and this could be a possible explanation for the mistake. Another possible explanation might be that the shape of the letter *ъ* is more similar to *e* than to *y* (cf. Boles and Clifford 1989; Gilmore et al. 1979). Also a semantic priming towards objects in nature might have influenced the participants' answers, for the list contained more names of trees and plants (10), animals (12) and other non-living objects in nature (10) and only few body parts (8) (cf. Collins and Loftus 1975).

4.5. Grapheme adaptation probability, surprisal and entropy

Using the Levenshtein algorithm to measure orthographic distances between the selected Slavic languages, we found that Bulgarian and Russian are orthographically closer to each other than Czech and Polish (see diagram 2). However, this string similarity measure is completely symmetric and cannot capture any asymmetries between related languages (cf. Frinsel et al. 2015, Moberg et al. 2006). Asymmetries, however, are something we expect. For example, in our test material, the Russian grapheme <a> (which occurs 175 times) corresponds exclusively to the Bulgarian grapheme <a> (which occurs 194 times).[4] Conversely, however, the Bulgarian grapheme <a> may correspond to the Russian graphemes <a> (175 times), <o> (15 times) or <я> (4 times). In such a case, we can expect a Russian reader to have more difficulties to correctly guess which graphemes in Russian correspond to the Bulgarian one he/she is confronted with. Using a set of aligned cognate words allows to model the adaptation process statistically, which reveals such asymmetries. The probability of translating grapheme g2 from the foreign language L2 into grapheme g1 from the native language L1 is given by:
4: Grapheme adaptation probability is calculated with the following formula:

$$P\left(L1 = g1 \mid L2 = g2\right) = \frac{count\left(L1 = g1 \land L2 = g2\right)}{count\left(L2 = g2\right)}$$

Thus, for our example above, we would get P(BG=<a> | RU=<a>) = 175/175 = 1.0, while P(RU=<a> | BG=<a>) = 175/194 ≈ 0.9, P(RU=<o> | BG=<a>) = 15/194 ≈ 0.07, and P(RU=<я> | BG=<a>) = 4/194 ≈ 0.02. In other research, another closely related information-theoretic concept called *surprisal* has been shown to

4 The grapheme adaptation probability, surprisal and entropy for Bulgarian and Russian were calculated on the basis of the 291 successfully transformable cognate pairs (identical + successfully transformed, doublets excluded), (see section 2).

oftentimes correlate better with various metrics of success, such as e.g. reading times in eye-tracking experiments (cf. Smith and Levy 2013). Surprisal is defined as the code length of an optimal prefix-free code for a given probability distribution and thus has an inverse logarithmic relation to the probability values themselves (cf. Shannon 1948). Surprisal values are given in bits and depend heavily on the used probability distribution. In our setting, we get *grapheme adaptation surprisal* from our grapheme adaptation probability.
5: Grapheme adaptation surprisal is calculated with the following formula:

$$surprisal(L1 = g1 \mid L2 = g2) = -\log_2 P(L1 = g1 \mid L2 = g2)$$

Grapheme adaptation surprisal values allow to quantify the unexpectedness both of individual letter correspondences and of whole cognate pairs. We can compute overall word adaptation surprisal by summing up the grapheme adaptation surprisals of the contained graphemes. This gives a quantification of the overall (un)expectedness of the correct cognate. For example, the Russian-Bulgarian cognate *дуб – дъб 'oak'* contains the correspondences *д:д* (transformation surprisal: 0.0 in both directions), *у:ъ* (surprisal BG-to-RU: 0.978, RU-to-BG: 1.974) and *б:б* (0.0 surprisal in both directions). Thus, *дуб – дъб* gets a word adaptation surprisal of 0.978 or 1.974 with a predicted advantage for Russian readers. We will analyse the potential of both individual grapheme adaptation surprisals and full word adaptation surprisal in our web-based experiments. Surprisal is closely related to *entropy,* which is the mean of surprisal. Its formula is:
6: Entropy is calculated with the following formula:

$$H(X) = -\sum_{x \in X} P(X = x) \log_2 P(X = x)$$

Entropy gives a quantification of the overall uncertainty involved in making a choice. In our setting, we can do multiple things with entropies. We can consider the entropy involved in transforming a specific grapheme, or the entropy involved in transforming any grapheme. With the definition:
7: The grapheme adaptation entropy of grapheme g2 is given by:

$$H(L1 \mid L2 = g2) = -\sum_{g1 \in L1} P(L1 = g1 \mid L2 = g2) \log_2 P(L1 = g1 \mid L2 = g2)$$

We can express overall conditional grapheme transformation entropy as follows:
8: Overall orthographic entropy between languages L1, L2 is given by:

$$H(L1|L2) = -\sum_{g2 \in L2} P(L2 = g2) H(L1|L2 = g2)$$
$$= -\sum_{g1 \in L1,\, g2 \in L2} P(L1 = g1 \wedge L2 = g2) \log_2 P(L1 = g1 | L2 = g2)$$

Here, H(L1|L2=g2) is the uncertainty involved in transforming grapheme g2 from language L2 (foreign language), e.g. Bulgarian, into any grapheme of language L1 (native language), e.g. Russian. H(L1|L2) then is the overall uncertainty in guessing any grapheme of the native language L1 given knowledge of the corresponding grapheme of the foreign language L2. Since these adaptation entropies are based on a *conditional* probability distribution, previous work has mostly referred to them simply as *conditional entropy* (cf. Frinsel et al. 2015, Moberg et al. 2006). Using these entropies, we can quantify both the uncertainty in the overall adaptation process as well as that in adaptation of individual graphemes. In our example above, the grapheme adaptation entropy of the Bulgarian grapheme <a> is 0.54 and the grapheme adaptation entropy of the Russian grapheme <a> is 0.0. This would indicate higher uncertainty for Russians than for Bulgarians when confronted with this grapheme. Again, we can apply this measure to individual graphemes or as an aggregate measure for entire words: For our example Russian-Bulgarian cognate *дуб – дъб* '*oak*', we would get individual grapheme adaptation entropies of 0.0 for <д> and <б>, but Bulgarian readers adapting the Russian grapheme <у> would be predicted to face lower uncertainty (0.818) than Russians trying to adapt <ъ> (1.462).

The full conditional entropy between two languages, H(L1|L2) then allows to measure the complexity of the *entire* mapping between these two languages. It reflects both the frequency and regularity of orthographic correspondences between two languages and can reveal asymmetries in overall adaptation difficulties, as it did for Swedish and Danish in Frinsel et al.'s 2015 study. Moberg et al.'s (2006) hypothesis was that high predictability improves intelligibility, and therefore a low entropy value should correspond to a high intelligibility score. They concluded that this is the case for Danish, Swedish and Norwegian, and Frinsel et al. concluded the same for Danish and Swedish (cf. Frinsel et al. 2015, Moberg et al. 2006).

We calculated the full orthographic entropy for those Bulgarian and Russian cognate pairs that proved to be transformable by the orthographic correspondences gathered in the previous study (including pairs with identical words, see section 2) and found that there is hardly any difference in the entropies for both directions (0.26 Russian for Bulgarian and 0.27 Bulgarian for Russian) with a very small amount of asymmetry (0.01). This means that

Russians reading Bulgarian are predicted to deal with hardly more uncertainty than Bulgarians reading Russian. Orthographic entropies between Czech and Polish, however, reveal a very clear asymmetry: the entropy for Czech given Polish (0.71) is much higher than for Polish given Czech (0.60).[5] This means that a Czech reader may have more difficulties reading Polish than a Polish person reading Czech. In addition, the orthographic entropy for Czech and Polish is in both cases higher than the orthographic entropy for Bulgarian and Russian. The orthographic correspondences between Bulgarian and Russian are more regular and less numerous than the orthographic correspondences between Czech and Polish in our selected test material. The low orthographic entropy for Bulgarian and Russian can be explained by a higher number of orthographically identical (163) than orthographically not identical items (128) in the material for these two languages. According to Moberg et al. (2006), at least 800 words are needed to reach stable entropy measures. Therefore, for a representative study of orthographic asymmetry we must expand our test material. However, in general it can be assumed that the mapping between the Czech and the Polish orthographic system is more difficult than the mapping between the Bulgarian and the Russian orthography.

The orthographic entropy may reflect the difficulties humans encounter when mapping one orthographic system to another. More importantly, it measures only the regularity of correspondences and does not measure the similarity between two languages (cf. Frinsel et al. 2015). Nonetheless, such regularity could very well have an effect on reader's ability to understand a related language (cf. Frinsel et al. 2015). The exact predictive potential of grapheme adaptation surprisal, individual grapheme adaptation entropies, and overall orthographic entropy for the intercomprehension process is an open question, which we will explore in our upcoming experiments.

5. Discussion and outlook

Intercomprehension scenarios reveal a remarkable tolerance of human language processing mechanisms to deviations in linguistic encoding. Our research aims to formally model the processes of intercomprehension and to provide a systematic investigation into mutual intelligibility from the point of view of information

---

5 The conditional entropy for Czech and Polish was calculated on the basis of 346 cognate pairs (identical + successfully transformed words from the previous transformation experiment – see section 2). Duplicates were removed from the formerly three separate lists.

being encoded and decoded at different linguistic levels. The present work focuses on the role of orthography in reading intercomprehension. Here, a reader fluent in one language is trying to decipher a text written in an unknown, but related language. In this setting, the first challenge is to decode the encountered strings of characters into meaningful units in order to form a coherent understanding of the encoded information. Thus, orthography critically affects the success of transmitting information across languages: unsuccessful or incomplete decoding of orthographic representations in an unknown language may lead to a situation where even cognate words become incomprehensible.

We explore cross-lingual orthographic correspondences as an experimental variable in reading intercomprehension of individual words, modeling orthographic intelligibility between related languages from an information-theoretic perspective. Previous research has shown that intelligibility of (closely) related languages can be predicted by linguistic distances, in particular by means of the Levenshtein algorithm. However, orthographic distance measures, as a rule, do not differentiate between regular and irregular orthographic correspondences. Correspondences themselves, as well as factors such as their frequency, their nature or their position can be expected to perform well as predictors of mutual intelligibility. Beyond this, we consider additional factors such as word/letter frequency, word length and neighbourhood density, as well as the overall frequency and regularity of orthographic correspondences as measured by means of conditional entropy and surprisal as potential explanatory variables.

In future research, we will refine the entropy and surprisal model in several ways. We will extend the experiments with measurements based on bigrams or trigrams, focusing on the position of orthographic correspondences in cognates as well as on their nature. We will also expand our test material in order to get statistically significant results. While our upcoming analysis will shed light on the degrees of transparency of the different orthographic correspondences, it remains to be seen which other factors are likely to play a role in mutual intelligibility. In order to model orthographic intelligibility accurately, we expect that additional aspects must be incorporated into the analyses. Some of these are the etymological heritage of words (e.g. internationalisms vs. inherited lexicon), syllabic differences between cognates, as well as phonetic/phonological characteristics of the individual languages.

References

Beijering, Katrin, Charlotte Gooskens, Wilbert Heeringa. 2008. "Predicting intelligibility and perceived linguistic distance by means of the Levenshtein algorithm." *Linguistics in the Netherlands*: 13–24.

Bidwell, Charles E. 1963. *Slavic Historical Phonology in Tabular Form*. The Hague: Mouton & Co.

Boles, David B. and Clifford, John E. 1989. "An upper- and lowercase alphabetic similarity matrix, with derived generation similarity values." *Behavior Research Methods, Instruments and Computers* 21(6): 579–86.

Carlton, Terence R. 1991. *Introduction to the Phonological History of the Slavic Languages*. Ohio: Slavica Publishers, Inc., Columbus.

Colins, Allan M. and Loftus, Elizabeth F. 1975. "A spreading-activation theory of sematic processing." *Psychological Review* 82 (6): 407–28.

Comrie, Bernard and Corbett, Creville G. 1993. "Introduction." In *The Slavonic Languages*, Bernard Comrie and Greville G. Corbett (eds.). London/New York: Routledge, 1–20.

Elert, Claes-Christian. 1981. "Kvantitativa mått på språklikhet. En jämförelse mellan färöiska, norska och svenska." In *Internordisk språkförståelse. Föredrag och diskussioner vid ett symposium på Rungstedgaard utanför Köpenhamn den 24–26 mars 1980*, Claes-Christian Elert (ed.). Umeå: University of Umeå, 85–101.

Fischer, Andrea, Tania Avgustinova, Roland Marti, Dietrich Klakow, Klára Jágrová and Irina Stenger. 2015. "An Orthography Transformation Experiment with Czech-Polish and Bulgarian-Russian Parallel Word Sets." In *Natural Language Processing and Cognitive Science 2015 Proceedings*, Bernadette Sharp, Wiesław Lubaszewski and Rodolfo Delmonte (eds.). Venezia: Libreria Editrice Cafoscarina, 115–26.

Frinsel, Felicity, Anne Kingma, Femke Swarte, Charlotte Gooskens. 2015. "Predicting the asymmetric intelligibility between spoken Danish and Swedish using conditional entropy." *Tijdschrift voor Slandinavistiek* 34(2): 120–38.

Frost, Ram. 2012. "Towards a universal model of reading." *Behavioral and Brain Sciences* 35(5): 263–329.

Gilmore, Gover C., Harry Hersh, Alfonso Caramazza and James Griffin. 1979. "Multidimensional letter similarity derived from recognition errors." *Perception and Psychophysics* 25(5): 425–31.

Gooskens, Charlotte. 2005. "Linguistic determinants of mutual intelligibility in Scandinavia (NWO Vidi, 2006–2011)." *Project Proposal*. http://www.let.rug.nl/gooskens/?p=project. Accessed 11.07.2016.

Gooskens, Charlotte. 2007. "The contribution of linguistic factors to the intelligibility of closely related languages." *Journal of Multilingual and Multicultural Development* 28(6): 445–67.

Gooskens, Charlotte. 2013. "Experimental methods for measuring intelligibility of closely related language varieties." In *Handbook of Sociolinguistics*, Robert

Bayley, Richard Cameron and Ceil Lucas (eds.). Oxford: Oxford University Press, 195–213.

Jágrová, Klára, Irina Stenger, Roland Marti, Tania Avgustinova. 2017. "Lexical and Orthographic Distances between Czech, Polish, Russian, and Bulgarian – a Comparative Analysis of the Most Frequent Nouns." *Proceedings of the Olomouc Linguistics Colloquium 2016.*

Kučera, Karel. 2009. "The Orthographic Principles in the Slavic Languages: Phonetic/Phonological." In *The Slavic Languages. An International Handbook of their Structure, their History and their Investigation. Volume 1*, Sebastian Kempgen, Peter Kosta, Tilman Berger and Karl Gutschmidt (eds.). Belin/New York: Walter de Gruyter, 70–6.

Kürschner, Sebastian, Renée van Bezooijen and Charlotte Gooskens. 2008. "Linguistic determinants of the intelligibility of Swedish words among Danes." *International Journal of Humanities and Arts Computing* 2(1/2): 83–100.

Ljaševskaja, Ol'ga N. and Šarov, Sergej A. 2009. *Častotnyj slovar' sovremennogo russkogo jazyka*. Moskva: Azbukovnik.

Luce, Paul A. and Pisoni, David B. 1998. "Recognizing spoken words: The Neighborhood Activation Model." *Ear and hearing* 19(1): 1–36.

Mahowald, Kyle, Evelina Fedorenko, Steven T. Piantadosi, Edward Gibson. 2013. "Info/information theory: Speakers choose shorter words in predictive contexts." *Cognition* 126: 313–18.

Mel'ničuk, Aleksandr S. 1986. *Istoričeskaja tipologija slavjanskich jazykov*. Kiev: Naukova dumka.

Moberg, Jens, Charlotte Gooskens, John Nerbonne and Nathan Vaillette. 2006. "Conditional entropy measures intelligibility among related languages". In *Computational Linguistics in the Netherlands 2006: Selected papers from the 17th CLIN Meeting*, Peter Dirix, Ineke Schuurman, Vincent Vandeghinste and Frank Van Eynde (eds.). Utrecht: LOT, 51–66.

Penzl, Herbert. 1987. "Zur alphabetischen Orthographie als Gegenstand der Sprachwissenschaft." In *Orthography and Phonology*, Philip A. Luelsdorff (ed). Amsterdam/Philadelphia: John Benjamins, 225–38.

Shannon, Claude E. 1948. "A mathematical theory of communication." *Bell System Technical Journal* 27(379–423): 623–56.

Sgall, Petr. 2006. "Towards a Theory of Phonemic Orthography." In *Language in its multifarious aspects*, Petr Sgall (ed.). Charles University: Karolinum Press, 430–52.

Smith, Nathaniel J. and Levy, Roger. 2013. "The effect of word predictability on reading time is logarithmic." *Cognition* 128(3): 302–19.

Townsend, Charles E. and Janda, Laura A. 1996. *Common and Comparative Slavic: Phonology and Inflection with special attention to Russian, Polish, Czech, Serbo-Croatian, Bulgarian*. Ohio: Slavica Publishers, Inc., Columbus.

Vanhove, Jan and Berthele, Raphael. 2015. "The lifespan development of cognate guessing skills in an unknown related language." *International Review of Applied Linguistics in Language Teaching* 53(1): 1–38.

Vanhove, Jan. 2015. "The Early Learning of Interlingual Correspondences Rules in Receptive Multilingualism." *International Journal of Bilingualism*, http://homeweb.unifr.ch/VanhoveJ/Pub/papers/Vanhove_CorrespondenceRules.pdf. Accessed 11.07.2016.

Vasmer, Max. 1973. *Etimologičeskij slovar' russkogo jazyka*. Moskva: Progress.

Vitevitch, Michael S. and Rodriguez, Eva. 2005. "Neighborhood density effects in spoken word recognition in Spanish." *Journal of Multilingual Communication Disorders* 3(1): 64–73.

Zipf, George K. 1949. *Human Behavior and the Principle of Least Effort: An Introduction to Human Ecology*. Cambridge, MA: Addison-Wesley.

Žuravlev, Anatolij F. (ed.). 1974–2012. *Etimologičeskij slovar' slavjanskich jazykov. Praslavjanskij leksičeskij fond*. Vol. 1–37. Moskva: Nauka.

Potsdam Linguistic Investigations
Potsdamer Linguistische Untersuchungen
Recherches Linguistique à Potsdam

Edited by / Herausgegeben von / Edité par
Peter Kosta, Gerda Haßler, Teodora Radeva-Bork, Lilia Schürcks,
Nadine Thielemann and / und / et Vladislava Maria Warditz

Band 1 Peter Kosta / Lilia Schürcks (eds.): Linguistics Investigations into Formal Description of Slavic Languages. Contributions of the Sixth European Conference held at Potsdam University, November 30–December 02, 2005. 2007.

Band 2 Lilia Schürcks: Binding and Discourse. Where Syntax and Pragmatics Meet. 2008.

Band 3 Christiane Hümmer: Synonymie bei phraseologischen Einheiten. Eine korpusbasierte Untersuchung. 2009.

Band 4 Svetlana Friedrich: Definitheit im Russischen. 2009.

Band 5 Matthias Guttke: Strategien der Persuasion in der schriftkonstituierten politischen Kommunikation. Dargestellt an Parteiprogrammen der Neuen Rechten in Polen. 2010.

Band 6 Peter Kosta / Lilia Schürcks (eds.): Formalization of Grammar in Slavic Languages. Contributions of the Eighth International Conference on Formal Description of Slavic Languages – FDSL VIII 2009. University of Potsdam, December 2–5, 2009. 2011.

Band 7 Roman Sukač (ed.): From Present to Past and Back. Papers on Baltic and Slavic Accentology. 2011.

Band 8 Diego Gabriel Krivochen: The Syntax and Semantics of Nominal Construction. A Radically Minimalist Perspective. 2012.

Band 9 Teodora Radeva-Bork: Single and Double Clitics in Adult and Child Grammar. 2012.

Band 10 Anja Hennemann: A Context-sensitive and Functional Approach to Evidentiality in Spanish or Why Evidentiality needs a Superordinate Category. 2013.

Band 11 Diego Gabriel Krivochen / Peter Kosta: Eliminating Empty Categories. A Radically Minimalist View on Their Ontology and Justification. 2013.

Band 12 Christina Behme: Evaluating Cartesian Linguistics. From Historical Antecedents to Computational Modeling. 2014.

Band 13 Kathleen Plötner: Raum und Zeit im Kontext der Metapher. Korpuslinguistische Studien zu französischen und spanischen Raum-Zeit-Lexemen und Raum-Zeit-Lokutionen. 2014.

Band 14 Marion Eva Ernst: Produktnamen der Lebensmittelindustrie. Eine empirisch-strukturelle Untersuchung. 2014.

Band 15 Stefanie Wagner: Eine „unbekannte" Sprache lesen *oder* Von der Entdeckung des Nissart durch Interkomprehension. 2015.

Band 16 Nataša Todorović: The Indicative and Subjunctive da-complements in Serbian: A Syntactic-Semantic Approach. 2015.

Band 17 Vladislava Warditz / Beatrix Kreß (eds.): Multilingualism and Translation. Studies on Slavonic and Non-Slavonic Languages in Contact. 2015.

Band 18 Nadia Varley: Optionality and overgeneralization patterns in second language acquisition: Where has the expletive ensconced *it*self? 2015.

Band 19 Verónica Böhm: La imperfectividad en la prensa española y su relación con las categorías semánticas de modalidad y evidencialidad. 2016.

Band 20 Roland Wagner: Reflexivität im tschechisch-deutschen Sprachvergleich. Möglichkeiten und Grenzen einer Prognose. 2016.

Band 21 Ray C. H. Leung: Institutional Construction of Gamblers' Identities. A Critical Multi-method Discourse Study. 2017.

Band 22 Markéta Ziková: Licensing of Vowel Length in Czech. The Syntax-Phonology Interface. 2018.

Band 23 Ludmila Veselovská: Noun Phrases in Czech. Their Structure and Agreements. 2018.

Band 24 Carmen Conti Jiménez: Complejidad lingüística. Orígenes y revisión crítica del concepto de lengua compleja. 2018.

Band 25 Nadine Thielemann / Nicole Richter (eds.): Urban Voices: The Sociolinguistics, Grammar and Pragmatics of Spoken Russian. 2019.

Band 26 Forthcoming

Band 27 Davide Fanciullo: Temporal expression in nominals: tripartite deictics in the Bulgarian Rhodope dialects. 2019.

Band 28 Olga Flug: Russisch und Ukrainisch im Wandel. Eine korpusbasierte Untersuchung zur Destandardisierung am Beispiel der Anglisierung in der Werbesprache nach 1985. 2019.

Band 29 Teodora Radeva-Bork / Peter Kosta (eds.): Current Developments in Slavic Linguistics. Twenty Years After (*based on selected papers from FDSL 11*). 2020.

www.peterlang.com

Lightning Source UK Ltd.
Milton Keynes UK
UKHW010147120422
401421UK00002B/24

9 783631 676738